SPHERE HISTORY
OF LITERATURE

AMERICAN
LITERATURE
SINCE 1900

SPHERE HISTORY
OF LITERATURE

This series was first published in the 1970s. Volumes 1, 2, 4 and 8 were revised and republished in 1986, and Volumes 3, 6, 9 and 10 in 1987. Some material has been reworked or replaced and some new material has been added. The bibliographies have been updated. Volumes 5 and 7 are entirely new and will be published in 1988.

AMERICAN LITERATURE SINCE 1900

·

EDITED BY

MARCUS CUNLIFFE

SPHERE REFERENCE

First published in Great Britain in 1975 by
Sphere Books Ltd
27 Wrights Lane
London W8 5TZ
Revised and republished 1987
© Sphere Books 1975, 1987

Sphere Reference

Set in Linotron Ehrhardt

Printed in Great Britain by
Billing & Sons Ltd., Worcester

CONTENTS

INTRODUCTION

In its newly revised form this book covers about ninety years. During those decades literature in the United States has evolved from a mainly defensive position, either gauche or genteel, to an aura of superpower magnitude and ease. One aim of the volume is to show how and when the shift began. The starting date of 1900 is of course not precise. As the contributors suggest, it is possible to argue that the unmistakable American accent could be heard long before that – even perhaps as early as the seventeenth century. So if we are to look for the start of 'modern' writing, there is a case for going back to 1890. There is also a case for assigning 1912 or 1913 as the point of departure; and another for seeing 1917–18 as the moment when the old American innocence yielded to the new sophistication. The division is bound to be arbitrary. 1900 is as convenient a date as any. Readers wishing to push the inquiry further back in time are recommended to lay hands on the previous volume in this series, *American Literature to 1900*, by the same editor, and in particular to consult the final essay of that collection, by Malcolm Bradbury, which can then be linked with his opening essay in the post-1900 survey.

A more difficult problem from that of where to begin is where to call a halt. Any attempt to supply the very latest information would be out of date before it could come into print. Nothing looks so outmoded as last year's modishness. Fashions change in literature as in dress; and the pace of change has accelerated. Reputations have soared and been superseded like rockets in some prodigal firework display. The first edition of *American Literature Since 1900* could only take the story to about 1970 – give or take a few years in individual essays. Some of the essays, such as those by Arnold Goldman and Leslie Fiedler, stand as admirable evocations, and prophecies, which both define and embody the liveliest thought of their era. Such essays have accordingly been left intact, sometimes with minor changes and additions. Dennis Welland's account of the famous inter-war era in American fiction, for example, is as before, except for an assessment of some of Ernest Hemingway's post-humously published material, and for bibliographical updating.

Likewise, Aleksandar Nejgebauer's examination of the major poetry of 1945–60 has been left essentially unchanged; the editor has merely supplied additional comments on Robert Lowell, and augmented the bibliography.

Other revisions have been more substantial. Malcolm Bradbury has rewritten his chapter, 'The American Risorgimento', so as to incorporate his own fresh thinking on its themes. Eric Mottram has substantially enriched and augmented his detailed guide to post-1960 vanguard poetry. Irving Wardle (drama critic of the London *Times*) has supplemented his interpretation of 'American Theatre Since 1945'. Ursula Brumm ('William Faulkner and the Southern Renascence') adds to her previous treatment of Faulkner's *Sartoris* and *Go Down, Moses*, and also to her broad analysis of Southern life and literature.

There are two entirely new chapters. Jean-Pierre Mileur follows chronologically upon Marshall Van Deusen. Together their essays clarify the complex history of twentieth-century literary criticism in the United States, with its interfusion of indigenous and of imported systems. Van Deusen, for instance, weighs the origins, techniques and achievements of the so-called 'New Criticism'; Mileur deals with the spectacular subsequent emergence, initially in large part from French sources, of the movements known as Structuralism, Post-Structuralism and Deconstruction.

In the other new chapter, Jerome Klinkowitz takes further the essays on fiction by Dennis Welland, Arnold Goldman and Ursula Brumm. His concern is with 'postmodern' forms as they have developed since 1970. Finally, Marcus Cunliffe, in 'Literature and Society', considers aspects of what may be called the sociology of literature – the socio-economic circumstances within which it is produced; distinctions between different 'levels' of writing; 'phases of the *Zeitgeist*', namely, successive intellectual climates; and certain distinctive features of recent and current American thought and feeling (the status of black and 'ethnic' self-expression, the flourishing of writing by and about women, 'gay' literature, the blending of fact and fiction as exhibited in the 'New Journalism', the vogue for 'conservative' theory and outward conduct, and so on).

As in the pre-1900 volume each contributor has expressed his or her own opinions. The editor has not sought to homogenize. One colleague happens to be from Yugoslavia, one from Germany. Our Anglo-American essayists include an Englishman domiciled in America and an American domiciled in England. There are differences of opinion between the contributors. Thus Leslie Fiedler uses 'Modernism' as a term of reproach, whereas for Marshall Van Deusen it is, more neutrally, a central term in establishing the formal critical categories of the period 1900–65. Again, the poet Robert Lowell is treated respectfully by Aleksandar Nejgebauer and less so by Eric Mottram. This is as it should be. The object of our collaboration is not collusion, but the provision of information and views on a huge mass of writing, in various genres, the vitality of which has found room for plenty of disagreement between author and author, group and group, generation and generation. The creative spirit of the now old twentieth century has of itself nurtured controversy.

An instance is the conflict, central to several of our essays, between the Risorgimento's Modernism and the latter-day repudiations in the name of Post-Modernism. For Post-Modernists in literary criticism, the codifications of a bygone age appear not merely as dead letters but as errors and nuisances. The gap might be compared to that between seadivers of the old school, with screwed-on helmets, air-lines and lead-soled boots, and the aqualunged frogmen of a newer dispensation. If so, of course, a retort might be that the old type of diver had a heavy job to do, and is still needed for the big and the deep stuff, where the frogman usually operates on light tasks near the surface. Certainly it is not easy to deliver firm or final opinions about very recent literature; and the critic may understandably prefer to swing with it rather than at it. Whereas Post-Modern creative writing is often candidly subversive of the conventional wisdom and far removed from the solemnities associated with 'literature', the very claim to be a critic threatens to align one with the prosecution instead of the defence. Remember Randall Jarrell's wittily deadpan definition of a novel as 'an extended piece of prose narrative that has something seriously wrong with it'.

Perhaps the debate does not matter in the old way. There is, after all, a new principle of obsolescence in the arts as already in other features of the consumer economy. The commodity may no longer be meant to last. The old *momentum aere perennius*, a monument sturdier than bronze, may in our century have been replaced by objects inherently perishable – cardboard or biodegradable artefacts. The writer's gain in such a scene consists in immediacy. A surfrider upon nowness, the author is often acutely attuned to material and audience. Whether the audience is big or tiny, their joint, generational knowledge is intimately shared. The risk for such a surfriding improvizer is of missing the next wave, coming a cropper, being consigned to yesterday, and either forgotten or put as an exhibit in some literary Hall of Fame. Or perhaps Modernism and Post-Modernism are not after all so fundamentally opposed. 'Making it new' was the aim of writers long before 1960. Possibly what we are witnessing is the ironical unfolding of the very concept of modernness: novelty turning brown at the edges, a rebellion against the successful rebels of Ezra Pound's era, to be capped inevitably by a further insurrection. Time will show; or usually does.

MC

1

THE AMERICAN RISORGIMENTO: THE UNITED STATES AND THE COMING OF THE NEW ARTS

Malcolm Bradbury

'What happened in those early years. A great deal happened.'
Gertrude Stein, *The Autobiography of Alice B. Toklas*

'Scenes from the Younger Generation were freely enacted.'
Carl Van Vechten, letter to Mabel Dodge

I

'So the twentieth century had come it began with 1901,' wrote Gertrude Stein, with her usual plain sagacity, in her late book *Paris France* (1940); and, give or take a year, she was perfectly right. But to Stein the twentieth century was not a mere fact of the calendar, but a new historical attitude, which meant a new view of art. She herself virtually embodied it: 'I was there to kill what was not dead, the nineteenth century which was so sure of evolution and prayers,' she once observed. The twentieth century did not come everywhere. It happened in France (she was almost there at the time, having expatriated to Montparnasse in 1903), and it happened to America, and to Americans (Miss Stein had an advantage there too). When it came, the French took it in their stride, for 'what is was and what was is, was their point of view of which they were not very conscious'. As for the British, they consciously refused it, 'knowing full well that they had gloriously created the nineteenth century and perhaps the twentieth was going to be one too many for them'. In saying all this, Gertrude Stein, who may have been an expatriate but was also a staunch patriot, was offering an old and honourable American conviction – that the United States was a nation with a very special disposition toward progress and a distinctive relation to the future, and that with her democratic social order, her technological innovations, her advanced life-styles and her favoured alliance with history, the nation was intended to lead the way into and through the modern world. In the sphere of social and technological development, this was becoming more and more evident, as American industrial capacity boomed, outrunning global competition; it was becoming equally clear in geo-politics. In words that John Dos Passos would later use ironically at the start of his fictional trilogy *USA* (1937), Senator Beveridge announced, as the new century turned, 'The twentieth century will be American . . . The regeneration of the world, physical as well as moral, has begun . . .' Stein, with the assurance of the developments of forty more years behind her, was arguing yet more; Americans not only possessed the moral and physical domination of the new age, but led the way into the modern arts as well. Like other radical figures of her time – we could call the whole thing the Harriet Monroe Doctrine – she considered that, while Modernism had European roots and was born from Europe's intellectual, political and artistic tensions and contentions, it was the natural possession of Americans, of a piece with their modernizing change. They nurtured, developed and eventually transported the tendency, and in the measure of history it was they to whom the modernity of modern art belonged.

In suggesting all this, Gertrude Stein was offering a twentieth-century version of an already well-established American doctrine. American literature had always promised to be the literature of the future – the more so since it had little of a past and an always unstable present. Melville saw the nation itself as an avant-garde, advancing through the world of untried things; it was natural that its arts should be avant-garde as well. Whitman, too, viewed the experimental note of his verse as an expression of the experimental spirit of American life, a reflection of its new democratic relations and encompassing hope for the future. But, though not novel, Stein's view was sharpened by her own capacious identification with the new century itself, and her intuition for what its new forms would be: an art of experiment, abstraction, consciousness, the changed space–time continuum. Admittedly the roots and origins of these arts did not necessarily lie in the American tradition, and American culture did not automatically support them. As Stein put it herself: 'And so in the beginning of the twentieth century when a new way had to be found naturally they needed France.' Settling in Paris in 1903, and remaining there as an American patriot ('America is my country and Paris is my home town'), she became a kind of aesthetic American ambassador to the court of Cézanne,

Picasso and Matisse, stimulating activity, funding aesthetic terrorism and always sending reports home; she was, amongst other things, one of a significant new generation of American patrons of the new European avant-garde who helped fill the art collections of Americans with the most novel developments (we can see the benefits of their enterprise in American art museums today). She was also one of many American writers who found that the best way to be experimental was to take America at a distance; like James and Edith Wharton, Ezra Pound and T. S. Eliot, she helped guide an essential artistic transition that allowed the major art movements of the new century to step westward across the Atlantic and, it could be fairly argued, reach their point of richest and ripest growth there.

This partial detachment becomes very comprehensible when we examine the cultural spirit and character of the United States at the beginning of the century. The nation was indeed venturing on the new century with a fresh confidence, supported by that explosion of power and energy that Henry Adams identified in *The Education of Henry Adams* (1907) – the ironic autobiography which can justly be seen as one of the great works of the new century – as the modern motor of history, the Dynamo that had replaced the Virgin. But, most observers agreed, the nation that had a high claim on modernity and modernization did not yet have Modernism, or anything like it. Adams pointed to the dilemma: the coming of the twentieth century marked the coming of a whole new age in the history of force. In 1900 'the continuity snapped' and 'an avalanche of forces had fallen on [the human mind] which needed new mental powers to control ... It must merge in its supersensual universe, or succumb to it'. The modern 'multiverse' had been born, and it displaced all past educations – including Adams's own. And Adams's ironic view of the United States as a land of force without culture, energy without intellect, was to last long in twentieth-century American cultural self-analysis. In literary and artistic matters, the America of the early twentieth century was still dominated by the Genteel Tradition, the lineage of Bryant, Longfellow and Lowell, by Mark Twain and Howells, provincialism and 'innocence', by a sense of cultural seclusion that, Henry F. May suggests in *The End of American Innocence* (1959), really only began to disappear after the First World War. Even then, many writers of the 1920s found the spirit of Puritanism and Prohibition, materialism and Middletown, defeating, and followed Stein to Europe.

The America of 1901 was not an artistic country; it was, said

James Gibbons Huneker, a land of bathtubs, not bohemia. When Henry James revisited his native land in 1904–5 and recorded his impressions in *The American Scene* (1907), he saw power and mass growing without recognizable culture. To Ezra Pound, who became a power in London Modernist circles much as Stein did in the Parisian ones, the United States was 'a half-savage country, out of date'. According to George Santayana's famous essay on 'The Genteel Tradition in American Philosophy' (1911), the American mind was divided between Will and Intellect; the will inhabited the skyscraper, the intellect the colonial mansion. 'Human nature in America exists on two irreconcilable planes, the plane of stark intellectuality and the plane of stark business,' Van Wyck Brooks was still complaining in 1915. Brooks, now, was sensing a change, the beginning of America's 'coming-of-age'. But the notion of a society split between the material and the cultural, the provincial and the cosmopolitan, the genteel and the raw social fact, was repeated again and again into the twenties. Art seemed displaced, its capitals elsewhere, in Europe. In his companion studies *The Ordeal of Mark Twain* (1920) and *The Pilgrimage of Henry James* (1925), Brooks represented the American writer as pressed into either vulgarity or exile. In *Civilization in the United States* (1922), a collection of essays by leading intellectual figures edited by Harold Stearns, most contributors concluded that there was none. Indeed Stearns's brutally simple advice to young American artists, 'Get out!', was taken by many of the leading talents of the new literary and artistic generation of the post-war years, many of whom expatriated, for a time at least, to Paris – and the influence of such figures as Gertrude Stein and Ezra Pound.

Here there is a paradox. In retrospect, we can see that over this period a major modern literature was growing in America – perhaps the literature that has most dominated literary culture in this century, pointed many of its main directions and raised many of its fundamental aesthetic questions. The two or three generations that now emerged contained many extraordinary talents, and this was one of the most productive periods the American arts have had. 'A second flowering,' Malcolm Cowley called the 1920s, comparing it with the 'American Renaissance' of Melville, Hawthorne, Emerson, Thoreau and Whitman just before the Civil War: the great achievement that in the 1920s suddenly became what Van Wyck Brooks called 'a usable past', displacing the dominant Genteel Tradition. It was Cowley who emphasized the spirit of exile that drove expatriates to Paris in the 1920s, but, as he stressed, they did return again, and while in Paris they related experimental European influences to themes and issues distinctly national. For though in the 1920s American culture remained mercantile and often profoundly provincial, the culture of what H. L. Mencken gleefully called 'the booboisie', the experience of European war and the excitements of the era that followed it – when, said F. Scott Fitzgerald, the author who most exactly caught the mood of the time, 'something subtle passed to America, the style of man' – made the new arts appear all of a piece with the new speed of life, the new spirit of jazz, the flapper and the new woman, the lure of the city, the break with the farm. The 1920s was a decade of conflict between the old and the new, a conflict dramatized in many of its most spectacular events: the Red Scare, the Scopes trial, the trial and execution of Sacco and Vanzetti. What was clear, however, by the end of that decade, when Sinclair Lewis was awarded the Nobel Prize for Literature, the first American author to achieve that honour, was that if America frequently outraged and offended its literary talents, it was nonetheless amazingly capable of producing them.

The paradox leads to a conflict of interpretation, very evident in the arts of the first twenty years of the new century. There was Gertrude Stein's patriotic, positive view: the new arts began in America because they were in the American spirit, but they needed to go to Europe for blessing and confirmation. There was a darker account, expressed by Ezra Pound: the 'half-savage country, out of date', was a materialist and provincial society that always exiled its artists, forcing them abroad to learn how to read, construct a usable past, discover the new *paideuma*, and then seek to reflect back to the United States news it could not comprehend. Similar views came from Adams, James, Stearns, Brooks, Mencken and many more, the great cultural critics of early modern America. But, as Pound came to acknowledge, the American 'Risorgimento' for which he called did, marvellously, happen, and took on its own distinctive energies and its own American character. It now appears to us the more remarkable because in the short history of American literature this twentieth-century component is central, important in a way that modern literature cannot quite be in nations with longer lines of artistic inheritance. At the same time, it cannot be explained on native grounds alone, as a product of what Hugh Kenner has called, in a book of the same title, 'the homemade world': as he puts it, America 'got, want it or not, its own modernism, a homemade variety'. But, like so much in modern American culture, it came from heterodox and plural sources, expatriate borrowings as well as the development of native funds. Yet, as Kenner says, it had a homemade aspect; and the result was something more than a simple assimilation of the European modern arts. Hence it calls for a double explanation – one that looks both to the developments of international experimentalism, and to the driving forces that were, despite the scepticism of the contemporary cultural critics, changing American artistic culture itself.

II

To look back now to the America of 1901 is indeed to look back to a culture that was in many ways basking in its own innocence, as critics like Henry F. May and Larzer Ziff have proposed. Ziff suggests in his *The American 1890s* (1967) that even the radical stirrings of the 1890s (when the American arts seemed to carry the weight of a *fin de siècle* aestheticism, as well as a new desire for liberation, social, sexual and psychological) were fading by the century's turn. Several of the major figures of the new tendencies driving toward naturalism and aestheticism – Stephen Crane, Frank Norris, Kate Chopin – died around this time. The most important book consecutive to their achievement, Theodore Dreiser's extraordinary *Sister Carrie* (1900), was, symbolically, half-hidden and virtually suppressed by its publisher, who had taken it on Norris's recommendation. The arts of the Genteel Tradition still exercised their dominant power, and would do so until well into the 1920s. The stirrings of *fin de siècle* bohemianism that had grown in the late nineteenth century – in Ambrose Bierce, Lafcadio Hearn, Richard Hovey, Henry Harland, Stuart Merrill and James Gibbons Huneker – seemed to weaken, and the experimental spirit of the new arts seemed remote from the America of Theodore Roosevelt. If there was a strong radical tradition, fed by populism and progressivism, it bore all the marks of American provincialism. The spirit of realism and naturalism deposited by the previous generation turned into a form of practical journalism, exemplified by Upton Sinclair's *The Jungle* (1906), which Jack London described as the *Uncle Tom's Cabin* of wage slavery. The newer writers called themselves 'muckrakers' and 'reformers', and their virtues lay less in their aesthetics than in their polemics and adventurous progressivism.

Yet the aesthetic and theoretical ideas that had shaped the new American arts – the self-questioning forms of realist naturalism that had grown in the work of Crane and others in the 1890s, the poetic heritage of Whitman, the philosophical weight of American Pragmatism – had not entirely faded. William James, Henry's brother, drove home the concept of what he called the 'pluralistic universe', a view of the contemporary epistemological and philosophical situation which resembles Henry Adams's assumption of the mind confronted with an avalanche of transformation in the face of the modern multiverse. But where Adams saw the individual self as the swamped victim of historical forces external to the self, William James worked in another direction: the direction of that pragmatism that was to be such a strong power in the evolution of a modern American philosophy, making consciousness rather a response to outward events and inner purposes than a transcendental viewer. James's pragmatic psychology deserves our full attention. He not only influenced some important writers, including his own brother and Gertrude Stein, who studied with him, but also those who, in the manner of Theodore Dreiser, aimed to examine human awareness as a product of social causes and pressures. The pragmatic enterprise was intended to unify rather than to separate the relation between the self and the external world; it was to some degree an attempt to resolve that crisis of intellect that men like Adams, who felt their aesthetic and intellectual abilities displaced by the gross materialism and practicality of American life, represented. But pragmatism's key emphasis on psychology and consciousness made it a form of modern awareness that could open out toward both a high aesthetic insight and an analysis of consciousness that led the way toward Bergson and Freud. Pragmatism also made much of the 'experimental' disposition, and this too was an important heritage from the 1890s that was to stimulate and feed the generation that emerged into the new century.

Here we might consider the example of Miss Stein herself, that self-conscious prototype of the new woman who went to the Harvard Annex (later Radcliffe College) to engage with the original minds at work there in experimental psychology and philosophy – including William James, Josiah Royce, and George Santayana. She found enough there, mostly from William James, to learn to distrust the neo-Darwinian and evolutionary views of determinism that had shaped many of her literary predecessors, and her sceptical views of causation and conventional chronicity led her to write in the manner of anti-realism. Her experimental attitude really began in medicine, and she was soon developing her own theories of causality in consciousness. She went on to the new graduate medical school at Johns Hopkins, and again found herself in a place of new opportunities. Such schools represented – especially for a self-consciously new woman like Stein – a fresh possibility for the living of the intellectual life in the United States, and, if experimentalism means, as frequently it does, the opportunity to seize upon and extend opportunities so far closed, then we can see the logic of her step from there to Paris in 1903. She went there then with her brother Leo, a Harvard aesthete and art-collector who was very much in the tradition of Bernard Berenson and George Santayana, and moved from medicine to an experimental writing done in the manner of the most modern painting.

Part of the story of the new spirit of modern writing is, then, of the growth of a new intelligentsia, benefitting from an expanding American educational system and the stimulus of new intellectual opportunities. Another important location is the world around the University of Pennsylvania, *circa* 1901–5, when three of the important new poets of the coming age, Ezra Pound, Hilda Doolittle and William Carlos Williams, were reading widely both in the European and the Oriental literatures. Again, there was the clear intellectual vigour of Harvard near 1909, when (independently of what was now going on around Pound and T. E. Hulme in London) young poetic undergraduates like T. S. Eliot and Conrad Aiken were enjoying the cult for Japanese *haiku* and the French symbolists, whose powerful influence radiates through the new poetry. The excitement of the new arts was spreading, under the influence of important figures like the photographer Alfred Stieglitz, and bohemias were growing in New York's Greenwich Village, California and Chicago. Indeed the Middle West was to be particularly well-represented in the burst of new artistic activity that, as Europe moved towards war, began to surge in Western literary, artistic and intellectual culture, as if in prescience of the historical fracture that was to come.

The stir in Europe had been more or less continuous from the 1890s, with major movements growing up in the first decade of the century: Cubism, Expressionism, Futurism and many more. In the United States the key time of change is later, around 1912–13, when the waves of new Modernist thought from Europe – Ibsen and Dostoevsky, Shaw and Wells, Bergson and Sorel and Freud – suddenly began to penetrate American life with remarkable speed. In 1912 (the year when all three principal presidential candidates affirmed a version of the Progressive ticket, Woodrow Wilson being elected to office) came the foundation of Harriet Monroe's important magazine *Poetry (Chicago)*, and other major 'little magazines' – *The Masses, The Seven Arts*, Margaret Anderson's *Little Review*, Alfred Kreymbourg's *Others* – were soon hosting the new spirit. In 1913 the Armory Show, the exhibition of Post-Impressionist and Cubist painting (analogous to that which had shaken the literary world of London in 1910, when, Virginia Woolf said, 'human nature changed') came to New York, Chicago and Boston, and crossed with the American 'Ashcan' school of neo-Naturalism to generate a major breakthrough in American painting. The change was paralleled in literature; Sherwood Anderson recognized Gertrude Stein as the prose equivalent of the new painting, and acknowledged her impact on his work. The expanding bohemias of Greenwich Village and Chicago opened up to the new sense of artistic opportunity, and the numbers of hopeful artists and self-liberators were soon driving rents above conventional levels for bohemian poverty. By 1916 there was enough Village emancipation around, in the form of artistic experiment, radical politics, Freudianism and feminism, to become material for familiar parody (as in Don Marquis's *Hermione and Her Little Group of Serious Thinkers*). The new campaigns and causes both in politics and the radical arts were clustering together, bringing new life-styles and patterns of behaviour, justifying the view that the evolutionary wheel had taken a turn, and that the 'progressive spirit', which was not quite Progressivism, had united a new, spirited and vitalistic principle of political, artistic and experientially radical experience.

By the time the United States entered the war in 1917 this whole new generation had already made its mark, and taken on the precarious cohesion *of* a generation. They included many major figures – Pound, Eliot, Aiken, Robert Frost, Williams, Hilda Doolittle, Wallace Stevens, Marianne Moore, Lindsay, Sandburg, Edgar Lee Masters and others in poetry; Stein, Dreiser, Willa Cather, Sherwood Anderson and Sinclair Lewis in fiction; Van Wyck Brooks, Randolph Bourne, and H. L. Mencken in critical thought – and expressed a new sense of opportunity. 'Looking back on it now,' wrote Mabel Dodge Luhan, one of the public figures of the period (she was drawn in prose by Gertrude Stein, reported her psycho-analysis in the Hearst press, and was to pursue D. H. Lawrence and marry an Indian), in her four-volume autobiography aptly called *Movers and Shakers* (1933–7), 'it seems as though everywhere, in that year of 1913, barriers went down and people reached each other who had never been in touch before; there were all sorts of new ways to communicate as well as new communications.' This is familiar revolutionary lore, but it refers to a truly prodigious transition. Over a short span of years America underwent a remarkable stylistic change and expansion, in the styles of life as well as styles of art, which rapidly took on international influence. The coming of the modern seemed to pass rapidly through the nation, of a piece with the automobile age, the time of new household technologies, the new flappers, the new young.

Was it importation from Europe, or the bursting out of a homemade tradition, that moment of outright breakaway from the European arts that fulfilled the long-standing American ideal of a declaration of literary independence? The argument was a schism, one that has lasted on in American writing ever since, as well as in critical interpretation of American literature. The two views each had powerful advocates: Pound and Eliot on one side, Stein and William Carlos Williams on the other. Pound read the essential tradition back into the international, comparative history of human culture, writing and reading, constructing a carefully selected historical and contemporary tradition. When in 1912 Harriet Monroe drew him in as foreign correspondent for her new Chicago magazine *Poetry*, he agreed in characteristic style. 'Are you for American poetry or for poetry?' he asked her, '. . . If I can be of any use in keeping you or the magazine in contact with whatever is most dynamic in artistic thought, either here [London] or in Paris – as much of it comes to me, and I do see nearly everyone that matters – I shall be glad to do so . . .' He declared that some boosting of American poetry was perfectly acceptable 'provided it don't mean a blindness to the art' and added: 'Any agonizing that tends to hurry what I believe in the end to be inevitable, our American Risorgimento, is dear to me.' But, he held, the new Risorgimento would come not from sentimentalism, traditionalism or collusion with provincial and genteel audiences, and his own proposals for the magazine were a study-session in the arts of the new:

I think if our American bards would study Rémy de Gourmont for rhythm, Laurent Tailhade for delineation, Henri de Regnier for simplicity of syntactical construction, Francis Jammes for humanity, and the faculty of rendering one's own time; and if they would get some idea of intensity from Tristan Corbière (since they will not take their Villon in the original) there might be some hope for American poetry.

This view did not, however, go down well with *Poetry*'s editors, still less its readers. It was certainly not where Monroe's hopes of poetry lay, for she came out of a different tradition of the new. She was former Laureate of the Chicago World's Columbian Exposition of 1893, where her 'Columbian Ode' had been declaimed to brass band accompaniment. Her aim for poetry was to generate a Chicago Renaissance; her ideal modern epic was one celebrating the building of the Panama Canal, and she regarded Joyce Kilmer's 'Trees' as one of her publishing triumphs. Her magazine took its feeling from the belief that the American mind was characteristically progressive in temper, and so she tolerated, without much liking, the experiments of Pound, Eliot, HD, Yeats, D. H. Lawrence and others that Pound provided (she famously wished to cut down 'Prufrock'); thus the magazine became the American bearer of the 'Imagist Manifesto'. But *Poetry* attracted a flood of new American poets, including William Carlos Williams, Wallace Stevens, Sara Teasdale, Edna St Vincent Millay, Marianne Moore, Vachel Lindsay and Carl Sandburg, the last two of whom, being Middle-Western, were much supported by the magazine. As her assistant editor Alice Corbin Henderson explained in a sharp retort to W. B. Yeats in an editorial of June 1914, after Yeats had told a *Poetry* dinner in Chicago it was too far away from Paris:

Mr Lindsay did not go to France for *The Congo* or for *General William Booth Enters Into Heaven*. He did not even stay on the eastern side of the Alleghenies ... He is realizing himself in relation to direct experience, and he is not adapting to his work a twilight zone which is quite foreign to him, as it is, generally speaking, to the temperament of the nation. He is working out his salvation in his own way. It will be his salvation at any rate, and therefore worth more to him than if he trundled in on the coat-tails of English or French credentials, and much more worth while to the nation.

What justified *Poetry* to itself was indeed this conviction of the experimentalism of the national temper itself, and in this it was largely parallel in mood to native agrarian radicalism. In other words, the spirit the paper was celebrating was that of 'provincial' Modernism, and this too played a large part in the American tradition. There were poets who skilfully cultivated it, including William Carlos Williams, who spent a significant period in France but who insisted always on the native base of his discoveries. 'I knew I could not live as Pound lived, and had, besides, no inclination to experiment,' Williams was to record in a somewhat ambiguous sentence in his *Autobiography* (1951). Yet Williams, who insisted that he wrote 'in the American grain', evidently owed much to Imagism, which in turn owed much to the British and European debates of the previous decade; so did Stevens and many more of the new American poets.

The American modern tradition, so central to the modern arts, was thus made of many sources and constructed from schisms and crucial dissents, in this resembling the experience of Modernism in Europe. 'Critically Eliot returned us to the classroom just at the moment when we felt we were on the point of escaping into matters much closer to the essence of a new art form itself – rooted in the locality which should give it fruit,' William Carlos Williams complained of *The Waste Land* in his *Autobiography*. But Williams was wise enough to realize the value of what was taught in the classroom, much of it the essence of the modern poetic arts. There can be no doubt that the new arts in America owe much to the European tradition and the influences that, in a classic American fashion, were assimilated by the expatriate writers of the pre-war years, most notably Stein and Pound. Yet so central became the American contribution that it grew reasonable to make large claims for their domination in the project. Modernism was, suggested Stein, the American way in art; said Pound, 'All the developments in English verse since 1910 are due almost wholly to Americans.' But they drew on European roots, and came from a divided tradition, both expatriate and native. Indeed the American enterprise of the first quarter of this century was largely concerned with reconciling the elements of this double tradition.

III

Thus, if we follow the development of the modern American novel through from the rather dull years before the First World War to the wonderful excitements of the 1920s, when a major generation of writers emerged, we can see these oscillations between the now nativized Naturalist tradition and the new lore of experiment playing a central part in its evolution. Up to about 1917, the year in which the United States entered the War, American fiction was dominated by largely social preoccupations. The important figures were writers like Upton Sinclair and Jack London, Edith Wharton and Ellen Glasgow, and the novel seemed largely a documentary genre. The late novels of Henry James, some of the most essential work of Modernism, appeared merely eccentric, and so indeed did the work of Gertrude Stein, whose move to Paris was really the occasion for becoming a prose writer. She had carried with her a novel-in-progress, *Quod Erat Demonstrandum* (not published until 1951, posthumously, as *Things As They Are*). But it was the experience of settling, with her brother Leo, who was collecting, in the middle of the Post-Impressionist, Fauvist and Cubist adventures of modern painting that were to transform and irradiate the twentieth-century arts that really made her an author. She began acquiring Cézannes, Matisses and Picassos; Picasso's portrait of her became a work on the way to Cubist abstraction, and the French and Spanish new painters became protégés and friends. When she began the adaptation of some stories by Flaubert that became *Three Lives* (1909), there were strong American influences, from the experiments in automatic writing of William James and others, and the late fiction of his brother Henry. But above all there was the impact of the new art, the manners of which she attempted to reproduce in fiction; *Three Lives* is notable for its central story *Melanctha*, a work of instantaneous consciousness which she explained by saying that 'there was a marked direction of being in the present although naturally I had been accustomed to past, present and future, and why, because the conception forming around me was a prolonged present...' The same prolonged present, and the same strong Cubist influence, underlay her next book, a massive work of fiction called *The Making of Americans* (written largely between 1906–8, though not published until 1925), which attempted a vast recuperation of American history seen in the 'continuous present'. She then turned to many painterly prose pieces, most notably those collected in *Tender Buttons*, which appeared in 1913, happily coinciding with the Armory Show. Sherwood Anderson, then just beginning writing, recognized in it a bareness of composition, a selective relevance, a concern with language as a power in its own right, that was, he said, 'vital for the artist who happens to work with words as his material'.

Anderson was one of many younger writers who, seeking a new way in American writing, chose to sit at the feet of Stein. And if the best American writing of the next generation, the novel of the 1920s, tends toward a conscious thinning of the naturalistic surface and a much more precise economy of word and stance, this has much to do with the tutorial influence of Paris and Stein. 'Begin over again – and concentrate,' she told Hemingway, when, after the war, she had become mentor to a whole new generation. Wise and influential as the advice was, her own work often seems to lack the concentration she commended; her verbal manner is both distilled and *loose*, freely associative in the spirit of the principles of automatic writing, and her modernism frequently a matter of repetitious mannerism, the world behind it being very domestic and uncomplicated, certainly lacking that sense of crisis and modern exposure to history as force which is so clearly present in the work of

Anderson, Hemingway, Scott Fitzgerald and William Faulkner, all of whom assimilated her impact. But in her work, doubly influenced by Pragmatism and Cubism, we can see a fundamental dissolution of realism and naturalism, a new species of fictional perspectivism growing, based on the conviction of a supreme contemporaneity – 'the new space–time continuum' – which has spatialized the temporal, the realistic and the historical sense. Her conviction of living in a world of fundamentally transformed relations, a new scenario of consciousness ('the composition in which we live makes the art we see and hear,' she said, explaining that everyone had become contemporary with modern composition) is what makes her a modern. Her work implied a dissolution not only of plot, character and conventional mimesis, and familiar structures of logical chronicity, but also the rigorous application of the authorial consciousness to the material it treats.

In all this, she appears to diverge a long way away from the naturalism of less urbane writers like Upton Sinclair, Jack London, Theodore Dreiser and 'muckraking' writers, many of them trained in journalism or what they would call 'the school of life', which largely marked the direction of the novel back home. Using Stephen Spender's distinction, we might see them as the 'contemporaries' by contrast to 'moderns' like Henry James or Stein herself: less concerned with aesthetic form than social material, less devoted to literature than life, less cosmopolitan than rootedly local and provincial. It would be hard to say of Dreiser, the most interesting of them all, what Anderson said of Stein, that he 'worked with words as his material'; his words seem rough-hewn, often ill-used, and they spread around or after the events they 'describe', as a journalist's do. The work of the newer naturalists thus feels bound to a flat, materialist view of society and history, a view that for Stein had been exploded by the Pragmatists' and the Cubists' sense of a plural universe, in which no single version of reality stands intact. Yet in some of the newer work of the American Naturalists, from Dreiser to Anderson, we can also see a significant dissolution of the solid material face of the world under the pressure of consciousness, displaying the same focus on the peculiarity and instability of the workings of the mind in relation to the material that is refined in Henry James or Stein. Certainly these two writers do continue some of the experiments discussed in the last essay of *American Literature to 1900* (Vol. 8 in this series), above all those of Stephen Crane, for whom the basis of the realist attempt to deal with the multiplied world – the world of the modern city, the modern world of life – required a new kind of novel, where prolixity and abundance pass beyond easy reconciliation.

Stein herself owed something to Naturalism; the Naturalist tradition in turn seems to owe something, either directly or indirectly, to Stein. At the same time, one difference between her and the newer 'muckraking' Naturalists is the engaged relationship they had with the problems they sought to explore, and the changing face of modern American life. Their major experiment seems one of subject-matter – Dreiser's treatment of sexuality, Sinclair's of the brutalities of the Chicago stockyards and the meatpacking industry – rather than form, their force that of having released into American writing, from first-hand experience, the proliferating detail and modern massing of the new industrial America. Their characteristic means and metaphors had been largely constructed for them in the fiction of the 1890s, in the work of Crane, Norris and Garland; the Naturalism of Jack London's *Call of the Wild* (1903) or Upton Sinclair's *The Jungle* (1906) now seems totally familiar; the underlying images of life as jungle, whether in the world of nature or the world of the city, now a commonplace. Journalism was always close to hand. In his *People of the Abyss* (1903) London ventures to the city of London, or rather to its East End and the almost unplumbed world of the unseen poor, while Sinclair's *The Jungle* functions as a dramatization of knowable facts, exploring the shocking conditions of the stockyards and their exploitation of immigrant labour. Here the writer leads the way, introducing the reader to what the author *saw*. In London, Jack London stalks supreme, a superman hero in a world of survivors and victims, sharing their situation but not their helpless despair; he is the investigator, waiting to act. So is Sinclair, though he writes without London's animal vigour of style. *The Jungle* is a fictionalized documentary, what we might now call a 'non-fiction novel', a savage detailing of the killing pace of factories and slums where the immigrants were forced to live for the short term of squalid lives. But, by making Jurgis both his hero and a representative victim, Sinclair is forced toward melodrama. Jurgis's victimization seems excessive, and his late conversion to the view that the solution lies in a socialist redistribution of power gives the novel a polemical rather than a dramatic resolution. Social radicalism does not necessarily generate literary radicalism, and London's and Sinclair's works last essentially because of their subject and their attitude.

But Theodore Dreiser is different, suggesting the larger potential that Naturalism was to have in the history of the modern American novel. He was consciously a 'new' writer, and he wrote with a lasting political urgency, but also an engrossed fascination with the material energies of American life. Like Stein, he came from an immigrant background, as more and more of the newer writers were to, though from a different, less urbane and cosmopolitan, social level of it. His father, German in origin, was a mill superintendent threatened with poverty through illness. Dreiser himself grew up among German-speaking Catholics in small-town Indiana, and he went to Chicago to work as a janitor. After a year of university education, he went on to become a successful newspaperman and magazine editor; his own social progress and liberation, as well as its constraints and imprisonments, is the essential story he tells. In this few rules of artistic discretion prevail, and when he seeks them they become grotesque art-gestures; and in most of his work he remains a dweller within, rather than an artistic observer of, the naturalistic world. The force of his work lies in that embodiment, presenting it as a total frame for existence. His novels live Naturalism, in all its aspects, as an efficient view of life. They encompass Naturalist failures (as in the defeat of Clyde Griffiths in the late work *An American Tragedy*, 1925), but also success, often won through acceptance of the animal vigour in this world. Not surprisingly Dreiser too is usually discussed in terms of his content; his new world of hotels, offices, factories, skyscrapers, of workgirls, salesmen, and contemporary 'types'. It is in fact when he reverts to the Naturalist laboratory of the 1880s, setting his characters into the web of character, heredity and environment ('Primarily, there were conditions under which she was brought to fifteen years of age,' begins his story *Sanctuary*), or when he interprets behaviour according to biological theories of human nature (the 'chemisms' and 'katastates' of *Sister Carrie*), that he seems most old-fashioned. But it is when he follows out, stage by stage, the detailed economy of want and desire, that he seems most modern and impressive as a writer.

There were many signs in the 1890s, I have suggested, that the world of realism and naturalism was being transformed by new views of consciousness; and Dreiser remarkably continues that development, not by the self-consciously abstract artistry of a Stein, but through his vision of a world in which consciousness is a kind of energetic machine, a countervailing force to the web of forces constituted by the animated world of the city and the social process. William James had given modern writing one of its most important metaphors in suggesting that consciousness was 'a river, or a stream', a continuum of mind in a world of flux (though he also suggested that the mind is a term without a referent, dependent on habit and external pressure to function). Dreiser's dominant image of consciousness was of a form of mechanical energy, of what he calls the 'clock' of thought. In *Sister Carrie* (1900), his greatest novel, the world of personal relationships is discounted, and we are concerned with the drifting of individuals within vast systems of force. Character is negligible, moral competence irrelevant, culture a gloss on success; what is central are the spiralling social ascents and descents of human existence. The ascent is Carrie Meeber's, as she runs away from her small-town home to Chicago, loses her virginity, and profits as a result, moving on from her free and easy lover Drouet to the more sophisticated Hurstwood, and finally becoming a stage success. The book is really an education of Carrie, conducted by the collective mass of common America and its material goods and possessions ('The voice of the so-called inanimate!'), an education that eventually and belatedly leads her toward an 'artistic' sense of 'culture' at the hands of an asexual young man who opens up her mind. But for Carrie, and essentially for Dreiser too, culture is the felt, instantaneous material life of America; each item of property, each event, is sufficient to itself, until its energy drains, the magic goes, and it is cast aside. The descent is Hurstwood's, caught as he is in a reverse spiral in which palsy of the will (Dreiser explains this chemically, in his familiar use of semi-science) ensures his downward social progress and a pauper's grave. Without irony or artistic detachment, Dreiser lives with each of his characters, creating society as solid, a fabric of energies and satisfactions in which human existence is immersed.

Dreiser's is a very pragmatic Naturalism, in which the material goods of society are talismans and hieroglyphs, generating the energy and animation of his characters. Hence the power of will in his superman hero Cowperwood, the hero of *The Financier* (1912), *The Titan* (1914) and *The Stoic* (1947, posthumous), a man of unmitigated desires, whose energy is celebrated as a naturalistic fact just as Clyde Griffith's murderous conflict of loyalties is seen as a chance collision of forces in *An American Tragedy*. By 1925, when it appeared, in the same year as *The Making of Americans* and *The Great Gatsby*, Dreiser's Naturalism seemed heavy and dated, but his unmistakeable force as a writer remains. By now, Dreiser and Stein appeared to represent contradictory literary impulses, one populist and one cosmopolitan, one concerned with the radical force of society, the other with the radical force of form. Yet both embody principles of consciousness founded on discontinuity, and both construct an energetically novel world of fiction. Indeed Dreiser's Naturalism shows well against more formal and refined kinds of the same impulse, like that to be found in some of the work of Edith Wharton (*Ethan Frome*, 1911) or Ellen Glasgow, writing of the experience of the stoic, defeated South (*The Deliverance*, 1904). Naturalism had indeed become part of the American literary temper, and was to leave its lasting mark on writers to follow, from Sherwood Anderson, who interestingly tries to reconcile the two modes, to Ernest Hemingway, John Dos Passos and John Steinbeck. In a broad sense modern American fiction has sought to bring together these two streams: one coming from the Naturalist tradition, dealing with the world of biological energies, urban life, social pressures and drives, and one coming from the Modernist preoccupation with form and consciousness. Yet there is a Naturalist aspect to Stein's work – in her portrait of Melanctha, in her sense of the fundamental tropisms of consciousness – as there is a Modernist face to Dreiser's, in his portrait of energy driving life and moving toward final entropy. Other notable novelists emerged in the period – most notably Edith Wharton, writing in another part of Paris of a social world that has a surface of culture and an underlying base of economics. Lily Bart, in her *The House of Mirth* (1905), is a highly specialized product who finds that it 'certainly simplified life to view it as a perpetual adjustment, a play of party politics, in which every concession had its recognized equivalent; Lily's tired mind was fascinated by this escape from fluctuating ethical estimates into a region of concrete weights and measures'. But in different modes Stein and Dreiser display the world where ethical estimates indeed fluctuate and consciousness faces reality directly in ways that point to the sensibility of a good deal of later, postwar American fiction. By the 1920s, with Anderson, Hemingway, Fitzgerald, Faulkner, Dos Passos, the modern and modernized American novel was an assured form. And by now, too, both Dreiser, the arch-Naturalist, and Stein, the arch-experimentalist, had become essential parts of its heritage.

IV

And in the years before the 1920s a somewhat similar heritage was growing in American poetry.[1] Once again a significant centre of the

---

[1] See also Chapter 4, by Geoffrey Moore, for a discussion from a different angle.

change was Europe, and this time Britain – to which, in 1908, Ezra Pound came, by way of Venice, searching, he said, for W. B. Yeats, and hoping to 'make it New'. Pound's arrival coincided with a ferment of poetic change which had begun during the 1890s, owed much to the impact of French symbolism, and led slowly toward what C. K. Stead has called 'the new poetic'; with that change, Pound himself, his London friend and compatriot T. S. Eliot, and other American visitors – Hilda Doolittle, John Gould Fletcher, and to some degree Robert Frost – were much involved. That transition of style and sensibility has become an exemplary case of Modernist development, with the dying away of the Victorian poetry of spiritual aestheticism and public oration, the rise of post-lyrical techniques of hardness and of free verse forms, and the general displacement of the Romantic tradition. 'Let us agree to call it [the new spirit in poetry] classicism,' suggested T. E. Hulme, and Eliot took up the word, associating it in due course with Anglo-Catholicism and Royalism. But if, as Hulme, Pound and others suggested, a new hardness and detachment were essential to the modern sensibility, that sensibility was made from complex sources. It drew on the British revolt against Victorianism, and its underlying Romanticism, on the ironic modes *and* on the opaqueness of French symbolism, on the intellectual and witty poetry of Donne, on the brevity of *haiku* and other Japanese forms, the coarse vernacular impulse of Villon, and the symbolist metaphysics of Yeats and the Celtic revival. Pound, who himself had a strong Romantic streak when he arrived in London, was to regard what he called the 'Forgotten School of 1909' as the key source in his personal history of the new arts, which moved toward the Imagist movement of 1912. The School's history was largely based on recent British developments from the 1890s onward, with decisive figures being Yeats, Edward Storer, T. E. Hulme, F. S. Flint, and more. James Joyce and D. H. Lawrence were more distantly related to these developments, but there was, largely thanks to Pound, an ever increasing American component; indeed, rarely before had British and American verse seemed so close together, and the intimacy affected both traditions, if in very different ways. Eliot became in effect a British poet and a powerful influence; Pound retained a strong contact with the American scene, proclaimed the Risorgimento, and finally, the War over, gave up London in disgust for the rival expatriate centre of Paris.

The question of the relative contributions of different poets to the making of the modern tradition remains contentious, in part because the view from London still remains different from that from New York. The British adopted Eliot and Pound, and to some degree Frost, but were and remain less acquainted with the American wing that developed partly by extension from London activities, partly in revolt against them. Poets like Williams, Wallace Stevens, Marianne Moore and later Hart Crane owe much to the distillation of an Anglo-American poetic Modernism that Pound achieved, through his delineation of Imagism, and his collection of the Imagist anthologies, in the two years before European war broke out. But they were making their own assimilation from similar influences – Wallace Stevens in effect posed in his early work as a French symbolist, and submitted poems to *Poetry* under the name of 'Peter Parasol' – and, as the spirit of cultural despair increased after Pound's publication of *Hugh Selwyn Mauberley* (1920), duly followed by the shattering impact of Eliot's great poem of modern sterility and dismay *The Waste Land* (1922), from an increased feeling of revolt against the pessimism of the European-based Moderns. English critics have largely tended to see the essential revolution occurring in American poetry, so leaving British poets with a sense of relation to the tradition through Hardy and Yeats; American critics have seen the main line as continuously American, running from Whitman through to William Carlos Williams, Hart Crane and then onward to more modern poets like Charles Olson, with Eliot and Pound as something of an aberration.

But neither account seems sufficient to explain the fundamental transformation that lies behind the modern forms of poetry, nor the emergence of the radical new aesthetic, philosophical and linguistic theories that have transformed twentieth-century poetics. Pound, undoubtedly, was a central figure, without whom the Anglo-American modern movement would probably not have cohered. This was not solely because of his intellectual or his poetic contribution, but because of his organizational energy. In some ways a traditional poet, he also acted as arch-innovator, the embodiment of the avant-garde ideal in a Britain where the avant-garde had never been strong, stirring London to action. In the arts he was, Wyndham Lewis said, a Baden-Powell, always trying to get artists under canvas, and schooling the young writers of the time in the principles of the new art. He single-handedly created much of the scenario for poetic Modernism, tackling the task as a military enterprise, a matter of campaigns, wars and revolutions, as indeed the avant-garde analogy insisted. It was he who invented movements (having Hilda Doolittle sign her poems

'HD, Imagiste'), took over magazines British and American, issued manifestos of modern dos and don'ts, promoted the major new writers, including Joyce and Eliot, and secured funds to support them. His remarkably generous campaign for the Risorgimento is one of the formative events of modern poetry and literary culture, which changed London and, largely through the mails, the United States. Pound's view of poetry was that it was fundamental to the politics of culture; this view fed *The Cantos*, his great work, drove him from London to Paris, Paris to Rapallo, constructed his support for Mussolini, and brought him at last to St Elizabeth's Hospital in Washington, unfit to plead on a treason charge. All this was the cosmopolitan – in the end the too cosmopolitan – Pound, who picked up the heritage from French symbolism and the Celtic twilight, transformed it under new intellectual pressures into Imagism, and generated a radical theory of modern culture and tradition.

Pound's sense of tradition, reflecting his education in comparative literature, was a massively eclectic, and some would say an autodidactic, one. It could also be considered, as could Eliot's, profoundly American. Tradition was not derived but created; it was not instinctively possessed, but sought with great labour; it was a search for new forms out of the chaotic imprint of the past and the claim modernity asserted in the present. It was misprision, a new way to read, an experimental enterprise. With various cautious qualifications, we can propose that Pound did not simply assimilate the European tradition in his London years, but also encouraged and browbeat his British and Irish contemporaries into acknowledging an American one. Certainly he struck those contemporaries as intensely American, and when he met Gertrude Stein in Paris she shrewdly observed him as the traditional American crackerbarrel philosopher ('a village explainer, excellent if you were in a village but if you were not, not,' she said in *The Autobiography of Alice B. Toklas*, 1933). Though he grew up mainly in the East, Pound came from Hailey, Idaho, and the Western background showed, not least in his economic theories. Going to the University of Pennsylvania (where at the age of fifteen he met Williams and Hilda Doolittle), he took his Master's degree in Comparative Literature in 1906, an education deriving in part from the earlier classic period of American cosmopolitanism represented by Ticknor, Cogswell and Longfellow – who himself wrote on Provence and translated the subject of Pound's thesis, Lope de Vega. Pound's early poetry, suffused with the troubadour spirit,

owed something to the poet-wanderer tradition celebrated by
Whitman and Richard Hovey. Also behind his work was a
pseudo-medieval spirit that had had its attractions in late
nineteenth-century America, as well as the *japonaiserie* fascination
of Whistler, Lafcadio Hearn and others. It was these traditions
Pound amended to relate himself to the lineage of 'classicism'
coming from influences like T. E. Hulme and the German
aesthetician Wilhelm Worringer.

Shortly after arriving in London, Pound put down some notes on
Whitman:

He *is* America. His crudity is an exceeding great stench, but it *is* America
... He is disgusting. ... Entirely free from the renaissance humanist ideal
of the complete man or from Greek idealism, he is content to be what he is,
and he is his time and his people ... And yet I am but one of his 'ages and
ages encrustations' or to be exact an encrustation of the next age. The vital
part of my message, taken from the sap and fibre of America, is the same as
his.

Pound's quarrel with Whitman preoccupied him greatly during the
London period, though he acknowledged that 'Mentally I am a Walt
Whitman who has learned to wear a collar and a dress shirt
(although at times inimical to both)'. We can see the classicism and
cultural elitism of his poetry as a revolt against Whitman's
egocentric subjectivism, and his rejection of a history of culture.
Whitman had celebrated America freely – its technological and
imperial growth matched his own democratic poetic imperialism.
Pound regarded poetry as an antithesis to materialism, and required
that culture be a cleansing of the usurious damage done to language
and the image. Nonetheless, as he was promoting Imagism in the
pages of *Poetry*, he was considering Whitman again: 'I make a pact
with you, Walt Whitman – / I have detested you long enough / ...
We have one sap and one root – / Let there be commerce between
us,' he wrote in his poem 'A Pact', a declaration of his connection
with a radical American poetic tradition. 'One main contrast between every page of my verses, compared with establish'd poems',
Whitman wrote in his *A Backward Glance*,

is their different attitude towards God, towards the objective universe, and
still more (by reflection, confession, assumption, &c) the quite changed
attitude toward the ego, the one chanting or talking, towards himself and
his fellow-humanity. It is certainly time for America, above all, to begin the
readjustment in the scope and basic point of view of verse, for everything
else has changed.

Whitman was the poet of 'make it new', and so was Pound himself.

Yet Pound was always to distinguish himself from much of the new American poetry that flew the Whitmanesque banner, especially from those *Poetry* poets who apparently took their Whitman straight, without benefit of European intercession:

> Hog Butcher for the World,
> Tool Maker, Stacker of Wheat,
> Player with Railroads and the Nation's
>   Freight Handler;
> Stormy, husky, brawling,
> City of the Big Shoulders,
> They tell me you are wicked and I believe them, for I
>   have seen your painted women under the gas lamps
>   luring the farm boys . . .

Whitman's populism clearly underlay Carl Sandburg's 'Chicago Poems', which appeared in *Poetry* in 1914. Vachel Lindsay's 'General William Booth Enters Into Heaven' came in January 1913, and in 1915 the magazine took up Edgar Lee Masters, who had just published his *Spoon River Anthology*. All Illinois-born, they carried mid-Western tonalities and vernacular into their verse, filled it often with the regional oratorical or tent-meeting temper, and were, like Whitman, 'content to be what one is'. For Lindsay, races, creeds and personalities blend into the fortunate onward progress of the race, everything swaying forward in a loose, vigorous, celebratory language fed with the rhythms of popular songs. For Sandburg vitality links nature and the urban world, so that in 'Skyscraper', one of his *Chicago Poems* (1916), nature and building fuse in the interaction between its structure and 'the sun and the rain, the air and the rust', which 'play on the building inside and use it'. Like Hart Crane, later, the modernity of the modern world did not produce cultural rage and despair, as it had for Pound, but a new Romanticism. In his portrait of the two hundred or so characters of *Spoon River Anthology*, Masters at least wrote something comparable in character to Sherwood Anderson's notable *Winesburg, Ohio* (1919), the collection of stories in which art comes out of human failure, isolation and solitude in an emptily Puritan culture. Masters's characters – all from the same small-town community, and all dead – have been trapped like Anderson's, by meaningless marriages, accidents at work, personal enmities, economic exploitation. Yet it is appropriate to the sentimental, all-inclusive Whitmanism that attracted many poets and writers of the time, that Masters attempts to unify the experiences, placing them in a world of opposed forces yearning for unity. Like Edwin Arlington Robinson and Robert Frost, he is saved by a residual naturalist bleakness, a sense that romantic fulfilments are not easily to hand. It can fairly be claimed that it was in that essential resistance *to* the modern that Pound feels most like a great modern poet, and his hardness, rejection of the tempting image or the sentimentalizing adjective, his sense of the fragmentation of culture, his awareness of a world that will not cohere, is what makes his work a fundamental expression of modern vision, which does not favour Whitmanesque inclusions, for good historical and experimental reasons.

The resistance is what helped construct a major tradition of modern poetry in America, one in which poets like Sandburg and Lindsay seem now small figures by comparison with far greater ones. Wallace Stevens, who seemed to begin as a playful symbolist quoting French symbolist verse and alluding constantly to French Cubist paintings, became through a slow evolution one of the great philosophers of Modernist poetry, a devout and exacting examiner of the nature of the modern imagination. William Carlos Williams, to my mind a far lesser poet than Stevens or Pound, also sustained a painterly enquiry into the nature of the modern image and the modern myth, an image and myth he steadfastly sought to domesticate and bring into the American grain. Hart Crane, like Sandburg, saw the task of the modern poet as to harmonize and poeticize the mechanical age, though his extraordinary late venture *The Bridge* (1930) poses to itself the difficulties of a modern romantic and mythical sensibility. Both Williams and Crane viewed themselves as antitheses to Eliot and Pound, seeing the twentieth-century American poet not in a condition of cultural crisis, but able to be a Modernist because, after all, America herself is new. Modernism may have been an international movement bred, in part, from the social, philosophical and cultural crises of Europe; but in America it could have a special place, reconciling itself to the modern American landscape, and to a native tradition written into the record and bred in the bone. In Europe largely a mode of despair, expressing the conflicts and anxieties of the prewar era and the anguish of the postwar one, founded on the disappearance of the creative and transcendent impulse from culture and history, on the displacement of the word, it could be for some American poets the discourse of hope and gratified perception. Pound sought to reconstitute the image as the antithesis to a debased culture; for

Williams the image itself was largely enough, and poetry grew not from the energetic resistance in the image but from the domestication of the familiar and the local, from inherent principles of growth in things and men. And Modernism could be got not from Paris or learning the new *paideuma* but from the experience of 9 Ridge Road, Rutherford, New Jersey.

There was, of course, a profound art in Williams's classic innocence, as there was even more in Wallace Stevens's. Nonetheless, Williams's belief that the American language itself embodied the nature of the new poetic ('For under that language to which we have been listening all our lives a new, more profound language, underlying all the dialectics offers itself'), and was an expression of the open fertility of local and national life, restated the promise that America was indeed the locus of poetic radicalism. American language, mediated through the mouths of Polish mothers, was the clue, and Whitman the guide – the Whitman who 'always said that his poems, which had broken the dominance of the iambic pentameter in English prosody, had only begun his theme. I agree. It is up to us, in the new dialect, to continue it by a new construction upon the syllables'. The view was congenial to many American moderns – to Stevens ('the poem is the cry of its occasion'), Frost, Hart Crane and E. E. Cummings, constituting a tradition still usable in the present. In that evolution, the European sources and connections of this apparently American impulse have grown more distant and remote. Yet the modern American poetic tradition retains its double heritage, one which remains its long-term challenge.

V

The cosmopolitan *and* national construction of the modern American tradition in fiction and poetry over the first two decades of the century, which is my theme here, was to reach its greatest point of enrichment during the 1920s. Inescapably related to the extraordinary transformation of the arts that passed through the Western nations from the 1890s to the period of reassessment that followed the First World War, it acquired, by selective assimilation and emendation by American myths and American versions of tradition, its own flavours. These had to do with a different experience of history, a different attitude toward myth, a different view of the prospect of the future; they had also to do with that endeavour to recover a usable American past which would allow the

American arts to break free of European dependences. But the result of the contact with Europe, direct or indirect, was a relation to international modern style which has been a decisive aspect of the modern American arts. In some ways a literature more native than it had ever been, finding a relation to its own, recovered literary past in Melville and Hawthorne and Twain, in Poe and Whitman and Emily Dickinson, it was also part of the international spirit of the modern arts. In due time, American writing, which at the beginning of the century seemed on the fringes of the Modern movement, came closer and closer to its centre. When American writers arrived in Paris in the 1920s, a confident new generation, they in turn took much from European Modernism, from Joyce, from Proust, from Mann; they equally seemed to contribute much to the Modernist spirit and its radical events, such as the 'Revolution of the Word'. In general it was not the specific movements that drew them, but the radical climate of style-making itself, and the atelier instruction they could gain from Stein, Pound and the other leaders of the great seminar of the modern.

The Modern impulse in America owed much not only to the European Modern movement but also to what had been assimilated earlier, especially the Naturalism of the 1880s and 1890s. But the transition of the American arts from nineteenth- to twentieth-century culture was conducted without the revolutions and upheavals that had marked the similar process in Europe. The new arts outraged some, but they won a relatively rapid acceptance, and in the 1920s a writer like Hemingway could move from being an avant-garde to a popular figure with considerable speed. The American writer seemed always to have been the prophet of a future to come. Certainly in the 1920s the obstacles persisted, the Genteel Tradition and the Puritan heritage had by no means died. But the change to the new arts was assisted, paradoxically, less by the aesthetic struggles of writers in conflict with their culture than by the change and development within America itself, as technological and material advance speeded, life-style changed and experimentalism in art complemented a sense of historical experimentalism in life. The outstanding writers of the American 1920s – Anderson, Fitzgerald, Faulkner, Hemingway and Dos Passos in fiction, Pound, Eliot, Stevens, Crane, Moore, Williams, Cummings and Edna St Vincent Millay in poetry, Eugene O'Neill and Maxwell Anderson in drama – established a tradition of the new which was assimilated, with sudden changes of fortune, into American culture, and they constructed a major tradition. When, after the Second World War, a darker sense of history and a changed view of form, the relation of the perceiver to the thing perceived, began to reshape American culture, it seemed natural, in time, to speak of this movement as Post-Modernism, a logical development of the American line. Like what went before, it owed much to influences outside, but it seemed at home in the nation that was bringing modernizing change to the world. In 1946 Gertrude Stein died, having said that the atomic bomb did not interest her; and Pound was tested for insanity. The reputations of Hemingway and Faulkner remained high; the work of Fitzgerald, who had died in 1940, was revived. Poetry extended the tradition of Williams, and in poets like John Ashbery the heritage persists. American writing spread in international influence, as an aspect both of power and artistic force. Stein's prophecy for the American arts proved curiously true.

2

THE LANGUAGE OF AMERICAN FICTION
BETWEEN THE WARS

Dennis Welland

I

In 1940, in 'East Coker', T. S. Eliot looked ruefully back over
what had been for him 'Twenty years largely wasted, the years of
l'entre deux guerres'. It seems perverse to borrow the phrase as a
description of what is more usually considered a period of remarkable development in the American novel, and yet the
achievements of the inter-war years are in some ways diminishing
in impressiveness as they recede. Extended, however, the
quotation from Eliot highlights with particular clarity the parallel
between him and the novelists, for they too were 'trying to learn to
use words' and for many of them every attempt seemed both 'a
wholly new start, and a different kind of failure'.

Sherwood Anderson, for example, in *A Story Teller's Story*
(1924) tries to dramatize the excitement of literary creativity:

Now for the pen or the pencil and paper and I shall make you feel this
thing I now feel – ... just the dark, brooding thing in the soul of that
laborer going homeward under those trees. He is getting old and was
born an American. Why did he not rise in the world and become the
owner or at least the superintendent of a factory and own an automobile?

Aha! You do not know, but I do. You wait now, I shall tell you. I have
felt all, everything. In myself I have no existence. Now I exist only in these
others.

I have run home to my room and have lighted a light. Words flow.
What has happened? Bah! Such tame, unutterably dull stuff! There was
something within me, truth, facility, the color and smell of things. Why, I
might have done something here. Words are everything. I swear to you I
have not lost my faith in words....

There is no reason at all why I should not have been able, by the
instrumentality of these little words, why I should not have been able to
give you the very smell of the little street wherein I just walked.

The affectation of artlessness and the overtones of Walt Whitman make the passage seem further removed from the sophisticated prose fiction of the period than in fact it is. It exemplifies conveniently four characteristics of that fiction: its concern with the everyday life of ordinary people; its desire, in Whitman's words, 'to prove this puzzle the New World, / And to define America, her athletic Democracy'; the conviction that the artist's task is to render the physical facts of experience, not merely to describe his own emotional response to those facts; and the realization that these concepts, however clear to the novelist's imagination, will defy ready translation into words.

The passage is thus Anderson's equivalent to the much better-known statement of Hemingway in *Death in the Afternoon* (1932) speaking of himself in the 1920s:

I was trying to write then and I found the greatest difficulty, aside from knowing truly what you really felt, rather than what you were supposed to feel, and had been taught to feel, was to put down what really happened in action; what the actual things were which produced the emotion that you experienced . . . ; but the real thing, the sequence of motion and fact which made the emotion and which would be as valid in a year or in ten years or, with luck and if you stated it purely enough, always, was beyond me and I was working very hard to try to get it.

Neither Anderson nor Hemingway denies the legitimacy of the writer's concern with emotion: what both are wary of is the bogus emotion that a facile writer can generate by too uncritical a use of language. Both are moving along their own lines towards Eliot's idea of the 'objective correlative'. 'Trying to learn to use words' involved, for that generation especially, the recognition of what words *not* to use because they had already been debased. Aware that he was, by his nature, 'a word fellow, one who could at most any time be hypnotized by high-sounding words', Anderson saw words as vulnerable to two particular enemies:

During the World War did we not see how even the very government went into the advertising business, selling the war to the young men of the country by the use of the same noble words advertising men used to forward the sale of soap or automobile tires?

In the same spirit Hemingway, in Chapter 27 of *A Farewell to Arms* (1929), makes his soldier-hero condemn the degradation of language for purposes of propaganda, and protest that 'Abstract words such as glory, honour, courage or hallow were obscene'. 'All our words from loose using have lost their edge', he said on another occasion. E. E. Cummings used the same image, suggesting that such words

> like Gillette Razor-Blades
> having been used and reused
> to the mystical moment of dullness emphatically are
> Not To Be Resharpened.

Sharpness of rendition the novelist certainly wanted but he also followed Ezra Pound's advice to 'Make it new'. Probably at no previous time had the novelist come so close to the poet in the nature of his concern with the words he used: he shared the responsibility 'to purify the language of the tribe'.

At the same time he was even more certain that it was the language of the *tribe* with which he was concerned. A contradiction that worried Anderson was this:

Did it come to this, that Americans worked, made love, settled new western states, arranged their personal affairs, drove their Fords, using one language while they read books, wanted perhaps to read books, in quite another language?

Disillusioned with the aftermath of the First World War, the United States was tempted to withdraw into itself, and one form of withdrawal was for its writers to dissociate themselves from the literary language of England, the language in which the war propaganda had been couched. In 1919 H. L. Mencken had published *The American Language*, a provocative and massive piece of erudition that had tried to see in contemporary American usage an equivalent to the fertility, vitality and innovating energy of Elizabethan English. Conscious that an American Shakespeare would have enhanced the plausibility of his argument and unable to identify one, Mencken often falls back upon special pleading, but the notion of American as a suitably creative literary language had an undeniable appeal to many writers. That it gained strength among Americans living and writing in Europe – this is, of course, the great period of the expatriate writer – is less paradoxical than it seems, for in Europe they came particularly under the influence of Gertrude Stein. Her theories of language, less chauvinistic and more literary in their sophistication than Mencken's, attracted Anderson, Hemingway, Fitzgerald and many more. All of them, with varying degrees of self-assertion, came to feel that they could make their own way without her, but the ways they made led in directions to which she had pointed. In saying 'I am servant to the words' Anderson was paralleling Gertrude Stein's 'feeling of words doing as they want to do and as they have to do when they have to live'. When a critic says that for her 'the word had to have not its romantic or literary meaning but the immediate meaning it had to the contemporary using it, a literal axiomatic meaning confined to the simple situations of the average life', he could be describing the linguistic aims of many novelists.

To render 'the simple situations of the average life' was a challenge that could best be met by a judicious use of the simple language of the average life. 'Suppose,' Anderson speculated, 'everyone in America really hungers for a more direct and subtle expression of our common lives than we have ever yet had and that we are all only terribly afraid that we won't get it.' This is what his *Winesburg, Ohio* had attempted in 1919; that a similar impulse underlay Joyce's *Dubliners* or the work of D. H. Lawrence is a salutary reminder that the Americans had no monopoly in this territory. Both could have subscribed to Anderson's plea for 'a more direct and subtle expression of our common lives'; so, on his own terms, could Hemingway. The reconciliation of the direct with the subtle is a characteristic of the fiction of the age and one to which Gertrude Stein, among others, contributed.

Convinced that America had discovered the twentieth century and that 'the past did not matter', she tried repeatedly to define America and to differentiate between Americans and other nationals. Beneath its occasionally deceptive cosmopolitanism American fiction of this period is similarly preoccupied, though often with less buoyant optimism than Miss Stein. John Dos Passos, whose trilogy *USA* has been rightly called 'one of the saddest books ever written by an American', ends his introductory attempts at definition with the assertion 'But mostly *USA* is the speech of the people'. In the novels of the inter-war years the American vernacular took on the stature of a tradition, and when Hemingway made his over-quoted observation that 'All American literature comes out of one book by Mark Twain called *Huckleberry Finn*', this was no doubt one of its characteristics that he had in mind. But the vernacular is important in *Huckleberry Finn* less for its novelty than as an expression of the limited sensibility and restricted awareness of its narrator. It acquired a similar importance in fiction between the wars.

'Sometimes', said Somerset Maugham once, 'the novelist feels himself like God . . . sometimes, however, he does not; and then he . . . grows less and less inclined to describe more than his own experience has given him. The first person singular is a very useful device for this limited purpose.' American novelists seem especially susceptible to the Emersonian doctrine of 'Only so much do I know as I have lived', and none more so than the novelists of this period. Their manipulation of narrative, either by the first person singular or by a point of view carefully focused through one character's vision, may be shown to derive in part from Conrad and Henry James, but more importantly it reflects a changing outlook on life and on human personality. Eliot's J. Alfred Prufrock, in his self-depreciation, epitomizes the role of many fictional protagonists: 'No, I am not Prince Hamlet nor was meant to be.' Even the 'tough' hero of Hemingway's fiction – if he is not, as so often happens, to be over-simplified by his readers more than by his creator – must be recognized as sharing in the non-heroic vulnerability of the ordinary man which became increasingly the preoccupation of the novelists in this period and which is as much reflected in their styles and their techniques as in their plots and their subjects.

II

The ordinary man in 'the simple situations of the average life' looked as though he had come into American fiction in the pages of Sinclair Lewis's *Main Street* (1920) or *Babbitt* (1922). The real-estate agent of the later book bumbles in goodnatured bewilderment from one familiar experience to the next, learns little in the process, but remains self-consciously aware of some of his own inadequacies and consoles himself with dreams of his fairy-girl like Prufrock with his mermaids. It was Lewis's achievement to have created in Babbit a character not so much in the fictional sense as in the sense in which Elizabethan writers like Earle and Overbury created 'characters' by encapsulating in stylized prose a type familiar to their age. Babbitt's name passed into the common language to denote the type, and from it Mencken gleefully coined the abstract noun Babbittry, while declaring with satisfaction that he knew 'of no American novel that more accurately presents the real America'. E. M. Forster was to make a similar point in 1929 more critically, suggesting that Lewis had helped 'to lodge a piece of a continent in our imagination' by having 'brought down some snapshots to show us and posterity'. The image catches the essentially static and descriptive nature of the book; plot and story give way to episodes, set pieces and 'characters' caught with all the externally accurate fidelity of the camera and giving the pleasure of recognition afforded by the snapshot or its modern successor, the holiday slide. Its immediate popularity might have indicated its true quality, for the popular novel is usually the one that gives a slightly new twist to an established pattern rather than the one that strikes out with experimental daring. As much 'the Story of a Simple Soul' as *Kipps*, *Babbitt* is an H. G. Wells social novel in an American setting, underpinned with the same sort of observation of external details that Virginia Woolf censured in Arnold Bennett; but, as E. M. Forster complained, we are 'never even given as wide a view as Arnold Bennett accords us of his Five Towns'. Saved by its episodic nature from the strained coincidences that the necessity of story imposed on *The History of Mr Polly*, it lacks also the bursts of inventive humour, Dickensian in their exuberance, that enliven Wells's novel. Indeed, what looks like comic invention may be seen in truer perspective if the world of *Babbitt* is compared with the sociological study of Muncie, Indiana, published in 1929 as *Middletown* by Robert and Helen Lynd. The ground covered by the two works is so similar, individual scenes are so closely parallel, that, had *Middletown* appeared before *Babbitt*, Lewis would have been suspected of using it as a source. Mencken spoke prophetically in hailing *Babbitt* as 'a social document of a high order'. In almost identical words Henry James had praised the work of William Dean Howells as 'in the highest degree *documentary*'. For all the scorn with which he affected to regard Howells, Lewis had not advanced the novel much beyond him. He had not focused his subject-matter clearly enough, and what to a superficial reader looked like robust satire was on close inspection seen to be a rather sentimentalized tribute to conformity. In an unpublished introduction to *Babbitt* he had written revealingly 'there are those of us who hesitated about being drafted into the army of complacency'. *Babbitt* is exactly that – a hesitation. It could have been a step forward but Lewis, like Babbitt, consented to being drafted. As Forster put it, 'In Mr Lewis, curiosity about the universe has never been very strong'.

Sherwood Anderson had 'the feeling that Lewis never laughs at all, that he is in an odd way too serious about something to laugh'; with his 'amazing attention to the outer details of lives' he has 'found out a lot of things about us and the way we live in our towns and cities, but I am very sure that in the life of every man, woman and child in the country there are forces at work that seem to have escaped the notice of Mr Lewis'. It was these forces that Anderson sought to evoke in *Winesburg, Ohio*: his 'curiosity about the universe' extended to people ordinary in a sense very different from

Babbitt. Their inadequacies, more deep-seated and more disturbing than his, are wounds, not foibles, sources not of comedy but of pathos and even, at times, of tragedy. Their incomprehension worries them in ways that do not trouble Babbitt. They are not sheltered by the middle-class affluence into which he can retreat, and they are ill-equipped by their upbringing to cope with their inbuilt hereditary failings. In the terms of Anderson's introduction they are, in their blinkered and desperate clutching at what they believe to be truths, grotesques. A rudimentary psychology, perhaps, but a psychology nonetheless, and the success of *Winesburg, Ohio* lies in its memorable capturing of the significance, in ordinary lives, of the insignificant; an event, trivial to anyone else, becomes, to the person experiencing it, an adventure. These epiphanies are embodied in short stories of varying length, uneven in their attempted lyric delicacy, but at times evocative and disturbing. A formal unity is given to the whole not merely by their taking place in Winesburg and by a carry-over of characters from one tale to another, but by the writer's imagination and vision.

For the 1920s, Anderson was a seminal writer in a way in which, it is now clear, Lewis was not. Perhaps Anderson was too eagerly and too sympathetically responsive to the extraordinary elements in the ordinary man and woman; his attempts to put them into words can be gauche and embarrassing in their confusion between simplicity and *simplesse*; but these are limitations less inhibiting than Lewis's, just as his experiments with language, if not wholly successful, were more adventurous than the pedestrian competence of Lewis's prose. Lewis's ear for ordinary speech has been rightly but sufficiently praised. Anderson, relying less on his ear than on his heart and imagination, is, for all his unevenness, the more stimulating and original writer. Though crediting him with 'scarcely any ideas at all', Scott Fitzgerald praised enthusiastically his 'brilliant and almost inimitable prose style'. Hemingway frankly admitted taking *Winesburg, Ohio* as his pattern when he began writing, but by 1926 felt he had outgrown the influence sufficiently to parody it in *The Torrents of Spring*; the parody is amusing, trenchant, but ungenerous.

Though his feelings for Winesburg are equivocal, Anderson is not an out-and-out opponent of small-town life, but neither does he exhibit the sentimentalized affection for it residual in *Babbitt* and *Main Street*. Both Lewis and Anderson know the America with which they deal, Lewis from observation, Anderson more from intuitive speculation. In these respects both draw on their own experiences, but not as nakedly, as exhaustively and as narcissistically as some others. Receiving the Nobel Prize for Literature in 1930 (the first American to do so), Lewis spoke of a younger writer, Thomas Wolfe, as 'a Gargantuan creature with great gusto of life' whose novel, *Look Homeward, Angel* (1929), he thought 'worthy to be compared with the best in our literary production'. Wolfe stands in many ways at the opposite end of the literary spectrum from Lewis, but the contrast between them must not be distorted, because of the accident of chronology, into the over-neat suggestion that fiction in the 1920s progressed from the socially-oriented objectivity of *Main Street* to the poetic subjectivity of *Look Homeward, Angel*. As early as 1922 E. E. Cummings had produced, in *The Enormous Room*, a book as subjective as Wolfe's, even more original and just as difficult to define. To it might have been applied the words Wolfe used in circulating his typescript to the publishers:

I have never called this book a novel. To me it is a book such as all men may have in them. It is a book made out of my life, and it represents my vision of life to my twentieth year.

The experiences of which Cummings writes are more unusual than Wolfe's: for Cummings had been imprisoned during the First World War in a French concentration camp because a friend and compatriot of his in the ambulance unit was accused of having written letters critical of France, and the book describes the process by which he comes to terms with his confinement and his heterogeneous and frequently villainous co-prisoners. Totally devoid of self-pity, it manifests 'great gusto of life' as vigorous and creatively energetic as Wolfe's, while its use of *Pilgrim's Progress* as a framework gives the book a humane spirituality, humility, and a discipline of form that Wolfe's lacks. Its exploration of the resources of language is at once less derivative and more controlled than Wolfe's though not every reader will accept readily the poetic flights of either.

Like *The Enormous Room*, *Look Homeward, Angel* comes directly out of the author's own experience and is instinct with the wonder, curiosity, exuberant intemperance and agony of youth – all of them qualities with which Lewis shows no depth of familiarity. It is the story of the early life of Eugene Gant, child of parents who belong to Sherwood Anderson's 'grotesques' but of whom we are given a view more extended and more penetrating than any Anderson achieved. Wolfe's transitions, in speaking of Eugene, from the third

to the first person and back are at once indicative of the fluidity of
form in the novel and of his sense of identity with the character.
'The most literal and autobiographical part of the book', he said, 'is
its picture of the buried life. The most exact thing in it is the fantasy
– its picture of a child's soul.' This concern with the buried life is in
part the product of an enthusiasm for Freudian patterns of thought;
it finds its expressions in a prose influenced by the Joyce of *Portrait
of the Artist* – and by a lyric impulse that can achieve real beauty and
equally real turgidity. There are moments comparable with Hart
Crane at his best and moments, also like some of Crane's, of
portentously self-conscious rhetoric and romanticization. A desire
to use language creatively and a wish to explore the realities of the
inner life are commendable but are not enough in themselves to
produce great fiction unless there is a tighter artistic control
operating than Wolfe has mastered. Visualizing the helplessness of
the baby he writes:

He was in agony because he was poverty-stricken in symbols: his mind was
caught in a net because he had no words to work with.

The unsympathetic reader may feel the grown writer to be handicapped by a plethora of symbols, caught in a net because he has far
too many words to work with and is intoxicated by them. Intended
as a plangent threnody to the irrecoverable innocence of the human
condition, the novel relies too heavily on the repeated incantatory
cadences of its epigraph:

O waste of loss, in the hot mazes, lost, among bright stars on this most
weary unbright cinder, lost! Remembering speechlessly we seek the great
forgotten language, the lost lane-end into heaven, a stone, a leaf, an
unfound door. Where? When?
O lost, and by the wind grieved, ghost, come back again.

III

The transition of the adolescent from innocence to experience was
also the theme of another work that enjoyed a considerable reputation at the time; if this is compared with Wolfe's it is not difficult
to see why his has lasted better. James T. Farrell's 'Studs Lonigan'
trilogy (1932, 1934, 1935) traces the dissolution of a young Catholic
in lower-middle-class Chicago. Its Marxist economic determinism
is characteristic of the thirties and of fiction in the Naturalist
tradition, and its bleak cheerlessness is the product of a felt experience as intense as Wolfe's. Wolfe's poetics are no less suspect

than Farrell's polemics, and both writers could, with advantage, have compressed their books considerably. Farrell's method is apparently more objective and his forthright treatment of sexual brutality and gang violence might seem ahead of his time, yet he has less to offer the present day reader than Wolfe has. Wolfe is the more imaginative writer, and his characters have a vitality that Farrell's lack; he involves the reader with mankind in a way that Farrell, for all his worthiness and concern, does not.

Fiction in this period, then, oscillates between the detached commentary of social observation and the imaginative rendering of sensitively-apprehended experience, between attempts at the Great American Novel pinning the continent down between its covers, and the search for the buried life of the private individual overwhelmed by the accelerating pace of the century. Yet, it hardly needs saying, no worthwhile novel fits strictly and exclusively into either category. Indeed, at least two distinguished novels – *USA* (1930–6) and *The Grapes of Wrath* (1939) – make almost schematic attempts at bridgebuilding between the two extremes. Both intersperse a fictional narrative with characters of a different, non-fictional nature as though to widen the references and increase the validity of the novel as a literary form. In the later and less complex of the two John Steinbeck tells a story of dispossessed Oklahoma farmers during the Depression migrating hopefully westwards towards the fertility symbolized by the vineyards of California and finding that the grapes are not the grapes of plenty but of wrath. By its suggestion of Julia Ward Howe's 'Battle Hymn of the Republic' the title glances ironically at an aspect of the American Dream. The narrative of the Joads' disillusioning migration alternates with the rhetoric of chapters positing against a modern background values akin to Jeffersonian agrarianism, the Emersonian doctrines of the Oversoul and the conviction that 'we the people' are the strength of America and the only basis for hope for the future. There are also some excellently managed inset scenes from modern American life such as the used-car lot, the hamburger stand, and the gas-station.

Dos Passos's tone is less shrill than Steinbeck's, his expectations are less hopeful, and his technique more ambitious and varied. Interweaving through the trilogy the stories of a larger number of fictitious characters of different social levels, he varies narrative with three other forms of prose, all showing more virtuosity and less didacticism than Steinbeck's. One of these, the 'Newsreel', is a collage of newspaper headlines, snatches of popular songs, advertisements and clippings from news-stories. These juxtapositionings are not infrequently ironic, thus constituting an implicit commentary on the events they recall and the atmosphere they evoke. Irony is even more apparent in the 'Biographies'. Here the lives of the saints of commercial, industrial and political America (Thomas Edison, Henry Ford, Woodrow Wilson and others) are mordantly compressed into racily satiric sketches while a briskly vernacular hagiography is extended to such proletarian heroes as Joe Hill, Big Bill Haywood and Eugene Debs. In complete contrast, the 'Camera Eye' introduces another element of semi-fiction in a series of first-person *monologues intérieurs* conducted by a sensitive but essentially passive character who is to some degree a *persona* for Dos Passos. The monologue develops contemporaneously with, but without touching, the central narrative which is too extrovert and deterministic to allow development of the characters' inner lives: the monologue may not be a wholly acceptable alternative, but the novel would be the poorer without it.

Towards the end of the trilogy Camera Eye 50 focuses the generic indignation of the book on the case of Sacco and Vanzetti, the anarchists whose trial, imprisonment and eventual execution caused such distress to the American conscience in the 1920s. For Dos Passos it marks the end of American innocence, an irreparable split in American society ('all right we are two nations') and the final betrayal of the American dream. The formulation of this anger is symptomatic: 'America our nation has been beaten by strangers who have turned our language inside out who have taken the clean words our fathers spoke and made them slimy and foul.' This feeling for language is unfortunately not paralleled by any sustained imaginative power in the writing that might counterbalance the doctrinaire anger and basic despair at human inadequacy. In *USA* and *The Grapes of Wrath* the novelist urges the need for regeneration but the tale denies the possibility of it: the experimentation with form compels admiration but falls short of complete persuasion. In the political atmosphere of the thirties Dos Passos is perhaps over-reacting against the aestheticism which, like many of his contemporaries at Harvard in the early war-years, he had inherited from the 1890s. His undergraduate feeling that '*The Yellow Book* . . . seemed more important, somehow, than the massacres around Verdun' is excessive, yet subsequent indignation at what those massacres represented need not have so entirely swallowed up the earlier concern with art. The attack on 'strangers who have turned our language inside out' reflects hatred of the strangers more than love of the language, and Dos Passos would have disdained

Anderson's description of himself as 'a word-fellow'. Yet Yeats in the nineties had declared 'Words alone are certain good' and in *Last Poems* (1936–9), as a 'wild old wicked man', could still claim 'Words I have that can pierce the heart.' For Dos Passos words are only as good as the ideas they represent; though they have still some persuasive power over the rational mind they all too seldom pierce the heart, even when every allowance is made for the difference between prose fiction and poetry.

IV

Dos Passos published on the First World War more promptly than any other major American novelist; *One Man's Initiation – 1917* appeared in 1920 and *Three Soldiers* the next year. The latter marks the last flourish of his Harvard aestheticism in John Andrews, the most important of the trio, who deserts from the American expeditionary force for a bohemian life in Paris as a composer. Diffuse and in some respects self-indulgently sentimental, the novel nevertheless adumbrates two significant themes: the GI who makes 'a separate peace', and the fascination with 'how Paris was in the early days when we were very poor and very happy'. Both phrases, of course, are Hemingway's and with these themes Hemingway achieved his greatest reputation; yet that reputation rests even more on his style which gave American prose a distinctive energy and spare directness. Most of his work and all that is best in it is a transcript of experience so straightforward that it became difficult to disengage the work from the man or to separate either from the legend that was to do so much harm to both. As boxer, hunter, fisherman and *aficionado* of bull-fighting Hemingway did not fit the conventional stereotype of the sensitive artist; wounded in the First World War, he was again active in the Second and had also been involved in the Spanish Civil War in the thirties. A one-time journalist, he himself led an incident-packed life that, down to his suicide in Idaho in 1961, always attracted the headlines. The temptation to inflate him into a real-life prototype of the rugged Hollywood hero proved as irresistible to the press as, it must be admitted, to Hemingway himself on occasion. His concern with physical prowess was one manifestation of the contemporary aesthetic of the artist-as-man-of-the-world rendering the realities of physical existence in a harsh environment, but with unfortunate inevitability he and his heroes came to be identified as tough, uncomplicated creatures of few words and fewer feelings – 'The Dumb Ox' as Wyndham Lewis entitled his 1934 essay on him.

To counter this by emphasizing him as a literary figure can be equally unfortunate and misleading. His relations with Gertrude Stein,

Sherwood Anderson, Scott Fitzgerald, Ezra Pound, T. S. Eliot and others become a tangled account of petty animosities, literary debts acknowledged and later repudiated churlishly in overt parody and malicious anecdote, and a brashly narcissistic self-confidence un-attractive in its arrogant assertiveness. He must, however, be judged finally on his art, not on his big-game hunting in Africa or in the literary salons.

The 'dumb ox' syndrome is peculiarly unjust to Hemingway as an artist, and particularly to the subtlety of his deceptively simple use of language. Sometimes praised as though he were a dictaphone, recording with mechanical fidelity whatever he hears, he may seem to resemble J. M. Synge: 'I got more aid than any learning could have given me from a chink in the floor of the old Wicklow house where I was staying, that let me hear what was being said by the servant girls in the kitchen.' Synge's advantage in writing of a region 'where the imagination of the people, and the language they use, is rich and living', may prompt disparaging contrasts with the language Hemingway overheard, but the simple truth is, of course, that both writers relied on the creative imagination just as much as on the ear. Hemingway's ear for vernacular speech is undeniably good. His first published book was *Three Stories and Ten Poems* (1923) but more interestingly original was *In Our Time* (1924). This comprised eighteen very short prose passages (Carlos Baker appropriately calls them 'miniatures'), sixteen of which were to reappear as 'inter-chapters' between the short stories in *In Our Time* (1925). All of these have in their compression a virtuoso quality, but two in particular are remarkable as vignettes of the First World War rendered impeccably in the vocabulary and the idiom of a British army officer of the time. The colloquially laconic under-statement is so inadequate to the violent events it conveys as to suggest a gentle satire, but the original reader, to whom the idiom was less dated than to us, would have seen it more neutrally. All eighteen miniatures, in fact, are exercises in the coolly objective presentation of the brutality and violence of modern life: the reader is left to react to it as he will.

In the expanded *In Our Time* of 1925, however, these miniatures give added point to the stories with which they are juxtaposed – and from what has been said already it will be apparent that in prose fiction of this period juxtaposition is often as significant and as illuminating as in, for example, *The Waste Land*. The two 'British officers' miniatures (they are really dramatic monologues) frame a story called 'The End of Something' in which a boy and a girl quarrel on a nocturnal fishing expedition in Michigan. The girl returns home alone and the boy is then joined by a friend whose almost prurient enquiries ('Did she go all right? . . . Have a scene? . . . How do you feel?') make it clear that the break was deliberate. To the alert reader this should have been already apparent: not only has the boy been unusually on edge throughout, but the quarrel is precipitated by a calculated misunderstanding on his part. This, however, is given no artificial prominence in the story. It occurs when, in answer to his remark, 'There's going to be a moon tonight', the girl says simply 'I know it.' In Middle-Western usage the phrase has no necessarily assertive force, indeed is little more than an expression of agreement. Nick must know this but chooses to interpret it otherwise: '"You know everything," Nick said' and despite Marjorie's poised refusal to be drawn into the recriminatory argument that he wants he has created grounds for rejecting her. There is no authorial comment, no explanation of motive (that occurs incidentally in another story later), yet the significance of Nick's perversity is unobtrusively established by a rare stage-direction in the form of an adverb: '"I know it," Marjorie said *happily*' (my italics). It is indicative of Hemingway's style that there is only one other adverb in the whole story: 'happily' leaves no room for suspecting Marjorie of provocation even if the reader is unfamiliar with her idiom, but the dialogue can carry alone the whole weight of the story. A delicate, almost pastoral study of adolescent love, the tale gains a new dimension from its juxtaposition. The British officer is using everyday language to minimize the outrageousness of violence in war, to come to terms with something otherwise intolerable, but the reader knows the violence is real. Nick's vernacular is similarly a civilized alternative to violence in the war of the sexes, but his treatment of Marjorie has its own brutality nonetheless, and the reader becomes aware of it.

In other stories in the book Nick Adams is himself exposed to and victimized by violence in various forms; he becomes the prototype of the wounded hero who throughout Hemingway's work confronts, with all the stoicism he can muster, situations not of his own choosing which threaten his destruction. In the final story, on a fishing trip, he is engaged in the archetypal American quest for spiritual renewal in solitary contact with nature in the woods. His preoccupation with process – even a process so trivial as frying beans and spaghetti – is not the preoccupation of a mindless and unemotional moron but of a man in search of the primal sanities, cautiously regaining control over mind and feelings lacerated by the brutality of experience. The characteristically simple but meticulous rendering of uncomplicated physical activity demonstrates well how a 'sequence of motion and fact' can evoke in the reader an emotion that needs no description. In some respects Hemingway never wrote anything better: his later heroes in this situation are seldom so convincing. *To Have and Have Not* (1937) – structurally his weakest book – leads to a conclusion which the rest of his work belies: 'a man alone ain't got no bloody chance'. In *Across the River and into the Trees* (1950) – his weakest book thematically – Colonel Cantwell never adequately embodies the battle-scarred maturity with which the story credits him and the writing is self-indulgent in its affectation of a wise serenity. *The Old Man and the Sea* (1952) is better written, the felicitously less sophisticated protagonist shows more effectively 'what a man can do and what a man endures', and the fable cogently establishes the belief underlying the whole canon: 'A man can be destroyed but not defeated.' Many readers, however, will find its portentous Christ-symbolism self-conscious and gratuitous while others are uneasy at what they regard as its whimsical *simplesse*. His most successful book, *For Whom the Bell Tolls* (1940), has not worn well, partly because of the sentimental falseness of the love-affair that originally seemed so boldly frank, partly because its attempted anglicization of Spanish peasant idiom is quaint rather than satisfying and calls into question the extent of his real affinity with Spain and the Spanish. It suffers too by comparison with the much more masterly *A Farewell to Arms* (1929).

If Robert Jordan's espousal of the Spanish cause is imperfectly realized, the dramatic strength of Frederic Henry rests on his indifference to causes. If Maria is sentimentalized into unreality, the idealization of Catherine Barkley is not inconsistent with the first-person retrospective narration. As in the earlier work the ear for the rhythms of speech is infallible, the dialogue is capable of sustaining the narrative dramatically, and the emotively un-emotional language of Henry's narration works perfectly. It is a powerful war-novel, but not an anti-war novel. The reader cannot ignore the horror, waste and futility of the war, but these are presented as historical fact external to the hero and from which he can contract out. E. M. Forster once expressed the view that, if forced to choose between betraying his country and betraying his friend, he hoped he would have the courage to betray his country. Henry is not even called upon to make this choice for, as Catherine reminds him, 'It's only the Italian army' from which he is deserting. His loyalty to her is not seriously challenged. Yet, if he is fortunate in being able to 'make a separate peace', the war is nonetheless omnipresent as a background to and even a condition of the love-affair which is the central theme. Part of their love-play involves the unpinning of Catherine's hair 'and it would all come down and she would drop her head and we would both be inside of it, and it was the feeling of inside a tent or behind a falls'. The image symbolizes aptly the only security the wartime lovers can know: if their relationship seems idyllic and imperfectly developed it is not solely because of its brevity but because for both it is a refuge from the pressures of a hostile reality that they can tolerate no longer. Fragile and temporary, it is nonetheless real for them while it is available, but it is totally different from the slowly ripening adjustment of peacetime domesticity. Hemingway's inability to handle that type of relationship is a limitation; so, it used to be said, was Jane Austen's failure to reflect the Napoleonic Wars; but both deserve credit for doing so well what they can do. In novels and short stories Hemingway's strength lies in depicting man's capacities in the face of the violence of life in our time, the desperation with which man seizes such anodynes as are accessible, and the surprising endurance with which such slender consolations can endow him. To this theme his controlled, laconic prose can, at its best, give dimensions surprisingly close to tragic.

'There is a fourth and fifth dimension that can be gotten,' he wrote in *The Green Hills of Africa* (1935). 'It is much more difficult than poetry. It is a prose that has never been written.' Where he comes nearest to this is in the dramatization of action in the novels, and in the power of suggestion in that and in his dialogue. The following statement has a dignity and a truth that are not contemptible, but it has none of the richness and emotive complexity of *A Farewell to Arms*, despite its obvious connection with that novel:

All stories, if continued far enough, end in death, and he is no true-story teller who would keep that from you ... There is no lonelier man in death, except the suicide, than that man who has lived many years with a good wife and then outlived her. If two people love each other there can be no happy end to it.

The statement lacks the resonance of the dramatization by leaving less to the imagination and by formulating as a general proposition something of which the novel presents one vividly realized instance. Though both are products of the writer's knowledge the novel seems empirical where the statement is theoretic.

If a writer of prose knows enough about what he is writing about he may omit things that he knows and the reader, if the writer is writing truly enough, will have a feeling of those things as strongly as though the writer had stated them. The dignity of movement of an iceberg is due to only one-eighth of it being above water.

Death in the Afternoon (1932), from which these extracts come, is, like *The Green Hills of Africa*, a not wholly successful attempt to combine Hemingway's interest in literature with his love of action in the bullring or on safari. Some of its insights, however, are valuable, and parallel discussions that were taking place elsewhere. In 1937, for example, Scott Fitzgerald wrote to Thomas Wolfe on the necessity for rigorous selection by the novelist; he received a reply in which Wolfe sided aggressively with what he called 'the putter-inners' as distinct from the 'taker-outers'. Fitzgerald, like Hemingway, preferred the dignity of the iceberg.

V

'Scott Fitzgerald and Hemingway, the obligatory double act of the twenties and thirties': thus, disparagingly but irrefutably, a Sunday reviewer. Obstinately they remain, with William Faulkner, the giants of the period, but, while Faulkner can more easily be isolated, they demand joint consideration. Their friendship was uneasy: Fitzgerald regarded Hemingway in 1934 as 'the only man writing fiction in America that I look up to very much', but Hemingway's published comments on Fitzgerald, especially in *A Moveable Feast* (1961), are usually contemptuous. A remark in Fitzgerald's notebooks suggests that he almost invited this: 'I talk with the authority of failure, Ernest with the authority of success. We could never sit across the same table again.' There was some truth in this, for when Fitzgerald died in 1940 not one of his books was in print, and the final years of his life were in some respects a greater tragedy of self-destruction than Hemingway's suicide. Like Hemingway he sustained a streak of romantic heroism in his attitude and in his fiction, but he could envisage defeat more unflinchingly than Hemingway. His own ambitions had received an early setback when academic failure at Princeton was closely followed by an idolized girl-friend's rejection of him: the tone and direction of his work were largely governed by these experiences. The gay insouciance that he felt to be the response appropriate to his situation never entirely overcame 'the smouldering hatred of a peasant' that he frankly recognized in himself, and it is this tension that he was so effectively to dramatize in his fiction. By birth a Middle–Westerner, he was fascinated by the leisure class of the Eastern seaboard in whose presence he felt as 'uncivilized' as his narrator Carraway dining with the Buchanans in *The Great Gatsby*. Yet Hemingway's sneer at him in *The Snows of Kilimanjaro* as 'poor Julian' (in the first version Fitzgerald's name had been used instead of this soubriquet) is as unfair to Fitzgerald as it is unworthy of Hemingway. In the novels illusions such as 'Julian's' that the rich 'were a special glamorous race' are checked and dispelled by an uncompromising awareness of the corrupting power of money, and it is this that gives critical point to T. S. Eliot's praise of *The Great Gatsby* as 'the first step that American fiction has taken since Henry James'.

That novel, published in 1925, is, in its remarkable compactness, a masterpiece of the moral imagination. Carraway, confident in his own honesty, looks out over New York at night from Buchanan's top-floor apartment and feels himself 'within and without, simultaneously enchanted and repelled by the inexhaustible variety of life'. It is Fitzgerald's own position, just as much as Fitzgerald might have echoed Carraway's remark 'almost any exhibition of complete self-sufficiency always draws a stunned tribute from me'. Out of this dualism Carraway acquires a degree of self-sufficiency and comes to recognize the true relative worth of Gatsby and the Buchanans. The final dismissal of the latter as 'careless people' is an understatement that conveys an acute moral judgment on a complete way of life, just as, in *The Portrait of a Lady*, Isabel's dismissal of Madame Merle does: 'She made a convenience of me.' Like James, though without James's intellectual sensibility, Fitzgerald has a high ideal of civilization and of what a civilized way of life could be yet often so tragically is not.

Inevitably there are hints of social satire and comedy of manners in the treatment of the parasites who throng Gatsby's parties; the catalogue of names which opens Chapter IV is particularly well handled. As a millionaire, Gatsby is appropriately realized in terms of his material possessions (his clothes, his automobile, his library). Less expected is the use Fitzgerald makes of place as an instrument of criticism. When Carraway first enters the Buchanans's drawing room he walks into a vision of light, airy grace and opulence brilliantly evoked by a few images ('the frosted wedding-cake of the ceiling', 'the wine-coloured rug', curtains 'like pale flags'), by 'open-space' references to wind, grass and sea, and by a rhythmically cadenced prose which, by its movement, contributes to the felt vitality of the scene and the richness of life it communicates. In the same vein he comments approvingly of Jordan Baker 'there was a jauntiness about her movements as if she had first learnt to walk upon golf-courses on clean, crisp mornings'. If this cool, clean crispness were all that Fitzgerald associates with the rich they might seem the 'special glamorous race' that Hemingway accused him of making them, but these qualities are dramatically undermined in three ways. There is the hint of conspiratorial corruption that Carraway so quickly detects beneath the surface sophistication and poise of the two graceful girls in the drawing room. There is the hot, fetid atmosphere of the Manhattan city summer in which most of the action takes place and which contrasts vividly with the natural, cool freshness of the West Egg shore. Most impressively, there is also the description of the valley of ashes with which Chapter II opens. Here language and image are used surrealistically to build up a nightmare impression of arid desolation dominated by the manmade eyes of Dr T. J. Eckleburg brooding sightless over the desecrated landscape. This no-man's-land between West Egg and Manhattan is not only the arena for the novel's catastrophe but a moral comment on the unlovely lovelessness and the sterility of its occupants and a scathing condemnation of the carelessness of the rich.

At the end of the novel, in a much-praised lyrical coda, Carraway visualizes 'the old island here that flowered once for Dutch sailors' eyes – a fresh green breast of the new world'. The pastoral scene and the eyes of the sailors, 'face to face for the last time in history with something commensurate to [their] capacity for wonder', contrast powerfully with the valley of ashes and the unseeing eyes of the oculist's advertisement to make yet another comment on the arid world of the rich. It is this imaginatively poetic use of language and imagery that enlarges the narrative into dimensions of myth. Lionel Trilling's recognition that 'Gatsby, divided between power and dream, comes inevitably to stand for America itself' opens another aspect of this, so that there is a case for seeing this work as a version of 'the great American novel' so long desiderated. *The Great Gatsby* has a disciplined tightness of control that was missing from Fitzgerald's earlier novels (*This Side of Paradise*, 1920, and *The Beautiful and the Damned*, 1922) and which he never wholly recaptured.

In 1925, before *Gatsby* was published, he began on another novel. In July of that year Hemingway also started work on one, completing the first draft by September; a completely rewritten and drastically compressed version went to the publisher in April 1926 and appeared in the same year as *The Sun Also Rises* (or, in England, as *Fiesta*). 'There is only one thing to do with a novel,' he told Fitzgerald in 1929, 'and that is to go straight on through to the end of the damned thing.' Fitzgerald cannot have been heartened by 'the authority of success' in this instance, for his own novel was running into difficulties and was not, in fact, to appear until 1934. *Tender is the Night* took Fitzgerald nine years as against Hemingway's nine months for *The Sun Also Rises*, and even after publication dissatisfaction kept him revising it.

One thing he feared was that it might show too much of Hemingway's influence, 'but I did every damn thing I could to avoid that', he told him. For a year and a half he had even stopped re-reading Hemingway, 'because I was afraid that your particular rhythms were going to creep in on mine by process of infiltration'. In *The Great Gatsby* the rhythms of Daisy's speech, with its patterns of incremental repetition, suggest Hemingway's less than they anticipate those of the opening scene of Eliot's *The Cocktail Party*; and although *Tender is the Night* treats, with a similar sensitivity to idiom, the same sophisticated expatriate set as *The Sun Also Rises* it preserves its individuality. Despite some fine dramatic scenes, Fitzgerald relies less exclusively than Hemingway on dialogue for his effects. In non-dramatic narrative his manner is more traditional than Hemingway's; more expansive, at times more poetically imaginative, but at times more over-written as well. *Tender is the Night* is structurally less confident than *The Sun Also Rises*, although ironically Fitzgerald seems to have influenced Hemingway's decision to tighten the form of that novel by cutting a lengthy introductory passage in favour of its present key-note starting point.

Like *The Great Gatsby*, *The Sun Also Rises* gains by its first-person narration an advantage over *Tender is the Night* that highlights Fitzgerald's peculiar and unexpected difficulty with that novel, the determining of a point of view. In 1951, working from Fitzgerald's papers, Malcolm Cowley produced an edition of the novel drastically reorganized and with the implications of this explained in a sensitive introduction. Briefly, instead of the uneasy divisions of focus between Rosemary Hoyt and Dick Diver, the main effect of this version was to concentrate attention more firmly on Dick. Diver, the psychiatrist, is a twentieth-century Lydgate, George Eliot's *Middlemarch* doctor who allows his social aspirations to prejudice his career and his sense of vocation. By describing him as 'a spoiled priest', Fitzgerald shows an acute prescience of the role of the psychiatrist in the modern world, but a wholly adequate ex-

ploration of the Lydgate theme demands a knowledge of professional psychiatry outside Fitzgerald's range; the potential tragedy
is diminished partly by Dick's frequently unprofessional attitude,
partly by the author's other preoccupation with him as playboy
symbol of the wealthy American expatriate.

This aspect brings the novel closest to *The Sun Also Rises* and was
of course so emphasized by its original structure as to excuse some
of the feeling in 1934 that it was outdated. Had Fitzgerald been less
dilatory in its completion it might have challenged comparison with
Hemingway's book as the definitive statement of the lost generation
and gained credit for its greater complexity and humanity. It is
concerned as much as Hemingway's with the deracinating effect of
post-war Europe on the American leisured class, but is more
troubled by it. Unlike Hemingway's bohemians, Dick has a role in
society and a definite concept of the responsibility involved in
personal relations. The process of his corruption is shown in
greater extension, as is his victimization by others who, recognizing
the generosity of his impulses, make a convenience of him. His
creator's experience had been similar. However, tracing his own
disintegration in 'The Crack-Up' (1936), Fitzgerald had recorded a
friend's suggestion that the flaw might not be in him but in the
world: '"The crack's in me," I said heroically.' Where Hemingway
invites sympathy for the emasculated Jake Barnes as a man in-
capacitated by external chance, Fitzgerald insists on Dick's inner
inadequacy. Their differing concepts of irony are relevant.
Hemingway's approximates to Hardy's: it is inherent in what life
does to you, and the novelist records it faithfully with the grim relish
apparent in the anecdote of the ants and the log in the final chapter
of *A Farewell to Arms*. With Fitzgerald irony is a literary device, a
means of moral criticism of his character's shortcomings or even –
as in the 'heroically' just quoted – of his own. Jake approaches this
only in his final exchange with Brett: to her 'Oh Jake, we could have
had such a damned good time together,' he replies 'Yes, isn't it
pretty to think so?' Jake in his cynical realism has less room for
self-pity than Dick Diver or Fitzgerald himself but, controlled, that
self-pity is a part of their essential humanity. 'A strange thing is,'
said Hemingway, 'that in retrospect his *Tender is the Night* gets
better and better.' Malcolm Cowley praised it as an attempt 'to
discover and even create values in a society where they had seemed
to be lacking'. Both comments could also be applied with justice to
The Sun Also Rises, though Fitzgerald's novel has the deeper concern with the implications of this sterility for the larger society.

Fitzgerald had begun novel-writing in order to earn enough money to marry Zelda Sayre, a glamorous Southern belle for whom his feelings were as romantic as Gatsby's for Daisy. The need for money was made chronic by the extravagance of their way of life and by the cost of the medical treatment necessitated by her tragic mental breakdown. To meet these demands Fitzgerald turned out short stories of very unequal merit and made several attempts to succeed as a Hollywood script-writer. How much of his experience was transmuted into his fiction may be seen from a biography such as Arthur Mizener's. In the 'Pat Hobby' short stories he burlesqued his own role as a Hollywood hack in a way that is frequently embarrassing, but another story, 'Crazy Sunday', maintains a skilful tension between admiration for the imaginative energy of a Hollywood director and criticism of the society in which he moves. To this theme (its parallel with *The Great Gatsby* is obvious) he returned in the novel uncompleted at his death, *The Last Tycoon*. This exploration of Hollywood as symbol of the failing American Dream is powerfully and promisingly done, yet here again Fitzgerald had been in part forestalled. In 1939 Nathanael West published his Hollywood novel, *The Day of the Locust*. If his presentation of the loneliness of the pathetic Homer Simpson derives directly from Sherwood Anderson's grotesques (notably Wing Biddlebaum), his exploitation of bizarre images owes much to Fitzgerald's technique in, for example, the eyes of Dr T.J. Eckleburg, but West's indictment of American civilization is more savagely satirical and more hopelessly nihilistic than Fitzgerald could have been. This is not because Fitzgerald was – as is sometimes suggested – flabby, intellectually confused and sentimental. With one of those flashes of self-knowledge that irradiate his work more illuminatingly than do Hemingway's sneers at him, he told his daughter, 'I guess I am too much a moralist at heart, and really want to preach at people in some acceptable form'. The forms of preaching were changing and faith in it was to diminish. The future of American fiction was heralded less by Fitzgerald than by West whose nightmare vision of an absurd world in *The Day of the Locust* is recognizably closer to the idiom of today. Nevertheless, Fitzgerald continues to claim attention and respect as an artist for his imaginative perception of the schism in the soul of modern man, his passionate concern with it beneath the brittle, sophisticated surface of his fiction, and the acceptability of the form in which his best preaching is cast.

In the years since his death (in 1940), Fitzgerald has continued to charm a widening circle of readers in many countries. Hemingway's heavier reputation and influence still outweigh those of the author of *Gatsby*. This effect has no doubt been heightened by the appearance, as if from beyond the grave, of various posthumous Hemingway works. Of these, *Islands in the Stream* (1970) remains a substantial novel even after cuts of unspecified severity made by his widow Mary Hemingway and his publisher Charles Scribner Jr. Another novel, *Garden of Eden* (1986), skilfully – it seems – abridged by a young editor, was respectfully reviewed by John Updike among others. The old master, they intimated, was still formidable. In the closing words of *Garden of Eden*: 'He wrote on a while longer now and there was no sign that any of it would ever cease returning to him intact.'

Time will show whether the magic of such phrasing is intrinsic, or imparted by the Hemingway legend of heroism and disaster. What these novels do both reveal is the extent to which his life and his fiction had become entwined. The protagonist of *Islands in the Stream*, purportedly a famous painter, talks and behaves very much like the Ernest Hemingway of the 1930s and 1940s – disconcertingly so for anyone acquainted with the author's life-style in Key West and Cuba. *Garden of Eden* is a more complicated matter. Admirers point out that the central figure, an American named David Bourne, becomes involved in more intricately submissive sexuality than in the stereotypical, macho Hemingway tale. On the other hand, David is a novelist, living in France in the 1920s in circumstances very close to those of Hemingway. The story can be interpreted – indeed, is hard not to interpret – as *a* version of the author's first marriage, its breakup, and his subsequent justifications of his own conduct. There is an interpolated inner story based on David's own supposed adolescent hunting experiences with his father in East Africa. Magnificently Hemingwayesque in tone, it is nevertheless a curious piece of fiction within fiction, or perhaps of self-imitation. It and *Islands in the Stream* make one wonder whether Hemingway's instinct to leave them unpublished was not wiser than that of his executors.

3

AMERICAN THEATRE: THE AGE OF O'NEILL

David Morse

The extraordinary explosion of young America in the theatre, poetry and fiction in the aftermath of the First World War made the twenties a decade unparalleled in American literature since the 1850s. It is popularly assumed that the American theatre did indeed begin with Eugene O'Neill and while obviously this is not strictly true the statement has a measure of accuracy. It was no easy task to create an American drama. Foreign plays were preferred both for snobbish and for practical reasons: they had the advantage of being pre-tested; there was less likelihood of financial risk. American playwrights were slow in appearing. Bronson Howard (1842–1908) was the first to establish himself as a professional dramatist, Clyde Fitch (1865–1909) the first to make any real money out of it; but O'Neill was certainly America's first dramatist of importance and the man who alerted the world to the existence of a native American theatre. Between the wars O'Neill towered over his rivals. If this survey begins and ends with him it merely reflects the magnitude of his achievement.

As in most European countries, serious drama developed largely outside the confines of the commercial theatre, although O'Neill and others were able to make the transition to Broadway. The Provincetown Players, who launched O'Neill, were succeeded by the Theater Guild (which put on many, better, plays from Europe); in the thirties it was the Group Theater, a closely knit association of actors, writers and directors, which came to the fore, while from 1935 the Federal Theater, though inhibited by political consider-ations from launching worthwhile new plays, at least brought many classics to towns that had had no legitimate theatre since the great Shakespearean actors of the nineteenth century toured the con-tinent. In these interstices the new drama thrived, but it nevertheless encountered many obstacles, the most formidable of which was the double or even triple standard employed by dramatic critics. Critics, then as now, were less severe on 'entertainment'. Yet a serious dramatist like O'Neill was castigated either because his work appeared to diverge from the moral standards deemed suitable for a middle-class audience, i.e. for portraying proletarian characters, for showing racial inter-marriage or for flouting puritanical notions of decency, or else, when it had become accepted that he was the great white hope of the American drama, because his vernacular idiom seemed insufficiently dignified placed alongside Aeschylus, Sophocles and Shakespeare.

The originality of O'Neill's early work has often been exaggerated. The main tradition of the American theatre, in the hands of David Belasco and James A. Herne, had been melodrama modified by more naturalistic styles of acting and production, and it was this that O'Neill continued, although it had already been out-dated by the Ibsenite well-made play, and, on a more fundamental level, by the drama of Chekhov. O'Neill was able to invest this melodrama with a psychological credibility which it had hitherto lacked, as a play like *Welded* (1924), which points prophetically forward to his later work, clearly demonstrates; but *Welded* also shows how much of a handicap the native tradition was to O'Neill, how consistently it impeded his effort to give his plays the power of true feeling as distinct from surefire theatrical effect. O'Neill had to discover for himself how to create dramatic situations that were both powerful and complex.

O'Neill came from a theatrical family. His father, James O'Neill, had been a well-known Shakespearean actor but ended up as a stereotyped mediocrity – playing his most successful part, the Count in *The Count of Monte Cristo*, over and over again. Eugene grew up in New London, Connecticut, but after the failure of an early marriage in 1909, when he was only twenty-one, he became a sailor and travelled all over the world. After a period in a sanatorium recovering from tuberculosis in 1913, he attended Professor George Pierce Baker's drama workshop at Harvard, where his career as a dramatist began. His first plays were written for a group of amateur actors, which was to become the Provincetown Players.

O'Neill's early plays deal with the experience of homelessness, of alienation, above all with the discrepancy between different levels of feeling experienced simultaneously. In *The Dreamy Kid*, Dreamy, a young Negro gangster, is obsessed with making his escape from the police and prepares to make his last stand while his old mother lies dying in the same room. To all appearances his behaviour is heartless, but he is thinking of the imminence of his *own* death:

Dey don't git Dreamy alive – not for de chair! Lawd Jesus, no suh!

This play crystallizes in dramatic form O'Neill's sense of the apartness of human beings: in the final analysis every man is on his own and his experience is inaccessible to others, whether they are sympathetic or indifferent. O'Neill emphasizes the pathos of this in *In the Zone* (1917) through a joke that turns out not to be funny: Smitty, an English sailor, has his love letters read out and his secret turns out to be not that he is a spy but that his girl-friend has finally broken with him. Olson's drunken confession of his homesickness and his resolve to go back in *The Long Voyage Home* (1917) is merely the cue for the inmates of the bar to rob him of his last cent and to add, on top of that, a bill that will keep him at sea for a long time to come. In *Bound East for Cardiff* (1916) Driscoll's agonizing moment of death is incommensurable with the uneventful routine of ship-board life; it is something that none of them can quite rise to, not even Driscoll himself. *The Moon of the Caribbees* (1918) most subtly creates a theatrical mood of leisureliness and well-being, ruffled only by our faint consciousness that even here the sailors are slightly uneasy and out-of-place, and hence unable to enjoy themselves quite as much as they would like. Smitty's refusal of Pearl, the most attractive of the West Indian girls to come on board, may strike us as snobbish or puritanical; but if, for many of the sailors, such experiences are the source of pleasant memories, for Smitty they are a source of unease, a reminder of the expense of spirit, the draining away little by little of personality in episodes which insofar as they are transitory involve a death of the self. Implicit in the very act of going to sea seems to be an urge to self-destruction: Edith accuses Smitty of having ruined both his life and her own and this is equally true of Captain Keeney in *Ile* (1917). Keeney is afraid of being made fun of if he returns from his whaling expedition without oil, so he carries on with his futile voyage, although his wife is aboard, and they are surrounded by the ice of the northern seas. There is nothing heroic about this search; it is monotonous, soul-destroying and brutalizing to the point where the Captain seems to have lost all human feeling. The conclusion, in which Mrs Keeney, apparently mad, sits hypnotically playing at the organ, is melodramatic but it constitutes a vivid image of death in life – madness, death, life: in O'Neill's eyes there is no difference once a man has nothing left to live for. O'Neill's drama reaches always to fundamentals; it is concerned not simply with motives, actions or intentions but with the sources of life and of the will to live itself.

It is this that is at the core of his full-length plays, *Beyond the Horizon* (1920), *The Straw* (1921) and *Anna Christie* (1921). *Beyond the Horizon* is set in a remote farmhouse, *The Straw* in a tuberculosis sanatorium; both are seen as prisons for the spirit, places of oppressive confinement in which the impulse to live dries up and withers away. Robert Mayo, of *Beyond the Horizon*, who has 'a touch of the poet in his make-up' is torn between his desire to see more of life and explore what lies 'beyond the horizon' and his love for Ruth Atkins, who is also loved by Andrew, his more pragmatic brother. Although the family has generally accepted that Ruth will marry Andrew, when it becomes clear that she really loves Robert, Andrew takes over his brother's passage on a ship bound for Yokohama. Predictably Robert fails to make a success of farming and the love which Ruth had felt for him is gradually destroyed. The implicit choice here between life and death and O'Neill's awareness of the interaction of subjective and objective factors is dramatized more explicitly in *The Straw*, where the sanatorium has a ruthless policy: patients must gain weight within six months or leave, probably to die. The degradation of institutional life is fully registered, from Dr Stanton's remark, 'Yes, we're strictly anti-Cupid, sir, from top to bottom', to the quiet observation of the writer, Stephen Murray:

Listen to them laugh. Did you ever notice that – perhaps it's my imagination – how forced they act on Saturday mornings before they are weighed?

Murray succeeds as a writer and leaves the sanatorium cured, but Eileen Carmody, who loves him without being loved in return, steadily deteriorates. In both of these plays O'Neill relies rather too heavily on counterpoint and on the mystical life-affirming optimism that overtakes tubercular patients in their last stages; one wishes that he could have learnt from Chekhov or Gorki the art of rendering the tone and atmosphere of a specific milieu. O'Neill's first real achievement is *Anna Christie*, a play which, despite the apparent banality of its theme, nevertheless deploys the developing complexity of his personal vision without seriously compromising it. Life is seen as repetition, as constituting a closed circle of possibilities from which it is impossible to escape. The characters struggle to break out and discover new hope. They find that what seemed to be different is in fact the same; which leads either into a desperate attempt to blot out one's consciousness of repetition and degradation in some alcoholic or other oblivion, or to a fatalistic acceptance of the situation without any illusions.

Fog, fog, fog, all bloody time. You can't see where you vas going, no. Only dat ole davil sea – she knows!

says Chris Christopherson, Anna's father, at the end of the play. The fog stands for the genuine obscurity of life, but also for the subjective world of unreality, the optimistic blurring of consciousness that persuades people to believe that things are other than what they are: so that Chris can believe his daughter is a nice girl who drinks sarsaparilla and not a prostitute who favours whisky; so that Mat Burke, the handsome, brawny stoker, can believe she is something other than the counterpart of the girls who, in other ports, have been primarily concerned to separate him from his money. But their hope has meaning; for just as contempt for oneself reinforces contempt for others, so belief in others and their personal worth feeds back into the ego, enhancing the individual's image of himself. Mat Burke, O'Neill's first real pipe-dreamer, would prefer that Anna should lie to him than face the truth, since that would mean the collapse of the structure of human dignity which they have so tenderly built up. And this is to come through to the other side of the fog, and see in it no longer the possibility of hope, but only a ground for false hope and imaginary freedom of action. The fog is life as obscurity, repetition, monotony and futility and Chris Christopherson's bafflement seems to be vindicated.

With *The Emperor Jones* (1920) O'Neill unmistakably established himself as a playwright of importance and at the same time inaugurated his Expressionist phase of the twenties. However, O'Neill's work shows that to postulate a diagrammatic antithesis between Naturalism and Expressionism is misleading. In fact both develop out of a preoccupation with the radical cleavage between the individual and society, which had characterized the modern theatre from Ibsen onwards. With Pirandello the discrepancy between the way in which the individual perceives the world and the way in which it is perceived by others became the basis for a new theatricality; with O'Neill the alienation of the individual demanded a more clearcut and dramatically heightened statement of his predicament. Expressionism was not only a more powerful means of theatrical expression; it signified that the rupture between the individual and his social integument was virtually complete and beyond the possibility of mediation.

Thus, in Expressionism, we find a paradoxical duality. On the one hand character and even individuality are de-emphasized and the hero becomes a generalized figure who is described purely in terms of a particular social role – the clerk of Kaiser and Rice, O'Neill's Yank, the proletarian, even the 'Emperor' Jones. On the other hand Expressionist theatre is very much more concerned with expressing emotions, moods, subjective states of mind which cannot be contained in ordinary verbal discourse. The ponderously furnished bourgeois parlour, which in post-Ibsen drama was so often presented as a prison for the human spirit, is for that very reason no longer seen as an adequate arena for the drama. Stage sets become increasingly abstract and symbolic; lighting and music (the darkness and drums of *The Emperor Jones*) are used to convey changes of mood; the hero is placed no longer by his cosy fireside but against the threatening impersonality of the universe – Kaiser's bank clerk stands alone surrounded by a wilderness of snow, the Emperor Jones flees desperately through the forest. The Expressionist hero is a cypher who struggles against his fate. In *The Great God Brown* masks are used to demonstrate the roles society imposes; in *Strange Interlude* the constrictions imposed on the personality by social discourse are highlighted by allowing the characters to express their private thoughts. The perspective of 'ordinary reality' disappears, precisely because reality is felt to be *abnormal*.

In *The Emperor Jones*, and later in *All God's Chillun Got Wings*, O'Neill took the American Negro as the type of the alienated man. Divorced from his original tribal culture and perhaps even contemptuous of it, he is even more lost and hopeless in the world of the white man, where he is rejected and despised and where the attempt to assimilate its values and become successful leads only to a loss of self. Jones uses a combination of the white man's cynical lore and native superstition to keep his people in subjection. Significantly he has accumulated his wisdom as a Pullman car attendant:

You heah what I tells you, Smithers. Dere's little stealin' like you does, and dere's big stealin' like I does. For de little stealin' dey git you in jail soon or late. For de big stealin' dey makes you Emperor and puts you in de Hall o' Fame when you croaks. (*Reminiscently*) If dey's one thing I learns in ten years on de Pullman ca's listenin' to de white quality talk, it's dat same fact. And when I gits a chance to use it, I wind up Emperor in two years.

Jones has no illusions about the duration of his tenure; he is in the Emperor business simply to make out of it what he can while he can. The accelerating pace of the second half of the play, as Jones flees from his pursuers into the jungle, on a stage darkened or lit by a pale and unreal light, to encounter phantoms from his past, while the drum beat gradually increases its momentum, has the character of a ritual incantation, in which Jones's black magic and the world of unreality, of sham civilization which he has built around himself, finally collapses.

The Emperor Jones adopts alien values as a means to power; Jim Harris of *All God's Chillun* (1924) as the way to self-respect, but

Harris's voluntary self-alienation only provokes the pathological hatred of the white girl, Ella Downey, who has dared to marry him. Only in fantasy and at the price of denying reality can they remain together. O'Neill's subject is not primarily the problem of colour. It is part of a continuing exploration of the potentialities of freedom. To attempt to escape from one's background, family, environment means alienation and the loss of identity; yet to remain within it may mean that that identity is threatened, stifled and suffocated.

With *The Hairy Ape* (1922) O'Neill's work assumes the form of a radical social critique. Yank is the heroic proletarian of the technological age, a stoker, conscious of himself as the motive power of industrial civilization and contemptuous of the idle leisure class which occupies the first-class cabins of his ship:

What's dem slobs in de foist cabin got to do with us? We're better men dan dey are, ain't we? Sure! One of us guys could clean up de whole mob wit one mit. Put one of 'em down here for one watch in de stokehole, what'd happen? Dey'd carry him off on a stretcher. Dem boids don't amount to nothin'. Dey're just baggage. Who makes dis old tub run? Ain't it us guys? Well den, we belong don't we? We belong and dey don't. Dat's all.

The steel steamship is Yank's element. This makes him very different from Paddy the old sailor, who looks back nostalgically to the days of sailing ships, when 'a ship was part of the sea and a man was part of the ship, and the ship joined all together and made it one'. According to Yank this is a 'dope dream', 'Hittin' de pipe of de past'. Yank is not conscious of being alienated. The false consciousness with which he regards the liner as 'home' derives from the fact that he has no real home and the word itself means nothing to him:

Home? Home, hell! I'll make a home for you! I'll knock yuh dead. Home! T'hell wit home! Where d'yuh get dat tripe? Dis is home, see? What d'yuh want wit home? (*Proudly*) I runned away from mine when I was a kid. On'y too glad to beat it, dat was me. Home was lickings for me, dat's all.

The love–hate which Yank conceives for Mildred Douglas, a steel heiress, triggers off a wider hostility which places him in open opposition to the system and compels him into an inarticulate rejection of the whole capitalist order. O'Neill sees Long, the populist-cum-communist, and even the IWW (a militant labour union, widely feared because it advocated the use of violence), as insufficiently radical. Their preoccupation is with language and rhetoric rather than action. O'Neill, like George Bernard Shaw, rapidly became disillusioned with the talk-shops of the Left. Yank represents everything that is totally opposed, totally unassimilable. But Yank's self-image has been destroyed:

Dat's me now – I don't tick, see? – I'm a busted Ingersoll, dat's what. Steel was me, and I owned de woild. Now I ain't steel, and de woild owns me.

Identity is linked to belonging – and Yank belongs nowhere, not even in the gorilla's cage, where he retreats from the manmade world, only to be crushed to death by the beast.

O'Neill's later Expressionist plays are less successful but none of them is without interest. We find him reaching out to extend his mastery of the stage. At the same time he is involved in a personal transvaluation of values: in a devastating assault upon the American enshrinement of the Protestant ethic and an attempt, most explicitly in *Lazarus Laughed* (1928), to find something to put in its place. Directly or indirectly the plays are concerned with religion. O'Neill concludes that whatever he may ostensibly worship, the deities venerated by Western man are money and power. In *The Fountain* (1925) the degraded search of Juan Ponce de Leon for the mythical land of Cathay ends somewhat bathetically in the swamps of Florida (we should bear in mind here the Florida land boom of the twenties and the cult of Miami, 'The Magic City'); yet it achieves nobility in its very failure, for dreams of gold and glory are left behind and Juan is able to experience a renewed sense of the wonder of life. This also is the spirit of Lazarus's gospel – a repudiation of bondage to work and money in order to live more fully. In *The Great God Brown* (1926) O'Neill shows how materialistic civilization denies the life-giving impulses and destroys the genuine artist, cannibalizing his talent, which it needs for its own purposes. *Marco Millions* (1928) is O'Neill's *Babbitt*, a satire on the American businessman, of whom the thrusting, go-getting Marco Polo was the original prototype. Marco is totally indifferent to the values and traditions of the East, which are flattened and obliterated under the crushing weight of his slick, self-important, vulgar pragmatism. For Marco, like the American businessman, takes himself very seriously and is wholly contented with himself. He achieves everything that he desires. The only question – asked by Kublai, the Eastern Emperor, but not by Marco himself – is whether this man has a soul? *Marco* is probably the most successful of the plays, *Dynamo* (1929) the weakest, but here again the theme is the utter absence of genuine values, in the atheist engineer's submission to the total power of the Dynamo, a god without meaning, a religion without spirituality.

O'Neill's converging social, psychological and philosophical perspectives had come to point in the direction of nihilism.

Standing somewhat apart is *Desire Under the Elms* (1924), in which O'Neill returns to the stifling provinciality of *Beyond the Horizon* and fulfils its sombre promise. The bleak, barren New England farm, worth little in itself, yet for which Ephraim Cabot married, for which Abbie marries Ephraim at seventy-five, and for which Eben, the youngest son, sullenly waits, is the focus of the action and dominating symbol. The giant elms which 'brood oppressively' over the farmhouse are emblems of the human spirit, able to live only insofar as it is engaged in oppressing and grinding down the lives of others. Ephraim, Abbie, Eben, each is a negation; together they cancel each other out. But the erotic passion of Abbie and Eben is creative. Paradoxically they can demonstrate that this is so only by a destructive act; they must free themselves by a gratuitous gesture which will demonstrate their indifference to everything they have lived by and even everything they have become capable of: the death of their child, which they have palmed off as Ephraim's. Yet even their romantic denial of worldly priorities is undercut by the final words of the sheriff, which show how universal is the greed which their sacrifice negates:

It's a jim-dandy farm, no denyin'. Wished I owned it.

Desire Under the Elms develops through striking scenic images: the set itself, the delayed theatrical entry of Ephraim with his young bride, Eben and Abbie separated by a wall, the moment when, as Ephraim finishes his exuberant dance at the party and pours himself a whisky, Eben stands silently staring at the cradle. Poetry *of* rather than in the theatre.

Strange Interlude (1928) recapitulates and consolidates O'Neill's experience of two decades of playwriting. O'Neill brings together a multitude of dramatic concerns: the struggle of life against death (civilized social existence); the separation between the official outward appearances of conventional dialogue and the turbulent thoughts and desires that may not ordinarily be spoken, but which in this play are (distinguished from normal speech in the original production by being delivered in a preoccupied, trance-like manner); the pull towards, and the desire to escape degradation, which was the theme of *Anna Christie*; the woman who bears a child to a man who is not her husband. Nina Leeds is loved by many men: her father; Gordon Shaw, an athlete and pilot who was killed in the First World War, and to whom she feels guilty for having not married him or given herself to him; Charles Marsden, a writer, who is interested in her but unable or unwilling to press his claim; Sam Evans, whom she marries and who becomes a successful businessman; Edmund Darrell, by whom she has a child, since Sam's mother has warned her of a record of insanity in their family; lastly the child himself, whom she names Gordon. O'Neill is at his best when he can portray characters whose lives are inextricably linked together and in *Strange Interlude* it is through Nina's child that he tries to create the sense of a common predicament. However, melodrama undermines the psychological subtlety which O'Neill intends and while many of his interior monologues contain real insight, others have the effect of over-simplifying by making everything too explicit. Nevertheless, the total vision of *Strange Interlude* is complex. The repressive character of civilization is directly linked to individual psychological drives. People live wasted lives partly because they are forced by social pressures to suppress what lies within them. The inexorable psychological logic by which each person becomes implicated in the lives of several others, necessarily creates unhappiness, division and tension, jealousy, conflict. Thus there can be no genuine fulfilment in life, which is a 'strange interlude' of 'trial and preparation', 'in which our souls have been scraped clean of impure flesh and made worthy to bleach in peace'.

Mourning Becomes Electra, an ambitious trilogy loosely based on the *Oresteia* of Aeschylus, must rank as O'Neill's most substantial contribution to the drama of the thirties since, although it was written in 1929, it was not actually performed until 1931. His choice of model enabled O'Neill to confront more directly those repressed incestuous feelings which had assumed such importance in his work. Lavinia, like Nina Deeds, is the central character who is pulled in different directions: she is going to be married to Peter, but she is strongly attracted towards her father, Ezra Mannon; to Adam Brant, her father's half-brother who strongly resembles him and who is also loved by her mother, Christine Mannon; to her brother Orin and even to a ship's officer, Wilkins, who reminds her of Brant. O'Neill puts these incestuous feelings completely in the open: significantly Orin does not so much resent the fact that his mother has poisoned his father (his hated rival) as that she loves Adam Brant, who is thus a more serious challenger for her affections. In accordance with these psychological compulsions O'Neill does not allow Orin to kill his mother, as in Aeschylus, since this would be too repugnant to him. Instead Orin shoots Brant, whereupon his mother kills herself. Adam Brant, like Dion

Antony of *The Great God Brown*, is an embodiment of creative energy, his vitality is contrasted with the Mannons' obsession with death, his 'Blessed Isles' in the South Seas, where it is possible to forget 'all men's dirty dreams of greed and power' stands in opposition to the mausoleum where Lavinia walls herself up. In *Mourning Becomes Electra* guilt itself is charged with eroticism; it is a way of obtaining power over another person, of binding them to oneself for ever. Christine says to Adam:

You'll never dare leave me now, Adam – for your ships or your sea or your naked Island girls – when I grow old and ugly!

and Orin, who holds the same threat of revelation over his sister, tells her: 'I love you now with all the guilt in me – the guilt we share.' The theme of the play is the impossibility of ever making a fresh start. Ezra's hope that his homecoming might be a new beginning is destroyed, while his children, Orin and Lavinia, are trapped in a process of repetition, in which they seem doomed to act out the roles of their parents over again. Lavinia wears her mother's green dress and virtually becomes her; Orin feels his father's jealousy and when he kills Brant it is as if he had killed his father:

This is like a dream. I've killed him before – over and over.

The Mannons are life-denying. They deny each other happiness instead of seeking it for themselves. They cannot love because they are consumed by jealousy and hate and the desire to punish others as much as they have been punished themselves. For the Mannons the Blessed Isles can only symbolize passions that must for ever be taboo.

O'Neill was not the only dramatist to be caught up by the mood of theatrical experimentalism which had been fanned by the excited European reports of Huntley Carter, Oliver M. Sayler, Kenneth MacGowan, Robert Edmond Jones – who was to become America's leading stage designer – and Hallie Flanagan, later to direct the Federal Theater Project. New ground was broken by Elmer Rice with his Expressionist play, *The Adding Machine* (1923), by John Howard Lawson with his *Processional* (1925), subtitled 'A Jazz Symphony of American Life in Four Acts', and by E. E. Cummings with *Him* (1927). Making a radical departure from the well-constructed melodramas which had occupied him previously, Rice satirized with a theatrical directness that went well beyond the affectionate ribbing of Sinclair Lewis the monotony and banality of the lives of ordinary Americans. Mr and Mrs Zero are the cyphers of mass society and their friends are numbered from one to six. Zero has been working as a clerk for twenty-five years, waiting for the day when the Boss comes to announce that he is to be promoted for his good work. The Boss finally comes – to tell Zero that he is to be replaced by an Adding Machine – whereupon Zero kills him. When Zero gets to heaven he is told that he will have soon to return to earth, since souls are used over and over again until they wear out. Rice despairingly contemplates the waste and pointlessness of life in a frame of mind that recalls the Shaw of *Back to Methuselah*. Zero is told:

You'll be a baby again – a bald, red-faced little animal and then you'll go through it all again ... You'll learn to be a liar and a bully and a braggart and a coward and a sneak. You'll learn to fear the sunlight and to hate beauty. By that time you'll be ready for school. There they'll tell you the truth about a great many things you don't give a damn about and they'll tell you lies about things you ought to know – and about all the things you want to know they'll tell you nothing at all. When you get through that you'll be equipped for your life work. You'll be ready to take a job.

Life is deprived of significance before it is even begun and Zero's monotonous, alienated labour seems a feeble culmination of thousands of years of evolution.

E. E. Cummings's *Him* shows a similar concern with problems of identity and with the nature of mass society. The play is a boisterous, multi-faceted extravaganza, whose farcical surface cannot wholly conceal an underlying seriousness. The theatre itself becomes a metaphor for the human personality: is it indeed a four-sided room, a prison in which the self is trapped, or is there one wall open through which we make contact with reality? 'Him', the writer, and 'Me', the girl who is expecting his child, have to lose their self-preoccupation, symbolized by the mirrors, visible and invisible, into which they peer, and come to terms with each other. 'Me' has to accept the imaginative side of 'Him', identified with the circus and the 'Queer Folk' whom she does not wish to see; 'Him' has to accept the child. Cummings explores the hubris of the artist, who, in his desire to play God in his fear of being like everyone else, cuts himself off from others and from authentic being. 'Him' envies 'Me' the sense of security and self-possession which she has:

I mean you have something which I supremely envy. That you are something which I would supremely like to discover: knowing that it exists in itself and as I have never existed.

In theory it is art which is capable of grasping the specificity of the universe; in practice 'Him' the artist, in his disdain and preoccupation with the aesthetic, remains imprisoned within his own subjectivity. Successive scenes depict his guilt and anxiety: his urge to self-destruction appears in a farcical scene in which Bill and Will, business partners, shoot themselves/each other; his guilty feelings towards 'Me' in the Frankie and Johnnie episode, in which his double is emasculated, because 'he was her man and he done her wrong' and in the scene in which an Englishman is accosted by a plainclothes man in a hotel, because he is carrying a trunk on his back (his unconscious), apparently containing the body of a woman ('Me'); his lack of social conscience in a scene in which a Gentleman with a loaf of bread is pursued by a starving mob. But 'Him' is unable to break through the fourth wall of his own consciousness and follow 'Me' into the real world.

Equally fantastic was *Processional*, in which John Howard Lawson attempted to reflect the glitter and diversity of American life by imitating that classic and unique American institution – vaudeville. 'All around me,' Lawson wrote,

I see the grotesque of the American environment, the colorful exaggeration of the American language – these are Rabelaisian in their intensity.

Lawson saw America as a racial melting pot, a place where there were people of every imaginable race, creed and colour, and he affirmed the value of this heterogeneity against those who insisted on conformity. So his play has a jazz band of striking miners, a Buffalo Bill style sheriff, the Ku Klux Klan, soldiers maintaining law and order, a naïve, gold-digging female, a 'Man in a Silk Hat' as the representative of capitalism and so on. The harmony with which *Processional* ends is deliberately ludicrous: employers and workers come together before the assembled radio microphones, the Sheriff marries Jim, a miner blinded by the KKK, to Sadie, the eternal feminine, with a document sealed by the blood of a Negro. But the essential dialectic is between the tolerant, internationalist, communist outlook of Psinski, the leader of the miners' band and a soldier, prophetically named MacCarthy, who proclaims:

Uncle Sam's gonna keep order here, any guy doubts it goes underground with lead in him, that's the law an' order program, savvy, 'cause the place is lousy with foreigners that don't understand American freedom.

The critique of America offered in these plays was conducted primarily from the perspective of mass society and it was only after the brutal fact of the Great Crash that a more authentic socialist consciousness emerged. But an important step along the way was the New Playwrights Theater, which, from 1927 to 1929, with some financial support from Otto Kahn, a patron of the arts who had also helped Hart Crane, put on a series of plays that included Upton Sinclair's *Singing Jailbirds*, Dos Passos's *The Garbage Man* and *Airways Inc*, Lawson's *Loudspeaker* and *International*, Paul Sifton's *The Belt*. They were succeeded by a host of left-wing plays: John Wexley's *Steel* (1930) which enjoyed a great success in the Soviet Union, Paul and Claire Sifton's *1931*, staged by the Group Theater, which was to be the focus of the most vital theatre of the thirties, and from the Marxist Theater Union, two important plays, *Peace on Earth* (1933) by George Sklar and Albert Maltz, and *Stevedore*, written by Sklar in collaboration with Paul Peters. It was the Theater Union which was most explicitly committed to the view that the theatre was a weapon to be used in the class struggle.

At the same time the American theatre went through bewildering changes in style, so that it seemed as if whole decades of theatrical history had been telescoped into a period of five years. These changes can be charted by examining the development of Lawson and Rice. With his plays for the New Playwrights Lawson modulated into a style using Constructive sets and based on the Russian example of Meyerhold, while Rice, with his *Street Scene* (1929), a lyrical evocation of the rhythms of daily life in a seedy walk-up apartment house in New York, recreated a Chekhovian poetic realism, which was to be the pervasive tone of the work of Clifford Odets, but which here was flawed by melodramatic concessions to conventional notions of theatrical effectiveness. In the thirties Lawson and Rice showed a parallel concern with the failure of success – Lawson's *Success Story*, Rice's *Counsellor-at-Law* (both 1931) – and with the success of failure – Lawson's *The Pure in Heart* (1934) and *Marching Song* (1937), Rice's *We the People* (1933), but in style these were perfectly conventional, naturalistic Broadway plays. Ironically Rice's *We the People* was at once a compendium of themes from the new left-wing drama and, with its final courtroom scene, a return to the traditions of his first success, *On Trial* (1914). *Plus ça change. . . .*

It would be easy but wrong to assume that these 'propaganda' plays of the thirties have become impossibly dated. The issues they raise: freedom of speech; academic freedom and the complicity of university administrators in the interlocking structure of capitalism, militarism and imperialism; the perversion of justice whereby radicals and Negroes are framed for crimes they did not commit, while police forces can commit legal murder with relative impunity; the dehumanization of the worker on the assembly line – these are as relevant now as they were then. Then as now liberalism was under attack. Sherwood Anderson commented on *Peace on Earth*:

The play itself is vital and alive. It is full of the curious dramatic realism of everyday American life right now. There is the pathetic hungryness of the kindly intentioned man – author, college professor, liberal – dramatically set over against the realism of men shot, broken heads – the thing so likely to happen when men and women stand up against the combined little fears of a frightened society.

Nevertheless, there was something essentially conservative about American radicalism, for Americans have always tended to look backward to the traditions of the Founding Fathers rather than forward to the creation of a new order. So, in *Peace on Earth*, a radical leader is arrested for reading from the Declaration of Independence; and this return to fundamentals is pitted against the mechanical conformity of the closing tableau, in which the singing of 'Onward Christian Soldiers' and the swearing of allegiance to the flag gives way to a runner with a sign reading 'Wheat is $2.10', to a blues singer who chants 'I wanna man with a uniform on', to a Recruiting Officer whose message is 'Join the army ... the army builds men.' American radicalism focused invariably on issues of legal injustice. Two famous trials, of Sacco and Vanzetti and of the Scottsboro boys, were made into successful plays by Maxwell Anderson and John Wexley respectively, while the emphasis made by Upton Sinclair in his Postscript to *Singing Jailbirds* (1927), about an IWW strike in California, may be taken as characteristic. Sinclair disassociated himself from the IWW programme as such, but added, referring to himself:

But he stands for the right of all groups of men and women to voice their political and social opinions; and his play is an appeal to the American people to re-establish the most fundamental of constitutional rights, free speech, free press and free assemblage.

The most celebrated left-wing play – perhaps the most completely successful agit-prop play ever written – was Clifford Odets's *Waiting for Lefty* (1935). To begin with it is a brilliant theatre piece with a compelling rhythm of its own, so that the transition of mood from the casual, menacing opening as Harry Fatt, the crooked union leader, tries to talk the men out of going on strike, as his gunman stands by, to the overwhelming solidarity and commitment of the final 'Strike, Strike, Strike!' is both rapid and inevitable. Above all, Odets's play does not deal in generalities. This is the speciality of Harry Fatt, who invokes the remoteness of Philadelphia, where a similar strike of cab-drivers is going on, by asking, 'Where's Philly? A thousand miles away? An hour's ride on the train?' and who tries to mystify his audience by talking about trends. But the chickens come home to roost when a man he calls on to set the record straight about the situation in Philadelphia is exposed by the man's own brother as a company spy. The episode called 'The Young Hack and his Girl' about Sid and Flor, who can't afford to get married, deals with a commonplace experience, yet one which is sharply particularized and moving even in its brevity. The sound of the record that carries on scratching round after they have finished dancing to 'a cheap, sad, dance tune' seems to symbolize the dearth of possibilities that life offers them. More than this, the play embodies a sense of individual responsibility that goes beyond such apparent fatalism: it is no good relying on corrupt union leaders or even 'waiting for Lefty', people must take action themselves if they want to change society.

However, the most characteristic and important plays of the Depression period, Odets's *Awake and Sing* (1935) and Paul Green's *The House of Connelly* (1931), are not directly political. In Odets's words, their concern is with 'a struggle for life amidst petty conditions'. In accordance with our still stereotyped picture of the thirties it might have been expected that the drama of the decade would be full of vague, generalized social conflicts, focused on large-scale social issues and padded out with abstract rhetoric. Undoubtedly plays of this kind were written, but on the whole it is in the twenties that we will find the optimism and imaginative boldness to make big dramatic statements about society. The dramatist of the thirties is restrained, cautious, suspicious of rhetoric, inclined towards the small subject rather than the large one. There is a possibly surprising but quite unmistakable emphasis on the *individual*, on the small group, on the problems of day-to-day living. This tendency was reinforced by the influence on theatre directors of Stanislavsky, who placed more emphasis on character and whose identification with Chekhov suggested a drama in which moments of laughter and hope are set alongside defeatism and sadness – the alien world of Tsarist Russia had evoked a shock of recognition.

The characters of Green and Odets are preoccupied with the sheer difficulty of living, in relation to which neither pessimism nor optimism seems an entirely adequate response. As it happens, Odets's play is hopeful, Green's despairing – yet originally *Awake and Sing* had been a good deal less positive, while *The House of Connelly* was altered in performance in order to make a more affirmative statement. Hope out of despair was, inevitably, the standard rhetorical trope. The endings of both plays have been criticized, but they are necessarily arbitrary in relation to a vision of life as frustrating and intractable, in face of the recognition of the many ways in which the human spirit can be worn away.

All the characters of *Awake and Sing* are blocked and thwarted. Bessie Berger is disappointed in her children and her husband, Myron; while Myron himself, who never made anything out of his two years at law school, is a broken man, living in the past, on his memories of Teddie Roosevelt and of the singer, Nora Bayes. Jacob, an old Jew who gives haircuts, still nurses his dreams of revolution, but he is mocked by Uncle Morty, a successful garment manufacturer, and squashed by Bessie. Moe Axelrod, who lost a leg in the First World War, and who loves Hennie Berger against the odds, conceals his feelings behind a coarse, sardonic vein of humour. Ralph, the son, has never had a life of his own; even now he works in his uncle's business and has to hand over virtually everything he owns to his mother. She strongly opposes his marrying the girl he loves on the grounds that she is an orphan! Essentially it is Bessie who grinds the others down. She leaves them with no respect or dignity and takes it for granted that she shall manage their affairs. So when Hennie becomes pregnant she persuades her to marry Sam Feinschreiber, whom she does not care for, in order to make it respectable. Gradually we come to recognize that the cynical pleasantries which the characters exchange are a measure not of their intimacy but of their distance from each other. They reflect the degree to which the Bergers' immersion in the day-to-day business of living deprives them of any perspective upon it. Bessie's confident rejoinder to everything, 'Go fight City Hall!' is in reality a confession of despair. Only Jacob with his books, his records, his faith in socialism has this perspective: it is suggested when he puts on a record of Caruso:

From 'L'Africana' . . . a big explorer comes on a new land – 'O Paradiso'. From act four this piece. Caruso stands on the ship and looks on a Utopia. You hear? 'Oh paradise! Oh paradise on earth! Oh blue sky, oh fragrant air –'

Bessie smashes the record and Jacob, who seems to have no reason to go on living, kills himself, leaving behind an insurance policy for Ralph. Death sharpens the sense of life: Jacob's sacrifice gives Ralph and Hennie the courage to make a fresh start, to finally break free from the stifling hopelessness that is 'home'.

Paul Green was born in 1894 in North Carolina and not surprisingly the past casts even longer shadows in his plays of the South than it did in the Bronx of Odets. For Green the bond that makes all men brothers in the South is the sense of disillusionment and defeat. Black or white, whether he be Abraham McCranie of *In Abraham's Bosom* (1926) or Will Connelly of *The House of Connelly*, it is hard enough for any one man to try to make a fresh start, even if he can summon up the will to do so. And when he does there are countless obstacles: narrow and perverse traditions, skeletons from the past, resentment or indifference on the part of others against which effort is gradually dissipated. For Green there is no rigid separation to be made between the races, for whatever may have been the theory, the *practice* of white Southerners was very different. Abraham is a mulatto who tries desperately to rise in the world and then, blocked and defeated, takes out his overwhelming sense of frustration on the white brother who denies him by choking and strangling him to death. This theme is paralleled in Langston Hughes's *Mulatto*. In *The House of Connelly* retribution is exacted by the Negro field women, Big Sis and Big Sue. The curse of the House of Connelly is that General Connelly condemned his own mulatto son to death. Will Connelly tries later to atone for it by inviting his mulatto kin to sit and eat at the same table, but such a gesture is too little and too late. Will is himself split in his attitude towards women: he has a Platonic relationship with Virginia Buchanan, a well-bred Southern lady, he is sexually attracted to Essie, the mulatto house-servant, while his involvement with Patsy Tate, the pushing daughter of one of his tenant farmers, is determined primarily by his sense that she has the drive to make the plantation prosperous. Even their love, if that is what it is, is corrupted by the desire to possess and dominate. But Green, through the dark warnings of Sue and Sis, through the counterpoint of Negro fieldsongs and Uncle Bob's mumbled Latin tags, has built up an overwhelming sense of fatality: there are to be no fresh starts, not for anybody; the house of Connelly is left deserted and Sis and Sue smother Patsy in a sacking bag.

Although Maxwell Anderson's Pennsylvania origins may have expressed themselves in his homage to George Washington in

Valley Forge (1934) and in his faith in the value of American institutions and traditions, he might perhaps be ranked as an honorary
Southerner. He is attracted to unfashionable values: defeat that
interests him rather than success – and the heroic obduracy that will
accept it rather than compromise. Anderson's work poses in a
critical form questions regarding the viability of a contemporary
poetic drama. In attempting to write a poetry that approximates
fairly closely to normal speech he ends up with something which
lacks the rhythmic energy, suppleness and complexity of verse, yet
which is starved of the inflection, tone, colour and vitality of
ordinary speech. This verse, as much as the subject matter, is
responsible for turning Anderson's plays into stiff, wooden,
essentially lifeless costume dramas. *Night Over Taos* (1932) is less
starchy than the rest and its theme, the sexual and political rivalry
between Pablo Montoya and his sons as New Mexico is threatened
from without by US forces, is genuinely engrossing. But the
aphorism of the heroic Montoya –

For wisdom and justice we must depend on the young; for madness in
devotion to a cause, for all madness you must go among their elders...

– is given a more pessimistic emphasis in Anderson's play of
contemporary life, *Winterset* (1935). Harking back to the Sacco–
Vanzetti case, it deals with the attempt of a young man, Mio, to
vindicate his father who has been framed on a murder charge and
reveal the truth. Gangsterdom has no liking for the truth and he and
his girl are machine-gunned. Anderson implies that justice (the one
thing which should not be bought and sold) is unattainable; that the
cunning of old age only leads to adjustment to an impossible world;
that youthful idealism must inevitably be destroyed. *Winterset* is a
Measure for Measure in which the Duke has left, never to return.

In the context of so much theatrical experimentalism the work of
Lillian Hellman may, at first sight, appear relatively conventional.
But Hellman is a real dramatist and the extent of her achievement
can best be measured by comparing her drama with that of Sidney
Howard and Philip Barry, who established themselves in the
twenties as leading purveyors of the well-made play to Broadway.
Neither makes much pretence at dealing in anything but the most
generalized theatrical types and obvious situations. Thus Barry's
Paris Bound features an adulterous husband and a virtuous wife, and
defends the institution of marriage, while Howard's *The Silver Cord*
is about weak sons and their possessive, dominating mother. And
when Barry tries something more ambitious in *Hotel Universe* he

succeeds only in being at once pretentious and trivial. The characters of Howard and Barry lack individuality – not even their long, cumbersome and unconvincing soliloquies can save them. By contrast Hellman's characters are individual and clearly realized, both in themselves and in relation to one another; her sense of theatre and the effects she achieves through *mise-en-scène* are infinitely more subtle. The picture of life and human nature which she builds up in her plays is not a very attractive one but neither is it melodramatic. Quietly and unassertively an atmosphere of evil is established, which seems, in the final analysis, to be unlocalizable. It is not the consequence of a single action but of many. Unfortunately because her plays are so immediately effective on the stage it is easy to misconstrue them and underestimate their complexity.

The Children's Hour (1934) is concerned with two schoolteachers who run a small school. Karen is proposing to marry Dr Joseph Cardin but says that she will nevertheless go on teaching. Martha is strongly against the marriage, ostensibly because it will damage the school, in reality because she feels a strong attraction towards her sister, the nature of which she does not entirely recognize. However, this is thrust into the open when Mary, the spoilt, unscrupulous child of a wealthy family, overhears something and accuses the sisters of lesbianism, whereupon all the parents withdraw their children from the school. Inevitably attention tends to focus on Mary and especially on the cruel way in which she blackmails another girl to silence. Nevertheless Mary is only a child, who does not comprehend the full significance of her actions; real responsibility lies with the malicious, thoughtless gossip of Mrs Lily Mortar and, above all, with Mary's grandmother, Mrs Tilford, who jumps to such damaging conclusions. Martha, though 'guilty', is innocent; and Hellman's indictment, like Fitzgerald's, is reserved for the rich, who carelessly smash up other people's lives.

Political attitudes have prejudiced verdicts on her next play, *Days to Come* (1936). It is by no means a failure, for the sense of corruption that overtakes a hitherto peaceful mid-Western town, when Andrew Rodman, a factory-owner in financial difficulties, brings in mobsters to break up a strike, is unquestionably convincing. The casual killing of one of the gangsters by another makes possible the framing of a labour organizer and this leads to the outbreak of violence in which the child of a worker is killed. However, Hellman's attempt to nail responsibility on to the Rodmans only seems to trivialize what has happened, which seems to go far beyond their own moral dilemmas. More successful is *The Little*

Foxes (1939), where the ethical dimension virtually disappears. Hellman paints a damning portrait of those who live only in order to exploit others – in this instance, the Hubbards, who collaborate with a financier from Chicago to bring cotton milling to the south and so undercut Northern labour. Their brutality and unscrupulousness does not leave their personal relationships unaffected. Oscar Hubbard has only married Birdie because his brother Ben wanted her cotton and she says: 'In twenty-two years I haven't had a whole day of happiness.' Her plight is paralleled by Horace Giddens, a dying man, who has grown tired of the Hubbards' ways. When he refuses to put up some bonds for the cotton deal they are stolen from him and he is then virtually murdered by his own wife, who keeps his medicine from him when he has a heart attack. When Alexandra, his daughter, asks Ben and Oscar if they loved him, they have no answer. Love is not a word in their vocabulary.

Thornton Wilder's sunny optimism is a long way from the blackness of Lillian Hellman and perhaps equally far from American reality. In his *Franklin D. Roosevelt and the New Deal* William E. Leuchtenburg says:

In early 1938 many Americans once more neared starvation – in Chicago children salvaged food from garbage cans. . . .

and it seems hard to believe that February of the same year also saw the first New York production of *Our Town*. But, of course, it is particularly in times of hardship and insecurity that people look for consolation and reassurance, to be distracted and amused. If the Depression period raised political awareness through the Federal Theater's living newspapers, it also saw George S. Kaufman's *Of Thee I Sing* (with music by Gershwin), where politics are taken a good deal less seriously and where a Presidential candidate campaigns on a 'Love' platform. Kaufman's high-spirited humour was displayed in many plays written in collaboration and was only rivalled by the more elegant S. N. Behrman. In the thirties Behrman produced interesting work, but like Odets with *Golden Boy* and *Rocket to the Moon*, he was never quite able to recapture the freshness and spontaneity of his earliest theatrical ventures. *The Second Man* (1927), a play about a second-rate writer who, with the best will in the world, is capable of neither loving nor writing well, succeeded in being both serious and funny, while *Serena Blandish* (1928) revealed a talent for Shavian paradox. Behrman's strength and weakness is that he seems a straight dramatist manqué. In *The*

Second Man the combination clicked, but with *Rain from Heaven* (1934) and the aptly named *No Time for Comedy* (1939) even Behrman found it difficult to keep up a comic front. Perhaps the failure was an honourable one. For Wilder's optimism seems facile. His reduction of life to a complacent involvement in trivialities (criticized by Odets), his inability to postulate any other prospect of social betterment than a society in which the diligent would rise to the top as the idle sank to the bottom, his celebration of families that are completely interchangeable, makes *Our Town* a panegyric to one-dimensional man. Wilder's aim was to portray the universal, but he failed to realize that great art conveys universality through the specific; and it is in the specifics of America, whether of 1938 or 1901, that *Our Town* is deficient. Its most striking device, the return of past inhabitants of the town from the dead, was taken directly from Irwin Shaw's anti-war play, *Bury the Dead* (1936). In his later *The Skin of Our Teeth* (1942), the saga of the survival of a universal Joycean family, the Antrobuses, through ice ages, wars and numerous catastrophes of world history, Wilder was forced to put back much of what he had left out of his earlier play, but even so his fundamental complacency was unshaken. A better guide to the pre-war mood is the work of one of Wilder's disciples, Robert Ardrey's *Thunder Rock* (1939), in which a man shuts himself away in a lonely lighthouse and, from his imaginary intercourse with the passengers of a ship which was wrecked there a century earlier, draws the inspiration which will enable him to carry on even when things seem at their darkest. It is a fairly obvious message play but at least it has the quality of personal involvement. Wilder's chief rival in spreading euphoria was William Saroyan, whose message was that the earth was a good place and that everyone should have a good time – like Jasper MacGregor, who in *My Heart's in the Highlands* (1939) gladdens the hearts of everyone with his melodious bugle playing. Saroyan took developments in *mise-en-scène* to the point where plot was no longer necessary. In *The Time of Your Life* (1939), set in Nick's waterfront bar in San Francisco, everyone simply does his own thing. A typical stage direction reads:

Each person belongs to the environment, in his own person, as himself: Wesley is playing better than ever. Harry is hoofing better than ever. Nick is behind the bar shining glasses. Joe is smiling at the toy and studying it. Dudley, although still troubled, is at least calm now and full of melancholy poise. Willit, at the marble-game, is happy. The Arab is deep in his memories where he wants to be.

With so much going for them why do people want to make trouble and come out on strike? They should go to a movie, take a drive on Sunday! There is something bullying about Saroyan's good-time gospel, and something repellent about Joe, his pseudo-Gatsby, the realizer of dreams, who spends the day winding up clockwork toys, drinking champagne, redeeming prostitutes and sending out his sidekick in search of different flavours of chewing gum.

During the thirties O'Neill was silent save for *Ah, Wilderness* (1933) and *Days Without End* (1934). The writing of them was essentially an act of exorcism. In the former, an uncharacteristic comedy, O'Neill undercut and qualified the figure of the adolescent rebel much as Joyce qualified Stephen in *Ulysses*. In the latter he made his peace with Catholicism by depicting a character who returns to the faith. In the late thirties O'Neill was at work on a massive cycle, to be known as 'A Tale of Possessors Self-dispossessed'. Only two plays from it have survived. *More Stately Mansions* most clearly suggests the significance of this title – the way in which the desire to dominate debases and perverts all relationships – and is valuable because it indicates how O'Neill made the transition from *Mourning Becomes Electra* to his later work. But it cannot really be subjected to critical appraisal since it is clearly a rough draft, which O'Neill explicitly asked to have destroyed. *A Touch of the Poet* is an important work, but it will probably always be underestimated because O'Neill worked out its themes with greater complexity in *The Iceman Cometh* and *Long Day's Journey into Night*, for which it appears to be a preparatory sketch.

Like *Our Town*, *The Iceman Cometh* is set in the period before the First World War; like *The Time of Your Life* it deals with a miscellaneous crowd of people hanging about in a bar and their wonder-working benefactor (Hickey); but there resemblances end. For *The Iceman Cometh* is a masterpiece, arguably the greatest work of the modern theatre, a complex, ironic, deeply moving exploration of human existence, written out of a profound insight into human nature and constructed with such skill and logic that carping criticisms of its length seem incomprehensible. The characters who sit drinking day after day in Harry Hope's bar live on their 'pipe dreams' – a phrase which immediately suggests an analogy with the 'life lie' which Dr Relling prescribed for his patients in *The Wild Duck*. The analogy is deceptive, however, because O'Neill's sense of the role which pipe dreams play in the lives of individuals is richer than Ibsen's and it developed organically out of his own dramatic concerns. As O'Neill sees it, man's essential problem is to come to terms with himself. Perhaps, ordinarily, we might think of this as 'facing the truth' but that is to put the matter too abstractly. The truth is always at a third remove. No one can be sure that they have faced it because man has an inexhaustible capacity for self-deception. The truth of existence is the truth that enables one to survive: so that Larry's belief that he has no pipe dream is, in reality, the illusion which he goes on living. A man, in O'Neill's view, cannot be other than fallible and imperfect; what is decisive is the attitude he adopts towards himself – self-respect or self-contempt. While O'Neill ironically qualifies the pipe dreams of the characters in the bar (of returning home, of getting back in the police force, of being elected counsellor and so on) insofar as they offer a basis for self-respect, there is more dignity in the pipe dream than in the overpowering self-contempt of Don Parritt, who has betrayed his revolutionist mother to the police, and of Hickey, the travelling salesman, who finally kills his wife Evelyn because he can no longer endure being forgiven for his casual adulteries. Parritt is locked into a downward spiral of self-loathing that eventually leads to suicide. His low opinion of himself leads him to despise others also; but he would prefer to admit that he betrayed his mother in order to spend money on a whore than confess that he hated her because she felt that she had something to live for. Parritt and Hickey are oppressed by the sense of their own emptiness. They can only free themselves of it by striking at the one person in life who matters most to them, for this is to destroy the last thing they have. Just as when Major Melody shoots his horse in *A Touch of the Poet* and crushes all that remains of his own best self, so when Hickey kills Evelyn this is tantamount to an act of self-destruction. Hickey, significantly, was the son of a preacher, and in this way O'Neill expresses his sense of the failure of America and of the Protestant ethic: a destructive, vengeful idealism that cannot be at peace in the world, in whose cheery optimism is concealed a latent death–wish. Hickey's arrival in the bar creates a feeling of unease. Its sacred rituals are disturbed, as Hickey boasts that he needs neither alcohol nor pipe dreams, and incongruously provides flowers, a birthday cake for Harry Hope, the proprietor, and champagne instead of the customary cheap whisky. He tries to force the inmates to face reality and make their pipe dreams concrete. They leave the bar momentarily, only to return without even the last shred of self-respect and resentful of Hickey for taking it away. They themselves know well enough what their pipe dreams are. In fact they do not at all confuse them with reality. But they prefer to keep them, just as Pearl and Margie prefer to think of themselves as tarts rather than whores and Rocky regards himself as a bartender rather than a pimp. Subconsciously they recognize that the peace which Hickey brings them, the end of all hopes and pipe dreams, is nothing less than death – the iceman. And just as Hickey tries to fill the drinkers at Harry Hope's with his own negativity, so they revenge themselves by declaring him mad; for this is the only way they can retain their self-respect. In other words, they choose life.

Long Day's Journey Into Night, written a year later in 1940, is equally impressive. The Tyrones are based fairly closely on O'Neill's own family but are seen in a light transfigured by art – only a dramatist as experienced as O'Neill could have attempted to write so close to his own experience. The play spins endless circles of mutual recrimination and self-accusation. James Tyrone, the father, a successful actor, seems most to blame: it was as the result of his meanness that his wife became addicted to morphine, since he would never pay for the best medical attention despite the fact he could easily afford it; now, although his son Edmund is dying, he will only send him to the State sanatorium. But it is also clear that his early poverty has left an indelible mark upon him, making him habitually mean, although his insecurity simultaneously leads him to invest his money recklessly in land. Much of the time the Tyrones are concerned with themselves. They shut themselves away and respect one another's privacy. The fog, as in *Anna Christie*, symbolizes the oblivion of evasion and self-deception. Mary Tyrone says:

I really love the fog. It hides you from the world and the world from you.

Existence is pain. The Tyrones try to exonerate themselves of guilt through mutual accusations. Always they try to look on their own experiences in the most favourable light. They are filled with self-pity and regret. Jamie, the cynical elder brother, a failed actor who spends his time with prostitutes, excoriates his mother for her inability to break her dependence on morphine because he recognizes in her his own failure; like Hickey, he tries to awaken his brother to unpalatable 'truths'. Yet this hostility cannot conceal the genuine affection and concern the Tyrones have for each other even in, perhaps because of, their weakness.

In *The Iceman Cometh* the pipe dream provided a reason for going on living; in *Long Day's Journey* dream progressively invades and overpowers reality, until, in the extraordinary theatricality of Mary Tyrone's final speech, when she speaks of her youthful ambition to become a nun, while the others listen as if in a trance, dream seems to be the only thing that is real. Such a moment in the theatre is beyond definition, but it can be illuminated to some extent by referring back to *Strange Interlude*, whose title it recalls. In the earlier plays also, subjective dreams and desires were seen as incommensurable with surface reality, but the disjuncture there has been transformed into subtle interpenetration and counterpoint. The greatness of *Long Day's Journey* is the product not of instant autobiography, but of hard-won art.

O'Neill in his sheer persistence and capacity for development was a law unto himself. In these late plays the enormous promise of the American theatre, which at times had seemed as if it might never be more than a series of hopeful beginnings, was fulfilled. With O'Neill's genius established as unquestioned, the other figures, Rice, Odets, Green, Hellman, and a host of others, begin to compose around him into a satisfying pattern of achievement. Even so, it would be idle to pretend that this serious drama was more than marginalia in the pages of the commercial theatre. The impression made on Americans by the Provincetown Players seems small enough if it is measured against the Ziegfeld Follies or *Abie's Irish Rose* – immensely popular and profitable Broadway hits of the 1920s. 'Show Business' is a significantly American phrase. Already at the turn of the century the American theatre, under the 'Syndicate' of Klaw and Erlanger, began to be organized on a basis which aligned it with cartelization in other spheres. The theatre business did not merely back artistic horses to win; increasingly it was concerned with maximizing financial return and with eliminating uncertainty and risk. Thus, the American dramatist was (and is) squeezed between the high-risk, high-cost, high-profit musical and the low-risk, low-profit foreign play. Moreover, the Theater Guild did little to help in this situation, since although it put on some excellent plays, the majority of them were European. Hollywood was a powerful rival to the theatre, not only because of the competition provided by the cinema, but because so many talented people – MacGowan, Odets, Lawson – left to work in the movies. After two decades the position of the American dramatist was as problematic as it had been when O'Neill made his first ventures in the theatre. But, in the interstices, miraculously, was a solid record of achievement.

4

AMERICAN POETRY AND THE ENGLISH LANGUAGE, 1900–1945

Geoffrey Moore

QUESTIONNAIRE

1. Is it nonsense to talk of a typical American poem? If not, what, in your opinion, are the qualities which tend to distinguish a poem as American?
2. Do you consider that the language of American poetry (vocabulary, use of vocabulary, metric, cadences, syntax, punctuation), differs notably from that of English poetry? Is this difference (if any) fortuitous, or does it correspond to some underlying difference of sensibility?[1]

Plato the purple swine advocated the expulsion of 'poets' (he may have meant Eddie Marsh's gang or the blokes who write in the *Observer*) from his projected republic but he failed to *specify* that he meant sloppy poets. He was, as I have already said, a 'prose poet', that is a rhapsodist who shirked verse technique (musical technique).[2]

It would have been interesting to have Pound's reply to Rajan's questionnaire. The poets interrogated – Marianne Moore, Robert Penn Warren, Wallace Stevens, Horace Gregory, Allen Tate, James Laughlin, William Carlos Williams – produced some oddly unilluminating responses, mainly because they refused to get down to details. There *are* differences and they arise, as Wallace Stevens pointed out, from the fact that 'we live in two different physical worlds and it is not nonsense to think that that matters'. But it is from closely observed differences in the areas which Rajan specifies – from induction rather than deduction – that the truth might emerge.

    Pound's personal aside, typical of the acrimonious and sporadic *aperçus* of the *Guide to Kulchur*, subsumes a whole line of criticism *vis-à-vis* American poetry. We have all heard it so often that we take

[1] B. Rajan, ed., *Modern American Poetry* (London, Dobson, 1950), p 182.
[2] Ezra Pound, *Guide to Kulchur* (New Directions pb, 1968), p 128.

it for truth, perhaps without as much examination as we might have given these axioms. *Nota*: American poetry in the twentieth century is better than English poetry. *Nota*: It all began in the years before the First World War, when Harriet Monroe perceived what was best in the new American poetry and, in the pages of *Poetry*, published a catholic collection of American poets whose work was as far from the thin Romanticism of Richard Hovey and Bliss Carman as it was from the Georgian pipings of 'Eddie Marsh's gang'.

But what do we actually find when we compare the first volume of *Georgian Poetry, 1911–1912*[1] with *Poetry: A Magazine of Verse* (Vol. I, October–March, 1912–13)? We find, for one thing, that the latter volume begins with a contribution by one Arthur Davison Ficke ('a graduate of Harvard, who studied law and entered his father's office in Davenport, Iowa'). It is called 'Poetry' and the first verse runs:

> It is a little isle amid bleak seas –
> An isolate realm of garden, circled round
> By importunity of stress and sound,
> Devoid of empery to master these.
> At most, the memory of its streams and bees,
> Borne to the toiling mariner outward-bound,
> Recalls his soul to that delightful ground;
> But serves no beacon toward his destinies.

Miss Monroe's chatty notes further inform us that another contributor, Mrs Roscoe P. Conkling, is a resident of the state of New York; her poem is 'Symphony of a Mexican Garden'. The contents list contains many non-American names – from W. B. Yeats (five Celtic Twilight poems), Rabindranath Tagore, Alfred Noyes, Ernest Rhys and Alice Meynell to Richard Aldington. Of the vaunted American new guard there is precious little – Pound's 'To Whistler, American' and 'Middle Aged' (both unpreserved in his *Collected Shorter Poems*) and Vachel Lindsay's 'General William Booth Enters into Heaven'. For the rest, it is a sad *mélange* of such as Witter Bynner, Madison Cawein, Fannie Stearns Davis, Lily A. Long, Mrs Schuyler Van Rensselaer and Ridgley Torrence.

The Georgian anthology, on the other hand, contains five poems by Rupert Brooke, including 'The Old Vicarage, Grantchester', de la Mare's 'Arabia', 'The Sleeper' and 'The Listeners' (among

[1] The Poetry Bookshop, Theobalds Road, London, December 1912.

others), poems by Flecker, W. W. Gibson, John Masefield and James Stephens, and D. H. Lawrence's 'The Snapdragon'. What price *Poetry* (Chicago)? All in all, it seems an amateurish affair, with, apart from a few Poundian nuggets, a peculiar kind of American poetasting, which might be found as distasteful as the mandarin style of the English. 'Sloppy poets' some of 'Eddie Marsh's gang' may have been – but not all.

Let us call a roll of some of the more usually cited American books of verse in the early years of the twentieth century.[1] Vachel Lindsay's volume containing 'General William Booth Enters into Heaven' appeared in 1913, and *The Congo and Other Poems* in 1914. Robert Frost's *North of Boston* came out in the same year (albeit published in England), Edgar Lee Masters's *Spoon River Anthology* in 1915, Sandburg's *Chicago Poems* and Edwin Arlington Robinson's *The Man Against the Sky* in 1916. It is a fair enough contribution. However, Lindsay, Sandburg and Masters achieved as much fame by being heralds of a so-called 'Middle-Western Renaissance' as by being poets of intrinsic literary importance. Robinson is revealed on close examination to have a peculiarly 'for them' (Americans that is) validity. And Frost – even Frost at his best – can hardly approach the glorious felicities of Yeats. Whitman was another matter but, certainly, the transatlantic fireworks of the early years of the twentieth century now seem a little damp.

We must look elsewhere for the greatest poetic contribution by Americans in the early days of the twentieth century. They are two-fold. The first is the extraordinary impetus given to modern poetry as a whole by the pioneering achievement of Pound and Eliot. By 1920 Pound had published eleven books, the last of them *Hugh Selwyn Mauberley*. Three more were to appear before *A Draft of XVI Cantos* in 1925. Eliot brought out *Prufrock* in 1917, *Ara Vos Prec* in 1919, *Poems* and *The Sacred Wood* in 1920, and *The Waste Land* in 1922. The second great poetic contribution is the Imagist movement (although it was not *wholly* American in origin).

It is in the six principles of Imagism, rather than in the less-than-first-class talent displayed in the anthology *Des Imagistes* (1914) and the three volumes of *Some Imagist Poets* (1915, 1916 and 1917), that there may be found the core of that new hardness and clearness which was to inform the best work of Pound, Eliot and, later, Williams:

[1] See L. Untermeyer, *Modern American Poetry* (1950), Preface, p 13.

1. To use the language of common speech, but to employ always the *exact* word, not the merely decorative word.
2. To create new rhythms – as the expression of new moods. We do not insist on 'free verse' as the only method of writing poetry ... We do believe that the individuality of a poet may often be better expressed in free verse than in conventional forms.
3. To allow absolute freedom in the choice of subject.
4. To present an image (hence the name 'Imagist'). We are not a school of painters, but we believe that poetry should render particulars exactly and not deal in vague generalities, however magnificent and sonorous.
5. To produce poetry that is hard and clear, never blurred or indefinite.
6. Finally, most of us believe that concentration is the very essence of poetry.

However, I do not believe that Imagism as such – that is, the simple, if skilful, setting down of images in a style which might be compared with the *haiku* – ever produced great poetry. Two examples from Pound might be adduced in evidence:

> The apparition of these faces in the crowd;
> Petals on a wet, black bough.

and

> Crushed strawberries! Come, let us feast our eyes,
> Green arsenic smeared on an egg-white cloth.

These are offered as poems, but poems they are not. They are, if you like, brilliant gestures, bold experiments, attempts to clear away the rubble of Victorian over-describing. In prose, they might be compared with the contribution which Hemingway made when he too 'used the language of common speech' and employed 'always the exact word, never the merely decorative word', when he substituted the dryness of 'he said', 'she said' for the pseudo-eloquence of, say, 'he expostulated violently'. 'Don't "talk about", "present",' said Henry James, and although his work is not an ideal example of using the language of common speech, one may applaud his sentiments. Even Williams's notorious experiments in the Imagist manner leave something to be desired – for example:

> so much depends
> upon
>
> a red wheel
> barrow
>
> glazed with rain
> water
>
> beside the white
> chickens

Those who were most possessed by Imagism, like HD (Hilda Doolittle), never became more than good minor poets. That the movement was for Pound, Eliot and Williams a stepping-stone towards their own personal goals, indicates their stature. What I find it interesting to enquire is what that stature was. All the great American poets, it has been said, have been either preachers or experimenters, or both. Not for them the modes of men 'content with the connotations of their masters'. This statement applies no doubt to Pound, Eliot and Williams – as it did to Whitman – but how far down the scale does it go? To examine the proposition carefully may not only provide a certain perspective but also enable tentative answers to be given to the first part of Rajan's questionnaire.

For the sake of clarity (and perhaps of comparative enlightenment) a list of twentieth-century American and British poets placed roughly in the decades in which they were most important might be attempted:

	American	*British*
1900s	Edwin Markham William Vaughn Moody E. A. Robinson Trumbull Stickney	Rudyard Kipling G. K. Chesterton Laurence Binyon Thomas Sturge Moore A. E. Housman
1910s	Robert Frost Carl Sandburg Vachel Lindsay Edgar Lee Masters Amy Lowell	G. M. Hopkins (posthumous) Robert Bridges Rupert Brooke Wilfred Owen Siegfried Sassoon John Masefield W. B. Yeats Edward Thomas W. H. Davies Walter de la Mare
1920s	Emily Dickinson (posthumous) Conrad Aiken Ezra Pound T. S. Eliot	D. H. Lawrence Edith Sitwell Robert Graves James Stephens W. J. Turner

	American	*British*
1920s	E. E. Cummings	
	Wallace Stevens	
	William Carlos Williams	
	HD	
	Stephen Vincent Benét	
1930s	Hart Crane	W. H. Auden
	Marianne Moore	Stephen Spender
	John Crowe Ransom ⎫	Louis Macneice
	Allan Tate ⎬ 'Fugitives'	Cecil Day Lewis
	Robert Penn Warren ⎭	William Empson
	Robinson Jeffers	David Gascoyne
	Archibald MacLeish	
	Richard Eberhart	
	Kenneth Fearing	
1940s	Delmore Schwartz	Dylan Thomas
	Karl Shapiro	Roy Fuller
	Muriel Rukeyser	Lawrence Durrell
	Elizabeth Bishop	Vernon Watkins
	Randall Jarrell	W. S. Graham
	John Ciardi	W. R. Rodgers
	Theodore Roethke	George Barker
	Robert Lowell	Henry Reed
	Richard Wilbur	Sidney Keyes
	John Berryman	Alun Lewis
	Kenneth Patchen	John Heath-Stubbs
	Winfield Townley Scott	David Wright
	Peter Viereck	John Betjeman

I choose Housman to compare with Robinson in the first decade since although, like Yeats, he spans a greater period, it was in the early years of the twentieth century that his poems had most impact. Like Robinson, too, he published his first book in the nineties. Both were classicists; both were pessimists.

A comparison of Robinson with Housman produces a conclusion which may be extended – through later comparisons – from the particular to the general. The English poet is conventional in form and (at least publicly expressed) morality, but the professionalism is superb and the music is all. Yet it is not music in the sense of

Swinburnian lilt or the thundering metres of Newbolt – and certainly not of Moody, Richard Hovey or Bliss Carman.

Housman's sense of touch – seemingly so bland – has a cutting edge and an element in it of that effectiveness, pertinence and happiness of phrase which Helen Gardner found in Chaucer compared with Langland:

> But Chaucer's 'divine fluidity' ... his unerring sense of *verbal melody*, his *skill in verse paragraph*, the range of his vocabulary and his discretion in the use of it ... the union in his poetry of grace and strength – these all make him a poet who has in a high degree what Langland lacks: what Mr Eliot has called 'auditory imagination'.[1]

Eliot's definition of 'auditory imagination' was:

> the feeling for syllable and rhythm, penetrating far below the conscious levels of thought and feeling, invigorating every word; sinking to the most primitive and forgotten, returning to the origin and bringing something back, seeking the beginning and the end. It works through meanings, certainly, or not without meanings in the ordinary sense, and fuses the old and obliterated and the trite, the current, and the new and surprising, the most ancient and the most civilized mentality.[2]

Does Housman possess 'auditory imagination'? In 'Reveillé' the extended image of the first stanza:

> And the ship of sunrise burning
>   Strands upon the eastern rims ...
> Wake: the silver dusk returning
>   Up the beach of darkness brims, ...

is far from being that of a conventional poetaster, although at first glance it might seem to be such. Rhythm and sense go hand in hand with an urgency that is sustained by the change of pace in the third stanza:

> Up, lad, up, 'tis late for lying:
>   Hear the drums of morning play ...

Finally, the last verse wrings the heart (in spite of ourselves?) with the felicity of its word-choice:

> Clay lies still but blood's a rover;
>   Breath's a ware that will not keep.
> Up, lad: when the journey's over
>   There'll be time enough to sleep.

---

[1] Helen Gardner, *The Art of T. S. Eliot* (E. P. Dutton pb, 1959), p 4.
[2] T. S. Eliot, *The Use of Poetry* (1933), quoted by Gardner, op. cit., p 6.

Kiplingesque echoes ('If you can keep your head when all about you . . .')? But what is wrong with these virtues, if expressed acceptably? Nor is it merely the young soldier's duty that Housman is underlining. The moral applies to us all.

A similar felicity attends 'With rue my heart is laden'. 'Golden friends' and 'rose-lipt maidens' may not be the contemporary poet's idea of original imagery. But backward-looking though Housman may be in vocabulary and technique, there is no pastiche here (as there is, very obviously for example, in the work of Edna St Vincent Millay).

There is a memorable quality about the typical Housman phrase:

> When I was one-and-twenty
> I heard a wise man say . . .

– memorable, that is, in a mnemonic sense. This kind of verse is for repeating, as in:

> In summertime on Bredon
> The bells they sound so clear . . .

or

> Loveliest of trees, the cherry now
> Is hung with bloom along the bough.

The final stanza of 'Loveliest of Trees' is trite enough in its sense: but although the *carpe diem* note is sad, it is not banal. Housman has used a traditional instrument and traditional imagery to express his own individual choice.

Let us take, for comparison, one of Robinson's best-known poems:

> Miniver Cheevy, child of scorn,
> Grew lean while he assailed the seasons;
> He wept that he was ever born,
> And he had reasons . . .

What is most noticeable is the difference of tone. Not only is Housman a singer; he can be sung. It would be difficult to sing Robinson. His metres, like his thought, are tough. The abrupt change of the four-stress line to a two-stress one is disconcerting – and is meant to be so. Robinson is an ironist; none of the well-controlled glamour of Housman for him. A 'down-East' dourness pervades even the most 'mystical' of his lyrics:

> No more with overflowing light
> Shall fill the eyes that now are faded
> Nor shall another's fringe with night
> Their woman-hidden world as they did ...

or

> She fears him, and will always ask
>   What fated her to choose him;
> She meets in his engaging mask
>   All reasons to refuse him:
> But what she meets and what she fears
> Are less than are the downward years,
> Drawn slowly to the foamless weirs
>   Of age, were she to lose him.

Housman would never have been guilty of the lack of ear which led to the third rhyme on the same sound in line seven. It is an error into which Poe more often fell; one would not have expected it of a poet of Robinson's desperate honesty.

But it is not only to the lyric Robinson or the Robinson of those pre-Spoon River pen-portraits that we must look if we are to gauge his quality. Most commentators dwell on the much-anthologized poems ('Eros Turannos', 'Mr Flood's Party', 'For a Dead Lady', 'Flammonde'). However, the bulk of his work consists of long narrative poems. After his first twentieth-century book, *Captain Craig* (1902), he published five such poems of book length, using Merlin or Lancelot or Tristram or 'King Jasper' as subjects.

Perhaps it was the fact of living in the United States, its context, its demands which made him approach the large subject and since – as a realist as well as a profound pessimist – he could not bring himself to write a new *Columbiad*, the impetus of his not inconsiderable talent frittered itself away. It was not even buried, like Melville's, in the holy ground of a *Clarel*, but maundered on into a world he never knew and with which he had little sympathy. When, occasionally, he succeeds in the long poem it is where he can identify himself passionately with the subject. An example (although it is by no means as long as the poems I have mentioned) is 'Ben Jonson Entertains a Man from Stratford'. This poem conveys that fascination with the 'otherness' of the English world – that mysterious world of hallowed literary names – which enabled John Livingston Lowes to write so penetratingly about Chaucer, or Thomas Wolfe to make a meal of such large chunks of Robert Burton and the Elizabethans. The almost-conversational blank verse line carries a wealth of knowledge and, above all, feeling for the greatest figure of that European literary heritage which Americans of Robinson's stamp hold so dear:

> You are a friend then, as I make it out,
> Of our man Shakespeare, who alone of us
> Will put an ass's head in Fairyland. . . .

It is clear, then, that we must not look in the work of Edwin Arlington Robinson for the delight in words and memorable phrases that we find in the English poet. It is like looking in the world of Hawthorn or Melville for the domesticated character-studies and warm-blooded sentiments of a Dickens or a George Eliot. And if Robinson has indeed a 'for them' significance, it is because Americans are accustomed to looking in their own literature for another kind of thing and not simply because, by being there, by being all there is, he *has* to be made much of. Indeed, if one spends as much time with Robinson as one is forced, by English education and chauvinism, to spend on English poets, he grows in stature. The amateurish quality in much of his verse tends to obscure its dry wit and homely honesty. Here is a clapboard carpenter, not an artist in Sheraton. But he thinks, he feels. He may not possess the quality of 'auditory imagination', but his eye is on the highest; he is at the farthest remove from the kind of poet who uses words for words' sake.

How true this is also of Frost, the most outstanding American poet of the next decade. He builds on the same substance as Robinson but accomplishes a great deal more, partly because of the advantage of publishing at a later period and partly because of his exposure to that 'other place' which Robinson knew only through books. Although there were only five years between their birthdates, Robinson began publishing in 1897, whereas Frost's *North of Boston* did not come out in England until 1914. In *Poetry and the Age*, Randall Jarrell tells of teaching Frost in Germany. German audiences, he says, found it difficult to accept Frost because he had none of the mannerisms they expected of a *Dichter*. One would assume, therefore, that it would have been easier for the English, who have Wordsworth in their inheritance. And so it has been. Edward Thomas admired Frost, and Cecil Day Lewis wrote an introduction to the Penguin selection of his work. Yet there have still been reservations. No English critic has been quite as enthusiastic as Jarrell. We are indebted to Jarrell for pointing out the bareness and hardness of Frost's sentiments (a point later made

with less admiration by Lionel Trilling). But we must also insist on
that element of whimsicality which occasionally mars Frost's work
and which Jarrell conveniently ignores. It is true that Frost is much
more than a good High School poet, a laureate of the *Saturday
Evening Post*, but the cracker-barrel philosopher with the elfish grin
breaks through a little too often for us to suspend all reservations.
Let us take two examples, one from 'Mending Wall':

> We keep the wall between us as we go.
> To each the boulders that have fallen to each.
> And some are loaves and some so nearly balls
> We have to use a spell to make them balance:
> 'Stay where you are until our backs are turned' ...
> Something there is that doesn't love a wall,
> That wants it down. I could say 'Elves' to him,
> But it's not elves exactly. ...

the other from 'Birches':

> ... Such heaps of broken glass to sweep away
> You'd think the inner dome of heaven had fallen ...
>
> You may see their trunks arching in the woods
> Years afterwards, trailing their leaves on the ground
> Like girls on hands and knees. ...

But it is not only Frost's whimsicality and preciousness which get
in the way. There is a sort of knowingness even in the narrative
poems which no doubt led Kenneth Koch to write his parody
'Mending Sump':

> 'Hiram, I think the sump is backing up.
> The bathroom floorboards for above two weeks
> Have seemed soaked through. A little bird, I think
> Has wandered in the pipes, and all's gone wrong.'
> 'Something there is that doesn't hump a sump,'
> He said ...

When Jarrell made his arbitrary and dramatic choice of Frost's
best poems most critics were too impressed by Jarrell's acuity to
raise questions. Frost, misled by Jarrell's choice of 'The Witch of
Coös' (among others), was moved to read it on the Library of
Congress recording. The result is bathetic, for 'The Witch of Coös'
brings out those qualities of the village poet and sententious
moralizer which occasionally mar even the successful 'Death of the
Hired Man' and 'Home Burial'. It is difficult to understand how any
reader could keep a straight face at the recital of how the bones

marched up and down the stairs. Enter Ralle the Sioux control; mother and son talk to each other in the third person; even the name of the protagonist – Toffile Lajway – adds to the unreality of the poem. 'The Witch of Coös' bears the same relation to the best of Frost as Hemingway's *Across the River and into the Trees* bears to *The Sun Also Rises*.

What *is* best in Frost may be seen the more clearly by comparing him with his English friend and mentor, Edward Thomas. There is a bookish, a 'literary' quality about Thomas, a clinging not merely to accepted metrics, but to the conventions and imagery which go with a 'poetic vocabulary' (nineteenth century, of course). This is Thomas:

> Out in the dark over the snow,
> The fallow fawns invisible go
> With the fallow deer
> And the winds blow
> Fast as the stars are slow. . . .

or

> The new moon hangs like an ivory bugle
>   In the naked frosty blue.
> The ghylls of the forest, already blackened
>   By Winter, are blackened anew. . . .

It is competent enough stuff; it has a ring and a lilt, but it lacks that edge of hardness and truth which enables us to forgive an obvious clinging to the conventions in the case of Housman. Let us consider one of Frost's many rhyming poems – for we must not be misled by the frequency with which the dramatic poems are quoted. The tone is more personal, the vocabulary simpler than Thomas's – for example, in 'To Earthward':

> The hurt is not enough:
> I long for weight and strength
> To feel the earth as rough
> To all my length.

This is very different from Thomas's world of 'Jenny Pink's Copse', of 'Cockham, Cockridden and Childerditch/Roses, Pyrgo and Lapwater'.

Frost's countryside is full of death, dangers, disasters, sudden accidents:

> The leaves got up in a coil and hissed
> Blindly struck at my knee and missed. . . .

Even when he is at his simplest and seemingly most pastoral there is a threat, a sadness, a hint of life's burden:

> The woods are lovely, dark and deep,
> But I have promises to keep,
> And miles to go before I sleep,
> And miles to go before I sleep.

In any list of important poets in the twentieth century, regardless of nationality, Frost commands a place; the same cannot be said of the poets of the so-called 'Middle-Western Renaissance'. The fact that Sandburg, Lindsay and Masters wrote about people and places they knew well, places them several notches above the 'birds and flowers' school of lady poets who had flourished in a region given over until then exclusively to pioneering, industry and commerce. But the poetic instrument with which they were endowed was of a lesser order than Frost's.

Sandburg is, for the most part, watered-down Whitman. Consciously or unconsciously, he modelled his style on Whitman's long line, his lists, his enumeration of American scenes and objects. But in the process something was lost. Even in his 'catalogues' Whitman sings to the reader. Whitman's lines are liturgical:

The pure contralto sings in the organ loft,
The carpenter dresses his plank, the tongue of his foreplane whistles its
    wild, ascending lisp,
The married and unmarried children ride home to their Thanksgiving
    dinner,
The pilot seizes his king-pin, he heaves down with a strong arm,
The mate stands braced in the whale-boat, lance and harpoon ready. . . .

In this extract, taken at random from 'Song of Myself', the word-choice, apparently so simple, is on closer scrutiny arresting: 'pure', 'dresses', 'tongue', 'wild, ascending lisp', 'stands braced'. The lines are taut with movement. By comparison, Sandburg is prosy:

I know an ice handler who wears a flannel shirt with pearl buttons the size
    of a dollar,
And he lugs a hundred-pound hunk into a saloon ice-box, helps himself to
    cold ham and rye bread,

Tells the bartender it's hotter than yesterday and will be hotter yet
    tomorrow, by Jesus,
And is on his way with his head in the air and a hard pair of fists. . . .

Every word is usual, unremarkable. To say that it echoes the voice
of the people is to fall into the fallacy of imitative form. In his
most-often-quoted poem, 'Chicago', the tone is expostulatory,
blustering:

> Hog Butcher for the World!
> Tool Maker, Stacker of Wheat,
> Player with Railroads and the Nation's Freight Handler
> Stormy, husky, brawling,
> City of the Big Shoulders, . . .

This is 'talking about', enunciating; the sensibility is not, to put it
conservatively, of the highest order. Where Sandburg is at his best,
in *The People, Yes*, the most interesting writing is to be found in the
'stories':

> Six feet six was Davy Tipton
> and he had the proportions
> as kingpin Mississippi River pilot
> nearly filling the pilothouse
> as he took the wheel with a laugh:
> 'Big rivers ought to have big men' . . .

and not in the flat statements which make up so much of his verse:

> The people will live on.
> The learning and blundering people will live on.
> They will be tricked and sold and again sold. . . .

Edgar Lee Masters is better because he is dramatic and laconic at
the same time; he does not try to put ideas into the reader's head:

> And down I came with both legs broken
> And my eyes burned crisp as a couple of eggs. . . .

> The Circuit Judge said whoever did it
> Was a fellow-servant of mine, and so
> Old Rhodes's son didn't have to pay me.
> And I say on the witness stand as blind
> As Jack the Fiddler, saying over and over,
> 'I didn't know him at all' . . .

Lindsay, who once seemed like a joke, is probably the best of the
three. He did not try to catch the 'voice of the people' with a prose
line (when did 'the people' ever read Sandburg and Masters?). He

went to the people with a ballad metre that roused them and succeeded thereby in rousing us. In the 'Negro Sermon' entitled 'Simon Legree' he hits just that note of hyperbole which communicates the comedy-in-terror of the subject. In 'Bryan, Bryan, Bryan' and, especially, in 'General William Booth Enters into Heaven' the style fits the subject. Best of all is the note Lindsay struck in:

> But the flower-fed buffaloes of the spring
> Left us, long ago.
> They gore no more, they bellow no more,
> With the Blackfeet, lying low
> With the Pawnees, lying low
> Lying low.

The achievement is in the tone, communicated with simplicity and without bravado. How quietly effective its feeling for America is may be seen by comparing it not only with the bluster of Sandburg but also with the hollow professionalism of Stephen Vincent Benét:

> I have fallen in love with American names,
> The sharp names that never get fat,
> The snakeskin-title of mining-claims,
> The plumed war-bonnet of Medicine Hat....

But all this is a prelude to the great age of American poetry – the twenties and the thirties. Four great names dominate the period between the end of the First World War and the beginning of the Second: Eliot, Pound, Stevens and Williams.

I should like, first of all, to consider the contribution of Pound, Stevens and Williams. Eliot is another matter. I have mentioned their indebtedness to Imagism, but we must go beyond Imagism to Imagism's principle, the *'Ding an sich'* of which Stevens spoke, but which Williams, more than any of them, practised. This is the touchstone of the American psyche, that urge towards facts, things, objects, the mapping of a continent, a world, which is responsible for such diverse phenomena as Whitman's verse, the pragmatism of William James, and the dry notations of the sexologist Alfred Kinsey. It is in the air of the country, the intellectual atmosphere which made Stevens speak of English and American poets 'living in two different physical worlds'. It is no accident, also, that all of them wrote long poems. A further quality links them: the degree to which they used verse in order to advance ideas, attitudes of mind. The effect of this is to make their verse often seem stubborn and deficient in that quality of charm and memorability of diction characteristic of good English poetry. When Williams's poetry began to be well-known in England, a younger English poet complained that it 'tasted like sawdust in the mouth'. Pound's verse is similarly fragmented. What mellifluousness it has, in some of the early *Cantos*, is sweepingly rhetorical, but not musically memorable. G. S. Fraser, in comparing Stevens's contribution with Yeats's, said:

What is it that one misses? Partly, or perhaps mainly, the whole area of life that lies between detached aesthetic perception and philosophical reflection on it; and as chief corollary to that, the urgency of ordinary human passion, the sense of commitment and the moment of final concentration.

Fraser is near the mark. The American poets offer us few sweets. Like the novelists of the nineteenth century they live in a harder world, their eye is on the object. Only the bad ones try to lull us – and they say nothing because they rarely achieve the quality of 'auditory imagination'. The good ones are either telling us something as directly as possible, or describing succinctly. They live in a much more visual world; their words do not so often chime in the mind's ear. In this they are in the vanguard of contemporary verse. One has only to read an anthology such as Donald M. Allen's *New American Poetry* or Berg and Mezey's *Naked Poetry* to see how far the American insistence on direct communication has been taken. In this process much has been lost – although younger readers do not feel the loss, perhaps because they have never really been committed to, or because they have no ear for memorability of diction. The contemporary reader is impatient to 'know what the poem means' and there are more of him than in the days when Archibald MacLeish could write that 'a poem must not mean but be' or Stevens say that a poem must 'defeat the intelligence almost successfully'. Even Stevens himself who, at first sight, seems the odd man out in the trio I have selected uses words in a way that no English poet has ever used them. His titles are surrealist, his world as unlocated as Poe's, his ontology of his own making. Only now, with the perspective given to us by time can we see the real significance of Pound, Williams and Stevens. Paradoxically, difficult as they are, they point the way to a world unrealized because unimagined by 'Eddie Marsh's gang'. It is not a comfortable world, but it is a challenging one.

Only Eliot, one of the great ones in the between-wars period, stands out as being different, and that because he is the most traditional of all – not merely because he emigrated to England, became 'classical, royalist and reactionary', and joined the Anglican Church; but perhaps because he achieved at times that quality of 'auditory imagination' which he himself defined and which few other American poets have. There is a little of it in Poe ('meretricious' according to Eliot), more in Whitman and Emily Dickinson.

It is possible to pick out the 'American' references in Eliot's verse, but these are superficial compared with the deep currents of his writing. One can point to the use of American turns of phrase in the early verse – 'one night cheap hotels', 'sawdust restaurants with oyster shells', 'butt-ends', 'a toast and tea'. In 'Portrait of a Lady' the protagonist 'reads the comics and the sporting page'. In 'Preludes' there are 'dingy shades' (not 'blinds'), a 'city block' and 'vacant lots'. The river in 'The Dry Salvages' is the Mississippi and the sea is the Atlantic off Cape Ann. We can show how, in the American tradition, Eliot preferred the long poem, the 'epic'; how like a good Harvard scholar he went for his references to Hinduism as well as Christian mysticism; how much of a teacher and preacher he was (also in a great American tradition); how much – like Pound and Williams – he uses visual imagery. All these things are demonstrable. Nevertheless, in addition, Eliot has that power of verbal memorability without which there can be no sense of 'auditory imagination'. Perhaps it is partly because by including so much of the writing of others he strikes a chord in the memory.

> A cold coming we had of it
> Just the worst time of the year for a journey
> And such a long journey. . . .

or

> What are the roots that clutch what branches grow
> Out of this stony rubbish?

But it is not merely that. What he did not invent for himself he made over into his own voice:

> April is the cruellest month, breeding
> Lilacs out of the dead land, mixing
> Memory and desire . . .

or

> Because I do not hope to turn again
> Because I do not hope
> Because I do not hope to turn
> Desiring this man's gift and that man's scope....

Compare this with the opening of one of the most poignant of Williams's poems:

> It is myself
>   not the poor beast lying there
>   yelping with pain
> that brings me to myself with a start –

or Pound's

> Lynx-purr, and heathery smell of beasts
>   where tar smell had been,
> Sniff and pad-foot of beasts,
>   fur brushing my knee-skin,
> Rustle of airy sheaths. . . .

or even Stevens's:

> It was something to see that their white hair was different
> Sharp as white paint in the January sun;
> Soothing to feel that they needed another yellow,
> Less Aix than Stockholm, hardly a yellow at all. . . .

Williams is communicating directly, without benefit of any ornament. It is not merely rhyme that he has discarded; there is no rhythm other than the sound of his spoken voice. Even when it is read aloud, his verse has the flat sound of prose. In Pound there is rhythm, but it is the rhythm of chanting, of *The Seafarer* or *Piers Plowman*. In Stevens the communication is again direct, but cultivated, refined, measured, ordered. None of these poets has the sheer memorability of Eliot, because Eliot immersed himself in another tradition, a tradition as alien to Stevens and Pound as it was to Williams ('I had to watch him carry my world off with him, the fool, to the enemy').

It is perhaps not easy to accept that the tone, the poetic world of Pound and Williams may be the voice of the future. But just as it has become clear – as Charles Feidelson, Jr, told us in *Symbolism and American Literature* – that the writers of the 'American Renaissance', because of a conjunction of historical and intellectual circumstances, anticipated certain developments in European literature in the twentieth century, so it has become increasingly apparent that the fragmented, directly spoken yet elliptical, communication of Pound and Williams speaks to the young contemporary reader more clearly and more nearly than gorgeous webs of Shakespearean blank verse, the 'marvellous conceits of Donne', or the conspiracies of Keats or Dylan Thomas. In a world in which every man will be his own poet any kind of obvious artifice, however controlled or magnificent, will be the undoing of the artificer. It was for this reason that Robert Lowell, among the greatest of contemporary poets, and acutely sensitive to the currents of his time, turned from the involuted word-weaving of his early verse to the no less cunning but more intimately direct verse of recent years.

Herbert Read put his finger on the pulse of our time when in *The True Voice of Feeling* he traced a 'line of sincerity'. Increasingly, as time goes on, and the number of readers and writers of verse grows greater, the proportion who have that special sensibility which enables the trained reader to enjoy words for what they connote as well as what they denote will grow less. In an age in which art is for everyman, everyman will dictate its canons; and everyman has no ear. He looks above, below, beyond, through the verse: resonance of phrase gets in his way. He wants to feel but he cannot feel through the texture of words. He demands his emotions straight, flung on to the page as an action-painter commits paint to canvas.

Williams is the easiest model, Stevens the most difficult. There can be no 'school of Stevens', for Stevens is the most subtle, the most abstruse, the most complicated poet of modern times. The 'essential bravura' may be there, but not for Stevens the heady delights of word-play for its own sake. A sober, serious thinker, the most accurate of poets in his use of words, he is also the most bewildering because the world of his imagination is at once so logical and so advanced. Two themes occupied him throughout his life: the nature of appearance and reality, and the question of belief. Feeling that organized religion was a matter – as Rupert Brooke said – of 'This life cannot be all they swear/For how unpleasant if it were', he moved from the stated doubts of 'Sunday Morning' to the philosophical musings of 'Notes Toward a Supreme Fiction'. Different as he was, in tone and intention, from Williams, however, his eye was on the same object – the celebration of the things of this world. In fact, there is a common theme which links Pound, Williams and Stevens, and that is the praise of Man – what man can do in this world, not as a vale of tears but as the repository of all our hopes and fears, our be-all and end-all, in which:

> Death is the mother of beauty; hence from her
> Alone, shall come fulfilment to her dreams. . . .

for

> The tomb in Palestine
> Is not the porch of spirits lingering.
> It is the grave of Jesus, where he lay.
> We live in an old chaos of the sun. . . .

or, as he put it in 'Notes Toward a Supreme Fiction':

> It feels good as it is without the giant,
> A thinker of the first idea. Perhaps
> The truth depends on a walk around a lake. . . .

and, most beautifully of all, in 'Credences of Summer':

> Now is midsummer come and all fools slaughtered
> And spring's infuriations over and a long way
> To the first autumnal inhalations, young broods
> Are in the grass, the roses are heavy with a weight
> Of fragrance and the mind lays by its trouble.

'The fidgets of remembrance,' says Stevens, 'come to this/It comes to this and the imagination's life.'

Stevens's contribution – immense as it is – brings up a matter which must be mentioned because of its importance in any assessment of the *nature* of American poetry compared with British. As G. S. Fraser put it, when comparing Stevens's work with Yeats's, poetry was for Yeats a matter of 'the sense of commitment and the moment of final concentration'. What I would suggest is that the 'different physical world' in which Yeats lived – or Lawrence, or Dylan Thomas, or Shakespeare for that matter – was a world whose peculiar literary heritage arose out of a *Gestalt* of circumstances which made it possible for him to write with more evidence of 'ordinary human passion' than did the cultural world out of which Stevens came. However felicitous their images, however skilful their metrics or the dedication of their souls, there is a peculiar 'thinness' about American poets, an intellectuality which sometimes moves the mind more than the heart. From Edward Taylor through Poe, Emerson, Whittier, Longfellow to Stevens and Ransom a line of worthy high-minded American poets contribute their concerns to their world, yet fail to move. Even Pound, that most cosmopolitan of men, suffers from the same disease. It is in vain for Dr Leavis to tell us what a great poem *Hugh Selwyn Mauberley* is; we do not feel it.

We come to honour, our heads bowed with awe, and we go away disappointed, feeling that the experience is just round the corner. We can follow the *oeuvre* all right (with a crib), but it is the sentiments and the bravura which we are left. We are not completely engaged by the verse in the act of reading.

I should like – to complete my perspective – to mention the work of three poets who, although less important than Eliot, Pound, Williams and Stevens, are important enough – and uniquely American: namely, E. E. Cummings, Hart Crane and Marianne Moore.

Bad things have been said about Cummings. R. P. Blackmur, one of the most penetrating and intelligent of American critics, counted 'flower' forty-eight times in *Tulips and Chimneys* and twenty-one times in *Etcetera*, each time in a different context, and concluded that the word must 'contain for him an almost unlimited variety and extent of meaning . . . The question is whether or not the reader can possibly have shared the experience which Mr Cummings has had of the word.' There is also a great use of vague emotive adjectives ('thrilling', 'delicious', 'bright'). Nevertheless, despite these undoubted facts, Cummings at his best has a capacity to communicate, more nearly than most modern American poets, a sense of delight in the present, a lyric celebration of life. It is true that Cummings is nearly always at his best in his first lines ('I thank you God for most this amazing', 'my father moved through dooms of love', 'anyone lived in a pretty how town', 'all ignorance toboggans into know', 'what if a much of a which of a wind', 'as freedom is a breakfastfood') but here and there stands out a single achieved poem. For example, although 'I sing of Olaf' and 'take it from me kiddo', are faulty in their sense and syntax, 'my sweet old etcetera' and 'plato told' are not. 'She being Brand' is an undergraduate exercise, but poems like 'buncha hardboil guys from duh A. C. Fulla' are successful because they exactly catch the accents of the Lower East Side and do not pretend to be more than they are. In 'Chanson Innocente' and 'this little bride and groom' Cummings gives us an insight into a peculiarly American world.

But perhaps most significant of all, in the light of contemporary developments in poetry, are the typographical experiments. A poem for Cummings consists of poem-plus-typography and not in any extractable 'meaning' which can be separated from the total construct of the poem. The way the words *look* is as important as the way they sound. In fact, in a poem like the one on the grasshopper, the sense is subservient to what the eye perceives:

```
                        r-p-o-p-h-e-s-s-a-g-r
                      who
        a)s w(e loo)k
        upnowgath
                 PPEGORHRASS
                                    eringint(o-
        aThe):l
            eA
            !p:
        S                                        a
                     (r
        rIvInG    .gRrEaPsPhOs)
                                    to
        rea(be)rran(com)gi(e)ngly
        ,grasshopper;
```

In the *Collected Poems* of 1938, one finds ample evidence of Cummings's unconscious drift towards the implications of concrete poetry. Numbers 48, 52, 74, 99, 205, 221, 222, 262, 263, 265, 270, 275, 276, 277, 290, 294, 295, 299, 302, and 303 – among others – would make equally good illustrations. It is possible that, before the end of the century, these logo-visual experiments will prove a satisfaction in themselves, where now they seem to be only steps in a certain direction.

I should like, at this point, to distinguish two aspects of the non-rational, intimately connected and both to be found in Cummings; one is the typographical experiments which are the antecedents of concrete poetry, and the other *a manner of writing* (compare Cummings's 'my father moved through dooms of love' with W. S. Graham's 'O gentle queen of the afternoon', Dylan Thomas's 'If I were tickled by the rub of love' or Hart Crane's 'Where icy and bright dungeons lift'). If one were reaching for the antecedents of concrete poetry one would, presumably, at least refer to the 'hour-glass' or 'wings' experiments of the seventeenth century, but, more recently to Apollinaire's *Calligrammes*, Mallarmé's 'house of words', the look-upon-the-page effects of Pound, and Dylan Thomas's experiments with 'shapes'. Even Williams's plain-patterns as in (for example) 'so much depends' would be part of the movement in which Cummings's experiments might be placed. At the end – so far as we know it – are the plain or complicated patterns of 'concrete' and 'sound' poetry, and the kinetic world of modern art.

The 'manner of writing' to which I have referred is connected with, but does not necessarily appear in conjunction with, those typographical and other experiments which produce a penumbra of significance beyond the world of linear communication. The typographical experiments might be expected to have more immediate impact in a post-Gutenberg age in which High School students play 'three-dimensional tick-tack-toe' against computers.[1] The 'manner of writing' has been going on for a much longer time and is a linguistic extension of that exploration of the boundaries of communication which is at the heart of Romanticism. The antecedents of the language experiment (of which, it might be remembered, Whitman said he was a part) are to be found in Blake, some of Shelley, Coleridge of 'Kubla Khan', les Symbolistes, Jarry, Dada and Surrealism. Dylan Thomas is part of the movement and so, in their own way, are Cummings and Hart Crane.

Crane is a true American phenomenon. Poor Crane – if only he had not had so much explaining to do. All those letters to Harriet Monroe and Otto Kahn spelling out painfully what he meant by 'adagios of islands'. It had all been done before; the battle had been fought and won somewhere between 1880 and 1920, but Crane, the maverick Middle Westerner, the little-boy-lost of Garrettsville, Ohio, secretly dressing up in his mother's clothes, had to fight the good fight against Comstockery, the League of Decency and the Daughters of the American Revolution. 'Absolute poetry' was an un-American activity. And so Crane turned from the 'verbal music' (so much more substantial than the thin impressionism of a John Gould Fletcher) of White Buildings to an ambitious attempt to deal with the 'Myth of America'. It was a worthy ideal and no one but an American would have undertaken it. After all, Whitman had done it in Leaves of Grass, and Joel Barlow in The Columbiad. Pound had begun to take the whole civilization as his subject and Eliot had written a diatribe against Western moral values. The time was ripe for a new Whitman, 'Christopher Newman' Crane, who would present 'an organic panorama, showing the continuous and living evidence of the past in the inmost vital substance of the present'. The structure would be based on America: the Conquistadors, Captain John Smith, Pocahontas, Rip Van Winkle. From the myths of America in 'Van Winkle', Crane turned to The River – a figurative psychological 'vehicle' for transporting the reader to the Middle West. 'The rhythm is jazz. Thenceforward the rhythm settles down to a steady pedestrian gait, like that of wanderers plodding along.' Among the various sections of this long poem, 'The Tunnel' was to

[1] The Reader's Digest (March 1970), p 15.

be 'a kind of purgatory in relation to the open sky', 'Cape Hatteras' a 'kind of ode to Whitman'.

With all his heart Crane tried to do the right thing by his banker angel, by his country, by his art, by his ambition, by his poet's sense of that 'absolute music' which he felt in his soul. It was a good idea; the only trouble was that it *was* an idea. Crane laboured manfully, but the result is fragments, moments of felicity. The curious thing is that one does not feel the need to apply the same strictures to Pound. Pound's work is also fragmentary, but there is a power behind it which is positive. However cranky Pound's world-view, however personal and eccentric the currents of his preoccupations, it all makes sense somewhere in his brain. He was not impelled by an outside idea, a worthy motive. It is the same with Whitman. America, 'these States', the all-embracing more-than-egotistical 'I' are for him part and parcel of the voyaging spirit. What he felt comes through the verse with a kind of defiance which is characteristic also of Pound. With Crane the honourable motive almost subverts the talent. Positive, however, despite the curiously disjointed idiom and slightly old-fashioned high style is a heady power over words, and a passion which few other American poets have. It is there in *The Bridge*:

> O caught like pennies beneath soot and stem,
> Kiss of our agony thou gatherest . . .
>
> And this thy harbour, O my city I have driven under,
> Tossed from the coil of ticking towers. . . . Tomorrow,
> And to be. . . . Here by the River that is East –
> Here at the water's edge the hands drop memory. . . .

But even more, tenderly and much more successfully, the note of triumph is in 'Voyages':

> Bind us in time, O Seasons clear, and awe.
> O minstrel galleons of Carib fire,
> Bequeath us to no earthly shore until
> Is answered in the vortex of our grave
> The seal's wide spindrift gaze toward paradise.

And so we have sailed the seas and come – to the magic city of Marianne Moore. Not for her the headiness of Crane's rhetoric. It was not for nothing that she won the accolade from Eliot; the tone is clear, learned, witty, wise, full of common sense. She was an experimenter of the first order – an experimenter in her strange collocation of facts and abstruse references, and an experimenter in her syllabic counting. Eliot, in his introduction to the *Selected Poems* (1935), described her as a 'descriptive' poet, a label which might be more acceptable if he had not made a comparison with 'Cooper's Hill', 'Windsor Forest' and Gray's 'Elegy'. A comparison in these terms is a little far-fetched. Miss Moore's voice is direct; the concentration is on the *Ding an sich* and the meditation is part of that concentration. A friend of Williams and a one-time editor of *The Dial*, she subscribes to the doctrine of 'no ideas but in things'.

The 'syllabic counting' is a rather confused issue. Everyone knows that it is supposed to exist and most critics refer to it. But few explore the facts behind the phrase. Two recent histories of American poetry, R. H. Pearce's *The Continuity of American Poetry* (1961), and H. H. Waggoner's *American Poets from the Puritans to the Present* (1968), seem to avoid the main issue. Waggoner, who comes nearest to some kind of helpful comment, merely says 'Attempts have been made to reduce this "syllabic" but "non-accentual" verse to a system; but the fact of the matter seems to be that the nature of language is such that nothing distinguishes, or can distinguish, the sound of verse in English from the sound of prose but some kind of pattern of recurrent *stress*.' Perhaps so, but this begs the question. If Miss Moore does depend on syllabic counting, let us find out how it works and leave it to the reader to decide whether or not the method succeeds.

'The fact of the matter' seems to be that Miss Moore gets as near as possible to equating the number of syllables in the first line of a verse with the number of syllables in the first line of the next verse, and so on through the verse – except that she will occasionally vary the system. In her best known poem 'Poetry' for example:

I, too, dislike it: there are things that are important beyond all this fiddle.
Reading it, however, with a perfect contempt for it, one discovers in
it after all, a place for the genuine.
Hands that can grasp, eyes
that can dilate, hair that can rise
        if it must, these things are important not because a . . .

I make the number of syllables 19, 19, 11, 5, 8 and 13, and this is followed with slight variations in the second verse, which begins

high-sounding interpretation can be put upon them but because they are
    . . . (19)

and proceeds with a count of 21 (because of the awkward 'intelligible' – Miss Moore is disinclined to break up words), 12, 5, 8 and 13. A similar exact or approximate system of syllabic-patterning is followed in 'To a Steam Roller', 'The Fish', 'The Monkeys', 'Critics and Connoisseurs', 'Peter', 'Part of a Novel, Part of a Poem, Part of a Play', 'No Swan so Fine' or 'In Distrust of Merits'. However, in poems like 'When I Buy Pictures' or 'The Labours of Hercules', where there is no stanza construction, the syllabic counting has to be abandoned. Waggoner is hard on such an artificial ordering of a poem, insisting that there is nothing to distinguish such 'poems' from prose. But Miss Moore's method, like the non-sonnets of her namesake Merrill Moore, has a validity of its own. Miss Moore's patterning has in fact a hoary lineage in Welsh verse. True, in the various varieties of *englynion*, relying mainly on syllabic counting, there are also internal rhymes, but we are in another country, and another century. If a Melville or Joyce can break up the structure of the conventional novel, a Marianne Moore is entitled to respect for any device she chooses.

Before making a summary of the general points to emerge from this attempted 'reassessment' of twentieth-century American verse we might look briefly at the kind of poetry which emerged in the forties. It can be argued that only five of those poets have 'lasted': Lowell, Richard Wilbur, Theodore Roethke, John Berryman and Randall Jarrell. Of the others, Karl Shapiro is perhaps the best. His smoothly ordered carefully wrought poems were models for that generation of fine writers which emerged in the fifties, to be enshrined by Donald Hall, Robert Pack and Louis Simpson in their first selection of *New Poets of England and America*. Most of the Americans in that volume – Hall himself, Meredith, James Merrill, W. S. Merwin, Moss, Pack, Simpson and Wright – wrote so well yet so urbanely as to be almost indistinguishable from one another. However, Shapiro must not be damned by his imitators; they had other models, too – Wallace Stevens, for example, who was as much the hero of the early fifties as Williams was to become of the sixties. Shapiro, and Randall Jarrell, were at their best as war poets, of which there were precious few in the United States.

How different this is from the English poetic scene during the Second World War, when every other combatant seemed to be a potential contributor to *Poems from the Forces*. Sidney Keyes, Alun Lewis, Henry Reed, Gavin Ewart, and many others, wrote remarkably good poems about the personal impact of war. One's conclusion must be that, for a time, American poetry had gone into the doldrums. Delmore Schwartz, who was included by F. O. Matthiessen in the *Oxford Book of American Verse* (1950), comes nearest to that combination of the personal and lyric which marks the best of the verse of the late forties and fifties. He had a gift of phrase which strikes a sad echo in the mind ('All of us always turning away for solace', 'All clowns are masked', 'The heavy bear who goes with me'). One other poet with a similar gift is Kenneth Patchen, who wrote that remarkable poem 'The Character of Love seen as a Search for the Lost':

> You, the woman; I, the man; this, the world,
> And each is the work of all.
>
> There is the muffled step in the snow; the stranger;
> The crippled wren; the nun; the dancer; the Jesus-Wing. . . .

But of the rest who were so often in the public eye in the forties – Muriel Rukeyser, John Ciardi, Winfield Townley Scott, Elizabeth Bishop – their work seems a rather unimportant moment in history. In the fifties and sixties American poetry was to experience a new 'renaissance', but in the forties – with the exception of the few I have mentioned – it was the older Americans who were most significant. Pound for example published *Cantos LII–LXXI* in 1940 and *The Pisan Cantos* in 1948; Robinson Jeffers *Medea* in 1946, *Be Angry at the Sun* in 1941, and *The Double Axe* in 1948; Marianne Moore *What are Years?* in 1941 and *Nevertheless* in 1944; Eliot *Four Quartets* in 1943; and Cummings *50 Poems* in 1940 and *1 × 1* in 1944. Crane had died in 1932, and there seemed no more recent American counterpart to Dylan Thomas. American Romanticism seemed to have become buried under the fat of opulent and highly competent writing which struck no fire and raised no hopes.

To recapitulate, in the first twenty years of the century – despite Harriet Monroe's and Amy Lowell's well-meaning encouragement of a 'poetic spirit' – there were inadequate grounds for asserting that American poetry had achieved major stature. The quality of English poets up to the end of the First World War is such that one cannot label them all as merely members of 'Eddie Marsh's gang'. Housman, Brooke, Owen, Sassoon, Yeats – even Masefield – wrote extraordinarily well, with a power of tradition behind them which triumphed over the fact that, generally speaking, they look back to the nineteenth century in their style and mannerisms. Compared with them Robinson, Frost, Sandburg and Masters could be called amateurs. That, at least, is one way of putting it.

In the twenties, however, the American talent which had shown promise before the First World War came to fruition. Frost published *New Hampshire* and *West-Running Brook*; Pound, having given birth to *Hugh Selwyn Mauberley*, began the *Cantos*; Eliot rocked the world of literature with *The Waste Land* (1922); Williams showed in his fourth book of verse, *Spring and All*, that if one could not exactly make speech out of the language of 'Polish mothers' one could at least fashion a new kind of verse based on one's own speech rhythms; Stevens, in *Harmonium*, produced yet another kind of American language, showing to later generations that, far from being – as Louis Untermeyer asserted – 'unrelated to any human struggle', it held perhaps the greatest significance of all.

By the thirties, the work of Marianne Moore, Jeffers, the 'Fugitives', Cummings and Hart Crane showed clearly the distinctive characteristics of the American voice.

In attempting a brief summary of those characteristics, those underlying correspondences and similarities, which mark American poetry in the twentieth century off from the English, we cannot help being dependent upon that perspective which the achievement of the twentieth century gives to the *whole* of American poetry. In his introduction to *The Faber Book of Modern American Verse* (1956), W. H. Auden made the statement that 'there is scarcely one American poet, from Bryant on, who can be mistaken for an Englishman'. The tradition goes back even further than that.

From the seventeenth century on, there has been apparent in American poetry a quality which it is only possible to define by a conjunction of descriptions. It is partly a 'homeliness' of reference, a not unattractive amateurishness – like the art of the 'limners' – and partly a high seriousness which borders on the portentous. Bradstreet, Taylor and Wigglesworth are all of a piece, despite the disparity of their styles. They produced for a purpose. Set beside the wealth of English poetry from Donne, Vaughan, Herbert, Herrick, Marvell and Milton to Dryden, Traherne and Rochester, the comparison – if it were set up for chauvinistic purposes – would be as laughable as it is unfair. Small pioneering colonies cannot compete with great nations. But therein lies the seed of the difference. 'We live', to repeat Stevens, 'in two different physical worlds, and it is not nonsense to think that that matters.' And with the different physical worlds there go historical, intellectual, religious and economic worlds. The note of 'do it yourself' set in the seventeenth century is traceable through to the twentieth. Not until the Second World War do we see in American poetry that easy competence with words and modes that characterizes English poetry – and even then the tone, the level of communication is flatter.

This is connected with the 'intellectuality' noticeable in that great line of sober, serious, dedicated Americans which runs from Taylor through Emerson and Longfellow to Wallace Stevens and is present in differing degrees in many other American poets. It has also something to do with the predominantly *visual* quality of American imagery compared with the English. Where the words of the English poet will chime in the mind's ear, those of the American – from the rhetoric and the catalogues of Whitman to the courteous meditations of Stevens – will appeal to the eye, to the sense. There is a point to be made and the American has his mind on it. One's thoughts go back to Cotton Mather, who, in the *Manuductio ad Ministerium* (1726), gave it as his opinion that:

There is a *Way of Writing*, wherein the Author endeavours, that the Reader may have *something to the Purpose* in every Paragraph. There is not only a *Vigor* sensible in every *Sentence*, but the Paragraph is embellished with *Profitable References*, even to something beyond what is *directly spoken*. Formal and Painful *Quotations* are not studied; yet all that could be learnt from them is insinuated. The Writer pretends not unto *Reading*, yet he could not have writ as he does if he had not Read very much in his Time; and his Composures are not only a *Cloth of Gold*, but also stuck with as many Jewels, as the Gown of a Russian Embassador. . . . [sic]

All of which is not to say that the American poets of the nineteenth and twentieth centuries perused Mather's manual, but rather that qualities in the cultural air, the 'données' of the American scene, forced the poet – as indeed they did the novelist too – through a process of intellectual osmosis, to turn towards high seriousness and unhumorous dedication. In Stevens's very playfulness there is something artificial; the incredible dexterity – like the unbearable convolution of Henry James – is part of the *persona*. The American literary artist is indeed a masked man.

From these preoccupations it is but a short step to the 'no ideas but in things' theory of Williams, which is itself related to the 'hardness and concreteness' of Imagism. Whether the American poet chooses to write in a form of the colloquial like Frost or Williams, or in the more elaborate style of Stevens or Wilbur (the Twain–James dichotomy of American literature) there is something earnest in his attitude. If he cannot get his message across in any other way he will communicate – as D. H. Lawrence pointed out –

in a high scream. A comparison of Robert Lowell and Philip Larkin – if I may go briefly beyond the period I have chosen – reveals the difference in tone, not only between two individuals but between representatives of two different cultures. For all the craftsmanship which is so apparent behind the seemingly unformed verse, there is a note of hysteria in Lowell which is part of a sensitive man's response to the electric atmosphere of his country and culture. Lowell confesses; Larkin professes. In Larkin, all is downgraded; the occasional shock-tactic metaphor given with the one hand is taken away with the other. 'Come off it,' says Larkin; 'I am serious,' says Lowell.

The English poet rarely preaches. He will moralize, but shamefacedly. The Americans have always been preachers, as they have been teachers; and in their teaching they are often teaching themselves. The mangle of *vates* suits a Whitman, a Pound, a Stevens. Not even Wordsworth was as ambitious as this. His messages were comparatively parochial and particular; he did not self-consciously direct his voice across a continent, a culture. Not man under the aspect of eternity, but man as a social creature, is the burden of the English poet – as it is of the English novelist.

Nor has the English poet been so much of an experimenter as the American; he has not needed to be. The extravagance and wildness of the American is part of his scene. It is part of the process of mapping the country, identifying the nation. 'What is an American?' asked Crévecoeur. Let us find out by writing an epic, say Barlow and Whitman, Pound, Williams or Hart Crane. And behind it all is the relentless search to find out more about Man himself. Americans are accused by Europeans of being chauvinistic because they write about American things. But few artists, in any culture, could be more resolutely high-minded than the American.

From an artificial and embattled nation like the United States, founded on high-minded theories and ideals, there might be expected that self-questioning, that interminable restless casting about for self-identification, ways and solutions which has in fact characterized its literature. It would be as well to end with a quotation from Stevens. His theme runs deeply but strongly below the surface of those considerations of style, tone, vocabulary, metric and cadences which, following Rajan's line of inquiry, have occupied the major part of this attempt to suggest a few of the differences between American and English poetry in the first half of the twentieth century. 'The major abstraction', says Stevens:

... is the idea of man
And major man is its exponent, abler
In the abstract than in his singular,
More fecund as principle than particle,
Happy fecundity, flor-abundant force,
In being more than an exception, part,
Though an heroic part, of the commonal. ...

5

POETRY 1945–60: SELF VERSUS CULTURE

Aleksandar Nejgebauer

Poets may be the unacknowledged legislators of the world, but not its chroniclers. In the USA, they failed to respond to the Second World War with anything approaching the greatness of its impact on the destiny of mankind, in spite of the appearance of significant books of war poems, like Karl Shapiro's *V-Letter and Other Poems* (1944) and Randall Jarrell's *Little Friend, Little Friend* (1945), of anthologies – *The War Poets*, edited by Oscar Williams, and *War and the Poet*, edited by Richard Eberhart and Selden Rodman (both 1945) – and of numerous individual poems. Conversely, the war failed to affect the core of the poets' creative powers. For one thing, it was unoriginal – the re-enactment of an earlier international massacre, less shockingly senseless, and poetically assimilated by the generation of Siegfried Sassoon and Wilfrid Owen. Besides, the tradition of post-Symbolist 'Modernism' in poetry as practised by Pound, Eliot, Yeats and Stevens, and theoretically sanctioned by the New Criticism, was still very much alive, as were many of its original exponents. With minor exceptions, the new war poetry became an extension of the rhetorical poetry of progressive social ideas of the thirties. But the ship of naïve and unpractical Western leftism was sinking fast: Auden and Spender abandoned it, trying to save their poetical lives on the same shore where Eliot had been busy salvaging fragments of Culture some twenty-five years earlier. They were joined by younger American poets in their retreat from the traumas of socially organized horrors into individual psychology, classical mythology, mysticism and 'pure' art.

Strangely enough, this trend did not lead to an assertion of individualism. The elitist cultural orthodoxy which Pound and Eliot had been advocating was, on the contrary, a mode of escape from personality, from its malaise in a baffling world. Ultimately Eliot's Roman Catholicism and Pound's Fascism were authoritarian frameworks intended to save the Western cultural heritage from disintegration. Yet in the end of such conservatism was the beginning of a new poetry, with its unmistakable development, in spite of coexistence with the old: from a revolt of the self against the culture – the European heritage, as well as the American way of life and death – through an assertion of the self, destructive or constructive, to a search for a new culture – on an import basis (England excepted), or else drawing on available subcultures in the United States. The major poets whose reputations were established between the end of the Second World War and the beginning of the sixties were mostly caught up in the first two of the three phases of development suggested. The master-mode of their awareness corresponds to post-war existentialist nausea in Western Europe, but the awareness itself is uniquely American. Here the Existential open was not a sudden void in place of age-old tradition but a return to the only true American traditon – starting from Paumanok again, towards a new Frontier, in a quest for new identity.

RICHARD WILBUR, born in 1921 in New York City, is the youngest of the poets who rose to prominence in the first decade and a half after the war, but culturally the most conservative. His conservatism is grounded not so much in admiration for, and kinship with, favourite poets of the past like George Herbert or Emily Dickinson, and some not quite fashionable twentieth-century poets like Crane and Stevens, as in his adherence to the aesthetic, and implicitly the impersonal high culture theory, of the Modernists.

I've always agreed with Eliot's assertion that poetry is not the expression of personality but an escape from personality,

Wilbur wrote in 1964, finding this position 'temperamentally convenient' and taking the classicist, and New Critical view of the poem

... as 'a box to be opened' [May Swenson's phrase], a created object, an altar-cloth, Japanese garden or ship of death. Not a message or confession.
(*The Contemporary Poet as Artist and Critic*)

He has also pleaded for complexity, irony and paradox – the stock-in-trade of the New Critics – as well as for the use of strict poetic forms, including rhyme, and for clever artificiality, in the belief that

... limitation makes for power; the strength of the genie comes of his being confined in a bottle.
(*Mid-Century American Poets*)

Some critics have taken a different view of limitation in Wilbur's poetry, accusing him of being too much confined by formal ingenuities, and by his serene aloofness, eschewing the tragic, the painfully personal. The idea reveals the critics' blind spot for the cultural context. Wilbur's poetry is not limited; it is different – an anachronism in an age of cold war and nuclear threats, of disenchantment of the best minds with the physical and moral aspects or urban civilization. He is a seer and maker of the beautiful; each of his poems is meant to be, and most often is, a thing of beauty and a source of pleasure. In this, he is more traditional than either Eliot of Pound: unlike their troubled search for firm values in a world hostile to high culture, his is an optimistic one for beauties to be discerned and enjoyed here and now.

Wilbur can be said to be wedded happily and wealthily to his Muse (to whom alone, in his own phrase, his poems are addressed). True, his first poems were written '... in answer to the inner and other disorders of the Second World War', when he served with the 36th Infantry Division in Europe, but his ordering of raw events into poetic experience has proved highly successful, quite in keeping with the general tenor of his life. He was educated at Amherst College and Harvard, where his academic career began in 1950, leading up to a professorship at Wesleyan University in 1959. His first three books of poetry, *The Beautiful Changes* (1947), *Ceremony* (1950) and *Things of This World* (1956), earned him several awards and fellowships. The fourth, *Advice to a Prophet* (1961),[1] stirred up considerable disagreement among critics: while some deplored its 'lack of force' and 'triviality', others hailed a more personal tone, a deeper human involvement.

The essence of Wilbur's poetry can perhaps be best understood by exploding the stereotype notion of it according to which Wilbur, fascinated by objects, finds intellectual beauty in them and presents it to the reader in a clever and elegant manner. He is far from such trifling in splendid isolation. His poetry does have a significant central dilemma – how to live in this world without being degraded by its material nature, how to cultivate the life of the spirit without losing touch with reality. In 'A Baroque Wall-Fountain in the Villa Sciarra' (*Th*) there is more than a beautiful description of two splendid fountains in Rome: the one symbolizes pleasure enjoyed in unfulfilled desires – 'the dreamt land/Toward which all hungers leap, all pleasures pass' (reminiscent of Keats's Grecian Urn, but

[1] Further referred to as *BC*, *C*, *Th* and *A* respectively.

more alive), the other the drive towards achievement, the rise ending in a fall. In 'A World Without Objects Is a Sensible Emptiness' (*C*) the confrontation is even sharper. 'The tall camels of the spirit' (abstract, ascetic) who 'long to learn and drink/Of pure mirage' are called 'connoisseurs of thirst', i.e. experts in frustration. The poet exhorts them to turn from the desert to 'the spirit's right/ Oasis, light incarnate', implying that the world around us is largely a desert for a man of spirit, but that his search should be for exceptional values within it, not for illusions beyond. Fortunately, St Augustine has taught him that 'Love Calls Us to the Things of This World' (*Th*) in spite of 'the punctual rape of every blessèd day'. This lovely poem about laundry seen at waking as 'angels' ends with the soul's cry:

> Bring them down from their ruddy gallows;
> Let there be clean linen for the backs of thieves;
> Let lovers go fresh and sweet to be undone,
> And the heaviest nuns walk in a pure floating
> Of dark habits,
>   keeping their difficult balance.

Wilbur is also absorbed in the question of what it means to be a poet. Of the several poems dealing with the art of vision, or visual art ('Museum Piece' (*C*), 'L'Etoile', 'Objects', 'A Dutch Courtyard' (*BC*), etc.) the most pregnant, perhaps, is 'Ceremony' (*C*), where the relation of art to nature (including that of poetry to life) is seen not as conflict but as tension and interaction, with a heightening effect. The 'feigning lady' in a 'striped blouse' (in a painting by the French nineteenth-century painter Jean Frédéric Bazille) would have a less rich appeal if seen in the nude, without the 'ceremony', i.e. formality, artificiality of dress and pose or, generally speaking, art. 'I am for wit and wakefulness' the poet says; artificiality cannot shut out nature; on the contrary, 'What's lightly hid is deepest understood.'

Paradoxically Wilbur, the happy poet (at least by contrast to the *poète maudit*, doomed poet type like Baudelaire or Rimbaud), is rather uneasy, sometimes resigned about the poet's lot. Merlin, the poet-magician, who had given spiritual substance to the Arthurian era by his dream, is enthralled by the Siren's daughter Niniane, his creation, i.e. lulled by his own success ('Merlin Enthralled', *Th*). 'The mind is like a bat' and all its ingenuity is spent within the confines of life's dark cave ('Mind', *Th*). The much applauded poet-juggler 'Swinging a small heaven about his ears' is lonely and tired after the show ('Juggler', *C*). The address to a fire-truck, image of efficient action, implies a sadly ironic recognition of how different it is from the engine of poetry:

> Beautiful, heavy, unweary, loud, obvious thing!
> I stand here purged of nuance, my mind a blank.
>
> ('A Fire-Truck,' *A*)

Wilbur's two main themes – the spiritual man's dilemma and the poet's plight – run through a wide range of poems which are ostensibly concerned with subjects ('Altitude', 'Love Calls Us . . .', *Th*; 'Someone Talking to Himself', *A*), objects ('The Melongene', 'Objects', *BC*; 'Driftwood', *C*; 'A Hole in the Floor', 'Junk', *A*), philosophic problems ('Epistemology', *C*; 'Lamarck Elaborated', 'A Chronic Condition', *Th*), or nature description ('In the Elegy Season', *C*; 'Fall in Corrales', *A*). Though without a 'program', he is by no means an occasional poet, as these leitmotifs demonstrate.

At times Wilbur has also assumed the role of poet-citizen. Some of his early war poems are moving, thanks to the personally experienced sympathy ('Mined Country', 'Place Pigalle', *BC*). But public poems like 'Still, Citizen Sparrow' (*C*) and 'Advice to a Prophet' (*A*) heavily depend on reasoning and rhetoric. So does his speech 'For the New Railway Station in Rome' (*Th*), though with far more grace. Modern evils rarely appear in Wilbur's verse. His main gift is to praise, not to denounce.

Wilbur's affirmation of the beautiful is made possible by shutting out large areas of modern experience: not only politics and economics but also the American cultural structure as a whole, American cities, men and women, even his own life, except in ethereal distillation. His oasis is in the beauties of the European cultural heritage: Italian architecture, Italian, French and Dutch painting, the teachings of St Augustine and Bishop Berkeley, the allegory and symbolism of plants and animals, the uses of *paysage moralisé*, French literature and the whole range of English poetry, from the Anglo-Saxons to Auden. He remains a poet who has gone on collecting the driftwood of Western civilization 'In a time of continual abdications/And of damp complicities' ('Driftwood', *C*) illumining 'these emblems/Royally sane' with a noble mind and making his readers aware of 'the beauty of/Excellence earned'.

*

RANDALL JARRELL (1914–65)

> 'I am myself still?' For a little while, forget:
> The world's selves cure that short disease, myself,
> And we see bending to us, dewy-eyed, the great –
> CHANGE, dear to all things not to themselves endeared.
>   ('Children Selecting Books in a Library')

This is one of the numerous quotations from Jarrell which suggest themselves as a motto. There would also be choices if one tried to label him: academic poet, war poet, poet of change, bat-poet (his own metaphor), lost *Wunderkind*, new Browning, culture elegist, Romantic *manqué*. Contraries meet here: scientific education and subjective humanism, highbrow arrogance and democratic radicalism, brilliant wit and sentimental compassion. In sketching his career, we may choose to view him as a successful poet-professor and eminent critic, or else as an obsessed seeker of a lost self who could neither immerse in the destructive element nor follow the dream.

Randall Jarrell was born in Nashville, Tennessee, and graduated from Vanderbilt University. After the Second World War, in which he served as combat pilot and navigator in the Air Force, he eventually taught at the Women's College of the University of North Carolina. He was poetry critic of the *Partisan Review*, and other magazines, Consultant in Poetry at the Library of Congress, and a member of the National Institute of Arts and Letters.

Precocious and brilliant, he was impatient of ignorance, uncompromising in his judgments – whether enthusiastic or vexingly censorious – *and yet* (a key phrase in his poetry) this swift angel of cultural justice was unsure of himself to the point of helplessness; in his frenzied enthusiasms for new areas of specialized knowledge, *change* – another guise, another chance – was the ruling principle. Some objects were areas of lasting interest with him: German culture (especially Romantic), anthropology, Renaissance painting, psycho-analysis, Romantic composers. Even more typicl were periods of intensive concern with individual culture-heroes – Goethe, Proust, Rilke, Chekhov, Wagner, Mahler, Ingmar Bergman – and things like technical details about war planes, sports cars, *Road and Track* magazine, L.L. Bean catalogue items, professional football. . . .

And then there was the drive towards metamorphosis, or impersonation. As Mrs Randall Jarrell (née von Schrader) has noted, he decided to grow a beard because he thought he would thus resemble Chekhov. He was fascinated by his 'Other' – reflected images of himself. Sometimes he would study for minutes 'the old friend who lives in [his] mirror'. Once he performed for his wife and this 'friend' 'a pantomime of Tsar Nicholas turning into Rasputin and Mephistopheles turning into Faust'.

Some of his weaknesses at the centre of strength are characteristic. He thought himself ill-educated because he knew only one language, but insisted that 'It is by trust, and Love, and reading Rilke/Without *ein Wörterbuch*, that man learns German', his 'favorite country'. He was liable to ignorant prejudice, on a large scale against England because of differences with some English academics; later, finding England culturally delightful, he dismissed the French as pushing and disorderly, after a weekend visit to Paris.

Jarrell the man of letters was racked between the role of an advocate of culture and critic of civilization, and the predicament of a poet of private suffering and fantasy. Roughly speaking, the former concern predominates in Jarrell's first book of poems (*Blood for a Stranger*, 1942), in the first part of *The Seven-League Crutches* (1951), 'Europe', and in his prose; the latter partly in *Little Friend, Little Friend* (1945) and *Losses* (1948), and completely in *The Seven-League Crutches* part two, 'Children', as well as his later verse – *The Woman at the Washington Zoo* (1960), *The Lost World* (1965).[1] Though the two broad themes coexist throughout Jarrell's work, especially in his war poems, each is at the heart of a peculiar poetic world, and the shift of emphasis from the one to the other forms the pattern of the poet's development, as well as part of the larger pattern of change in post-war American poetry.

Jarrell's idea of true culture was fundamentally the same as the Modernists' – a Europe-saturated, humanistic high culture (though differently compounded from Pound's or Eliot's model), as opposed to mass culture, or what he called 'the Medium'. But under the influence of Auden and other liberal and would-be leftist poets of the thirties he adopted a democratic anti-authoritarian, non-elitist attitude to culture. Before and during the war, his emphasis was on anti-Fascism, anti-Stalinism and a general abhorrence of the impersonal State. Later, it shifted to anti-institutionalism in public life (including higher education and literature) and to a kind of New Enlightenment, the belief that the average 100 per cent American should be taught to appreciate and enjoy the wealth that Proust, Rilke, Chekhov, Liszt, Mahler and so many other great Europeans can offer.

[1] Further referred to as *BS*, *7LC*, *LF*, *L*, *WWZ* and *LW* respectively.

Already·in *Blood for a Stranger*, a largely imitative and experimental first book, the outlook is mature and more comprehensive than in the later work, ranging over war, revolution, betrayal
of ideas and decay of the West. The subject of many poems is pain
and alienation, but the poet's commitment is mainly theoretical, his
creative response rather cerebral and general.

Apart from the war poems, which stand in a class by themselves,
Jarrell's post-war concern with civilization became less far-ranging
but more penetrating in its frustration. *Pictures from an Institution*
(1954) is a witty satiric novel dealing with the institutionalized
sterility of academic life. In his famous essay 'The Age of Criticism'
he accused the 'appallingly influential' flood of (New) Criticism of
stifling creative writing. But his own poetics was half-heartedly New
Critical. His greatest grievance was that in this age 'the poet is a
condemned man for whom the State will not even buy breakfast',
and that the man who vacantly relishes the *Reader's Digest* cannot
read the *Divine Comedy* ('The Obscurity of the Poet').[1] In this
hierarchical approach to potential readers he *was* elitist, though
perhaps through no fault of his: the academic writers' isolation
tended to develop a new institutionalism, a new Establishment.

The feeling of being misunderstood or ignored by one's inferiors
is responsible for the cultural resignation, arrogance, or ex-
hibitionism in some of Jarrell's important poems. In the
neo-Faustian 'Conversation with the Devil' (*7LC*) the two speakers'
fates and images merge wittily and sadly into one. But the culture
criticism here is less venomous than in the well-known poem 'A
Girl in a Library' (*7LC*), about a student of Home Economics and
Physical Education, asleep over her book. The insults hurled at her,
like 'One sees in your blurred eyes/The "uneasy half-soul" Kipling
saw in dogs' betray the poet's irritation at the girl's superior, though inarticulate vitality. 'An English Garden in Austria'
(*7LC*), Jarrell tells us in the Introduction to *Selected Poems* (where he
tries to tease the common reader into a game of cultural
hide-and-seek),

is a poem about neo-classicism changing into romanticism, the eighteenth
century changing into the nineteenth. Someone going home from an
Austrian performance of *Der Rosenkavalier* thinks the poem – thinks it when
he comes across an English garden, the first outpost of romanticism there
on the Continent.

It is not hard to guess who the 'someone' is, parading his learning in

[1] Both essays are in *Poetry and the Age*, 1953.

a pot-pourri of references to European art and history. In its pure form, the civilization theme did not produce Jarrell's finest poetry; but it underlies all of his writing and so has a share in his finest achievements.

In Jarrell's war poetry the cause of civilization has dwindled to the vague promise of a 'Different World' in the name of which the impersonal State imposes dehumanizing army routine, pain and mechanized death on helpless individuals. Glory is no longer statistically significant: 'When we lasted long enough they gave us medals;/When we died they said, "Our casualties were low".' The soldier 'learns to fight for freedom of the State' with the result that 'his dull torment mottles like a fly's/The lying amber of the histories'. Writing mostly about air-force personnel, planes and carriers, Jarrell combines military and verbal expertise. But the real strength of these poems lies in the juxtaposition of man and machine, or the whole machinery of war from the bewildered individual's point of view. The fateful encounter between bomber and fighter is too mechanized, too remote to be experienced in fully human terms: 'Under the leather and fur and wire, in the gunner's skull,/It is a dream: and he, the watcher, guiltily/watches the him, the actor, who is innocent' ('Siegfried', *LF*). To preserve human values in this war means to be mentally deranged, like the pilot who still searches, in dreams, for his lost comrade ('The Dead Wingman', *L*). Often the soldier is compared to a child or beast, the deadly machines to toys: 'The soldier ... Is lied to like a child, cursed like a beast.' Parachuting, a pilot sees 'a child's first scrawl, the carrier's wake' and 'the little blaze' [on the carrier]/'Toylike as the glitter of the wing-guns'. The soldier's only real world is 'in letters and dreams'; and of course, back in the States, 'The thing about you is, you're *real*.' The ultimate message of Jarrell's war poems is that the war experience is unreal, a meaningless nightmare, a second, deeper fall of man.

It did not make him write his best poetry, because here his subtle humanistic imagination was engaged self-defeatingly. To him the numbing ordeals of war were a temporary escape into a helplessness for which the world was to blame, not the self. Probably no other American poet has written a more impressive body of war poems. But only a handful, like 'Death of the Ball Turret Gunner', 'Second Air Force', 'A Lullaby' (*LF*), 'The Dead Wingman', 'Eighth Air Force', 'The Dead in Melanesia' (*L*), reach unqualified greatness.

Little Friend, Little Friend (1945) is a war book; already in *Losses* (1948) only about half the poems are about war, while the others announce his inward turning, the self's escape from the vanity of culture and civilization. In his fable *The Bat-Poet* (1964), Jarrell defined his creative dilemma. The curious bat who ventures out into the Apollonian world of daylight writes his most important poem – about a mother bat and her baby flying through the dark; but when he returns to the barn, he forgets it and goes to sleep with the other bats. The question is not 'whether to be a bat or a poet', but what can a bat-poet do. Jarrell's answer is, Be a poet of bathood. In 'The Märchen' (*L*) he brings into focus his mature theme of the suffering self in terms of the child and his world. Using Grimm's Tales as an allegory of 'our own hearts, the realm of dark' he presents the Enchanted Forest and 'the eternal sea' as the real world, governed by Necessity, 'the blind untroubled Might/Renting a destiny to men on terms', while 'the dreaming Hänsel' unites the figures of Everychild, Everyman and Christ, whose vitality lies in the ability to wish, i.e. in the creative imagination. The 'kingdom' of 'men', the ordered human existence, is surrounded by 'giants, warlocks, the unburied dead/Invulnerable to any power' – the irrational forces of the world. The lesson to be learnt from those Tales is 'neither to rule nor to die' but 'to change', the ideal proclaimed being neither power nor defeatism, but creative escape.

'The Märchen' is a key poem to Jarrell's later poetry, concerned with the peace time crisis of humanity, the one that really counts. His central, mythic figure becomes the child, rather unlike Blake's innocents, Wordsworth's child as father of the man, Rilke's uneasy *Kinder* waiting till their time comes, though the kinship is evident, particularly with Rilke. Jarrell equates the relation of the grown man to the world with that of the child to the equally inscrutable and frightening world of adults, fairy-tale, dream and fantasy. The second part of *The Seven-League Crutches* is largely based on this equation. His child is brother of the man and a valid source of understanding adult experience, its subjective meaning, himself being the hero's prototype, and the unfulfilled great promise of his childhood the ultimate theme.

Jarrell's subjective later poems show *change* to be an ambivalent motif – the metamorphic escape, but also the trap of decay and death, just as the child is an ambivalent figure with its potential of wishes and growth, but also its bondage and helplessness. Several of his important dramatic monologues deal with the consciousness of ageing women, their vanishing beauty and identity ('The Face' *7LC*; 'The Woman at the Washington Zoo', *WWZ*; 'Next Day', *LW*). Robert Lowell has observed that Jarrell's speakers, mostly women, are 'unlike Browning's, very close to the author'. But the difference is in the range of empathy and in outlook – wistful diffidence as against the older poet's expansive optimism. The drive towards impersonation is the same, coming from the lack of centripetal egotism, of Romantic self-assurance. For this reason Jarrell, with all his dream/fancy escapism remains a Romantic *manqué*, but develops a dramatic vitality comparable to Browning's and an even superior living voice in a new and pure conversational idiom, fitted with ease into iambic pentameters or 'sprung rhythm'.

Jarrell's late poetry, *The Woman at the Washington Zoo*, and especially *The Lost World*, works towards the completion of the child myth. With play and make-believe as his 'real life', 'The child is hopeful and unhappy in a world/Whose future is his recourse.' Having travelled through time to his childhood (in the title-sequence of his last book), to recapture that old hope and belief, he finds that 'age is like it', that 'our end copies/Its beginning'. The child's imaginary wish-fulfilment is all the fulfilment there ever will be. Hence it is wise to accept one's status of a child in the enchanted forest and to go on wishing.

The concluding lines in Jarrell's last book – 'I hold in my own hands, in happiness,/Nothing: the nothing for which there's no reward.' ('Thinking of the Lost World') – may sound nihilistic; but he was not through as a poet. The vision of every man as child and every woman as mother (disturbing, threatening: 'Hope', 'Woman', *LW*) was developing in the direction of precise, poignantly humane humour, a kind of brittle strength. This, too, was part of an unclamorous revolt of the fleeting true self against the solid but unreal world.

JOHN BERRYMAN (1914–72) makes one wonder about the validity of classifications according to period and dominant trend. He began his career as a poet of the thirties, with a heavy debt to Auden and a variety of Modernist influences. His major work was published in the sixties; doggedly personal, it is in some ways akin to the recent 'confessional' fashion. In spite of frequent obscurity, which has exasperated certain critics, his awareness, idiom and form are unmistakable: he walked through more than three decades of general and poetic history and remained himself, wherever we try to place him. Yet the opposite claim can be advanced, that Berryman is one of the most time-marked (though not dated) modern poets in America, with a sensibility of the forties and fifties, and that his originality lies precisely in giving expression to one variant of the complex state of mind of his generation.

The years of apprenticeship to middle and late Yeats and to

trumpeting young Auden were marked by technical experimentation and fashionable, rather abstract complaints about the
failures of civilization, about the alarming pre-war atmosphere. But
already in the short poems later collected in *The Dispossessed* (1948)
we find such stuff as Berryman's 'dreams' are made of – tormented
personal multiplicity and passionate, guilty sex. Some poems foreshadow Berryman's gift of trenchant phrasing (e.g. 'the evil waste of
history/Outstretched' in 'Winter Landscape'), his later mastery in
shifting aspects of identity ('The Ball Poem'), in modelling the
idiom and syntax after the flux of feeling and breath: 'If (Unknown
Majesty) I not confess/praise for the rack the rock the live sailor/
under the blue sea, – yet I may You bless/always for her . . .' ('Canto
Amor').

The sequence slyly entitled *Berryman's Sonnets*, written in the
forties but not published (except No. 25) until 1968, displays his
first mature poetic formula: traditional form and personal
experience in a modern idiom. The 115 sonnets in the Italian
rhyme-scheme deal with an illicit 'knock-down-and-drag-out love'
between the poet (called by his name in No. 84) and Lise, 'A reckless
lady', in the form of a loose chronicle. Berryman beats his 'modern
breast' rather too hard in No. 26, for bits of the conventional
repertory of Petrarch's imitators are still good enough for him: the
lady's eyes resemble lightning (2); she is 'sunlight' (27) and has a
'sun-incomparable face' (77); she 'thrives' where he 'pines' (35); he
is the sacrifice 'led/Burning to slaughter', she the 'priestess' (19);
he oscillates between hope and despair (89), unworthy to sing her
praises (32). He also imitates the cadences of Shakespeare's
sonnets (43, 8–9; 84, 1–2; 101, 1–3) and the central passage in
Donne's 'The Good Morrow' (36, 9–11).

Still, *Berryman's Sonnets* are basically modern in awareness and
idiom. A metaphysical conceit is built round a 'suicide/From the
Empire State falling on someone's car' (7); we catch glimpses of the
boring office routine with the poet as '*Eremiteamateur* in the midst of
boobs' (53), of a depressing city bar (13), of a house-party (115).
The erotic descriptions are precise and fresh: 'nude upon some
warm lawn softly turn/Toward me the silence of your breast' (2); 'A
darkness dreams adown her softest crotch' (77), the kisses
(poetically) masterful: 'Teeth click, suddenly your tongue like a
mulled wine/Slides fire' (4). But referring to the sex act (3, 13; 46;
67; 70, 12; 104) Berryman settles for neutral definitions ('writhing',
'heaving') or for evasive witticisms ('Ah, to work underground/
Slowly and wholly in your vein profound', 34). This is in keeping

with the moral assumption of adulterous sex as 'sin', 'crime' or 'wickedness'. Though the poet-lover asserts that 'Our law too binds', and 'I met my soul', he calls himself an 'evil clown'. The hostile and deadening culture is not rebelled against: 'this town/My tomb becomes a kind of paradise .../How then complain?' (74). Within this limiting framework, *Berryman's Sonnets* are rich and strange, ultimately personal in that they deal, not with what happens to the poet but with how it happens in his mind.

Following his growing affinity for long forms Berryman worked for four-and-a-half years on *Homage to Mistress Bradstreet* (1953; as a book, 1956), an impressive narrative poem in fifty-seven eight-line stanzas, featuring the first American poet, Anne Dudley, born 1612 and married to Simon Bradstreet – with vivid or (lurid) detail, wrenched syntax, tense, rather affected diction and arresting rhythms:

> Outside the New World winters in grand dark
> white air lashing high thro' the virgin stands
> foxes down foxholes sigh
> surely the English heart quails, stunned.
> I doubt if Simon than this blast, that sea,
> spares from his rigour for your poetry
> more. We are on each other's hands
> who care. Both of our worlds unhanded us. Lie stark ...
>
> (Stanza 2)

Berryman's *persona* ('I') and Anne talk, fall in love and come desperately close to adultery in the central part of the 'historical' poem. From the very beginning it is not only, not even primarily concerned with 'pock-marked' Anne – her repressed eroticism, domestic joys and sorrows, diseases and approaching death. She is like a ghost summoned by the alienated poet as an ally, to help him overcome 'the almost insuperable difficulty of writing high verse at all in a land that cared and cares so little for it'.[1] Perhaps she is a zombie, or a newly stitched Bride of Frankenstein; after all, he is 'appalled' by her 'bald abstract didactic rime'. 'I did not choose her – somehow she chose me,' Berryman assures us; she is his excuse, his Muse, made to serve well past the invocation. He paints in black Anne's fairly cheerful crossing in the *Arabella*, 1630, her happy marriage to *not* 'so much older Simon', her satisfactory environment and status as poet, in a compulsive need to dig at the

---

[1] In *Poets on Poetry*.

roots of the poison tree of Puritan knowledge that flesh is evil. What may seem a romantic escape from an oppressive present is prying in the depth of a sore that will not heal. Hence the *pathophilia* of Anne's pleased exclamation when the poet agrees to touch her smallpox scars, the sado-masochism of the gripping description of childbirth, the chronicle of living decay: if sex is a disease, disease may be sex.

77 Dream Songs (1964) is the second book on which Berryman's reputation was founded. When first offered as 'one version of a poem in progress' (Books I–III) in 'sections' of three six-line stanzas each, varying in the number of feet and use of rhyme, many critics found it too chaotic to view as a whole. But the claim was made good in more than quantity when 308 more 'dream songs' were published as *His Joy, His Dream, His Rest* (1968). Here the poet's Note offers clarification to those who 'went . . . desperately astray' in the maze of the seventy-seven:

The poem . . . is essentially about an imaginary character (not the poet, not me) named Henry, a white American in early middle age and sometimes in blackface, who has suffered an irreversible loss and talks about himself sometimes in the first person, sometimes in the third, sometimes even in the second; he has a friend, never named, who addresses him as Mr Bones and variants thereof.

The 'Note' on the hero's divided self is both authoritative and misleading. Berryman had earlier[1] spoken of 'the "I", perhaps of the poet', which 'disappears into Henry's first and third persons'. The 'I' is always the poet's; Henry is a character rather than a *persona* modelled on the poet's stream of verbal consciousness. And it is the 'friend' with his minstrel-show talk, his plantation-Negro dialect who mostly accounts for the blackface effects and sardonic wit, playing a kind of Mephistopheles to a non-Faustian, rather martyr-like hero without a story. We watch a fragmented nightmare with suffering as the keynote, in an idiom characterized by often rudely distorted syntax and colloquial speech, with infusions of affected literary expressions and dialect. Not unlike Gerard Manley Hopkins in his 'terrible sonnets', Henry Pussy-cat is 'pried open' (1), tortured and castrated (8), skinned and displayed (16). He is 'at odds wif de world & its god' (5); 'God's Henry's enemy' (13); Lucifer torments him with madness (17), life with boredom and loneliness. Henry is weighed down by a sense of guilt, of a crime he

---

[1] In *Poets on Poetry*.

thinks he has committed, maybe murder (19, 29, 39). The broad themes of crime and punishment, and of unheroic reality contrasted with the heroic past or with great art and thought give unity to apparently disparate topics. Sex is treated as untranscended lustfulness (4, 15, 44, 69) which causes disgust ('the great flare & stench'). The myth of Christ's Passion (48) and the 'Next World' (55, 56) as well as Arthurian legends are referred to with a bitter, taunting ambiguity which reflects Berryman's mixed feelings about himself as Christ-figure or modern knight-errant. After a long hovering between hysteria and sullen self-pity, Henry gives up his idealistic belief in 'Kyoto, Toledo, Benares – the holy cities' and Cambridge, Paris, Siena which 'do not make up/for ... the horror of unlove' and 'pulling together' settles for catering to the pleasure principle – 'tasting all the secret bits of life' (74).

Henry Berryman, 'a human American man', moves protesting but not rebelling through a modernized version of the Waste Land located in his country: his protest and disgust are ego-ridden and fragmentary, but authentic. His words, too, are certainly good: not merely unforgettable phrases ('We betrayed me'; 'He lay in the middle of the world, and twitcht'; 'He felt like shrieking but he shuddered') and brief passages, but the whole poetic world he creates, hauntingly more real for being at one remove from waking reality, in songs about bad dreams come true.

The additional 308 Dream Songs (4 × 77 in Books IV–VII) are both a continuation and a fresh start – unlike *Short Poems* (1967), a pot-pourri of Berryman's characteristic themes and motifs. The hero is still 'impenetrable Henry, goatish, reserved,/whose heart is broken' (297), and the same three-stanza form is skilfully applied throughout; but the nightmare intensity is gone and we get a daylight chronicle instead. The unnamed 'friend' appears but rarely; Henry's position and awareness are radically changed and a curious Passion-Death-Resurrection pattern emerges. His 'pulling together' and substitution of ordinary pleasures for exalted pain at the end of *77 Dream Songs* is seen to be the death of Henry Agonistes, the idealist; the new volume opens with *Op. posth.* (Book IV). At the end of these creepily witty poems Henry is 'returning to our life/adult & difficult', 'with a shovel/digging like mad, Lazarus with a plan/to get his own back'. His Resurrection is a fall into worldliness: thirsting for women and alcohol, *making it* as a writer, commenting on the culture, politics and literature with a new, 'comfy' detachment, recording his quotidian experiences. Yet the shadow of real death is cast over the new life from the start: Book V opening with a 'confessional' group of poems from a hospital, the 'race with Time', the approach of sickness and old age, deaths of literary contemporaries, especially the moving elegy for Delmore Schwarz (154–158), add up to a sombre countercurrent.

The frequent treatment of the sex theme, ranging between simple lust ('Hey: an empty girl./Fill 'er up, pal.' 250) and crime (222, 237) features Henry rather boastfully as *homme fatal* (371). Guilty goatishness is only transcended in a few poems displaying sympathy for women suffering for love (358, 372, 375), and, quite exceptionally, 361, where the defeat of the Spanish Armada is celebrated as a great love-in.

Henry's socio-politico-cultural chronicle is spun out from an academic observer-consumer's point of view. He sports his European culture talk (258, 347–9) and his White House invitation (302, 304); is casually critical of cocktail-party relationships and bad writing (98), the New York Police Force (110), US postal services (167), 'Rich Critical Prose'; deplores the crazy respect for 'guns/ (not persons)' (135), the lack of 'holy cities' in his country (210), the corrupt elders' criticism of American youth (216), the 'stupidity' of J. F. Kennedy's administration (245), the American involvement in Korea (217) and Vietnam (162), remaining 'a shameless patriot' (339) facing 'the faceless monsters of the Soviet Unions' and preferring 'lovely & sane' American show-biz sex, for 'as we all know,/the peoples in the East/have no sexual problems, have no problems/but housing & food & ideology' (363). Characteristically, the protest of the earlier book has disappeared, the disgust become tolerable. Unlike Jarrell's regressive escapism, Berryman's response to the fifties and sixties has been a limiting readjustment. Henry's 'winning tributes, given prizes, made offers, & such', and his complacent chat about academic life and travel in Ireland show that his protest was essentially not against the culture, but against the buffets it had dealt to his loyally aspiring ego. Unlike Eliot, he calmed down without a religious conversion, succumbing to success and middle age. Ultimately, Berryman fails to qualify as a tragic culture-hero, to resolve the self versus culture dilemma of his generation by transcending the 'normal' self. As an artist, he succeeds by portraying this failure.

KARL J. SHAPIRO (b. 1913) has described himself in relation to the Literary Establishment of his generation as 'an outsider, or one who was constantly battling to get on the outside'. But he has been professor of English in well-known universities, Consultant in

Poetry at the Library of Congress, editor of prestigious magazines, *Poetry* (Chicago) and *The Prairie Schooner*. Elected a member of the National Institute of Arts and Letters, he professes to have tried to decline, and to have been snubbed into acceptance. On not receiving an invitation to the public ceremony at Yale University to honour the memory of Randall Jarrell (1966) he 'had a blood-boiling moment of suspicion or paranoia that the Bollingen Committee or Professor Pearson or Robert Lowell had blackballed [him] from the club'. A few months later he used his lecture on Jarrell delivered at the Library of Congress to advertise himself and to accuse Lowell of uninspired one-upmanship in poetry.

According to Shapiro, 'only inferior poetry battles against society'; true poetry 'exists in a dimension outside civilization'. He rejects the Pound–Eliot concept of a 'Culture which is the substitute for religion', disgusted with artists and intellectuals who 'backslide' into religion and with 'the Greco-Judaic-Christian thingamajig'. His message to poets is 'Get off the Culture Waggon'. And yet, in many of his best-known poems there is hardly anything but venomous battling against the society he lives in: 'The Dome of Sunday' (deploring 'Rowhouses and row-lives'); 'University' (where 'To hurt the Negro and avoid the Jew/Is the curriculum'); 'Drugstore' (where 'Youth comes to jingle nickels and crack wise' ... 'And every nook and cranny of the flesh/Is spoken to in packages with wiles'); the mock-dithyrambic 'Buick'; 'Auto-Wreck', leading up to the question of collective responsibility (in *Person, Place, and Thing*, 1942); the 'rage and rat's logic' of 'Emporium'; 'Boy-Man' (in *Trial of a Poet*, 1947: a portrait of the average American male as vulgarly optimistic and ignorantly pushing). These are poems of a social and cultural moralist, mostly presented as objective but really based on humane, though ostentatiously superior participation.

The Greek heritage is practically absent from Shapiro's verse (though Plato and Aristotle are not outside his scope in criticism); the 'Judaic-Christian' complex, however, provides the basis for his own culture religion. In the Introduction to *Poems of a Jew* (1958) he constructs a culture myth of the Jew as a prototype of modern man, reduced to his existential basis – 'the primitive ego of the human race', an uneasy, disillusioned seeker of God, 'neither hero nor victim' but 'man left over, after everything that can happen has happened'. Here, as well as in *V-Letter and Other Poems* (1944) several poems are built around this thesis. The realistic humanism of the Judaic faith is contrasted approvingly with the romantic high promise of Christianity ('Synagogue'), and stubborn humanity is shown as the essence of tragic greatness ('The Murder of Moses'). On the other hand, the holy beggar in 'Messias' is a shocking and sad substitute for romantic illusion. Besides, Shapiro did backslide into very orthodox, very organized religion himself in his brief conversion to Roman Catholicism, with poor poetic results, except for the unusually gentle poem 'The Convert'. Nor is his mockery of Christianity ('The Confirmation', 'Teasing the Nuns') and criticism of its practice ('The Jew at Christmas Eve') very impressive, for a reason found already in his preface to *V-Letter and Other Poems*: 'I try to write freely, one day as a Christian, the next as a Jew, the next as a soldier who sees the slapstick of modern war.' With neither creed is his involvement very deep; moreover, his concept of Judaism is 'virtually beyond religion' and his identification with it improbable: for his ego is far from primitive, his alienation deeply imbedded in the American intellectual's way of life.

Shapiro's denunciations of Modernist poets (Pound, Eliot, Yeats and Stevens) and of the 'New Criticism' are notorious. His main thesis is that the Pound–Eliot 'culture Orthodoxy', anti-democratic in politics, anti-romantic in letters, ritualist and dogmatic in religion, has produced a third-rate impersonal poetry of ideas. As for modern criticism, he vowed as early as 1941 to destroy its 'dictatorship', and has persisted in the belief that it stands between the audience and poetry, and prevents the poet from writing from within his creative self. But his reputation in the forties and fifties was founded on poems which the New Critics praised – poems sparkling with ironic wit, cerebral, pontifical; in the sequence 'Adam and Eve' he even tried his hand at the typically Modernist reinterpretation of ancient myth with the help of modern depth psychology. And Shapiro himself said about his 'initiation into criticism', after his first successes in *Poetry* and *Partisan Review*: 'From then on I took it for granted that I was expected to write essays or reviews when asked and I almost never refused.'[1] It is only fair to add that his scathing criticism of Pound, Yeats and Eliot must needs stand between an unwary audience and their poetry.

Having learned from Auden to revere prosody, Shapiro has made numerous pronouncements on the relationship between poetry and prose (most affectedly in the *Essay on Rime*, i.e. on poetry, 1945, written in iambic pentameters, which he professes to abhor). These embrace both the assertion that poetry and prose are antithetic

[1] In *Defense of Ignorance*, 1960.

modes of experience and expression, and its opposite: 'There is no borderline between poetry and prose. Even verse (meter) is no distinction', with a variety of intermediate positions. In practice he has ranged from prosaic, metrically bolstered verse in all his books to the ingenious prose poems of *The Bourgeois Poet* (1964), where he 'break[s] free of the poetry trap'.

Paradoxes or incompatibles seem to be the very essence of Karl Shapiro's literary theory and practice. But what are we to think of them? Dismiss him as a hopeless eclectic who could not make up his mind, or made it up too often? Ignore his criticism and simply enjoy some of his poems? Or accept his contradicting himself because like Whitman, the patron saint of his maturity, he 'contains multitudes'?

Shapiro cannot be dismissed as either poet or critic because at his best he is very good, and his entire production is significant for the understanding of the first post-war generation of American poets. Like so many others, he grew up in the shadow of the Modernists. Then he was converted to the belief in the Marx–Freud–Auden Trinity. The things he learned from Auden – how to make socio-cultural problems his personal concern and how to 'think his emotions' in poetry, i.e. to translate feeling into intellectual realization – are firmly embedded in Shapiro's most successful performances, such as 'The Dome of Sunday', 'Scyros', 'Washington Cathedral', 'Full Moon: New Guinea', 'Christmas Eve: Australia', parts of 'Elegy for a Dead Soldier' and of 'Adam and Eve', practically all of *The Bourgeois Poet* (1964) and about half of *White-Haired Lover* (1968). During the fifties 'the first white aboriginal', Whitman, prophet of the self as body-soul, with a 'cosmic consciousness' became his idol; he also expressed admiration for D. H. Lawrence, Henry Miller and W. C. Williams, and an interest (rather abstract) in Wilhelm Reich, mysticism, Zen Buddhism and the *I Ching*. If unlike the Beats, the Black Mountain group and other poets of the late fifties and sixties, Shapiro was incapable of 'making a wholesale return to the anarchy of experience', it was because he had undertaken the Faust-like task of tasting every bit of the poetic and cultural experience in his lifetime, while his sensibility and up-bringing enabled him to move gracefully only along the border-line of self and culture in conflict.

Intellectual control and non-idealizing detail are counterweights to yearning and near-sentimentality in 'V-Letter'; bristling wit and verbal poise are complementary to the Whitmanesque catalogues and ramblings across the American culture scene and the poet's own tastes and needs in *The Bourgeois Poet*; colloquial idiom is matched with strict meters, erotic subject-matter with urbane utterance in *White-Haired Lover*. Exceptionally, we find little triumphs of another kind: the direct excitement of 'Israel' (in *Poems 1940–1953*), the vital visual imagery of 'The Alphabet' (*Poems of a Jew*), the sensuous use of words in 'There is Gray in My Eyebrows' (*White-Haired Lover*, VII). In some respects, Shapiro's work is reminiscent of older English poets: the elegiac sentimentalism of Thomas Gray ('Conscription Camp', 'Elegy for a Dead Soldier'), the 'negative capability' of Keats's 'chameleon poet', himself 'the glory, jest and riddle of the world' like Pope, that Romantic *manqué* ('Longing for the Primitive, I Survive as a Modern, barely'). To the inert reader, Shapiro has suffered a 'confession' posing (not unreasonably) as a man of compromise, a complacent Bourgeois Poet whose dualism of values is close to duplicity: 'I am an Atheist who says his prayers./I am an anarchist, and a full professor at that. I take the loyalty oath.' But this is too easy. Though he never really questions the basis of his own existence, Shapiro is completely absorbed in his tight-rope dance of the American way of life and poetry writing (with the academic safety-net below). He sees the culture to be evil but it has become part of his own self. Inside the culture trap he is doomed to wander, as an American in the classic search for identity rather than as a Jew.

THEODORE ROETHKE (1908–63)

'One has said a thing as best one can in the poem . . . why debase it or water it down to a didactic prose for a lazy modern audience?' Roethke's snap at the middlemen of literature seems particularly appropriate in relation to his own poetry. What, for example, may be interesting to say after these lines from 'Cuttings (later)'?

> This urge, wrestle, resurrection of dry sticks,
> Cut stems struggling to put down feet,
> What saint strained so much,
> Rose on such lopped limbs to a new life?

The answer is simple – what the poet said, working backward and downward to 'that anguish of concreteness':

> I can hear underground, that sucking and sobbing,
> In my veins, in my bones I feel it –
> The small waters seeping upward,
> The tight grains parting at last,
> When sprouts break out,
> Slippery as fish,
> I quail, lean to beginnings, sheath-wet.

Even the poet's own prose statement of his central theme in *The Lost Son* (1948), which includes this poem, is flat by comparison: '. . . a kind of struggle out of the slime . . . a slow spiritual progress; an effort to be born, and later, to become something more' ('Open Letter'). Learned definitions of vegetal and sexual imagery, psychic regression, identification with lower forms of life as employed here would be even less exciting, far from the energy of suffering and hope which the poem has captured for us.

Unfortunately, even in reading Roethke's poetry of the nascent self the world is too much with us. The judgment passed by Randall Jarrell in his role as advocate of culture is characteristic:

. . . plants and animals, soil and weather, sex, ontogeny and the unconscious swarm over the reader, but he looks in vain for hydrogen bombs, world wars, Christianity, money, ordinary social observations, his everyday moral doubts.

('Fifty Years of American Poetry')

This had been said in 1962, before Roethke's most explicitly religious poetry was written (it was published posthumously in *The Far Field*, 1964); besides, the ambivalent father cult in his earlier work had a clear, though less prominent religious parallel in basic Christian terms. What matters, however, is the implied dissatisfaction with the absence of historical, social and moral interest in Roethke. His poetry has been called too narrow in scope, being wholly absorbed in his own self as subject-matter. Some critics admit the originality and power of his 'greenhouse poems' in *The Lost Son* and of his explorations of the pre- and sub-conscious in *Praise to the End!* (1951) while finding nothing but undigested imitation and decline in the later books. And then there is the long list of poetic influences, often invoked to raise the question of Roethke's creative status: Yeats most disapprovingly, with Léonie Adams, W. H. Auden, William Blake, Louise Bogan, John Clare, Emily Dickinson, John Donne, T. S. Eliot, Stanley Kunitz, Walter Raleigh, Christopher Smart, Wallace Stevens, Dylan Thomas, Thomas Traherne, Walt Whitman, William Wordsworth, and others. To these must be added the psychoanalysts – Sigmund Freud, C. G. Jung, as well as the theologians and mystics Jacob Boehme, Martin Buber, St John of the Cross, Søren Kierkegaard and Paul Tillich, whose teachings became Roethke's major interest by the mid-fifties. Hence the kind of critical consideration Roethke requires in the first place is an antidote to confusing and damaging criticism, to make room for enjoyment of the poetry.

Roethke's first book of poems, *Open House* (1941) bears amazing negative testimony to his development as artist. Here we find 'a sense of total participation in life', allegedly lacking from his own work as a whole, but no sense of total participation in poetry. The prevailing mode is rational and metaphysical, with a variety of rhetorical effects. 'Everyday moral doubts' are frequently discussed ('Epidermal Macabre', 'Reply to Censure', 'The Auction', 'The Favorite', etc.), social satire is in full swing ('Academic', 'Ballad of the Clairvoyant Widow', 'The Reckoning'). The nature descriptions are either pointless or vaguely moralistic. What betrays the immaturity most is the diction – insipidly general, genteel, correct. Only the title poem touches the core of Roethke's inspiration:

> I'm naked to the bone,
> With nakedness my shield.
> Myself is what I wear:
> I keep the spirit spare.

After this, *The Lost Son* came as a miracle: it could just as well have been entitled *The Found World*. Together with *Praise to the End!* (1951), it forms the most unusual part of Roethke's quest for spiritual identity. The 'greenhouse poems' in Section I, featuring with uncanny insight the world of the poet's father, a florist from Saginaw, Michigan, are but the *medium* (microbiologically speaking) in which the poetic *culture* of the origins of a consciousness is grown. Roethke's tragic personality – his sense of physical clumsiness, an almost babyish helplessness and agonized need of protection, combined with recurrent psychotic crises throughout his adult life within a broader manic-depressive pattern which made him oscillate between self-loathing jealousy and exultant love-radiation – begins its incantatory, magical reconstruction by entering the natural world of 'the minimal', by studying 'the lives on a leaf: the little/Sleepers, numb nudgers in cold dimensions,/ Beetles in caves, newts, stone-deaf fishes ...' as well as plants, stones and waters. The lowest organic forms and the inorganic, from childhood memories, are one source of the wisdom he seeks, asking What is life and How to live it. The other source is his own inner world: the father–son relationship, the infantile to adolescent awareness (Section IV), and later (*Praise to the End!*) an imaginary journey even further back, in the realm of nativity, prenatal existence and conception. The poetic innovation is in the idiom as much as in the regressive range of subject matter. The reader joins Roethke in Wonderland, a primitive animistic world, by way of a language purged of intellectualism and syntactic connectives, bare in vocabulary, infinitely rich in symbolic associations. The literary examples of James Joyce and Dylan Thomas, the psychological theory of individuation advanced by Jung, are in close kinship with this kind of poetry but cannot explain it away. However simple the basic mechanism of sexual awakening and filial guilt, or the alternating patterns of protective unconscious darkness and the promise of light, of consciousness and spirituality, the effect is complex because it is both less and more than personal, below the formed ego level and beyond its exclusiveness. And even more exciting than the threats of this surreal universe of primordial vitality is the joy and sympathetic humour which breaks through in moments of affirmation:

> For you, my pond,
> Rocking with small fish,
> I'm an otter with only one nose;
> I'm all ready to whistle;
> I'm more than when I was born;
> I could talk to a snail;
> I see what sings!
> What sings!
>   ('O Lull Me, Lull Me')

Poems outside the protagonist's spiritual history, with social and moral aspects of contemporary civilization ('Dolor', 'Double Feature'; 'Judge Not') became exceptions; the main line of Roethke's poetic development continued with his love lyrics in *The Waking* (1953) and *Words for the Wind* (1958). In this genre, so rare in our century and particularly in the period under consideration, Roethke wrote some of his happiest and finest poems. Some are a direct continuation of his 'spiritual history', with the beloved as both part of nature (earth, air, light) and an extension of the protagonist's self; though tighter in meter, they speak in the voice of the previous two books:

> Loving, I use the air
> Most lovingly: I breathe; ... The wind's white with her name,
> And I walk with the wind ... I ... see and suffer myself
> In another being at last ...
>   ('Words for the Wind')

Love poems of the same type recur in *The Far Field* (1964), though there they are saddened by the sense of approaching death and some are dramatized, presented from the woman's point of view.

On the other hand, the sequence of love poems 'Four for Sir John Davies' is an introduction to Roethke's late poetry.'To become something more' than a born self, he was 'struggling to put down feet' in areas other than the human body and non-human nature. Here he combines the idea of cosmic dance as elaborated in Davies's long philosophical poem 'Orchestra' (1954) with Yeats's motif of the dancer and the dance, the two poets' use of stanzas in rhymed pentameters, and Dante's journey into the spiritual through the sensual, in an effort to elaborate his own love, to transcend its bi-personal confines. The method is new but less original in the Romantic sense of the term; rather, it relies on the Renaissance idea of imitation as creative traditionalism. The admission 'I take this cadence from a man named Yeats' has been over-interpreted by numerous critics who ignore the line which follows: 'I take it, and I give it back again.' Why should T. S. Eliot's 'stealing' with authority of fragments from other poets (partly parodied) to be 'shored against [his] ruins' be legitimate, and Roethke's creative dialogue with them, partly in their own terms, be viewed as exhaustion, as capitulation? Poets who have achieved greatness by creative assimilation, from Spenser and Shakespeare to Eliot and Yeats, give the lie to this theory of originality. We may regret (unreasonably) that Roethke did not become a new kind of poet in his maturity without outside help, as it were. But the crux of adverse criticism of his late work is in the confusion of his creative process and some of its results.

While Roethke's love poetry constitutes the middle phase of his spiritual autobiography, his late poetry is concerned with a desperate struggle against the idea of approaching death. His 'long journey out of the self', begun as erotic expansion, soon turned into a series of excursions into the dramatized consciousness of other persons faced with non-being, and into attempted transcendence of the self through mystical 'oneness' with the womb-like universe or with the Christian God-as-father principle.

The first direction, resulting from the urge to *give* understanding and sympathy, operates from the mother image ('Old Lady's Winter Words' in *The Waking*, 'Meditations of an Old Woman' in *Words of the Wind*) and the complex image of Yeats as spiritual father and the poet's biological father ('The Dying Man', in *Words for the Wind*). It is tempting to speculate on all the women in these two books as representing Jung's idea of the *anima*, 'an inherited collective image of women ... in a man's unconscious', but Roethke's poetic use of them is twofold – as the beloved, within the natural order of life, and as mother, moving towards the unnatural chaos of death. Existentially, these poems succeed because unlike T. S. Eliot's baffling mixture of 'memory and desire', they display memory (filial, literary, philosophical) as a key to intense and far-ranging awareness, the closest one can come in a lifetime to the unattainable fruit of eternity. Poetically, they succeed too, for the dialogue with Yeats's Byzantium poems ('The Dying Man') and Eliot's 'Ash Wednesday' and *Four Quartets* not only goes beyond their own statements in emulation rather than imitation, but works within Roethke's unique sensibility and a blend of his earlier diction with experiments in rival idioms he makes his own.

The second direction of Roethke's late quest for a superself, in *The Far Field* (1964), is regressive and overprotective. In a cultural vacuum, with rare, disgusted references to the day-to-day American way of life, he strives to *receive* understanding of life's final phase through contemplation of natural scenery on a grand scale and sympathy with his *timor mortis*. In the 'North American Sequence', accurate nature description combined with the symbolic uses of earth as body and death, and water as soul and life (temporal river, eternal sea) leads to mixed results. The landscapes are authentic and moving as a vast metaphor of a rich departing life; but the symbolism of the archetypal journey seems somewhat too obvious, the assurances won merely declarative ('I am renewed by death, thought of my death'; 'And I stood outside myself,/Beyond becoming and perishing,/A something wholly other'). The long, discursive line already explored in 'Meditation of an Old Woman' under the influence of *Four Quartets* expands and contracts in supple pulsation; but the interplay between self and world, between perception and idea, is not nearly as convincing as in the earlier work, not owing to a loss of poetic power, but simply because Roethke attempts the impossible – to solve the riddle of dying by using words.

The impasse is even more tragically apparent in 'Sequence, Sometimes Metaphysical', where poetry is made to present achieved communion with God, or to demonstrate the validity of 'mystical experience'. Theological glosses of lines like 'Godhead above my God, are you there still?' or 'Sweet Christ, rejoice in my infirmity' are poetically irrelevant, just as the technicalities of Milton's cosmogony have no bearing on the vitality of *Paradise Lost*. Roethke must have been aware of this, and of what he could really hope to achieve apart from verbal wish-fulfilment: 'Brooding on God, I may become a man.' His late absorption in religious texts was actually more damaging because he was beginning to dilute his diction with their poetically trite jargon ('Love begets love. This torment is my joy', etc.). And yet, whenever this 'perpetual beginner' controlled his existential range within packed, end-stopped pentameters, as in the magnificent poem 'In Dark Time', or wisely made the best of his dangerous inclination to unstructured line-writing, as in 'The Infirmity', or worked towards a new, mellowed sympathy and humour with 'All things innocent, hapless, forsaken' ('The Lizard', 'The Meadow House', in 'Mixed Sequence'), he showed that these late triumphs were partial because he was still learning to sing his final song.

The history of Roethke's poetic becoming leaves us 'free in the tearing wind', exposed to the humour and terror, to the exultation and despair of a poetry which is personal in the sense that it is born out of the disordered, vulnerable, at times abnormal obverse side of a man's self, out of his efforts as creator and preserver of the deepest, most fundamental values of personal experience. His search was not for autobiographical fixation but for infinity in a handful of dust. That he did not write about public issues, except very early in his career, or occasionally in purgatory invectives under the pseudonym of Winterset Rothberg, does not prove that his range was limited. Rather, it is the great subversive gesture of an alienated modern self, a daring to root all exploration in its Yes and No, an implicit accusation hurled at the culture because it had offered too little to one who strove to 'proclaim once more a condition of joy'.

ROBERT LOWELL (1917–77) is the most impressive, perhaps the most obtrusive, poetic figure of his generation. Beside him Wilbur may appear insipidly graceful, Jarrell fretfully escapist, Roethke solipsistically babyish. Like a black granite rock, Lowell's work jabs into a storm-lashed ocean. He displays courage to face the horrors of our century on a larger scale than Karl Shapiro, the horror of his own self with more unsparing directness than Berryman.

Inevitably, a comprehensive grasp of modern reality entails complexity, or incongruity. In Lowell's case, these assume the form of warring opposites: a Calvinist New England tradition and Europe-oriented Roman Catholicism; orthodox Christianity and a man-monstered godless universe; the spirit of public service and self-laceration; helplessness before life and vaulting literary ambition; discipleship to the New Criticism and Southern Agrarian conservatism, replaced by confessional poetry and liberal-to-radical politics. His reputation, too, has ranged from labelling the post-war period as 'the Age of Lowell' to assigning him the place of an overpublicized minor poet.

Aristocratic family pride was manifest in Lowell's most rebellious public gesture, when revolted by the Western Allies' bombing of civilians in Europe he declared himself a conscientious objector in 1943, for the Lowells and the Winslows (on his mother's side) were among the oldest New England families and had produced generations of eminent teachers, officers, preachers and poets. The justice of the position involved is questionable – 'the USSR, a totalitarian tyranny, committed to world revolution', rather than the Fascist powers, was seen as the chief enemy. One thing is certain – Robert Traill Spence Lowell, Jr made his 'manic statement,/telling off the state and president' (Roosevelt, in an open letter) in the spirit of passive resistance to family and national authority. He remained true to the family tradition of public service; but his values were changed. Despite all awards and honours, wide publicity, professorships, including Kenyon College and Boston University, his chosen, but perhaps inevitable position was outside and against the power structure of the State, while firmly rooted in the East Coast main culture. In order to act out his share, he found it necessary to expose what was rotten, dying or dead in his heritage – the inhumanity of modern warfare, New England Calvinism and Capitalism, the human failures of his parents and his own.

Land of Unlikeness (1944), dominated by the first two themes, views the USA as a country in which the divine image, man's likeness to God, has been lost through Puritan materialism (especially in Lowell's native Boston and New England) and un-Christian bloodshed in the war. A general influence of T. S. Eliot's *Waste Land* is obvious, but Lowell was affected more directly by the anti-urban conservatism of John Crowe Ransom, his teacher at Kenyon College, Allen Tate, another early guide, and by his own recent conversion to Roman Catholicism.

In condemning the war, Lowell wields his new faith like a fire-brand, violently, sometimes almost blasphemously. The anti-Puritan theme is burdened with Biblical symbolism: Boston as Babylon, 'Mammon's unbridled industry', the Last Judgment, recurrent images of Christ and Cain. No less contrived is the supporting apparatus of classical allusion (the fall of Troy, Charon and the Acheron, etc.) and of historical learning ('Napoleon Crosses the

Berezina'). Lowell himself was dissatisfied with the 'messy violence', with 'too much twisting and disgust' in this book. But the true source of its weakness, apart from the superimposed Catholic ideology, is the imperfect use of the symbolists' combination of jagged imagination and strict form. Lowell's correct meters and stanza forms clash with the shocking diction, baroque imagery and strained rhetoric, which, of course, are also parts of the formal pattern.

The poetry of *Land of Unlikeness* was given a second chance in *Lord Weary's Castle* (1946), where about one-third of the best poems were reprinted, many in largely revised form. The grim prophetic prose recurs ('to Peter Taylor on the Feast of the Epiphany', 'As a Plane Tree by the Water', 'The Dead in Europe', 'Where the Rainbow Ends'), resulting in the same kind of prefabricated symbolism and rhetoric: '. . . only Armageddon will suffice', 'Babel of Boston where our money talks/And multiplies the darkness of a land', '. . . the scythers, Time and Death,/Helmed locusts, move upon the tree of breath'. The poet's obsession with a sense of sin and damnation in Puritan New England, past and present, is far more fruitful where his invectives are based on a historical vision, concrete imagery and a secular idiom. These were already present in some of the poems taken over from the previous book: 'Our fathers wrung their bread from sticks and stones/And fenced their gardens with the Redman's bones' ('Children of Light'; also, in 'Salem' and 'Concord'). They are most conspicuous in 'The Quaker Graveyard in Nantucket', one of the best poems in Lowell's early, densely textured manner. The massacre of contemporary warfare is juxtaposed with the Quakers' slaughtering of whales – both seen as un-godlike and futile – in dynamic images of great verbal energy.

The elegy is vitiated, however, by its religious element, and so are many other poems in the book. Section VI flatly describes an old Catholic shrine in England and ends in an easy prophecy: '. . . and the world shall come to Walsingham'. This is religious wish-fulfilment, substituting unlived doctrinal material for poetic evidence. Lowell's first attempt to find a positive alternative to a culture seen as doomed is limited to conventional hints at Christian salvation, with Jesus as water-walker, fisherman, kingfisher or bridegroom.

The genius of *Lord Weary's Castle* is negative, the poetic triumphs are realizations of failure: religious ('Mr. Edwards and the Spider', 'After the Surprising Conversions'), in the family ('In Memory of Arthur Winslow', 'Mary Winslow') and obliquely personal ('Between the Porch and the Altar', 'The Death of the Sheriff'). The mixture of censure and sympathy in the poems on the deaths of the poet's grandparents and the themes of adulterous guilt, incest, painful inefficiency, hallucinations, insanity, homicidal and suicidal tendencies foreshadow the exposure of family and self in *Life Studies*. While continuing to be intellectually complex and highly allusive to Biblical and classical lore, these poems are also experiments in fragmentary narrative and dramatic monologue.

It seems in keeping with Lowell's own insistent and partly blasphemous use of religious symbolism to call his next book, *The Mills of the Kavanaughs* (1951), a Fortunate Fall. No patent salvations are offered any more: the religious element, heavily reinforced with Greek mythology, becomes a vehicle of nightmarish though highly artificial dramatic monologues on the themes tackled in 'Between the Porch and the Altar' and 'The Death of the Sheriff'. When a naval officer's sister-mistress turns on her gas burners, there is just enough time for her to combine acute observation, religious and psychological symbols, and historical judgment into highly formal verse ('Her Dead Brother'). Thwarted adulterous lust, murderous and suicidal drives and insanity are equally dominant in 'Thanksgiving's Over' and the long title poem. In the latter, personal inspiration is apparent not only in the decay of a famous New England family (Henry Kavanaugh is a retired naval officer like the poet's father) but also in details of a disastrous marriage, which coincide with those in a story written by Jean Stafford, Lowell's first wife. It is not the collapse of religious faith which harms the book but the inappropriateness of the method applied to the new matter. One might put up with the melodramatic tone of 'Thanksgiving's Over', but hardly with the over-ingenious symbols and allusions. The inward turning, the passionate portrayal of the self within a decadent culture, is ill supported by the pseudocharacters who speak in Lowell's voice and idiom, and by the European mythological apparatus. To create images of his mind's hell, Lowell needed the help of fact, not fiction.

Life Studies (1959) was hailed and admired largely for the wrong reason. What caught the reader's and critic's eye was the title group of poems dealing with the pathetic inefficiency and humiliations of the poet's father, the dissolution of a pretentious family tradition, loss of the poet's childhood world, his material troubles, alcoholism, mental disease and social apathy – the speaker in these dramatic monologues being unmistakably Robert Lowell, not a character or *persona*. The 'confessional' writing (though actually closer to a mixture of satiric exposure and memories) was viewed by some as 'clinical' and 'therapeutic', as eliciting an embarrassing personal response which must somehow be 'transcended'. This personal poetry in the nude, just as nude acting, was too provocative for untrained sensibilities.

The breakthrough after a creative crisis between 1951 and 1959 was real, however, in cultural and poetic terms. Here was a poetry of rebellious culture-conscious self, made out of the familiar materials of American life instead of superimposed religion and mythology, in approach not unlike Allen Ginsberg's 'Howl' (1956) and W. D. Snodgrass's *Heart's Needle* (1959). The 'confessional' material, itself doctored for artistic reasons, was used as part of the book's larger pattern – following the harshly secular, objective culture criticism of Part One, the rich prose satire on the poet's family in Part Two and the sympathetic *in memoriam* for four writers and spiritual fellow-sufferers in Part Three. The idiom is de-poetized, modelled on educated American speech, partly under the influence of a series of poetry readings on the West Coast, in direct contact with appreciative audiences. The escape from tight forms, the broken meters varying between a ghost of an iambic pentameter and phrase-lines may have something to do with Lowell's early free verse modelled on William Carlos Williams.

This is not to deny existential substance to the poetic innovations in *Life Studies*. The morbid fascination with social vivisection is now fixed on the poet's self and family environment. He is not attempting a recovery of his past or laying a groundwork for a personal mythology, but demythologizing his bankrupt heritage in the name of painful honesty. Lowell accuses his father of 'impotent optimism' and himself of impotent pessimism: 'These are the tranquillized *Fifties,*/and I am forty' ('Memories of West Street and Lepke'). The disloyal chronicle of losses includes those dearly loved: grandfather Winslow, long dead, and the poet's little daughter, to whose charming world he is a stranger.

'Waking in the blue' of a godless, man-monstered universe, Lowell sets out in search of a positive alternative, a secular salvation. In the destructive-reductive tenor of *Life Studies* there *is* a preserving countercurrent: the poignant, tender compassion in spite of disgust, the perspective of humour earned by one's own involvement. Instead of the earlier hateful snake-images of sin, this book is dominated by 'a mother skunk with her column of kittens' who 'swills the garbage pail . . . and will not scare' ('Skunk Hour') – a vision of limited affirmation, shocking and amusing. And yet in the midst of 'confession' ('My mind's not right') Lowell *pretends* to be nothing but an individual on the defensive, content with stoic endurance in the skunks' 'rich air'. His imaginative, verbal and formal grasp on existential decay is aggressive and hopeful. The salvation glimpsed is a tragic triumph of art over tainted survival.

The glimpse is turned into a deliberate search in *Imitations* (1961). More clearly than in the earlier adaptations of other poets' work, the element of translation is of secondary importance here. The effort is more similar to that in Macpherson's *Ossian* and Sir Walter Scott's *Minstrelsy of the Scottish Border*: exploration of a literary heritage as a cultural frame of reference. Lowell's eighteen European poets are a genealogy of alienated fellow-sufferers: their example shows how the iniquities of history and human misery can be creatively overcome by the artist's tragic vision. Kinship of sensibility and talent has lifted some of these 'imitations' (or rather 'appropriations') above the rest: Villon's sinful Christianity, Baudelaire's polished urban disgust, Montale's graphic moments of awareness come to life, as Homer's universals and Pasternak's nuances of idiom do not.

For the Union Dead (1964) combines the personal lore of *Life Studies* (now more lyrical, imaginative, fragmentary, the family album left behind) and the lessons of *Imitations* into a formula of *memory and satire* – a parallel to T. S. Eliot's 'memory and desire' in *The Waste Land*. Failures of love, deaths, existential misery, degradation of gods, men and animals, dark views of 'the unforgivable landscape' and its decadent history present a sinister panorama; and yet the overall effect is disturbing, not depressing. 'What can be salvaged from your life?' ('Caligula') is the question. The self, operating through memory ('remember' is the key word in several poems), finds that fragments shored against one's ruins will not do – for the elements are cold, things change owners, buildings crumble under 'dinosaur steamshovels'. The only firm ground in the cyclic flux of existence is memory, the guardian of the self's continuity: 'we are where we were. We were!' ('The Lesson'). But since the outside world seems to produce nothing lasting or worth keeping, it is the fruits of imagination which count – even if grotesque ('The Severed Head'), or pathetic and laughable by the world's standards ('Hawthorne', 'Jonathan Edwards in Western Massachusetts') and Ovid, the banished poet, can utter the boast of immortality: 'I shall never die.'

The three one-act plays which constitute *The Old Glory* (1964) and the poems in *Near the Ocean* (1966) are dominated by satire.

Lowell brings poetic drama even closer to dissected prose than Eliot, with a similar effect – the texture is less difficult than in the non-dramatic verse but also less satisfying. The intended unfolding of character and destiny is often too declarative or almost banal, even in *Benito Cereno*, the best of the three ('If you look into your hearts, we all want slaves'; 'They think America is Santa Claus'). In *Near the Ocean* both the subject-matter and the poetic process are much more complex and subtle. The ocean of the title sequence – the time-tormented destructive element we survive in for a while – is paralleled with 'The Ruins of Time', adaptations of poems by Quevedo and Góngora; the surreal brutality and corruption of contemporary America are juxtaposed with those of imperial Rome, especially through Lowell's version of Juvenal's Tenth Satire. Within the title sequence itself two themes coexist. One develops through the epigrammatic insights of an American humanistic in-tellectual – about 'small war on the heels of small/war', because 'top-heavy Goliath in full armor' intends 'until the end of time/to police the earth', about the President's 'ghost-written rhetoric', criminal violence matched by the 'deterrent terror' of the police, the decay of religion and spiritual life. This is reinforced by the lyrically treated theme of threatened sexual potency and of the sterility of modern sex. Lowell's enduring sense of sexual guilt has given way to fear and unrest. Culturally and erotically speaking, he is still a moralist, but without a moral code.

In spite of its sombre content, *Near the Ocean* has a bracing tone. The harsh four-foot couplets of the original poems, echoing Andrew Marvell in form and wit, lend structure and perspective to the poet's 'fierce, fireless mind', and the painful lyricism achieved is just like the 'stiff quatrains shovelled out four-square' in the 'Bible chopped and crucified/in hymns'; for 'they sing of peace, and preach despair;/yet they gave darkness some control,/and left a loophole for the soul'.

The brilliant but limiting satiric finality and formal finish of *Near the Ocean* are absent from Lowell's next book of poems, *Notebook 1967–68* (1969), through which a stream of poetic consciousness flows, carrying both public and personal matter. While the point of view is basically the same as in the earlier works, the attitude is new. Lowell's resignation before the evils of the Western world has led to enlightenment, mellowed though unforgiving.

The change is even greater in the poet's private world. Memory becomes more than the vehicle of creative triumph over the irrecoverable flux of negative experience; the renunciation of hopes for a public role worthy of his human stature has permitted Lowell to develop his potential for love, tenderness and appreciation. These are felt to radiate from a new family feeling, especially for his daughter. Meaningful existential moments are the raw material for the poet at fifty, particularly in the short sequences ('Harriet', 'Long Summer', 'Mexico').

Thanks to the cumulative existentialism and open form of a deliberately structured journal written in equal sections (unrhymed sonnets), *Notebook 1967–68* turned a new leaf in Lowell's varied poetic career. But the fruitful method is undermined by the very attitude which has made it possible. This variant of 'wise passiveness' does not take any risks. The personal balance gained results in a lack of urgency, vividness and humour. Too often the blank verse sections leave things merely well said. There is not enough 'instress', as Hopkins used to call the shaping energy. This is not secular imitation of Christ through art because there is no acute drama, no suffering. Rather, we seem to watch a well-programmed poetic sensibility respond to the proper range of stimuli with great precision and in detail. We are impressed and moved, but not shocked into fresh awareness.

Lowell's poetry is essentially committed to the European tradition on which the bourgeois main culture in the United States is based – rebellious, 'disloyal still', but tied up with it inextricably. In this he differs from the 'new new' poets who have rejected this tradition; but in his later work he approaches their romanticism in taking the self and its positive longings, instead of the world as it is, as the measure of things. But Lowell is more than a transitional poet, or an influential exponent of 'confessional' poetry, or a 'representative' public poet: his idiosyncratic sensibility, brutally tender tone and potentially tragic stance have made him a poet of more than one generation.

The six poets discussed are by no means the only ones who achieved prominence in the first post-war decade and a half. Insights and beauties are perhaps equally present in the work of Elizabeth Bishop, Richard Eberhart, Jean Garrigue, Stanley Kunitz, Delmore Schwartz, Louis Simpson, and several others. These, however, are less crucial to the outlined shift in the relationship between the poet's self and an increasingly unsatisfactory, inherited culture, which was then taking place. It could be argued that with this criterion in mind, William Carlos Williams is to be considered *the* poet of the period. But in spite of the late fruits of his plea for a joyous poetry of the self in the American grain, his flowering period was between the World Wars, whereas the early achievements of his disciples – the Black Mountain Group and the Beats – are only chronologically within the period; genetically, they belong to the next phase in the development of American poetry.

6

LITERARY CRITICISM TO 1965

Marshall Van Deusen

I

BACKGROUND

The literary critics of the late years of the nineteenth century understood that post-Civil-War America was a new world. After all, they could hardly help noticing that Ulysses S. Grant was not George Washington and they were not likely to confuse the new industrialism with Jefferson's pastoral vision of an agrarian republic. But noting such changes did not mean they could so naturally as Emerson define a role for literature in the new New World. Some of the difficulty may have been that Emerson and Jefferson were now part of the American past. At any rate the criticism of these years seems in retrospect to have been on the whole inept. And yet a very brief glance at its failures may be in order, if only to suggest a partial explanation for the intensity of feeling which erupted in the years following 1900.

In his famous essay on 'The Genteel Tradition in American Philosophy', delivered in the summer of 1911 at the University of California in Berkeley (reprinted in *Winds of Doctrine*), George Santayana offered what has since been taken as a classic metaphor for the American intellectual situation at the end of the nineteenth century. 'The truth is,' said Santayana, 'that ... one-half of the American mind, that not occupied intensely in practical affairs, has remained, I will not say high-and-dry, but slightly becalmed; it has floated gently in the back-water, while, alongside, in invention and industry and social organization the other half of the mind was leaping down a sort of Niagara Rapids.' Or to change the figure: 'The American Will inhabits the skyscraper; the American Intellect inhabits the colonial mansion. The one is the sphere of the American man; the other, at least predominantly, of the American woman. The one is all aggressive enterprise; the other is all genteel tradition.'

Santayana himself was to leave the United States for good two years after he spoke these words. His own definition of beauty in *The Sense of Beauty* (1896) as 'pleasure objectified', and his later discussions of aesthetic essences in *Reason in Art* (1906), in *The Realm of Essence* (1927), and in 'The Mutability of Aesthetic Categories' (published in 1925 in *The Philosophical Review*), caused no ripple in the back-water and certainly did not divert Niagara. His discovery in 'Proust on Essences' (collected in *Obiter Scripta*) that his theory provided a rationale for the work of Marcel Proust suggests its irrelevance to the America he had described.

Nor were Henry James's definitions of artistic intelligence apposite in that world. He proposed a discipline too subtle and too rigorous for the ladies in the parlour and too absurd for the men in the skyscrapers. Acutely sensitive to the problems of delicate balance posed for the artist in the post-Civil-War world, James championed the cause of realism and free experimentation in the novel in his famous essay of 1884 on 'The Art of Fiction'. But he understood that to deal with raw experience in all its insistent immediacy is also to enter confusion. And so when he argued that fiction must 'really . . . represent life', we understand that the aim is to *re*-present life through aesthetic form, and that the form will be a kind of judgment: 'the moral sense and the artistic sense lie very near together'.

James's constant effort was to mediate between art and life. He understood that freedom in choice of subject is granted the artist provisionally until we can see what 'he makes of it'. His success or failure will be recorded in the execution, because, as James wrote to H. G. Wells, 'it is art that *makes* life, makes interest, makes importance'. But though the artist works through 'selection', 'it is a selection whose main care is to be typical, to be inclusive', to be as 'intelligent' and unprejudiced as possible, to offer as 'complete' a version of life as the artist is capable of bringing to reality. And yet 'intelligence' in this same sense is apt to be ironic; it is registered in the technical resourcefulness of the artist's expression, which is at once the definition and the result of intelligence. The narrow partisanship of Zola and his fellow-Naturalists is thus technically and morally a deficiency, if measured, for example, against the larger and more resourceful achievement of Turgenev. And Maupassant's realism has simply left out 'the whole reflective part of his men and women – that reflective part which governs conduct and produces character'. Such a failure too is a failure of artistic intelligence. It is a failure to tell the truth, to be 'complete'.

James's whole critical argument, from such early volumes as *French Poets and Novelists* (1884) and *Partial Portraits* (1888), to the prefaces he wrote for the New York edition of his novels (1907–17), is extremely subtle and resourceful in reconciling inclusiveness and selection, content and technique, the real and the aesthetic, the aesthetic and the moral, in short experience and the mind. *In toto* it is a major critical achievement; but unfortunately it had no major importance or influence for American critics at the turn of the century or for those who occupied the centre of the stage in the 'teens and twenties. And James's contemporary, William Dean Howells, for all his labours on behalf of realism and the new critical approaches it demanded, and for all his rejection of the aristocratic cultural ideal of his special *bête noire*, Matthew Arnold, could not free himself sufficiently from Victorian inhibitions to escape being grouped by younger critics with the genteel apologists for sentimental ideality whom he sought to oppose.

Howells was sensitive to new currents: he read the French Naturalists and the Russian Realists; he knew the work of Mill, Comte and Spencer; and he encouraged young American authors like Stephen Crane, Hamlin Garland and Frank Norris. He insisted in *Criticism and Fiction* (1891) that the novelist must deal with life as it is in 'fact', not with romantic or sentimental illusion; he knew also that 'when realism . . . heaps up facts merely, and maps life instead of picturing it, realism will perish too'. But Howells's critical vocabulary is not nearly so resourceful as James's, and when he attempted, for example, to mediate between inclusiveness and selection, he tended to justify his exclusions, not in terms of the novelist's technical responsibility to his calling, but in terms of his moralistic (or propagandistic) relation to his audience. Thus certain sexual indiscretions might best be avoided because the American novel-reading public included large numbers of 'young girls'. Howells reconciled such restrictions with his insistence that the novel be true to life by arguing that in America it was the novelist's responsibility 'to front the everyday world and catch the charm of its work-worn, case-worn, brave, kindly face'. For in America 'the more smiling aspects of life' are the truest. Even Howells's advocacy of the work of Crane, Garland and Norris seems less a contradiction of such cheerful recommendations than a confirmation of a basic critical assumption that literature was a social instrument. His own pleas for social reform, which he regularly published along with his literary reviews in 'The Easy Chair' in *Harpers*, suggest as much.

Howells's progressivism and his interest in social reform should perhaps have recommended him to later critics bent on restoring vigour to criticism. But his genteel squeamishness condemned him in their eyes instead to the company of such critics among his own generation as Richard Henry Stoddard, E. C. Stedman and Richard Watson Gilder, and allied him with younger critics like George Edward Woodberry, William Crary Brownell, Hamilton Wright Mabie, Brander Matthews and Henry Van Dyke. Many of these critics too strove to be up to date. Stedman, for example, wanted to give a sympathetic hearing to theories of pure art. He also insisted on the need to make criticism 'scientific' and protested his admiration for the environmental methods of Hippolyte Taine (as did Mabie and Matthews). But even more, Stedman wanted to preserve a moral function for literature, and he defended the notion of original genius as a usable explanation for artistic expression. Similarly Woodberry was the early mentor of J. E. Spingarn, yet drew back from Spingarn's advocacy of a kind of autonomy for art, preferring an older idealism in which the ethical dimension of literature is primary. And Brownell, while admitting that '"Realism" . . . is fundamentally consonant with the current phase of the Time-Spirit', suspected that in the timeless book of final judgment Walter Scott might turn out to be more realistic than Balzac.

There were great differences among these critics. Stedman's work in *The Nature and Elements of Poetry* (1892), *Victorian Poets* (1875), *Poets of America* (1885), and in his *Victorian Anthology* (1895), and *American Anthology* (1900), is distinctly superior in range and substance to that of Stoddard in *Under the Evening Lamp* (1892) and Gilder in his pieces for *The Century*. Woodberry, who edited the works of Shelley (1892) and, with Stedman, the works of Poe (1894–5), shows in *Studies in Letters and Life* (1890), *Heart of Man* (1899) and *The Torch* (1905), a sensibility of finer grain than that displayed in the intellectual opportunism of his colleague at Columbia, Brander Matthews, who wrote numerous books and articles on fiction and on drama and the theatre. And Brownell's critical position, which has affinities with neo-Humanism, is more subtle and precise in *French Traits* (1889), *Victorian Prose Masters* (1901), *American Prose Masters* (1909), *Criticism* (1914) and *Standards* (1917) than the fatuous emptiness of Mabie in such works as *My Study Fire* (1890) and *Backgrounds of Literature* (1903) and the

tedious effusions in the eighteen volumes of the *Works* (1920–7) of
the Reverend Professor Van Dyke.

But despite differences between them, and despite their recurrent sense that they were facing a new world, these critics strike
us now as ineffectual. Their detachment seems, for the most part,
nostalgic and backward-looking, genteel in Santayana's sense of the
term. Their efforts to be engaged seem provincial and naïve. They
made, however, the perfect foil for a new breed, who looked back in
anger and whose provincialism was aggressively disillusioned.

II

1900–30

Writing a 'Footnote on Criticism' in 1922, H. L. Mencken gleefully
welcomed 'the revival of acrimony in criticism' as one of the 'most
hopeful symptoms of the new Aufklärung in the Republic'. J. E.
Spingarn, no mean polemicist himself, writing in the same year on
'Scholarship and Criticism', was much less sanguine than Mencken
about the benefits of what Spingarn called the 'guerrilla warfare' of
American criticism. But the question of enlightenment aside,
Mencken's phrase points to two circumstances which governed a
good deal of the diverse critical activity of the first thirty years of the
twentieth century in the United States. Criticism at the turn of the
century *had* been bland to the point of irrelevance; and those critics
who sought to reinvigorate it with a new sense of purpose were
often, in their different ways, as much concerned with the general
cultural life of the Republic as with literature itself.

Spingarn, who persisted valiantly for years in his effort to
domesticate the idealistic aesthetic of Benedetto Croce among the
hustling pragmatic Americans, argued in the essay cited above
(published in Harold Stearns's *Civilization in the United States*) that
the first need of American criticism was greater discipline and
greater coherence in aesthetic theory; but he made it clear that the
need had a special urgency because of 'the benumbing chaos and
the benumbing monotony of American art and life'. In America, he
said, 'are more hearts empty and unfulfilled and more restless
minds than the world has ever before gathered together'. He explained in 'The Growth of a Literary Myth' that it was this situation
which had led him to try 'to make use of Croce for the benefit of my
countrymen', and finally he confessed in 'The American Critic' that

the 'chief duty' of 'the critics of America' was 'to justify the ways of the artist to Americans'.

Mencken was at the other extreme from Spingarn in that he was sceptical of all aesthetic or critical theory, favoured a catch-as-catch-can method, and insisted that in his own criticism he was 'wholly devoid of public spirit', seeking only 'for his own ego the grateful feeling of a function performed, a tension relieved, a *katharsis* attained which Wagner achieved when he wrote "Die Walküre", and a hen achieves every time she lays an egg'. But Mencken's iconoclasm has the reformer's ring, as his generous trumpetings on behalf of Theodore Dreiser testify. And even in his 'Footnote on Criticism', in the third series of his *Prejudices* (1914–27), from which the dicta quoted above are taken, he hopes he may convince the healthy American male to take aesthetic matters as seriously 'as he takes business, sport, and amour'.

Mencken's early model, James Gibbons Huneker, was not himself a social reformer. Rather he was a cosmopolitan and free-ranging impressionist, an amateur of experience and an elegant bohemian, recording his own personal responses, somewhat after the fashion of Anatole France, to the work of a wide variety of painters, musicians and writers, Continental and British as well as American. In a long series of articles and books, including *Iconoclasts* (1905), *Promenades of an Impressionist* (1910), *Ivory Apes and Peacocks* (1915), Huneker discussed the latest fashions, whether gastronomic or intellectual, with a cheerful zest and charm that must have been refreshing in his day. Mencken's own impressionism, on the other hand, became increasingly *un*cheerful and he repeatedly attacked the American 'booboisie' for its social and political stupidities as well as for its aesthetic and intellectual ignorance. His noisy preoccupation with the provincialism of his environment is not only a symptom of 'the revival of acrimony in criticism', but, like Spingarn's muted patriotism, a sign of a deeply serious revival of national cultural self-consciousness.

Henry James's sensitive probing, in his life, in his art and in his criticism, of the uneasy relations between the general cultural scene in the United States and the life of the aesthetic sensibility has persuaded many in our time of the complications, social and psychic, of those relations. But self-consciousness about the national cultural life goes back a long way in the United States. Mencken and Spingarn (and James) were inheritors of a tradition which began at least as early as Sydney Smith's famous query over a hundred years before in *The Edinburgh Review* for January 1820: 'In

the four quarters of the globe, who reads an American book?'
Fenimore Cooper's dogged fight for a copyright law to protect
American authors from the pirating of the works of more popular
established British writers was one way to remedy the situation
Smith described; and though he was often amused and sometimes
irate at the nationalistic excesses of some of his compatriots' responses to Smith's jibe, Cooper's fiction as well as his social criticism
make it clear that he thought the establishment of a native American
literature a matter of the first importance for the cultural life of his
homeland. Emerson's Phi Beta Kappa address on 'The American
Scholar' was, as Oliver Wendell Holmes rightly saw, a cultural
declaration of independence and Melville's hyperbolic praise of
Hawthorne was at least as much a patriotic expression of hope and
faith as a considered critical evaluation of literary achievement.
Whitman's criticism was occasionally downright chauvinistic. Mark
Twain's sometimes bumptious, sometimes defensive, concern with
the 'problem of Europe', and especially with what sometimes
seemed to him the absurdities of effete European literary and
artistic conventions, testifies again to a provincial American
tendency to merge aesthetic considerations with considerations
touching the national honour, as does also the growing
preoccupation during the last decades of the nineteenth century
with the problems of 'the great American novel'. One may remember too that in the early years of the twentieth century the
Pulitzer Prizes in Journalism and Letters were established for the
'encouragement of public service, public morals, American
Literature, and the advancement of Education'.

Howard Mumford Jones has argued in his *Theory of American
Literature* (1948) that much of the early nineteenth-century pleading
for a distinctively American literature was a reflection, not of 'naïve
patriotism', but of 'European theories of the nature of literature and
of its relation to society'. But Professor Jones does not comment on
the *tone* of the American pleading, which often *was* chauvinistic, and
in any event both doctrine and tone, whatever their ultimate origins,
do seem to survive in the arguments and voices (sometimes
querulous, sometimes plaintive) of many of the American critics of
the early decades of the twentieth century. Critics of various and
opposing persuasions assumed that a healthy national literature
would affect the quality of the national life and they also seemed to
agree that the growth of such a literature depended in some measure
on social and cultural reform. These critics, therefore, characteristically became general critics rather than literary critics.

Thus Irving Babbitt, Professor of French at Harvard and a man of considerable erudition, was also the sharpest controversialist in what came to be known as the neo-Humanist movement, and in his first book, published in 1908, he addressed himself to the general problem of *Literature and the American College*. In his long polemic against the self-indulgent irrationalism and egalitarianism which he thought the moderns (especially the Naturalists) had inherited from Romanticism, a polemic early elaborated in *The New Laokoön* (1910) and *Rousseau and Romanticism* (1919), Babbitt was never far from such contemporary American problems as those he discussed in *Democracy and Leadership* (1924). He was fond of free-ranging surveys of intellectual history – Greek, Christian and Oriental – and he found in such study confirmation for his professed discovery in experience itself of the need for an 'inner check' on man's natural impulses, if man's most distinctively human experience, his ethical life, was not to collapse into meaningless mechanism or animal automatism. In this argument, he had his eye on the contemporary American scene.

Babbitt argued that Naturalism on its scientific-utilitarian side threatened to overwhelm the ethical imagination in gross materialism and on its sentimental-romatic side to seduce the moral sense into emotional indulgence and a flabby humanitarianism in which truly humanistic discriminations of value and difference would be lost. The literary naturalism of the twentieth century combined, in the work of a writer like Dreiser, scientific pretensions with emotional debauch. It was, thus, a literary and moral disaster: it was 'Romanticism on all fours'.

Opposing the 'aristocratic' implications of Babbitt's emphasis on the 'classic' virtues of decorum in literature and prudent restraint in life was the early work of Van Wyck Brooks, leader of the 'literary radicals'. Brooks too was interested in the past (especially the American past), and he could even see the usefulness of a literary 'remnant'. But in such books as *The Wine of the Puritans* (1909), and in a steady stream of essays like those collected in *America's Coming of Age* (1915) and *Letters and Leadership* (1918), he argued that the job of American critics was to discover a 'usable past' which would encourage the development of a socialist future in which the true liberal spirit of America could free itself from its Puritan bondage to the practical life. In Brooks and in many of his followers, there was often an assumption that this liberation might be encouraged by recapturing the free spirit of 'romanticism', an attitude which seemed to them not incompatible with their sponsorship of 'realism'. Walt Whitman suggested a model for the synthesis.

Brooks and others of the liberal persuasion often thought of Randolph Bourne as their patron saint. Brooks collected and published in 1920 a selection of Bourne's papers under the title of *The History of a Literary Radical.* (James Oppenheim had made a collection of Bourne's pacifist writings in *Untimely Papers* in 1919.) Bourne had concentrated on political and social criticism, and following his friend's lead, Brooks also focused in his early criticism on large social and cultural problems. Following Santayana, he diagnosed the American malady as a split between 'highbrow' and 'lowbrow', between abstract intellect on the one hand and brute, practical acquisitiveness on the other. The split could perhaps be traced back as far as the figures of Jonathan Edwards and Benjamin Franklin, but it was certain, Brooks thought, that during the nineteenth century, Emersonian idealism had become more and more attenuated and less and less relevant to the vulgar business world of John D. Rockefeller, however much the new powers might invoke the old morality in justification of their exercise of raw energy. Between the two, the writer who sought the wholeness of life was lost. The old morality was become only an habitual gesture, Brooks said, inapplicable in the new world, though it was easily perverted in Puritan America to reinforce business materialism. The new energy was full of possibilities in what it promised for democratic society, but it needed more responsible direction than was provided by monopoly capitalism. Without a reintegration of the divergent tendencies of American life, the story of the artist's victimization or alienation, which Brooks had recounted in *The Ordeal of Mark Twain* (1920) and *The Pilgrimage of Henry James* (1925), was bound to be repeated.

Brooks seemed to hope that a kind of literary élite might help in re-establishing a meaningful relation between spirit and matter by facing the raw facts of American life, attacking the inhibiting taboos of American culture, and vigorously propagandizing for the implementation of the principles of humanitarian democracy, thus socializing 'culture' and refining society. It is to be doubted that Theodore Dreiser and Sinclair Lewis were equal to such a task even had they cared to attempt it; but Brooks and his fellow radicals welcomed their campaigns for freedom in literature and against repression in society as hopeful signs.

Babbitt and Brooks are representative. Whether 'conservative' or 'liberal', most of the critics of these years seemed to be bent on reforming American life through the agency of literature or improving American literature through moralistic or sociological reform. Certainly the criticism of the liberals was not very literary, though often it pretended to be historical. John Macy, like Brooks, sought to discover *The Spirit of American Literature* (1913) in the past and, like Brooks, was disappointed in what he found; his sociological orientation became explicit in *Socialism in America* (1916). Waldo Frank's *Our America* (1919) and *The Rediscovery of America* (1928) are also versions of the socio-historical metaphors which Brooks had suggested, and in 1930 Matthew Josephson, in *Portrait of the Artist as an American*, repeated Brooks's thesis that capitalist, industrial America had thwarted the free development of the artistic careers of such as Henry James, James Whistler and Ambrose Bierce. Lewis Mumford, a good friend of Brooks, had, in *Golden Day: a Study in American Experience and Culture* (1926), traced the problems of American culture back to disintegrative changes initiated in Europe in the Renaissance! And in *Herman Melville* (1929) he attempted to illustrate the oft-repeated complaint about the inhospitality of materialistic, business-dominated American society to the spiritual aspirations of the creative artist.

History was a mode of critical and social argumentation in those years. The most ambitious 'scholarly' effort (that is, by a professor) to discover the American literary tradition was Vernon Louis Parrington's *Main Currents in American Thought* (1927–30), which was recommended for publication to Harcourt, Brace and Company by Brooks. Parrington approached his task almost entirely in terms of politics and economics, and his main critical instrument was a somewhat Romantic and sentimentalized version of what he conceived as the tradition of Jeffersonian liberalism. It is not surprising that he had very little helpful to say about such artists as Hawthorne or James.

Even J. E. Spingarn, a genuine scholar whose *History of Literary Criticism in the Renaissance* (1899) and *Critical Essays of the Seventeenth Century* (1908–9) are still consulted, made use of synthetic historical generalizations for the purpose of clarifying his aesthetic theory. Spingarn's critical polemics on behalf of Croce's idealistic aesthetic, especially his famous 'radical' lecture in 1910 on 'The New Criticism', but also his 'conservative' manifesto to 'The Younger Generation' published in 1922 in Brooks's journal, *The Freeman* (both collected in *Creative Criticism*, enlarged edn, 1931), led his contemporaries, liberal and conservative, to accuse him of wanting to isolate art from life. In 'Scholarship and Criticism' he called for a plague on both houses. But in his six lectures on *Literature and the New Era*, delivered at the New School for Social Research in 1931, Spingarn undertook to explain that Western history revealed an alternation between theory and practice, with practical activities becoming more and more dominant in the nineteenth and twentieth centuries. Spingarn's distinctions were borrowed from the philosophy of Croce, but they bear some resemblance to Brooks's historical metaphors. And in any event it is clear in these lectures (one of which was published posthumously in *The Atlantic Monthly* in 1941 as 'Politics and the Poet'), as it should have been clear in the tone of all he had written, that Spingarn's interests were not narrowly literary: he was too deeply concerned with the danger to the general spiritual life in America of American concentration on mastery of the material world.

Much of the work of the liberal critics was, thus, an effort (in a way traditional enough) to discover, or invent, America, complete with normative metaphors for her history and sociological prescriptions for her future; it was often vaguely Marxist. But overtly Marxist criticism of the twenties and thirties was not more helpful in interpreting and evaluating individual literary works or exploring peculiarly artistic problems. It too concentrated to a surprising extent on the 'problem of America', past and present, as in V. F. Calverton's *The Newer Spirit* (1925) and *The Liberation of American Literature* (1932), Granville Hicks's *The Great Tradition: an Interpretation of American Literature Since the Civil War* (1933; rev. edn, 1935), the anthology of *Proletarian Literature in the United States* (1935), edited by Hicks and others, and Bernard Smith's perceptive *Forces in American Criticism: a Study in the History of American Thought* (1939).

As the comparison above of Brooks and Babbitt may suggest, the 'conservatives' too spent a good deal of time and energy describing, defining and diagnosing the American cultural situation at large. Paul Elmer More, along with Babbitt one of the two most formidable of the neo-Humanists, published as his first book in 1900 a life of Benjamin Franklin. And though he was learned in Sanskrit and classical literatures, and taught both subjects briefly at Harvard (1894–5) and Bryn Mawr (1895–7), More often returned, throughout his long series of *Shelburne Essays* (1904–21) and *New Shelburne Essays* (1928–36) to a discussion of the shortcomings of nineteenth-century American authors like Whitman and twentieth-century villains like Dreiser and Sinclair Lewis. He explained in *The Drift of Romanticism*, published in 1913, the year Babbitt brought out his *Rousseau and Romanticism*, that the moderns were suffering from a disease which had begun much earlier. As he put it in 'Victorian Literature' (*Shelburne Essays*, Seventh Series), the trouble came historically from an uncritical acceptance of a philosophy of the flux: the seemingly hostile temperaments of the scientist, who is committed to 'a hard materialism or a dry intellectualism', and that of the sentimental romanticist, 'who dreams and loses himself in futile revery', sprang up together as a result of the failure of moral standards. When the scientist leaves his whirling world of 'fact', he easily becomes an impressionist. And thus 'the harshest egotism and the most sentimental sympathy', 'self-developing individualism and self-developing socialism' (each with its 'admixture of humanitarian sympathy'), *laissez-faire* economics and égalitarian social theory, even the 'elective system' in American education, all derive from 'the same surrender to the philosophy of change'. More, like the other neo-Humanists and like their liberal opponents, was a social critic. He was more willing than Babbitt to seek in religion a stay against the invading flux in literature and life. But religion often seemed to him a social necessity; as he explained in 'A Revival of Humanism', printed in *The Bookman* for March, 1930, and reprinted in *On Being Human* (1930), 'there can be no great and simple and sincere art without ideals of greatness and simplicity and sincerity prevailing in society'. Such a premise would not be unacceptable to the Marxists.

More, like the Marxists and the other liberals, and like Babbitt and the other neo-Humanists, agreed that the literary critic was primarily concerned with content. In 'The Humility of Common Sense', which appeared in *The Demon of the Absolute* (1928) and was reprinted in *Humanism and America*, a symposium edited by Norman Foerster in 1930 (the same year in which Hartley Grattan edited *The Critique of Humanism*), More rehearsed his attack on 'the romantic glorification of uncontrollable temperament' and the 'realistic theory of subjection to the bestial passions', and added that the consequent modern attempt to represent life 'as an unmitigated flux' had led to Crocean theories of self-expression which emptied literature of substantial content in an effort to arrive at 'pure art'. Though More was sometimes a more sensitive critic than Babbitt, like Babbitt he seldom attended to the formal details of literary expression. Yvor Winters, who sturdily defended the importance of content in literature, is said to have remarked that Babbitt's insensitivity to formal elements betrayed his misunderstanding of how meaning gets into literature. The remark could be applied to More as well (in lesser degree) and to the younger neo-Humanists like Robert Shafer (*Paul Elmer More and American Criticism*, 1935) and Norman Foerster (*American Criticism*, 1928; *Towards Standards: a Study of the Present Critical Movement in American Letters, 1930*), though Foerster sensed the difficulties of the problem in his later essay on 'The Esthetic Judgment and the Ethical Judgment', published in Donald Stauffer's *The Intent of the Critic* (1941). But in that essay Foerster is anxiously conceding a point to the 'new critics', who are sandwiched in uncomfortably close to him between the covers of Stauffer's anthology. The earlier critics, whether conservative or liberal, seem pretty generally to have assumed that literary judgments could be made on the basis of the argument of a given literary work without attending to the structural or formal implications such a term raises.

But perhaps general critics of whatever party must concentrate on content if their own arguments are to be heard. Stuart Sherman, for example, who began as a neo-Humanist, but who deserted the fold for something like liberal Rotarianism, was, early and late, fond of extracting moral nuggets (or dross) from whatever literary veins he happened to be mining and then exhibiting them as proof of the values of rather large non-literary claims. In *On Contemporary Literature* (1917), Sherman argued that 'The great revolutionary task of the nineteenth-century thinkers was to put man into nature. The great task of twentieth-century thinkers is to get him out again.' The American Naturalists, of course, had betrayed their trust. In *Americans* (1922) and *The Genius of America* (1923), Sherman continued to slip 'spiritual gold pieces' into the hands of his countrymen as a hedge against moral and cultural bankruptcy, but the nativist strain in Sherman's criticism began to wane in *Points of View* (1924); and in *Critical Woodcuts* (1926), he had reversed himself on Dreiser. As Sherman's sense of crisis weakened, however, his criticism also became less interesting, even as Van Wyck Brooks's work, after his defection from militancy, tended towards agreeable impressionism, charming antiquarianism and petulant conservatism in such books as *Emerson and Others* (1927), *Sketches in Criticism* (1932), the several volumes of his *Makers and Finders* series (1936–52), *On Literature Today* (1941), and *The Opinions of Oliver Allston* (1941).

In the first thirty years of the twentieth century most serious critical questions *were* referred to a sense of American cultural crisis, real or imagined. For example, though Paul Elmer More wrote books on *Platonism* (1917), *The Religion of Plato* (1921),

Hellenistic Philosophies (1923), *The Christ of the New Testament* (1924) and *Christ the Word* (1927), he was for many of the critics of the 'teens and twenties a symbol of the repressiveness of twentieth-century American society. Ludwig Lewisohn, for one, whose social concerns came to full flower in the Romantic Freudianism of *Expression in America* (1932), described in the 'Introduction' to his anthology, *A Modern Book of Criticism* (1919), *his* sense of crisis and of More's responsibility for it. As captain of a company of 'shivering young Davids' who, 'slim and frail but with a glint of morning sunshine on their foreheads', were marching out to 'face an army of Goliaths', Lewisohn addressed the enemy in the person of More as follows:

I love beauty in all its forms and find life tragic and worthy of my sympathy in every manifestation. I need no hierarchical world for my dwelling-place, because I desire neither to judge nor to condemn.

This was pretty heady stuff; and even for more jaded or cosmopolitan modern palates there is fun in sampling the earlier provincial vintage. For those who concocted it, however, there were all sorts of after-effects. One was the conviction that the in-hospitality of America to the free creative spirit left no alternative for the artist (and the would-be artist) but expatriation. Writing in 1922, in his 'Preface' to that 'famous inquest over American culture, sardonically entitled *Civilization in the United States*' (to borrow Alfred Kazin's description), Harold Stearns complained that the 'most moving and pathetic fact in the social life of America today is emotional and aesthetic starvation'. Stearns was here echoing the mournful conclusion of his 'America and the Young Intellectual', published the year before in *The Bookman* as a reply to Stuart Sherman's article in that year in *The Atlantic Monthly* on 'The National Genius'. Sherman, said Stearns, was forcing the

younger generation [to] make our plans for leaving the country of our birth and early affections. We do not want to cut ourselves off from our national life, but we are inexorably being forced to do it – many of us shall probably starve when we go to some alien country, but at least we shall be able, spiritually, to breathe.

Sherman's answer in the New York *Evening Post, Literary Review* (14 January 1922), to what he called Stearns's 'fatuous and hackneyed Menckenisms and Dreiserisms' was as follows:

When Mr Stearns runs on in this lugubrious vein, . . .I no longer feel that he is an Intellectual; I feel only that he is very young, which, after all, is not quite the same thing. . . .

Stearns modified his tone of martyrdom when he reprinted his remarks as the title essay in *America and the Young Intellectuals* (1921). That collection and Malcolm Cowley's later *Exile's Return* (1934) make clear what Stearns confessed in the 'Preface' to *Civilization in the United States*: the whole controversy over expatriation was part of an effort to establish, nearly a hundred years after Emerson's 'American Scholar', a 'genuine nationalistic self-consciousness'. Elizabeth Sergeant, in 'A Tilt with Two Critics', in *The Bookman* (June 1921), understood the dispute between Stearns and Sherman in these terms. On the whole she sided with Stearns, but of his threat of expatriation she said:

by his forlorn gesture, [he] simply throws the key of . . . [the] future into the Atlantic Ocean. . . . This weak conclusion . . . is enough to make the ghost of Randolph Bourne rise from his grave. . . . When Mr Stearns is drinking his *petite verre* on the boulevards, feeling very proud that he has circumvented Volstead, he may dimly hear, above the rumble of the traffic, . . . profoundly native voices – and . . . he will then suddenly, nostalgically, take ship for New York.

Perhaps Sherman was right: Stearns *was* young. So also was Sherman. And so was American criticism. The time seems long ago now, but condescension is not the right attitude to take towards Babbitt, More, Bourne, Brooks, Mencken, Spingarn and the others. Issues were being prepared; the ground was being cleared. Especially did the debate about the artist's role (at home or abroad), the effort to 'justify the ways of artists to Americans' (to repeat Spingarn's phrase), imply questions about the nature of art and its mode of discourse. Though the stridency of those earlier disputing voices gave way to the somewhat subtler modulations of more sophisticated critics, and though these later critics more sharply defined more fundamental questions, the transference of critical debate from the noisy public forum to the relative quiet of the study did not necessarily result in either greater geniality or vastly increased general wisdom. The *Aufklärung* was still in the future and criticism seemed likely to continue yet a little longer.

III

1930–65

Most American critics of the first thirty years of the twentieth century were general critics rather than specifically literary critics. They were, traditionally enough, aware of America as a special case, and they often described her situation in more or less elaborate historical metaphors. Their sense of cultural crisis was frequently focused on the alienation of the artist in both the spiritual and geographic senses of the term. The problems these critics engaged and their manner of approaching these problems characteristically led to treating literary works as though they were equivalent to brief summaries of their paraphrasable content; their approach did not encourage the development of systems of formal or technical analysis, sensitive to contextual relations within literary works.

Furthermore, appropriately enough, these earlier critics were not primarily academics. Their criticism tended to be journalistic, and virtually all of them held editorial positions with newspapers or magazines addressing a general audience: the Baltimore *Evening Sun* (Mencken), the New York *Herald Tribune* (Sherman), the New York *Evening Post* (More), *The American Mercury* (Mencken), *The Freeman* (Brooks), *The Nation* (Macy, Lewisohn, More), *The New Republic* (Cowley). Babbitt was, as Yvor Winters has pointed out in *The Function of Criticism* (1957), for some young men of the twenties, 'the Professor in person'; but the university literature departments in that day were mostly interested in philology and *Quellenforschung*, and so, as Winters said, among his academic colleagues, 'Babbitt was a professor largely on sufferance'. Academics like Carl and Mark Van Doren were important in the critical scene because of their editorial work on *The Nation*. Another professor, Henry Seidel Canby of Yale, gained prominence largely as literary editor for the New York *Evening Post* and subsequently as a founder and long-time chief editor of *The Saturday Review of Literature*.

After 1930, the year of the final flare-up between the liberals and the neo-Humanists, the situation began to change. Criticism began to move into the universities, where a lively battle developed between the 'New Criticism' and traditional literary scholarship. Critics like John Crowe Ransom, Allen Tate, R. P. Blackmur and Yvor Winters, all of whom were also poets, held university posts and from within the walls mounted an attack on the biographical and bibliographical bookkeeping of their colleagues. Tate, in 'Miss Emily and the Bibliographer', collected in *Reason and Madness* (1941), and W. K. Wimsatt and M. C. Beardsley (also academics), in their often-reprinted essay on 'The International Fallacy' (*Sewanee Review*, 1946), argued that the collection of extrinsic information about literary works was at best preliminary to the central task of interpreting the texts themselves in their full rhetorical complexity. For the 'New Critics' the formal characteristics of literary works were the means through which both artist and critic discovered and defined literary meaning. Wimsatt's later book on the *Verbal Icon* (1954) is an impressive exploration of the nature of such meaning.

In *God Without Thunder* (1930), *The World's Body* (1938) and *The New Criticism* (1941), Ransom recognized that the meaning of a poem is not so simple a thing as the sociological critics or the neo-Humanists thought. He described poetry as a 'logical structure' or 'argument' enormously complicated by a 'texture' which, though 'it "depends" from the logical argument', is 'not closely determined by it'. The literary critic will be especially interested in aesthetic texture, because the relationships of this 'curious increment of riches' to the structure which supports it will yield the meanings the artist is peculiarly called upon to recover: the sense of the individual particularities and the contingent, qualitative richness of experience so easily sacrificed in the world of conceptual argument, practical utility, and quantitative scientific generalization.

For Ransom the end of poetry appears to be knowledge, knowledge of particulars. But the meaning of such an end for critical judgment is obscure. And Ransom's various provisional justifications of textural 'irrelevance' are not very helpful: it satisfies a civilized interest in the precious; it is an expression of man's inborn love of play, his love of objects and ideas without respect to their utility; or it may even be, metaphorically, a product of the *id*'s working on substance provided by the *ego*. In any event, its full appreciation requires of the critic special technical attention to the formal characteristics of the literary work. And Ransom's sense of dualistic tension between structure and texture leads him to a preference for the wry irony and sceptical wit associated with the metaphysical poets of the seventeenth century; his special aversions are the emotional excess and formal looseness associated with the Romantics.

In *Reactionary Essays* (1936), *Reason in Madness* (1941), *The Hovering Fly* (1945) and *The Forlorn Demon* (1953), Tate devoted a good deal of effort to attacking the idea that critical problems can be solved by easy reference to accumulations of scholarly 'facts', sociological doctrine, or moral precept. He also attacked psychological criticism, like that of I. A. Richards, because it conceives literature as a kind of therapy for regulating the nervous states of author or reader; and he attacked positivist theories of language. He argued that literature gives us the completest knowledge we can hope for by catching the 'extensional' and 'intensional' aspects of experience in the 'tension' of metaphoric language. Like Ransom, Tate wants to redeem human knowledge from the realm of quantitative scientific 'objectivity' on the one hand and indulgent Romantic 'subjectivity' on the other; and like Ransom he insists that the insights of the undissociated sensibility must be sought, not in some detachable paraphrasable content, but in the contextual interaction of all the linguistic and literary conventions which discover the meanings of any particular verbal structure. Tate's literary preferences are similar to Ransom's, though again the operational relationship between literature's final cause and critical judgment is not as clear as it might be. Some clues to the relationship are suggested in *The House of Fiction*, published by Tate and Caroline Gordon in 1950. In an attempt to extend the new critical approaches to prose fiction, Tate pretty clearly shows an affinity between his own contextualism and the critical theory of Henry James.

The drift of the New Critics' contextualism is even clearer in the work of Cleanth Brooks, whose series of textbooks – especially *Understanding Poetry*, done in collaboration with Robert Penn Warren in 1938 – has had enormous impact on the teaching of literature (poetry, drama, and fiction) in colleges and universities. In these books and in *Modern Poetry and the Tradition* (1939) and *The Well Wrought Urn* (1947), Brooks seems to argue that literary language is non-referential: 'what [a poem] "says" can be rendered only by the poem itself'. Brooks's special method for getting at the untranslatable 'meanings' of poems is to search out the 'irony' and 'paradox' which he takes to be characteristic of poetic discourse. Though Brooks suggests that irony is a mark of intelligence in something like the Jamesian sense of the word, the tracking of the currents and countercurrents of paradox leads him to view the poem as a more or less self-contained dramatic structure to be judged by its success in accommodating its internal complexities to some principle of internal coherence. This notion recalls Richards's idea of a poem as a balance of competing 'interests' and Kenneth Burke's elaboration of a 'dramatistic' theory of criticism. But Brooks's view is determinedly literary, whereas Richards's view is overtly psychological and Burke's approach merges linguistic forms with the worlds of 'political' and religious behaviour.

The formalist emphasis of the New Critics and their rejection of referential theories of language in favour of linguistic contextualism made them vulnerable to the charge that they had separated literature from common experience. Walter Sutton strongly argued this view in two articles published in *The Journal of Aesthetics and Art*

Criticism in 1948 and 1961 and he continued to urge it in *Modern American Criticism* (1963). There may be something in what Sutton said, but the emphasis Ransom and Tate and Brooks put on the cognitive function of literature certainly shows they had not intended to be advocates of art for art. Wimsatt and Beardsley had specifically rejected hedonism and escapism in 'The Affective Fallacy', published in *The Sewanee Review* in 1949; and in R. P. Blackmur's persistent advocacy of pluralistic criticism in *The Double Agent* (1935), *The Expanse of Greatness* (1940), *Language as Gesture* (1953) and *The Lion and the Honeycomb* (1955), there was also abundant evidence that the new criticism did not wish to 'understand literature solely by literary means'. As Blackmur put it in 'The Enabling Act of Criticism' (in *American Issues*, Vol. II, ed. Willard Thorp, 1941), everything 'that can be made to bear, bears'. In his later work, Blackmur's earlier technical emphasis gave way more and more to an emphasis on literature's cultural relations.

But in most of the New Critics there *was* fuzziness in explaining what these relations were, what kind of knowledge literature made available. Murray Krieger, who had published *The New Apologists for Poetry* in 1956, undertook to clarify the issues in a reply to Sutton published in *The Journal of Aesthetics and Art Criticism* in 1962, and he discussed them in *The Play and Place of Criticism* (1967). Eliseo Vivas also replied to Sutton in *The Artistic Transaction* (1963), which developed the position he had defined in his earlier *Creation and Discovery* (1955). The burden of Vivas's argument is that genuinely creative poetic language brings to clarity ideas and attitudes that were previously unavailable to ready reference, and that it is therefore constitutive of our experience instead of being merely a reflection of it, as referential language is. The meanings of creative art are perhaps immanent, but they are, by virtue of that very characteristic, even more intimately entwined with our general experience than the conceptual abstractions we may derive from them. On the literary side of this argument, we may hear echoes of Henry James, and on the philosophical side, we may hear the voices of Coleridge, Kant, Benedetto Croce, and most clearly, Ernst Cassirer. The difference between contextualistic and referential language in this tradition is the difference between language conceived as symbol and language conceived as a system of signs.

That distinction, however, is not the only basis for describing the literary language. Yvor Winters proposed a simpler and perhaps more usable approach. Accepting language as a referential system and rejecting the notion of a realm peculiarly aesthetic, he argued in the three short volumes collected in *In Defense of Reason* (1947) and in *The Function of Criticism* (1957), that the technical resources of literary language, from meter to the conventions of genre, are simply instruments for extending the range and precision of our general language so that it may discover, define, explore and criticize the rational and emotional dimensions of general human experience with greater fullness and subtlety than can be managed by the various partial, technical languages devised for the treatment of various specialized fields of knowledge. Literature is thus for Winters an enriched means of moral contemplation in the broad sense of that term. The critic must understand rhetorical subtleties in their full contextual complexity in order to understand literary meanings, and Winters has given impressive evidence in his own criticism of his ability to locate the manifest and latent content of literary works through rhetorical analysis. But finally the critic must be prepared to judge these meanings not as special symbolism but as human truth. The problem of mediating between immanence and reference will not be greater in such a judgment than it is in human experience generally and it will not be helped by assigning to one or the other kind of meaning a predominant role in literary experience.

Winter's last work, *Forms of Discovery* (1967), is a kind of grand reference work, sometimes elliptical in argument and petulant in manner, in which are recorded the particular literary judgments to which he was led by his vast reading in English (and other) poetry. These final judgments, especially his harshness on the Romantics and Victorians, have, like his earlier judgments, maddened critics of more conventional tastes, but even in this volume, the critic who is willing to suspend disbelief may discover a body of neglected poetry and rediscover more familiar verse in a way which enlightens individual works and also defines an approach to the historical development of poetic forms. More important, all these discoveries are also discoveries about the forms of the human sensibility.

The formalist emphasis of the New Criticism *was* new. And yet this criticism had connections with the battles of the twenties. Ransom, Tate and Robert Penn Warren were leading contributors to *I'll Take My Stand* (1930), a famous collection of essays in which an overwhelming sense of cultural crisis was defined in terms of a conflict between technological industrial capitalism and traditional Southern agrarianism. In his foreword to *In Defense of Reason*, Yvor Winters recorded *his* impression that 'our literary culture (to mention nothing more) appears ... to be breaking up'; its 'rescue',

he said, was a matter of the greatest moment. And Winters confessed that one of the sources of the new critics' distrust of
Romanticism was Babbitt's work. Furthermore, the New Critics, like
the critics of the 'teens and twenties, tended to treat history as
metaphor. The South of *I'll Take My Stand* is surely an imaginary
realm. Tate's biographies of *Stonewall Jackson* (1928) and *Jefferson
Davis* (1929) are almost novelistic in technique, even as his novel,
The Fathers (1938), has a strongly historical tone. And in various
essays Tate has specifically linked the historical sense with the
literary and religious imagination in language that recalls Spingarn's
Crocean view of history as an imaginative projection of the present.
As Frederick Pottle pointed out in 1953 in *The Yale Review*, 'the
standards of ... [the new] criticism are not really derived from a
study of seventeenth-century literature. They are the definition of
[a] modern sensibility'. Finally, the formalist emphasis of the New
Criticism was itself prepared for by the earlier debate about the
special role of the artist in a practical and pragmatic world.

Other influences, general and specific, also prepared the way for
the New Critics. Croce's 'expressionistic' aesthetic and his idea of
history as art were part of the general background; and Ernst
Cassirer's definition of man as a symbol-making animal lies behind
Vivas's theory of literary language. Closer to home, however, were
the work and example in the twenties of Ezra Pound and T. S.
Eliot. Their expatriation dramatized the alienation of the artist in
America and pointed to the need to 'justify the ways of the artist to
Americans'. Pound, in *The Spirit of Romance* (1910), in his 'translations' from Classical, Provençal and Oriental literatures, and in
the extensive borrowings of his own verse, and Eliot in his similar
borrowings and in his notion of all literature as a timeless order or
constant present, supplied both example and precept to the New
Criticism in its view of history. Eliot especially encouraged a taste
for the metaphysical poets and, drawing on the work of T. E.
Hulme, a distrust of the Romantics. But most important in the work
of Pound and Eliot in the twenties was their insistence on the need
for renewed attention to the *craft* of the poet. Pound, in *Pavannes
and Divisions* (1918), *Instigations* (1920), *Irritations* (1920), *How to
Read* (1931), *The ABC of Reading* (1954) and *Make It New* (1934),
and Eliot, in *The Sacred Wood* (1920), *For Launcelot Andrewes* (1928),
Selected Essays: 1917–1932 (1932) and *The Use of Poetry and the Use
of Criticism* (1933), both repeatedly called for a fresh and active
confrontation of specific literary texts, and for a more sensitive
awareness of the poet's linguistic medium. Eliot tried to explain, in

his famous (though confusing) definition of the 'objective correlative' in his essay on *Hamlet* and in his equally famous discussion of 'Tradition and the Individual Talent' (both in *The Sacred Wood*), that attention to individual literary structures and to the conventions of literary tradition provided one means of escape from the marshy ground of affective criticism and the cult of personality.

The emphasis of Pound and Eliot on craft helps account for the tendency on the part of the leading liberals of the twenties, interested as they were in sociology rather than literature, to discount Pound and Eliot, though Eliot's conservatism in politics and religion seems to have had something to do with Van Wyck Brooks's special antipathy to him and Pound's 'reactionary' politics would certainly not have recommended *him* in liberal circles. But the conservatives of the twenties were not sympathetic either. Though Eliot may have learned something about Romanticism from Babbitt at Harvard, *his* emphasis was literary not moralistic. Those who did listen to Pound and Eliot in the twenties were the young men who were to develop the new rhetorical criticism of the next decades. Though neither Pound nor Eliot developed systematic methodologies for criticism (Pound was far too enthusiastic and Eliot too urbane), they both urged a scrupulous regard for technique as an antidote to hasty summaries of content on the one hand and emotional impressionism on the other, and they both cited individual poems which they thought worthy of technical scrutiny. As Yvor Winters has put it in *The Function of Criticism*, Pound 'showed us fine poems which we had overlooked, whereas Babbit all too often misunderstood fine poems with which we were familiar'.

The problem of the artist's special means and function had been set by the general critical debate in the first thirty years of the century. And in those years Pound and Eliot had suggested the terms of its solution in their emphasis on craft. The New Critics applied the terms to the problem.

During the thirties and forties the New Critics routed the journalists and solidified their own position within the academy. It is true that Edmund Wilson, a critic of independent genius, in *Axel's Castle* (1931), *The Triple Thinkers* (1939), *The Wound and the Bow* (1941) and in other books, managed to carry on the tradition of general criticism outside the walls. Lionel Trilling at Columbia continued to emphasize the connections between literature and broad sociological concerns in *The Liberal Imagination* (1943) and *The Opposing Self* (1955), and in frequent contributions to the *Partisan Review*, as did F. O. Matthiessen of Harvard in *American*

Renaissance (1941) and *The Responsibilities of the Critic* (1952). But Wilson and Trilling and Matthiessen combined their awareness of larger systems, especially those of Marx and Freud, with a fine sensitivity to the formal aspects of literary structure. Indeed no genuine critic in these years, no matter how general his reference, could avoid confronting the problem of the artist's special function and his appropriate language.

The work of Kenneth Burke is a case in point. He has written the most ambitious general criticism of the period in such books as *Counter-Statement* (1931), *Permanence and Change* (1935), *Attitudes Toward History* (1937), *The Philosophy of Literary Form* (1941), *A Grammar of Motives* (1945), *A Rhetoric of Motives* (1950), *The Rhetoric of Religion* (1961) and *Language as Symbolic Action* (1966). Burke's aim in these books has been nothing less than the development of a kind of master language by which to measure the 'dramatistic' nature of other languages – aesthetic, philosophical, psychological, political, religious or whatnot. He has sought to see all thought and behaviour as a series of 'strategies' which are describable in more or less literary terms. Burke's work has taken him well beyond 'literature', while at the same time giving to all human experience 'symbolic' significance. In this sense, his work, though certainly general, has also been most persistently formal.

Perhaps the most impressive efforts to expand the reference of literary studies while yet describing the peculiarities of literary form have been made by the myth critics. Such diverse writers as Francis Fergusson, in *The Idea of a Theater* (1949), Philip Wheelwright, in *The Burning Fountain* (1954) and *Metaphor and Reality* (1962), and Stanley Edgar Hyman in 'The Ritual View and the Mythic' (in T. A. Sebeok's *Myth: A Symposium*, 1958) and *The Tangled Bank* (1962), have agreed that myth and ritual are historically and psychologically associated with literature, that they constitute a language different from conceptual argument or the language of science, and that the recognition of mythic and ritualistic elements in literature will therefore enable critics to explore the latent patterns natural to the literary mode and estimate also the value of mythic displacements in any given work. In the interplay between model and example lies the peculiar power of literary meanings.

Though myth critics have borrowed heavily from anthropology, especially from the Cambridge school as represented by Sir James Frazer's *The Golden Bough* and Jane Harrison's *Themis*, and though they have made use of Freud's *Totem and Taboo* and Carl Jung's *Psychology of the Unconscious*, they have not needed to endorse

Frazer's anthropological assumptions or Jung's theory of racial memory; for their interest is in the structural principles of *literature*. Northrop Frye's enormously important *Anatomy of Criticism* (1957) makes clear that *for the literary critic* myth is form, not content, and that the literary mode, as studied by critics, is in some sense autonomous, and its 'meanings' non-referential. In this sense and in their ability to follow the intricate inner workings of individual literary texts, the myth critics are participators in the movement inaugurated by the New Critics. But Frye certainly seems more catholic than the New Critics in his eagerness to accept philology, social and intellectual history, philosophy, psychology and anthropology as contributory approaches. And yet in his eagerness he does not forget to emphasize that these approaches must be transformed in the service of literature, which is something else. What it is, in its own autonomy, is as difficult for him to make clear as it was for the New Critics to define literature's peculiar cognitive functions. The study of ritual and myth may offer clues, but myth is not of course a synonym for literature. In literature myth has no extra-literary meanings. For Wheelwright the 'depth language' of literature is different from the 'steno language' of referential discourse, but the archetypes of literature look very much like those of religion. What are the differentia of literature? And how is the nature of literature (or religion) to be made clear in the steno language of criticism? Perhaps this last problem is insoluble. Perhaps we must be satisfied with hints. Frye seems to suggest that referential discourse itself cannot include the idea of external reference except as an internal assumption.

Nineteenth-century symbolism is certainly part of the complex background for myth criticism, as it was also a source for the work of Eliot and Pound. But for Frye at least, the Romantic movement, as he tells us in the 'Introduction' to *Fables of Identity* (1963), lies behind all modern speculations on literary theory, including those of the anti-Romantics. His own study of William Blake's '*Fearful Symmetry*' had suggested as much in 1947. Such an interest in Romanticism implies what used to be called an interest in the transcendental which is contrary to the New Critics' professed interest in the particularity of the world's body. And myth critics have also been interested in the longer literary forms – in the novel and the epic – which the narrower rhetorical emphasis of the New Critics had tended to slight. Frye has elaborated a very suggestive theory of correspondences between ritual and narrative, oracle and imagery, both enclosed by the master structures of myth. And he has discovered correspondences also between certain mythic patterns and various literary genres: romance, comedy, pastoral, tragedy and satire. The only one among the New Critics who has addressed the problems of literary genres at all is Yvor Winters.

The neo-Aristotelians of the so-called Chicago school, led by R. S. Crane, Richard McKeon, Norman Maclean and Elder Olson have made tentative efforts at genre criticism in their discrimination of the different 'forms' (each with its own peculiar *dynamis*) governing individual literary works. They have differed from the New Critics in their willingness to consider such elements as plot and character as more important than language in developing their formal analyses. Crane has argued persuasively in his *The Languages of Criticism and the Structure of Poetry* (1953) that language is only the medium or material of poetry, not its 'essence'; the final cause of a given literary work, says Crane, is not 'meaning' but the realization of the constructive rationale imposed on its making by the 'hypothetical necessities' of the formal principle (tragic, comic, epic, lyric, etc.) governing its constitution as a 'concrete whole'. Thus one important task for critics is to refine and extend inductively the vocabulary available for analysing *ex post facto* the poetic forms made manifest in actual literary productions. The practising critic needs such a vocabulary in order to help judge if particular poems succeed in realizing their own concrete natures.

Though Crane is careful to insist that *mimesis* is not an 'abstract' principle for *all* 'poetic' productions, he tends to think of it as a peculiarly literary principle – didactic or argumentative 'poems', for example, falling under rhetorical (or oratorical) canons. And his effort to reconcile the principle of 'imitation' (which applies even to lyrics) with the idea that poems are autonomous wholes suggests how pervasive is the influence of the New Critics, felt even in the standard anthology of the Chicago group's work, *Critics and Criticism* (1952), though this book is in a sense directed *against* the New Critics. (For Crane, *plus arabe que l'Arabe*, even non-imitative poems are autonomous: though 'constituted of some particular thesis, intellectual or practical', they are not to be measured by their 'meaning' or truth but only by the sufficiency of the means employed in 'the artful elaboration and enforcement' of their theses.) Finally, though Crane insists on the plurality of possible critical languages and viewpoints, his own tendency to imply that a peculiarly literary criticism will be centrally concerned with 'emotional effect' (as a quality or power of the object) seems a less satisfactory way of mediating between the autonomy of poetic

productions and their external references than the halting efforts of
the New Critics to discover a peculiar kind of cognition as literature's
final cause.

The need to cut through such epistemological tangles was presumably a principal motive behind the development of
phenomenological criticism, which draws directly on the work of
such philosophers as Edmund Husserl and indirectly on the
attitudes of modern existentialism. For the phenomenological
philosopher, interested in bridging the gulf between subject and
object, reality truly consists of its 'appearances' as these are
reflected in consciousness. For the phenomenological critic, the
literary problem becomes not the analysis of a literary object, but
the exploration of the consciousness of the author as it reveals itself
throughout the corpus of his *oeuvre* and in other areas too. This
criticism as represented, for example, by the work of Georges
Poulet of the so-called Geneva school, is anti-formalist, and
seemingly sympathetic to Romantic notions of a pre-verbal or
supra-verbal mental world, perhaps 'subjective', but existentially
validated as 'intentional act'. In these ways phenomenological
criticism, more clearly than the criticism of the Chicago school or
that of the mythographers, contradicts the thrust of American 'new
criticism'. The counter thrust is seen in Geoffrey Hartman's studies
of Wordsworth, Hopkins, Valéry and Rilke in *The Unmediated Vision*
(1954) and in the astonishing virtuoso performance of J. Hillis
Miller in *Charles Dickens: The World of His Novels* (1959), *The
Disappearance of God* (1963) and *Poets of Reality* (1965). In these
works Miller ranges freely and sometimes bewilderingly through
the total work of Dickens, De Quincey, Browning, Emily Brontë,
Arnold, Hopkins, Conrad, Yeats, Eliot, Thomas, Stevens and William Carlos Williams, in pursuit of what might be called the
metaphysical biography of these authors; and more than that he
charts in the three books taken together the development of literary
consciousness from the Romantics to the moderns. Miller's aim is
not to describe autonomous literary structures; and yet he is
certainly more willing than Poulet to engage in formal analysis as a
means of defining the consciousness he seeks. Especially in *Poets of
Reality* he implies that the end of literature is knowledge, perhaps
peculiarly in our day a kind of direct knowledge of acquaintance.
Miller's work, like Frye's, thus suggests the pervasiveness of the
influence of the New Critics even over those who are not of their
persuasion.

Miller's work, like all the important American criticism of the last fifty years, testifies to an enormous increase in critical sophistication over the work of the first thirty years of the century. Sometimes the abstruseness of recent critical theory may make us think wistfully of the provincial simplicities of an earlier time. We may remember the remark attributed to Albert Einstein concerning one of Kafka's novels: 'the human mind isn't that complex'. But the complication and the abstruseness are likely to remain – as least as long as criticism is dominated by academics addressing other academics. In any event, the resourcefulness of recent criticism in dealing with the formal characteristics of literary art has surely increased our power of analysis and response. And the slowly converging interest of a variety of critics in defining literature's final cause as in some sense cognitive may yet provide a firmer basis than we now have for the exercise of those powers, even as recent definitions of the varieties of literary forms have increased the range of their applicability. In addition, the myth critics and the phenomenological critics opened negotiations with a wider cultural world. With a firmer base, increased range and a greater interest in allied disciplines, literary criticism may again become general criticism.

7

WILLIAM FAULKNER AND THE SOUTHERN RENASCENCE

Ursula Brumm

I

CIVIL WAR AND AFTERMATH

Since we left Chester – solitude. Nothing but tall blackened chimneys to show that any man has ever trod this road before us.

This is Sherman's track. It is hard not to curse him.

I wept incessantly at first. 'The roses of these gardens are already hiding the ruins', said Mr. C. 'Nature is a wonderful renovator.' He tried to say something.

Then I shut my eyes and made a vow. If we are a crushed people, crushed by aught, I have vowed never to be a whimpering pining slave.

Thus Mary Boykin Chesnut, wife of a South Carolina senator and Confederate general, wrote on 2 May 1865 in her diary, published in 1905 under the title *A Diary from Dixie*. The complete text of this diary is now edited by C. Vann Woodward as *Mary Chesnut's War* (1981).

This 'crushed people' has emerged as a strong force in twentieth-century American literature; it produced one of the greatest writers of our time: William Faulkner. In view of this surprising development some people may wonder what makes great literature: progress, pursuit of happiness, the acquisition of material well-being, or perhaps, hardship, defeat, tears and suffering. But, of course, the question is too simply put and cannot be answered in this fashion. Literature is the result of a peculiar and immensely complex imaginative response to experience and circumstance, and is in its greatest achievements unexplainable. It is impossible to establish conditions of creativity with any amount of certainty; however, conditions can be examined and the story outlined by pointing to its major elements and stages.

There is, first of all, this peculiar part of the United States, 'the South', a regional as well as a historical definition. Historically, as the 'Old South', it comprised the states Virginia, North and South Carolina, Georgia, Alabama, Tennessee, Louisiana, Arkansas, Mississippi, Florida and Texas which united into a confederacy and fought against the rest of the country from 1861 to 1865; different from the rest by its climate, social structure and a way of life, which depended, in good part, on the main reason for this war: the great 'burden' and guilt of slavery. Except for a short period during and after the American Revolution when patriots and intellectual leaders like Jefferson or Patrick Henry were prominent in the great national cause, the South has been, up to the 1920s, intellectually and culturally overshadowed by the rest of the country, specifically by New England. Although 'The College of William and Mary' had been established at Williamsburg in 1693, Southern society had not been vitally interested in intellectual progress.

The hot and humid climate, the fertile land of the coastal regions called for a leisurely life on the great plantations where the work was done by Negro slaves. This quasi-aristocratic life of the leading families received hard blows during the Civil War and went into decline during the 'reconstruction' period which followed it. It had, however, established itself as a myth of powerful archetypal ingredients: there was the big plantation mansion with its shining front of Greek pillars, the home of a large family and the centre of a web of relations to other families on similar plantations, and this called for tribal gatherings on visits, dances, parties, weddings and funerals, prepared and served by an army of black slaves. Some of those were recalcitrant and rebellious, but others marvellously able and secretly dominant. To set off and surround this kind of life, there were small independent farmers with few or no slaves and at the lower end of the social spectrum the crude poor white farmer on the stony arid hillside land.

The South, then, the 'Old South', is a way of life in the Confederate States, arranged towards the amenities of life, graced with the ideals of a gentlemanly existence and courteous manners, but burdened with the sin of slavery. It was awakened from its leisure into a four-year heroic effort when in the Civil War it was fought by the rest of the country. Military defeat and its economic consequences destroyed this form of life, but also established the conditions for its imaginative rebirth. The war, suffering and defeat strengthened the awareness of solidarity and created the feeling of a peculiar and unique experience which set the Southerner off from the rest of the country. Defeat created the myth of the South, which for some time manifested itself in Southern writing as a nostalgic and cheaply sentimental picture of mansions, magnolias, pure women and splendid gentlemen: Margaret Mitchell in her immensely popular romance *Gone With the Wind* (1936) added dramatic vigour and a dash of caprice, but on the whole confirmed the literary convention. It was Faulkner who transformed this myth into parables of human existence, unique in its mode and at the same time representative of the human possibilities towards the good and the bad: bravery, endurance, constancy and generosity as well as greed, violence, weakness or dishonesty.

By the middle of the 1930s, after the publication of Faulkner's great novels *The Sound and the Fury*, *As I Lay Dying*, *Light in August*, *Absalom, Absalom!*, the South is firmly established on the literary map of the United States. This is the achievement of one literary genius. But at the same time, he is dependent on the life he transforms, on his experiences, sources, predecessors and contemporaries and has thus to be seen in a literary and cultural tradition, as part of a historical and literary development.

If this history cannot be reported fully, it can be traced by pointing to some significant steps. The Civil War, the watershed separating Southern history into an ante-bellum and a post-bellum period, functions as the major force in the formation of post-bellum Southern cultural identity. The war, however, did not immediately produce significant results. The most important novel about the war which came from personal observations, John William De Forest's *Miss Ravenel's Conversion from Secession to Loyalty* (1867) was written by a Union officer and expresses the Northern point of view. There were corresponding Southern works, yet they were hardly noticed by the rest of the country. John Esten Cooke who had also participated in the war – he had served as staff officer with Stonewall Jackson and Jeb Stuart – soon after the war produced romances which were vastly popular in the South: *Surry of Eagle's Nest, or the Memoirs of a Staff Officer Serving in Virginia, edited from the Mss of Colonel Surry* (1866, republished 1968) and *Mohun, or the Last Days of Lee and his Paladins. Final Memoirs of a Staff Officer Serving in Virginia. From the Mss of Colonel Surry of Eagle's Nest* (1869, republished 1968). Cooke provided a mixture of war reporting based on his own experience with elements of dashing romance which helped to form the Southern view of the war. The lasting influence of these novels is acknowledged by the fact that Faulkner used Cooke as a source, notably in *Sartoris*.

To the North, however, the defeated Southern past seemed silent from exhaustion, shame or wounded pride; its only major literary talent, Samuel Langhorne Clemens, assumed another name (Mark Twain) and changed over to the North. During this time it is predominantly the Northerner who explains the South: Albion W. Tourgée, a somewhat dubious reconstruction official, describes post-war conditions there. On a higher level, George Washington Cable, born in New Orleans as the son of a New Englander and therefore always something of an outsider, conveys the charms as well as the dark side of Louisiana life, which is enriched by an admixture of French and Spanish immigration, in the stories of *Old Creole Days* (1879) and his novel *The Grandissimes* (1880). Creole themes were also treated in the short stories of Kate Chopin who came to Louisiana through marriage. She reached her greatest literary achievement with her novel *The Awakening* (1899) which created a scandal because it candidly treated the thoughts and passions of a woman seeking self-fulfilment outside a conventional marriage.

Toward the end of the century, a writer from the border state of Maryland, Francis Hopkinson Smith, presented what he considered typical Southern characters in his novel *Colonel Carter of Cartersville* (1891). It is not a great or even a good novel, but it was very popular, and also highly successful as a drama. It is a part of popular culture, and it is significant for the general response in the North as well as for its intentions. *Colonel Carter of Cartersville* is an attempt to reconcile the two parties by taking the best of each – Southern graciousness and Northern practicality – and uniting them in action. As such, it is a Northern usurpation of the myth of the South; it presents a cheap Northern version of Southern ideals and characters, made palatable to Northern taste and expectations.

Colonel Carter, the hero of the novel, is an elderly, mild, well-mannered gentleman who has moved to New York, where his faithful and shrewd Negro servant provides for him on credit established among the shopkeepers with marvellous tales about 'de. old fambly place in Cartersville'. Carter is the pet Northern idea of a Southerner, graceful but emasculate: 'his voice is soft and low and tempered with a cadence that is delicious'; he is 'frank and tenderhearted', 'happy as a boy; hospitable to the verge of beggary; enthusiastic as he is visionary, simple as he is genuine'. In other words, he is a child in the practical matters of life, particularly in things financial, commercial, industrial. While he entertains his friends – 'to dine well was with him an inherited instinct' – he reveals his outmoded family pride and naïvely undemocratic social arrogance. He has come to New York to find support for a railroad scheme, which proves impracticable, but is in the end helped by shrewder Northern friends who discover coal on his run-down family possessions. The Colonel's former rigid views of honour and duelling are also reshaped; and we leave him with the assurance that his family place will be restored and that the natural resources of the backward South will be industrially utilized.

It is understandable that this attempt to reconcile the more innocuous Southern virtues – represented by elderly, solitary, childless Southern characters – with the practical abilities of the North could not satisfy the defeated party. The first articulate revolt against such Northern tutelage came after the First World War from a group of poets, writers and critics who called themselves 'Fugitives' and published a journal of the same name during the early twenties. They regarded themselves as voluntary fugitives from the present state of American society, and also as victims who suffered from severe disadvantages in a country which was controlled, including the press and the publishing trade, by the Northern point of view.

The 'Fugitives' and another related group, the 'Agrarians', presented themselves proudly and defiantly as reactionaries; as Southerners they felt ploughed under by the push and drive of a materialistic American civilization. Thus they stood up for tradition and individual attachment to family, kinship, place and region. As defenders of an agrarian society they expressed their experience of 'how difficult it was to be a Southerner in the twentieth century' and attacked the failings of modern industrial civilization.

To the 'Fugitives' belonged poets and critics of the first order, like Allen Tate, John Crowe Ransom and Robert Penn Warren. The 'Fugitive' group had started among students of Vanderbilt University who met to discuss their own poetry, and it is in the field of literary criticism that they had their greatest, nationwide, even worldwide, influence. Ransom, Tate and Warren contributed substantially to the movement of the New Criticism. As men of erudition they turned to literary traditions which appealed to their sense of order, decorum, precision and concreteness: especially to the Elizabethans and the Metaphysical poets of the seventeenth century. Here, their taste concurred with that of their colleagues from other parts of the country – as, for example, that of T. S. Eliot. Together they formulated the rules which instructed a whole generation in the principles of poetry: the exploration of language, techniques of paradox and gentlemanly wit, and the function of images. The 'Fugitives' are something unique in the American scene: intellectuals who rebel against the industrial civilization – not only as other critics, against its undesirable consequences – but to profess an anti-progressive credo.

The 'Southern Manifesto' *I'll Take My Stand* expressed the Agrarians' and Fugitives' critique of the dehumanizing consequences of industrialism. It was heavily criticized both in the North and the South at the time, while some of its warnings foreshadow the concerns of contemporary ecologists. A true Southerner was still a man who was rooted – or, at least, wished to be rooted – in the soil and who had a deep suspicion of technical and industrial progress. Faulkner, although fascinated by aeroplanes, hated machines, cars and other technical contraptions. Attachment to family, to a clan of relatives and to place and region has been a characteristic of Southern writing, as the lack of these ties became a theme of tragic alienation.

For this reason, Southern literature from its re-emergence till now has often been seen under the somewhat condescending designation of 'regionalism'. It is, however, not the concreteness of, or restriction to, a specific place or region which makes a work of literature 'regional' in the limiting sense, but a preponderance of a purely local theme rather than one of larger human impact. Ellen Glasgow (1874–1945) in her numerous novels wrote about human problems between the old order and the advancing industrialism in her native state of Virginia. Born of an 'aristocratic' family of the South she was acutely aware that the genteel tradition of the Old South was doomed, and she undertook to present the social and political changes in her home state Virginia in a series of novels which followed each other at intervals of two or three years between 1902 and 1925. In several of them, the female protagonists are the victims of these changes; *Barren Ground* (1925), the most successful of her works, is concerned with the theme of female self-realization. The heroine is the daughter of a poor white farmer and, through affliction and disappointment, learns to question her romantic delusions. After a trip to the North she redeems the barren ground of the family farm with the advanced agricultural knowledge she has acquired. It has been said that with this novel realism entered Southern literature, the realism which Ellen Glasgow applied in her later novels to Richmond high society. Like *Barren Ground*, *Vein of Iron* (1939) was again set in rural Virginia. The heroine, daughter of an impoverished schoolteacher, is formed by the 'vein of iron' in her character. Ellen Glasgow is the first Southern novelist of the twentieth century to win a respectable place in the roster of American literature. She is, however, not a force in modern literature, nor has she blazed a trail or established a style of her own.

The first writer to achieve outstanding popular success in writing about the South was Erskine Caldwell (born in 1903). His great period was in the early days of the Depression, when his novels about poor white sharecroppers were taken for highly entertaining social criticism. His best books, *Tobacco Road* (1932) and *God's Little Acre* (1933) – folksy, bawdy tales about some very lusty, primitive characters – are burlesques which in their own way are just as schematized as the nostalgic romances about ante-bellum plantation life. *Tobacco Road* in its dramatized form had a spectacular success on the stage and a continuous run of more than 3000 Broadway performances. The most prolific and versatile of modern Southern writers is Robert Penn Warren (born in 1905) who belonged to the 'Fugitives' as a student and later had a distinguished career as poet, teacher and critic. Warren wrote a number of novels, some on historical subjects, and all of them searching investigations into the moral problems of the South. But the South for him, as for Faulkner, may not differ fundamentally from the rest of the United States. This was made clear by his most important novel, *All the King's Men* (1946) which portrayed the rise and fall of a Southern back-country demagogue, modelled on Senator Huey Long of Louisiana, yet an *American* portent.

It is, perhaps, today a handicap to be a Southern writer and to deal with the matters of the South because of being measured against the towering figure of William Faulkner. On the other hand, it can be said that Faulkner paved the way for a number of younger writers who can now move with ease in a territory which Faulkner has made familiar to the reading public. Since the 1940s at least five writers have emerged who have produced an *oeuvre* characterized by specific themes and style. Of these, Tennessee Williams (1911–83) is mainly a dramatist; Truman Capote (1924–84), who started his career with stories of poetic sensitivity (*Other Voices, Other Rooms*, 1948), more recently applied his talents to what he considered a new and significant form: the non-fiction novel. *In Cold Blood* (1968) purports to recreate an actual case of a sensational murder.

There are several women among recent Southern writers who have explored characters in rural or small-town life. Eudora Welty (born in 1909) deals with small-town or plantation life in her home state Mississippi. She prefers the shorter literary forms in which she explores the inner lives of a great variety of people: ordinary, eccentric or abnormal, and from many different walks of life, planters as well as the poor black or white sharecropper. About all of them she writes with close attention to delicate emotions and submerged passions, in her mode of presentation linking the real to the fantastic, or dream to myth. Abnormal and handicapped characters – half-wits, deaf-mutes, dwarfs – populate the fiction of Carson McCullers (1917–67); she also writes about children, cripples, people who suffer from unusual sensibility. Her most successful novel, *The Member of the Wedding* (1946), which was turned into a play and even a musical, is a moving story about a small girl's loneliness and her confusions and pains in growing up. In company with writers like Capote, Tennessee Williams, Flannery O'Connor, and Faulkner, Carson McCullers has in some of her other work made use of what has been termed 'Southern Gothic'. Images of the grotesque, the horrible and the violent have served her and these other writers to project the anomalies in a society afflicted by racial problems and the psychological distortions which were the long-term consequences of the Civil War. Violence plays a dominant role in the works of Flannery O'Connor (1925–64) whose great talent is of an even harsher grain. *The Violent Bear It Away* (1960) – namely the kingdom of heaven – is a revealing title for her writing which is intensely concerned with the rebirth of religious consciousness in our century. Searching for this consciousness among the backwoods farmers and fundamentalists of her region, Flannery O'Connor created a world of violent action and burning intensity of feeling.

Two writers fascinated by psychological problems of modern existence are Walker Percy and William Styron. Their themes are not necessarily Southern in a specific or restrictively regional sense but rather the anxieties and alienation of contemporary life. This in ta sense is an indication that Southern life has ceased being significantly different from that of the North; it has lost its predominantly agrarian nature; urbanization and industrialization have reduced the differences. Walker Percy's first and most successful novel *The Moviegoer* (1961) centres on New Orleans; the protagonist's addiction to movies is analysed as life lived at second-hand. In as much as the egocentricity and narcissism of man, the sickness of the modern world, becomes the dominant theme of modern Southern fiction, it ceases to be uniquely Southern. William Styron also deals with alienation, ennui and despair, most impressively in his first novel *Lie Down in Darkness* (1951) which traces the tragically solitary life of a Southern girl in New York. He was less successful in his attempt to recreate the voice of the black rebel in his *Confessions of Nat Turner* (1967), an effort which was violently criticized by black writers and critics.

It is a measure of Southern cultural and literary rehabilitation that the South has found access to the literary market-place as well as generally to the intellectual life of the nation. Southern writers have moved North or West in order to accept academic positions, or because they felt that the country as a whole was open to them. As a consequence, their work may not any more be entirely focused on Southern characters or localities. This does not necessarily mean that Southern literature as a separate entity has ceased to exist; it becomes increasingly difficult, however, to determine the Southernness of some of the writers and their work.

Even earlier and for different reasons, often because of racial discrimination, some of the black writers who were born in the South had moved North. This is true for Richard Wright who went to Chicago and then to Paris. His contribution to American literature is discussed in Chapter 10 of this volume.

II

WILLIAM FAULKNER

Since the 1950s William Faulkner (1897–1962) has become the most frequently and intensely interpreted writer of modern American literature; his work is a text endlessly searched for meanings. However, this high estimation is of relatively recent date: Faulkner is a difficult author, and critics have been slow to discover his true stature behind the involvements of his form and content.

When in 1929 Faulkner published *The Sound and the Fury*, his fourth novel and first masterpiece, he received almost no critical attention. During the thirties while his major works appeared, he found no sympathy from the dominant trend of social criticism. The few critics who paid attention took him for a rather extreme kind of Naturalist who indulged in horror, violence, nihilism and decadence. Larger recognition came only after the Second World War. In 1946, when most of Faulkner's works were out of print, Malcolm Cowley in a Viking Press volume presented Faulkner as the historian of the South, or rather, as the man who converted Southern history into a legend:

Briefly stated, the legend might run something like this: The Deep South was settled partly by aristocrats like the Sartoris clan and partly by new men like Colonel Sutpen. Both types of planters were determined to establish a lasting social order on the land they had seized from the Indians (that is, to leave sons behind them). They had the virtue of living single-mindedly by a fixed code; but there was also an inherent guilt in their 'design', their way of life; it was slavery that put a curse on the land and brought about the Civil War. (p 13f.)

If this is a somewhat simplified version of Faulkner's intentions, it served well as an introduction; it was shortly afterwards supplemented and improved by another explanatory essay, by fellow-Southerner Robert Penn Warren, who furthermore pointed to and interpreted such essentials in Faulkner's work as nature, humour and the role of the Negro. When in 1950 Faulkner received the Nobel prize, the great run of critics on Faulkner began. His work was analysed for its time structure; its narrative structure; the use of imagery, myth or archetypes; the use of religious elements, of gothic elements; for patterns of images or motives; for patterns of movement, or polarities of motion and stasis; for the recurrent phenomena of arrested motion; for the dualism of light and shadow, of good and bad. A pioneer study of Faulkner's difficult style by the poet Conrad Aiken showed that the long-winded hypotactic sentences and the complicated narrative technique served the purpose of 'deliberately withheld meaning'. While the critical exegesis is still in progress, a new phase of lexicographic treatment has begun; several 'Who's Whos' of Yoknapatawpha County have appeared; there are now glossaries and 'Reader's Guides' to Faulkner which try to unravel the complicated time structure of his novels by arranging them in chronological order, but thereby impairing them as works of art. Concordances to some of his works have been prepared and several of his books have been edited from typescripts and publisher's copies.

For the *Viking Portable Faulkner* Cowley had cut up and rearranged pieces from various works – a dubious method – in order to make his anthology serve to document the history of Yoknapatawpha County, Faulkner's representative Southern district, from 1820 to 1940. This, in spite of its arbitrariness, had the merit of apprehending Faulkner's main works as an epic universe formed by that imaginary–real territory Yoknapatawpha County in the State of Mississippi where all his stories about the South take place. For the first time, Faulkner's work could be seen for what it is: a great vision of Southern history – and, as such, of human history – in which the aspirations, passions, greed and guilt of man found their very specific manifestations.

The man who created this world tried to remain invisible behind his work. 'What I have written is of course in the public domain and the public is welcome; what I ate and did and when and where, is my own business,' he wrote to Cowley when questioned about his biography. All he cared to admit was in the form and brevity of a *Who's Who* paragraph:

Born (when and where). (He) came to Oxford as a child, attended Oxford grammar school without graduating, had one year as a special student in modern language in the University of Mississippi. Rest of education was undirected and uncorrelated reading. If you mention military experience at all (which is not necessary, as I could have invented a few failed RAF airmen as easily as I did Confeds) say 'belonged to RAF 1918'. Then continue: Has lived in same section of Miss. since, worked at various odd jobs until he got a job writing movies and was able to make a living at writing.

(The Faulkner–Cowley File, p 77)

He had not been in France during the war, as earlier biographies reported, nor had he been shot down and wounded: scornful of the publicity frenzy of his age and country he simply did not care to comment on the mistake. He was a shy man, highly sensitive to any intrusion into his privacy. The important facts about his life were that he was born in 1897 into a prominent Southern family which for several generations had been active in the political life of the region. His great-grandfather William T. Falkner [sic], had been an army officer, banker, railroad builder and had written novels besides. If one can trust Faulkner's own account, he drifted into literature when in New Orleans, where during Prohibition he earned his living as a rum runner, met Sherwood Anderson and liked the way Anderson lived: writing in the morning, walking around New Orleans in the afternoon, drinking all night. Actually, Faulkner had by then already published some poetry. His earliest sketches appeared in a student annual together with drawings by him which were heavily influenced by Beardsley and the art of the English Decadence. His first novel *Soldiers' Pay* (1926) was on the returned-soldier theme; *Mosquitoes* (1927) gave an ironic picture of life among bohemians at New Orleans. Except for the short-lived friendship with Anderson, Faulkner kept apart from colleagues and literary circles. He came into his own when he decided to make use of the world he knew best: the places and people in and around

Oxford, Mississippi, in Lafayette County, where he had grown up. This region he transformed into the mythical Yoknapatawpha County with the county town Jefferson, Miss. The first two novels from that world, *Sartoris* and *The Sound and the Fury*, appeared in 1929, to be followed in the thirties by a flow of major works: *As I Lay Dying* (1930), *Light in August* (1932), *Absalom, Absalom!* (1936), *The Wild Palms* (1939), *The Hamlet* (1940). In addition, there were collections of short stories, and two novels which have the form of a short-story novel, that is they consist of stories which are thematically interwoven: *The Unvanquished* (1939) and *Go Down, Moses* (1942).

It appears from the letters to Cowley in *The Faulkner–Cowley File* that Faulkner was quite resigned to have done with his literary career when Cowley contacted him after the Second World War. Only one of his numerous works had been a financial success, the sex-and-violence thriller *Sanctuary* (1931), and it was mainly due to this book that Faulkner had been hired to write scripts for Hollywood and consequently was able to buy himself a farm and house at Oxford, Miss.

The renewed interest in his work, which also stimulated his publisher, started him again. There is thus a second phase in his career which also brought forth a number of remarkable novels, although none reached the level established by his best earlier work. With *Intruder in the Dust* (1948), Faulkner took up threads from *Go Down, Moses*, and with *The Town* (1957) and *The Mansion* (1959) he continued a story of the new upstarts, the Snopeses, which he had begun in *The Hamlet*. *Requiem for a Nun* (1951), part narrative, part dramatic dialogue, dealt with the later life of the heroine from *Sanctuary*. The only work which moves beyond the boundaries of Yoknapatawpha is the allegorical First World War novel *A Fable* (1954). Finally, in the year of his death (1962) he published a comedy of reminiscence, *The Reivers*.

In spite of his reticence, William Faulkner emerged as a public figure in this late period after he had received the Nobel Prize. Faulkner became a national celebrity and was persuaded to appear at parties and in classrooms. He gave interviews and answered questions about his work at a Japanese university and the University of Virginia. The records of these discussions, published as *Faulkner at Nagano* (1956) and *Faulkner in the University* (1959), are a marvellous source for the personality of Faulkner, and also, in a characteristically limited way, for his work and its intentions. Two reasons account for the limitations: first, the poor quality of many of the questions asked, and secondly, Faulkner's inability to treat his novels as definite and completed works on the printed page. When asked about persons and events in his novels, to clear up obscurities, inconsistencies, discrepancies – and such is demanded in the majority of questions – he would answer not from the book but from the living knowledge in his imagination. He was, in fact, quite unable to tell a story twice in the same way. When presented with a challenge of facts, his imagination would set to work to spin them into a new yarn. *The Sound and the Fury*, as it is now available, is printed with a twenty-page 'Appendix. Compson 1899–1945', which provides a pre-history as well as explanatory details for the main characters. This was written on Cowley's request fifteen years after the novel appeared – and, as we are told by Cowley, by an author who refused to re-read the novel and who at the time did not even own a copy of it. As a result, the appendix did not really fit the novel as published in 1929, but it helped to clarify it. It was another attempt of Faulkner at the Compson story 'that lived and grew in his imagination'.

For the anthology of 1946 Faulkner drew a map which is now reprinted with several of his novels. It was inscribed 'Jefferson, Yoknapatawpha Co., Mississippi. Area, 2,400 Square Miles – Population Whites, 6,298; Negroes, 9,313. William Faulkner, Sole Owner and Proprietor.' It covers an uprightly rectangular territory bordered in the North by the Tallahatchie and in the South by the Yoknapatawpha Rivers. At the intersection of two straight roads, running North–South and East–West, lies Jefferson, county seat, surrounded East and West by pine hill country. On this map, Faulkner has marked the places where significant incidents from his novels take place: the Sartoris Plantation; Sutpen's Hundred; the 'sawmill where Byron Bunch first saw Lena Grove'; 'where old Bayard Sartoris died in young Bayard's car'; 'Bridge which washed away so Anse Bundren and his sons could not cross it with Addie's body'; and many others.

This map contains the exact topography for the novels and stories from Yoknapatawpha; they are part of a coherent world, complete with rivers, hills, town, courthouse, jail, churches, plantations, country stores and people. Yet, even if not only places but persons and events reappear in his work, his novels are independent units, not part of a *roman-fleuve*. Their independence is a requirement of content and form; indeed, no great author has so scrupulously and ingeniously developed specific forms for his novels from the nature of their thematic structure. For this reason, Faulkner is one of the greatest practitioners in formal experimentation, an innovator of the novel in our century. His style can be described as a unique mixture of the folksy and the avant-garde, because he combines oral with highly sophisticated modern techniques of narration.

This was already obvious, even if then not noted, when in 1929 Faulkner published two novels: *Sartoris* (the first to appear but probably written later, actually a shortened version of *Flags in the Dust* which now has been published in its entirety), and *The Sound and the Fury*, which is an amazing break-through to his own style and one of the great novels of the twentieth century. By turning to his own region, his true inheritance, a creative power was released which made this novel very different from and very much superior to his earlier work. *Sartoris*, however, bears some features of transition. Its basic situation, a young soldier back from the war who is unable to accept his home and the post-war world, is similar to that of *Soldiers' Pay*. But by drawing now from family history and memories, an abundance of themes is introduced which receive full treatment in later novels.

Sartoris was the first attempt in American literature to project a version of Southern society which in every way avoided the traditional clichés. At the same time *Sartoris* is significant as Faulkner's first attempt to deal with the Civil War as part of Southern consciousness. The memories of the Civil War are a legacy within the Sartoris family which determine the mood and the fate of the contemporary Sartoris twins who serve in the First World War. This first Yoknapatawpha novel is also the only place in Faulkner's work where major historical Civil War personalities make an appearance – if only in the protagonists' memories: Old Bayard (who as a boy and young man reappears in the stories of *The Unvanquished*, 1938) and his aunt Miss Jenny bring their memories into the twentieth century. Miss Jenny, a Civil War widow, has many times told her story of Civil War bravery, 'and as she grew older the tale itself grew richer and richer, taking on a mellow splendor like wine'.

The story, therefore, is presented as it lives on in the mind of one of the women of whom Faulkner said 'they had never surrendered'. It concerns another Bayard Sartoris, a cousin who serves as aide-de-camp to General Jeb Stuart, the most glamorous of the Confederate war heroes. Bayard accompanies Stuart on a night raid in which they surprise and put to flight General Pope of the Union forces, plunder his food supplies and capture one of his staff officers. When this officer, who is treated with exquisite if slightly ironic politeness by his captors, expresses his conviction that 'No gentleman has any business in this war ... He is an anachronism, like anchovies' (which Stuart has failed to capture), he touches the Southern nerve of honour and prompts Bayard to ride back to the enemy's commissary tent, where he is shot, not by a soldier but by the cook who had remained hidden among his supplies.

Faulkner derived the basic features of this episode from John Esten Cooke who in *Surry of Eagle's Nest* describes a night raid in which Stuart captured military plans from General Pope's tent. He embellished the story with typically Faulknerian hyperbolic touches, thereby converting it into a significant psychogram. What on the surface appears as a spectacular incident of supreme courage and recklessness is Faulkner's subtle interpretation of Southern war neurosis. Bayard's spontaneous attack is not so much an example of military heroism as an act in which the youthful drive to excel is blended with an infantile streak of vanity. The Southern boy who feels superior to his Northern brethren and enemies by his sense of valour and honour feels impelled to risk his life in a purely symbolic act. The whole attack, performed with excessive courage at the ultimate danger of death for in-significant gain, characterizes the psychological condition of the South in facing an enemy of superior material resources and advanced military technology. Jeb Stuart, 'the beau ideal of a cavalier', as Cooke calls him, proves an old-fashioned chivalric bravura, in actions of doubtful military value, conducted in the stoic fortitude of a soldier who foresees ultimate defeat and by heroic contempt of death tries to ensure immortality.

Although *Sartoris* contains brilliant writing in some of the episodes which present the character mentality of the First World War generation of the Sartorises, Faulkner did not quite succeed in fusing the parts into a wholly satisfactory aesthetic unity; it has not yet the mastery of his maturity. Nonetheless, *Sartoris* provides a key to the Yoknapatawpha novels, even if it does not have the magnificent, aesthetic abstraction from personal problems or in-volvement which is characteristic of Faulkner's best work.

The Sound and the Fury, although deeply compassionate, has this cool perfection of feeling objectified into art. The novel demands an extraordinary effort on the part of the reader: the willingness to read it several times, to consult interpretative help from criticism, or perhaps to penetrate to its meaning intuitively by reading it like poetry. Its four parts are arranged in order of difficulty; they successively become clearer and easier to understand; thus the reader is subjected, among other things, to an exercise in detective discovery. *The Sound and the Fury* is a novel four times told, and Faulkner has often explained why, as in an interview given to Jean Stein for the *Paris Review*:

It began with a mental picture. I didn't realize at the time it was symbolical. The picture was of the muddy seat of a little girl's drawers in a pear tree, where she could see through a window where her grandmother's funeral was taking place and report what was happening to her brothers on the ground below. By the time I explained who they were and what they were doing and how her pants got muddy, I realized it would be impossible to get all of it into a short story and that it would have to be a book ... I had already begun to tell the story through the eyes of the idiot child, since I felt that it would be more effective as told by someone capable only of knowing what happened, but not why. I saw that I had not told the story that time. I tried to tell it again, the same story through the eyes of another brother. That was still not it. I told it for the third time through the eyes of the third brother. That was still not it. I tried to gather the pieces together and fill in the gaps by making myself the spokesman. It was still not complete, not until fifteen years after the book was published, when I wrote as an appendix to another book the final effort to get the story told and off my mind, so that I myself could have some peace from it.

(*The Faulkner–Cowley File*, p 38f.)

'I couldn't leave it alone, and I never could tell it right.' 'I wrote it five separate times, trying to tell the story, to rid myself of the dream which would continue to anguish me until I did.' These and other confessions attest to Faulkner's deep involvement with the story: 'the tragedy of two lost women' within the theme of a family disintegration and the still larger theme of the decline of the South.

Faulkner presented the story in a unique way. He told it four times, or rather he had it told in four different ways, by four persons and at four different dates: 'April 7, 1928' by Benjy, the youngest son of the Compson family and an idiot, on 'June 2, 1910' by Quentin Compson, then a Harvard student, on 'April 6, 1928' by Jason Compson, and finally on 'April 8, 1928' by the author's narrative voice which is focused on Dilsey, a Negro servant of the Compsons. There is thus a provocative disregard of the con-ventional sequence of time in favour of an individual experience of time. The greatest provocation, however, and the reason for the novel's difficulty, is the author's sovereign disregard for the reader.

In 1910, Thomas Mann in *Buddenbrooks* could still narrate the decline of a family – and this is an individual as well as a social phenomenon – in the traditional way, by the voice of an omniscient author. Faulkner presents the same story, Southern fashion, by having it not told but experienced – that is, lived and felt – by those who by doing so create it: the three Compson sons who are the end of the family line, because by reason of idiocy, suicide and sterile egomania they are without hope for offspring. Their futility is contrasted by the person who keeps the disintegrating family together, the Negro servant Dilsey.

No other novel except Joyce's *Ulysses* so radically and at the same time to such advantage abolishes the novelist's traditional regard for the reader: he is not helped in his understanding by introductory information, explanatory descriptions or narrative summaries, all of which are conceptual stratifications and thereby falsifications of something ineffable which happens at the very sinews of life. By the reader being forced to share in the effort of assembling the story by participating in the characters' flow of consciousness and thus in the story at its creation, understanding reaches a level deeper and more immediate than in the traditional narrative.

The first chapter of *The Sound and the Fury* is the greatest challenge to the reader. The stream of consciousness of the 33-year-old Benjy, presented as an uninterrupted tape, reaches over a period of thirty years and consists, as has been established by patient scrutiny, of ninety-nine shifts between the present and different scenes from memory. This flow of consciousness presents the events without any attention to chronological order, but constitutes a composition which in its own way is as beautiful as it is cryptic. By verbal or sensory association the idiot's empty mind weaves particles of memory into his experiences of April 1928, when on his thirty-third birthday he watches the golf players on the adjacent course. This first scene and its images establish the mood and the basic situation of the novel: the idiot looks through the fence into the golf course, laid out on land which was sold in order to pay for Quentin Compson's Harvard education. He hears the players call for their caddie, and this sound, mistaken for the name of his sister Caddy, evokes a string of memories which start with that other symbolic scene, when on that evening of the grandmother's death in 1898 Caddy climbs a tree in order to look into the room and tell the other children what is going on. She is the only one with enough guts to do this, and in the proceedings she gets her pants dirty.

Caddy, although not represented directly with her thoughts and feelings, is the central figure in this novel. She is one of 'the two lost women' (together with her daughter Quentin) Faulkner said he wrote the novel about, and according to another quotation, she is 'his heart's darling'. She emerges from the chapters of her brothers as a moving, lovable and pathetic character: the figure of a twentieth-century girl lost between tradition and freedom. Southern tradition, which worshipped at the altar of the pure woman, has become too weak and too empty to support her; modern freedom she is too weak or too sensuous to sustain. In her and her daughter's fate Faulkner has centred the theme of dislocation of love which is basic to the whole novel. The two women get 'lost' because they are unable to focus and define their love. It is love out of balance or a disproportion of love, of the ability to love or to accept love, which is at the root of the family's decline. Jason Richmond Compson, the father, is unable to convert the understanding and sympathy he feels for his children into helpful guidance; his wife is a neurotic whose self-centredness greatly contributes to the family's disintegration. Among the children, Benjy is capable of recognizing his sister Caddy's kindness and attention, but being an idiot he is unable to express his own feelings for her except by a pathetic bellowing and moaning. In the two other sons, Quentin and Jason, disproportion of love is, as it is for Caddy, linked to the larger disproportions of the time. Quentin is gifted with extraordinary sensibility, but he is emotionally so locked within the walls of family and tradition – both of which are incapable of satisfying his high expectations – that he is unable to accept the progression of time which propels him into adult life. On the day of his chapter, 2 June 1910, he commits suicide when he realizes that by his refusal he has also betrayed his own code of honour and ideals; he has intensified his childhood attachment to Caddy into incestuous fantasies.

In contrast to his brother Quentin, Jason only too well understands the spirit of the time. The third chapter of the novel is the monologue to a colossal egomania which feeds on the materialistic allurements of the time. Jason has, however, little luck in his stock-market speculations, and in the end, for all his trickery, he is the dupe as his niece gets away with the money which he in turn embezzled by keeping it from his family. He is a man incapable of love and therefore entirely corrupt, cynical and barren. In having barred his sister Caddy from her home and in driving away her illegitimate child, his niece Quentin – named by Caddy after her brother who committed suicide three months before the child was born – Jason has completed the disintegration of the house of

Compson, which had been one of the prominent families at the time of the Civil War.

Dilsey alone is capable of a well-balanced love, even in the highest form of disinterested love. She humours Mr Compson's inane complaints and caprices, she takes care of Benjy, she defends Caddy and her unhappy daughter. On 8 April, 1928, she takes Benjy with her to attend the Easter Sunday Service where a black minister preaches on a sentence derived from Revelations: 'I got the recollection and the blood of the lamb.' She is deeply moved and it is evident that she alone of all the characters in *The Sound and the Fury* is able to understand and respond to the supreme form of love, the divine love of Christ for sinful man.

Dilsey made no sound, her face did not quiver as the tears took their sunken and devious courses, walking with her head up, making no effort to dry them away even. 'Whyn't you quit dat, mammy?' Frony said. 'Wid all dese people lookin. We be passin white folks soon.'

'I've seed de first en de last,' Dilsey said. 'Never you mind me.'

This account of Faulkner's great novel has concentrated on main aspects of form and meaning; it could not do justice to Faulkner's sovereignty of inventing, placing and connecting images and motives. After all, the really decisive endowment of a literary genius remains unexplainable: the supreme quality of the imagination, namely the power to create characters, situations and events which are the unique, exact and absolutely convincing projections of his intentions. They not only convince us of their true existence but at the same time expand our awareness of the possibilities of life.

When asked which was his favourite novel, Faulkner sometimes named *As I Lay Dying*. It was written in six weeks and Faulkner claimed that he did not change a word of the original draft. Again, it is a novel about a family, this time of poor white farmers from the hill country around Jefferson. Thus, their life is outside the grander dimensions of history. As in *The Sound and the Fury*, Faulkner attempts to get at the very core of action by seeking it in the immediate experience of the participants. *As I Lay Dying* is the story of Addie Bundren's burial and it is reported in rotation by fifteen persons, the members of her family who perform this difficult enterprise, and by some friends and outsiders who watch the much impeded procession. More than in any other novel, Faulkner here gives free reign to his strong sense of the paradoxes and incongruities of human existence. The novel's cumbersome action is set in motion by an immobilized dying woman whose putrescent corpse dominates the procession which forms the plot of the novel. This dominion of the terrible, however, is counterpoised by the urgent, the petty or the merely ridiculous matters of life.

To Addie Bundren 'living was terrible' and to be alive was merely a duty. She has given sons and a daughter to her husband, and one son to a lover, but has remained a stranger in her family, isolated by a deeper, more demanding sense of life and the knowledge that true understanding is unattainable. Words to her are 'just a shape to fill a lack'. 'I would think how words go straight up to a thin line, quick and harmless, and how terrible doing goes along the earth, clinging to it, so that after a while the two lines are too far apart for the same person to straddle from one to the other.' She has accepted her father's credo that 'the reason for living was to get ready to stay dead a long time', and it is in a rebellious effort to give meaning to an otherwise meaningless or unfathomable universe that she requests her family to bring her body to Jefferson and bury her there. The procession from the hills to the town is a ritual enactment of this belief. Anse Bundren and his sons and daughter are called to consecrate her long stay in death by a long and toilsome journey which by its very pains and troubles attests to the power of death in life.

The members of the family are thus asked to engage on a quest which to common-sense opinion is absurd and almost impossible to fulfil. The Bundrens carry their burden through water, flood and heat. The corpse is almost more difficult to preserve than life: it has to be rescued from fire and annihilation and maintained through ordeals of odour and ridicule. In keeping their promise to the dead woman and interring her body at the prescribed place, the family has shared in a quest of mythic proportions. They have accepted the task not only as a duty of piety but as a symbolic action in which man achieves dignity by expressing in toil and troubles his sense of life and death.

If this describes the heroic aspect of the undertaking, there is also an all-too-human side. Faulkner has imposed the task on ordinary, poor and naïvely selfish people, that is, on the common man who is the true protagonist of American democracy. The result is a mixture of primitive–heroic with grotesquely comic elements; of the ridiculous and the sublime, the pathetic and the extraordinary. This mixture is a true expression of Faulkner's view of life. It was not his intention in this novel, as some critics submit, to present human existence as an absurd joke, but to give an exemplum which shows 'fragile man trying to do the best he can in a universe put together

by coincidence'. In this effort, man's most essential quality is endurance, his capacity for suffering, his patience and persistence.
Without these qualities he would not have survived in history,
because he is also stupid, stubborn and inclined to all sorts of
caprices and dissipations.

No Southern writer can ignore the largest, indeed the determining factor in the social life of his region: the issue of black
and white. It is present in almost everything Faulkner has written
and he confronted it full-force in his two great novels *Light in
August* (1932) and *Absalom, Absalom!* (1936). During the last years
before his death he was sometimes accused of advocating an unduly
slow progress toward desegregation. Actually, he had never been so
much concerned with the political as with the human aspect of the
problem; but this he illuminated with unequalled penetration and
sympathy.

The South, Faulkner suggests, is primarily a state of mind; at
least, that is how he presents it in *Light in August*. In this novel, the
mental landscape of the South is portioned into three separate fields
on which operate representatives of three different attitudes
towards life. Two of the attitudes are plainly obsessions, represented by male characters as main protagonists. It is the obsession with
the past, the defeat of the South, which freezes the Reverend
Hightower into mental and emotional stagnation, and it is the
obsession with blood or race, the victims of which are Joe Christmas, the man under suspicion of Negro blood, and, in a reverse
sense, Joanna Burden, the white philanthropist, which result in
violence and murder. The third attitude contrasts with the other
two in almost every respect: it is a feminine one, represented by the
humble and patient Lena Grove (supported by the gentle Byron
Bunch), who is concerned solely with bringing forth and preserving
life.

Faulkner has explained that the cryptic title of this novel refers to
Lena: she is 'light in August' when she gives birth to her child. As
the novel opens Lena Grove, nine months pregnant, is walking from
Alabama to Jefferson in search of the father of her child. In
Jefferson she is referred to Byron Bunch whose name resembles
that of her faithless lover; she finds in him a kind and helpful
companion. As they meet, the fire can be seen which signals that the
final phase of Joe Christmas's life has begun. He has killed his
benefactress and mistress Joanna Burden and has put fire to the
mansion which her grandfather, Calvin Burden, built when he came
during the period of Reconstruction to help the Negro to be free.

Joe Christmas's life has been an alternation of anguish and violence. Born under the suspicion of Negro blood, he is consequently condemned to an orphanage where he is named Christmas for the day of his arrival. Raised by a religious fanatic, he is continuously prevented from achieving his identity. The powers which wrench this life from a sane and natural course and drive a sensitive mind into violence have an evil alliance with religion, more specifically with various creeds derived from the stern Calvinist conviction of election or damnation. *Light in August* gives a whole spectrum of such beliefs and their effects on the minds of followers. It confirms this role of religion in Southern society when Joe Christmas is finally cornered in the house of the Reverend Gail Hightower whose faith has degenerated into absolute sterility because it has become fixed on a battle scene from the Civil War. In the minister's house he is emasculated and killed by his pursuer. His death is horribly elevated to a crucifixion which opens the hope towards salvation and resurrection, as his life had borne resemblance to the passion of Christ:

He just lay there, with his eyes open and empty of everything save consciousness, and with something, a shadow, about his mouth. For a long moment he looked up at them with peaceful and unfathomable and unbearable eyes. Then his face, body, all, seemed to collapse, to fall in upon itself, and from out the slashed garments about his hips and loins the pent black blood seemed to rush like a released breath. It seemed to rush out of his pale body like the rush of sparks from a rising rocket; upon that black blast the man seemed to rise soaring into their memories forever and ever. (p 407)

Since the characters of his novels had a living existence in Faulkner's imagination, he allowed some of his favourites to appear in more than one novel. Quentin Compson, the over-sensitive hero from *The Sound and the Fury*, was revived to serve as protagonist in *Absalom, Absalom!* Yet the reader must be warned that a character only exists in one novel; the Quentin of *Absalom, Absalom!* is in subtle ways different from that Quentin who loved his sister in *The Sound and the Fury* and consequently committed suicide.

After the straight narrative progression of *Light in August*, *Absalom, Absalom!* is once more a staggeringly difficult novel, characterized by involutions of narrative structure which express corresponding complexities of meaning. In this novel, Faulkner took up the challenge of history full scale. History had loomed in the background since he had begun to write about Yoknapatawpha;

it had cast its shadow on Bayard Sartoris and Quentin Compson, grandsons of Civil War heroes. In *Absalom, Absalom!* (1936) Faulkner started his story in the year 1833, and carried it through Civil War and Reconstruction into the twentieth century. Already between 1934 and 1936 he had published a number of short stories from the Civil War which later became chapters of *The Unvanquished* (1938). Their hero, Bayard Sartoris, is grandfather 'Old Bayard' of *Sartoris* rejuvenated: Faulkner had moved his characters back into the history which formed them. *The Unvanquished*, one of Faulkner's slighter novels, still in the tradition of Southern patriotism, with a slightly ironical touch celebrates the bravery and ingenuity of the weak, of women and children, *vis-à-vis* adversity.

Absalom, Absalom! is of a completely different cast: it is an intense search of conscience into the materials of history. In this novel, the challenge which history poses to the American imagination has been wholly accepted. The opening scene of *Absalom, Absalom!* – Quentin Compson summoned to Miss Rosa Coldfield who wishes to tell him her story – illustrates just this: the American imagination, represented by Quentin, is forced to take up the challenge of history, imposed on him by Miss Rosa. Quentin is both eager and afraid to invade this dark and haunted land, history, in order to find out what happened to Thomas Sutpen and his family in and around the time of the Civil War. Thus, innocence, the American mind in meditation, sets out to investigate guilt, brought about by the will in action.

But *Absalom, Absalom!* deals not only with Southern history; it is concerned with history in an even more comprehensive way. *Absalom, Absalom!* is immensely complex, for it is two kinds of novel at once: a 'historical novel' and, at the same time, a novel about history as an epistemological problem. As a novel of history it is about the South, the Civil War, or, more specifically, about the fate of Thomas Sutpen, who tried to become a plantation owner and the father of a dynasty, establishing himself among the social elite of the South. As a novel about history, *Absalom, Absalom!* discusses history as a problem of the mind: as a composite of experience, of immediate participation, of the records and reporting of this experience and participation, of transmitted tales, confessions, documents, monuments and, finally, as an artefact of imagination. This second novel within the novel is represented by Quentin Compson's effort to reconstruct the story of what happened to Thomas Sutpen, and why Sutpen's son Henry shot his friend Charles Bon at the gate of Sutpen's Hundred when they came back from the war.

Consequently, the novel has two protagonists: Thomas Sutpen and Quentin Compson, who are two generations apart and who have never met because Sutpen was killed more than twenty years before Quentin was born. It also has two plots: one around the man of action (and history), Thomas Sutpen; the other around the man of thought (and historian), Quentin Compson. In this bi-focal structure, the historian is in the foreground. On a September afternoon of the year 1909 Rosa Coldfield summons Quentin and tells him her story:

Because she wants it told, he thought, so that people whom she will never see and whose names she will never hear and who have never heard her name nor seen her face will read it and know at last why God let us lose the war . . .

But as Rosa tells her story, which is mainly that of Sutpen, Quentin discovers that she burdens him with an apocalyptic version of the past, in which Sutpen appears as the great monster, the beast. Rosa is a witness, a participant in the events of history, and as that a primary source, but also, and because of that, a partial witness and a doubtful historical source.

It thus becomes Quentin's task to check, complete and re-check the story of Thomas Sutpen, who in the year 1833 suddenly appeared in Jefferson; bought land for a plantation which he called 'Sutpen's Hundred'; built a mansion, married Ellen Coldfield, a sister of Rosa, and had two children with her, Judith and Henry. Judith wants to marry Charles Bon, a friend of Henry; Sutpen prevents the marriage; Henry Sutpen renounces his father and goes to war with Bon. When they return from the war, Henry shoots Bon at the entrance to Sutpen's Hundred and disappears. Sutpen begins to restore his war-ravaged property and attempts to have another son; he is killed by a farm labourer whose daughter has a daughter by Sutpen and is rejected by him. These are the bare outlines which emerge from Quentin's efforts in reconstructing the events of history: from the reports he has from Rosa and then from his father, who tells him what he in turn got from his father, General Compson, who was a friend of Sutpen. General Compson tells his son what he knows about Rosa, what he learned from the town people about Sutpen, and finally what Sutpen himself told him. The story which emerges is that of a great design: Sutpen, a son of poor hill-country farmers who migrated into the rich river-bottom land, decides to become a plantation owner and establish his family among the society of the South, but is defeated in this ambitious plan. The story, derived from so many different reports, still contains blank spots, which Quentin together with his father unsuccessfully tries to fill out by ingenious conjectures. It remains a mystery why Sutpen prevents his daughter's marriage with Bon and why Henry shoots his friend, until Quentin learns that Bon is Sutpen's son from an earlier marriage. As a son who is part Negro he is unable to serve in Sutpen's grandiose scheme of founding a plantation dynasty and is therefore rejected by his father. With this information Charles Bon emerges from the obscurity which surrounded him. Thus, his role in the scheme of things has to be established. Quentin undertakes this new and unexpected task when on a wintry day in Cambridge, Massachusetts, together with a Canadian friend he re-examines the Sutpen story. For lack of reports or other sources, the two historians in their effort to reconstruct what cannot be known by historical research have to rely on empathy and imagination.

As the result of their joint speculations and conjectures, justice is finally done to Charles Bon as a historical figure and a tragic character. They discover in him the true counterpart to Sutpen: the abandoned son who at the risk, and indeed the loss, of his life tried to provoke his father into recognizing him as the eldest son and heir. Sutpen's refusal of recognition reveals the guilt inherent in his great enterprise. As he renounced his eldest son, he not only failed as an empire builder but also morally as a human being. In this failure he is inescapably linked with Southern society and its refusal to recognize the black man as a human being: a society which went to war in order to preserve the moral shame of slavery and paid for it with defeat.

In completing the story of Thomas Sutpen's rise and fall Quentin has also ended, even transcended, his historiographic activity. It is only by empathy and imagination, even by identification with the unhappy son of Sutpen, that Quentin is able to rescue Bon's tragic fate from oblivion. Thus, in this supreme effort to solve the mysteries of history, the historian has to transform himself into seer, poet. In regard to the innermost secrets, to the lost motifs of history, the historian like the writer has to rely on his imagination and his knowledge of the human heart: the historian becomes artist.

Since the early thirties, Faulkner had published in magazines short stories which he collected into various volumes and finally into a comprehensive edition of *Collected Stories* (1950). Grouped according to place and time – they appear under the six headings 'The Country', 'The Village', 'The Wilderness', 'The Wasteland',

'The Middle Ground' and 'Beyond' – they testify to the inner coherence of Faulkner's imaginative world. Unlike Hemingway, Faulkner was not greatly interested in the form and technique of the short story. He therefore did not experiment with it, nor try to reform or innovate the genre. His short stories are part of his activity as a story teller and thus share in the fictional projects of his imagination. Many of his favourite characters first appeared in short narratives to be later developed at greater scope in his novels; several of his short stories have been incorporated into novels.

Go Down, Moses of 1942 shows how Faulkner in his later years developed and completed themes and characters which had occupied his imagination for some time. Five of its seven chapters had already appeared as short stories and were now incorporated into a larger unit which Faulkner rightly regarded as a novel. Since its chapters retain high independence as separate stories, *Go Down, Moses* should perhaps be called a short-story novel. Not, however, in the sense of a compromise of convenience: there is a definite gain in this unusual form, for the individuality of the chapters greatly extends the scope and possibilities of the novel's grasp on life. If Faulkner is not an experimenter in the short form of fiction, he very much is one in respect to the novel, indeed one of the most daring and most successful in this country. Each of his great novels – *The Sound and the Fury, As I Lay Dying, Light in August, Absalom, Absalom!* – was an experiment in form and a unique achievement in the realization of particular themes.

Go Down, Moses is in a sense a companion piece to *Absalom, Absalom!*, but at the same time another and very different attempt to deal with the Southern reality of land, family and the plantation as a form of life. The Sartorises, the Compsons, and Thomas Sutpen had already figured in this complex of themes. Now the McCaslins and their entourage were added to the great families of Yoknapatawpha County. As in *Absalom, Absalom!*, this calls for the dimension of history. Here is a family extending over several generations; it is a plantation dynasty which has a white as well as a black lineage. This seems to necessitate epic breadth and an involved plot. But Faulkner knew that the old plot structure of the nineteenth-century novel was dead and could only be used at a loss. It was exactly in order to escape the artificialities of plot and the danger of being trapped into a bulky, crammed family history that Faulkner chose to present his material in this way. In doing so, he did not introduce a completely new idea but modified the form which had been applied already by Turgenev for a very similar purpose in his *Sportsman's Diary* (1851) and had been used in different ways in this century by writers like Sherwood Anderson for his *Winesburg, Ohio* (1919) and Ernest Hemingway for *In Our Time* (1925). The self-contained unit of the short story within the novel permitted Faulkner to range from the comic to the tragic, from the present back into pre-historic times, and to present the white McCaslins as well as their black cousins in their specific characters, ambitions and mode of existence.

Again, the reader is made to do part of the work. Relations and connections between characters, their position in time and context, are often only given by slight hints from which the reader has to get his bearings in genealogy and family history. *Go Down, Moses* deals with the moral abomination of slavery and the human entanglements which result from it. In this novel Faulkner illuminates the problem of black and white in Southern society as a close-knit destiny of blood brotherhood. Lucius Quintus Carothers McCaslin, the founder of the dynasty, has produced black as well as white descendants. The amorality of slavery has led him to commit incest with his own black daughter; her grandson Lucas Quintus Carothers McCaslin Beauchamp claims his share in the McCaslin property, which for lack of male white descendants in later decades has passed to a female line. It is actually the black descendant Lucas Beauchamp, by incest twice a McCaslin, who in his pride and will-power most closely resembles his white ancestor. In him, a strong self-esteem is coupled with business shrewdness, which, however, because of racial restrictions is forced into clandestine enterprises, even, literally, underground. He operates a whiskey still and digs for hidden gold treasure. At the same time, he powerfully asserts his manhood to his white cousins, a secretly respected member of the clan. The ancestor's one white grandson, Isaac McCaslin, on the other hand, is a much humbler person, a sensitive young man, afflicted by self-doubt and the scruples of conscience, so that when coming of age he repudiates his inheritance for its burden of sin. He takes upon himself his grandfather's guilt and comes to realize:

They are better than we are. Stronger than we are. Their vices are vices aped from white men or that white men and bondage have taught them: improvidence and intemperance and evasion – no laziness: evasion: of what white men had set them to, not for their aggrandisement or even comfort but his own –. (p 294)

Isaac McCaslin is the protagonist of 'The Bear', the book's longest and most complex story of almost short-novel dimensions, in which the view is extended beyond history, to the beginnings, to mythic time. A hunting story about shooting an old crafty bear, fierce symbol of the timeless freedom of the wilderness, is expanded into an epitome of human history. The hunting party moves back to primeval time and to the sources of life when it invades the forest:

... that doomed wilderness whose edges were being constantly and punily gnawed at by men with plows and axes who feared it because it was wilderness, men myriad and nameless even to one another in the land where the old bear had earned a name, and through which ran not even a mortal beast but an anachronism indomitable and invincible out of an old dead time, a phantom, epitome and apotheosis of the old wild life which the little puny humans swarmed and hacked at in a fury of abhorrence and fear like pygmies about the ankles of a drowsing elephant; – the old bear, solitary, indomitable, and alone; widowered childless and absolved of mortality – old Priam reft of his old wife and outlived all his sons.

'The Bear' is written from God's perspective of human life, and from this august perspective Southern history is a parable of human history and part of its recurring pattern of greed, conquest, dominion and destruction. Isaac McCaslin recognizes that the plantation land was already cursed by rapacity before his grandfather bought it from an Indian chief; he reads the big ledger of the plantation as a 'chronicle which was a whole land in miniature'. It is the book of God's reckoning with the people to whom he promised a new land – a land they tainted with the curse of injustice and slavery.

If history shows a repetitive pattern of rise and fall and the recurrent rise of newcomers by ambition and greed, the twentieth century must have its own kind of empire builders. Faulkner had been aware of this new type of man from the beginning of his writing career. In his imaginary region they appear as the Snopeses, a clan of traders, sharecroppers or bank clerks (as Byron Snopes in *Sartoris*) who prefer the monetary trades because it is with money instead of land that they make their fortune. They are much less likable than their predecessors who, for all their failings, had established and maintained standards of honour, generosity and pride. Members of the the Snopes family had already appeared in several of Faulkner's earlier works and in *The Hamlet* (1940) they finally invade Yoknapatawpha in full force.

Their entrance is well chosen: they reach Jefferson by way of the 'hamlet' Frenchman's Bend which lies between the hill country of the poor whites and the rich land of the plantations around

Jefferson: a region of small farmers without Negroes which is ruled by Will Varner who owns the store, most of the good land, and holds mortgages on most of the rest. Faulkner is always precise in laying the social and economic foundations. It is by their reputation as arsonists that the Snopeses bully their way into Varner's dominion. Flem Snopes, the most coldly rapacious of the tribe, establishes himself as clerk in Varner's store. He marries Varner's daughter Eula who is with child by another man, not in order to start a family but only as a step on the social and financial ladder towards power in Jefferson.

Perhaps this sterile marriage of Flem Snopes and Eula Varner is almost too patently symbolic to be absolutely convincing: the man without any feeling but with an uncanny sense of money is impotent; he marries the woman of supreme passion and irresistible sexual attraction, Eula, the fertility goddess of Frenchman's Bend, whose life is blighted by this marriage. This is not so much a problem in *The Hamlet* as in its lesser sequels *The Town* (1957) and *The Mansion* (1959). In *The Hamlet* the Snopes story is only one in a number of tales – grotesque, earthy, raucously funny (as in the story about the 'Spotted Horses'), and touching or tragic; in the later volumes the Snopeses are the main protagonists. In *The Town* Flem Snopes rises in Jefferson to bank president and owner of an antebellum mansion, while Eula becomes involved in a love affair and commits suicide; in *The Mansion* Flem is killed in revenge for his treachery, by a member of his own clan who by this act destroys a life which is a monstrous monument to the unmitigated acquisitive qualities of man.

Faulkner's first novel after the Second World War was *Intruder in the Dust* (1948) which continues the career of Lucas Beauchamp from *Go Down, Moses*. This proud and aristocratic black man, who is one of Faulkner's most admirable characters, comes under suspicion of murder, from which he is rescued by the joint efforts of a boy, Chick Mallison, and an old spinster. This very readable but slight work, a detective novel in which the good party is in the end gloriously exonerated and victorious, was taken by some as a political pronouncement of the author: Faulkner's favourite lawyer, Gavin Stevens, always advocate of the good and innocent – he helped to save Lucas Beauchamp from a lynch mob and in the Snopes trilogy served as Eula's friend and adviser – advances the claim that the South should be allowed to solve its problems in its own time.

Gavin Stevens also figures in *Requiem for a Nun* (1951), an experiment in form which combines dramatic dialogue with narrated sections. This novel continues the story of Temple Drake from Faulkner's early shocker *Sanctuary* (1931). Once more it is evident how characters live and develop in Faulkner's imagination in order to carry new meaning. In the sensational earlier novel the spoiled girl 'Temple' Drake, symbolically representing the South, was raped with a corn cob by the impotent criminal Popeye, and under his influence sank into complete moral corruption. In *Requiem for a Nun* her child is murdered by her Negro maid; under the impact of this tragic loss she finally becomes ready to face her moral eresponsibilities.

The magnum opus of Faulkner's later years undoubtedly is *A Fable*, the only work of his later period which moves outside the territory of Yoknapatawpha: a philosophical book and a great allegory of human history. *A Fable*'s involved allegorical plot is concentrated on a week in the spring of 1918 when a French regiment in the front lines during the First World War, led by a corporal and his twelve disciples, decides to lay down arms and refuses to attack. With this refusal they rebel against the power of the military, led by the Supreme Commander, and try to do their duty towards achieving peace on earth. It is thus a dualism between a party of peace, represented by the corporal as the leader and the meek and simple men, and a party of war, led by the Supreme Commander, which is the party of the ambitious and the conquerors, to which belong the founders of state, the creators of art and the promoters of civilization and scientific progress. Human achievement, always so inextricably mixed with human weakness in Faulkner's Yoknapatawpha world, has here been isolated from the amiable qualities of humility, patience and endurance. The corporal, a reincarnation of Christ in our century, has his antithesis in the Supreme Commander, who is his father and unsuccessfully tries to win him over to the party of authority and power. The corporal is executed for his rebellious activity, but his body is 'resurrected' by an explosion and finally buried in the grave of the Unknown Soldier in Paris. Human existence, Faulkner tells us, is ruled by the dualism of the meek and the rapacious, and both of them have their share in the history of the race.

For all its serious and honest engagement in the cause of humanity, *A Fable* is not one of Faulkner's most convincing achievements. His creative potentialities did not so much respond to theoretical impulses and considerations as to the concreteness of life seen and experienced. His truly original vision of life was not a matter of allegorical construction but of imaginative condensation. The fictions of Yoknapatawpha County were filtered from real events, memories, stories told at the family gatherings or at county drug-stores. Thus, Yoknapatawpha remains his unique territory of which he is not only 'sole proprietor' but sovereign king.

When at the University of Virginia Faulkner was asked, apparently in reference to his Nobel Prize speech, 'Mr. Faulkner, when you say man has prevailed do you mean individual man has prevailed or group man?' Faulkner replied: 'Man as a part of life.' This is a basic law in Faulkner's universe.

8

AMERICAN THEATRE SINCE 1945

Irving Wardle

When the American theatre returned to peacetime business in 1945 its situation in some ways resembled that of the British theatre after the Puritan Revolution. A link had been cut. The pre-war play-wrights (with the stupendous exception of O'Neill) had shot their bolt, and were now either slowing down or silent – fled to Hollywood, like Odets; institutionalized, like Archibald MacLeish; or writing sour accounts of what went wrong in the thirties, like Elmer Rice. As Robert Ardrey said, looking back on the time, 'It was as if the band of playwrights who had created a broad vital theater in the twenties and thirties had never returned from the war.'

Things were no better in the sphere of theatre organization. Broadway continued on its accustomed course, marked by the contrary spirals of mounting costs and collapsing buildings: but there was little sign of the energetic counter-force which had opposed 'Trade theatre' in the previous decades. Its two strongest champions both died at the outbreak of war: the Federal Theater Project, killed by Congress in 1939; and the Group Theater, dis-rupted by internal cliques in 1941. The fervent years were over, and in their wake came only real estate and manifestos – on one hand New York's City Center of Music and Drama, opened in 1944 and housing 'icetravaganzas'; and on the other (in 1946) the short-lived American Repertory Company (founded by Cheryl Crawford, Eva Le Gallienne and Margaret Webster) which went broke within a couple of years, and the abortive scheme of the American National Theater and Academy (ANTA) to establish forty regional centres for professional performance.

Fifth-century Athens excepted, war is always bad for the theatre. In this case, the impact of Pearl Harbor was to intensify the 42nd Street policy of happy shows for people, and to bring social and psychological inquiry to a halt. Morale had to be kept up. The dramatists who rose to the top were Thornton Wilder and William Saroyan who applied their considerable skills to putting over the idea that no matter how lousy things may look all will be well in the end. It was also the war that gave birth to the modern musical, inaugurated by *Oklahoma!* which had a solid run from 1943 to 1948, and launched the still potent mirage of a national art form in which the American theatre could find its soul without any sacrifice at the box office.

If the war stunted theatrical growth, its atomic aftermath proved no less hostile. The declension from the thirties to the mid-fifties can be traced in the career of a popular writer like Irwin Shaw who made his debut in 1936 with *Bury the Dead* – a pacifist fantasy, hailed at the time as 'better than Odets', about six dead soldiers who refuse to be buried and march off against those who had sent them out to be killed. Leaving the theatre, he produced his heroic war novel, *The Young Lions*; and then, early in the fifties, his deeply pessimistic *The Troubled Air*, showing an allegedly 'controversial' hero progressively stripped of his job and his family by the poisonous climate of the time. Shaw's hero is a mass-communications man, and his fate, proclaiming the impossibility of heroism, reflects that of the Hollywood Ten, the Seattle Six, and the many other demoralized survivors of the fervent years whose past drove them into silence or aesthetic and personal betrayal from the beginning of the Cold War to the downfall of Joseph McCarthy in 1954.

Earlier in the century, the American theatre had passed through phases of Labour, Federal, repertory and regional organization: perhaps not achieving anything to stand comparison with the great European companies, but presenting continuous opposition to the commercial system and sustained by powerful ideals of what the theatre could be. You get this visionary aspiration at full strength, say, in George Cram Cook's 1916 manifesto for the Provincetown Players, who launched O'Neill; or in the white-hot reporting of Kenneth MacGowan and Robert Edmond Jones, passing on the gospel of Continental stagecraft to American readers in the twenties: 'It is hard to escape the belief that this ferment means something. ... Something immensely important to the sense of godhead in man which is life and art together, and life and art fecundating one another.' Nobody spoke like that during the period under review: the period of the 'silent generation' when the general spirit of faceless social conformity was matched by timidity inside the theatre – not only in Broadway's readiness to let its scripts be vetted in advance by the Play of the Month Guild, but also in the country's booming university theatre programmes (growing at an annual rate of 20 per cent to a total of 7000 courses involving over 15,000 students by 1966), with their productions of *Auntie Mame* and *Brigadoon*; and where visiting lecturers like Herbert Blau found aspirant professionals to be mainly interested in salaries and working conditions.

Reduced to its simplest terms, the situation marked a tyranny of 'professionalism' in the most blinkered sense. Opposition theatre, frozen up since the outbreak of war, had no living link with the post-war scene (except in the case of Elia Kazan, the one major director to survive with full creative vigour); while Broadway – relying increasingly on outside backers to foot the bill for inflated star salaries, union featherbedding, and soaring midcity rents – was passing more and more into the hands of the yahoos. Taken together, these two factors seem to form a deadly equation. However, Broadway is always escaping death with the assurance of a serial heroine roped to the railway track; and if its theatres have dwindled from eighty in the pre-talkie golden age to barely thirty in the mid-sixties, it can still offer its investors a handsome return or a useful tax deduction. (One survey estimates that an investor who supported all the shows between 1948 and 1958 would have profited by 19.5 per cent a year.) As for the opposition theatre, it is a rule – applying equally to Europe and America – that the most influential work is often begun under the most hopeless conditions: a fact acknowledged in Herbert Blau's memoir of the San Francisco Actors' Workshop, *The Impossible Theater*. Blau's organization, along with others that have taken root outside the world of ticket-scalping and star-billing, was begun in poverty and run by near-amateur enthusiasts (like the Vieux-Colombier and the Moscow Art Theatre). In their two decades of life they have established a powerful counter-atmosphere, far richer and more varied than the social theatre of the thirties: it presents a spectrum bounded at one end by purely sensory events deriving from graphic art and the drug experience, and at the other by the passionately political work of the Black Arts theatre network, and the agit-prop *commedia* of the San Francisco Mime Troupe and the Californian Teatro Campesino (whose main purpose is to incite strikes among the Mexican-American grape-pickers). Although these developments often took place under the shadow of European cultural models, there has been a strong positive feedback, and at the end of the sixties America was a more pervasive presence in the European theatre than ever before. In surveying the period it is an advantage at least to the writer that most of this work started from scratch.

Playwrights are not the heroes of the story, but the post-war theatre got off to a resounding bang with the arrival of two of the best playwrights the country has ever produced: Tennessee Williams and Arthur Miller. They appeared almost instantaneously: Williams with *The Glass Menagerie* in 1945; and Miller a year later with *All My Sons*. Both moved straight on to Broadway and have stayed there ever since. Bracketed together as eternal opposites, Miller and Williams invite all kinds of dualistic comparison: North and South; the intellect and the senses; social and personal; tribunal and confession; male and female. In some general way they do occupy antithetical positions, but most of the detailed contrasts break down under examination; for instance, the 'feminine' Williams excels in the creation of male animals; and the whole range of American drama has no more nakedly personal confession to offer than the socially-conscious Miller's *After the Fall*. Looked at in the twenty-year perspective, the differences between the two writers are less important than their similarities.

Both grew up in the Depression and underwent the common collapse of family fortunes. Miller's father lost a sizeable clothes-manufacturing business in Brooklyn, and Miller paid his way to college by working for two years in an automobile-parts warehouse; Williams, when troubles overtook his hated salesman father, was transplanted from rural Mississippi to a St Louis slum (producing 'a shock and rebellion that have grown into an inherent part of my work'). Both established some contact with the pre-war progressive theatre: Miller by leaving college to work with the Federal Theater Project; and Williams by collecting a Group Theater prize in 1939 for *American Blues*. And in a curious way, each suggests a character that the other might have created. Just as the marriage of Miller the intellectual to Marilyn Monroe might have furnished Williams with a plot, so Williams's solitary fugitive life illustrates Miller's preoccupation with those (like the hero of *Focus*) who barricade themselves from the world.

The world, for both men, is the American world. Williams may use exotic settings, but they serve to lend magnification and intensity to local themes. Miller, even more, is attached to his own place and time: when he discusses his work he only talks about European influences – but for him, Ibsen seems to have been filtered through Sidney Kingsley and Lillian Hellman, just as

'German' Expressionism seems to have reached him via Elmer Rice and John Howard Lawson. (Nowhere does Miller show himself more provincial than in pieces like *After the Fall* and *Incident at Vichy* where he attempts to escape his national boundaries and speak for the whole of Western civilization.)

The correct, if question-begging, explanation of these two writers' pre-eminence in the post-war theatre is that they had more talent than anyone else of their generation. But their talent is inseparable from their attunement to the mood of the time. Both children of the thirties, they shared an ability to articulate what many Americans were feeling – and any playwright who can do that acquires a mesmeric hold over his audience. What they managed to capture was a turning point in national consciousness: a move from confidence to doubt. In the land of success, they wrote, obsessively, about the unsuccessful; they met the entrenched myth of virility with sexual ambiguities, and showed the solid conformist majority as self-cheating automata with the potentialities of a brutal mob. In this respect, the difference between them is mainly one of degree. Miller, still with a stake in the old socialist faith, surveys the immediate scene against the distant vision of the just city, and his indignation stems from the assumption that men could act better than they do. No such faith colours Williams's view of society which is shown simply as a jungle – either overshadowing the background (like the shoe-factory in *The Glass Menagerie*) or embodied in such mammoth-like characters as the Gooper family in *Cat on a Hot Tin Roof* and Boss Finley in *Sweet Bird of Youth*. Accordingly Miller's heroes are those who stand their ground; and Williams's are those who respond to their hopeless environment by taking flight (or, as he put it in *Camino Real*, 'making voyages').

Both postures, however, show the continuation of American tradition shorn of its American certainties: in particular the dream of a lost paradise that haunts Williams's characters in their fragile sanctuaries and runs through Miller's *Death of a Salesman* as an off-stage flute melody. As much as anything, these plays are allegories: quests, however, not so much for a happy land as for a place where the dramatic hero can regain human dignity. Great drama usually sweeps in on a great idea, and even lesser drama finds it hard to function without some organized estimate of man. Previously, drama had had Freud and Marx at its disposal: but, as Robert Ardrey notes, the war years had precipitated human actions 'which could be explained by neither aim-inhibited eroticism nor the weary dialectics of the class struggle'. Ardrey, best known for

Thunder Rock (1939), but also the author of the indignant Civil Rights piece *Jeb* which appeared some twenty years ahead of its time in 1946, himself withdrew from the theatre to seek a new estimate of the human animal in the new biology (whence Territorial Man, the protagonist of *African Genesis* and *The Territorial Imperative*, but not as yet a hero who has made much headway on the American stage). For Williams and Miller the only available figure was the 'little man' of old Expressionist drama and film comedy whose stature had been steadily diminishing since his debut in the aftermath of the First War (a process hastened, according to one source, by the shocking results of a series of mass-scale IQ tests conducted by army induction centres revealing the average American male to possess a mental age of thirteen). Following the Second War, the playwrights' task was somehow to equip Mr Zero with personal identity and significance: and we should wonder not at the contortions through which he was put but the extent to which he did develop these qualities and offer some kind of resistance to the other-directed gigantism of the modern world. Whatever their weaknesses, Williams's outsiders – 'my little company of the faded and frightened the difficult and odd and lonely' – are not sleep-walkers. And while Miller's requiem for Willie Loman may be as wide of the mark as the salesman spectator's remark, 'That New England territory never was any good', Willie himself undoubtedly enforces attention: and when he first appeared, playing to tearfully sympathetic audiences of out-of-town buyers who would doubtless have fired him instantly had he been on their payroll, he must have commanded an almost epic size.

There is another reason for admiring what these playwrights achieved. American drama characteristically prefers action to speech (critics as widely divergent as Walter Kerr and Mary McCarthy have assailed their country's playwrights for verbal poverty and the prevalent habit of running speeches to ground on a row of dots). Yet the post-war theatrical spirit was one of stalemate. How was it possible to reconcile the taste for action with the belief that there was nothing to be done? Miller found one solution in *The Crucible* by commenting on the present from the vantage point of historical melodrama – thus, without any intellectual sacrifice, reviving America's most robust form and returning to a period when heroes could still be heroes. But the usual approach was to construct a plot enmeshing past and present. Technically, this meant superimposing non-realistic devices on an essentially realistic tradition. And the trick was to show vigorous actions taking place between characters whose lives were finished before the curtain went up. A roll-call of the leading characters of the time – Willie Loman, Blanche DuBois, Joe Keller, Maggie the Cat – mainly shows people leading posthumous lives. The same holds good as we move on into the fifties and sixties, with the two office workers ageing thirty years in the course of a single day in Murray Schisgal's *The Typists*; and with George and Martha undergoing their life sentence in the marital torture chamber of Edward Albee's *Who's Afraid of Virginia Woolf?*

These non-realistic devices are all methods of releasing theatrical time from the simple linear chronology of Naturalism. They include Miller's simultaneous expressionism in *Death of a Salesman* and his use of a retrospective tribunal in *A View from the Bridge*; and Williams's dream narratives and compulsive symbolism. There were also borrowings from the cinema, particularly the flashback which in lesser hands produced any number of action-halting scenes showing a character drifting moodily off to gaze through the window and say, 'It wasn't always like this. Do you remember the time when . . .'

The curse of the past was no doubt partly a legacy of O'Neill to America's post-war playwrights. Certainly none of them handled it quite as perfectly as he did in his greatest play, *Long Day's Journey into Night*, which finally reached the stage in 1956, three years after his death. But his successors started something of their own, however encapsulated they may now appear to be within the period of their first success. Miller, antiquated 'good-guy liberal' though he may seem to subsequent critics, succeeded in forging a link between the old social drama and his own more complex and sceptical society, and in restoring moral authority to the stage when it was hardly to be found anywhere else outside the banks. Critics who complain against his contradictions and evasiveness are merely acknowledging the complexity of his task. Williams, the more prophetic writer of the two, exercised a double influence. Robert Ardrey sums it up:

First, he showed that the sympathies and emotions of an audience need not be enlisted to secure the success of a play, but attention may be held by a series of shocks, if only new and more remarkable shocks can be devised to replace old, outworn ones. And second, he demonstrated that any concern for man which may have disturbed the philosophies of the older playwrights was quite unnecessary. A playwright must have his estimate of man, without doubt, but it need contain no concern whatsoever.

The outside factor that contributed most to the success of Williams and Miller (not to mention such lesser playwrights as William Inge, Paddy Chayefsky and Robert Anderson) was the high quality of American Naturalistic acting. Although it was a specifically national style, it derived from a foreign source and provides a classic example of America's repeated attempts to absorb transatlantic cultural models. The creators of the three dominant production styles of modern Europe – Stanislavsky (psychological realism); Copeau (revitalized classicism); and Brecht and Piscator (epic theatre) – had all worked in America and implanted seeds that continued to grow after their departure. Of these, unquestionably the greatest influence was Stanislavsky's: partly through the Moscow Art Theatre's post-Revolutionary tour of America, and partly through the work of three members of the MAT who stayed behind to form the American Laboratory Theater under the leadership of Richard Boleslavsky. Among its pupils in the 1920s were Harold Clurman, Lee Strasberg and Stella Adler who went on to found the Group Theater and apply the Stanislavsky System to the contemporary American repertory. During this process the System somehow got reborn as the 'Method', and by 1937 – according to Clurman – its battle had been won: Method schools (notably Sanford Meisner's Neighborhood Playhouse) were springing up, and an increasing number of leading players, such as Franchot Tone, were making it a part of their normal professional equipment.

However, it still belonged mainly to the experimental scene; and not until after the war did it become fully entrenched on Broadway as the *lingua franca* of American acting. This was the strongest link with the thirties, and it was composed of an indefinable number of separate strands. But at least two of them can be identified. First was the emergence of Elia Kazan from the Group Theater chrysalis to his unchallenged position as Broadway's most powerful post-war director. Second was the formation in 1947, in a disused church on West 44th Street, of the Actors' Studio. Originally it was set up under Kazan, Cheryl Crawford (another Group veteran) and Robert Lewis. At the end of the first season only Miss Crawford survived from the triumvirate, and the studio did not assume its permanent form until the appointment of Strasberg at the end of 1949.

The studio was not designed as a theatre school or as a production unit. It aimed to give actors of proved talent a sanctuary from the commercial theatre where they could exercise their craft in a spirit of aesthetic concentration and continuity. Such a sanctuary was certainly needed; and its rules were sensible and strict. Casting directors were not admitted; members qualified on talent alone, and nobody could butt his way in. Uncontaminated by money or professional influence, it lived up to Kazan's description as 'the one clean place in the theater'.

Under Strasberg, however, the studio became something more than a professional retreat. It also became a shrine to Stanislavsky – or rather to Strasberg's interpretation of him; and as time went by, the church setting became increasingly apt. Studio sessions followed a fixed pattern, in which participating actors would offer a prepared scene, comment on their intentions, and then sit back to hear Strasberg's verdict. The approach remained that of a master-class; but this leaves open the question of whether Strasberg was a master.

His declared purpose was to free the actor to handle his body as a musician handles his instrument; discovering his resources so as to use them at will and understand how to repeat effects. To this end, a great battery of exercises – some Stanislavsky's and some his own – are wheeled into position: sense memory, affective memory, one-word and three-word improvisation, the private moment, animals, gibberish. These can all be strongly defended; but somehow the prospect of public performance retreats further and further into the distance (admittedly the same could be said of Stanislavsky's own work in his final years).

What went wrong? According to Robert Lewis, the studio's failure is that the Method ignores half of the Russian System. In his witty book *Method – Or Madness?* he claims that American Method is based on Stanislavsky's early book *An Actor Prepares* to the exclusion of its sequel *Building a Character* which was not translated until after the war. The central exhibit in Lewis's argument is a tattered chart, dictated by Stanislavsky to Stella Adler in 1934, in which the actor's techniques are laid out in the shape of a pipe organ: one bank of pipes relating to inner processes, and the other to external techniques of expression. The second group, says Lewis, has been ignored by the studio. And the published transcript of its tape-recorded sessions, *Strasberg at the Actors' Studio*, bears him out: there is hardly a word about placement of the voice, external tempo, fencing, acrobatics, dancing, how to walk, or the other external skills on which Stanislavsky laid such stress.

The book exudes a sense of paralysis, in which the personality problems of the actors are exactly matched by rehearsal methods encouraging them to concentrate exclusively on themselves. Here is a characteristic sample:

Strasberg: If the directors knew they could depend on your *mañana* they would let you go, but there is too much *mañana* in the theater that never gets there at all.

H.H.: But if they don't know whether I can do it tomorrow, how can they find out if they won't let me?

Strasberg: That's right. Your talent has not yet been worth it. Why should they?

H.H.: Well, why shouldn't they?

Strasberg: You are a young person just starting in, and you want to work as only a finished actor has the right to work.

H.H.: Right. But should I have two methods? I ask the director, 'Can I do something?' And he doesn't like that. He just says to do it again.

Strasberg: Darling, I don't want to get involved with any experiences you may have had, but I tell you this, since you are speaking personally. You make such a bad impression that no director could possibly have any faith in you.

A formidable number of good actors have thought it worth their while to attend the studio's sessions. Why, one wonders, if they have to sit through that sort of thing. We can discount the crude criticism of Strasberg as a would-be analyst who positively encourages slovenly performance. To a large extent (particularly in the latter days of the studio after its honeymoon phase with Marlon Brando, Julie Harris and Marilyn Monroe), he is the victim of an undeveloped cultural environment: the younger actor's contempt for traditionally disciplined skills in favour of down-to-earth simplicity and guts; and the excessive appeal exerted by intro-spective techniques upon the members of an extrovert society.

The long-term failure of the Method is really that it betrays the aims of Stanislavsky. Instead of developing ensemble companies it bred Broadway stars. And instead of serving as a grammar for the performance of any play, it lent itself entirely to the style of the post-war dramatists, creating a breed of three-dot plays. This was demonstrated by Strasberg's disastrous studio production of Chekhov's *Three Sisters* in 1965 (after which the studio lost its Ford Foundation grant); and by Kazan's Lincoln Center production of Middleton's *The Changeling* in the previous year which drew this comment from Robert Brustein in the *New Republic*:

The blame for this particular event must be spread ... among those who have dictated the direction of our stage for the past twenty-five years. The social–psychological theater of the thirties, which culminated in the Actors' Studio and the Lincoln Center, has now proved itself utterly incompetent to deal with a serious work of the imagination, or anything other than Broadway and Hollywood commodities. And the American theater will never find itself again until all these outmoded methods and limited visions have been swept away.

Brustein delivered this judgment as a prelude to announcing that renewal was already under way at another address: to be exact, at the American Place Theater (another converted church) which was then staging Robert Lowell's *The Old Glory*, a double-bill adapted from stories by Hawthorne and Melville and directed by an Englishman, Jonathan Miller. But when the more substantial of the two pieces, *Benito Cereno*, appeared subsequently in London under the same director, it was hard to see what all the fuss was about. The piece struck British reviewers as a stiffly academic exercise in poetic melodrama: opera, as it were, without music. It was not even an original work. American intellectuals, perhaps, fell for the piece because it was undoubtedly, ostentatiously, literate (its unsuitability for Broadway probably ranked as another point in its favour): and because it marked the attempt of an eminent author to create a serious work from national legend (the plot concerns a Yankee merchant captain's murderous confrontation with the African rebels who have seized command of a Spanish slave ship). American history and myth is a recurring obsession in the period under review: very occasionally it has yielded lasting work like Miller's *The Crucible*; more often it has produced aberrant directionless pieces like Paul Foster's *Tom Paine* and Arthur Kopit's *Indians* (a critical reworking of Wild Western folklore in terms of Buffalo Bill's Wild West Show, which somehow manages to get the white men off the genocide hook). Such plays seem to spring from the American theatre's over-susceptibility to academic theory. Because, say, Greek and Elizabethan theatre rose to greatness by expressing national myth; because Nietzsche recommends it in *The Birth of Tragedy*; then America should follow the same prescription. Obviously, in the largest sense national culture implies a sense of temporal continuity ultimately involving contact with some mythical root. But what we are facing here is something cruder; a symptom of the aspirin society; the idea that a sick theatre can be doctored up by regular dosages of national legend. And also the idea that by this means the theatre can pull itself up by its own bootstraps to the level of the European Olympus.

'Greatness' is the fatal keyword here. And just as heavyweight

American writers, like Hemingway and Mailer, have cast themselves as pugilistic contenders for a world literary championship, so
the champions of the American theatre have thought of knocking
out Mr Shakespeare and Mr Sophocles. The process is seen at its
full absurdity in O'Neill's attempt to take care simultaneously of
Aeschylus and the American Civil War in *Mourning Becomes Electra*.
If this kind of material is often swallowed it is because there is as
strong a hunger for the great American play as for the great
American novel. From all sides, the infant American theatre is
urged on to claim its mighty inheritance. The daily reviewers behave like doting aunts, gushing over every step it takes. 'With this
play the American theater comes of age.' 'In this play the American
theater grows ten feet tall.' Critics like Brustein view the child from
the opposite angle of a headmaster writing ferocious term reports.
Foundations and other private patrons club together for the darling's benefit, setting up bursaries and production schemes for
hopeful playwrights (like the post-war Shubert Foundation
Fellowship, the New Dramatists' Committee, or the two APT's, one
of which launched Mr Lowell); and bestrewing the country with
civic arts centres in which the youngster can come to manhood
before triumphantly claiming his place in New York. (Dating from
about 1963, this development was dubbed the 'Cultural Explosion'
by *Life* magazine: otherwise known as the Edifice Complex.)

So far it hasn't worked. It rather suggests the fairy-tale of an
idolized baby prince growing up, to the Palace's horror, into a
hulking moron. Perhaps they are the wrong gifts; or perhaps some
changeling had been substituted for the true prince. The fairy-tale
exists in both versions, and when we come to the question of
explanations it loses its specifically American relevance. In America
as in the European theatre, the true prince always turns up in the
humble woodcutter's cottage which, of course, then changes into a
desirable piece of real estate forcing the prince of the next
generation to move further out into the forest.

Where playwrights are concerned there have been very few
seriously considered pretenders. In fact only two have really established themselves on Broadway since the generation of Williams
and Miller. These are Edward Albee and Neil Simon, a complementary couple who bound the opposite poles of the legitimate
stage.

Albee, a most fastidious stylist with a deadly ear for American
speech, is usually classed as an 'absurdist'. This is only partly true.
He has certainly been affected by the French avant-garde (*The*

American Dream might have been written as a deliberate exercise in the manner of Ionesco), and the mere fact that he handles language with such unconcealed sensitivity sets him apart from American stage tradition. But if he has any obvious forerunner it is the arch anti-stylist O'Neill with whom Albee shares a taste for melodrama and thunderous insult, and for such themes as marital imprisonment (linking, say, O'Neill's *Welded* with Albee's best play, *Who's Afraid of Virginia Woolf?*) and the doomed family (for all its echoes of Eliot and Beckett, Albee's *A Delicate Balance* still recalls *Desire Under the Elms*). Albee also repeats O'Neill's achievement as the only other American playwright to have raised his personal legend – that of an orphan outsider spying balefully on the smug social majority – into a public myth.

Simon is a Bronx comedian who, in a time of unusually resounding flops, scroed a record of unbroken successes from *Come Blow Your Horn* to *Plaza Suite*. His plays are all Manhattan folktales, never exceeding by a fraction the blinkered taste of the Manhattan playgoers. But where other writers solicit this public with craven calculation, Simon seems genuinely to share its taste: never practising self-censorship or writing for any other motive than sheer fun. As a result, in the midst of all the restrictions of Broadway, he appears as a free man: and his thriftily workmanlike plays have done something to uphold the good name of the commercial theatre as well as its box-office take.

These two exceptional figures apart, theatrical vitality has moved away from the commercial centre in successive waves. The process began immediately after the war with the development of Off-Broadway. The definition of Off-Broadway is any theatre not in the concentrated area between 41st Street and 52nd Street, in the Broadway theatre district. It came into being for strictly financial reasons. Up to 1950, the average production cost for a Broadway play was in the region of $70,000: Off-Broadway, the average budget was $5000. (Equity also allowed Off-Broadway to pay its actors less than the union minimum, on the agreement that they could abandon a production in the event of finding a more profitable engagement: casts, for this reason, were apt to change like lightning.) Off-Broadway consisted of about thirty little theatres, often situated in adapted buildings (the De Lys was an old cinema, the Cherry Lane a converted stables), and departing from proscenium design. Here, if anywhere, new playwrights had a chance to emerge, but those who did do not add up to a particularly impressive total. Albee had his American debut Off-Broadway (though after a well publicized German première of *The Zoo Story*): so did Murray Schisgal (previously performed in London); Arthur Kopit (with his celebrated parody of Tennessee Williams, *Oh Dad, Poor Dad, Mamma's Hung You in the Closet and I'm Feelin' so Sad*); Jack Richardson (a conventionally literate specialist in social pleasure of the individual, variously shown in *Gallows Humor* and his reworking of the *Oresteia*, *The Prodigal*); and the two house dramatists of the Living Theater (to which we shall return), Jack Gelber (*The Connection* and *The Apple*) and Kenneth Brown (*The Brig*).

Off-Broadway earned its name more as America's first springboard for the post-war Continental avant-garde: Beckett, Ionesco and Genet; and as a home of classical revivals. If as a movement it had any character of its own, this came out mainly in low-budget musicals like *The Fantasticks* and *The Wayward Way* (adapted from the Victorian melodrama, *The Drunkard*) which featured a local variety of innocently camp charm which continued to flourish until the end of the sixties in shows like the Manhattan rock-group raid on *Twelfth Night, Your Own Thing*.

Melting-pot though New York may be, its theatres thrive on ghettoes: black, Jewish, homosexual or addictive. And nothing protected Off-Broadway so effectively as the indifference of the Broadway public, who form a separate ghetto in themselves. Even during the actors' strike of 1960, when Broadway went dark, Off-Broadway's house figures remained unchanged. Production costs, however, did not. Virtually ignored by the critics during its first few years, Off-Broadway found its place on the theatrical map in 1952 when Brooks Atkinson (doyen reviewer of the *New York Times*) bestowed his approval on a revival of Tennessee Williams's *Summer and Smoke* in a converted night-club in Sheridan Square. This event launched the actress Geraldine Page and the director José Quintero: it also brought other critics out to Off-Broadway and led to the rapid growth of new theatres in Greenwich Village and downtown Second Avenue. From this moment, in other words, Off-Broadway started to get smart. Opportunistic and near-amateur managements began moving in, costs started mounting, and the success-ethic began to make its customary demands on a fledgling avant-garde that was neither strong enough to resist them nor professional enough to deliver the real commercial goods. As a result, according to the producer Richard Barr, 'Off-Broadway began to imitate Broadway. Productions that used to cost between five and seven thousand dollars began to cost seventeen, twenty-seven, and, in the case of Kopit's *Oh Dad, Poor Dad*, over fifty thousand dollars. One cannot survive Off-Broadway under those circumstances'.

Off-Broadway has survived, and has also managed to preserve a character of its own. Originally a counter-force, it has settled down as a counter-attraction to Broadway, specializing in the modest little musicals and the assimilated styles of yesterday's avant-garde. Tennessee Williams launched new work here (like *In The Bar of a Tokyo Hotel*, 1969), and when it produces a new writer, like Israel Horovitz (*The Indian Wants the Bronx*, 1968), he is most likely to succeed by the skill with which he re-states familiar themes. Off-Broadway's complementary role was clearly defined in its two biggest hits of the late sixties – Barbara Garson's *MacBird!* and Bruce Jay Friedman's *Scuba Duba*: the first a Shakespearian pastiche aligning the careers of Macbeth and President Johnson, and the second a farce about adultery between a middle-class white wife and a Negro skin-diver. Both plays touched on strong pre-judices and taboos, and dropped the mask of obligatory cant which would have camouflaged or excluded them from Broadway. But they were still addressed to much the same middle-class audience: and what they offered was a safety-valve for ingrained but publicly unacceptable attitudes. The characteristic response they invited was one of guilty laughter in the dark.

As Off-Broadway was settling into peaceful coexistence with Times Square, the action was moving on elsewhere. The process began early in the sixties, and it took two clear directions – into the lofts, cafes and churches of New York's East Village, and out of New York altogether. The first development came to be known as Off-Off-Broadway (a phrase coined by the *Village Voice* critic Jerry Tallmer), and the second the aforementioned 'Cultural Explosion' in which the profits of post-war reconversion were siphoned off into cultural foundations as tax reductions, permitting the spread of civic arts centres and state arts councils (growing in number from three in 1962 to fifty-four by 1967) across the country.

Both movements had roots in the past, and in particular in the two main companies that flourished as the polar extremes of Off-Broadway – The New York Shakespeare Festival, and the Living Theater: respectively created by Joseph Papp, and by the marital partnership of Julian Beck and Judith Malina. As pioneer ventures led by passionately single-minded individuals and standing well above the ebb and flow of temporary fashion, they deserve sections to themselves.

*

As much in his life as in his work, Joseph Papp occupies an almost anachronistically heroic position in the post-war American scene. Born in 1921 in Williamsburg – one of the toughest sections of Brooklyn – he had a classic first-chapter upbringing as one of the four children of working-class immigrant parents. (His father was a Jewish trunk-maker of Polish extraction; 'Papp' being an abbreviation of Papirofsky which Joseph subsequently made to fit the limited space of CBS schedules.) As a boy he belonged to the neighbourhood Jewish gang, but he was increasingly alienated by street fights and the other brutalities of the environment and decided that life must have something better to offer: which he found at the local library in the plays of Shakespeare and Sean O'Casey. After leaving school, with no money for college, he worked for a laundry before enlisting in the navy where, through involvement in troop shows in the South Pacific, he discovered he had theatrical talent and organizing ability. On demobilization in 1946 he joined the Los Angeles Actors' Laboratory under the GI Bill of Rights. He went on to direct plays at the Laboratory and to become a member of its executive board, and to teach acting at the California Labor School.

The laboratory was important to Papp for two reasons. As an outgrowth of the Group Theater it gave him a link with the crusading social theatre of the thirties; and as a democratically administered institution which ultimately fell apart through internal quarrels (much as the Group Theater itself had done), it left him with a lasting belief that any effective theatre must be run by a single boss. And as his own theatre developed it followed the paradoxical principle familiar in Europe (Meyerhold, Brecht, Vilar) but new to America, that the more a stage devotes itself to the popular democratic ideal, the more authoritarian is the role of its director. Papp's theatre takes its favourite slogan from Emerson: 'An institution is the lengthened shadow of one man.'

His real work began in 1952 with his return to New York and his formation of the Shakespearian Theater Workshop in a Presbyterian church on the Lower East Side. With the help of a businessman patron, Leo Brody, who wanted to bring drama (including some of his own) to the locality, he managed to equip the 185-seat theatre for next to nothing (Brody had contacts with a Bronx wrecker) and rehearse an impoverished but professional cast in *Romeo and Juliet* in what spare time he had from his job as a television floor manager. At this period – with Shakespeare festivals in their first North American bloom – Papp's main interest was in evolving an American approach to classical texts. Rejecting Method as an appropriate style, he wrote, 'The future of our theater lies in creating a new style of playing that will combine the vitality and humanity of the modern actor with the discipline, grace, and eloquence of the classical actor.'

More originally, at that time, he was pledged from the start to the principle of theatrical subsidy. In 1954 no theatre in the United States received any subsidy. But this did not discourage Papp from incorporating his workshop and then applying to the New York State Department of Education for a charter certifying it as an 'educational, nonprofit institution'; a qualification making it eligible for tax-exemption and financial aid from sources themselves seeking to reap income tax cuts by means of charitable donation. Such charters are now common among Off-Broadway groups and regional theatres. But in the early fifties they were rarely granted, as the production of plays was not held to be either of educational or social benefit. However, Papp was granted his charter, and moved on to his next phase: the establishment of an annual Shakespeare Festival.

Coinciding with Mayor Wagner's 'New York is a Summer Festival' campaign, Papp's first season opened in June 1956 at the East River Amphitheatre on the Lower East Side. The unique feature of this three-month event (subsequently established in a 2000-seat concrete amphitheatre overlooking Belvedere Lake in Central Park) is that all the seats were given away free. In Papp's words, it was 'a theater for everybody – for those who can afford it and those who cannot'; and the first of his indefatigable tactics to undercut the financial and racial barriers of the city and attract the 'great dispossessed audience'. It opened with *Julius Caesar*, and the howling entrance of the Roman commoners met with answering howls from the public. 'It sounded,' Papp says, 'like Ebbets Field during a pre-game warm-up. Frankly, I was scared to death. Obviously most of the people out there had never seen live actors before. They might stone us to death for all I knew.'

It was also the most precarious moment in his career from a financial point of view. His budget had been raised from private gifts. The big foundations contributed nothing (to date Ford and Rockefeller have steadfastly refused him any support); and the reasons for this illuminate the whole question of American patronage of the arts. First, it was felt that Papp's enterprise was uncomfortably close to socialism and that people did not appreciate what they got for nothing. Secondly, it was objected that the money would be spent on producing plays; works, that is, that would leave behind no tangible evidence of the expenditure: hence the phenomenon, astonishing to the European visitor, of sumptuous buildings like the Lincoln Center, erected to leave conspicuous testimony of public-spirited investment, but denied any sustaining grant to keep them in the business for which they had been put up to begin with.

As a director Papp has often been criticized (and from the start he has engaged other men, like Stuart Vaughan and Gerald Freedman, to direct a large proportion of his productions). But no one has ever questioned his genius as a fund-raiser. He has consistently gone ahead with new projects – tours of schools and the congested neighbourhoods; and the bilingual Mobile Theater which was the second main spearhead of his audience crusade – before having the money to pay for them. He excelled in getting people to work for nothing (distributing vanity titles – like 'Transportation Coordinator' for the truck driver); and in conjuring handouts from the unlikeliest sources. This was more than a knack: it was one of the strengths deriving from his socially impassioned approach to the whole enterprise; his refusal to draw any dividing line between art and economics, and his belief that everything – the manner of fund-raising no less than the manner of staff recruitment – feeds the play.

It was evidently the suspicion of socialism, so alarming to the big foundations, which also caused the two subsequent big rows of the Festival's first years. First Papp was summoned by the House Committee on Un-American Activities to answer questions on previous political affiliations. He denied membership of the Communist Party, but declined to say whether he had been a member before 1955 – whereupon he was instantly dismissed by CBS. However, when the case was submitted to binding arbitration, the ruling was that he should be reinstated because CBS had known of Papp's associations before the hearing. Papp's fears that the festival might be killed by this smear proved groundless; but it did come in handy as a weapon for his future antagonists, including the Park Commissioner Robert Moses, who tried to compel the festival to make admission charges on the grounds that Papp's audiences were wearing the grass thin. After a two-month battle Moses was defeated, and majority opinion was summed up in the *Herald-Tribune's* comment: 'Free Shakespeare is an even rarer commodity in this world than non-eroded grass.'

With the turn of the sixties, the Festival was well established with regular grants from the Board of Education and the City, and support from the labour unions. Opinion on the quality of its productions is divided; and it is hard to see how any critic could bring solely aesthetic criteria to bear on shows liable at any minute to be interrupted by rainstorms or showers of rocks from the neighbourhood gangs. What is true is that Papp has an extraordinary flair for picking talented new actors (his discoveries include George C. Scott, Colleen Dewhurst and James Earl Jones): and that his policy of matching the multi-racial audience with a 'racially richer company' (including the Puerto Rican director Osvaldo Riofrancos and the Negro directors William Hairston and Robert Hooks) stimulated the separate development of Spanish and Black theatre in the second half of the decade. The Mobile Theater (alias El Teatro Movil), softening up the toughest ghettoes with preliminary 'pacifying programmes' before 'hitting people who respond because they don't know how the play ends', similarly paved the way for the spread of street and 'guerrilla' theatre towards the end of the sixties.

Still maintaining all this work, Papp in 1967 returned to the Lower East Side and opened a new headquarters in the Astor Library in Lafayette Street. As the city's first free public library it was an apt choice, though the nature of the operation was not to house free shows. Renamed the Public Theater, it was planned to complement the Shakespeare Festival. It was an expensive project (an estimated $2.5m was needed to buy the building and equip it with two theatres: one thrust stage, and the other an end-arena). There was to be no Shakespeare there, no mass audience and no free admission (though seat prices were kept down with the aid of a grant from the National Endowment for the Arts). Its relationship to the festival corresponded to that between the Royal Shakespeare Company's two theatres in Stratford and London: a relationship of reciprocal nourishment between classical and significant contemporary work. In the first season, although Papp broke his own rules by putting on a cut-up version of *Hamlet* at the Public Theater (featuring a Puerto Rican grave-digger, and the drop-out Prince as a peanut vendor), he certainly started something with his opening production – the tribal love-rock musical, *Hair.*

Touching a vast number of people and mingling art with social engineering, the effect of Papp's work is incalculable. It is much easier to assess the influence of the Living Theater, since – at least during the twelve years before its departure into European exile – it was a small-audience, avant-garde house better known to theatrical practitioners than to the general public. It started regular performances in 1951 – roughly coinciding with Papp's beginnings; it took a stand against Method acting, and it declared war on money: otherwise there are no parallels between the two.

The Living Theater began as a product of the New York Jewish intelligentsia. Julian Beck came from a well-to-do middle-class family of teachers. Judith Malina, born in Kiel, was the daughter of a rabbi and an actress. Before their marriage in 1948 (both in their early twenties) Beck had exhibited paintings under the patronage of Peggy Guggenheim (through whom he discovered the French Surrealists and the American Abstract Expressionists); while Malina was a student of Brecht's co-founder of Epic theatre, Erwin Piscator, at the New School's Dramatic Workshop. Thus, their first intention in forming a theatre was to catch up with the European stage and the visual arts of their own country. As Beck put it: 'We wanted the theater to undergo the same revolution that had convulsed the other arts: music, painting, sculpture.' And to begin with, their chief purpose was to develop a fresh acting style, particularly in the approach to language. In place of the naturalistic texts on which the Method flourished, they wanted to create a theatre for modern poetic drama.

Playing to begin with in their own apartment, then in a loft, and finally in a converted shop on 14th Street (1957–63), they built up an uncompromisingly individual programme from plays by Gertrude Stein, Paul Goodman, Brecht, Lorca and William Carlos Williams, creating, incidentally, the only repertory theatre then operating in the United States. Their main preoccupations at that time were with Oriental stagecraft, verbal experiment, automatism, poetry and anarchism: though during their early years that overcrowded list underwent two important modifications. First, although their original concern had been with the word, they found (particularly after unhappy collisions with Sophocles and Racine) that their range did not include verse-speaking. Secondly, their anarchism (first expressed in their choice of the Goodman plays) developed to take up as much of their concern as the theatre. Both were repeatedly arrested for pacifist activities, and their administration of the Living Theater – having to balance the books while believing money to be inherently evil – became a mounting nightmare that reached its climax in October 1963 when their premises were seized by agents of the US Internal Revenue Service for failure to pay back taxes of $28,000.

The full story of the Living Theater, leading on to its tribal wanderings through Europe and its ultimate destruction of all dramatic categories in *Paradise Now*, has no parallel in the history of the theatre. Here we are only concerned with its relatively conformist period, still somehow coexisting with the society which it later renounced. But even before going into exile the troupe had gained international recognition by playing in Europe and winning numerous foreign awards (including the Grand Prix de la Recherche of the Théâtre des Nations, never previously given to an American company). This process began in 1959 with the production of Jack Gelber's *The Connection*, a piece which exactly answered the prevailing concerns of the company. Entirely ignoring the usual dramatic requirements, it shows a group of heroin-addicts awaiting the arrival of the man with the dope. Apart from the moment when one of them gives himself a nearly fatal overdose, there are no events: under the cameras of a Pirandellian film-director, they simply fill in the time until the connection arrives by talking and listening to a jazz group. The work related equally to society and to stage technique. Unlike other plays of that time, it passed no judgment on the drug habit: it viewed drugs partly as an addiction neither better nor worse than an addiction to work or money; and partly – like jazz – as a method of release from conventional life. Addicts and audience were alike members of the human family (a point underlined by the undifferentiated mingling of black and white actors). Technically the production undercut the sense of theatrical make-believe by putting the jazzmen up on the stage with the junkies: since the musicians were undoubtedly 'real', might not the actors be real-life addicts too? As spectators often fainted during the overdose scene, the trick undoubtedly worked.

The paradox is that tricks were the outcome of pursuing the literal truth. The Becks have been consistently preoccupied with the need to establish an honest relationship with the spectator. But the attempt precipitated a kind of actuality show far exceeding the Naturalism against which they originally reacted. It also led (in Europe) to the discarding of all theatrical 'distance' for a head-on assault against the audience which their opponents have condemned as near-fascist paranoia. As Malina put it in a 1969 interview:

If I say, 'I'm Hedda Gabler and I've had a very unhappy life,' that's one kind of lie; but if I say, 'Now, I am not speaking as Hedda Gabler, now I am speaking as Judith Malina and I'm saying somebody else's words written for me,' then it's a much worse lie . . . because I've compounded the distance between myself and the spectator.

The Becks' isolated position, as devout anarchists in a devoutly capitalist society, certainly yielded a pattern of compulsive self-victimization hard to distinguish from paranoia. But in New York they were at least still addressing their own people in their own language, and there is no need to resort to any clinical analysis of their farewell American production of Kenneth Brown's *The Brig*. In the interval between *The Connection* and this piece, the Becks had discovered Artaud who, among other things, gave authority to their verbal blind-spot (henceforth the Word became a 'barricade': another enemy like Wall Street and the Pentagon); and licensed them to use stage violence as an inoculation against the real thing. Based on its author's experiences in a US Marine prison, *The Brig* projects Naturalism to the point of ritual. Again, there is no plot: merely a literally formalized display of the routine barbarities by which the guards humiliate and terrorize the prisoners into so many cowed automata. Seen through the wire mesh of Beck's set, it was literally a vision of hell – designed to expand in the spectator's memory to apply to other rigid social and mental structures within his personal experience (the image was subsequently taken up again in the company's *Frankenstein*, played on a steel scaffold subdivided into small cages). In performance guards and prisoners exchanged roles from night to night; and Malina's rehearsals (relying extensively on the *Guidebook for Marines*) were conducted with the full rigour of military drill. This was a direct reversal of the normal company ethic. Beck at that time summed up his anarchist programme under three headings: emphasis on the sacredness of life; increase of conscious awareness; destruction of walls and barriers. Even in America, the quality of community life inside the troupe ranked equal in importance to the quality of their public performances; while subsequently the urge to create an ideal community and transmit its doctrine to the outside world has altogether eclipsed any limited concern with art and talent.

The Living Theater casts a long shadow over the great upsurge of fresh activity that spread through New York's East Village in the sixties. The only points of general agreement on Off-Off-Broadway is that while the movement itself was full of life, most of its work was bad (though no one can have seen more than a fragmentary part of its unnumerable shows). But amid all the diversity, the legacy of the Becks is felt in several ways: in the movement's fear of financial contamination (most of the shows operated on a voluntary contribution system); in preferring visceral impact to reason; in dismissing the whole apparatus of American Naturalism; and in 'getting the audience', much as George and Martha got the guests in *Virginia Woolf*. You can see the temptations. Perhaps they were most clearly exposed in the first rash of 'hate whitey' plays where white spectators turned up to be verbally flayed by black actors; and even white performers in the troupes were liable to be beaten up by their black colleagues. Given intelligent reasons for doing so, the theatre may be justified in renouncing intelligence. Beck, for instance, speaks sensibly of desiring to leave an expanding 'stain' on the spectator's memory rather than purveying an instantly comprehensible message: similarly Albee, when I questioned him on his apparent distaste for explicit dramatic resolutions, said:

I get criticized for not having the catharsis in the body of the play. I don't think that's where the catharsis should be any more. I think it should take place in the mind of the spectator some time afterwards – maybe a year after experiencing the play.

That is one thing: but all too easily it becomes an excuse for not thinking at all, and abdicating from all artistic responsibility apart from the infantile impulse to make a noise in public. Strasberg's Method generation, intent on self-expression at the expense of every other dramatic component, were not so different from the 'happenings' generation for whom everything was theatre – a burning pile of old automobile tyres, a man carried through Grand Central Station wrapped in tin-foil.

In a curious way, despite its avant-garde posture and determined pursuit of 'loft economy', Off-Off-Broadway often strikes the outside observer as anything but an opposition theatre. The whole spectrum, from showbiz to the experimental ghetto, rather suggests a snake biting its own tail. At both extremes you get the same emphasis on communal togetherness concealing the same aggressive careerism; and the same clearance sale on values – which is especially surprising to the visitor who comes expecting underground theatre to be debating the American crisis of conscience, only to find it offering mixed-media light shows and would-be Dionysian grope-ins. (From Stanislavsky, through Artaud, Grotowski and Cornford's theories of the Attic stage, you could write a history of the modern American theatre in terms of its misunderstanding of European models.)

To one group, at least, the Becks did pass on some of their ethical fervour. This is the Open Theater, formed in 1963 by a like-minded group of actors under the leadership of Joseph

Chaikin, himself formerly a member of the Living Theater troupe. Although, like the Becks, Chaikin had engaged in political dissent, his company had no interest in direct radical exhortation. They banded together as fellow refugees from a sick theatre in a sick society; and (the inoculation principle again) one of their aims was to find ways of dramatizing the virus which they felt was poisoning them. This involved, in Chaikin's words, 'developing a vocabulary to refer to nameless things that happen'. Chaikin was extremely well equipped for the task, for he excels as an inventor of acting exercises (which have been widely adopted by other directors). The exercises served at once to assist the group towards its goal as an 'exemplary community' and to examine the texture of familiar American life. There were exercises, for instance, for 'Perfect People', consisting of improvised discussions between idealized figures from advertisements; glamorous, two-dimensional secretaries and doctors conversing strictly in proverbs, clichés, and marketing slogans. And there were 'Transformation' exercises (based on the idea that anybody can be anybody else) in which, say, a trial improvisation would be interrupted and the judge, victim and prosecutor would change roles. This style of work has called a new school of drama into existence. Either writing in sympathy with the actors, or working directly from their inventions in rehearsal, playwrights like Megan Terry and Jean-Claude van Itallie have produced some dazzling material that amounts to a theatrical equivalent of pop art.

The Open Theater's first phase yielded some sulphurous social comedy (as in the TV section of van Itallie's *America Hurrah*); but with time Chaikin felt this was becoming too glib. As he put it when I interviewed him: 'There was a danger of the group turning into an ensemble who were very deft at a type of satire; but if we aimed at pleasing, we were in complicity with what we were attacking.' Increasingly since then the Open Theater has moved on to an examination of Western myth: approached not psychologically (psychology is generally unpopular Off-Off-Broadway) but as an intersection point between the everyday self, the dream self and the buried community of myth. The first full expression of this was in van Itallie's *The Serpent* (1968), a reworking of Genesis cutting between the Garden of Eden and the Kennedy assassination, and written from the inside out; taking its verbal form entirely from the starting ideas of Chaikin and the improvised actions of the company in rehearsal.

Despite European assumptions to the contrary, this is not the common practice Off-Off-Broadway. Most of the playwrights who made their names there – Sam Shepard, Rochelle Owens, Leonard Melfi, Paul Foster, Rosalyn Drexler – were authors in the full old-fashioned sense. And their profession is treated with the greatest respect by those who first accepted their work for production. Here, however, we come upon another paradox of the American experimental theatre.

Among the many stages of Off-Off-Broadway, it was a handful that set the pace. These included the Café Cino, Theater Genesis, the Café La Mama and the Judson Poets' Theater. The Judson Memorial Church was one of the original centres of the movement – a Baptist foundation with a long record of social service (it was the first New York church to install a gymnasium) and no interest in proselytization. Just as it took in waves of Italian immigrants and Depression victims, so in the 1950s it took in young artists who had nowhere else to work; and it was here that Jim Dine, Allan Kaprow and Claes Oldenburg had their early showings. These painters were the originators of the 'happenings' movement which was a theatrical extension of the graphic arts; with the result that when the church set up its Poets' Theater in 1961 (followed by a Dance Theater) it established a point of aesthetic cross-fertilization. Off-Off-Broadway was born out of such cross-currents, but only at the Judson were they all gathered under one roof.

The church itself stipulated only that there should be no censorship, and no religious plays. The architect of this policy was the Rev. Al Carmines whose purpose was to help new playwrights, and to learn from them as 'secular prophets' of the city: and in six years he presented some seventy new works. This is where the paradox comes in. In spite of its open policy, and in spite of exposing itself like an Aeolian harp to any wind that happens to be blowing through New York, the Judson Theater is known as a house with a strong character of its own: specializing in 'campy' productions like Rosalyn Drexler's *Home Movies* and Ronald Tavel's *Gorilla Queen* (in which King Kong is unmasked as homosexual); and in Carmines's own pastiche mini-operas taken from Gertrude Stein (in *Circles*) and the sayings of Chairman Mao.

Even more does this division between theory and practice apply to the Café La Mama. In a charming set speech before every performance the club's remarkable founder, Ellen Stewart, rings a little bell and informs the audience that her experimental theatre is dedicated to the playwright. At one time she was putting on a new play every week; her writers had control over production decisions, and were given a choice of directors. And yet again, when the club began to win an international name it was not through the quality of its plays but through the La Mama Troupe's acting style – which was the creation of its star director, Tom O'Horgan, whose productions are most striking in their capacity to conjure up an electrifying stage action from the thinnest of texts.

When the Off-Off-Broadway movement falls into historical perspective, I suspect that most of its plays will be seen as disposable works whose main purpose was to feed a new performance style. There is nothing surprising in this. Broadway, too, has generally viewed plays as perishable material. And the anti-verbal atmosphere of the East Village theatre was no place for the full growth of what will always be primarily a verbal art. The business of the new playwrights was to supply scenarios celebrating the urban environment – finding theatrical equivalents for the drug experience, the pressure of technology, the sexual explosion that accompanies the divorce from natural surroundings – and entrust actors and directors to bring these to full theatrical life with jazz-based choreography, the use of words for sound value, psychedelic lighting and the other devices of the environmental theatre.

What verbal achievements there have been lie much more in the developing Black Theater movement which ran a parallel course to that of Off-Off-Broadway; equally determined – though for totally different reasons – to build up a repertory of its own as fast as possible. Unlike their white counterparts, the black writers had something definite to say, and an idiom of their own which had not been staled either by literature or advertising copy. Hence, in the plays of writers like Ed Bullins and LeRoi Jones (the militant founder of the Harlem Black Arts Repertory, progenitor of the nationwide Black Arts theater network), you find – as in the crusading drama of the thirties – that the main emphasis is on verbally expressed conflicts of character, with only a minimal interest in experimental production techniques.

Standing apart from all its neighbouring East Village groups and making them seem frivolous by comparison, is the Bread and Puppet Theater, a Christian Socialist collective who specialize in street theatre and 'walking plays' in the city's slums. Their founder is Peter Schumann, a German sculptor, who began his American career as a solitary showman-evangelist with a travelling puppet theatre. Installed in an old court-house on the Lower East Side, his troupe combine the crafts of musicians, printers, actors, puppet-makers and manipulators. Their collectively evolved texts express social and political dissent from a basis of New Testament charity; but the real glory of their work is in the dolls, grotesque and seraphic presences, some over twenty feet high, which take on a life of their own in performance. Ranging between the carnival and the sacramental ceremony, their shows suggest a modern revival of medieval street drama.

This survey is anything but a comprehensive account of American theatre since the war. I have dwelt less on the conspicuous landmarks than on points of new growth. As a result there is more about lofts than about the Lincoln Center. I have discussed the Shakespeare Festival, but not the APA's venture into classical repertory in New York; the Black Arts Movement, but not the more moderate Negro Ensemble.

The biggest omission is that of the resident theatres across the country, now some thirty in number and absorbing a good deal of talent from the city. Tyrone Guthrie, who did much to advance this movement and lent his name to one of its first buildings (the beautiful open-stage Guthrie Theater in Minneapolis, opened in 1963), foresaw a dramatic renaissance in the American provinces. So far it does not seem to have happened. There have been some bold originating managements, like the Theater Company of Boston, the Washington Arena Stage and the San Francisco Actors' Workshop (whose directors, Herbert Blau and Jules Irving, assumed control of the Lincoln Center after the collapse of the Kazan administration). But to judge from the production schedules of the Theater Communications Group very little new work is being hazarded on local audiences; and there are numerous cases of rows and dismissals when this does happen. As in Britain, the mirage of a healthy tributary theatre flourishing at a safe remove from the metropolitan rat race, has haunted the American stage. Back in the thirties, the designer Lee Simonson was saying that the Broadway theatre was a boarding house and the community theatre a home. Set against this the comment made to me by Peter Zeisler, the steely-eyed managing director of the Guthrie Theater: 'You could name on the fingers of one hand the people who are out here because they want to be.' For better or worse, it seems that the American theatre still means the theatre in New York.

Such was my conclusion in 1975 when this essay first appeared. Ten years later the balance has shifted and the theatrical map needs to be redrawn. New York still occupies the central position, but it has lost its power as an irresistible magnet. Its public can no longer sit tight in the comfortable assurance that everything of interest will be delivered to their doorstep.

One cause of this decline is the energetic and widespread growth of repertory theatres elsewhere. Sadly, this revival does not include the Guthrie. Originally planned as a flagship for American classical production (a sister house to Guthrie's Festival Theater in Stratford, Ontario), it has surrendered to box-office pressures and turned to presenting runs of commercial hits. There remain, however, a great many other resident theatres that have held out against this soft option. Theater Communications Group's directory of nonprofit professional theatres lists some 160 theatres in eighty-five towns and cities: many of them engaged in classical revivals, European transfers and new work; and some achieving an international reputation with no help from New York.

One conspicuous example is the Actors' Theater of Louisville, Kentucky, which began its life in a 100-seat converted loft in 1964. Two years later it had moved to an abandoned railway station where the critic, Julius Novik, saw a performance of George M. Cohan's *The Tavern* which 'had been entirely sold out to a local high school, but the house was half empty: an ominous sign'. ATL then acquired a new producing director, Jon Jory, who set about building a subscription audience and raising corporate funding: which, by the mid-seventies, had catapulted the organization into a $1.7m theatre complex (including a main house and a studio) with a policy heavily weighted in favour of American world premieres and new European work. One of Jory's early discoveries was the Pulitzer-Prize winning *The Gin Game.* Since then, ATL has gone on to run an annual festival of new American plays (launching such writers as Marsha Norman, Beth Henley, John Pielmeier and William Mastrosimone). For foreign visitors it is quite a shock to find local citizens queuing up *en masse* for programmes of totally unknown work. It is a sight that you do not encounter in New York.

Some of these plays vanish without trace; but a fair proportion go on to lead a healthy life in other resident theatres without the patronage, and sometimes in conscious defiance, of Broadway. Too often, plays that do reach Broadway meet with an instant death that also kills their chances of finding future productions anywhere else. Why should a playwright take that suicidal gamble when his work can pick up a profitable living in Houston, Cincinnati and Los Angeles?

The spread of such new platforms for the writer has left America in possession of two parallel theatre systems, each deriving from a separate European tradition. There is the old commercial circuit, centred on New York, which developed from the raffish Anglo-Saxon model of star-billing and cut-throat competition. Side by side with this, there is now the resident theatre circuit deriving (as America's orchestras always have done) from the ultra-respectable German model of an ensemble integrated into a particular community. The first offers entertainment to the crowd; the second dispenses culture to a select public.

The advantages of the Germanic system are obvious: instead of the commercial jungle, it offers a stable working environment where actors and writers alike can develop and make mistakes without fear of being thrown on the scrap-heap. However, as Germany found out long ago, 'Civil Service theatre' also has its drawbacks. If a theatre builds up a loyal subscription audience, that means that its trust must not be violated; which, in turn, is apt to enforce a tyranny of middlebrow taste.

Where America is concerned it seems no accident that this development has taken place in the conservative aftermath of the Vietnam War. In the theatre, as everywhere else, the wild days are over. And in place of the iconoclasts and instant artists of the sixties, there is a cautious generation of young theatre workers 'learning their craft' as interns in organizations like ATL, in college drama departments, and in the sessions of the O'Neill Playwrights' Convention at Waterford, Connecticut. Play writing has given way to 'play-development', which, at its worst, has bred a school of small-scale, creepingly naturalistic domestic drama, marked by the effects of 'scene study' (in which aspirants compose single-scene exercises instead of writing a play). Good writers have emerged from this background, but with the exception of 'magic realism' (as practised by Adele Edling Shank in plays like *Sand Castles* and *Sunset/Sunrise*) it has yielded no visionary departures.

In New York, likewise, the avant-garde ferment is over. The Living Theater and the Open Theater have disbanded, leaving no successors. The annual Albee play, regularly savaged by the reviewers and swiftly withdrawn, has vanished from the scene. And the experimental crusades promoted by Stanislavsky and Artaud were formally wound up by the deaths of Strasberg (1982) and Julian Beck (1985). Another chapter ended with the death of Tennessee Williams (1983) after a final burst of spurned productivity. Awakening like Rip Van Winkle from what he called his 'stoned age', Williams remained marooned in the memory of the

Broadway he had dominated in the days of Elia Kazan. Arthur Miller, by contrast, adapted to theatrical change, and has sought platforms outside New York for his recent work, which itself has shown a similar flexibility: both in extension of international range (as with East European politics in *The Archbishop's Ceiling*), and in formal innovation (as with his 'mural' of the Depression years, *The American Clock*).

In the period under review two successors to Williams and Miller have appeared in the persons of Sam Shepard and David Mamet: another pair of eternal opposites who happen both to have been born in Illinois during the 1940s.

Shepard grew up in California and arrived on the scene (as much as a rock-drummer as a playwright) in the lofts and church halls of Off-Off-Broadway; where, as a child of the time, he took everything on board – drugs, astrology, science fiction, detective films and the racetrack. However, his spiritual territory is the American West, and his work amounts to a pilgrimage towards that ever-retreating El Dorado. 'I'm pulled towards images that shine in the middle of junk,' he once wrote, 'like cracked headlights shining in a deer's eyes.' The collective image that arises from his plays is of a rural oasis in a desert of intersecting freeways.

Mamet, although he studied in New York, has built his career in his native Chicago, as a playwright and as founding artistic director of the St Nicholas Theater Company and (with Gregory Mosher) of the Goodman Theater where he first attracted national attention with *American Buffalo* (1975): a thieves'-kitchen piece showing a group of junkshop cronies plotting a robbery they are incapable of carrying out. They define Mamet's chosen territory: benighted city-dwellers, like rats in the Paris catacombs, whose lives are entirely bounded by the struggle to retain control of their own squalid little patch of ground. Their very inarticulateness and total concentration on the tactics of survival are the means by which Mamet (as Michael Billington wrote) indicts a society 'in which the business ethic is used as a cover for any kind of criminal activity'. When Mamet pursued this theme into the world of legitimate business in his best play, *Glengarry Glen Ross* (1983), the picture was blacker than ever.

As with Williams and Miller, Shepard and Mamet invite dualistic comparison: between landscape and city; visionary and critic; improvisation and structured composition. The vastly prolific Shepard gives the impression of never having read a book. Mamet's much smaller output is the product of a highly literate intelligence with a conscious debt to Harold Pinter. And where Shepard assembled a fantastic world and a synthetic language from his cultural junkyard, Mamet found his voice through giving heightened realism to the precise locations and speech-habits of smalltime crooks and real-estate men.

As with the two elder writers, though, detailed comparison discloses a subterranean bond between the younger pair. Shepard is famous for his excursions into American 'myth'. In *Operation Sidewinder* (1970) an Army computer in the shape of a sidewinder rattlesnake is transformed into the actual snake during a Hopi Indian religious ceremony. In *The Tooth of Crime* (1972) two rock stars enact a style duel in a Las Vegas mansion which becomes a Frazerian battleground where a young warrior defeats an ageing tribal king. Precisely the same vein of national mythology underlies the realist shell of Mamet's work: from the rare old coin that gives its name to *American Buffalo* to the strips of useless swampland which the salesmen in *Glengarry Glen Ross* unload on their gullible customers as the pastoral America of their dreams: the very place for Shepard to ride out to in the sunset.

Like leading playwrights of the past, Shepard and Mamet regularly exhibit their work on Broadway. Amid the soaring ticket prices and make-or-break reviews, their plays still have the muscle to survive; and they have done something to preserve New York's name as a theatrical capital at a time when the scene consists mainly of musicals and darkened houses. The musical itself has recovered some of its self-respect: thanks, above all, to the uncompromisingly independent output of Stephen Sondheim – whether in taking Victorian horror to the limit in *Sweeney Todd*, or staging a Seurat painting in *Sunday in the Park with George.* Of New York's recent drama, Neil Simon emerges amid the encircling gloom, pursuing his own line in a series of increasingly sombre comedies which continue to please everybody. But the general level of expectation can be gauged from the fact that the greatest hit since 1980 has been Harvey Fierstein's rambling four-hour *Torch Song Trilogy* whose claim to fame is that it established homosexuality as a red-blooded subject in the central theatre district.

Good new work does continue to appear at such off-centre addresses as Playwrights' Horizons (which has nurtured the gently original talent of A. R. Gurney), and at Joseph Papp's now massively entrenched New York Shakespeare Festival, a complex of performance spaces which amounts to the closest thing America has to a national theatre. Given the blank history of the Lincoln Center and the abortive opening season of the self-styled American National Theater in Washington DC (launched at the Kennedy Center in January 1985 and suspended in the following year) the vitality of Papp's enterprises gives redoubled confirmation to the advantage of one-man over committee-led institutions.

What makes for Papp's unique achievement in the context of New York is his ability to detect pathfinding and seemingly uncommercial new writers, and then market them like sliced bread. Of those who have benefited from his support, two must be singled out: David Rabe (b. 1940), combat veteran and author of *Sticks and Bones* and *Streamers* in which the American stage first learnt to digest the experience of the Vietnam War; and David Henry Hwang (b. 1957) who gave a theatrical voice to the Chinese-American community in pieces like *FOB* ('fresh off the boat') and *The Dance and the Railroad* which treats the life of immigrant construction workers in the style of Peking Opera, setting their raw impoverished present against their ancient civilized past.

Papp's interests are not confined to New York; besides launching American writers, he has supplied a platform for East European dissidents, not to mention initiating an exchange programme with London's beleaguered Royal Court Theatre including an annual grant of $50,000. If the West End meets the same fate as Broadway, he may be bailing us out as well.

9

AMERICAN POETRY, POETICS AND POETIC MOVEMENTS SINCE 1950

Eric Mottram

I

A brief account of some of the origins of current poetics in America can begin with the words which Jonathan Williams places in his poem on Whitman, 'Dangerous Calamus Emotions' (1969 version in *An Ear in Bartram's Tree*):

W.C.W. – 'him and that Jesuit, them with the variable feet – they changed it'.

To Williams's sense of the point of change in the nature of poetic measure we can add a selection of other acknowledged recognitions: the paragraphic line in Blake's 'prophetic' books and Christopher Smart's line in 'Jubilate Agno', for Allen Ginsberg's poetry; the lyric and improvisatory continuity of line in the horns of Lester Young and Charlie Parker in the 1940s and 1950s which combine with Thomas Wolfe's piling articulations in Jack Kerouac's *Mexico City Blues* (1959); the various effects of cubist and Dadaist dislocations and reassemblages which constitute a resource in innovative literature from the 1920s onwards; and the ways in which Kerouac, William Carlos Williams, Ezra Pound, Zukofsky and others use American speech cadences and rhythms as basic measures for their lines. Pound acknowledged his 'pact' with Walt Whitman in *Lustra* in 1917: 'It was you who broke the new wood, / Now it is time for carving.' But he began to consider the possibilities of new spatial organization in poetry earlier, while reading Ernest Fenollosa's 'The Chinese Written Character as a Medium for Poetry' shortly before the American scholar's death in 1908. In his 1915 article, 'Imagisme and England', Pound indicated the 'two sorts of poetry' which concerned him: lyric poetry in which melody moves into speech, and a poetry whose form is nearer painting and sculpture, the Imagist – 'we have sought the force of Chinese

ideographs without knowing it'. His first Chinese poem came out in
Poetry, March 1915: 'Exile's Letter'.

But contemporary American poetry has a further resource, indi-
cated in Kenneth Rexroth's 'The Influence of French Poets on
America' (*Assays*, 1961; see also *Revolution of the Word*, ed.
Jerome Rothenberg, 1975, and Rene Taupin, *The Influence of French
Symbolism on Modern American Poetry*, 1985). For Rexroth,
American poetic Modernism begins with Alfred Kreymborg's
magazine *Others* (1914–19) printing Williams, Marianne Moore,
Stevens, Eliot, Mina Loy, Conrad Aiken and others. Pound transmuted Laforgue's interplay of animate and inanimate, and his
syllabic forms, into American currency, and from him Aiken derived his 'inadequate spleen-ridden and troubled narrators', and
from Valéry Larbaud, his long-packed line. Williams's *Kora in Hell*
(1920) 'shows familiarity with Max Jacob and Fargue' and other
French writers – Williams had lived in France for extended periods,
had translated Phillippe Soupault and was a friend of Larbaud
(Bram Dijkstra, *Cubism, Stieglitz, and the Early Poetry of William
Carlos Williams*, 1969). His poetry confers unprovincial forms on
the New Jersey scene within which he writes:

Williams could be said to belong in the Cubist tradition – Imagism,
Objectivism, the dissociation and rearrangement of the elements of concrete reality, rather than rhetoric and free association . . . His long quest for
a completely defenseless simplicity of personal speech produces an idiom
identical with that which is the end product of centuries of polish, refinement, tradition, and revolution.

From Man Ray's *Self Portrait* (1963) it is clear that French art
penetrated far into innovative American work. He saw Cézannes at
Stieglitz's gallery before the Armory show of 1913, and his 1913
portrait of 'Donna' contains elements from Picasso and Matisse –
painted at Ridgefield, while Williams was living in Rutherford not
far away. He knew of Brancusi's golden birds through Stieglitz, and
Lautréamont and Apollinaire's *Calligrammes* through his wife's
interest. Before Man Ray went to Paris in 1921, he had contacted
Marcel Duchamp (1915) and Picabia, and through them the
Dadaists in Paris – in fact, Tristan Tzara gave 'mock authorization'
for the New York Dada magazine (1921). Williams met Duchamp
during his Grantwood years (*Autobiography*, ch 23) and entertained
both him and Man Ray at Rutherford in 1916 (ch 26; and see *A
Recognizable Image: William Carlos Williams on Art and Artists*, ed.
Bram Dijkstra, 1978).

The American scene was, therefore, not at all provincial. Mayakovsky was translated into American before French. Carl Sandburg wrote a poem to Brancusi. Yehoash made Yiddish versions of *haiku* and transmuted Apollinaire's ideas into Yiddish verse, long before American poetry in English took them up. Walter Arensberg, whom Man Ray also knew, wrote imitations of Mallarmé and the Dadaists. The little magazines, themselves the centres of innovation, moved internationally. The *Little Review* began in Chicago, moved to Paris, and died at what Rexroth calls 'Gurdjieff's dude ranch in Fontainebleau'. *Broom* was edited from Rome, Paris and Berlin, before dying in America. *Contact*, edited by Williams and Robert McAlmon, like many other magazines became increasingly integrated with European cultural life, an internationalism exemplified also by Eugene Jolas's *Transition* (1927) and Sam Putnam's *New Review*.

The counter-forces assembled predictably. Yvor Winters identified with the anti-Modernism of Valéry and Maritain, and became the most '*parnassien*' and formalist of American poet-critics: *Primitivism and Decadence* (1937) and *The Anatomy of Nonsense* (1943) summarize his position, and *Yvor Winters on Modern Poets* collects six of his probes (1959). At Vanderbilt University, Nashville, Tennessee, poets under the leadership of John Crowe Ransom adopted anti-Modernist positions associated with Daudet, Maurras, Pareto, Houston Stewart Chamberlain, Major Douglas, and ideas phrased as 'social credit', 'classless syndicalism' and 'new agrarianism'. These Southern Agrarians supported reactionary politics and worshipped T. S. Eliot the classicist, Anglo-Catholic and royalist – and Eliot himself derived a good deal of his attitudes from the aristocratic, Dantesque tradition manufactured and upheld by Harvard Jacobinism. The Southern 'Fugitives', as they called themselves, approved of some of Pound but not of his extended open forms. They were certainly racist when it came to 'nigras' and followed the political philosophy of Donald Davison, whose writings, in Rexroth's words, 'somewhat resembled those of a literate Senator Eastland'. They were also generally Christian and delighted in tight elliptical statements of melancholic irony for which the ideal reader would need special training in exegesis. Theirs was, in Karl Shapiro's summary phrase, 'criticism-poetry' (*In Defense of Ignorance*, 1960), and it became the standard poetry for the academic mind and the establishment reviewers between 1940 and 1950, the heyday of American criticism. Its imitators thrive because of the steady domination of publishers, reviews and university courses by the attitudes derived from this location.

Further to the Left, Walter Lowenfels lived in Paris for many years and contributed to *Transition*; his series of elegies on Lawrence, Hart Crane, Rimbaud and Apollinaire – to whom it was structurally indebted – was printed in Paris. E. E. Cummings lived in France after the First World War, but seems to have understood as little of European Modernism as did Henry Miller. More important, so far as invention was concerned, were the followers of André Breton who included Charles Henri Ford, Parker Tyler and Philip Lamantia, who together edited the vigorous Surrealist magazine *View*. Tyler's 'Granite Butterfly' employs procedures derived from Mallarmé's 'Un Coup de dés' – the assemblage of elements towards a spatialized philosophical reverie, a form also used by Lowenfels and Rexroth.

American little magazines and their poets in Europe introduced Cubist and Surrealist forms, as well as the writings of James Joyce and Gertrude Stein, to American writers who thereby had the opportunity to break from the trap of early twentieth-century bohemian or *parnassien* modes and attitudes by recognizing post-1916 innovations in form (ed. E. Anderson and M. Kinzie, *The Little Magazine in America*, 1978). As Robert Bly and James Wright observed in their 1967 introduction to Neruda's *Twenty Poems* (1967): 'the French Surrealist poets drove themselves by force into the unconscious because they hated establishment academicism and the rationalistic European culture'. With this penetration we can place Blaise Cendrars's and Matthew Josephson's appreciation of American popular movies, comic strips, advertisements, sky-scraper styles and Nick Carter dime novels as a way through snobbish academic rejection of popular culture and towards 1960s forms of pop art. Dada rejections of bohemian and bourgeois compromise, its contempt for 'cultivated' audiences and its pre-sentation of bad taste to counter the establishment's 'good taste' also had its salutary repercussions in the 1960s. Duchamp's con-ceptual art finally emerged as a major influence on the work of American writers in the 1960s in *C* magazine (1963) – Ron Padgett, Ted Berrigan and their associates – while Tristan Tzara and Dadaism moved in the writers within *Tzarad*, edited by the English poet Lee Harwood (1965).

These main lines are not difficult to record. For example: in the 1920s *Secession* published not only Hart Crane's poetry and Marianne Moore's appreciation of HD – the focus of Robert Duncan's *HD Book* in the 1960s – but also Malcolm Cowley's appreciation of Roussel's *Locus Solus*. Between 1961 and 1962, the poets John Ashbery, Kenneth Koch, Harry Mathew and James

Schuyler edited *Locus Solus*, which published among other materials Mathew's translation of Roussel's work and many of the *C* magazine writers. *Art and Literature* (1964–7), edited by Ashbery and others, continued this Franco–American relationship of developments out of Cubism into Abstract Expressionism, minimal and pop art, and poetry related to these art forms, and thence into the period of those extensions of Dada events, the happenings and multimedia events of the 1960s and the activities of Andy Warhol's workshop. (Already in 1952, at Black Mountain College, an event had been staged which included the music of John Cage and David Tudor, the poetry of Charles Olson, the dance of Merce Cunningham and the paintings of Robert Rauschenberg, in a multimedial action.)

One poet in particular stands at the centre of this field and in many ways exemplifies its activity. Frank O'Hara was deeply aware of the modern musical developments and as a curator at the Museum of Modern Art in New York produced major exhibitions of Robert Motherwell, Jackson Pollock, Ruben Nakian and Franz Kline. His appreciation of Larry Rivers ('Larry Rivers: A Memoir', 1965), is reflected in the style of his long poem 'Second Avenue' (1960) written in Rivers's studio (and the first edition had a characteristic cover by the painter). Among poets who read at The Club, where many of these artists met on East 8th Street, New York, were Ashbery, Barbara Guest, James Schuyler and O'Hara himself. But he also accurately appears in Elias Wilentz's *The Beat Scene* (1960) – a photograph shows him reading with Ray Bremser, LeRoi Jones and Allen Ginsberg at a benefit for Totem Press, an important little press in Greenwich Village. (Memoirs of O'Hara are contained in John Gruen's *The Party's Over Now*, 1972.) His poems in *Lunch Poems* (1965) and *Odes* (1969) (*Collected Poems*, 1971) articulate an essentially urban experience – luxuriant and socially sophisticated, exuberant and witty, and completely inside the New York scene of poets and painters, a world in which John Ashbery was an editor of *Art News* and Harold Rosenberg, one of the finest critics of American painting of the period, wrote for both *Locus Solus* and *Art and Literature*. This kind of continuity is further indicated by Pollock and Philip Guston reading *Transition* in 1928–9 while they were at Manual Arts High School in Los Angeles, and by the fact that Jasper Johns and Frank Stella were among the first subscribers to *C* magazine.

During the 1920s Pound's *Cantos* appeared in *Transatlantic Review* ('Three Cantos of a Poem of Some Length' had appeared in the private American edition of *Lustra* in 1917). It also carried art supplements with work by Picasso, Brancusi and Gris, and music supplements with work by Pound and Antheil, and on one occasion a song by Erik Satie. Jolas's *Transition* emphasized Joyce's 'structure of multiple planes' and 'polysynthetic language', the possible uses of Freud's dream materials, and the pleasures of Buster Keaton, Charlie Chaplin and Harold Lloyd. Jolas also drew on Blake and Rimbaud (a source also for Hart Crane, even if he spoke little French) in his manifesto, 'Revolution of the Word', in No. 16/17 (1929). At the same time there developed a poetry out of needs to clarify by simplification. Drawing on Pound's and T.·E. Hulme's criticism of romantic symbolism, together with the poems of HD, F. S. Flint, Amy Lowell and others, Imagism proposed concise visual clarity and highly simplified ideas and emotions. It produced little interesting poetry until its programme was taken up and modified in the poetry and poetics of William Carlos Williams and Louis Zukofsky and writers associated with the Objectivist Press. These included Charles Reznikoff and George Oppen, both still excellently active in the 1960s with poetry which takes their early styles into far more complicated areas of articulation (Reznikoff, *Complete Poems*, 2 vols, 1976–7; Oppen, *Collected Poems*, 1975).

Two major seminal works were written within the Objectivist orbit: W. C. Williams's *Spring and All* (1923) and Louis Zukofsky's *A 1–5* (1928–30). Their poetics, combined with certain aspects of the ideogrammatic form of the *Cantos* and the modifications of all three masters in Charles Olson's essay, 'Projective Verse' (*Poetry New York*, No. 3, 1950), form the primary poetics of the 1960s. In fact, Williams himself recognized the significance of Olson's essay by printing part of it in his *Autobiography* (1951). To his resources in American and French poetry, Williams added Lorca's response to his life in New York between 1920 and 1930 – *Poeta en Nueva York* (1940); his essay on Lorca and Whitman was written in 1939. A fairly representative summary of major writing in the early 1930s is Pound's *Active Anthology* (1933), which included work by Williams, Zukofsky, Marianne Moore, E. E. Cummings and the English poet Basil Bunting, who also worked on editing the volume.

Williams's example was effective right through the 1950s and into the 1960s – a long example by poetry and writing on poetry. In 1932 he wrote: 'the form of poetry is that of language' – that is, it is not the form of past poetry or of the criticism of poetry. Poetry for him and for all these poets was not simply personal lyricism and imitations of regular measures and stanzas: it was an innovating function of society. The line of speech is the basic measure, a form which 'excludes no possibility of intelligent resource'. The form is not 'free verse' but the measure and spatial control of cadential lengths, and the varied placing of a wide range of information. The peaks not only exemplify fine craftsmanship; they speak urgently of society – the continuously inventive forms of Williams's *Paterson* (in five books, 1946–58), the ideograms and lyrics of Pound's *Cantos*, and the nervous argumentative journals of Zukofsky's *A* (sections 1–21 appeared between 1928 and 1969). In 1948 Williams wrote of a poem as 'a field of action'; these works carry the sense of a constructed place to work, into which the poet's experience is continuously articulated, becoming synonymous with his life, rather in the sense of the alchemist engaged for life in his work (Eric Mottram, 'Open Field Poetry', *Poetry Information*, No. 17, 1977).

In his early short poem 'Paterson' (1926), Williams had already stated his credo: 'Say it, not in ideas but in things' – a procedure which resisted the transformation of experience into metaphors of something else. It was Pound who early commented on Williams's opacity, lucidity and refusal of symbolic language of the type that must be seen 'through' in order to reach its meaning. But the form of *Kora in Hell* has its sources not only in this insistence and in Max Jacob and Léon Paul Fargue, but in Rimbaud's *Les Illuminations*, and in that dislocation of objects, their reassemblage and metamorphosis, associated with the Cubist and Surrealist–Dadaist complex; in 'The Descent of Winter' (*The Collected Earlier Poems*, 1951), he also used developments of 1923 experiments with automatic writing.

Louis Zukofsky understood that, in comparison with typical early twentieth-century poetic styles, Objectivist verse tended fundamentally to exclude symbol and metaphor, and could be exemplified in Williams's *Spring and All*. In 'An Objective' (1930–1, reprinted in *Prepositions*, 1967), he wrote:

Emotion is the organizer of poetic form . . . the poet's image is not dissociable from the movement of the cadenced shape of the poem. A new cadence is a new idea.

Typography functions to 'tell how the voice should sound':

the poet is continually encountering the facts which in the making seem to want to disturb the music and yet the music or the movement cannot exist without the facts.

Zukofsky's *A 1–5* has exactly this kind of 'musical cohesiveness' (it is Charles Tomlinson's phrase), managing to incorporate a large range of information within a continuous play of motifs and sound patterns of considerable vitality and invention. Within a wider field of contemporary poetics, as Rexroth points out in *Assays*, Objectivism 'owed a good deal to Apollinaire and the Cubists and to the German *Neue Sächlichkeit*', and to those in France who, like the painter Léger, spoke of 'the return to the object'. As *A* gradually unfolded its twenty-four sections (published between 1959 and 1975), the shorter poems were collected (1965 and 1967) and the magnificent prose of *Bottom: On Shakespeare* was published (1963), Zukofsky's stature as one of the century's finest poets became clear (ed. Carroll F. Terrell, *Louis Zukofsky: Man and Poet*, 1980).

II

These poems and poetics, magazines and movements, helped to release poets writing after 1950 from the officialdom of New Criticism poetry, exegesis poetry and the poetry of snobbish cultural reference – poetry for the academic quarterlies and reviewers still hung up on shored ruins, dissociated sensibility and the bewitching trio: tradition, orthodoxy and heresy – the liturgical trinity of Eliot's 1930s scriptures. It was a release from the poetry and critical terminology of reactionary religion and politics, and from preferential prescriptions for poetry derived from seventeenth-century English poems and nineteenth-century French hermetic symbolism. Pound, Williams and Zukofsky were alive and well and writing as excellently as ever in the later 1950s when the Beat poets and the younger poets of Donald M. Allen's anthology, *The New American Poetry 1945–1960* (1960; ed. Donald Allen and George F. Butterick, *The Postmoderns: The New American Poetry Revised*, 1982), needed them as masters and as examples of persistence against officialdom. The appearance of Canto 85 in Pound's *Pisan Cantos* of 1948 demonstrated the kind of powers American poetry could exemplify: and the poet not only gained the Bollingen prize for his work but was incarcerated in St Elizabeth's asylum for his political views and behaviour. The *Cantos* were not only a compendium of poetic resources but demonstrated the ability to compose an epic poetry which placed the active self within a wide range of defining information. Pound's example became a constant for American poets defining their own embattled position in long poems during the politically and morally disastrous double decade from 1950 to 1970. As late as 1969, Pound's *Drafts and Fragments of Cantos CX–CXVII* showed how this great onward-going work remained the central act of poetry, containing the main interests of major American poets of a young generation: the renewal of the city, the renewal of language and poetic forms, the renewal of mythology, the destruction of a degenerate economic system, the placing of the Southeast Asian conflict within the historical conduct of America and the West, and the possibilities of strategies of survival without being overwhelmed by the defeats of compromise.

Pound's 1969 book reverberated with a sense of wonder at human achievement. His scorn for materialistic greed – at the heart of his analysis of the City – is as powerful as ever (especially in 'Addendum to Canto C') but it is now juxtaposed to remorse at his own behaviour and a search for personal charity. More than ever, the *Cantos* could be seen as the measure, both in their poetics and in their information, for the committed American poet. (It is significant that the pirated first edition of the last *Cantos* came from the centre of post-Beat anarchist poetry, the Fuck You Press, in 1967 – 'at a secret location in the lower East Side, New York City', with a cover by Joe Brainard, firm associate of the *C* magazine group.) Civilization 'without tyranny' had always been Pound's criterion, and now he defined the movement of peaceful, fertile pleasure – in art and in landscape – in three exemplary civilizations which harboured the wonderful ability of men. The effect in the poems is that of a garden which has the freshness and formality of an ideal city, imbued with the erotic myths of Orpheus, Endymion and Artemis. Beyond a brief locating reference to Quemoy in Canto CXI, providing a dateline for the Asian conflict, lie the strenuous definitions of 'serenitas', maintained throughout half a century of financial corruption and political cruelty. That 'clear discourse' for which Pound has always aimed, in Canto CXIII becomes once again the garden combination of man-made form and natural botany. Zukofsky's emphasis on clarity and the eye, and Robert Duncan's explorations of HD's Mediterranean world continually come to mind. The great light images of the *Cantos* seem even more urgent here, as the counter to the major sin of the whole century, the use of belief and usury against justice, to 'implement domination'. Canto CXIV reaches into a condition which would have been supported by the 1960s Movement itself, with a fine ideogram of the propertyless society, emphasizing men who have been 'still, uncontending – not to pos-session, in hypostasis'. The book concludes with statements distinctly for the 1960s: 'the young for the old/that is the tragedy' – and: 'To be men not destroyers' (see Peter Makin, *Pound's Cantos*, 1985, and ed. R. W. Butterfield, *Modern American Poetry*, 1984).

A passage in Charles Olson's *Maximus IV, V, VI* (1969) can be used to summarize Pound's example and relevance: 'An American/is a complex of occasions,/themselves a geometry/of spatial nature.' But academic critics and the reviewers seized on Robert Lowell as being the more relevant poet. He began as a disciple of the New Criticism poets, camping out in Allen Tate's garden, and then re-read Williams in an effort to shake himself reasonably free to articulate his sense of personal neurosis and a collapsed society that believed itself to be thriving. *Life Studies* (1959) is an exercise in secularized New England exhibitions of conscience as they enter the enforced anarchy of the American 1960s. Compared with the poems in Donald Allen's anthology, Lowell's incline to iambic boredom and uninteresting prosody; and Olson's *In Cold Hell, In Thicket* (1953) had already presented the material of New England under contemporary controls – 'An Ode on Nativity' moves far beyond Lowell's tourism of the ego. In David Antin's words, 'Lowell's New Englandism is merely an inversion of Tate's Confederacy' (Antin's essay, 'Modernism and Postmodernism: Approaching the Present in American Poetry', *Boundary 2*, 1972, makes the issues between Tate, Lowell and Olson clear). *For the Union Dead* (1964) and *Near the Ocean* (1967) consolidated Lowell's position as a self-consciously 'contemporary' academic poet, aristo-cratic and vulnerable, the foremost poetic witness of a charac-teristically bewildered and agonized liberalism, the staple fare of the American middle classes. Norman Mailer's portrait of him in *The Armies of the Night* (1968) is accurate, and Lowell himself has endorsed it. But his example persisted into the grimly popular 'confessional poets' of the 1960s – Plath, Sexton and the rest, with their nervous attempts to justify commonplace lives through com-monplace poetics.

Poetry as a totally invented field of action, not instantly con-sumable and confirmatory of the liberal 'status quo', required both energy and information in demanding proportions. In fact, by the 1960s American poetry of any consequence needed an attention beyond the consumerism of the amateur of the arts. For example, the poetics of 'Projective Verse', and the forms of Olson's *Maximus* poems, present 'composition by field, as opposed to inherited line, stanza, over-all form'. The poem invents its form and invites the reader to enter the area of invention rather than immediate recog-nition. The poem is an energy transference (Zukofsky had used a similar terminology earlier), 'at all points ... a high energy-construct' and 'energy-discharge'. Pound's 'musical phrase' as a unit of form is extended: 'form is never more than an extension of content' (a phrase from Robert Creeley's correspondence with Olson which went into the essay – see 'Robert Creeley in Conversation with Charles Tomlinson', *Kulchur 16*, Winter, 1964–5, and *The Review 10*, 1964 – Black Mountain poetry issue). Pound's structure of continuous and overlapping ideograms is a process now formulated as inheritable procedure and placed with Edward Dahlberg's dictum: 'one perception must immediately and directly lead to a further perception'. The juxtaposition of syllables as particles of sound articulates the mind's ear in action, towards that over-all melopoeia Pound had stressed. The unit (line of measure) is a set of these energies and its length is controlled not by mathematical metrics but by the breath of a man making his poem, an action which is partly the automatic or natural activity of his body, and partly the creative activity of play.

Olson's poetic structures play and dance rather than fulfil any puritanical prescription of obedience to a form. Units of energy (sound, social information, spatial size) are assembled on the page with their own dynamic interrelationships and intersections – as they are in *Paterson* (which explains Williams's interest in Olson's essay). The field of objects is neither syntactically nor metrically rigid, nor is it imitative. Olson states that he admires Hart Crane's 'arc of freshness', based on the word as a 'handle', and he understands how the arc needs reinforcement from Fenollosa's idea of the sentence as the 'passage of force from subject to object' and of the energy of 'the verb between two nouns'. Like Harold A. Innis (*The Bias of Communication*, 1951) and his pupil, Marshall McLuhan, Olson was aware of how manuscript and press can remove the voice from poetry, but he asserted the possibilities of the typewritten page as a set of controls equivalent to the notation of sounds in music. His theory and practice at this point are part of a general twentieth-century inclination towards the spatial rather than the linear: it is there in the influences of Alfred Korzybski's neo-Aristotelian logic (*Science and Sanity*, 1933), in the solutions to notational problems developed by John Cage in *A Year from Monday* (1967) and his anthology *Notations* (1969), and in the poetics of sound-text and concrete poetry, including typewriter poems or 'typestracts' (cf. *Open Poetry: Four Anthologies of Expanded Poems*, ed. Ronald Gross and George Quasha, 1973). As Olson observes, both Cummings and Williams 'used the machine as a scoring to their composing, as a script to their vocalization'. Space and time become, in compatibility with twentieth-century philosophy and science, space-time coordinates. Beyond Olson's 'projective verse', the twentieth-century poem may exist either in new notation, mechanically recorded voice, or video form, or in a single unrepeated performance. Silence is as much part of a poem's score as space: the space–time notation of Webern has its American poetic equivalents in the work of Aram Saroyan and other concrete and sound-text poets, and especially in the splendid performances of Jackson Mac Low (his *Representative Works: 1938–1985*, 1986, at least publishes the visual forms of his work).

'Projective Verse' in theory and in its many practices – which modified its origins again and again – place Objectivism and Imagism in a broader poetic with a wider range of application. Olson's aim was to reduce egotistical lyric sprawl and exegetical rhetoric so that 'the projective act, which is the artist's act in the larger field of objects, leads to dimensions larger than the man'. This is exactly the effect of *Paterson* (cf. Eric Mottram, 'The Making of Paterson', *Stand*, Vol. 7, No. 3, 1965; reprinted in *Profile of William Carlos Williams*, ed. Jerome Mazzaro, 1971; Benjamin Sankey, *Paterson*, 1971), the *Cantos, A 1–24*, and Olson's *Maximus Poems* (begun in 1950, completely in 1970, published complete in 1983) and later Robert Duncan's series of poems called 'Passages', embodied in *Bending the Bow* (1968) and *Ground Work: Before the War* (1984). In these large scale works (and there are others by Theodore Enslin, John Ashbery, Clark Coolidge, etc.), the varied articulations possible in the poet's voice unify his projected information, working to dramatize a wide range of objects and feelings. The resulting epic structure is the movement of a man in his own time and in history. The *Cantos* began to solve notational problems of how to fuse autobiography with history back in 1915 and evolved a syntax which was not bound to the traditional sentence, with its assumed social order and basis in linear logic. Nine years after 'projective verse', Olson returned, as poet and historian, to the difficulties of sentence and syntax in a letter to the English poet, then a student at Cambridge, Elaine Feinstein. The track through which the reader enters the propositions of the poem, Olson now says, is a course of speech rhythms which demonstrate 'the value of the vernacular over grammar' (and he is well aware of the example in Dante which this enacts). Since speech is both inherent and etymological, Olson, in common with a number of investigators into the relationships between nature and culture, became increasingly involved in linguistic scholarship and archaeology (*The Mayan Letters, 1953*, and *Letters for Origin 1960–1965*, 1969, suggest the double activity). He places the action of many poems in the small seaport fishing town of Gloucester, Massachusetts, and then anchors that auto-biographical locality in the historical and geographical world map. The action of himself in Gloucester is related at every point to the non-symbolic, euhemeristic reality of myths, especially creation myths used as descriptions of man's apprehensions of earth, sky, migration and ecology. The separate poems are events which project the self in the America of the 1950s and 1960s as a force for survival, through sensuous and intellectual understanding and the making of a distinctive poetics. The aim is steady, from the early poem 'An Ode on Nativity' (1951) through to the final *Maximus Poems*: to offer the forms and materials for a renewed life (see also *The Special View of History*, 1970, *Additional Prose*, 1974 and *Muthologos* Vols 1 and 2, 1979 and 1980). That this could be a useful launching basis for a younger poet, and not an impossible programme, is evidenced by the work of Edward Dorn in *Geography* (1965), *Gunslinger* (1968–72) and *Recollections of Gran Apacheria* (1974) (and see *Interviews*, 1980, *Views*, 1980 and ed. D. Wesling, *Internal Resistances*, 1986).

III

Olson showed poets opportunities of writing ontogenetically without losing a sense of urgency and without the pompous didacticism and dogma of the university poets or the ego-trips of 'confessional' poets (cf. 'The Limits of Self-Regard', Eric Mottram, *Parnassus*, Fall/Winter 1972). Naturally, he had slavish adherents, but works as widely different as Paul Blackburn's *The Cities* (1967), Robert Kelly's *Axon Dendron Tree* (1967) and Ted Berrigan's *Many Happy Returns* (1969), use projective field methods of placing information, with an excitement and virtuosity remote from discipleship. Paul Carroll's anthology of poets who emerged in the 1960s, *The Young American Poets* (1968), testifies to both the difficulty of release from the inter-war period's masters and the liberation into new styles which their example enabled.

'Composition by field' is also the poetic equivalent of Abstract Expressionist and action painting (which Harold Rosenberg was instrumental in defining in the 1950s) in its use of personal gesture made with a controlled spontaneity, the result of discipline within changing and risking inventiveness. Michael McClure's *Hymns to St Geryon* (1959) makes the connections explicit:

          ... GESTURE THE GESTURE   to make fists of it.
       Clyfford Still: 'We are committed to an unequalled act,
    not illustrating outworn myths or contemporary alibis.
                                            One must
       accept total responsibility for what he executes.
    And the measure of his greatness will be the depth of his
              insight and courage in realizing
       his own vision. Demands for communication are pre-
       sumptuous and irrelevant.'

Besides this direct implication of Still, a major American painter of the period, McClure cites Pollock and Kline in his poem, and makes his connection with Olson: 'To hit again, the foot is to kick with', a reference to an essay in *Human Universe* (1965) which itself quotes Pound's famous maxim: 'Prosody is the articulation of the total sound of the poem.' John Ashbery's 'The Skaters' (*Rivers and Mountains*, 1965), and 'Europe' (*The Tennis Court Oath*, 1962), are major field compositions which relate to contemporary American painting but belong to a completely different set of procedures to Olson's 'projective' methods. The action of 'The Skaters' consists of a moving collage of scenes, objects and reminiscences which illus-trates nothing: 'Poetry does not have subject matter because it is the subject!' (quoted in *The Poets of the New York School*, ed. John Bernard Myers, 1969). Ashbery practises what Pound calls 'con-centrare' – the presentation of events, rather than what the events are. He acknowledges the influence of John Cage's *Music of Changes* (1952) rather than other poets, and in a statement in *A Controversy of Poets* (ed. Paris Leary and Robert Kelly, 1965), says:

I originally wanted to be a painter, and did paint until I was eighteen years old, but I feel I could best express myself in music. What I like about music is its ability of being convincing, of carrying an argument through success-fully to the finish, though the terms of this argument remain unknown quantities. What remains is the structure, the architecture of the argument, scene or story. I would like to do this in poetry. I would also like to reproduce the power dreams have of persuading you that a certain event has a meaning not logically connected with it, or there is a hidden relation among disparate objects.

With Kenneth Koch's poems in *Thank You* (1962), and certain poems of the *C* magazine poets, 'The Skaters' belongs with a variety of compositional methods: Auden's narrative landscapes of the 1930s, the poetics of Max Jacob and Pierre Reverdy, and Gertrude Stein's Cubist works together with their critical explanation in her

1926 essay, 'Composition as Explanation' (*Selected Writings of Gertrude Stein*, ed. Carl Van Vechten, 1946). Ashbery's 'Europe' suggests the spatial dislocations of Cubist and post-Cubist painting, the montage methods of film, and the constellatory procedures of post-Webern music. Koch's poetics are related to the work of Paul Eluard, Henri Michaux, Pierre Reverdy, Max Jacob and Raymond Roussel, as well as to the local American actions of Whitman and the Marx Brothers. Ashbery, too, has used popular materials, notably Mickey Spillane, E. Phillips Oppenheim and the poems of Paul Engle. (Ashbery's later books include *Self-Portrait in a Convex Mirror*, 1975, *Houseboat Days*, 1977, *As We Know*, 1979 and *A Wave*, 1984; Kenneth Koch's work includes *When the Sun Tries to Go On*, 1969, *The Pleasures of Peace*, 1969, *The Duplications*, 1969 and *Days and Nights*, 1982.)

Ted Berrigan, an admirer of both Ashbery and Koch, and co-founder of *C* magazine, has used Henry Green's novels (on which Ashbery wrote his graduate thesis), and Westerns, as well as Breton and the Dadaists. Berrigan's stylistic eclecticism and range of humour, together with his use of existent works of art, is nearer to the painting and assemblage of Larry Rivers and Andy Warhol than to Ashbery's relatively classicist work (cf. 'Craft Interview with John Ashbery', *The New York Quarterly*, No. 9, Winter, 1972). The range of *C* magazine is summarized in *Bean Spasms* (1967), a significant work of the period, put together by Berrigan and Ron Padgett and illustrated by Joe Brainard, and exemplifying the Americanization of the European avant-garde which had been continuous since the 1920s. (*So Going Around Cities* (1980) is an excellent selection of Berrigan's poetry). The title of Padgett's *In Advance of the Broken Arm*, 1964, with drawings by Brainard, and published by *C* Press, is taken from the first Marcel Duchamp ready-made, dated '1915 New York'.) It is with Ashbery, Koch, Harry Mathew, James Schuyler and the younger New York poets in *C* and *Mother*, and later *Angel Hour* and *Paris Review*, that the relationship with French forms of *écriture* and conceptual art are maintained in America. As John Graham wrote in his *System and Dialectics of Art* (1937), 'the difficulty in producing a work of art lies in the fact that the artist has to unite at one and the same time three elements: thought, feeling and authentic *écriture*.' (See *An Anthology of New York Poets*, ed. Padgett and D. Shapiro, 1970.)

The breakthrough in formal education towards a sense of a common field of art work in any medium and the traditional humanities subjects came at Black Mountain College, North

Carolina, in the 1940s and 1950s. In 1953, Olson wrote to the poet and editor Cid Corman about 'a show by Kline, De Kooning, Tworkov, Guston (the space cadets, who have all been here the past two years . . .)'. This was in the influential series of letters through which Olson guided Corman's early editing of *Origin* in the 1950s, and 'here' was, of course, Black Mountain College, to which many of the finest painters, musicians and poets had gravitated since its foundation, and particularly since 1950. Founded in 1933 by John Andrew Rice, a liberal dissenting classics professor from Rollins College, Florida, it became, from the late 1940s onwards, the centre for an experiment in community within the competitive anti-community of capitalism and its educational manipulations. From the beginning, Black Mountain had utopian and regenerative purposes: but it did not teach overt sociology or a political or philosophical line (see Martin Duberman, *Black Mountain – An Exploration in Community*, 1973). Besides the painters Olson mentions, Josef Albers (with his Bauhaus background) became head of an art department which numbered also Rauschenberg and Esteban Vicente among its members. Besides Olson, who became the last rector of the college, in literature there were Edward Dahlberg, Eric Bentley, Paul Blackburn, Robert Creeley, Robert Kelly, Denise Levertov, John Wieners, Jonathan Williams and LeRoi Jones, either on the staff or among the students. *The Black Mountain Review*, which Creeley edited (1954–7), transmitted the main interests in literature which the college inherited from Pound, Williams and Olson himself (cf. Paul Blackburn, 'The Grinding Down', *Kulchur*, No. 10, 1963). Given the interaction between traditionally exclusive 'disciplines' at the college, it is not surprising, therefore, that John Cage was able to organize there the first event of the genre later called 'happenings' in 1952 (Richard Kostelanetz, *The Theater of Mixed Means*, 1968).

Multimedia events became common in the 1960s. Poetry, traditionally insulated in the West from other arts, frequently took place within an oral-visual-aural combine, an action which realized in a theatre performance Joyce's 'verbivocovisual on the word' (it is thoroughly examined in *Explorations*, No. 8, 1957, ed. Marshall McLuhan and Edmund C. Carpenter). It was not simply a matter of poetry with jazz (as a way of widening the audience for poetry and breaking literary insularities), but of using concrete and phonic sound and language elements within a dramatic combine which included space and movement, and yet was still not traditional theatre. Central to this movement – which later became a large range of 'performance arts' – were the Fluxus group of musicians, poets and artists, and indications of their work can be gathered from Dick Higgins's *Jefferson's Birthday/Postface* (1964) and *Foew&ombwhnw* (1969). The Great Bear Pamphlets (1965–7), also published by Something Else Press, indicate the international range of the artists involved in happenings and conceptual art (a form which again relates to Duchamp's definitions of art as choice); they include Allan Kaprow, David Antin, Jackson Mac Low, Claes Oldenberg, Al Hansen, Jerome Rothenberg (*Ritual: A Book of Primitive Rites and Events*, 1966, later included in his *Technicians of the Sacred*, 1968), Emmett Williams and Philip Corner (*Popular Entertainments*, 1967), all from America, together with Diter Rot, Nam June Paik, Wolf Vostell, the Zaj group from Madrid, Luigi Russolo, Robert Filliou and George Brecht. John Cage's *Change the World (You Will Only Make Matters Worse)*, 1967, was later incorporated into his *A Year from Monday* (1967). (A fuller range of examples of this whole group can be obtained from *Happening & Fluxus*, ed. H. Sohm, 1970.)

Conceptual art or information art is concerned with art as indication, choice, scenario for performance, and as such can be related to the strong advent of poetry performances developing throughout the 1950s and reaching a peak in the 1960s in America. Allen Ginsberg's performances would be preceded by chants adapted from the Hindu, to relax both poet and audience before the poems themselves. Michael McClure's *Ghost Tantras* (1964) again indicates the usage of Indian forms in the period (this would include Kerouac's *The Scripture of the Golden Eternity*, an American sutra, written in 1956 at the instance of Gary Snyder). It is a collection of phonic texts for oral performance, based on tantric principles of transformation of body–mind continuum through the performance of sound structures (which combine words and invented linguistic forms).

Concrete and sound-text poetry developed rather later in America than in the rest of the world. John Giorno's *Poems* (1967) reversed certain principles of Mallarmé and Joyce by transcribing newspaper materials into the shape of poems (that is, into familiar linear and spatial forms), to make 'found' poems, again related to Duchamp's ready-mades. (Ronald Gross's *Pop Poems* (1967) similarly used advertisements.) Giorno's book is still well within the New York poets' scene, however: the cover is by Rauschenberg and it was published at Mother Press by Peter Schjeldahl, himself a poet associated with *C*-group writers and *Art News*. Schjeldahl's *White*

Country (1968) contains his own poems, and those of his co-editor of *Mother* magazine, Lewis MacAdams, are in *City Money* (1967) and *The Poetry Room* (1970). Again indicating the inclination to performance, the last issue of *Mother* was a long-playing record made by McClure, Aram Saroyan, John Wieners, Ginsberg, Kenward Elmslie and others (1968). The most useful collections of concrete sound-text work which contain American poets are *Concrete Poetry: A World View* (ed. Mary Ellen Solt, 1968), *This Book is a Movie: An Exhibition of Language Art and Visual Poetry* (ed. J. G. Bowles and T. Russel, 1971), *Imaged Words and Worded Images* (ed. Richard Kostelanetz, 1970), and *An Anthology of Concrete Poetry* (ed. Emmett Williams, 1967).

All these events present both new and not so new solutions to our continuous investigations into form and notation: and it is exactly this which separates them from the conservative inheritors of the academy and the critical establishment reviewers. Frequently the result is a self-evident structure which holds its materials in a dynamic mobile equilibrium, without necessarily reaching after a finished synthesis of all its elements. It may resist definitions of completion in traditional terms of imitation and the fulfilment of recognized programmes. For example, the terminology of 'organic' approval has become tautological since the discoveries of biologists and zoologists represented in L. L. Whyte's *Aspects of Form* (1951) and George Kepes's *Value and Vision* (5 vols, 1955–6). Structural procedure is now understood as invention within a universal morphology of forms, and procedures are openly revealed in order to be part of the pleasure of participating in art. In Allen Ginsberg's terms, 'Mind is Shapely ... the message is: widen the area of consciousness.' The reader of poetry is invited into an event which takes place as part of the perceptual space-time of his period and place; the work may not necessarily record any fixity or boundary; the participant may be invited to contemplate the poem, meditate on its spatiality rather than track its lineality. To refer to McClure's use of Clyfford Still again: 'we are now committed to an unqualified act, not illustrating outward myths, or contemporary alibis. One must accept total responsibility for whatever he executes'.

That responsibility included political and social responsibility, responding to America's Southeast Asia wars, the anti-draft and Civil Rights movements, the Government's bombing of Hanoi and the Vietnam dykes, the murders of protesting students at Orangeville and Kent State – and later, to American intervention in Latin America and the Mediterranean, and the unrestrained development of nuclear energy and weaponry. Some of the poets' response is contained in Walter Lowenfels's anthology *Where Is Vietnam?* (1967), in Diane DiPrima's *War Poems* collection (1968) and in James F. Mersmann's study of this action, *Out of the Vietnam Vortex* (1974). As Mayakovsky observed: 'One condition indispensable for the production of a poem is the existence in society of a problem whose solution is unimaginable except by a poem.'

The effect on the teaching of poetry in universities of all these changes, and the political ones in particular, was salutary: 'Teachers and critics of literature could hardly escape the contrast between the sterility of their academic roles and the new sense of literary vocation discovered by writers increasingly active in the anti-war movement' (Louis Kampf and Paul Lauter, introduction to their *The Politics of Literature*, 1972, a collection of essays dedicated to the imprisoned black activist George Jackson). Denise Levertov read her poems in a sanctuary for draft resisters; Robert Bly publicly handed over his National Book Award money to young Americans defying the draft authorities; Allen Ginsberg led chants and songs at the Pentagon and in Chicago streets against the tyranny of government. Kampf and Lauter go further: it was, they claim, the anti-war poems of Muriel Rukeyser, Levertov, Bly, Galway Kinnell, Adrienne Rich and many others, and of course the war itself, 'not radical literary criticism, which helped break the claim that self-absorbed, academic poets had maintained (despite the popular success of Allen Ginsberg, for example) over literature classrooms and literary journals'. Most of the work of the distinguished black poets – including Baraka, Ishmael Reed, Clarence Major and David Henderson – 'had to be understood as weapons in a struggle for liberation, just as slave narratives, spirituals and work songs had been before them'.

IV

The contemporary American poet who works truly within the poetics of his own time renounces a single point of view, linear perspective and imitation. He respects Pound's sculptural ideal for the poet: 'he sees the in and the through/the four sides'. He understands Creeley's remark in 'Olson and Others – Some Orts for the Sports' (*Big Table*, No. 4, 1960; reprinted in *A Quick Graph*, 1970): 'Olson's emphasis is put upon prosody and not upon interpretation' (and he adds Pound's maxim, already cited here, that prosody is 'the articulation of the total sound of the poem'). Robert Duncan stands as a major poet whose extraordinary understanding of poetics articulates his political responsibilities. His deft summaries of the implications of objectivist and projective verse poetics in 'Notes on Poetics regarding Olson's *Maximus*' (*Black Mountain Review*, No. 6, 1956) and 'Ideas of the Meaning of Form' (*Kulchur*, No. 4, 1961), are activated in the movements between passionate denunciation of world tyranny, the nature of professional killing and the idea of community in 'Orders', 'Up Rising' and 'The Soldiers', the titles of 'Passages' 24–26 in *Bending the Bow* (1968). (Both the essays are reprinted in Donald Allen and Warren Tallman's essential *The Poetics of the New American Poetry*, 1973; see *Boundary 2*, Vol. VIII, No., 1980 – Duncan issue.)

Redefinitions of poetry away from academic exegesis and reactionary attitudes received further help from Jerome Rothenberg's magnificent *Technicians of the Sacred* (1968; revised and enlarged edition 1985). The title is Mircea Eliade's phrase for ethnic artists, functioning in tribal societies; the book collates a powerful 'range of poetries' from Africa, America, Asia and Oceania which demonstrates how 'primitive means complex', and that, as Noam Chomsky's concept of generative language and Lévi-Strauss's structural anthropology also indicate, indigenous poetry is a social function right across cultural frontiers and technological 'progress'. Rothenberg writes in his introduction:

it is a matter of energy & intelligence as universal constants &, in any specific case, the direction that energy & intelligence (=imagination) have been given. No people today is newly born. No people has sat in sloth for the thousands of years of its history. Measure everything by the Titan rocket & the transistor radio, & the world is full of primitive peoples. But once change the unit of value to the poem or the dance-event or the dream (all clearly artefactual situations) & it becomes apparent what all those people have been doing all those years with all that time on their hands.

Rothenberg's collection is both a counter to official imperialist policy and its support from anthropology and Darwinist racism, and a demonstration of ways in which contemporary American inventive poetry and happenings are traditional, in the sense that their forms have similar forms and procedures to those of 'primitive' ethnic complexities. The book concludes with a set of 'commentaries' which make these connections between ethnic and contemporary America by juxtaposing poetries 'carried by voice', poems with non-linear logic, including constellatory forms, poems as social rituals, random and found poems, composition by field, and various instances of bardic or shamanistic functions for poetry. Rothenberg shows similarities between a Seneca Indian eagle dance and the form of 1960s happenings, and relates Hugo Ball's sound poems of 1915, McClure's *Ghost Tantras*, Maori genealogical poems and Mac Low's *Light Poems* (1968). Bantu images and Robert Kelly's *Lunes* (1965), Aztec definitions and Gary Snyder's poems, Indian picture-writing and works by both Apollinaire and Kenneth Patchen (poems in *Hallelujah Anyway*, 1967, for example) are shown to partake of similar materials and forms, because they have a similar social function, or a similar human urge to make and shape. When Rothenberg's book is placed with Solt's *Concrete Poetry: A World View*, the implications are clear. They can be indicated by two passages in Rothenberg; the first is Ernst Cassirer on 'primitive man':

in his conception of nature and life these differences are obliterated by a stronger feeling: the deep conviction of a fundamental and indelible 'solidarity of life' that bridges over the multiplicity and variety of its single forms ... Life is felt as an unbroken continuous whole ... The limits between (its) different spheres are not insurmountable barriers; they are fluent and fluctuating ... By a sudden metamorphosis everything may be turned into everything. If there is any characteristic and outstanding feature of the mythical world, any law by which it is governed – it is this law of metamorphosis.

The second is from Mac Low:

The poet creates a *situation* wherein he invites other persons & the world in general to be co-creators with him! He does not wish to be a dictator but a loyal co-initiator of action within the free society of equals which he hopes his work will help to bring about.

Mary Ellen Solt's introduction shows how, within American culture, the configurations of Cummings, Williams, Olson, Henri Chopin's phonic poems, Zukofsky, Creeley in a poem like 'Le Fou' (*For Love: Poems 1950–1960*, 1962), Emmett Williams ('the first American poet who can be properly called concrete in terms of commitment and consistency of method'), and certain works of Jonathan Williams and Ronald Johnson, all indicate a precise consideration of composition by field, poetry as serious play activity, and poetry as revelatory function in society. The discussion on this kind of probing image is primarily in two essays of the period: 'Why Deep Image?' (*Trobar*, No. 3, 1961), and 'Deep Image and Mode', in which Rothenberg is joined by Creeley (*Kulchur*, No. 6, 1962). Rothenberg is a fine poet, as well as a promoter of poetry. He founded the Hawk's Well Press and the magazine *Poems from the Floating World*, and kept in circulation a wide range of European and ethnic poetries, helping to prevent American poetry from becoming parochial. His own poems are transcultural in reference and poetics (*Between: Poems 1960/63*, 1967), and he is particularly American in the very act of exploring the relationships between American cultural feeling and his own Polish–Jewish antecedents in some of his best poems – *Poland/1931* (1969) and *A Book of Testimony* (1971). A useful selection of his work appeared as *Poems for the Game of Silence* in 1971, and *A Seneca Journal* (1978) and *Vienna Blood* (1980) show an increasingly subtle poetics for his ethnic preoccupations.

Technicians of the Sacred, together with *Shaking the Pumpkin* (1971, revised and enlarged 1986), *A Big Jewish Book* (1978) and *Symposium of the Whole: A Range of Discourse toward an Ethnopoetics* (1983), are essential collections of documents in the steady development of hermeneutics and heuristic analysis of myth and culture which poets, among others, have taken into their work during these decades. It can be seen as an extension of the rather thinner platonistic definitions of 'major man' in the 1930s poems of Wallace Stevens – syllogistic iambic structures dedicated to imagining a sensuous aristocratic world without gods. Olson's 'human universe' (developed in a series of 1950s essays collected under that title in 1965), and Duncan's 'open universe' ('Towards an Open Universe', in *Poets and Poetry*, ed. Howard Nemerov, 1967), contain much more necessary information and a stronger sense of relationship to anthropology and physics. Stevens's poems formed 'sets' through which to determine the possible nature of an abundance society, a projected vision of mythless space–time (in 'Esthétique du Mal' and 'Credences of Summer'), a way out of inter-war ideologies, conflict philosophies and the Earth treated as an object of conquest in a state of scarcity. Stevens's morphology at least arises from a sense of ecology which resists philosophic myth and dogmatic religion. His 'supreme fiction' is close to Creeley's vision, but Creeley also uses Wittgenstein and the refraction of his philosophy of language through Zukofsky's huge compendium, *Bottom: On Shakespeare* (1963). It is as if Creeley's meticulous, wary procedures derived from techniques of founding a proposition laid bare in *Tractatus Logico-Philosophicus*; his poetry might be seen as an offspring of a statement in *Philosophical Investigations*: 'it is the field of force of a word that is decisive'. Like Stevens, Creeley is making his world so that it will not let him down at a time when confidence has been lost in the society he is raised in and works in. *Words* (1967) is a set of poems which gradually and warily explore the poet's situation as a number of events which yield basic proposi- tions. Their movement has no swing, none of Stevens's plausible confidence, and rather more of Zukofsky's hesitant, almost flin- ching poise. His poems define 'mind' – the word constantly recurs – and 'consciousness' in order to free the warmth of love to combat his sense of panic, of endless threat to a man's integrity while he lives in ad-mass America. *Pieces* (1969) is a continuity of separate poems whose information is now wider, less claustrophobic. Creeley searched here for definitions of law (especially in 'Numbers') – an American preoccupation from the beginning – and, in 'The Finger', the nature of the basic existential elements: light, patterns, the woman, the eye, the room, the fire, thinking, knowing. This poem is a masterly play with vital units in order to make them yield flexible securities for living rather than oppressive limits.

Pieces, A Day Book (1973) and *Hello* (1978) develop forms for a continuity of poetic presentation which he calls 'a common audit of days', 'ways in which the statement could include the diversity and variousness of experience rather than always choosing these moments of untensive crisis which tend to be singularizing and thus contained' (ed. Ekbert Faas, *Towards a New American Poetics*, 1978). But Creeley's ability to extend the shape and tone of his short poem is still clear in *Away* (1976), *Later* (1980) and *Echoes* (1982). His skills as an analyst and critic of poetry, which make him an ex- ceptional teacher, can be read in *A Quick Graph* (1970) and *Contexts of Poetry* (1973) (and see *Robert Creeley*, ed. Carroll F. Terrell, 1984).

The amount of information in the poetry of Olson and Duncan is much more ambitious. Their problem is to maintain 'total sound' throughout their complex fusions of personal instance and historical knowledge, to maintain the bodily nature of poetry throughout a structure which contains historicized vision, analysed myth, geographic locality, a critique of the City (in the immediate tradition of Pound), and an analytical use of etymology. Olson calls his means 'proprioception' – the body's reception of knowledge as its own, 'the data of depth sensibility' in a human universe (*Proprioception*, 1965). Duncan calls his means 'rime', defined in a numbered series of passages entitled *The Structure of Rime* intermittently throughout

The Opening of the Field (1960), *Roots and Branches* (1964), *Bending the Bow* (1968) and *Ground Work* (1984): 'correspondences, working of figures and patterns of figures in which we apprehend the whole we do not see . . . the plot we are to follow, the great myth or work, is a fiction of what Man is' ('Two Chapters from HD', *Tri-Quarterly*, No. 12, Spring, 1968). Both Olson's *Maximus* poems and Duncan's 'Passages' are open-ended (like *Paterson*, *A*, the *Cantos* and, at least by internal implication, 'Esthétique du Mal'), holding their accumulations in an encyclopaedic mobile field.

These poets are erudite in the Miltonic sense. They project sets of rapid notations, relevantly juxtaposed chronology and bibliography, felt in the body (the terms are Creeley's in 'A Foot Is To Kick With', *Poetry*, October, 1966). Their discourse is fairly rapid and its relationships have to be recreated in the reader's experience by slowing up the processes. Sometimes their work presents difficulty, through ignorance of their sources; but as Alain Robbe-Grillet once observed, 'art is not meant simply to reassure people'. The ambition of these poets is to recreate the City as the container, bearer and cultivator of a civilization that is not antagonistic to men. Therefore their opposition to official America is radical – it is overt, for instance, in Duncan's 'Passages' 21, 25 and 26, and in Olson's 'I, Maximus of Gloucester to You'. Their aim is like Blake's in *Jerusalem*, plates 98 and 99 – to contribute to the creation, for the first time, of the four-fold son of man 'creating exemplars of Memory and of Intellect,/Creating Space, Creating Time, according to the wonders Divine/Of Human Imagination', and creating 'the great City'. Their imaginative synthesis extends further than the provincial and national, outward to the global poem, the poem of Goethe's world-literature (cf. Thornton Wilder, 'Goethe and World Literature', *Perspectives*, No. 1, 1952).

V

America has frequently produced its arts in short-lived communities of common sympathy, beyond mere bohemianism and middle-class dilettante amateurism, or the isolated rogue artist. The huge land mass, the jungle of its cities and the ethos of competition militate against community. In fact, the common action of artists has been one of the few ways in which the culture has cohered at all. In the 1950s and 1960s poets grouped in New York around painters and musicians with whom they shared interests, or grouped at Black Mountain College. These focuses overlapped with three others: the Beat poets, the San Francisco 'renaissance', and the Minnesota *Sixties* campaign. More recently, resurgences in Philadelphia centred on *Contact* magazine (Jeff Goldberg), Telegraph Books (Victor Bokris and Andrew Wylie), *Paper Air* (Gil Ott) and *Tamarisk* (Dennis Barone), and in the San Francisco–New York activities of poets associated with some of the most radical and exciting developments focused in *L-A-N-G-U-A-G-E* magazine, and Hills, The Figures, Segue and other presses. Such designations immediately suggest more cohesion and planned decision than probably took place, but they hold firmly enough as limiting parameters of activity.

Out of younger poets associated with Black Mountain College – LeRoi Jones, Paul Blackburn, Joel Oppenheimer, Gilbert Sorrentino – and some of the Beat writers, Allan Ginsberg, Gregory Corso, Peter Orlovksy – there developed a poetry scene in New York in the later 1950s and early 1960s of considerable strength and variety. Their work constituted what Rexroth calls an escape from 'poet-professors, Southern colonels and ex-Left Social Fascists'. Ginsberg and Jack Kerouac were among those who rebelled against the Columbia University/*Partisan Review* dominance to which Rexroth is partly referring (more fully recognized in Seymour Krim's 'What's *This* Cat's Story?' in *Views of a Nearsighted Cannoneer*, 1961). They were joined by Orlovsky and Corso and by William Burroughs, ex-Harvard English major, student of anthropology, experimenter in states of consciousness, and novelist, whose work was to change American fiction. This loosely formed band of writers was immediately seized on by the press as good copy – a nicely scary potential threat to bourgeois assumptions of the clean and affluent American Way of Life – and Diana Trilling represented orthodox panicked reaction in the academies with her essay, 'The Other Night at Columbia – A Report from the Academy' (*Partisan Review*, Spring, 1959). As Rexroth wrote later (in *Information et Documents*, Paris, October, 1963):

For two generations, American intellectual life was controlled by a small group of intellectuals who had their fingers in foundations, grants, reviews, magazines, etc. ... This group was made up – and still is – of a strange compromise between the Roosevelt left, symbolized by *Partisan Review*, and semi-reactionary nationalist, certainly chauvinist, groups. The Beats were the first to make a break in this monopoly which distributed praise and blame and determined very often the success of a work.

(Further documentation is in John Clellon Holmes's novel, *Go*, 1952, and his essays in *Nothing More to Declare*, 1968; in John Tytell, *Naked Angels*, 1976; and in two anthologies: *A Casebook on the Beat*, ed. Thomas Parkinson, 1961, and *The Eastside Scene*, ed. Allen de Loach, 1969.)

Ginsberg's movement from suburban Paterson, New Jersey (his letters to William Carlos Williams at that time, as a struggling poet, appear in *Paterson*), to Columbia University, the Lower East Side of New York, San Francisco and to Naropa Institute in Boulder, Colorado, in itself represents the search for community and audience. But he found mates and a supportive hearing (cf. Jack Kerouac's *Vanity of Duluoz*, 1968, and Ginsberg's interview in *Gay Sunshine*, January–February, 1973, reprinted in *It*, No. 148, 1973, as 'Your Heart Is Your Guru – Interview'). The 1930s generation of Zukofsky, Lowenfels, Muriel Rukeyser and Williams was an active basis for a continuous cultural action (see Chapter 6 of *Nothing Else to Fear*, ed. S. W. Baskerville and R. Willett, 1985). Poets like Carol Bergé, Diane Wakoski, Rochelle Owens, John Keys and Theodore Enslin found at least some community within which to work and be heard, and a few shops – most outstanding were the Eighth Street Bookshop in New York, City Lights in San Francisco, and Asphodel in Cleveland – carried enough poetry to ensure sufficient distribution and visibility. In New York, regular poetry readings culminated in the Café Le Metro sessions, extending later to the St Mark's Poetry Project. Readings took place almost anywhere – bookshops, cafés, apartments – and little magazines, broadsheets and little presses flourished, all the more abundantly through what the poet and publisher Kirby Congdon called 'the mimeograph revolution'. Poetry sheets, circulating letters and pamphlets, mimeographed or cheaply printed, could be distributed at minimum price, or given away. Such freedom of choice made excellent inroads into the competitive publishing business, with its connections with the academic reviewers. The amount of poetry increased. As Denise Levertov wrote in the *Seventh Street Anthology*: 'they are not writing in competition with each other or with poets outside their groups, not pursuing status'. Kirby Congdon's *Magazine*, together with *Interim Books*, which he edited with his fellow poet, Jay Socin, exemplifies the essential productivity of the scene.

Paul Blackburn's significance for the 1960s is two-fold. Not only was he a fine poet (*Collected Poems*, 1986), but a new and crucial figure in poetry – a staunch instigator of readings for a large range of poets (including radio work) and the first poet to tape-record every reading he attended, the basis of the unique collection housed today in the University of California at San Diego. He pioneered what is today taken for granted: that the poet's recorded performance is part of his text.

Beat Generation writers were part of a wider action, therefore. The *City Lights Journal* of 1963 still witnessed to the continuity of values from the 1950s Beats into the 1960s. They were anti-academic and anti-establishment, attacking *Time-Life* as well as Columbia/*Partisan Review*. They were dedicated to 'projective' open forms and the perceptual space of reading with a living audience present and responding, rather than awaiting the approval of critical schools or posterity. Their way of life and their poetry was not simply literary: it gave access to the discovery of God through visionary experience rather than church organization, and through beatific states of consciousness of sometimes self-annihilating terror and joy. They were deeply concerned with non-puritan and non-bourgeois responses to the family, to the body, to love and to friendship. They devoted themselves to living with minimal accoutrements and were opposed to the characteristic American evaluation of life by property and formal educational achievements. Emerson's transcendentalist interest in oriental philosophy, nature mysticism and the Oversoul, Thoreau's civil disobedience and anarchistic pragmatism in social beliefs, and Whitman's sense of the open road, of the individual having 'all to make', and of the sensuality and sensuousness of men in contact with the Earth and each other in mutual joy – all these had a renewed life in the Beats and were reinforced by the use of marijuana as a method of reducing ego and relaxing consciousness, and, later, LSD, as a method of gaining access to states of consciousness which conventional training forbade. Beat anti-authoritarianism, in both literary and social forms, reached in some people a certain shapelessness and dispersal of energy, passivity as well as saintliness. The Beat mode, while necessary to break up an urban consumerist conformity, tended to its own stultifying mannerism and conservatism. But the major poets of the period changed and survived (cf. Allan Kaplan, review of *City Lights Journal*, No. 1, ed. Lawrence Ferlinghetti, *Kulchur*, No. 12, 1963; Eric Mottram, 'A Pig-Headed Father and the New Wood', *London Magazine*, December, 1962). The growth of the intense activity at Naropa is witness to the power of the writers still, as against the feebleness of academic dismissal of their work persistently since 1960.

The changes in the 1960–80 decades partly involved a culture already developed in the Northwest. Between 1940 and 1960, San Francisco and its environment – including the Berkeley campus of the University of California – became a major centre. To the North, in Seattle, the painters Mark Tobey and Morris Graves and the poets Theodore Roethke and Caroline Kizer formed part of a nucleus with the *Rocky Mountain Review* and the *Western Review* (Ray B. West was the organizer behind them), which later merged into *Contact*, edited from San Francisco (the first number was dedicated to William Carlos Williams). To the South, Yvor Winters wrote and taught at Stanford University. Lawrence Lipton, poet and representative of dissident radicalism, worked at Venice West, Los Angeles (his *Holy Barbarians*, 1959, was the first book to document the transition from traditional political commitment to Beat protest). Henry Miller had lived at Big Sur since 1944. But the concentration took place in San Francisco itself and centred in the first place on three influential poets: Kenneth Rexroth, Kenneth Patchen and Robert Duncan. The second impetus occurred from about 1944 onwards and included Catholic poets inclined to personalism and mystical states – William Everson, later to become Brother Antoninus, and Philip Lamantia. Everson (he left his order in 1970), worked during this period in a conscientious objectors' camp with a group whose Untide Press mimeographed protest poetry during the war. In 1968 he published his 1934–48 poems in *The Residual Years*, and a series of volumes followed – poems of inventive personal forms and rhythms which record intense experiences of natural landscape, marriage, moral concern with post-Depression America and crisis of religious faith. His centrality can be gauged by his account of the major Californian poet Jeffers (*Robinson Jeffers*, 1968), and by the fact that he introduced Bill Butler's first book *Alder Gulch* in 1961. Butler's work appeared in the San Francisco *Beatitude Magazine*, founded in 1959, but his own major work was written in England – including *The Discovery of America* (1966) and *Byrne's Atlas* (1970). (*Angel Dancing*, 1982, collects his major long poems.)

Philip Lamantia also appeared in *Beatitude* – a poet who bridges San Francisco, the Surrealism of *View* mentioned earlier, and the resurgence of drug experience for obtaining states and images beyond daily contingency: a long romantic poet tradition (*Erotic Poems*, 1946; *Narcotica*, 1959; *Ekstasis*, 1959; *Destroyed Works*, 1962; *Selected Poems*, 1967; *Meadowlark West*, 1986). One other magazine should be mentioned: George Leite's *Circle*, published from

Berkeley between 1944 and 1950. Then a third impetus arrived with the Beat poets in the 1950s, coming mainly from New York. They moved into a scene which, like Black Mountain College, included painting and music. At the California School of Fine Art, in San Francisco, Mark Rothko, Lawrence Calcagno, Clyfford Still and Richard Diebenkorn worked or taught, and Sam Francis, Hans Hofmann, and Robert Motherwell worked in the area in the late 1930s and the 1940s. Jazz-and-poetry was a 'natural' for an area in which poetry released itself from the genteel programmes of the academy. The 'cool' jazz of Gerry Mulligan and Dave Brubeck associated with the Bay Area was supported by great jazz men who played at the Black Hawk club which opened in 1957, the year Jazz Workshop opened and Rexroth and Lawrence Ferlinghetti held the highly popular jazz-and-poetry sessions at the Cellar. In 1953 Mort Sahl offered his satirical comedy at the *hungry i*, part of a local discrimination that also included the listener-sponsored radio station KPFA which transmitted a high level of literature and music. Public poetry readings reached the proportions of a major revival (*The San Francisco Poets*, ed. David Meltzer, 1971, contains interviews and poems from main writers of the area: Rexroth, Everson, Ferlinghetti, Lew Welch, McClure, Richard Brautigan).

But it was that third impetus which got the San Francisco 'renaissance' under way. Kerouac arrived in 1949. Ferlinghetti came in 1953 and took over the City Lights bookshop and the publishing concern associated with *City Lights Magazine* founded by Peter Marin in 1951 (he had printed Corso, Duncan, Antoninus and Ferlinghetti). Ginsberg arrived in 1954 and met up with Gary Snyder in Berkeley in 1955 (Snyder was born in San Francisco and lived as a boy north of Seattle; at this time he alternated between logging and forestry in the Northwest and studying Chinese and Japanese cultures at Berkeley). Corso followed in 1956. In 1955, Ferlinghetti began his Pocket Poets series with his own *Pictures from the Gone World*, which was followed by Rexroth and Patchen. Number 4 was Ginsberg's *Howl and other Poems* (1956), introduced by William Carlos Williams, a major signal of the quality of the poetry now emerging; it was, in Rexroth's words, 'the confession of faith of a generation that is going to be running the world in 1965 or 1975 – if it's still there to be run'. Corso's *Gasoline* was Number 5, and then came volumes by Levertov and Duncan. In 1958, Dave Haselwood's Auerhahn Press produced its first volume, Wiener's *Hotel Wentley Poems*, another major work of the period: Haselwood's second volume was Lamantia's *Ekstasis*, followed by McClure's

Hymns to St Geryon and poetry by Jack Spicer, Edward Marsh, Lew Welch and Philip Whalen (see *The Auerhahn Press, a bibliography*, 1976). In the *New York Times* in 1956, Richard Eberhart registered the awareness of the non-involved establishment:

Poetry here has become a tangible social force, moving and unifying its audience, releasing the energies of the audience through the spoken, even shouted, verse, in a way at present unique to this region.

The word spread to the rest of the world, in the first instance, through *Evergreen Review*, No. 2 (1957), which carried poems and articles by Rexroth, Ginsberg, Ferlinghetti, Antoninus, Duncan, Henry Miller, Spicer, Snyder, Whalen, Kerouac and McClure. This 'San Francisco Scene' issue was then backed by the recorded voices of eight of the poets on an LP entitled 'San Francisco Poets'.

Many of the Beats had returned to New York by the 1960s, and San Francisco settled for its own rather more local scene. But the foundations of a good deal of contemporary American poetry were secured there in the previous decade. Bern Porter published Duncan in 1947 and 1949, and Lamantia's *Erotic Poems* in 1946. Jonathan Williams began his Jargon Press series with McClure's *Passage* (1956). Discovery Press issued Meltzer's *Ragas* (1959). White Rabbit published Richard Brautigan, Duncan, Levertov, Olson and Spicer. *The Ark* magazine printed practically all the poets in the Bay Area; and there were *The Needle* (1959), *Nomad, San Francisco Review*, *Semina* and many more. In 1955, Duncan's play, *Faust Foutu*, was performed at the Six Gallery, and in 1962, the Poetry Center at San Francisco State College put on Ferlinghetti's *The Alligation*. Between these dates, there were theatre events in abundance. Response to the new poetry can be judged from the fact that when McClure's *The Blossom* was performed at the University of Wisconsin in 1967, it was closed after one performance by the Regents. (His *Pillow* appeared at the Off-Bowery theatre in New York in 1961, with plays by LeRoi Jones and Diane DiPrima.) In San Francisco itself, drama, jazz and poetry continued in spite of pressures from local forces of business, politics and education and their agents, police and censorship.

To Black Mountain, Lower East Side, New York and San Francisco scenes must be added the flourishing Chicago culture between the wars, described in detail in Rexroth's *An Auto-biographical Novel*, 1966 (long sections are included in *The Rexroth Reader*, ed. Eric Mottram 1972), and the work of Robert Bly and his *The Sixties* magazine, with its associated poetry books. Rather more significant than American poets in the *Sixties* group (the magazine operated from Minnesota, but contributors came from the whole country – Louis Simpson, Donald Hall, W. D. Snodgrass, James Logan, James Wright and James Dickey) – were the foreign poets in translation issued by Bly. Through Bly's enterprise and sense of the need, Neruda, Vallejo, Trakl, Benn, and some of the French Symbolists were widely available in translation largely for the first time, at least in the States. A number of the *Sixties* American poets took up the 'deep image' concept in order to bypass trite verbalizations and reach into non-verbal areas of experience and recognition – already practised by Trakl, Neruda, etc. The better flowering of this effort did not occur until the later 1960s: Louis Simpson's *At the End of the Road* (1964), Dickey's *Poems 1957–1967* (1969) and Bly's *The Light Around the Body* (1967). The imagic and lyrical procedures of these otherwise disparate poets are linked by what Paul Sweig calls 'a common resistance to the orthodoxies of American poetry since the Second World War' ('The American Outside', *The Nation*, 14 November 1966). He quotes Bly:

The fundamental world of poetry ... is the inward world. The poem expresses what we are just beginning to think, thoughts we have not yet thought. The poem must catch these thoughts alive, flexible and animal-like as they are.

Bly prefers Yves Bonnefoy's 'An interior sea lighted by turning eagles' to Pound's 'petals on a wet black bough'; he emphasizes the short poem of perceptions which have the power of resonance rather than the long poem of accumulated instances and continuities. Each issue of *The Sixties* contains an essay relevant to a contemporary poet and focusing this lyricist concern, and signed by 'Crunk'. Some of the discriminations are shrewd; the more abrasive and less valuable form of this criticism thrashes around in Dickey's *The Suspect in Poetry* (1964). Bly's recent work has modified his 1960s position. *The Teeth-Mother Naked at Last* (City Lights Pocket Poets 26, 1970) is a long poem against the condition of the Southeast Asian war, read throughout the country by the American Writers Against the Vietnam War (founded by Bly and David Ray in 1966); its form is nearer early Ferlinghetti and *Howl* than the *Sixties* poets. His essay, 'Looking for Dragon Smoke' (*The Seventies*, No. 1, Spring, 1972), is a fine piece of poetics, concerning 'the leap *away* from the unconscious, not *toward* it' in poetry of the Christianized West, and the possibilities of recovering 'conscious psychic substance' (see *Leaping Poetry*, 1975).

The only innovation of any strength, since the 1950s, which has urged itself into the lives of any majority as the Beats did, is focused in Richard Goldstein's *The Poetry of Rock* (1969), which includes lyrics by Tuli Kupferberg (of *Birth* magazine and the Fugs popgroup), Tim Hardin, the Doors and Bob Dylan. Dylan transformed the sentimental traditions of lyrics on disc with an outstanding range of songs, from simple and fairly conventional blues love lyrics, to the complex, multi-referential use of social comment and 'deep image' in 'Bob Dylan's 115th Dream' and 'The Gates of Eden' (*Bob Dylan Song Book*, 1966), and 'Visions of Joanna' (*Blonde on Blonde*, 1966). Bob Dylan, as the citation for his Princeton Honorary Doctor of Music degree stated:

based his technique in the arts of the common people of our past and tore his appeals for human compassion from the experience of the dispossessed. His music remains the authentic expression of the disturbed and concerned conscience of young America.

(*Time*, 22 June 1970)

Since Dylan and the West Coast rock groups of the sixties, there has been little development in this field apart from the extraordinary lyrics of Captain Beefheart, which make a good deal of our poetry seem tame and dull. Rock became big business and went into a trough of imitation and cheap thrills; poetry has never been big business but has been just as oppressed by government agencies as the rock artists and their festivals. Good examples of the post-Beat generation of poets forced underground by the hostile illiteracy of the great cities are the writers and little magazines associated with D. A. Levy in Cleveland. Poetry was central to the Civil Rights struggle in the 1960s. When Levy was arrested on spurious charges, a letter to a Cleveland newspaper said: 'Levy is alleged to have read poetry to juveniles. That being the case, the police have the right to arrest him.' In an editorial for his *Mary Jane Quarterly* (Vol. 2, No. 1, 1966 – other issues were entitled *The Marahwannah Quarterly* and other variants), Levy wrote: 'Cleveland died in 1930/died so quickly & quietly that no one seemed to notice.' He decided to challenge inertia by moving out from 'Cleveland's primitive west side' and in February 1963 began to publish poetry in extremely cheap but finely produced small editions – at first known poets like Carol Bergé, Allan Katzman, John Keys and Ed Sanders (with Edwin Morgan and Dom Sylvester Houédard from Britain), and later his own work and that of local writers including Douglas Blazek and

Kent Taylor. James Lowell's Asphodel Bookshop provided an important sales and publicity outlet in Cleveland. The city escalated its hostility to both Levy and Lowell, both of whom finally needed 'tribute' volumes to defray expenses of court procedures against them. Levy, born in 1942, founded the Renegade and 7 Flowers Presses, published three journals and a mass of other poets' work, and also found time to compose and read himself. He was arrested twice in 1967 on obscenity charges and was subjected to endless police harassment. According to an interview published that year, he planned to leave Cleveland in despair. As it turned out, he burned his poetry, sat in his apartment with a rifle, visited friends he had not seen in years, and finally committed suicide on 24 November 1968. As one columnist in a local paper observed: 'D. A. Levy was a threat to no one except those who are afraid of the truth.' He had come to believe that the country was 'programmed to fall apart', and that state of the nation reaches into his poems, many of which contemplate the possibility of suicide as the accurate response to the 1960s. Exile or outlawry were the only other alternatives and part of a long American tradition. Levy's *The North American Book of the Dead* (1966) and *Suburban Monastery Death Poem* (1968) are to the 1960s what Ginsberg's *Howl* was to the 1950s: documents of witness to cultural deterioration. This poetry is created within the disaster area and searches for some kind of viable private life to retrieve from public catastrophe. Levy worked in a wide variety of forms, including visual poems, but his most powerful poems are low-toned, direct, and use projective forms. His Buddhism is characteristic of his generation of poets investigating alternatives to the historic destructiveness of the official Christian state. ('D. A. Levy: Cleveland's Survival Artist', Eric Mottram, *The Serif*, December, 1971.) Thus his poetry stands in direct relationship to Snyder and the Beats, to later leaders like Timothy Leary, and to the ecological investigations in Paul Shepard and Daniel McKinley's *The Subversive Science* (1969) in which Lynn White substantiates his claim that 'Christianity made it possible to exploit nature in a mood of indifference to the feelings of natural objects'. Levy stood between Ed Sanders' 'amer-egyptian underground' (it is Levy's phrase) and the Cleveland poet's fellow-American writer, George Dowden, who works in Britain and whose best work, *Renew Jerusalem* (1970), has Sanders's energy and that sad indictment of the West exemplified in America which is characteristic of Cleveland's Renegade Press poets.

VI

The effort to resist pessimism by having a vision of a viable human city and a human universe repeatedly gains a resource in William Blake, central to Duncan and Olson, and the inspiring voice which Ginsberg heard one day in Harlem. But for Ginsberg inspiration not only came through Blake's voice and the long-breathed lines of his Prophetic Books, but through an essential sense of the poet as visionary bard. That concept of the poet still gains power in the States: it is there in Duncan, in Sanders, in Snyder and Kelly, and in the inherent policies of Clayton Eshleman's magazine *Caterpillar* (1967–73). It is present, too, in Eshleman's own poetry – a fine record of discovering a personal poetics for an intensely enquiring life: *Altars*, 1971; *The Gull Wall*, 1975; *Hades in Manganese*, 1981; *Fracture*, 1983 (see Eric Mottram, 'The Poetics of Rebirth and Confidence', *Poetry Information*, No. 7, 1974). His translations of Vallejo, Artaud and Césaire are exemplary in their keen sense of the transference of meaning into an appropriate poetics.

The poet's responsibility takes other forms. Ginsberg has always been aware of his messianism and deliberately checks it in a number of poems. The onwardgoing necessity of resistance to officials in America has directed his position as a leader, from the Eisenhower years to the 1986–7 White House fiasco (see the tributes for his sixtieth birthday in *Best Minds*, ed. B. Morgan and B. Rosenthal, 1986). He has had to come to terms with his public functions, with a vital division of energy between poetry, politics and religion, both in America and wherever he travels – in Cuba, Czechoslovakia, India, Hungary, the USSR and, most recently in China and Nicaragua. Ginsberg is an internationally respected presence.

Amazingly, he has found time to develop his writings as well. His measure is frequently a large inclusive line, reaching sometimes paragraphic proportions, a major inventive rhetoric of the time, and eminently suited to declamation. It incorporated Melville's sentence structure (especially in *Pierre*), Hebraic scripture, Blake's long lines and Whitman's chants. At the core of Ginsberg's work, poetry for public persuasion developed a new set of forms. The simple and exhilarating lament and excoriation of 'Howl' exemplified and partly created the Beat ethos of the 1950s, with its strategic avoidance of complex information, its passive protest and its descent into consciousness explored to the point of hallucination and madness, a response to and counterpart of the state of America. But the inspiration of Artaud and the concept of the *poète maudit* receded in Ginsberg's work as it became increasingly political. The elliptical imagery of Hart Crane, which provided a vertical take-off for emotion within the linear expansiveness of 'Howl', was curtailed and often discarded by 1968 and the poems in *Planet News*. He retained his swinging, improvisatory paragraphs – learned partly from Kerouac's prose of the early 1950s (cf. 'The Art of Poetry VIII', *Paris Review* 37, Spring, 1966). He outgrew Beat publicity and became a major transmitter of the American anarchist tradition. His poetic aim is two-fold: first, to create a counter-magic of language against the black magic of the state's electronic communications networks – TV, advertising, the manipulations of consumer capitalism and the methods of the Washington-Pentagon-high finance corporations against the American people, explicit in 'Wichita Vortex Sutra'. Like his contemporary Norman Mailer, Ginsberg's criticism of America is not based in political dogma but in a radical sense of socio-economic failure in the nation's controls, an analysis profoundly based today in a religious vision of experience. Secondly, therefore, Ginsberg needs to provide examples of the expansion and regeneration of mutual consciousness, the sense of touch and 'adhesiveness' which he inherits from Whitman, and that possible sense of unity across the huge landscape and centripetal forces of America – the grandeur of the epic impulse in *The Fall of America: Poems of These States 1965–1971* (City Lights Pocket Poets 30, 1972).

'Kaddish' (1961) described his response to the manic break-down of his mother under the pressures of being a socialist emigrant in the 1930s; she becomes the type of human being sacrificed to ideological catastrophe in this century. In 'Wichita Vortex Sutra' and 'Television Was a Baby Crawling Toward the Death Chamber' (*Planet News*), the poet is himself at the centre of the American vortex which threatens vision with madness. These long passionate poems project dense visionary counter-information against the System in order to stir readers and hearers towards revolutionary change. Their forms are 'directed meditations' which move from printed page into public performance. When they become flaccid, as in 'New York to San Fran' (*Airplane Dreams*, 1968), and parts of 'Ankor Wat' (1968), it is due to excessive repetitions of states of vulnerability and anxiety and to blasts at obvious political targets – although, to be fair, Ginsberg does call some of these works 'compositions from journals'.

In 1967, he produced 'Wales Visitation', a wonderful and meticulously detailed description of human oneness with the Earth, a basis which he has always needed, from which to move out into the urban and the political. The poem projects a field of physical 'earth relations' – 'one solemn wave' or mandala of ecstatic ecological wonder at the particulars of landscape, which the poet is still able to make even in this disastrous time. It is his 'Divine Poem on the physical world'. The non-human, natural world increasingly becomes a refuge in his poetry, such is the urgency of his resistance to the current official world – manifest, for example, in *Mind Breaths* (1978) and *Plutonian Ode* (1982). With the publication of *Collected Poems 1947–1980* (1985), and successive collections of letters and journals, his stature is grander than ever (see Eric Mottram, *The Wild Good and the Heart Ultimately: Ginsberg's Art of Persuasion*, 1978).

Ginsberg shares this feeling for landscape nature, and its ethical necessities for men, with Gary Snyder. They also share usages of Buddhist and other Asian religious and mythical writings and devotional practices (in particular, the modes of tantric art and the mantra in Ginsberg, and Zen forms in Snyder). This is in itself an American constant at least from Emerson and Thoreau onwards, part of the transcendental mode of philosophy and poetic actions since the nineteenth-century Romantics. Those poems which are gradually forming the open-ended *Mountains and Rivers* series (six sections were published together in 1965 and others have appeared in magazines), especially indicate Snyder's centrality in the 1960s: his usage of linguistic analysis, his enquiry into the relevance of world myths, his use of the page as a field for the action of an experience both sensuous and erudite (e.g. 'Lookout's Journal', *Earth House Hold*, 1969). His strength lies in balancing a sense of labour as a means to live, as well as a human action in itself, and meditation on the human condition, and in maintaining a light tension between 'discipline of self-restraint' and 'discipline of following desire', 'a careful balance of free action and sense of where cultural taboos lay'. He, too, uses Blake: 'if the doors of perception were cleansed, everything would appear to man as it is, infinite'. His own cleansing of perception takes place within the disciplines of Buddhism and the severely beautiful landscape of Northwestern America, between solitary meditation and a finely articulated pattern of love and friendship. He is constantly aware of Robinson Jeffers' example of misanthropic retreat into the Pacific seaboard ecology, and moves away from the city towards the open air with a sense of non-attachment to objects and with relief for its offer of relative freedom (*A Range of Poems*, 1966, and *Regarding Wave*, 1970). Snyder's public readings developed something of the leadership following that Ginsberg had earlier. This was partly due to his highly topical incorporation of both Asian, Indian and Japanese procedures and myths with the tribal inheritance of North American Indians (cf. 'Passage to More Than India' and 'Poetry and the Primitive' in *Earth House Hold*, and *Passage Through India* (1972, 1983). In issue 4 of *Alcheringa*, of which he is a contributing editor, he writes of a 'syncretism' through which to embody 'values of nature against those of technology' (see *The Real Work*, 1980).

The natural landscape, the city and the world map is the field of exploration for the major American poets of the 1960s as they move across large spaces and through violent cities, aware of their nation's predatory extensions abroad and into cosmic space, and trying to maintain still that old sense of America as a hub of world information (continuous since the 1840s), and the place where humanity always has a further chance. Their range of poetics and locatory materials is large and their imaginative invention demonstrates the extraordinary health of a literary culture within a disastrous social and political period in both domestic and imperialistic national behaviour.

Paul Blackburn's poems in *The Cities* (1967), *In.On.Or About the Premises* (1968) and *Early Selected Y Mas* (1972), project the New York experience with a control of cadence and rhythm unique in contemporary poetry, combining sardonic criticism of his time with a gentle passion for love and friendship in structures of deceptively lightly-held technique. His final *Journals* (1975) produced a closing dimension of existential fight against terminal illness and the treacherous times he had lived through. Philip Whalen's skills are even less exhibitionistic; he uses tantric and calligraphic forms, and highly developed projective verse structures, articulating his belief that 'art does not seek to describe but to enact'. His poems act out an exhilarating but wary and non-ideological stream of intelligence and receptivity to ideas and environments, making 'a continuous fabric (nerve movies)' of 'total attention and pleasure' (preface to *Every Day*, 1965), 'a picture graph of a mind moving, which is a world body being here and now which is history ... and you' (*Memoirs of an Interglacial Age*, 1960; his collected poems, *On Bear's Head*, 1969). Jonathan Williams also moves between landscape and city, and with a technique and wit unique in American poetry. His selected poems, *An Ear in Bartram's Tree* (1969), show his range – from what he terms 'the garrulous landscape nature that feeds on Brucknerian lengths' to 'the exactly contrary nature that yearns to be as laconic as Webern or a pebble'. His drastic political humour

('Lawless Wallace Über Alles/all ass, alas,/no arse–/nic, no/lace,/as well as no/solace', *Lullabies Twisters Gibbers Drags*, 1963) is aimed at the annihilation of anyone and anything which has no respect for ecology or privacy or visionary experience, the primary values which he dramatizes in, for example, 'Emblems for the Little Dells and Nooks, and Corners of Paradise' and a number of poems infused with Blake, Samuel Palmer, Henry Vaughan and the Appalachian and English landscapes he knows from first-hand and on foot. His recent work concentrates on the briefest poetic forms – clerihews, epigrams, *haiku*-like stanzas, into which he can exercise his wit. *Get Hot or Get Out* (1982) is a useful selection, and *The Magpie's Bagpipe* (1982) selects the essays of one of the wittiest prose writers in America.

Lawrence Ferlinghetti's poetry has deepened in tone since his 1950s San Francisco Beat days; the light ironical style of his 1955 and 1958 volumes darkened. His vision remained anarchist and undogmatic in its outrage at political and social victimization, but 'The Third World' (*El Corno Emplumado 29*, 1969) and *The Secret Meaning of Things* (1969) have considerably less gaiety – the work of a poet who can barely hope that there may be 'time in some later reincarnation/to lie down in silence, without cunning' and for whom 'every day the news gets more surreal' in its abject contingencies. Ferlinghetti retains his dry humour within satirical response, a cool absence of bitterness and a cutting edge in his resistance to resignation. But in his latest work, sad nostalgia has become a severe resource (*Over All the Obscene Boundaries*, 1984). Most recently, *Seven Days in Nicaragua Libre* (1986) consists of prose and photographic images. (*Endless Life: Selected Poems*, 1981; and see Larry Smith, *Lawrence Ferlinghetti, Poet-at-Large*, 1983.) A more painfully personal involvement is the action of John Wieners, America's foremost poet of the exposed and utterly vulnerable life, a true *poète maudit* as Ginsberg called him in 1960 after the publication of *The Hotel Wentley Poems* (1958). *Ace of Pentacles* (1964) and *Nerves* (1970), show how he has developed his ability to dramatize city pressures on the human body overcome with desire for love and desperately taking refuge in dreams and drugs. The pathos of his autobiographical witness is formed inside a highly skilful lyric prosody. ('John Wieners: Guide through the Suspended Vacuum', Eric Motram, *Contact*, No. 7, 1973; *Behind the State Capitol or Cincinnati Pike*, 1975). A more extrovert poet is Robert Kelly; his poetry yearns to digest any and every kind of intellectual and emotional experience. He probably tries for a too rapid transference of his appetite and enthusiasm to verse forms, but his recent work is central to the period in its inclusion of a wide range of etymological research and considerable usage of alchemy studies and the nature of the occult which reinforce his use of mythology and the surreal image (*Songs I–XXX*, 1968; *The Common Shore*, 1969; *Kali Yuga*, 1970). His poetry has developed in range not only of intellectual capacities but in its placing of personal experience within his characteristically omnivorous learning (*Kill the Messenger Who Brings Bad News*, 1979; *Spiritual Exercises*, 1981; *Under Words*, 1983).

Ed Sanders, one of the most emotionally and politically committed poets in America, was, in the 1960s, part of the bardic line of Ginsberg and Dylan. As organizer of the Fugs pop-group resurgent in the 1980s, he bridged the protest lyric of Bob Dylan and the sardonic humour of the black humorists of the period (*The Fugs Song Book*, 1967), and the group also set to music two of Blake's songs. *Poem from Jail* (1963) is the meditational protest of a scholar, poet and 'peace freak' jailed for his pacifist assault on a nuclear submarine – a double action which forms his 'total assault on the culture'. Sanders's best poems have an astonishingly direct sensuality in forms which combine classical myth and the language of the Lower East Side (partly invented by the poet himself). *Peace Eye* (1965) uses some of the main poetics of the 1960s but emerges as an entirely individual, anarchist rejection of the disastrous American status quo by insisting on the nakedness of the human body and its vital sensuality in a sun-centred cosmos. 'Song of the Eye-Heart-Mind' fuses the 'clear Eye' of poets like Zukofsky and Williams, the clear, crystal light which penetrates the *Cantos*, the Eye of Horus, which Sanders interprets as the Peace eye (cf. *Technicians of the Sacred*, p 361), and the Emersonian eye of human penetration into the cosmos. Sanders was instrumental in forming the Yippie movement of the later 1960s, and exposed the nature of American culture through the case of Charles Manson (*The Family*, 1972). His recent excursions into a committed poetics appear in *Investigation Poetry* (1976).

VII

No black poet could have afforded such languages and informational references if he wished to reach the black majority on the move during the Civil Rights period (1950–75). The inspirational black spokesmen were Malcolm X and Stokely Carmichael, with their rhetoric of revolt to meet violence with violence, and Martin Luther King, with his rhetoric of religion, reconciliation and civil disobedience – rather than the intellectual poet, the rock descendants of the blues singers and Tamla Motown or the black protest theatre in Off-Broadway playhouses. The problem for the black poet lies between M. B. Tolson and LeRoi Jones. In an interview of 1956, Tolson claimed his right to be both black and complex:

I am no soothsayer talking to Virgil's dark Aeneas, before his descent into the lower world of the black ghetto . . . I, as a black poet, have absorbed the Great Ideas of the Great White world, and have interpreted them in the melting-pot idiom of my people. My roots are in Africa, Europe, and America . . . My catholicity of taste and interests takes in the Charleston and the ballet, Mr Jelly Roll and Stravinsky, the Congolese sculptor and Phidias, the scop and the Classicist.'

(*Anger and Beyond*, ed. Herbert Hill, 1966)

But most Americans and certainly most black Americans do not have access to that range of cultural resources. Specifically 'black' poetry necessarily includes built-in reactions for that particular condition of black Americans which condemns them to second-class citizenship. Poetry written out of the 350 years of the main American civil conflict is bound to reflect what Bob Dylan calls 'philosophic disgrace' as well as the stereotypes of 'let my people go', and the passionate assault on any suggestion of imitating white American cultural attitudes. Conflict poetry has to be an instrument in the immediate cause of liberation, to tell it all exactly as it is, to change consciousness from resignation to action. It is pointless to judge such poetry in any other way. The exception would be poetry containing a complexity of material and controls of form not designed for immediate rhetorical consumption or weaponry against ghetto-living and Christian capitalist hypocrisy. As Charles E. Silberman put it in 1964, 'part of the price of being a Negro in America is a degree of paranoia' (*Crisis in Black and White*).

No black poetry approached the power of Malcolm X's autobiography (1967), and no black poet who wished to participate in the liberation of his people could risk separation from them. LeRoi Jones's career remains exemplary. In the 1950s he turned in good poetry with 'projective verse' poetics and the political concerns of the time, skilfully controlling his criticism of white society's limitations and editing one of the most significant poetry magazines of the period, *Yugen*, from 1957. The later development of his poetry, plays, and social action, recorded in *Home* (1968), moved him towards increased political involvement and a revolutionarily literary aim: 'the role of the black artist in America is to help the destruction of America as it now exists. If what he does – whether it's polemical or lyrical or however it functions – if it contributes to that destruction it is beautiful.' It is the black equivalent of John Cage's foreword to *A Year from Monday*: 'our proper work now if we love mankind and the world we live in is revolution'. Jones's *The Dead Lecturer* (1965) dramatizes distress and desperate irony as a preliminary to non-poetic action; the poems move from self-hatred, hysteria, the hypocrisy of art in the society of 'usura' and the injustice of corrupt Hollywood images of the Negro ('A Poem for Willie Best'), to the need to go beyond self-sacrifice ('Rhythm & Blues', dedicated to Robert Williams, the revolutionary black leader), and the struggle for a black identity. The shift to vengeance ('Short Speech to My Friend') concludes in the alchemy of a transformation into true blackness, 'Black Dada Nihilismus', the poetic equivalent to Jones's plays, *Dutchman* and *The Slave* (1964). The poet must stop substituting for the dead white lecturer of his Greenwich Village recent past, and take the Dada tradition into action for black liberation. His next work was polemical from within the citadel of 'black is beautiful' and the meaning of those words spoken by the black hero of *The Slave*: 'no social protest – right in the act!' He responded to the protest events of the late 1960s by moving to the Black Arts Repertory Theater in Harlem, by changing his name to Amiri Baraka, and subsequently to leading direct political action in Newark, New Jersey, his home region. (*The Autobiography of Leroi Jones/Amiri Baraka*, 1984). His poetry and plays continued to grow in polemical power, to use Marxist terms of analysis and agit-prop methods, but always confronting the problems of activist art (*Four Black Revolutionary Plays*, 1969; *Black Magic: Poetry 1961–67*, 1969; *Raise Race Rays Raze*, 1971; *In Our Terribleness*, 1970; *Hard Facts: 1973–75*; *Daggers and Javelins*, *Essays 1974–1979*, 1984; *Boundary 2*, Vol. VI, No. 2, 1978 contains a useful collection of criticism and an interview; see also Eric Mottram, 'Towards the Alternative . . .', in *Black Fiction*, ed. A. Robert Lee, 1980).

The poems of a first-rate black poet of the next generation, like, for example, those of David Henderson, are more relaxed and confident, even exuberant, within their free forms, black American language and social consciousness. Henderson's 'So We Went to Harlem', 'Boston Road Blues' and 'They Are Killing All the Young

Men' (*Felix of the Silent Forest*, 1967), represent the kind of achievement placing black American poetry beyond the immediacies and instrumentality of propaganda (see also Henderson's *De Mayor of Harlem*, 1970, and *Jimi Hendrix*, 1978).

Harlem Gallery: Book 1, The Curator (1965), the first part of a long work in progress, by Melvin Beaunoris Tolson, is outstanding and exceptional in black poetry. Tolson is a veteran of black literature. 'Dark Symphony' dates from 1944 and part of 'Libretto for the Republic of Liberia' (1953), was a commission received as poet laureate of Liberia in 1947. He writes within the tradition of multiple reference and complex structures associated with Pound and Eliot, and the tight movement of telescoped metaphors and parataxis found in Hart Crane. But his argument in *Harlem Gallery* is clear: the nature of Negro art in a white culture, 'a people's New World Odyssey from chattel to Esquire!'. His wit, analysis and sensuousness build towards a major criticism of racial cultures. Tolson has the courage and confidence to place himself within his own poetic and social structures as a possible 'Judas' who needs white and European cultures as much as he needs and understands the need to re-invent black America. Few of the poets in *New Negro Poets: USA* (1965, ed. Langston Hughes) reach either the heartfelt anxieties of LeRoi Jones or the complexity of Tolson. They are mostly too well-mannered and conventionally black, insufficiently complex and inventive, to carry black power into poetry. The exceptions are A. B. Spellman, Ted Jones, J. C. Oden, and Jones himself. The political and emotional strength of African poetry in English, or the work of Aimée Césaire, or blues lyrics, is hardly present. For that we turn to later work. Jones was right in 'The Myth of a Negro Literature' (*Home*): 'there has never been an equivalent to Duke Ellington or Louis Armstrong in Negro writing; even the best of contemporary literature written by Negroes cannot yet compare to the fantastic beauty of Charlie Parker's music'.

Nevertheless, Calvin Hernton's 'The Coming of Chronos to the House of Nightsong' (1964) showed the way towards a poetry 'practically and magically involved in collective efforts to trigger real social change' in the tradition of 'freedom fighters like the writer Ahmed Baba of Timbuktu, in the fourth century' and 'uganga (native medicine) ... the means to the structure of black consciousness' (Clarence Major's introduction to *The New Black Poetry*, 1969). In music, the parallels for black energy were John Coltrane, Sun Ra, Cecil Taylor and Pharaoh Sanders in jazz and Ray Charles and James Brown in rock. In revolutionary poetry the example was the work of South American and Caribbean poets – Guillen, Castillo, Cardenal, Vallejo. Ways in which these examples might be used can be read in the work of Len Chandler, Sam Cornish, Al Young, Tom Weatherly, Ishmael Reed and Nicki Giovanni. Their kinds of technical skill and revolutionary verve as collected in Neal's major book of 'Afro-American writing' 'aimed at the destruction of the double-consciousness' and the 'consolidating of the Afro-American consciousness' rather than the formation of a protest poetry. The collection reflects an inward turning of black Americans towards an examination of the possibilities of a culture which has survived slavery and ghetto and of the need for the poet to be a leader of liberation. The function of the poet in Western society is to restate the possibilities of personal and communal life against the claims of the reductive and authoritarian (*Black Fire*, ed. Larry Neal, 1968).

VIII

During the later 1970s and into the 1980s at least four developments in American poetry need to be briefly considered in conclusion. Cassette and videotape have made the audio-visual performance of poetry further available, and not simply by private or restricted library circulation, but advertised for public purchase. Thus no further excuse is possible for resistance to the poem as both printed text *and* aural-visual performance. The quantity and quality of poetry readings is partly responsible for this increase in recorded performance, and is properly documented – for example in: *Boundary 2*, Vol. III, No. 3, 1975 – 'The Oral Impulse in Contemporary American Poetry'; *The Poetry Reading*, ed. S. Vincent and E. Zweig, 1981; and *Talking Poetics*, Vols 1 and 2, 1978 and 1979, ed. Anne Waldman and Marilyn Webb.

Certainly for the distribution of certain forms of ethnic poetry, some kind of aural performance is necessary. A few native American performers have recorded dance-chants. Jerome Rothenberg has put his outstanding versions of native American works on cassette, and his collections of ethnic poetries, interfused with white American instances, have changed the vision of American poetry available. Techniques for translation are, of course, endlessly evolved to transmit one culture to another, but native American peoples have produced poets who write in English or are prepared to publish their own versions from their many languages, or both. Both native American and white American responses to such developments have been guided by new respects for and resurgences of local cultures, changes signalled, for example, by *Reinventing Anthropology* (ed. Dell Hymes, 1972) and Kenneth Lincoln's *Native American Renaissance* (1983), an essential account of the interplay between Western literary forms and writers and performers in tribal cultures, while *Sacred Narratives* (ed. Alan Dundes, 1984) assembles twentieth-century definitions of myth, including chapters on North American tribal cultural manifestations. The subtitle of David M. Guss's *The Language of the Birds* (1985) is 'Tales, texts and poems of interspecies communication', and his collection is mainly drawn from a wide range of native American sources – but includes (perhaps taking his stance from Rothenberg's *Technicians of the Sacred*) Mandelstam, McClure, Duncan, Snyder, Enzensberg and Rothenberg himself. It begins, then, to be clear how the outstanding inventiveness of poetic procedures in America in this century, briefly surveyed in this present essay, have offered examples for creative transmission in this field. *The Clouds Threw This Light: Contemporary Native American Poetry* (ed. Philip Foss, 1983) demonstrated as much, and the issues are even clearer in *Finding the Centre: Narrative Poetry of the Zuni Indians* (1972; the 1978 edition contains an interesting additional preface), translated by Dennis Tedlock 'from performance in the Zuni by Andrew Peyneysa and Walter Sanchez'. (Tedlock co-edited, with Rothenberg, *Alcheringa*, the key oral and ethnic poetry journal of these decades, founded in 1970.)

Thirdly, concomitant with the feminist movement since the early 1960s, women's genre poetry grew to be as widely written and published as black poetry during the period. (Gay poetry was less prominent until quite recently; the *Gay Sunshine Interviews* series – vol. 1 appeared in 1978 – is an excellent channel through which to discover this part of the field.) Elizabeth Janeway's chapter on women's literature in the *Harvard Guide to Contemporary American Writing* (ed. Daniel Hoffman, 1979) provides a brief introduction, and *The World Split Open* (ed. Louise Bernikow, 1974) is a fine collection of women poets from 1552 to 1950. *Coming to Light: American Women Poets in the Twentieth Century* (ed. D. Middlebrook and M. Yalom, 1985) is a key introduction to this work. But women's poetry is still mostly available in individual books from such excellent poets as Denise Levertov, Barbara Guest, Anne Waldman, Anne Lauterbach, Diane Ward, Alice Notely, Diane DiPrima, Adrienne Rich and Diane Wakowski. The growing power of a woman's voice, experience and sheer presence, before and during the ostensibly feminist movement, is superbly demonstrated in two major volumes of collected poems recently published – by Muriel Rukeyser (1979) and Louise Niedecker (*From This Condensery: The Complete Writings* . . . , 1985).

Lastly, the grouping of poets, primarily writing in the New York and San Francisco areas, under the aegis of *L-A-N-G-U-A-G-E* magazine, which first appeared in 1978 (the first three volumes are edited by two of the poets, Bruce Andrews and Charles Bernstein, in *The L-A-N-G-U-A-G-E Book*, 1984). Once again, it is not so much a school of poetics as a community of interests, ideals and practices, as the introduction to the latter collection suggests: 'The idea that writing should (or could) be stripped of reference' is, however, a primary consideration:

reference, like the body itself, is one of the horizons of language, whose value is to be found in the writing (the world) before which we find ourselves at any moment. It is the multiple powers and scope of reference (denotative, connotative, associational), not the writers' refusal or fear of it, that threads these essays together.

These poets' emphasis, partly directed from Russian Formalism, is towards complex surfaces and highly orderly structures of language. The politics of their criticism of the simplifications of popular referential poetry (and its tired academic exegeses) is clear enough: 'the project of poetry does not involve turning language into a commodity for consumption; instead, it involves repossessing the sign through close attention to, and active participation in, its production'. The relevant poems – by Andrews, Bernstein, Ron Silliman, Robert Grenier, David Bromige, Carla Harryman, Barrett Watten, Bob Perelman, Clark Coolidge and others – may be read, not only in their many individual volumes, but in three journals in particular – *Hills* (ed. Perelman), *This* (ed. Watten) and *Roof* (ed. James Sherry) – and in the finely produced issues from Tuumba Press (Lyn Hejinian), and the selection in *Legend*, published by another key press, the Segue Foundation, in 1980. The poetics are developed in *Talks* (*Hills* 6/7, 1980), *Poetics Journal* (ed. Hejinian and Watten), some of the chapters in one of the most important recent collections on poetry, *Code of Signals* (edited in 1983 by Michael Palmer, one of the most original poets in America today), and in the special edition of the British journal, *Reality Studios* (Vol. 2, No. 4, 1980), entitled 'Death of the Referent?'

The extraordinarily varied and powerful generation of American twentieth-century poetry continues. It is doubtful if any culture has ever produced such a range and quality of poetics and poems, and it forms a major resistant resource in the predominantly consumer-spectator orientations of mass society preoccupied with competition and conflict-winning, both domestically and imperialistically.

10

A REMNANT TO ESCAPE: THE AMERICAN WRITER AND THE MINORITY GROUP

Arnold Goldman

I

The call for a national literature in America is as old as the union of its states. It was sounded insistently through the nineteenth century but was shadowed by an equally consistent lament for the bareness of American life. A sense that the social texture in the country was too thin to support a complex civilization and a complex literature possessed not only conservatives like Cooper but democrats like Hawthorne and was echoed at the end of the century by Henry James.

In 1915, Van Wyck Brooks published his youthful summing-up of American literary culture, *America's Coming-of-Age*. For all the vitality of its language, the essay embodies a melancholy assessment. Part of the anti-Puritan current of its time, Brooks's polemic saw the baleful, restricting arm of the seventeenth-century Puritan ethos stretching out over the years, inhibiting the potentialities of national expression. Brooks communicates a profound disaffection from the American literary tradition, but he envisages nothing growing to reinvigorate or supersede it. Despite the optimism of his title, he is really at an impasse.

America's Coming-of-Age testifies to a significant loss of confidence and faith in the Anglo-American tradition of high culture, a tradition based on British culture and requiring no additional sources of strength. Brooks accepts that the horrors of a Gilded Age of political and commercial sham derive from the very well-springs of America's past. He instances brave cases of 'revolt' against the deadening hand of the past by individual American writers. But he considers that each failed, condemned to sterility for a lack of anything outside himself to attach to, any viable *social* forms in which his concrete plots and fables can be imagined.[1]

Herein lies the great attraction of 'minority' groups in the American literary mind: they might provide some new social model of that specific texture and depth long felt lacking in the majority culture. Van Wyck Brooks and his spiritual predecessors usually looked to specific sub-groups *within* an Anglo-Saxon hegemony for their 'Beloved Community':[2] to a civil service establishment to overcome the mere politics of national life, later to a society of 'engineers', technocrats who would rescue society from competing ideologies. One can see a change in the character of such valued groups over a passage of time. Attention shifts from the professional to the regional and then to the ethnic. The post Civil War flowering of a myth of the American South is another such 'saving remnant': if once there was a true civilization in America, albeit destroyed by a War, it may rise again. This is a conservative version of the function of a minority, nostalgic, founded on the feeling that the country has been diverted from its true direction. Its most articulate exponents accurately called themselves 'the Fugitives'.

As we move to more ethnic variants, there is a continuance of the historical shift away from those most closely resembling the original Anglo-Saxon stock, so that the formulation eventually can accommodate religious and then racial differences. The late nineteenth-century increase in immigration into the United States was accompanied by a gradual diversification of its sources (until immigration laws in this century checked the Southern and Eastern European flow). The first significant American authors to write out of this new balance came from the Western states and the earlier North European emigrations. More acceptable to national prejudices than other groups – the late nineteenth century witnessed an intellectual *rapprochement* between Anglo-Saxon and Teuton – their writers nevertheless mourned the passing of an older, Europeanized way of life in its transplanted setting. The novels of Willa Cather (1873–1947) are the outstanding refractor of the social transformations and the complex of feeling within these groups. In novels like *O Pioneers!* (1913) and *My Antonia* (1918), we

[1] The persistence and strength of this strain of analysis can be seen from Richard Poirier's *A World Elsewhere* (New York, 1966 and London, 1967). Poirier considers that American writers have responded by celebrating the individual consciousness, the interior landscape.

[2] William Wasserstrom, *Van Wyck Brooks* (Minneapolis, 1968), provides an excellent introduction to Brooks's thought and his place in American letters.

can trace the speed with which the new and 'American' way takes over from the older, here Scandinavian and Bohemian, texture of life. Willa Cather has little illusion that the older forms can maintain themselves in the new situation, nor is there much expectation that they might endow the national circumstance with a modicum of their qualities even as they dive into it. The immigrant group functions (like Rip Van Winkle) to demonstrate the swiftness of change in American life by bringing an older way of life into sharp contrast with the only too contemporary.

It was left to the literature based on other, later groups to form a more comprehensive alternative to American majority culture. The Jewish community in particular held out the hope of an *urbanized*, cosmopolitan focus which would have more leverage in the changing economic conditions than the earlier rural-agricultural Western American immigrants. A critic of Willa Cather's has noted what a small part Eastern European Jews play in her fiction, and he attributes the omission largely to her agrarian orientation.[1] In this view, what makes older immigrants a focus for the pastoral, 'natural', country-based myth of strength and virtue, makes the Jewish immigrant available for the counter-formulation in which the city is the home of the civilized basis of life. Certain possibilities for literary transformations within the American circumstance then follow. The possibility of seeing America anew is reinvigorated along with the importation of an urban, cosmopolitan sensibility. Exhausted stereotypes can be reversed and new life breathed in: instead of the American innocent loose in complex Europe, we can have a complicated European (Jewish) immigrant in a simpler America. What can be sought in the imagination and folkways of the minority group, or in its relations with the larger society, is precisely that denseness and complexity so long desired and found wanting on native grounds, that richness and specificity, context, tradition even, to oppose to an increasingly homogenized, bland 'big Anglo-Saxon total'.[2]

As many of the terms of the debate – denseness, complexity, tradition – were provided by Henry James, it is appropriate to use as illustration his own confrontation with the 'alien note' in American life. After a twenty-year absence he revisited America and felt

---

[1] James Schroeter, 'Willa Cather and *The Professor's House*', in Schroeter, ed., *Willa Cather and her Critics* (Ithaca, 1967). The essay contains a useful *resumé* of twentieth-century American writers' often hostile attitudes towards Jews.

[2] Henry James's phrase, in a letter to William James, 1888 (*Letters*, ed. Percy Lubbock, New York and London, 1920, Vol. 1, p 143).

equally repelled by the rampaging business culture of the late
Gilded Age and by the immigrant hordes of New York. As he put it
in *The American Scene* (1907), he felt doubly dispossessed. But if it
came to a choice, James knew where he would stand: anything
would be better than the 'refusal to consent to history' in the
commercial world, 'the so complete abolition of *forms*' in the 'in-
ordinate untempered monotony'. Faced with this horror he turns
directly to the 'alien' for his saving hope, in a hilarious, symbolic
description of an execrable 'Anglo-American' melodrama acted in
New York's Lower East Side before a Yiddish-speaking immigrant
audience:

I seemed to see the so domestic drama reach out to the so exotic audience
and the so exotic audience reach out to the so domestic drama. The play . . .
was American, to intensity, in its blank conformity to the convention, the
particular implanted convention of the place. . . . [T]he sense of the business would still have to reside in our ineradicable Anglo-Saxon policy, or
our seemingly deep-seated necessity, of keeping, where 'representation' is
concerned, so far away from the truth and the facts of life as really to betray
a fear in us of possibly doing something like them should we be caught
nearer. 'Foreigners', in general, unmistakably, in any attempt to render life,
obey the instinct of keeping closer, positively recognize the presence and
the solicitation of the deep waters; yet here was my houseful of foreigners
. . . confronted with our pale poetic – fairly caught for schooling. . . . Were
they going to rise to it, or rather to fall to it – to *our* instinct, as distinguished
from their own, for picturing life? . . . Or would it be their dim intellectual
resistance, a vague stir in them of some unwitting heritage . . . that I should
make out, on the contrary, as withstanding the effort to corrupt them, and
thus perhaps really promising to react, over the head of our offered
mechanic bribes, on our ingrained intellectual platitude?
  One had only to formulate that question to seem to see the issue hang
there, for the excitement of the matter, quite as if the determination were to
be taken on the spot. For the opposition over the chasm of the footlights . . .
grew intense truly, as I took in on the one side the hue of the Galician
cheek, the light of the Moldavian eye . . . and took in on the other the
perfect 'Yankee' quality of the challenge which stared back at them as in the
white light of its hereditary thinness. I needn't say that when I departed –
perhaps from excess of suspense – it was without seeing the balance drop to
either quarter.

Though James was to express his doubt 'whether there be, comparatively, in the vastly greater number of the representatives of the
fresh contingent, any spirit that the American does not find an easy
prey', his decision as to what, if anything, could save America from
its own 'hereditary thinness' did not waver.

The varieties of literary response to the hypothetical attractions of a minority culture are manifold. Many strike one as largely personal to the individual vision of a particular author, others as a response to historical changes in the position and status of the group, some as both at once. In this essay I have chosen six authors with varying relationships to two minority groups in American society, Jews and Negroes. In them may be seen the literary imagination recording and shaping visions of the newest America, in the struggle between what James called the 'elements of swift convertibility' and 'the unconverted residuum'.

American Negroes comprised the last great wave of American migration. Their 'Great Migration' from the South to the North in the years surrounding the First World War turned a rural people into a largely urban one, and the first Negro literary movement, the city-based and city-named 'Harlem Renaissance' of the 1920s followed closely thereon. Negro writing, by and large, has fulfilled the conditions of two major American themes, the conversion of an agrarian into an urban people and a physical migration into a hostile 'majority culture'. The work of the three Negro novelists selected for emphasis in this essay – Richard Wright, Ralph Ellison and James Baldwin – have the scenario of the Great Migration at the heart of their work.

There are writers of minority stock for whom the people of their birth has had little to no attraction as a literary subject. Jean Toomer's *Cane* (1923) is a cornerstone of the Negro Renaissance of the twenties and a book of astonishing assurance. It treats masterfully of the rural/urban shift in Negro life. After *Cane*, Toomer declared he wanted no more of the Negro situation in America, and took himself off from the national literary scene altogether. No Negro writer of real quality has so far left his race behind as a subject for fiction: the proposition may be tested against the two most well-known writers of Negro birth who have tried, Frank Yerby and Willard Motley. Whether the Negro community can provide any counter-cultural sustenance for authors or for the country itself is an important theme in American Negro writing.

The 'visibility' of the Negro-born may account for the lesser amount of melting into the national whole in literary terms as well as social. (The subject of 'passing for white', however, was a prominent theme in Negro writing for some thirty years from the beginning of this century.) Of writers of Jewish origin whose work either owes little to their ethnic background or whose use of it is so transformed as to require extremities of sophistication to make the connection, the work of Nathanael West (born Nathan Weinstein) and Norman Mailer may be singled out. West, as the change of name partly indicates, made a determined effort to put his Jewish origins behind him, and some third term is needed to connect the themes, characterizations and emotions of his novels, including *Miss Lonelyhearts* (1933) and *The Day of the Locust* (1939), to Jewish experience. Mailer's comment on what constitutes minority experience demonstrates how quickly he moves from the group to a larger frame of reference:

A member of a minority group is – if we are to speak existentially – not a man who is a member of a category, a Negro or a Jew, but rather a man who feels his existence in a particular way. It is in the very form or context of his existence to live with two opposed notions of himself.

What characterizes a member of a minority group is that he is forced to see himself as both exceptional and insignificant, marvelous and awful, good and evil. . . . What characterizes the sensation of being a member of a minority group is that one's emotions are forever locked in the chains of ambivalence – the expression of an emotion forever releasing its opposite. . . .

Mailer's consuming passion for the contemporary may well mean that the time in which he might have interested himself in his Brooklyn background has passed. As the Jewish group ceases to seem a potential focus for a counter-cultural position, it would hold little interest for a man whose passion to formulate the nature of benign power in America has been focused on the charisma of *individuals* (like President Kennedy) rather than groups. This view gives a certain tension to his reportorial books *Armies of the Night* (1967) and *Miami and the Siege of Chicago* (1968), where he began the search for the seeds of group alternatives to the 'cancer' of politico-military-industrial America.[1]

The waning of hope in the American Jewish community as a force upon American life has provided much of the focus for the energies of America's Jewish-born writers, not the least for the three writers examined in the pages that follow – Saul Bellow, Bernard Malamud and Philip Roth. The late Robert Warshow, in an essay which celebrates Clifford Odets's play *Awake and Sing!* (1935) as the foundation of Jewish-American writing, singled out particularly its depiction of the betrayal of the ideals and hopes of the younger generation. Warshow seems to share the play's intense

---

[1] Negro intellectuals today point to the supposed triumph of 'Jewish power' in America as they pursue ideas of group, or 'black power'.

feelings over the way in which the older generation has abandoned itself to crass American materialism – indeed inventing a particularly virulent form of it – and settling for an indoctrination in cynicism as the ethnic 'wisdom' to pass on to their children. As Warshow epitomizes their message: 'money is filth, but money is all you'll ever get'.[1] Thus the emotional core of American Jewish writing is often the reaction of the first generation American to the 'migration' made by his parents. Warshow's analysis is largely applicable to the finest Jewish-American novel written before the Second World War, Henry Roth's *Call It Sleep* (1934). There is a direct comparison to be made here with Richard Wright's description, in his autobiography *Black Boy* (1945), of the indoctrination in 'Tomming' which the Negro community (in the person of his mother) gave him. In each case, the older generation accompanies its lessons in cynicism with a lament for the attempts at 'assimilation' by the idealistic young, i.e., the effort to reject the limits set for them by their communities.

In the sections on individual authors which follow, comments have not been restricted to the question of the minority situation. Thus when it appears, it may be understood to reflect matters of central interest, and not the single-minded pursuance of a thesis. It is as important to note the latitude to remove themselves from this subject (or theme) available to the writers as the extent to which they deal with it more directly.

II

In a classification of character types, W. B. Yeats once wrote,

The mind that has shown a predominantly emotional character, called that of the *Victim*, through the *antithetical* [Subjective] phases, now shows a predominantly intellectual character, called that of the *Sage* (though until [a number of additional phases have] been passed it can but use intellect when true to phase to eliminate intellect); whereas the mind that has been predominantly that of the *Sage* puts on *Victimage*.

The terminology of 'victim' and 'sage' lies close to the heart of Saul Bellow's fiction. Yeats's analysis of the personality 'balance[d] between ambition and contemplation', who must beware of 'Self-

---

[1] 'Clifford Odets: Poet of the Jewish Middle Class' first appeared in *Commentary* (May, 1946) and was reprinted in *The Immediate Experience* (Doubleday and Co., 1962; Anchor paperback, 1964).

assurance' and 'The Temptation through Strength', provides a glossary of terms to approach Bellow and his protagonists.[1]

Dangling Man (1944), his first novel, is the diary of a man in the days before his call-up into the army. Free of the arbitrary ordering of his life which a civilian job has provided, Joseph drifts from incident to incident, day to day, looking for a new centre. He is dry, reserved, watchful. He does not forget himself or get carried away in passion. He has something of the protagonists of Sartre (Roquentin in *La Nausée*) and Camus (Meursault in *L'Étranger*) about him. He cannot bear 'to be held accountable for myself'; the condition of subjective 'freedom' is insupportable. Joseph is broken by the strain of life 'dangling' between external orders and his only approach to feeling is mustered in the partly-ironic last words:

> Hurray for regular hours!
> And for the supervision of the spirit!
> Long live regimentation!

One might argue that Joseph never shows himself halfway willing to come to grips with the outside, to impose himself upon life. He seems too weak to make a battle of it, and we find his collapse only too likely. To the extent that readers have felt Bellow to have been figuring in *Dangling Man* a general symbol for humanity they have often reacted adversely.

The cards are stacked against success by Joseph's reliance on the world's providing him with a self. But *Dangling Man* has a kind of minor perfection in integrity despite the many echoes of other writers (in addition to Sartre and Camus, Dostoyevsky, Kafka, the Melville of 'Bartleby the Scrivener'). That it survives this load is a testimony to its narrow but true strength.

Joseph is largely a victim of himself, locked in a prison of self. Asa Leventhal, the protagonist of Bellow's second novel *The Victim* (1947), is in a more complex relation to the world. Bellow is not strong at presenting involved human relationships: the solitary individual is at the centre of each of his books. But in *The Victim*, the Jewish Leventhal's strange relation to his Gentile *doppelgänger*, the derelict Kirby Allbee, is hauntingly portrayed.

Leventhal has more stomach for his loneliness than had Joseph, though he is convinced of its pervasiveness in human life. Bellow levies little on a Jewish background for the realistic basis of

---

[1] W. B. Yeats, *A Vision* (London and New York, 1938), pp 159, 157. The type, he also noted, 'comes to hate symbolism'.

Leventhal's melancholy. Leventhal is just better able to bear it than Joseph, but at the cost of a certain sensitivity. Allbee's claim that Leventhal has cost him his job and therefore shares a certain responsibility for the subsequent degradation of his life is met with incomprehension and denial. Through a series of episodes, Allbee obtrudes himself more and more upon Leventhal, who becomes shaken in his belief. The issue seems crucial to a man who has always sensed a sharp division between those who 'got away with it' and 'the lost, the outcast, the overcome, the effaced, the ruined'. Allbee threatens to drag him down into that other world.

Allbee is outrageously Gentile – a Jew's nightmare of a *goy* – in his copybook prejudices:

'When I was born, when I was a boy, everything was different. We thought it would be daylight forever. Do you know, one of my ancestors was Governor Winthrop. Governor Winthrop!' His voice vibrated fiercely; there was a repressed laugh in it. 'I'm a fine one to be talking about tradition, you must be saying. But still I was born into it. And try to imagine how New York affects me. Isn't it preposterous? It's really as if the children of Caliban were running everything . . . The old breeds are out. The streets are named after them. But what are they themselves? Just remnants . . . last week I saw a book about Thoreau and Emerson by a man named Lipschitz. . . .'

That Allbee's language does not strike the ear with total conviction only adds to the nightmare quality. For a moment the encounter between the two men swells to include the literary situation. The Jewish writer has ousted the native American. Perhaps just as Leventhal comes to accept his partial responsibility for Allbee's downfall (even though he must draw a line beyond which he will not sympathize or be imposed upon), the Jewish writer acknowledges a certain guilt by seeing that America has been to a degree his victim. For by the novel's end, it is not Leventhal alone who is the innocent victim of a persecutor, nor is Allbee's alternative version of guilt paramount. Wisdom is chastening, teaching man's mutual victimage. Leventhal's worst fears (symbolized by the ever-present thought of 'a black list') have come to pass, but he has lived through them and may be purged.

In *The Adventures of Augie March* (1953) Bellow next created a character who was to be nobody's shrinking violet, an antithetical figure of ambition and self-assurance. Augie is patently a picaresque figure, a roaring boy with great gusto and little consci-ence. In polar contrast to Joseph and Leventhal, Augie takes events almost too much in his stride:

I always heard from women that I didn't have the profounder knowledge of life, that I didn't know its damage or its suffering or its stupendous ecstasies and glories. . . .

She shot it off in my face that I wasn't mad enough about abominations or aware enough of them, didn't know how many graves were underneath my feet, was lacking in disgust, wasn't hard enough against horrors or wrathful about swindlers.

Bellow has been criticized for a dramatic failure in respect of Augie's insensitivity, though he obviously intended the characterization. It is the price he pays for the overcompensation, for having a character who does not count the cost or scrutinize himself so intently as his earlier heroes.

Augie March is plastic, unformed – 'nobody knew where I belonged'. As a result, however, his 'adventures' become a history of other people's efforts to mould him to their desires. Each claims the status of a sage, and as Augie heeds their wisdom, he becomes a victim without feeling for his condition. He may be 'the born recruit' – the metaphor makes him begin where Joseph ended – someone 'other people are always trying to fit into their schemes', but he resists being trapped utterly and, like a true picaresque hero, lives to be recruited another day. Latterly, Augie grows in an awareness that the currents into which he is sucked prevent him from being himself. One wonders, however, just where this interior self springs from, so categorically extroverted has Augie's presentation been.

The energy and even wastefulness, the copiousness of *The Adventures of Augie March* are a deliberate counter to Bellow's earlier sparer work, where he seems almost too careful a husbander of his talents. There is little resolution for Augie, whose final adventures are extraordinarily romantic and melodramatic. In fact, he moves back at the last towards the brooding characterizations of Joseph and Leventhal. The superimposition of a more questing, thoughtful, philosophical 'pilgrimage' on the outgoing, free-wheeling earlier portions remains mechanical.

In the two novels which succeeded *Augie March* Bellow first returned to the more sensitive, restricted canvas of *Dangling Man* and *The Victim* in *Seize the Day* (1956), and then launched further into the extravagant in *Henderson the Rain King* (1959). *Seize the Day* has been highly regarded, particularly by those who have found something false and forced in Bellow's more eupeptic performances. The novel certainly shows an advance in handling the figure of the sage who haunts almost every Bellow work, offering to the hero panaceas usually compounded of ethnic or tribal wisdom. The sage purports to offer an 'objective', communally sanctioned path to rescue the victim equally from his subjective self and the sham objectivity of 'the world's business'. In this novel the sage is *seen through*, as in the flanking novels he is not. *Seize the Day* is finally most ambivalent, however, and despite Bellow's maturity of talent, looks too much like a rewritten version of earlier books.

Henderson is an Augie with *angst*, the landscape of his pilgrimage not the American continent, but Africa, and the big game both lions and (almost equally literally) 'reality'. Bellow tries his arm at creating a sensitive Augie March, but to float the improbable compound must reduce the realism of his setting. Henderson's Africa is a mythical terrain. Henderson is a butt as much as a hero, as foolish in his questing as he is noble. An all-consuming irony is never very far off, as though Bellow were parodying his own deepest needs for search and discovery. Structurally, Henderson lives through a series of myth-situations which cast him as a ritual god-figure – only he botches them. Promising to secure a tribe its water supply, he blows up their well. Nevertheless, we take seriously his search for wisdom from African masters.[1] The comedy conveys a sense of unease: we don't quite know how to have it, and the suspicion grows that the freewheeling juggernaut is as much Bellow's way of holding difficulties in solution, laughing at them, but with a certain desperation, as of piercing them to a resolution. In the grey climate of the American fifties *Augie* and *Henderson* seemed daring releases of otherwise repressed forces in the national literary psyche. In retrospect Bellow's distaste for the risky, the formless, the longing, is more apparent.

The episodic, fragmentary, contingent universe of the adventure novels was finally wedded to the antithetical, contemplative, unself-assured world of the other three in *Herzog* (1964). Here, a college professor of the humanities broods over both his personal life and the civilization of Western Man and bewilders himself in an attempt to adjust the two. Personally, he feels victimized: his ex-wife now lives with his former friend. Life is treachery, betrayals. What is new in Bellow is the active way Herzog lays hands on his memories and thoughts. Some of this is comic, particularly the series of (unsent) letters Herzog writes to the famous (their characteristic form: Dear –, in your book you say . . . but I have personally found . . .).

[1] Norman Mailer was in these years turning more straightforwardly to the *American black man* as a counter-image. See his 'The White Negro'.

Herzog is clearly in as much of a *state* as Bellow's other protagonists. (Only Augie can take things easy and at the end even he alters.) As usual it is no intellectual synthesis which wins the hero respite – indeed it may only be exhaustion. But Herzog does exorcize one particular obsession, when he spies on his child being bathed by his ex-wife's lover, and his frenzied half-resolve to shoot the man evaporates. He acknowledges that love can exist outside his own desires. Herzog is further moved from his obsession by a contrasting episode, his arrest (for illegal possession of the gun he no longer intends to use) and a courtroom scene where sympathy for the misery of others can break in upon the walls of his ego.

For all its paraphernalia of intellect, *Herzog* is a profoundly anti-intellectual work. We depend not upon intellect but upon the fortuity and contingency of event. Herzog's mania is intended to sober, his logorrhea to silence. (Yeats called this the use of intellect to eliminate intellect.) 'A good five cent synthesis' is precisely what America does *not* need, and no combination of words will wake us from the nightmare of our needs and demands and restore us to ourselves. Bellow's own remarks in recent years (in interviews and essays) strike just this pugnacious and derogatory attitude towards 'the life of the mind', yet it is no wonder if he is approached by his readership for the secrets of how to live. All his heroes are just such seekers, and it is a narrow view which converts all Bellow's irony to criticism of them. They all live in the impasse, in an iron time: *Mr Sammler's Planet* (1970) is no exception; nor are *Humboldt's Gift* (1975) or *The Dean's December* (1982). In holding on to the bleaker emotional spectrum of the American thirties through a time of official cheer, Bellow has had little to apologize for subsequently. Where the alienated believe as much in the quick solution as the majority from whom they are disaffected, Bellow's growing refusal to sit for the wise man's portrait may leave many baffled. He has noted how the artist has in our society usurped or been handed the role held previously by the priest or teacher, with clear indications that he doesn't like the process and intends no part of it. How far he can opt out of it, or – perhaps more importantly – how much he can alter the situation by his own fiction, is another question.

III

The hoped-for return to inner harmony in Bellow is based on an awakened potentiality for love and selflessness. Bellow's characters search for and, we feel, should rightly be granted an end to their

inner torture. For Bernard Malamud's heroes such freedom is a
snare: purified suffering is itself the desired end, not something to
be passed beyond. Indeed, true suffering is a difficult state to attain
and carefully to be distinguished from the mere fretfulness of
romantic quandary.

The title story of the collection *The Magic Barrel* (1958) illus-
trates the pitfalls of the desire to be free, characteristically free of
the restraints of the older, Jewish way of life and the limiting bounds
it sets on existence. In the story, Leo Finkle, a rabbinical student,
goes to the marriage broker, Salzman, for a wife. This is fit and
proper. But, in a gesture of romantic revolt he hardly comprehends,
he determines to choose 'love' rather than a sanctioned practicality.
The broker attempts to hold Finkle back – there is a strong
suggestion he has selected a 'lost' woman – only to meet with
increased demands. Finally the broker (apparently the girl's father)
capitulates:

Leo was informed by letter that she would meet him on a certain corner,
and she was there one spring night, waiting under a street lamp. He
appeared, carrying a small bouquet of flowers, violets and rosebuds. Stella
stood by the lamp post, smoking. She wore white with red shoes, which
fitted his expectations, although in a troubled moment he had imagined the
dress red, and only the shoes white. She waited uneasily and shyly. From
afar he saw that her eyes – clearly her father's – were filled with desperate
innocence. He pictured, in her, his own redemption. Violins and lit candles
revolved in the sky. Leo ran forward with flowers out-thrust.

Around the corner, Salzman, leaning against a wall, chanted prayers for
the dead.

'The Magic Barrel' takes on a fairy-tale intensity (the revolving
violins and candles suggest the magical ghettoes in the paintings of
Marc Chagall). Finkle by his gesture towards freedom is 'lost' to the
older way of life and is mourned in traditional fashion.

Malamud's second novel, *The Assistant* (1957), almost precisely
reverses the pattern. A young Italian, Frankie Alpine, in penance
for having robbed an elderly Jewish storekeeper, returns to the shop
to offer his services. Gradually he becomes more and more like the
old, suffering Jew and at the novel's end he is painfully circumcised
to mark his conversion to Judaism. Considerable ambiguity hangs
over this progress, making it Malamud's most successful piece of
long fiction. The storekeeper, Bober, has a daughter, Helen. Alpine
falls in love with her, but after careful ingratiation alienates her by
making her succumb to his advances. Her reaction is in good part
guilt. He spends the rest of the novel doggedly trying to win back

her favour, a hopeless medieval knight and his now untouchable lady.

This affair and the general deterioration of the shop (it cannot maintain itself in competition with the new supermarket) give a strange and troubling undercurrent to the hero's quest. He accepts suffering, he rejoins a tradition and a community of suffering, though it is not his by birth. Does his romantic dedication undercut his path to purgation? Is that very path itself a dead end, the tradition he has chosen played out? It is hard not to agree with the salesman who early on advises Frankie to get out before the store 'buries' him. The novel concludes on a wonderfully troubled note of mixed bondage and freedom.

Almost all of Malamud's fiction takes place between the extremes of the romantic search for personal freedom and the willing acceptance of bonds. But the countercurrents are many and the emotional responses, at their most successful, extremely mixed. In *A New Life* (1961), S. Levin attempts to set behind him a 1930s New York, Jewish life of unspecified woefulness for a post-war, specifically Western American life of freedom and spontaneity. The comic imperfections of the college society in which he finds himself predispose us to more sympathy for him than is usual in Malamud. As long as the West is the subject, in the persons of Levin's colleagues, we are with him. When, on the other hand, we take his struggle seriously, we become critical. Then, in the Malamud morality, we see Levin struggling for the foolish freedom, the moth for the star. In this respect, the awfulness of 'Cascadia' only underscores Levin's futility – what is he doing looking for a 'new life' *there*? Levin is in the end faithful to his struggle, he sees it through. He leaves Cascadia saddled with the wife he has stolen from a colleague (the colleague is disconcertingly approving). She no longer holds any attraction for him, but he will soldier on, 'because he can'. Though the plot is, so to speak, against him, he seems neither elated nor depressed. His new burdens are not 'Jewish', but he seems to accept responsibility once again. Levin has, then, reverted from anti-type to type.

Subsequently, the two characters who have engaged Malamud's attention most are the two sides of Levin, a pure case of suffering and a comic freedom-reacher whose fingers had already been burned in earlier stories, the would-be artist Fidelman. The former, hero of the novel *The Fixer* (1966), is the Jewish victim of a Czarist pogrom. The historical fiction recreates an actual case of Russian persecution, and Malamud presents a *tour de force* of anxiety and hope destroyed. It is a classic nightmare of incarceration, the hero subjected to outer and inner torment, yet living through his despair to dignity. Ordinarily, we might ask what that avails when injustice prevails: Malamud has sidestepped the problem by the historical setting, whose repressions we need not concern ourselves with so strongly as with our own society's, leaving us free to concentrate on the inner life of the protagonist. At the same time a general equation of his hero with 'Jews' and Czarist Russia with 'America' can hover in the air. If in Malamud's comic posture, society's weaknesses only seem to underline his hero's impossible quests, in his more 'serious' writing, ways are found to obscure their social implications.

IV

Malamud has come more and more to picture the limiting past as freedom and the limitless future as a trap. Less and less does there hover any ambiguity (as in *The Assistant*) over the choice of a backward-oriented fate. He may represent the ideology of the past weakly ('all sufferers are Jews'), but in the concrete details of a traditional and sanctioned life his notations are sure and accurate. He seems unable to imagine an integrated existence without a specific framework of tradition, and he comes nearest of all the major Jewish-American writers to an essential sympathy with the 'old ways', in reaction to which most other writers have found their basic energies.

Of a younger generation, Philip Roth (b. 1933) demonstrates the continuance of tension between revolt and admiration. His first published work, *Goodbye, Columbus* (1959), consisted of a satirical novella and a handful of brilliant short stories. The novella traced an adolescent love-affair against the divergent background of the young lovers, both Jewish, one middle- and the other working-class. All the crassness belongs to the one, all the gentility to the other. But something of the hero's failure to 'hold' his girl stems from the larger, if cruder, energies lacking in the stream he inherited. Certain of the short stories, most notably 'Defender of the Faith', also show the divided stream of tradition. Roth exploits within a Jewish context a theme in the American grain, posing the intellectual, spiritual but febrile individual against the materialistic but energetic.

Roth's second novel, the lengthy *Letting Go* (1962), again deals with the scions of the dual strain of American Jewry. At first it seems that the descendant of the more energetic, 'modern' and affluent parents is the intelligence Roth will work through. It is even odd to find someone so well endowed as his narrator Gabe Wallach taking a mere college teaching position: the role better suits the nebbishy, past-haunted Paul Hertz. Intentionally or not, a complete reversal of roles is accomplished over the novel's length. Wallach takes on scruples enough to refrain from stealing Paul's wife Libby, but in fact he is losing strength throughout the novel. Roth is less successful at making Paul appear to be gaining strength. The title seems more to refer to 'losing one's grip' on life than 'letting things rip', overthrowing old inhibitions. And Roth's considerable comic talent is in abeyance throughout.

The reverse is the case in Roth's fourth novel, *Portnoy's Complaint* (1969), glossed medically as an acute conflict between idealism and sensuality. The opposition is hardly unique, but the composition of its features from the relationship of Jewish adolescent and mother strikes home with great force. Portnoy's mother is a great American Jewish evil genius, a direct descendant of Bessie in Clifford Odets's *Awake and Sing!* The portions of Portnoy's monologue dealing with his childhood are much more successful than that dealing with his present (as a supposed Commissioner for Human Opportunity in New York), and it is apparent that the negative energy which impels Roth's portraits of the constraining elder generation is a stronger force than the less satirical view of the here and now. Portnoy's agonies as a youth are brought to high art; as a man he seems absurd. The man may be absurdly tortuous as an adolescent, but the mere description of that experience does not account for present incapacities. It might have been better not to have given a present at all.

Something of this has been apparent throughout Roth's work – the best parts of *Letting Go* deal with the elders – and the irony is plain: it is still the vicious, whining, clever, grasping elders who outrank the younger generation by the sheer force of their characters. If this is Portnoy's problem, it is Roth's, too. Gabe Wallach looked like being an anti-Portnoy, but by the book's end he is an emotional, moral and physical invalid. One wonders if Roth will give him, or someone on his original side of the fence, another round.

In the 1970s and 1980s Philip Roth, spending much of his time in London and expressing support and admiration for such 'Iron Curtain' writers as Kundera, has richly experimented with native and foreign scenes and themes – the semi-Surrealist *The Breast*, for example, or flights of exasperated fantasy on President Nixon, *Our Gang*. Some of this goes far away from Portnoy-Roth. He returns, however, to the problems of a *succès de scandale*, repugnant to some fellow-Jews, in the *Zuckerman* trilogy (completed in 1985, with *The Counterlife*, 1986, as coda) – Zuckerman being a fictitious American novelist who has much in common with his creator. Roth's later writings have tended to bewilder that hypothetical creature, the 'general reader', but are much admired by fellow-authors who recognize the complexity of the professional problems he agonizes over, and the richly ironic wit with which he conveys them.

V

The grinding poverty of the thirties cuts like a sword across the optimism which had been the prevailing tone of American Negro writing. Writers in the Harlem Renaissance held so strongly to the possibilities of this new Negro community that they averted their eyes from the reckoning.[1] 'Last hired; first fired' – in the Great Depression American Negroes paid their dues for the years of hope.

Recent interest in the history of Negro American writing has thus not obscured the sense of a new beginning which comes with the work of Richard Wright. Wright's early stories are set in a rural South untouched by the boom-and-bust Northern pattern. Collectively titled *Uncle Tom's Children* (1938), their world is poised on the edge of change. In an introductory comment Wright contrasted 'reluctant toleration for the cringing type who knew his place before white folk' with the attitude of a younger generation. *Uncle Tom's Children* portrays the death-bed of the old way and the seed-bed of the new. The death is not an easy one, nor is the birth, and the process and means of maturation is in doubt. Scenes of violence punctuate each story, both black violence (usually in self-defence) against whites and white revenge upon blacks, its characteristic form the lynching.[2] The order of the stories suggests a shadowy chronology. At first Negroes become 'bad niggers' by chance, later, the history of persecution having been established by Wright, more by choice. If the individual agonies are not to be found meaningless, a social theory is necessary, and it is found first by co-operating with

[1] See, for example, Alain Locke, ed., *The New Negro* (1925). Reprinted Atheneum, New York, 1968.

[2] 'Did ever in history a race of men have for so long a time the same horror before their eyes?' *White Man, Listen!* (New York, 1957).

and subsequently by belonging to the Communist Party. Wright's sense of proportion never wholly deserts him, however. When white violence is confined to a whipping, the story can end with an exultant joining of black and white workers in industrial protest. When collaboration becomes active organizing and death is the punishment, only an individual act of revenge, and that self-immolating, is possible. At the last, it is not achieved social action which is depicted but individual confidence in the revolution to come. 'Bright and Morning Star' inverts the stereotype of the Black Mammy and converts the obsessive image of a lynching into a paradoxical rededication and rebirth.

Many years later Wright was to write that he did 'not hanker after, and seem[ed] not to need, as many emotional attachments, sustaining roots, or idealistic allegiances as most people' (*White Man, Listen!*), but his early works pivot on the emotional need for a sustaining faith or allegiance.[1] And a social faith which could satisfy the intellectual but not the ordinary man was not enough.

Wright's pre-eminent work, the novel *Native Son* (1940), demonstrates precisely the failure of attachments, roots or allegiances to claim the Negro *homme moyen sensuel*. Wright's protagonist Bigger Thomas, though he kills both a white and a black woman, is no monster. His actions have seemed to some so much the product of environmental forces as to align Wright with the school of the Naturalistic and Determinist novelists like Dreiser. (*Native Son* has certain obvious similarities with Theodore Dreiser's *An American Tragedy* of 1925, which was likewise based on an actual murder case.) In fact, the environmental explanation is the one Bigger's defence attorney Max uses during the trial.

Though many readers felt that the attorney's explanation was Wright's own – Max is a Communist, as Wright was for a time, but his argument is poor Marxism in any case – what is more important is that Bigger himself rejects it, and what Bigger himself will accept is the focus of interest in the novel's last part. Unlike Dreiser's Clyde Griffiths, who comes to accept the Governor's version of his significance, Bigger rejects, one after another, all explanations and dies in utter rejection, without hope.

There has only been one moment when Bigger felt differently and, paradoxically, it was in the moment of his becoming a murderer:

---

[1] See Wright's essay 'Black Boy' in R. H. S. Crossman, *The God That Failed* (London, 1949 and New York, 1950).

He had murdered and had created a new life for himself. It was something that was all his own, and it was the first time in his life he had had anything that others could not take from him. . . . His crime was an anchor weighing him safely in time; it added to him a certain confidence which his gun and knife did not. . . .

The hidden meaning of his life . . . had spilled out.

For a very short time Bigger can *see*, but *what* he sees points to the ironical brevity of his 'new life':

Buddy was soft and vague; his eyes were defenseless and their glance went only to the surface of things. It was strange that he had not noticed that before. Buddy, too, was blind. Buddy was sitting there longing for a job like his. Buddy, too, went round and round in a groove and did not see things. . . . He saw in Buddy a certain stillness, an isolation, meaninglessness.

The irony is that Bigger's new self cannot exist in time, in history. He murders again, as much to regain the extraordinary sense of freedom as for any practical reason of concealment, but this time his transcendent state lasts for even shorter time. Once a prisoner of the State, with its own notion of what such acts lead to (the 'chair'), he feels it no more.

Violence in Wright is thus far from gratuitous (James Baldwin, among others, has attacked him on this score), and it is fitting that the French Existentialists, Jean-Paul Sartre in particular, should have fastened upon Wright as a writer of the modern 'absurd' sensibility. But the discovery of new sight under stress is a classic *American* theme as well, as is the impossibility of social realizations for free states of consciousness.[1] *Native Son* is a tragedy because the transcendent act of freedom carries with it its own extinction. Subsequently, in settling for a life without attachments, roots and allegiances, Wright came to 'cherish the state of abandonment, of aloneness', and no later novel recaptured the tensions of *Native Son*.

It is clear from Wright's autobiography of his first twenty years, *Black Boy* (1945), that for him the act of writing was the act of violence which sufficed Bigger Thomas. His descriptions of the severe environmental restraints of his Mississippi and Tennessee childhood demonstrate how society, black as much as white, attempted to force him to play a particular role. For Wright, Negro 'culture' was merely a system of punishments to deter him from getting in bad with whites. That writing came to him as both an act of violence and a weapon is clear when he describes his discovery of the power of the written word:

[1] This is the theme of Richard Poirier's *A World Elsewhere*.

I opened [H. L. Mencken's] *A Book of Prefaces* and began to read. I was jarred and shocked by the style, the clear, clean, sweeping sentences. Why did he write like that? I pictured the man as a raging demon, slashing with his pen, consumed with hate, denouncing ... laughing ... mocking. ... Yes, this man was fighting, fighting with words. He was using words as a weapon, using them as one would use a club. Could words be weapons? Well, yes, for here they were. Then, maybe, perhaps, I could use them as a weapon.

'Art as a weapon' became a cliché of the Marxist idea of literature. Wright found the notion in his life and not on a page of polemic and it served him rather better than most. But something of the essentially destructive nature of the analogy clung to him throughout, taking a progressive toll on his work. With him is instanced that complex fate awaiting the Negro writer in America, whose experience puts him in the way of extreme and ultimate conditions very early and whose particular antinomies loom quickly up when many another writer is afforded a slower logic of development. The relatively static agony of the Negro situation in America likewise inhibits a largely altered emotional fabric in the work of the individual writer. Richard Wright struck quickly, and lived in his own shadow thenceforward.

VI

Ralph Ellison has described his Oklahoma youth as a unique moment in American life, with the undoubted inference that to the accident of it accrues perhaps his greatest debt. Oklahoma, though a Southern state, 'had no tradition of slavery, and while it was segregated, relationships between the races were more fluid and thus more human than in the old slave states'. Oklahoma Negroes had, he says, 'a tradition of aggressiveness' to help preserve their budding identity (compare Richard Wright's Mississippi childhood), and 'life there was not so tightly structured as it would have been in the traditional South – or even in deceptively "free" Harlem'. This early opportunity to stand forthright, to grow, to dream, later suffered traumatic shock, not only from the expected rebuffs of prejudice and discrimination – of whose psychological effect upon American Negroes Ellison has written movingly in 'Harlem is Nowhere' (reprinted in his essay collection *Shadow and Act*, 1964, from which come the quotations in this paragraph). Shocks to the very core of self-definition were insidiously provided by 'that feverish industry dedicated to telling Negroes who and what they are', by 'formulas through which historians, politicians, sociologists, and an older generation of Negro leaders and writers – those of the so-called "Negro Renaissance" – had evolved to describe by the group's identity, its predicament, its fate and its relation to the larger society and the culture which we share'. As a would-be writer, Ellison felt his problem was to reveal 'what he truly felt, rather than serving up what Negroes were supposed to feel, and were encouraged to feel'.

Ellison's single, massive novel, *Invisible Man* (1952), refracts these autobiographical conditions of struggle through a monstrous comic prism. Episodically, the unnamed protagonist moves through the stages of modern American Negro history: a deep Southern childhood; a Negro college supported by Northern philanthropy (Ellison himself attended Tuskegee Institute, founded by Booker T. Washington); industrial factory work in New York; exposure to the polar currents of Negro ferment in Harlem: a 'back to Africa' anti-colonialist movement and a communist-like organization called only 'the Brotherhood'; the 'hipster' scene. Ultimately the protagonist drops out almost literally: he ends, and he pens his memoir, in a fantastic underground retreat from which he meditates on the necessity of returning to the surface – but to what *new* phase of Negro experience? For it is crystal-clear that 'I couldn't return ... to any part of my old life'.

The events of that old life, comic extravaganzas on successive decades (more or less) since the turn of the century, were clearly a series of traps from which the gullible 'hero' is sprung only by accident – or the artistic necessity of moving him on to keep up the historical allegory. He usually wants nothing more than to fit in, to play the role demanded of him, but he always manages to put a foot wrong.[1] Then the forces of conformity to whatever immediate allegiance mass to expel him: 'keep this nigger running' is their motto. Squiring the wealthy philanthropist about the college campus, the 'Invisible Man' inadvertently shows him squalid quarters of the poor Negroes. Worse, he allows 'Mr Norton' to speak to an unrepentantly incestuous illiterate tenant farmer, the neighbourhood sideshow. For this the canting college president expels him. In his later career the protagonist displays more will and choice in his rejections: he is always suspicious of the white-hating, West Indian 'Ras the Destroyer', and his disillusionment with 'the Brotherhood' requires more decision on his part than have previous

[1] Compare Bellow's *Augie March*, which has a similar structure.

entanglements. Paradoxically, any increase in maturity or self-possession by the Invisible Man himself is cruelly negated by the absence of objective social opportunity. 'I'm coming out' of the cellar, he declares at the end, 'there's a possibility that even an invisible man has a socially responsible role to play'. But he has just previously been unable to answer his own question: 'but what *is* the next phase?'.

The Invisible Man is a kind of anti-Ellison, lacking his creator's exceptional childhood, his feelings for the values of a black heritage. If Ellison is critical of his anti-hero's amorphous, neutral personality – and he is a bit like the character of the Jewish *schlemiel*-figure in this respect – he is not wholly unsympathetic, and the truly awful proportions of what the Invisible Man is up against in Southern town and Northern metropolis leave the question of what *anyone* might have done in these circumstances the final taste in the reader's mouth. The force is so irresistible that the subject's mobility pales by comparison. For the caricatural exaggerations of the hostile environments function less to tell us that American reality is 'better' than as the hidden truth behind the bland façades of small town, campus and factory.

Thus the writer and his novel are not just polar opposites. The novel entertains possibilities of defeat and pessimism Ellison constantly refuses in his own voice. The writer's injunctions to study the Negro past (the 'shadow' whose scrutiny is necessary to the 'act' of writing) seem hardly available to the hero at the end of the line, rather a Gulliver after his travels. Marcus Klein, in an excellent essay on Ellison's novel[1] has noted both the repetitiveness of each of its sections and their tendency to state the whole condition of the Negro in America, each ending in a stark image of immobilization. I have indicated that *Invisible Man* does have recognizable internal stages, however, but what Klein says maintains a considerable force. Where does the hero, where does Ellison, go from here? In the years since the publication of *Invisible Man*, only the merest fragment of a new novel has appeared, and that most disappointing. The encyclopedic, cosmic urge of the American writer and the stages of American history appear to have converged to inhibit one of the largest talents of the mid-century: Ellison's silence is only less eloquent than his speech.

These comments appear still valid in the later 1980s. The segments

---

[1] In *After Alienation* (Cleveland and New York, 1964).

of the new novel have not coalesced into an entire work. Ralph Ellison has continued to publish occasional essays, and to receive some respectful responses to these. But in 1986, his reputation tended to be put in the past tense; and also, by both the more radically 'black' writers of the sixties and seventies and the new wave of black women writers, to be regarded as part of a male ancestry that might be as much handicap as inspiration.

VII

James Baldwin, unlike Wright and Ellison, is city bred and born (1924). The City is of course Harlem. If he is too young to have undergone the Great Migration, he is still a child of the great disillusionment, growing up in time to experience the fading of the promise of the New Jerusalem of the North. In this sense his fiction has mirrored a similar familial situation to Odets's *Awake and Sing!*,[1] where a younger generation's revolt is initially directed more against the failure of the older than against the larger society which precipitated it.

Baldwin's first novel, *Go Tell It on the Mountain* (1953), counterpoints a Harlem adolescence with the rural-to-urban memories and lives of his step-father, a turbulent and embittered store-front church preacher, his mother, and his aunt. In a pattern reminiscent of Joyce's *A Portrait of the Artist as a Young Man*, Baldwin's young protagonist strives to realize his own nature while others, older, point the way to dead ends. As Baldwin has said of all American Negro youth of his generation, the poles of the fictional John Grimes's options appear to be 'the church' or 'the street', his roles the preacher or the hipster-junkie-gangster. No middle ground seems available. To consider extremes is therefore the novel's realism. The 'street' is never presented as a real alternative for the sensitive John, however, and Baldwin assigns it to John's half-brother, Royal. Everything conspires to the end that John be 'saved', become one of 'the saints', gravelled by ecstasy and hysteria on the 'threshing-floor'. The novel's basic irony is that this promised end is ambiguously a defeat, stamping him in the mould of his fanatical step-father, *and* a victory, either for its spiritual rescue or for the psychological leverage he needs *against* his father. In a sense, the father, Gabriel, is the novel's real key character. The

---

[1] *Awake and Sing!* was originally titled *I Got the Blues*. The finest section of Philip Roth's *Portnoy's Complaint* is called 'The Jewish Blues'.

lines of his motivations, his experience, his bafflements come together in the novel's most complex and taut nexus of forces.

The path of 'sanctification' Gabriel sets for John is an ultimate exercise of his authority, yet its success is the greatest threat to that authority. Indeed, despite the wrought emotion of John's 'conversion', *Go Tell It on the Mountain*'s last section is anticlimactic after the moving complexities of the memory-monologues of the older generation, particularly Gabriel's, which form its central panel.

Baldwin became, in the years surrounding the publication of his first novel, the New York intelligentsia's foremost Negro commentator. This is ironic, in that a number of his early essays (collected in 1955 in *Notes of a Native Son*) attack the notion of his – or anyone's – wishing to become a spokesman for his 'people'. His most famous statement of this point of view is in the essay 'Everybody's Protest Novel' (1949), when he turns on his acknowledged literary father, Richard Wright, to claim that 'protest writing' is a dead end for artists.

One of Baldwin's most incisive comments is that there was no place in Wright's created world for a sensibility like the author's own. Wright wholly denigrated the culture out of which he sprang (as a part of the 'protest') and could never project how he came by his own sense of values and perceptions. (This seems unfair in the face of *Black Boy*.) And yet it has so far seemed that only in the world of Baldwin's own essays[1] has there been large room for Baldwin's own sensibility, for in the fiction there has remained a similar disjunction between his narrating voice and the actions and speaking voices of his characters. Mailer has called Baldwin's prose 'perfumed' in disparagement of its almost Jamesian decorated aspect, the intrusive fussiness and preciousness which constantly threaten to catch the action up into itself.

Another Country (1962) is a novel whose theme is panoramic – nothing less than the soul of America expressed through an anatomy of love relationships. It is structured (like E. M. Forster's *A Passage to India*) by a serial phasing of protagonists. The pairs of relationships run to both the inter-racial and the homosexual, in one case combined. Little of the past, is, however, available to his large cast, particularly after the early suicide of their potential link with it in the person of a Negro jazzman. The severance and deprivation seems Baldwin's point, though the characters are so

[1] A second collection, *Nobody Knows My Name*, was published in 1961, and a third, *No Name in the Street*, in 1972.

obviously striving for enlightenment and connection in the dense urban milieu. Their triumphs always appear undercut by their pretensions, their over-intense categorical elaboration and appreciation of the meaning of their involvements, and yet the reader can be confused as to whether Baldwin really provides a point from which one can assess them as either enlightened by their experience or evading its implications. Something of this is undoubtedly Baldwin's intent in choosing for his epigraph a comment of Henry James on the new non-Anglo-Saxon American travellers abroad:

They strike one, above all, as giving no account of themselves in any terms already consecrated by human use; to this inarticulate state they probably form, collectively, the most unprecedented of monuments; abysmal the mystery of what they think, what they feel, what they want, what they suppose themselves to be saying.

Alas, it is doubtful if Baldwin has done more than project these obscurities. He has done little to clear the darkness, and yet how otherwise to meet the challenge he threw down in his critique of Wright?

An apocalyptic light spreads over the novel's last section, 'Towards Bethlehem'. The Promised Land is becoming the Promised End. But it is hard to accept the bisexual actor, a white Southerner, as a Dionysiac saviour. Nor has the character who is an aspiring novelist been shaken loose from the despair which his affair with the dead Negro jazzman's sister has precipitated. Are these people unsalvageable, are they 'coming-of-age', are they carriers of a 'new life'? Who knows?

In common with many recent Negro American writers, Baldwin sometimes seems to be embroiled in 'Whitey'-baiting – as in, for example, his play *Blues for Mister Charlie* (1964). The figure of the white actor in *Another Country*, however, suggests that spiritual regeneration may come from the least expected quarter, the white South, and that by virtue of the idyllic relationship with a Negro boy in his rural youth.[1] (The thesis of Leslie Fiedler's *Love and Death in the American Novel* is relevant here.) The most substantial short story Baldwin has written, 'Going to Meet the Man' (title story of

---

[1] Eldridge Cleaver in *Soul on Ice* (New York, 1968 and London, 1969) considers that 'There is in James Baldwin's work the most gruelling, agonizing, total hatred of the blacks, particularly of himself, and the most shameful, fanatical, fawning, sycophantic love of the whites that one can find in the writings of any black American writer of note in our time'.

the volume published in 1965) underscores the point bizarrely and astonishingly. The story describes a lynching in a Southern community, not as had Richard Wright and many Negro writers from the inside, but from the 'white' side. By finding a hidden trace of sympathy within his loathing Baldwin carries the hideous spectacle beyond protest into art, showing and defining the precise measures of sickness and health in the perverse ritual, seeing it both in its degrading and – extraordinarily – its pacifying and restorative role in the white community. He has no illusion that the sickness will not recur, that even as it heals white psyches it institutes the vicious cycle again. With this story Baldwin reaches the heart of the matter: can he define his present, his Harlem and his New York, with equal precision?

The protagonist of *Tell Me How Long the Train's Been Gone* (1968), Leo Proudhammer, is a middle-ageing Negro actor of serious pretensions. When the novel opens, he has just suffered a heart attack, and much of the story is his reminscences during recuperation. The first-person narrative is closer to the tone of Baldwin's essays than in his previous fiction and conveys a surer sense of direction than *Another Country*. Here at last seems the attempt to get something of his own sensibility into a character. Precisely because he cannot appear to have too much of an investment in a Negro actor who has supposedly, in the 1960s, risen to the top of the profession to be universally admired by white America, Baldwin begins to draw away from Proudhammer as the novel proceeds. Some of the ambivalence of *Another Country* returns, notably in the character's (and novelist's) subservience to 'Black Christopher', the swinging militant black lover of the protagonist. As the novel shifts back into the present, the lack of examination of young Christopher rubs off on to Proudhammer, and Baldwin is ultimately unwilling to risk or carry through a definite evaluation of the protagonist and world he has created.

VIII

In fact, Baldwin has moved steadily (*pace* the thesis of Marcus Klein) towards alienation. In doing so, his fiction and latterly his essays (see particularly *The Fire Next Time*, 1963) have gone back on the posture he struck in 'Everybody's Protest Novel'. Like many of the younger Negro writers in America today, Baldwin now seems desirous of appearing specifically as a *black* artist.

LeRoi Jones, in the preface to his book of essays *Home*,[1] writes, 'By the time this book appears, I will be even blacker' – meaning more identified with race, more alienated from White America. (He now writes as Imamu Amiri Baraka.)

The conscious espousal of an intransigent minority position by Negro artists has come to them to seem liberating. This was the position of the participants in the first flowering of Negro culture in the twenties, but it was denied by both Richard Wright and Ralph Ellison (and by the young Baldwin). They maintained, even in the teeth of the profound alienations of their imaginative visions, that their status as Negroes had no essential bearing on the life of their art. They might choose Negroes as subject but their own authorial voice was colourless. Richard Wright's late novel, *The Outsider* (1953), slights the fact of the Negro hero's responses to cultural conditioning, and asserts for him a metaphysical status of alienation. This fracture in the chain between individual and universal significance is common in American writing, as Tony Tanner has noted in *The Reign of Wonder*.[2] Ellison has made dual claims for the inessentiality of his blackness and the vital sustenance derivable from the Negro community – something unproven on the showing of *Invisible Man*, which rejects a historical gamut of Negro life-styles. But, in fiction, he has been silent. For the moment, in literature as in politics, the militant blacks make all the news.

The dominance of ethnic cultures within America is presently a firm plank in the analyses of black sociology.[3] In this view, the United States is a volatile balance of power between heterogeneous congeries of ethnic groups (part religion, part race, part country of origin). For the proponents of this view it is the path of the Jews whose historic example the Negro must follow on the road to effective power. On this account, the intramural crises of the American Jewish community over ethnicity and assimilation mean nothing (to admit their reality would cause serious ideological problems). Ironically, American Jewish artists appear now not to believe that Jews as a group have contributed any element of creative

---

[1] New York, 1966 and London, 1968.

[2] Cambridge (England) and New York, 1965. The playwright Arthur Miller has been criticized for 'suppressing' a specifically Jewish background for his characters, particularly in *Death of a Salesman* (1949), in order to assert a more generalized picture of humanity. A similar complaint has been made against J. D. Salinger.

[3] See Harold Cruse, *The Crisis of the Negro Intellectual* (New York, 1967 and London, 1969).

diversity to majority culture – unless it be their own memorializations of the failure to do so.

Yet Jewish tensions between minority identity and assimilation bear striking resemblance to the Negro 'alternatives' of nationalism and integration. In the literary context it is clear that the accommodation to 'American' values and mores is the central subject in much minority fiction. In approaching it, various writers have put their own seal upon what constitutes those values, what constitutes alternatives, by what means and how we evaluate individual actions bounded by the general situation. It is difficult, though, to imagine much of a *future* for the central nexus of the Jewish situation. Something of the thirties has always hung over its literature and perhaps revealingly over the best work written out of it. Bernard Malamud, who has perhaps more feeling for the old ways than the others, has been driven back for it into an even deeper past.[1] Roth's Portnoy is as much a parody of earlier Jewish-American writing as a picture from life. The literary portrait of the Jew usually, as Marvin Mudrick has written, smacks of archaeology.

Attempts to link Jewish ethnicity with contemporary material success in the majority American community have been unfailingly diagnosed by liberal critics – with justice – as soothing clap-trap.

It is more characteristic that the lonely individual in Jewish-American writing is a fugitive from both the community of his birth and the larger American society. While his rebuffs, if nothing else, may occur by virtue of his Jewish background, they rarely give him a feeling of solidarity with it, particularly as the American Jewish community has ceased to be an under-class in the national life. The situation is not the same with the American Negro. What we have been witnessing of late is a determined effort by black writers to set aside any division which their education and imagination may have induced and to reassociate themselves with 'their people'.

In the morphology of intellectual adaptions, however, the new Negro strategy not only seems regressive but is acknowledgedly so to some of its writers: they are going back to an earlier formulation of American culture before they listened to the siren song of International Marxism or the Gospel of Integration – each a delusive 'colourless' universal.

---

[1] Jonathan Raban has pointed out to me that Yakov Bok, the persecuted hero of *The Fixer*, traverses the classic ground of the immigrant experience, journeying over water from a rural to an urban circumstance in which, contrary to expectation, he comes to be trapped. But instead of the geography involving a journey across the Atlantic, it all takes place within Russia.

History need not move logically, and the militant black may well impose his vision of America upon its culture. The theory courts Armageddon, as is obvious in the role which has replaced that of the 'hipster' (the very last temptation which Ralph Ellison's 'invisible man' resists), and which strikes the most contemporary pose, the black guerrilla resistance fighter.[1] In this figure we seem to have reached the furthest bounds of minority opposition.

Indeed a number of individual and group roles have been formulated lately to join the series of professional, regional and ethnic ones that have acted historically as remnants in American society. We have seen a revival of interest in the American Indian in precisely these terms.[2] Communitarian hippies are beginning to live out their separation from American society. But it would be as well to note in conclusion a phenomenon which in a sense by-passes the whole question of a need for individual or group outposts. This is the process of re-sanctification of the most mundane and ordinary features of neon and superhighway America which is found in the beatnik flowering of the fifties and mixes easily with the ironic aspects of Pop Art and the 'Pop Culture' phenomenon. 'If it moves, love it' is the motto, but how much easier when 'it' is vegetable or mineral. The glorification of Coca Cola and Ballantine Beer in a sense rounds out a long historical process in which the intellectual, sensing a yawning gulf between the 'business' of America and matters of the spirit,[3] has attached himself to and detached himself from roles which promise an arduous exodus but an ultimate Israel (or Mecca, as Harlem was called in the twenties). In the final term, a remnant need not be sought to leaven the national loaf when the entire American Hero Sandwich is found holy. Here the remnant is Everybody (Walt Whitman's dream come true): while elsewhere, as the century explodes about us, the 'red shift' from the chosen few who will save us all to the only escapees darkens annually.

[Comments on writing published after 1969 have been added by the Editor. For some supplementary comments on the themes discussed by Arnold Goldman, see the final essay in this volume, 'Literature and Society'.]

[1] See, for example, LeRoi Jones's play *The Slave* (New York, 1964 and London, 1965).

[2] See, for example, Edmund Wilson, *Apologies to the Iroquois* (New York and London, 1960) and Leslie A. Fiedler, *Return of the Vanishing Indian* (New York, 1968 and London, 1969).

[3] See Leo Marx, *The Machine in the Garden* (New York and London, 1964), especially the chapter 'Two Kingdoms of Force'.

11

LITERARY CRITICISM SINCE 1965

Jean-Pierre Mileur

The last twenty-five years have seen the fruition of the movement of criticism into the universities that began in the thirties. Through most of its history, criticism in the United States has been limited by its audience. Writing for mass-circulation newspapers and magazines encouraged a general, culture-oriented criticism, preoccupied with the traditional question of the American difference and quite naturally inclined to fret over the marginal status of the life of the mind in American society. Since the end of the Second World War, academic criticism has largely succeeded in forging an alternative audience, composed of thousands of professors, graduate students, and even English majors, capable of sustaining its own most esoteric efforts. This new audience has made possible vastly more complex and sophisticated forms of specifically literary criticism and pointed the way toward more subtle and demanding forms of general criticism as well. In particular, these years are marked by an emphasis on the theory of literature and of criticism that only a vast academic audience could sustain.

Openness to theoretical concerns has somewhat eased the anti-intellectualism of the primarily moral and literary American tradition and made it more receptive to the ideas and even the conceptual styles of intellectual/philosophical traditions like the German and particularly the French. As a result, this has been a period of extraordinary cosmopolitanism in criticism, in which the question of what is uniquely American has all but given way to a critical agenda largely derived (whether in affirmation or reaction) from continental sources.

Among these is Structuralism, based on the work of the Swiss linguist, Ferdinand de Saussure. Saussurean linguistics rejects the familiar conception of language as a system of references linking words to world. Language, Saussure argued, is a play of purely differential relationships – a structure – whose relation to the world is determined not by 'reality' but by its own nature. This means that a Structuralist critic approaches a literary text not by way of the world it purports to represent but by way of the linguistic structures it must employ in order to be a text at all. Literature is not treated as a privileged, unique kind of language; it can be apprehended in terms of the same structural elements that linguists use to describe everyday language. Language, not the individual subject, author or reader, is seen to be the determining factor in shaping the literary text and fixing the task of criticism.

Beginning with *Writing Degree Zero* (1953) and *Mythologies* (1957), continuing with *The Elements of Semiology* (1964), *S/Z* (1970) and *The Pleasures of the Text* (1973), among many others, the French critic, Roland Barthes, probably did more than any other individual to extend Structuralist premises to encompass literary criticism and the criticism of culture in general. Among Americans, Jonathon Culler's *Structuralist Poetics* (1975) is notable for combining a skilled appreciation of the full range and value of Structuralist thinking about literature with a critique of the Structuralists' tendency to oversimplify literary texts in order to accommodate them to linguistic categories. Culler nevertheless believes that, properly employed, Structuralism can be used to transform the study of literature. In *The Pursuit of Signs* (1981), he argues that instead of generating 'readings' of individual works, critics should aim at the intellectual rigour and disciplinary coherence that would come from concentrating on the conditions that establish the possibility of literary texts and on the rules governing their production.

As an idea, Structuralism has been enormously influential, both in its promise of a more scientific humanism and in switching the focus of critical attention to language as a text-making force in its own right. Yet there are relatively few American Structuralists. Another group of French critics, the Post-Structuralists, with their formidable interpretive skills, have been more readily absorbed into American critical practice.

Most influential of the Post-Structuralists are the psycho-analyst Jacques Lacan, the historian Michel Foucault and the philosopher Jacques Derrida, all of whom share the linguistic bias of Structuralism but extend it in ways that challenge any smug confidence in language as the basis of critical truth. Lacan's psychoanalysis attributes to the unconscious the structure and character of a language and proceeds from there to a revision of Freud. By means of what he calls an 'archaeology' Foucault's aim has been to describe the preconditions of knowing and the distinctive forms of knowledge that they make possible. He terms these complex structures of possibility and manifestation 'epistemes' and his most important book, *The Order of Things* (1966), traces the succession of epistemes that have determined and transformed the nature of knowledge since the sixteenth century.

Much more controversial and arguably more radical than any other individual influencing American criticism is Jacques Derrida, inventor of Deconstruction. Broadly speaking, Deconstructionism is an attack on the metaphysical bias of Western philosophy. In practice, it is an uncompromising scepticism, directed at any manifestation of the preference for 'metaphysical' positivities – for truth or reality as the ground of philosophy, for the immediacy of speech over the belatedness of writing, for the presence of the subject as the guarantor of the text over the anonymous text-generating capacities of language. In *Of Grammatology* (1967), Derrida criticizes Saussure himself for using the immediate reality of sound in speech as the implicit anchor of language in the world. Yet Derrida's aim is not to transcend the metaphysical bias or 'logocentrism' of our tradition. How can it be, since the tradition determines the very possibility of Deconstruction as a form of philosophy, as a mode of criticism, as a kind of writing? In Derrida's work, subtlety and perversity, profundity and the appearance of bad faith can be in richly challenging and uncomfortable proximity.

Predictably, these influences have by no means been universally (or even generally) welcomed. The emphasis on language at the expense of the subject has prompted strong reactions from a number of well-established critical constituencies. The case against the French has been made variously, in the name of Ralph Waldo Emerson, of Matthew Arnold, of T. S. Eliot, of the New Critics, and of the pedagogical role of critics in the universities.

The collective life embodied in the impersonal domain of linguistic structures and texts without authors is seen as an offence against the Emersonian preoccupation with the intensely personal question of how to be: how to be an American, how to be a moral being, how to be yourself. Arnold may be even more important to academic critics than Emerson, since their conception of the value of what they do and its role in society is still largely derived from him. Of key importance are his idealization of 'high culture' as the repository of enduring values and his complementary hostility to modern, industrial/technological society. The value-neutrality of

Structuralist 'language' and the Deconstructionists' tendency to view cultural ideals as tissues of self-deception undermine Arnoldian conceptions of cultural authority. The specialized language, scepticism and intellectuality of much of this Derridean and other criticism give it a decidedly technical, Modernist flavour that has moved some – Gerald Graff, for instance, in his widely-read *Literature Against Itself* (1977) – to accuse it of being anti-literary. The offence against Eliot consists largely in refusing to idealize the past at the expense of the present and in exploiting rather than deploring our dissociated sensibilities.

The new, continental criticisms aim at abstraction rather than specificity, elevating theory and the 'science' of text production over the close reading of texts. They show a relative lack of interest in the epistemological approach to the writer-text-reader relationship. In all these ways, they offend against the New Criticism. Additionally, New Critical techniques of close reading are essential to the American critic's conception of his pedagogical role since they provide a method for working with literature that does not require developed literary knowledge or a level of aesthetic sophistication that students are unlikely to have. The same cannot be said for many new forms of criticism, with their idiosyncratic jargon, high level of abstraction, and frequent references to philosophy, psycho-analysis, and linguistics.

It would be difficult to overstate the importance of the New Criticism in shaping the specific professional identity of academic critics, distinguishing them from culture critics and reviewers. Virtually all important critical theories of recent years start from or tend toward some critique of New Critical ideas, either extending or superseding them.

Good examples are provided by E. D. Hirsch and Stanley Fish, who came to prominence in the late sixties and have enjoyed enduring influence. Both men have tried to resolve the epistemological questions raised by the New Critics, engaging Wimsatt's and Beardsley's famous essays on the intentional and affective fallacies.

Hirsch's *Validity in Interpretation* (1967) has been a rallying point for defenders of the idea of stable meaning against Deconstruction. In that book, he argues that authorial intention is the indispensable ground of stable, communicable interpretation; and that an objective criticism can be based on a distinction between description, addressing the author's manifest intentions, and evaluation, which proceeds from the context of the work and the situation of the reader. In *The Aims of Interpretation* (1976), Hirsch elaborates his earlier theory with a new distinction between meaning – that which can be agreed upon and shared as the basis of an objective interpretation – and significance – that which, by its very nature, cannot be agreed upon.

Hirsch mounts a strong argument against those who facilely insist that description and evaluation, meaning and significance, are inseparable. Yet rendering interpretation philosophically respectable is not the same as giving an account of what makes it worthwhile. In separating meaning from significance, Hirsch also banishes from the realm of valid interpretation almost all of the questions that most engage the interests of critics. Hirsch's theories are profitably viewed in the context of a dream, quite compelling for many American critics, of grounding criticism in the prevailing rational positivism of the Anglo-American philosophical tradition. What Hirsch inadvertently shows, however, is that literary criticism is not a special case of the philosophy of interpretation, indeed that it is not governed by philosophy at all.

The New Critics argued that the author's intentions are unavailable, the reader's responses unreliable, and that only the text itself is the proper object and basis of interpretation. Hirsch tries to provide a solid philosophical underpinning for New Critical claims for the stability of the text (which the New Critics themselves were never able to do), by showing that the author's intention is, in fact, readily available and that it does not entice readers to reduce all aesthetic differences to matters of individual psychology, as the New Critics had assumed. Stanley Fish tries to achieve a similar rehabilitation of the reader, using an approach called affective stylistics or reader-response criticism.

Fish is one of the most brilliant theoretical polemicists of his day and his ideas have undergone a much richer evolution than Hirsch's. In his first book, *Surprised by Sin* (1967), Fish seeks to demonstrate in a reading of *Paradise Lost* that the text is not the sole or even the primary repository of meaning. He treats the poem as a series of traps or encouragements to error promoting a self-recognition and realization that only the reader can provide. The reader alone can complete the poem and manifest its meaning. Therefore, the structure and outcome of the reader's responses, not the formal structures of the poem, are the proper focus of interpretation.

In order to sustain this position, Fish had to meet the New Critical objection that the concept of the reader's response is inherently unstable – that there are potentially as many responses as readers. He tells us in *Is There a Text in This Class?* (1980):

I met that objection by positing a level of experience which all readers share, independently of differences in education and culture. This level was conceived more or less syntactically, as an extension of the Chomskian notion of linguistic competence, a linguistic system that every native speaker shares.[1] I reasoned that if the speakers of a language share a system of rules that each of them has somehow internalized, understanding will, in some sense, be uniform. The fact that the understandings of so many readers and critics were not uniform was accounted for by superimposing on this primary or basic level (identified more or less with perception itself) a secondary or after-the-fact level at which the differences between individuals make themselves manifest.

This is strikingly like Hirsch's meaning/significance distinction and it has analogous flaws. Most fundamental is the objection that although the responses of Fish's reader are quite complex, involving ideas and values, he seeks to guarantee their generality by appealing to an underlying consistency that cannot confidently be extended much beyond the level of basic perception.

To his credit, Fish eventually came to recognize the equivocation at the heart of his argument. On the one hand, he argues for the reader as the source of meaning; on the other hand, the generality of the reader's responses, their underlying uniformity, ultimately has to be underwritten by a stable text, held in common. In his own way, Fish realized, he was no less dependent on the text than Hirsch or the New Critics. Behind this continued dependence on the text, he concluded, was the Arnoldian fear of subjectivism – that without a stable text, interpreters can impose any meaning they choose.

In questioning whether this fear is justified, Fish found himself reversing the trend toward making fundamental distinctions between kinds of meaning or language. The reader is not a threat to the stability of the literary text or to the integrity of literary language because literature is a way of treating texts and their language – a convention:

In other words, it is not that literature exhibits certain formal properties that compel a certain kind of attention; rather, paying a certain kind of attention (as defined by what literature is understood to be) results in the emergence into noticeability of the properties we know in advance to be literary.

---

[1] Noam Chomsky – American linguist best known for his efforts to define a 'transformational' grammar, which would make explicit the rules governing the transformation of the structures of language into individual sentences, of competence into performance.

This is not the much-feared Subjectivist anarchy of interpreters, because they are not free agents but members of a community, bound by its conventions. Neither the text nor the reader is independent (i.e. purely subjective or objective); formal features are the products of the interpretive conventions brought to bear *but* those formal features are then produced as evidence in support of the conventions that privilege them. Even though Fish's argument contradicts Arnold in some ways, it is nonetheless appealing because, after granting so much to contemporary scepticism about the formalism upon which our sense of literary value has been based, it returns us to a renewed sense of a community of letters, of shared conventions and the values they imply.

Although Fish is not a Romanticist, the course of his thinking ultimately involves a critique of the subject–object language that has come down to critics primarily from S. T. Coleridge. Hirsch, Paul de Man, Geoffrey Hartman and Harold Bloom are Romanticists, and even more than Fish, they demonstrate the intimate relationship in contemporary criticism between theory and the reassessment of the Romantics.

The 'rhetorical criticism' or 'American Deconstructionism' of Paul de Man begins in 'The Rhetoric of Temporality' (1969) with a highly influential attack on the established view that the essence of Romanticism is the reconciliation of subject and object, mind and nature, by means of the faculty of imagination expressed in the language of the symbol. Beneath the symbolic reconciliation with nature, de Man finds the desire of man, completely immersed in mutability, to identify with the permanence at the heart of nature – in short, the desire not to die. The greatest of the Romantics, de Man argues, sooner or later confront their own difference from the world, their alienation from desire, and accept their 'genuine temporal predicament'. The sign of such an acceptance is a movement away from tropes engaged with the world, like mimesis or symbol, toward tropes of detachment, like allegory, irony and prosopopeia.

The pathos of our predicament seduces us into an inauthentic identification with the world and leads us to mistake desire for knowledge. Acceptance and detachment – ultimately the acceptance and detachment that might be associated imaginatively with the dead themselves – allow us to untangle desire from knowledge and to deconstruct the pretensions to the status of nature or reality of our intellectual creations. The point of de Man's Deconstructionism (and here he can usefully be distinguished from

Derrida) is not to tear down but to preserve. In his view, the moment that literature turns back to the world and tries to find itself there, it opens itself up to the brute, temporal fact of death. No human creation can preserve its sense of its own value in such a reductive confrontation. The result is that despair which is the dark complement of our tendency to idealize literature as the conjuction of the created and the real. The only reality to which literature refers is its own reality and it is in this sense alone that it is the privileged mode for expressing our alienated condition.

Nowhere is the value that de Man places on detachment more clearly expressed than in *Blindness and Insight* (1971) – the book which established him as perhaps the most widely admired critic of his generation. This collection of essays is characterized by cool intellectual brilliance and lapidary craftsmanship; it is also a collection of critical essays about critics – deplored by some as a movement away from literature as the 'natural' focus of critical interest, recognized by others as the next step in the movement of literature toward realizing its own literariness.

De Man credits the Structuralists with recognizing that their insights into literary language are not insights into phenomena but into language, and with creating a domain of meanings and the accompanying terms that cannot be reduced to common sense or paraphrased in everyday language. Having thus established the true distinctiveness of language, however, they betray it by confining it within the limits of a linguistics that leads from grammar, by way of logic, back to knowledge of the phenomenal world. Rhetoric, de Man feels, is a far better means of representing the distinctive literariness of language. Unlike grammar, tropes perform as persuasion as well as meaning: 'They are text-producing functions that are not necessarily patterned on a non-verbal entity, whereas grammar is by definition capable of extra-linguistic generalization.' In de Man's view, the tension between grammar and rhetoric gives rise to the problem of reading and hence to criticism.

His critique of Derrida's Deconstructionism focuses on the latter's treatment of Rousseau in *Of Grammatology*. According to Derrida, Rousseau's discussion of writing as an unnecessary supplement to the immediacy of voice is belied by his dependence on the literariness of his written language to establish that supposedly original presence. In deconstructing Rousseau's assertions about the nature of language, Derrida claims to be bringing to light what had previously been hidden.

Quite the contrary, de Man argues, Rousseau's text hides

nothing. The key question is not, as Derrida would have it, whether Rousseau has full awareness or control over 'the cognitive value of his language' – no such thing exists; instead, we must ask if the language, as language, conveys an adequate knowledge of its own nature. That the literariness of Rousseau's written language does indeed act, as Derrida insists, to remedy its own deficiency by inventing a 'voice' to embody it is the best evidence for this self-knowledge.

Derrida is not *wrong* about Rousseau's theory of language; according to de Man, he simply fails to grasp that there is a figural dimension to Rousseau's language that bespeaks an awareness of the status of its literal statement. That the figural inheres in the literal gives language its rhetorical character. When a language seems to know and exploit this rhetoricality, it becomes literary. Whatever the limitations of Rousseau's awareness, the literariness of his language continues to operate.

What is exposed here is the hubris of Derridean Deconstruction. Derrida assumes the stance of rectifier of errors, requiring Rousseau as a sparring partner. Literature and the literariness of language itself mark the limits of such a stance. De Man insists that a work of literature cannot be 'demystified' because it is already demystified. As in the case of Rousseau's *Confessions*, it takes off from precisely that knowledge of the nature of language that serves Derrida for a conclusion. A more profound Deconstructionist might recognize that the inevitable failure of literal statement to encompass its own figural dimension applies to himself as well and hopelessly compromises his pretensions to superiority.

This leads de Man to his celebrated notion of critical 'blindness'. In each of the critical texts he examines in *Blindness and Insight*, de Man identifies a level of insight that runs counter to the work's explicit assertions, a consequence of the literariness that critical language itself cannot escape. It is relatively easy to see why the literal statement and its figural dimension would be different; a less obvious claim is that they are necessarily contradictory. Yet de Man clearly feels that they are.

This is because literature begins in and takes flight from a state of demystification. Each literary progress contains within itself an inexorable regression back to that demystified state. For de Man, the ultimate form of this demystification from which all literature and, by implication, all language, proceeds is the nothingness of human things, the essential emptiness of desire. Fortunately, the literariness of language, its refusal to coincide with itself, prevents this final reduction from ever occurring.

De Man's Deconstruction traces a movement that exists in every text by virtue of the nature of language and what it does for us. Protecting us from reality, it reminds us of reality. Reminding us of reality in language, it protects us from reality as such. Everywhere in the works of this most intellectual of critics can be discerned a level of ethical concern, a sense of literature as a mode of coexisting with the nothingness of human things that promises to return us eventually to the Emersonian concern with how to be.

The other chief figure of American Deconstructionism and its chief polemicist has been J. Hillis Miller, who first gained prominence on the basis of his studies of the novel, influenced by the Phenomenologist Georges Poulet. In the seventies, under the influence of Derrida and de Man, Miller outlined a Deconstructionist literary criticism in the face of vigorous attacks by traditionalist critics. Indeed, one of Miller's more influential essays, 'The Critic as Host' (1979), appeared as a response to the accusation that a Deconstructive reading is 'parasitical' upon the 'obvious and univocal reading' which is all but indistinguishable from the literary text itself.

In a movement characteristic of Deconstructionist polemic, Miller proceeds to undermine the polarities on which the accusation is based. A philological and etymological investigation reveals an identity underlying the superficial antithesis between parasite and host. The opening up of apparently univocal terms like 'parasite' in order to reveal the figural and contradictory possibilities that inhere within them is, according to Miller, the essence of Deconstructive criticism. Pursuing the implications of this example, Miller argues that the univocal reading of the traditional critic is actually as multivocal and equivocal as any Deconstruction. Therefore, both kinds of reading are equally parasitical and the traditionalist reading's claim to stand closer to the text itself is an illusion.

But Miller does not stop there. Taking Shelley's *The Triumph of Life* as his proof text, he goes on to show that the literary text itself is so made up of echoes and allusions, so constituted by its equivocal relations with other texts and competing voices within itself as to efface its borders and undermine its sovereign identity. In short, Deconstructive and traditionalist reading and the literary text are *all* multivocal and belated in relation to other texts. Having thus compromised the distinctions between text and commentary, univocal and parasitical (i.e. responsible and perverse) modes of reading, Miller is now in a position to challenge the absolute distinction

LITERARY CRITICISM SINCE 1965

between the poet and the critic and the ritual elevation of the former over the latter.

The Triumph of Life, Miller argues, defeats a univocal reading because the poem itself is divided between Shelley's idealism and the scepticism triggered by his recognition of the role of projection in our lives. In Shelley's poetic practice, the assertion of the ideal evokes the sceptical countermovement and vice versa. Similarly, the critic's attempt to seize one thread or the other, idealism or scepticism, in order to unravel the text, only ravels it more tightly at the other end. This situation is not idosyncratic but representative, having to do with the nature of Western literature itself.

Miller approaches this level of generality by meeting the charge that Deconstruction undermines values and leads to nihilism. Nihilism is commonly treated as 'the parasitical stranger within the house of metaphysics' that sustains our conceptions of value. Once again, Miller asks if nihilism, like parasitism, isn't the name given by metaphysics to an aspect of its own being. Described from its own perspective instead of that of metaphysics, nihilism might be nothing more than 'rhetoric', or 'philology', or 'the study of tropes' – whatever must be condemned by metaphysics because it undermines values based on univocity. From this new perspective, however, metaphysics itself might be seen as nothing more than a 'phantom' generated 'by the play of language'. In the largest sense, this is the Deconstructive 'reversal'.

Generally associated with de Man and Miller as members of the so-called 'Yale School' are Geoffrey Hartman and Harold Bloom, neither of whom can be described accurately as a Deconstructionist. In *Deconstruction and Criticism* (1979), Hartman himself has eloquently described the difference:

... de Man and Miller are certainly boa-deconstructors, merciless and consequent, though each enjoys his own style of closing again and again the 'abysm' of words. But Bloom and Hartman are barely deconstructionists. They even write against it on occasion. Though they understand Nietzsche when he says 'the deepest pathos is still aesthetic play', they have a stake in that pathos: its persistence, its psychological provenance. For them the ethos of literature is not dissociable from this pathos, whereas for deconstructionist criticism literature is precisely that use of language which can purge pathos, which can show that it too is figurative, ironic or aesthetic.

Rather than regarding themselves as the Deconstuctors of a criticism focused on the subject and the pathos of his predicament, Hartman and Bloom prefer to see themselves as its 'Revisionists'.

Bloom and Hartman, more so than any of the others we have discussed, are brilliant readers. Both men were pre-eminent interpreters of Romantic poetry long before achieving their reputations as theorists. Hartman in particular continues to sublimate his theoretical concerns into individual acts of reading. His early manifesto, 'Beyond Formalism' (1966), admits a certain tendency in the formalism of the New Critics to isolate the aesthetic dimension of art from its human content. But he insists that it need not be so. For Hartman, formalism is the method of 'revealing the human content of art by a study of its formal properties'. In this sense, the New Critics were not formalist enough because they did not pursue literary forms to the point at which they open outward on larger human truths. New Criticism, Hartman argues, elevated exegesis to the status of be-all and end-all. The true value of explication, however, is to confront art with experience 'as searchingly as if it were scripture'.

Hartman's effort to place in their proper perspective attention to forms and the practice of close reading goes hand in hand with his attempt to broaden an overly-narrow, Arnoldian conception of the role of criticism. The persistence of this double project can be discerned in all of Hartman's major work from 'Beyond Formalism' through *Criticism in the Wilderness* (1980) – a book which also demonstrates Hartman's concern with developing a broader literary history than either Arnold or the New Critics could conceive.

Great historical learning imaginatively applied, careful attention to literary forms and unusually skilful close reading are the elements of Hartman's *Wordsworth's Poetry*, probably the best book written on that poet. But its special distinctiveness lies in the way these elements combine in a phenomenological portrait of Wordsworth's sensibility as a particular instance of the general human experience of traumatic separation from nature and fear of imaginative excess, of loss and alienation.

From all of this, it should be clear that the basic impulse of Hartman's work could easily be characterized as profoundly conservative. Hartman's reputation as a radical or avant-garde critic is partly based on the fact that he has been receptive to Deconstruction and other forms of Post-Structuralism as means of expanding the scope and refining the methods of American criticism. More than anything else, however, it is Hartman's critical style that leads his detractors to identify him with Derrida in particular. He is the most playful of critics, given to puns, etymologies, philological athletics – all of which both carry and hold open his argument to the point of coyness and perversity. Nowhere is this tendency more apparent than when Hartman engages Derrida's *Glas* in *Saving the Text* (1981).

The basis of Hartman's affinity for Derrida is not agreement with the programme of Deconstruction (Hartman's book declares itself, after all, to be 'For the Subject' – infuriatingly, another pun); rather it is in the use of these devices to open up the literary text and to hold it open to elicit what would otherwise be foreclosed by the anxious reaching after conclusions of more conventional argumentation.

Hartman differentiates himself from Bloom as a believer in authority is differentiated from a believer in priority. For Bloom, no imaginative or intellectual power is finally adequate to overcome the temporal priority of the precursors. For Hartman, the essential aspect of priority is authority, which is qualitative and not temporal. Seeking and gaining authority, we have a second chance against the tyranny of time. Bloom is infinitely more sceptical about the reality of second chances.

For Harold Bloom, as for Hartman and de Man, the question of Romanticism is never entirely distinct from central theoretical concerns. From *Shelley's Mythmaking* (1959), through *The Visionary Company* (1961) and *Blake's Apocalypse* (1963), to *Yeats* (1970), Bloom argued relentlessly against the traditional and ultimately trivializing view of the Romantics as nature poets, seeing in them instead a great visionary tradition, aiming at nothing less than the fundamental transformation of man and his world, the fulfilment of the romance tradition in English literature.

As was the case with the Romantics themselves, the very intensity of the demand made on poetry seems to have eroded Bloom's faith in its visionary powers. In any case, he certainly realized that if it was to have any credibility in this role, poetry would have to survive a much harsher testing than weakly idealizing critical orthodoxy had yet allowed. The result was the now-famous tetralogy, *The Anxiety of Influence* (1973), *A Map of Misreading* (1975), *Kabbalah and Criticism* (1975) and *Poetry and Repression* (1976). These present, respectively, a theory of poetry and poetic relations, the accompanying theory of reading, an account of the provenance in religious heterodoxy of the poet's (and critic's) stance, and, in effect, a history of the tradition since Milton.

Briefly, Bloom's argument is this. The poet is distinguished from other men by his greater rebellion against the fact of his own death, his refusal to settle for the compensations of normal life, and his consequent drive 'to be elsewhere'. This drive takes the form of a desire to surpass his precursors and achieve an originality so compelling as to transform the tradition in its image. For Bloom, the historical fact of our obsession with originality is linked to the individual's search for a satisfaction unique to him and sufficient to compensate even for the necessity of death – not death in general, but the intensely personal terror of his own death.

Unfortunately, the conditions of his election stand between the poet and the fulfilment of this ambition. Poetic identity originates in reading the poetry of a precursor. There the poet discovers the desire to write poetry and recognizes his own potential. Thus the relationship between poet and precursor is as inextricable as that of parent and child, and is equally governed by the Oedipal complexities of the Freudian family romance. The same stature that allows the precursor to stand for the poet's own limitless poetic desire also makes him the representative of the tradition's authority; he both nurtures and suffocates and the poet's consequent ambivalence is incurable.

Bloom traces the life-cycle of the poet through a progressive series of defensive stances designed to evade the influence of the precursor and assert the independent powers of the poet. No aspect of Bloom's theory has excited as much resistance as his sense of the poet's inevitable failure. According to Bloom, in the final stage of his development the strong poet

holds his own poem so open to the precursor's work that at first we might believe that the wheel has come full-circle, and that we are back in the later poet's flooded apprenticeship, before his strength began to assert itself . . . But the poem is now *held* open to the precursor, where once it *was* open, and the uncanny effect is that the new poem's achievement makes it seem to us, not as though the precursor was writing it, but as though the later poet himself had written the precursor's characteristic work.

Superficially, this resembles the wished-for, humane conclusion to the drama of poetic relations, in which the poet is reconciled with the precursor and with the tradition, which he can now afford to give their due. Yet Bloom seems finally unwilling or unable to assert the reality of this ending. The key moment, in which the poet becomes essential to the precursor and to the tradition remains in the realm of 'seems', an 'effect' rather than a reality. In the last, decisive moment, poetry falls short of desire.

This is not surprising since Bloom's poetic psychology and his literary history militate against the fulfilment of the poet's ambition. Because poetic identity is so closely tied to the precursor, any diminution of his status that is more than mere seeming involves a consequent diminution of the poet as well. For a variety of historical reasons, Bloom further argues that Milton was the last poet who could with any confidence assert the qualitative priority of the later over the earlier, and thus become his precursor's precursor.

From the idea that poetry and individual desire are permanently separated, it is only a short step to the conclusion that the entire project of literary humanism – to find and/or create in literature an embodiment of a perfected human desire, against which we can measure and adjust ourselves and our institutions – is doomed to failure, is already a failure. For Bloom, man, at least in so far as he is represented by the poet, is a creature who insists on what he cannot have, and the entire project of secular letters since the Romantics is infected with that desire. The result has been a chronic melancholy, perpetually threatening to deepen into despair.

But literary humanism does not exhaust the resources of literature any more than visionary aspiration exhausts the possibilities of Romanticism. With *Agon* (1982), Bloom turns away from British Romanticism to the distinctively American Romanticism he terms Emersonian pragmatism. 'Self-Reliance', stressing not truth but usefulness, is his text.

The Emerson of 'Self-Reliance' combines a thrust beyond institutional and traditional restraints with a pragmatic suspicion of the tendency to universalize and therefore depersonalize ideals. In this way, Bloom suggests, Emerson's pragmatism prevents him from becoming the victim of his own idealizations; he is never so driven to alienation or outrage that he loses faith that the available means, however tainted, are sufficient to construct a personal salvation. This Emerson represents a limitation that Bloom must impose on his drive toward a visionary absolute.

Although in a general sort of way Harold Bloom has been lumped together with other critics of the American avant-garde as a part of the new, French-inspired criticism, he has argued vigorously against the linguistic bias of Structuralism and Post-Structuralism on behalf of the individual psyche as the source of literary creation and the proper focus of critical study. Bloom is in many ways the most imaginative and characteristically American critic of his day, not least because, in his return to Emerson, he reopens the question of the American difference in a much more sophisticated form.

The accusation has been made, notably by Frank Lentricchia in *After the New Criticism* (1980), that the post New Critical movements we have been discussing all tend finally toward an aestheticist separation of literary activity from the larger life of society. Whether the motivation is self-involvement or a principled rejection of modern society, this inward-looking tendency may have left a vacuum, to be filled by more engaged forms of criticism. One of these is the feminist criticism that has gained ground steadily in American universities by using subtly fresh readings of individual works to build toward a sustained meditation on the plight of women writing within a male-dominated literary tradition. Sandra M. Gilbert's and Susan Gubar's *The Madwoman in the Attic* (1979) is a much-admired example.

Nor is it possible to ignore Marxist criticism, which has enjoyed a substantial revival in the seventies and continues to engage many bright younger critics. Far and away the most important American Marxist critic is Fredric Jameson, whose *Marxism and Form* (1971) and *The Political Unconscious* (1980) remain indispensable. Like the Deconstructionists, literary Marxists have worked to cultivate an audience receptive to theory and therefore able to absorb the work of influential Europeans like Theodor Adorno, Walter Benjamin and Herbert Marcuse. This attachment to theory, along with the position of Marxist critics in the university, promotes a certain as-yet-unresolved tension between the drive to develop a durable and engaged Marxist criticism and an essentially aesthetic impulse toward ever-more-refined versions of Marxist theory.

In the final analysis then, American criticism as it existed before 1965 has been transformed in three main directions:
1. Toward an openly engaged criticism, chiefly Marxist or feminist, challenged by its own aestheticizing tendencies;
2. Toward a theoretically sophisticated criticism, heavily influenced by European models, whose very sophistication threatens to deepen the isolation of literary activity from the rest of society;
3. Toward a criticism superficially like the second type, which turns aside from aestheticization and politicization equally in favour of a twentieth-century version of Emerson's 'Self-Reliance' and a renewed meditation on the American difference.

12

CROSS THE BORDER – CLOSE THAT GAP: POST-MODERNISM

Leslie A. Fiedler

To describe the situation of American letters at the end of the sixties is difficult indeed, almost impossible, since the language available to critics at this point is totally inappropriate to the best work of the artists who give the period its special flavour, its essential life. But precisely here is a clue, a way to begin: not with some presumed crisis of poetry or fiction, but with the unconfessed scandal of contemporary literary criticism, which for three or four decades now has vainly attempted to deal in terms invented to explain, defend and evaluate one kind of book with *another* kind of book – so radically different that it calls the very assumptions underlying those terms into question. Established critics may think that they have been judging recent literature; but, in truth, recent literature has been judging them.

Almost all living readers and writers are aware of a fact which they have no adequate words to express, not in English certainly, nor even in American. We are living, have been living for two decades – and have become acutely conscious of the fact since 1955 – through the death throes of Modernism and the birth pangs of Post-Modernism. The kind of literature which had arrogated to itself the name Modern (with the presumption that it represented the ultimate advance in sensibility and form, that beyond it newness was not possible), and whose moment of triumph lasted from a point just before the First World War until one just after the Second World War, is *dead*, i.e. belongs to history not actuality. In the field of the novel, this means that the age of Proust, Mann and Joyce is over; just as in verse that of T. S. Eliot, Paul Valéry, Montale and Seferis is done with.

Obviously *this* fact has not remained secret: and some critics have, indeed, been attempting to deal with its implications. But they have been trying to do it in a language and with methods which are singularly inappropriate, since both method and language were invented by the defunct Modernists themselves to apologize for their own work and the work of their preferred literary ancestors (John Donne, for instance, or the *symbolistes*), and to educate an audience capable of responding to them. Naturally, this will not do at all; and so the second or third generation New Critics in America, like the spiritual descendants of F. R. Leavis in England, the neo-neo-Hegelians in Germany, or the belated Croceans in Italy, end by proving themselves imbeciles and naïfs when confronted by, say, a poem, of Allen Ginsberg, or a new novel by John Barth.

Why not, then, invent a New New Criticism, a Post-Modernist criticism appropriate to Post-Modernist fiction and verse? It sounds simple enough – quite as simple as imperative – but it is much simpler to say than do; for the question which arises immediately is whether there can be *any* criticism adequate to Post-Modernism. The Age of T. S. Eliot, after all, was the age of a literature essentially self-aware, a literature dedicated, in avowed intent, to analysis, rationality, anti-Romantic dialect – and consequently aimed at eventual respectability, gentility, even, at last, academicism. Criticism is natural, even essential to such an age; and to no one's surprise (though finally there were some voices crying out in dismay), the period of early twentieth-century Modernism became, as it was doomed to do, an Age of Criticism: an age in which criticism began by invading the novel, verse, drama, and ended by threatening to swallow up all other forms of literature. Certainly, it seems, looking back from this point, as if many of the best books of the period were critical books (by T. S. Eliot and Ezra Pound and I. A. Richards, by John Crowe Ransom and Kenneth Burke and R. P. Blackmur, to mention only a few particularly eminent names); and its second-best, novels and poems eminently suited to critical analysis, particularly in schools and universities: the works of Proust-Mann-and-Joyce, for instance, to evoke a trilogy which seems at the moment more the name of a single college course than a list of three authors.

We have, however, entered quite another time, apocalyptic, anti-rational, blatantly romantic and sentimental; an age dedicated to joyous misology and prophetic irresponsibility; one, at any rate, distrustful of self-protective irony and too great self-awareness. If criticism is to survive at all, therefore, which is to say, if criticism is to remain or become useful, viable, relevant, it must be radically altered from the models provided by Croce or Leavis or Eliot or

Erich Auerbach, or whoever; though not in the direction indicated by Marxist critics, however subtle and refined. The Marxists are last-ditch defenders of rationality and the primacy of political fact, intrinsically hostile to an age of myth and passion, sentimentality and fantasy.

On the other hand, a renewed criticism certainly will no longer be formalist or intrinsic; it will be con-textual rather than textual, not primarily concerned with structure or diction or syntax, all of which assume that the work of art 'really' exists on the page rather than in a reader's passionate apprehension and response. Not words-on-the-page but words-in-the-world or rather words-in-the-head, which is to say, at the private juncture of a thousand contexts, social, psychological, historical, biographical, geographical, in the consciousness of the lonely reader (delivered for an instant, but an instant only, from all of those contexts by the *ekstasis* of reading): this will be the proper concern of the critics to come. Certain older critics have already begun to provide examples of this sort of criticism by turning their backs on their teachers and even their own earlier practices. Norman O. Brown, for instance, who began with scholarly, somewhat Marxian studies of Classic Literature has moved on to meta-psychology in *Life Against Death* and *Love's Body*; while Marshall McLuhan, who made his debut with formalist examinations of texts by Joyce and Gerard Manley Hopkins, has shifted to meta-sociological analyses of the mass media in *Understanding Media*, and finally to a kind of pictographic shorthand, half put-on and half serious emulation of advertising style in *The Medium is The Message*.

The voice as well as the approach is important in each case, since neither in Brown nor McLuhan does one hear the cadence and tone proper to 'scientific' criticism of culture, normative psychology or sociology attached to literary texts. No, the pitch, the rhythms, the dynamics of both are mantic, magical, more than a little *mad* (it is a word, a concept that one desiring to deal with contemporary literature must learn to regard as more honorific than pejorative). In McLuhan and Brown – as in D. H. Lawrence earlier, Charles Olson when he first wrote on Melville – a not-so-secret fact recently hushed up in an age of science and positivism is candidly confessed once more: criticism is literature or it is nothing. Not amateur philosophy or objective analysis, it differs from other forms of literary art in that it starts not with the world in general but the world of art itself, in that it uses one work of art as an occasion to make another.

There have been, of course, many such mediating works of art in the past, both fairly recent (Nietzsche's *Birth of Tragedy*) and quite remote (Longinus, *On the Sublime*), which make it clear that the authority of the critic is based not on his skills in research or his collation of texts but on his ability to find words and rhythms and images appropriate to his ecstatic vision of, say, the plays of Euripides or the opening verse of *Genesis*. To evoke Longinus or even Nietzsche, however, is in a sense misleading, suggesting models too grandiose and solemn. To be sure, the newest criticism must be aesthetic, poetic in form as well as substance; but it must also be, in light of where we are, comical, irreverent, vulgar. Models have appeared everywhere in recent years but tentatively, inadvertently as it were – as in the case of Angus Wilson, who began a review of *City of Night* some years ago (in the pages of an ephemeral little magazine), by writing quite matter-of-factly, 'Everyone knows John Rechy is a little shit'. And all at once we are out of the Eliotic church, whose dogmas delivered *ex cathedra* two generations of students were expected to learn by heart: 'Honest criticism and sensitive appreciation are directed not upon the poet but upon the poetry ... The mind of the mature poet differs from that of the immature one not precisely on any valuation of personality, not by being necessarily more interesting, or having "more to say", but rather by being a more finely perfected medium in which etc., etc.'

Unless criticism refuses to take itself quite so seriously or at least to permit its readers not to, it will inevitably continue to reflect the finicky canons of the Genteel Tradition and the depressing pieties of the Culture Religion of Modernism, from which Eliot thought he had escaped – but which he only succeeded in giving a High-Anglican tone: 'It is our business as readers of literature, to know what we like. It is our business, as Christians, *as well as* readers of literature, to know what we ought to like.' But not to know that such stuff is funny is to be imprisoned in church, cut off from the liberating privilege of comic sacrilege. It is high time, however, for such sacrilege rather than such piety; as some poets have known really ever since Dada, without knowing how to keep their sacrilege from becoming itself sacred; as the dearest obscenities of Dada were sanctified into the social 'art' of Surrealism under the fell influence of Freud and Marx.

The kind of criticism which the age demands is, then, Death-of-Art Criticism, which is most naturally practised by those who have come of age since the death of the 'New Poetry' and the 'New Criticism'. But it ought to be possible under certain conditions to some of us oldsters as well, even those of us whose own youth was coincident with the freezing of all the madness of *symbolisme*-Dada-*surrealisme* into the rigidities of academic avant-garde. In this sense, the problem of the ageing contemporary critic is quite like that of the no-longer-young contemporary novelist, which one necessarily begins to define even as he defines the dilemma of the critic.

In any case, it seems evident that writers not blessed enough to be under thirty (or thirty-five, or whatever the critical age is these days) must be reborn in order to seem relevant to the moment, and those who inhabit it most comfortably, i.e. the young. But no one has even the hope of being reborn unless he knows first that he is dead – dead, to be sure, for someone else; but a writer exists as a writer precisely for someone else. More specifically, no novelist can be reborn until he knows that in so far as he remains a novelist in the traditional sense, he is dead; since the traditional novel is dead – not dying, but dead. What was up to only a few years ago a diagnosis, a prediction (made, to be sure, almost from the moment of the invention of the novel: first form of Pop literature, and therefore conscious that as compared to classic forms like epic or tragedy its life-span was necessarily short) is now a fact. As certainly as God, i.e. the Old God, is dead, so the Novel, i.e. the Old Novel, is dead. To be sure, certain writers, still alive and productive (Saul Bellow, for instance, or John Updike, Mary McCarthy or James Baldwin), continue to write Old Novels, and certain readers, often with a sense of being quite up to date, continue to read them. But so do preachers continue to preach in the Old Churches, and congregations gather to hear them.

It is *not* a matter of assuming, like Marshall McLuhan, that the printed book is about to disappear, taking with it the novel – first form invented for print; only of realizing that in all of its forms – and most notably, perhaps, the novel – the printed book is being radically, functionally altered. No medium of communication ever disappears merely because a new and more efficient one is invented. One thinks, for instance, of the lecture, presumably super-annuated by the invention of movable type, yet flourishing still after more than five centuries of obsolescence. What is demanded by functional obsolescence is learning to be less serious, more frivolous, a form of *entertainment*. Indeed, it could be argued that a medium begins to be felt as entertainment only at the point where it ceases to be a necessary or primary means of communication, as recent developments in radio (the total disappearance, for instance, of all high-minded commentators and pretentious playwrights) sufficiently indicates. Students at any rate are well aware of this truth in regard to the university lecture, and woe to the lecturer (of whom, alas, there are many) who does not know it!

In any event, even as the 'serious' lecture was doomed by the technology of the fifteenth century, and the 'serious' church service by the philology of the eighteenth and nineteenth – so is the 'serious' novel and 'serious' criticism as well, by the technology and philology of the twentieth. Like the lecture and Christian church services, its self-awareness must now include the perception of its own absurdity, even impossibility. Since, however, the serious novel of our time is the Art Novel as practised by Proust, Mann and Joyce and imitated by their epigones, it is that odd blend of poetry, psychology and documentation, whose real though not always avowed end was to make itself canonical, that we must disavow. Matthew Arnold may have been quite correct in foreseeing the emergence of literature as scripture in a world which was forsaking the Old Time Religion: but the life of the New Scriptures and the New Time Religion was briefer than he could have guessed.

Before the Bible of the Christians and Jews ceased to be central to the concerns of men in Western society, it had become merely a 'book' among others; and this, indeed, may have misled the Arnoldians, who could not believe that a time might come when not merely *the* Book ceased to move men, but even books in general. Such, however, is the case – certainly as far as all books which consider themselves 'art', i.e. scripture once removed, are concerned; and for this reason the reborn novel, the truly New Novel must be anti-art as well as anti-serious. But this means, after all, that it must become more like what it was in the beginning, more what it seemed when Samuel Richardson could not be taken *quite* seriously, and what it remained in England (as opposed to France, for instance) until Henry James had justified himself as an artist against such self-declared 'entertainers' as Charles Dickens and Robert Louis Stevenson: popular, not quite reputable, a little dangerous – the one his loved and rejected cultural father, the other his sibling rival in art. The critical interchange on the nature of the novel to which James contributed 'The Art of Fiction' and Stevenson 'A Humble Remonstrance' memorializes their debate – which in the thirties most readers believed had been won hands down by James's defence of the novel of art; but which in the seventies and eighties we are not sure about at all – having reached a time when *Treasure Island* seems somehow more to the point and the heart's delight than, say, *The Princess Casamassima*.

This popular tradition the French may have understood once (in the days when Diderot praised Richardson extravagantly, and the Marquis de Sade emulated him in a dirtier book than the Englishman dared), but they long ago lost sight of it. And certainly the so-called '*nouveau roman*' is in its deadly earnest almost the opposite of anything truly new, which is to say, anti-art. Robbe-Grillet, for example, is still the prisoner of dying notions of the avant-garde; and though he is aware of half of what the new novelist must do (destroy the Old, destroy Marcel Proust), he is unaware of what he must create in its place. His kind of anti-novel is finally too arty and serious: a kind of neo-neo-Classicism, as if to illustrate once more that in the end this is all the French can invent no matter how hard they try. Re-imagined on film by Alain Resnais, *Last Year at Marienbad* speaks to the young; but in print it remains merely *chic*, which is to say, a fashionable and temporary error of taste. Better by far, and by the same token infinitely more pertinent is Samuel Beckett, who having been born Irish rather than French, finds it hard to escape being (what some of his readers choose to ignore) compulsively and hilariously funny.

Best of all, however, and therefore totally isolated on the recent French scene (except for the perceptive comments of that equally ambiguous figure, Raymond Queneau) is Boris Vian, especially in his most successful work of fiction, *L'écume des jours*, recently translated into English as *Mood Indigo*. Indeed, Boris Vian is in many ways a prototype of the New Novelist, though he has been dead for a quarter of a century and his most characteristic work belongs to the years just after the Second World War. He was, first of all, an Imaginary American (as even writers born in the United States must be these days), who found himself in total opposition to the politics of America at the very moment he was most completely immersed in its popular culture; actually writing a detective novel called 'I Will Spit on Your Grave' under the pen-name of Vernon Sullivan, but pretending that he was only its translator into French. In fact, by virtue of this peculiar brand of mythological Americanism he managed to straddle the border, if not quite close the gap between high culture and low, *belles-lettres* and Pop Art. On the one hand, he was the writer of Pop songs and a jazz trumpeter much influenced by New Orleans style; and on the other, the author of novels in which the thinly disguised figures of such standard French intellectuals as Jean Paul Sartre and Simone de Beauvoir are satirized. But even in his fiction, which seems at first glance quite traditional or, at any rate, conventionally avant-garde, the characters move towards their fates through an imaginary city whose main thoroughfare is called Boulevard Louis Armstrong.

Only now, however, has Vian won the audience he all along deserved, finding it first among the young of Paris, who know like their American counterparts that such a closing of the gap between elite and mass culture is precisely the function of the novel now – not merely optional as in Vian's day, but necessary. And though most of the younger American authors who follow a similar course, follow it without ever having known him, by a shared concern rather than direct emulation, he seems more like them than such eminent American forerunners of theirs as Faulkner or Hemingway (except perhaps in Hemingway's neglected early burlesque, *Torrents of Spring*, and Faulkner's self-styled 'pot-boiler', *Sanctuary*). Vian, unfortunately, turned to the form of the Pop Novel only for the work of his left hand, to which he was not willing even to sign his own name, writing in *L'écume des jours* what seems superficially a traditional enough love story to disarm the conventional critics; though it is finally undercut by a sentimentality which redeems its irony, and reflects a mythology too Pop and American for neo-neo-Classicists to bear.

The young Americans who have succeeded Vian, on the other hand, have abandoned all concealment; and when they are most themselves, nearest to their central concerns, turn frankly to Pop forms – though not, to be sure, the detective story which has by our time become hopelessly compromised by middle-brow condescension: an affectation of presidents and college professors. The forms of the novel which they prefer are those which seem now what the hard-boiled detective story once seemed to Vian: at the furthest possible remove from art and avant-garde, the greatest distance from inwardness, analysis and pretension; and, therefore, immune to lyricism, on the one hand, or righteous social commentary, on the other. It is not compromise by the market-place they fear; on the contrary, they choose the genre most associated with exploitation by the mass media: notably, the Western, Science Fiction and Pornography.

Most congenial of all is the Western, precisely because it has for many decades now seemed to belong exclusively to pulp magazines, run-of-the-mill TV series and class-B movies; which is to say, has been experienced almost purely as myth and entertainment rather than as 'literature' at all – and its sentimentality has, therefore, come to possess our minds so completely that it can now be mitigated without essential loss by parody, irony – and even critical analysis. In a sense, our mythological innocence has been preserved in the Western, awaiting the day when, no longer believing ourselves innocent in fact, we could decently return to claim it in fantasy. But such a return of the Western represents, of course, a rejection of laureates of the loss of innocence like Henry James and Hawthorne: those particular favourites of the forties, who despite their real virtues turn out to have been too committed to the notion of European High Art to survive as major influences in an age of Pop. And it implies as well momentarily turning aside from our beloved Herman Melville (compromised by his New Critical admirers and the countless PhD dissertations they prompted), and even from Mark Twain. To Hemingway, Twain could still seem central to a living tradition, the Father of us all, but being Folk rather than Pop in essence, he has become ever more remote from an urban, industrialized world, for which any evocation of pre Civil War, rural America seems a kind of pastoralism which complements rather than challenges the Art Religion. Folk Art knows and accepts its place in a class-structured world which Pop blows up, whatever its avowed intentions. What remain are only the possibilities of something closer to travesty than emulation – such a grotesque neo-Huck, for instance, as the foul-mouthed D.J. in Norman Mailer's *Why Are We in Vietnam?*, who, it is wickedly suggested, may *really* be a Black joker in Harlem pretending to be the White refugee from respectability. And, quite recently, Twain's book itself has been rewritten to please and mock its exegetes in John Seelye's *Huck Finn for the Critics*, which lops off the whole silly-happy ending, the deliverance of Nigger Jim (in which Hemingway, for instance, never believed); and puts back into the tale the cussing and sex presumably excised by the least authentic part of Samuel Clemens's mind – as well as the revelation, at long last, that what Huck and Jim were smoking on the raft was not tobacco but 'hemp', which is to say, marijuana. Despite all, however, Huck seems for the moment to belong not to the childhood we all continue to live, but to the one we have left behind.

Natty Bumppo, on the other hand, dreamed originally in the suburbs of New York City and in Paris, oddly survives along with his author. Contrary to what we had long believed, it is James Fenimore Cooper who now remains alive, or rather who has been reborn, perhaps not so much as he saw himself as in the form in which D. H. Lawrence re-imagined him *en route* to America; for Cooper understood that the dream which does not fade with the building of cities, but assumes in their concrete and steel environment the compelling vividness of a waking hallucination, is the encounter of Old World men and New in the wilderness, the meeting of the transplanted European and the Red Indian. No wonder Lawrence spoke of himself as 'kindled by Fenimore Cooper'.

The return of the Redskin to the centre of our art and our deep imagination, as we all of us have retraced Lawrence's trip to the mythical America, is based not merely on the revival of the oldest and most authentic of American Pop forms, but also projects certain meanings of our lives in terms more metapolitical than political, which is to say, meanings valid as myth is valid rather than as history. Writers of Westerns have traditionally taken sides for or against the Indians; and unlike the authors of the movies which set the kids to cheering at the Saturday matinées of the twenties and thirties, the new novelists have taken a clear stand with the Red man. In this act of mythological renegacy they have not only implicitly declared themselves enemies of the Christian Humanism; but they have also rejected the act of genocide with which our nation began – and whose last reflection, perhaps, is to be found in the war in Vietnam.

It is impossible to write any Western which does not in some sense glorify violence; but the violence celebrated in the anti-White Western is guerrilla violence: the sneak attack on 'civilization' as practised first by Geronimo and Cochise and other Indian warrior chiefs, and more latterly prescribed by Ché Guevara or the spokesmen for North Vietnam. Warfare, however, is not the final vision implicit in the New Western, which is motivated on a deeper level by a nostalgia for the Tribe: a form of social organization thought of as preferable both to the tight two-generation bourgeois family, from which its authors come, and the soulless out-of-human-scale bureaucratic state, into which they are initiated via schools and universities. In the end, of course, both the dream of violence in the woods and the vision of tribal life, rendered in terms of a genre that has long been the preferred reading of boys, seem juvenile, even infantile. But this is precisely the point; for what recommends the Western to the New Novelist is pre-eminently its association with children and the kind of books superciliously identified with their limited and special needs.

For the German, brought up on Karl May, the situation is quite similar to that in which the American, who grew up with Cooper or his native imitators, finds himself. What has Old Shatterhand to do with Art, asks the one, even as the other asks the same of Chingachgook. And the answer is *nothing*. The legendary Indians have nothing to do with Art in the traditional sense, everything to do with joining boy to man, childhood to adulthood, immaturity to maturity. They preside over the closing of the gap which aristocratic conceptions of art have opened between the joys that fulfil us at eight or ten or twelve and what satisfies us at forty or fifty or sixty.

In light of all this, it is perhaps time to look again at the much-discussed 'immaturity' of American literature, the notorious fact that our classic books are boys' books – our greatest novels at home in the children's section of libraries; in short, that they are all in some sense 'Westerns': accounts of an idyllic encounter between White man and non-White in one or another variety of wilderness setting. But suddenly this fact – once read as a 'flaw' or 'failure' or 'lack' (it implies, after all, the absence in our books of heterosexual love and of the elaborate analysis of social relations central to the continental novel) – seems evidence of a real advantage, a clue to why the Gap we now want to close opened so late and so unconvincingly, as it were, in American letters. Before Henry James, none of our novelists felt himself cut off from the world of magic and wonder; he had only to go to sea or, especially, to cross our own particular border, the Frontier, to inhabit a region where adults and children, educated and un-educated, shared a common enchantment.

How different the plight of mid-nineteenth-century English writers, like Lewis Carroll or Edward Lear or George MacDonald, who had to pretend that they were writing exclusively for the nursery in order to enter the deep wonderland of their own imaginations. Even in our own time, a writer like J. R. R. Tolkien found it necessary to invent the Hobbits in a book specifically aimed at children, before he could release the fearful scholarship (another device foreign to American mythologies) and presumably adult magic of the Rings trilogy. It makes a difference, after all, whether one thinks of the World Across the Border as Faerie or Frontier, fantasy or history. It has been so long since Europeans lived their deepest dreams – but only yesterday for us. And this is why even now, when we are at last sundered from those dreams, we can turn rotten-ripe without loss of essential innocence, be (what has become a model for the young of all the world, as Godard's *Weekend* testifies) decadent children playing Indians; which is to say, imaginary Americans, all of us whether native to this land or not. But to be an American (unlike being English or French or whatever) is to *imagine* a destiny rather than to inherit one; since we have always been, in so far as we are Americans at all, inhabitants of myth rather than history – and have now come to know it.

In any case, our best writers have been able to take up the Western again – playfully and seriously at once, quite like their ancestors who began the Revolution which made us a country by playing Indians in deadly earnest and dumping all that English tea into the salt sea that sundered them from their king. There are many writers still under forty, among them the most distinguished of their generation, who have written New Westerns which have found the hearts of the young, particularly in paperback form; since to these young readers, for reasons psychological as well as economic, the hard-cover book with its aspiration to immortality in libraries begins to look obsolete. John Barth's *The Sotweed Factor* represents the beginning of the wave which has been cresting ever since 1960; and which not only has carried with it Barth's near contemporaries like Thomas Berger (in *Little Big Man*), Ken Kesey (in both *One Flew Over the Cuckoo's Nest* and *Sometimes a Great Notion*), and most recently Leonard Cohen (in his extraordinarily gross and elegant *Beautiful Losers*) – but has won over older and more established writers like Norman Mailer whose novel, *Why Are We in Vietnam?*, is not as its title seems to promise a book about a war in the East as much as a book about the idea of the West. Even William Burroughs, expert in drug fantasies and homosexual paranoia, keeps promising to turn to the genre; though so far he has contented himself with another popular form, another way of escaping from personal to public or popular myth, of using dreams to close rather than open a gap: Science Fiction.

Science Fiction does not seem at first glance to have as wide and universal an appeal as the Western, in book form at least; though perhaps it is too soon to judge, for it is a very young genre, having found its real meaning and scope only after the Second World War, after tentative beginnings in Jules Verne, H. G. Wells, etc. At that point, two things became clear: first, that the future was upon us, that the pace of technological advance had become so swift that a distinction between present and future would get harder and harder to maintain; and second, that the end of Man, by annihilation or mutation, was a real, even an immediate possibility. But these are the two proper subjects of Science Fiction: the Present Future and the End of Man – not time travel or the penetration of outer space, except as these latter somehow symbolize the former.

Perhaps only in quite advanced technologies which also have a tradition of self-examination and analysis, bred by Puritanism or Marxism or whatever, can Science Fiction at its most explicit, which is to say, expressed in words on the page, really flourish. In any case, only in America, England and the Soviet Union does the Science

Fiction Novel or Post-Novel seem to thrive; though Science Fiction cartoon strips and comic books, as well as Science Fiction TV programmes and especially films (where the basic imagery is blissfully wed to electronic music, and words are kept to a minimum) penetrate everywhere. In England and America, at any rate, the prestige and influence of the genre are sufficient not only to allure Burroughs (in *Nova Express*), but also to provide a model for William Golding (in *Lord of the Flies*), Anthony Burgess (in *The Clockwork Orange*) and John Barth (whose second major book, *Giles Goatboy*, abandoned the Indian in favour of the Future).

Quite unlike the Western, which asserts the differences between England and America, Science Fiction reflects what still makes the two mutually distrustful communities one; as, for instance, a joint effort (an English author, an American director) like the movie, *2001: A Space Odyssey*, testifies. If there is still a common 'Anglo-Saxon' form, it is Science Fiction. Yet even here, the American case is a little different from the English; for only in the United States is there a writer of first rank whose preferred mode has been from the first Science Fiction in its unmitigated Pop form. Kurt Vonnegut, Jr, did not begin by making some sort of traditional bid for literary fame and then shift to Science Fiction, but was so closely identified with that popular, not-quite-respectable form from the first, that the established critics were still ignoring him completely at a time when younger readers, attuned to the new rhythm of events by Marshall McLuhan or Buckminster Fuller, had already made underground favourites of his *The Sirens of Titan* and *Cat's Cradle*. That Vonnegut now, after years of neglect, teaches writing in a famous American university and is hailed in lead reviews in the popular press, is a tribute not to the critics' acuity but to the persuasive powers of the young.

The revival of pornography in recent days, its moving from the periphery to the centre of the literary scene, is best understood in this context, too; for it, like the Western and Science Fiction, is a form of Pop Art – ever since Victorian times, indeed, the *essential* form of Pop Art, which is to say, the most unredeemable of all kinds of sub-literature, understood as a sort of entertainment closer to the pole of Vice than that of Art. Many of the more notable recent works of the genre have tended to conceal this fact, often because the authors themselves did not understand what they were after, and have tried to disguise their work as earnest morality (Hubert Selby's *Last Exit to Brooklyn*, for instance) or parody (Terry Southern's *Candy*). But whatever the author's conscious intent, all those writers who have helped move Porn from the underground to the foreground have in effect been working towards the liquidation of the very conception of pornography; since the end of Art on one side means the end of Porn on the other. And that end is now in sight, in the area of films and Pop songs and poetry, but especially in that of the novel which seemed, initially at least, more congenial than other later Pop Art forms to the sort of private masturbatory reverie which is essential to pornography.

It is instructive in this regard to reflect on the careers of two publishers who have flourished because somehow they sensed early on that a mass society can no longer endure the distinction between low literature and high, especially in the area of sex; and that the line drawn early in the century between serious, 'artistic' exploitation of pornography (e.g. *Lady Chatterley's Lover*) and so-called 'hard-core' pornography was bound to be blurred away. Even the classics of the genre straddle the line: *Fanny Hill*, for example, and de Sade's *Justine*, as do more recent works like John Rechy's *City of Night* or Stephen Schneck's *The Night Clerk*, whose sheer dirtiness may be adulterated by sentiment or irony but remains a chief appeal. This, at any rate, Maurice Girodias and Barney Rosset appear to have sensed; and from both sides of the Atlantic they have, through the Olympia Press and Grove Press, supplied the American reading public, chiefly but not exclusively the young, with books (including, let it be noted, Nabokov's *Lolita*, the sole work in which the pursuit of Porn enabled that emigré writer to escape the limitations of early twentieth-century avant-garde) exploiting, often in contempt of art and seriousness, not just Good Clean Sex, but sadism, masochism, homosexuality, coprophilia, necrophilia, etc., etc.

The standard forms of heterosexual copulation, standardly or 'poetically' recorded, seem oddly old-fashioned, even a little ridiculous; it is fellatio, buggery, flagellation, that we demand in order to be sure that we are not reading Love Stories but Pornography. A special beneficiary of this trend has been Norman Mailer, whose first novel, *The Naked and the Dead*, emulated the dying tradition of the anti-war art novel, with occasional obscenities thrown in, presumably in the interest of verisimilitude. But more and more, Mailer has come to move the obscenity to the centre, the social commentary to the periphery, until in *Why Are We in Vietnam?* the insistence on foul language and obsession with scatology are obviously ends in themselves, too unremitting to be felt as merely an assault on old-fashioned sensibility and taste. And even his earlier

Pop Novel, *An American Dream*, which marked his emergence from ten years in which he produced no major fiction, he had committed himself to Porn as a way into the region to which his title alludes: the place where in darkness and filth all men are alike – the Harvard graduate and the reader of the *Daily News*, joined in fantasies of murdering their wives and buggering their maids. To talk of such books in terms of Dostoevsky, as certain baffled critics have felt obliged to do, is absurd; James Bond is more to the point. But to confess this would be to confess that the old distinctions are no longer valid, and that critics will have to find another claim to authority more appropriate to our times than the outmoded ability to discriminate between High and Low.

Even more disconcertingly than Mailer, Philip Roth has with *Portnoy's Complaint* raised the question of whether 'pornography', even what was called until only yesterday 'hard-core pornography', any longer exists. Explicit, vulgar, joyous, gross and pathetic all at once, Roth has established himself not only as the laureate of masturbation and oral-genital lovemaking but also as a master of the 'thin' novel, the novel with minimum inwardness – ironically presented as a confession to a psychiatrist. Without its sexual interest, therefore, the continual balancing off of titillation and burlesque, his book has no meaning at all, no more than any other dirty joke, to which genre it quite clearly belongs. There is pathos, even terror in great plenty, to be sure, but it is everywhere dependent on, subservient to the dirty jokes about mothers, Jews, shrinks, potency, impotency; and Roth is, consequently, quite correct when he asserts that he is less like such more solemn and pious Jewish-American writers as Saul Bellow and Bernard Malamud, than he is like the half-mad Pop singer Tiny Tim (himself actually half-Arab and half-Jew).

'I am a Jew Freak', Roth has insisted, 'not a Jewish Sage' – and one is reminded of Lennie Bruce, who was there first, occupying the dangerous DMZ between the world of the stand-up comedian and that of the proper maker of fictions. But Bruce made no claim to being a novelist and therefore neither disturbed the critics nor opened up new possibilities for prose narrative. Indeed, before *Portnoy's Complaint*, the Jewish-American novel had come to seem a specially egregious example of the death of *belles-lettres*, having become smug, established, repetitive and sterile. But *Portnoy* marks the passage of that genre into the new world of Porn and Pop, as Roth's booming sales (even in hard-covers!) perhaps sufficiently attest.

It is, of course, the middle-aged and well-heeled who buy the hard-cover editions of the book, yet their children apparently are picking it up, too; for once not even waiting for the paperback edition. They know it is a subversive book, as their parents do not (convinced that a boy who loves his mother can't be all bad), and as Roth himself perhaps was not at first quite aware either. Before its publication, he had been at least equivocal on the subject of frankly disruptive literature; full of distrust, for instance, for Norman Mailer – and appears therefore to have become a Pop rebel despite himself, driven less by principle than by a saving hunger for the great audience, like that which moved John Updike out of his elitist exile towards bestsellerdom and relevance in *Couples*.

There is, however, no doubt in the minds of most other writers whom the young especially prize at the moment that their essential task is to destroy once and for all – by parody or exaggeration or grotesque emulation of the classic past, as well as by the adaptation and 'camping' of Pop forms – just such distinctions and dis- criminations. But to turn High Art into vaudeville and burlesque at the same moment that Mass Art is being irreverently introduced into museums and libraries is to perform an act which has political as well as aesthetic implications: an act which closes a class, as well as a generation gap. The notion of one art for the 'cultured', i.e. the favoured few in any given society – in our own chiefly the university educated – and another sub-art for the 'uncultured', i.e. an excluded majority as deficient in Gutenberg skills as they are untutored in 'taste', in fact represents the last survival in mass industrial societies (capitalist, socialist, communist – it makes no difference in this regard) of an invidious distinction proper only to a class-structured community. Precisely because it carries on, as it has carried on ever since the middle of the eighteenth century, a war against that anachronistic survival, Pop Art is, whatever its overt politics, *sub- versive:* a threat to all hierarchies in so far as it is hostile to order and ordering in its own realm. What the final intrusion of Pop into the citadels of High Art provides, therefore, for the critic is the ex- hilarating new possibility of making judgments about the 'goodness' and 'badness' of art quite separated from distinctions between 'high' and 'low' with their concealed class bias.

But the new audience has not waited for new critics to guide them in this direction. Reversing the process typical of Modernism – under whose aegis an unwilling, ageing elite audience was bullied and cajoled slowly, slowly, into accepting the most vital art of its time – Post-Modernism provides an example of a young, mass audience urging certain ageing, reluctant critics onwards towards the abandonment of their former elite status in return for a freedom the prospect of which more terrifies than elates them. In fact, Post-Modernism implies the closing of the gap between critic and audience, too, if by critic one understands 'leader of taste' and by audience 'follower'. But most importantly of all, it implies the closing of the gap between artist and audience, or at any rate, between professional and amateur in the realm of art.

The jack of all arts is master of none, professional in none, and therefore no better than any man-jack among the rest of us, formerly safely penned off from the practitioners we most admire by our status as 'audience'. It all follows logically enough. On the one hand, a poet like Ed Sanders, or a novelist like Leonard Cohen, grows weary of his confinement in the realm of traditional high art; and the former organizes a musical Pop Group called the Fugs, while the latter makes recordings of his own Pop songs to his own guitar accompaniment. There are precedents for this, after all, not only as in the case of Boris Vian, which we have already noticed, but closer to home: in the career, for instance, of Richard Farina, who died very young, but not before he had written that imperfect, deeply moving novel, *Been Down So Long It Looks Like Up to Me*, and had recorded a song or two for the popular audience.

Meanwhile, even more surprisingly some who had begun, or whom we had begun to think of, as mere 'entertainers', Pop performers without loftier pretensions, were crossing the line from their direction. Frank Zappa for example, insisted on being taken seriously as poet and satirist, suggesting that the music of his own group, The Mothers of Invention, has been all along more a deliberate parody of Pop than an extension of it in psychedelic directions; while Bob Dylan, who began by abandoning Folk Music with left-wing protest overtones in favour of electronic Rock-and-Roll, finally succeeded in creating inside that form a kind of Pop Surrealist poetry, passionate, mysterious and quite complex; complex enough in fact, to prompt a score of scholarly articles on his 'art'. Most recently, however, he has returned to 'acoustic' instruments and to the most naïve traditions of country music – apparently out of a sense that he had grown too 'arty', and had once more to close the gap by back-tracking across the border he had earlier lost his first audience by crossing. It is a spectacular case of the new artist as Double Agent.

Even more spectacular is that of John Lennon, who coming into view first as merely one of the Beatles, then still just another rock group from Liverpool, revealed himself stage by stage as novelist, playwright, movie maker, guru, sculptor, etc., etc. There is a special pathos in his example since, though initially inspired by American models, he tried to work out his essentially American strategies in English idioms and in growing isolation on the generally dismal English scene. He refused to become the prisoner of his special talent as a musician, venturing into other realms where he had, initially at least, as little authority as anyone else; and thus he provided one more model for the young who, without any special gift or calling, in the name of mere possibility insist on making all up and down America, and, more tentatively, perhaps, everywhere else in the world, tens of thousands of records, movies, collections of verse, paintings, junk-sculptures, even novels in complete contempt of professional 'standards'. Perhaps, though, the novel is the most unpromising form for an amateur age (it is easier to learn the guitar or make a two-minute eight-millimetre film), and it may be doomed to become less and less important, less and less central, no matter how it is altered. But for the moment at least, on the border between the world of Art and that of non-Art, it flourishes with especial vigour in proportion as it realizes its transitional status, and is willing to surrender the kind of 'realism' and analysis it once thought its special province in quest of the marvellous and magical it began by disavowing.

Samuel Richardson may have believed that when he wrote *Pamela* and *Clarissa* he was delivering prose fiction from that bondage to the *merveilleux* which characterized the old Romances; but it is clear now that he was merely translating the Marvellous into new terms, specifically, into bourgeois English. It is time, at any rate, to be through with pretences; for to Close the Gap means also to Cross the Border between the Marvellous and the Probable, the Real and the Mythical, the world of the boudoir and the counting house and the realm of what used to be called Faerie, but has for so long been designated mere madness. Certainly the basic images of Pop forms like the Western, Science Fiction and Pornography suggest mythological as well as political or metapolitical meanings. The passage into Indian Territory, the flight into Outer Space, the ecstatic release into the fantasy world of the orgy: all these are analogues for what has traditionally been described as a Journey or Pilgrimage (recently we have been more likely to say 'Trip' without altering the significance) towards a transcendent goal, a moment of Vision.

But the mythologies of Voyage and Vision which the late Middle

Ages and the Renaissance inherited from the Classical World and the Judaeo-Christian tradition, and which froze into pedantry and academicism in the eighteenth and nineteenth century, have not survived their last ironical uses in the earlier part of the twentieth: those burlesque-pathetic evocations in Joyce's *Ulysses*, Eliot's *The Waste Land*, Mann's *Joseph and his Brethren* or the *Cantos* of Ezra Pound. If they are not quite dead, they should be, *need* be for the health of post-Art – as, indeed, Walt Whitman foresaw, anticipating the twenty-first century from the vantage point of his peculiar vision more than a hundred years ago.

> Come Muse migrate from Greece and Ionia,
> Cross out please those immensely overpaid accounts,
> That matter of Troy and Achilles' wrath, and Aeneas'
>   Odysseus' wanderings,
> Place 'Removed' and 'To Let' on the rocks of your
>   snowy Parnassus,
> Repeat at Jerusalem. . . .

Pop Art, however, can no more abide a mythological vacuum than can High Art; and into the space left vacant by the disappearance of the Matter of Troy and the myths of the ancient Middle East has rushed, first of all, the Matter of Childhood: the stuff of traditional fairy-tales out of the Black Forest, which seems to the present generation especially attractive, perhaps, because their 'progressive' parents tended to distrust it. But something much more radically new has appeared as well: the Matter of Metropolis and the myths of The Present Future, in which the non-human world about us, hostile or benign, is rendered not in the guise of elves or dwarfs or witches or even Gods, but of Machines quite as uncanny as any Elemental or Olympian – and apparently as immortal. Machines and the mythological figures appropriate to the media mass-produced and mass-distributed by machines: the newsboy who, saying *Shazam* in an abandoned subway tunnel, becomes Captain Marvel: the reporter (with glasses), who shucking his civilian garb in a telephone booth is revealed as Superman, immune to all but kryptonite – these are the appropriate images of power and grace for an urban, industrial world busy manufacturing the Future.

But the Comic Book heroes do not stand alone. Out of the world of Jazz and Rock, of newspaper headlines and political cartoons, of old movies immortalized on TV and idiot talk-shows carried on car radios, new anti-Gods and anti-Heroes arrive, endless wave after wave of them: 'Bluff'd not a bit by drain-pipe, gasometer, artificial fertilizers' (the appropriate commentary is Whitman's), 'smiling and pleas'd with palpable intent to stay' – in our Imaginary America, of course. In the heads of our new writers, they live a secondary life, begin to realize their immortality: not only Jean Harlow and Marilyn Monroe and Humphrey Bogart, Charlie Parker and Louis Armstrong and Lennie Bruce, Geronimo and Billy the Kid, the Lone Ranger and Fu Manchu and the Bride of Frankenstein, but Hitler and Stalin, John F. Kennedy and Lee Oswald and Jack Ruby as well; for the press mythologizes certain public figures, the actors of Pop History, even before they are dead – making a doomed president one with Superman in the Supermarket of Pop Culture, as Norman Mailer perceived so accurately and reported so movingly in an essay on John F. Kennedy.

But the secret he told was already known to scores of younger writers at least, and recorded in the text and texture of their work. In the deep memory of Leonard Cohen writing *Beautiful Losers*, or Richard Farina composing *Been Down So Long It Looks Like Up to Me*, or Ken Kesey making *Sometimes a Great Notion*, there stir to life not archetypal images out of books read in school or at the urging of parents; but those out of comic books forbidden in schools, or radio and TV programmes banned or condescendingly endured by parents. From the taboo underground culture of the kids of just after the Second World War comes the essential mythology which informs the literature of right now. As early as T. S. Eliot, to be sure, Jazz rhythms had been evoked, as in 'O O O O that Shakespeherian Rag – It's so elegant, So intelligent. . . .', but Eliot is mocking a world he resents; and even in Brecht's *Threepenny Opera*, the emulation of Pop music seems still largely 'slumming'. In the newest writers, however, mockery and condescension alike are absent; since they are not slumming, they are living in the only world in which they feel at home. They are able, therefore, to recapture a certain rude magic in its authentic context, by seizing on myths, not as stored in encyclopedias or preserved in certain beloved ancient works, but as apprehended at their moment of making, which is to say, at a moment when they are not yet labelled 'myths'.

In some ways the present movement not only in its quest for myths, but also in its preference for sentimentality over irony, and especially in its dedication to the Primitive, resembles the beginnings of Romanticism, with its yearning for the naïve, and its attempt to find authentic sources for poetry in folk forms like the Märchen or the Ballads. But the Romantics turned towards the past

in the hope of renewal – to a dream of the Past, which they knew
they could only write not actually live. And, indeed, there persists in
the Post-Modernists some of that old nostalgia for folk ways and
folk rhythms, curiously tempered by the realization that the 'folk-
songs' of an electronic age are made not in rural loneliness or in
sylvan retreats, but in super-studios by boys singing into the
sensitive ear of machines – or even by those machines themselves
editing, blending, making out of imperfect scraps of human song an
artifice of simplicity only possible on tape. What recent writers have
learned, and are true enough children of the Present Future to find
exhilarating, is not only that the Naïve can be machine-produced,
but that dreams themselves can be manufactured, projected on TV
or laser beams with all the vividness of the visions of saints. In the
first wave of Romanticism, pre-electronic Romanticism, it took an
act of faith on the part of Novalis to be able to say, 'Life is not a
dream, but it can be and probably should be made one'. And
echoing his German progenitor, in the pages of both *Lilith* and
Phantastes, George MacDonald, maddest of the Victorian mad
visionaries, echoes the tone of desperate hope. But to the young in
America, who have learned to read MacDonald once more, along
with his English successors, Charles Williams and C. S. Lewis and
Tolkien, the declaration of faith has become a matter of fact.

The Dream, the Vision, *ekstasis*: these have again become the
avowed goals of literature; for our latest poets realize in this time of
Endings, what their remotest ancestors knew in the era of Beginnings, that merely 'to instruct and delight' is not enough. Like
Longinus, the new novelists and critics believe that great art releases and liberates as well; but unlike him, they are convinced that
wonder and fantasy which deliver the mind from the body, the body
from the mind, must be naturalized to a world of machines –
subverted perhaps or even transformed, but certainly not destroyed
or denied. The ending of Ken Kesey's *One Flew Over the Cuckoo's
Nest* expresses fictionally, metaphorically that conviction, when the
Indian who is his second hero breaks out of the Insane Asylum in
which 'The System' has kept him impotent and trapped, and flees
to join his fellows who are building a fishing weir on a giant hydro-
electric power dam. The Dam and Weir both are essential to post-
electronic Romanticism, which knows that the point is no longer to
pursue some uncorrupted West over the next horizon, since there is
no incorruption and all our horizons have been reached. It is rather
to make a thousand little Wests in the interstices of a machine
civilization, and, as it were, on its steel and concrete back; to live the

tribal life among and with the support of machines; to shelter new communes under domes constructed according to the technology of Buckminster Fuller; and warm the nakedness of New Primitives with advanced techniques of solar heating.

All this is less a matter of choice than of necessity; because, it has turned out, machine civilization tends inevitably to synthesize the primitive, and *ekstasis* is the unforeseen end of advanced technology, mysticism the by-product – no more nor no less accidental than penicillin – of scientific research. In the antiseptic laboratories of Switzerland, the psychedelic drug, LSD, was first developed, first tried by two white-coated experimenters; and even now Dow Chemical which manufactures napalm also produces the even more powerful psychedelic agent STP. It is, in large part, thanks to machines – the supermachines which, unlike their simpler prototypes, insist on tending us rather than demanding we tend them – that we live in the midst of a great religious revival, scarcely noticed by the official leaders of established Christian churches since it speaks quite another language. Yet many among us feel that they are able to live honestly only by what machines cannot do better than they – which is why certain poets and novelists, as well as Pop singers and pornographic playwrights, are suggesting in print, on the air, everywhere, that not Work but Vision is the proper activity of men, and that, therefore, the contemplative life may, after all, be preferable to the active one. In such an age, our age, it is not surprising that the books which most move the young are essentially religious books, as, indeed, Pop Art is always religious.

In the immediate past, however, when an absolute distinction was made between High Art and Pop, works of the latter category tended to be the secret scriptures of a kind of shabby, store-front church – a religion as exclusive in its attempt to remain the humble possession of the unambitious and unlettered, as the canonical works of High Art in their claim to be an esoteric gospel of Art itself, available only to a cultivated elite. But in a time of Closing the Gap, literature becomes again prophetic and universal – a continuing revelation appropriate to a permanent religious revolution, whose function is precisely to transform the secular crowd into a sacred community: one with each other, and equally at home in the world of technology and the realm of wonder. Pledged like Isaiah to speaking the language of everyone, the prophets of the new dispensation can afford to be neither finicky nor genteel; and they echo, therefore, the desperate cry of the Hebrew prototype: 'I am a man of unclean lips in the midst of a people of unclean lips.'

Let those to whom religion means security beware, for it is no
New Established Church that is in the process of being founded;
and its communicants are, therefore, less like the pillars of the
Lutheran Church or Anglican gentleman than they are like ranters,
enthusiasts, Dionysiacs, Anabaptists: holy disturbers of the peace of
the devout. Leonard Cohen, in a moment of vision which constitutes the climax of *Beautiful Losers*, aptly calls them 'New Jews';
for he sees them as a saved remnant moving across deserts of
boredom, out of that exile from our authentic selves which we all
share, towards a salvation none of us can quite imagine. Such New
Jews, Cohen (himself a Jew as well as a Canadian) adds, do not have
to be Jewish but probably do have to be Americans – by which he
must surely mean 'Imaginary Americans'; since as we have been
observing all along, there were never any other kind.

13

THE NEW FICTION

Jerome Klinkowitz

'Contemporary fiction' has always been a hopelessly fluid and amorphous term. The word 'contemporary' lives on, but any fiction so designated becomes a matter of history the next day. To complicate matters, in our day the term 'fiction' has been expanded to include works formerly ascribed to the genres of poetry (Michael Ondaatje's *Coming Through Slaughter*), journalism (Truman Capote's *In Cold Blood*) and the personal essay (Hunter S. Thompson's *Fear and Loathing in Las Vegas*), thanks to the era's penchant for blurring all distinctions between form and content, fantasy and fact.

A history of the period, however, can be constructed by considering the various names authors and critics have devised for the work most customarily referred to as 'the new fiction', a style beginning in the late 1960s and flourishing through the 1970s and 80s. That there was something else afoot besides the novel of morals and manners (Saul Bellow, John Updike) became clear to Bruce Jay Friedman and to Douglas M. Davis, who in their respective anthologies *Black Humor* (1965) and *The World of Black Humor* (1967) noted the work of several novelists who would become in subsequent decades the new mainstream of serious fiction: John Barth (b. 1930), John Hawkes (b. 1925), Thomas Pynchon (b. 1937), Joseph Heller (b. 1923) and Kurt Vonnegut (b. 1922). At the same time, Robert Scholes introduced these writers as *The Fabulators* (1967), a term he would eventually expand as *Fabulation and Metafiction* (1979), adding William H. Gass (b. 1924), Donald Barthelme (b. 1931), Robert Coover (b. 1932) and Ishmael Reed (b. 1938) at this later date. In the meantime, my own *Literary Disruptions* (1975) playfully suggested 'post-contemporary' as a term best suiting fiction still in the process of development and proposed 'disruption' as a measure of these writers' formal as well as thematic achievements. Over the past ten years readers have been given the options of using many other labels, from 'surfiction' (Raymond Federman on fiction which instead of creating a semblance of order offers itself for ordering) and 'exploded form' (James M. Mellard's description of limit-testing), through 'post-realistic' (Philip Stevick on transcending documentary conventions) and 'midfiction' (Alan Wilde on ironic parody), to 'transfiction' (Mas'ud Zavarzadeh on work which effaces the distinctions between fact and fantasy) and 'minimalist' (James Atlas on fiction which understates practical matters of character, action and theme). What one notes about these critical responses to the times is that American fiction since 1970 has swung away from the tenets of conventional mimesis only to re-embrace a new style of realism a decade and a half later. In no sense has this journey been in vain, since the exploration of fiction's nature by the writers themselves has given a new sense of formal depth to a genre once considered autodidactic and socially realistic in the simplest terms.

As the twentieth century moves into its closing decades, certain writers have kept pace with this development while others have not. Joseph Heller's and Ken Kesey's (b. 1935) later novels are much more conventional than their initial works, while Philip Roth (b. 1933) has stepped back from both formal and thematic shock-effects to compose more relaxed and even lyrical meditations on history and the writer's role. Of interest here will be the figures who have developed with the age, an unsettling time in which many traditions of and standards for behaviour were re-examined. Hawkes, Barth and Pynchon are the period's first major triad, grouped around Hawkes's belief that the enemies of the life of fiction are the outworn conventions of plot, character, setting and theme. Hawkes himself is the most traditional in his overthrowing of tradition, using the thematic devices of dream and perverse psychology as a way of relocating his narrative. His is a nightmare world, from *The Cannibal* (1949) through *The Lime Twig* (1961) to *The Passion Artist* (1979). His interest in unfettered sexuality as a counter-force to civilized (largely familial) claims helps shape *Virginie: Her Two Lives* (1982) and *Adventures in the Alaskan Skin Trade* (1985); in these works female protagonists respond physically and emotionally to the storytelling impulses of their master or father, a situation best envisioned by Sade. Hawkes's moral and psychological dislocations, however, prevent the novels from being read solely for their action; instead, nuances of language and clusters of imagery redeem Hawkes's fiction as art. John Barth's progress has been more spectacular, growing from intellectually comic, post-Existentialist novels in the 1950s, through extravagant literary experiments in the 1960s, to a merited self-indulgence in the joys of storytelling in his most recent works. His landmark essays, 'The Literature of Exhaustion' (1967) and 'The Literature of Replenishment' (1980), especially as collected in the company of his other critical statements in *The Friday Book* (1984), define both the need for his fiction and the form of response it has taken. Literary art in our times, Barth agrees with most theorists, can no longer follow the Aristotelian tradition of being an imitation of an action; but rather than take the Post-Modernist step into the world in which writing is a representation of nothing but itself, he prefers to follow Aristotle (albeit exponentially) as his self-reflective fiction dramatizes the imitation of an imitation of an action. Here Barth bridges the narrow gap between 'fabulation' (narration with an emphasis on the art of storytelling) and 'metafiction' (fiction which explores the conditions of its own making). Thomas Pynchon's work flourishes within this gap, as he writes what critics have praised as the 'mega-novel' or 'the novel of excess', in which a deliberate over-enlargement of all conventions (in the manner of Superrealist painter Chuck Close's massive close-up portraits) frustrates the reader's attempt to organize things. Instead, such mega-novels (as written by Pynchon, Don DeLillo, William Gaddis, Joseph McElroy and Robert Coover) encourage a sympathy for the formless chaos their authors believe characterize the period; Pynchon's *Gravity's Rainbow* (1973) remains the classic example of such narrative overkill.

With their reputations established in the 1950s and early 1960s, Hawkes, Barth and Pynchon pre-date the major breakthrough of innovative fiction which characterized the late 1960s and flourished during the first half of the next decade; in Ihab Hassan's scheme which contrasts the purposefulness of design and masterful hierarchy in Modernism with the playfulness of chance and the exhaustive anarchy of Post-Modernism, these novelists are squarely on the former side. A writer more willing to suspend the Aristotelian conventions was Kurt Vonnegut, whose first five novels were published in a critical and popular vacuum (1952–65), only to be brought back into print (and into wide academic acclaim) in the 1970s, following the success of *Slaughterhouse-Five* (1969). The key to Vonnegut's success on both popular and theoretical levels was his ability to integrate his own act of writing into the substance of his fiction. Beginning with the Introduction he added to the 1966 edition of his earlier novel *Mother Night* (1961), Vonnegut has clarified his own role as storyteller of everything he writes, fiction and non-fiction alike. Unlike the artificial (yet essentially mimetic) structures employed by Hawkes, Barth and Pynchon, Vonnegut's patently autobiographical devices place himself on the page as an equal to his creations, effacing the line between fact and fantasy which Post-Modernism has been unwilling to maintain. When the first words of *Slaughterhouse-Five* announce that 'All this happened, more or less', Vonnegut is referring not just to the novel's external action (which is centred around the Allied bombing of Dresden during the Second World War), but to his process of committing the tale to paper, a complex undertaking which occupies the first and last chapters and makes its presence felt throughout the novel.

Like most Post-Modern writers, Vonnegut is disarmingly honest about his methods and also instructively helpful in teaching his readers how to read such strange new works. *Slaughterhouse-Five* itself is written in the form of a 'Tralfamadorian novel', as a character from that planet explains to protagonist Billy Pilgrim:

> Billy couldn't read Tralfamadorian, of course, but he could at least see how the books were laid out – in brief clumps of symbols separated by stars. Billy commented that the clumps might be telegrams.
> 'Exactly,' said the voice.
> 'They *are* telegrams?'
> 'There are no telegrams on Tralfamadore. But you're right: each clump of symbols is a brief, urgent message – describing a situation, a scene. We Tralfamadorians read them all at once, not one after the other. There isn't any particular relationship between all the messages, except that the author has chosen them carefully, so that, when seen all at once, they produce an image of life that is beautiful and surprising and deep. What we love in our books are the depths of many marvelous moments seen all at one time.'
> (p 76)

To achieve this effect, Vonnegut scrambles all chronology so that the reader is discouraged from drawing any conclusions until the novel's picture is complete. Nor has there been any suspension of disbelief, as the author's process of assemblage has remained evident on virtually every page.

Among the other American fictionists who have written 'Tralfamadorian novels' are Donald Barthelme and Richard Brautigan (1935–84). Barthelme's *Snow White* (1967) is, like *Slaughterhouse-Five*, a primer for understanding innovative fiction; from time to time throughout its fragmentary retelling of the Snow White fairy-tale (recostumed for contemporary times) characters will discuss the use of language and the nature of quasi-mythic narrative, all in a comically accessible mode. Thanks to his regular appearance in the pages of *The New Yorker* magazine, Barthelme has educated a readership with his short stories, the most important of which are collected in his *Sixty Stories* (1981). His first and most important lesson is that language no longer communicates as it should, as is demonstrated by the military scientists and engineers of 'The Report' (first published in 1967), who have developed 'rots, blights, and rusts capable of attacking [the enemy's] alphabet', are working on 'the deadly testicle-destroying telegram', and are perfecting 'realtime online computer-controlled wish evaporation' which is crucial in 'meeting the rising expectations of the world's peoples, which are as you know rising entirely too fast'. Barthelme's second major concern is that most human intercourse takes the form of a self-serving system; like the Deconstructionist philosophers, he knows that 'signs are signs, and that some of them are lies'. This insight from his first published story, 'The Darling Duckling at School' (1961, later collected as 'Me and Miss Mandible'), is a far better motto for his fiction than the one usually cited, 'Fragments are the only form I trust'. Spoken by a middle-aged insurance adjustor suddenly and explicably returned in time to his place among a classroom of twelve-year-olds, this appraisal of how semiotics plays a cruel game with our ideals for life could have just as easily been an example fashioned by Roland Barthes or Jacques Derrida.

Richard Brautigan, the first of the 'new fiction' practitioners to die (by his own hand in 1984), accepted the same premise as Barthelme when it came to language, but instead of satirizing it thematically Brautigan preferred to embrace this circumstance for its creative potential. His *Trout Fishing in America* (1967) celebrates language as self-conscious play, deconstructing the referential connections of metaphor by stretching the distance between tenor and vehicle to previously-unthought-of distances; California's sylvan Big Sur, for example, is described as a 'thousand-year-old flophouse for mountain lions and lilacs', while an untended cemetery is introduced as having 'no trees and the grass turned a flat-tire brown in the summer and stayed that way until the rain, like a mechanic, began in the late autumn'. Brautigan's last novel published in his lifetime, *So the Wind Won't Blow It All Away* (1982), transposes his thoughts about language into the world of time. When his narrator puts himself back into the past for the occasion of writing this novel, he finds himself dealing with several layers of narrative existence, from the 1980s' present of writing through the

1940s' events narrated to the various objects of the past the
narrator-as-a-boy discovered back then, such as an ancient
perambulator:

> I walked very carefully over to the baby buggy. I didn't want to stumble
> over the past and break my present-tense leg that might leave me crippled
> in the future.
> I took the handle of the baby buggy and pulled it away from the 1900s
> and into the year 1947.
>
> (p 11)

To explain the nature of 'one's time and life on earth', Brautigan
employs his talent for exploding metaphors to contrast the implosive
nature of one's day-to-day progress through existence. Following
an uneventful morning his narrator can note, 'The sun had reversed
its boredom and now had grown interesting as it began its descent
which would soon open the beginning doors of night and the wind
had died down making the pond as still and quiet as sleeping glass'.
The anti-hierarchical nature of the conjunction *and* here establishes
the author's habit of letting poetic fancy and naturalistic observation
blend into one seamless texture of narration.

A far less sanguine view of art is presented by Jerzy Kosinski
(b. 1933 in Poland, emigrated to the US in 1955, and who writes in
English), whose celebration of imaginative power is put to
survivalist ends in *The Painted Bird* (1965) and *Steps* (1968),
functions as satire in *Being There* (1971), and from *The Devil Tree*
(1974) onwards degenerates into a self-aggrandizing orgy of
violence and glittery commercialization. The road not taken by
Kosinski's fiction, that of confronting the terrors of life with an
innovatively accommodating form, opened up instead to John Irving
(b. 1942), whose *The World According to Garp* (1978) presents a text
written by the protagonist (in Kosinski's mode) which the novel's
larger structure adequately critiques. Like Kosinski, Irving accepts
the technical superiority of art (and the imagination) over life, but
the younger novelist (a student of Kurt Vonnegut at the University
of Iowa Writers Workshop) wishes to underscore the difference
between fiction and life without purging the former of the latter.
Rather than subtract life in favour of a fully abstract form, Irving
adds it in all its contradictory varieties; but also rather than
surrendering to life's terror, he provides a vehicle – self-conscious
storytelling – by which existence can be allowed to make sense. In
one scene Garp tells his children a story, and then concludes it
(with striking modifications) for his wife. The kids assume it is

autobiographical, but Helen Garp (as an English professor) knows that it is mostly made up. Yet even she demands a coherent model: that in her husband's imaginative creation of the tale there be a certain standard of internal truth. Seeing so many parts change – as *The World According to Garp* itself changes before us as readers – confuses her. 'Which of it is true,' she asks, 'and which of it is made up?' Garp plays it as a game with her, always giving the same answer, which serves as a guide to Irving's own complex, multifaceted texts: 'Every part she believed was true; every part she didn't believe needed work.'

The vagaries of fact and fiction spill over from the works of those writers once labelled 'black humorists' into reportage published under the term 'the new journalism'. Although the first major example of it was Truman Capote's *In Cold Blood* (1966), the best explanation for this sub-genre's existence came from Tom Wolfe (b. 1931), whose own experiments in this high-bred field were included in his anthology (edited with E. W. Johnson in 1973), *The New Journalism*:

By the Sixties, about the time I came to New York, the serious, ambitious and, presumably talented novelists had abandoned the richest terrain of the novel: namely, the whole business of 'the way we live now,' in Trollope's phrase. There is no novelist who will be remembered as the novelist who captured the Sixties in America, or even in New York, in the sense that Thackeray was the chronicler of London in the 1840's and Balzac was the chronicler of Paris and all of France after the fall of the Empire. Balzac prided himself on being 'the secretary of French society.' Most serious American novelists would rather cut their wrists than be known as 'the secretary of American society,' and not merely because of ideological considerations. With fable, myth and the sacred office to think about – who wants such a role?

(p 29)

In reaction, Wolfe proposed that the conventions novelists had abandoned be employed by journalists in order to create a new form, which in time became known as 'the non-fiction novel'. Norman Mailer's account of the Vietnam War protest, *The Armies of the Night* (1968), fits this description, but the finest example of a supposedly historical work adopting characterization, development via dialogue, and imagery remains Hunter S. Thompson's (b. 1939) *Fear and Loathing in Las Vegas* (1972). Ostensibly a report on the journalist's attendance at a dirt bike race and then a drug-law enforcement convention in the gambling capital, this deftly control-led riot of misbehaviour and abuse succeeds not as conventional reportage (with its standards of distance and objectivity) but as fiction, sharing many techniques with the innovationists of Thompson's own generation. Like them, he makes the final subject of his book be himself, as he places his physical and emotional person at the centre of events and describes his own reactions. Moreover, the conditions of Thompson's own act of writing are, like Vonnegut's, made an integral part of the work itself. He thrives on the conditions under which he must compose: fighting deadlines, sending in his material on tape and in unedited notebooks (which are included in the book as such), and doing his actual writing in the constantly self-described context of drugs, alcohol and violence, until this manner itself becomes an essential part of his subject. There is no illusion that there is not a very real and stunningly idiosyncratic writer at the centre of this work. Like the innovationists, Thompson creates his own mythology, his own life of fiction, against which his subjects are tested and not just explained.

History, then – which in the hands of earlier writers had been such a problematic concern (one thinks of Faulkner) – becomes for writers in the 1970s and 1980s just one more convention to be played with and eventually purged. One of the most effective novelists in this regard has been Ishmael Reed, whose belief in the comparative, pluralistic values of 'multiculturalism' lends his fiction great authority in challenging any one person's view of the world. Far better than E. L. Doctorow's (b. 1931) *Ragtime* (1975), which relegates history to the status of a character acting within the reader's memory, Reed's novels do not so much tell a story as generate a language in which historical events become signs, semiotic entities which in a grammatical fashion are allowed to be themselves even as they are combined to form a new meaning. At one point in *The Terrible Twos* (1982), a futuristic novel which looks back upon the American present by reanimating its social and political signs, the ghost of President Dwight D. Eisenhower appears to explain a little bit of the past:

'If it hadn't been for Dulles,' he cried. 'That man had so much Bible and brimstone inside of him. The whole family – everybody but Allen was like him. They even had a fidgety woman preacher in the family. Dulles became haunted by that young black man. Said that when the young man, then a new leader of the Congo, visited Washington he sassed Dillon and the others. Swore up and down that Lumumba would bring the Communists to the Congo. Said that the Communism was the bitch of Babylon. Kept it up. Kept it up so much that I started smoking again, though I had sworn off the habit. And so one day, I was anxious to get out and play a couple rounds of golf at Burning Tree and they'd been pestering me all day about this Patrice Lumumba fellow, and so I stamped my foot and said, a guy like that ought to take a hike. I should have known when they started shaking hands and congratulating each other that something was up. I didn't mean for them to go and kill the man.'

(p 112)

Unlike Robert Coover, whose *The Public Burning* (1977) employs classic American myths (such as Uncle Sam, the Yankee pedlar) in order to construct a contemporary fable, Reed employs signs as they are used in everyday life to create a full-fledged fiction. The Secretary of State's fundamentalist Christian fire, the African leader's presumed impertinence, the President's muddling confusion – these are small icons once used as the lingua franca of the times, and which in Reed's narrative contribute to the language of fiction.

Fiction as language and language as fiction are the concerns of the central group of American innovators: Ronald Sukenick (b. 1932), William H. Gass, and Gilbert Sorrentino (b. 1929). Each has published a significant amount of literary theory (Gass and Sukenick hold PhDs from Cornell and Brandeis respectively), and all three have combined to move the novel significantly beyond the aesthetics of both 'morals and manners' and 'black humour'. Sukenick reveals the Post-Modern fascination with the theory when he begins his own successful novella, 'The Death of the Novel' (1969), with the following disclaimer, the strategy of which determines the form his fiction will take:

Fiction constitutes a way of looking at the world. Therefore I will begin by considering how the world looks in what I think we may now begin to call the contemporary post-realistic novel. Realistic fiction presupposed chronological time as the medium of a plotted narrative, an irreducible individual psyche as the subject of its characterization, and, above all, the ultimate, concrete reality of things as the object and rationale of its description. In the world of post-realism, however, all of these absolutes have become absolutely problematic.

The contemporary writer – the writer who is acutely in touch with the life of which he is a part – is forced to start from scratch: Reality doesn't exist, time doesn't exist, personality doesn't exist. God was the omniscient author, but he died; now no one knows the plot, and since our reality lacks the sanction of a creator, there's no guarantee as to the authenticity of the received version. Time is reduced to presence, the content of a series of discontinuous moments. Time is no longer purposive, and so there is no destiny, only chance. Reality is, simply, our experience, and objectivity is, of course, an illusion. Personality, after passing through a phase of awkward self-consciousness, has become, quite minimally, a mere locus for our experience. In view of these annihilations, it should be no surprise that literature, also, does not exist – how could it? There is only reading and writing, which are things we do, like eating and making love, to pass the time, ways of maintaining a considered boredom in the face of the abyss.

Not to mention a series of overwhelming social dislocations.

I walked into the cafeteria. I had been hired to teach an advanced honors seminar on The Death of the Novel. The kids from my class were sitting around...

(pp 41–2)

Thus the narrator, who is named 'Professor Ronald Sukenick', moves directly from theory to action, underscoring the novelist and theorist Ronald Sukenick's belief that art is not about experience, it is more experience. Rather than presenting the news, Sukenick's fiction provides a response to the news. By effacing the distinction between art and life, he avoids the biographical fallacy which might lead to a self-indulgent confessionalism – Sukenick is not writing 'about' anything, much less himself. But, from an honest confrontation with himself writing, a fiction is produced which yields all the requisite products of novelistic art: a rhythm to existence, a generative energy behind it and a sense of continuous flow which gives some intimation of the texture of life.

The distinctions among Sukenick, Gass and Sorrentino define the range of what truly innovative fiction can be. Gass, particularly in his *Willie Masters' Lonesome Wife* (1968), tries to reduce all fiction to language itself, aided by this critical principle established in his *Fiction and the Figures of Life* (1970):

It seems a country-headed thing to say: that literature is language, that stories and the places and the people in them are merely made of words as chairs are made of smoothed sticks and sometimes of cloth or metal tubes. Still, we cannot be too simple at the start, since the obvious is often the unobserved. Occasionally we should allow the trite to tease us into thought, for such old friends, the clichés in our life, are the only strangers we can know. It seems incredible, the ease with which we sink through books quite out of sight, pass clamorous pages into soundless dreams. That novels should be made of words, and merely words, is shocking, really. It's as though you had discovered that your wife were made of rubber: the bliss of all those years, the fears ... from sponge.

(p 27)

Gass is right: we are indeed 'so pathetically eager for this other life' that we tolerate all sorts of suspensions of disbelief in order to experience it vicariously, which is the substance of his novella about the sex-starved Willie Masters and the text which seeks his ravishment. But Sukenick's complementary *In Form: Digressions on the Act of Fiction* (1985), makes an important point:

Language is a self-contained system. Oui, monsieur. But the art of fiction and poetry lies precisely in opening that system up to experience beyond language. The obligation of fiction is to rescue experience from history, from politics, from commerce, from theory, even from language itself – from any system, in fact, that threatens to devitalize, or manipulate experience. The health of language depends upon its contact with experience, which it both embodies and helps to create. . . . The art field is a nexus of various kinds of energy, image, and experience. What they are, and how they interact, may in the long run be the most profitable area for criticism: the study of composition.

(p 11)

And so while Gass's fiction draws its substance from words, Sukenick's novels find creative, compositional energy in the imaginative confrontations within the writer's life and the text which results from it, most often a text following the imperative to create a Watts tower from that curiously intransitive verb, *to write*.

Gilbert Sorrentino's fiction bridges the narrow but important gap between Gass and Sukenick. His work can be fully abstract, such as the alphabetically organized *Splendide-Hôtel* (1973), yet it can also engage in biting satire both of its subject and of the writing act itself, as in the vitriolic *roman à clef*, *Imaginative Qualities of Actual Things* (1971):

One of my great problems with Anton Harley is that I can't make up enough terrible stories about him to make him totally unreal, absolutely fleshless and one-dimensional, lifeless, as my other characters are. I'm afraid that the reader may get the idea that some monster like this actually walks the earth. I assure them that although there are people who try to be Harleys, they can't quite make it. I'll do my best to make him totally unbelievable. I saw him on Second Avenue the other day. . . . It was seeing him that made me realize that I had to really stir this prose around to make sure that he doesn't walk around in this book with any degree of reality. That is, *his* reality. I want him to walk around in this book with my reality. Fiction. Fine.

(p 160)

Sorrentino's high moral ground for fiction is the area above and beyond semiotics – beyond the 'signals' which clutter novels, in his appraisal, pointing out too obviously the intended configurations in plot and character. Although such signals are reassuring and do create a climate of understanding, what the reader understands is only what he or she already knows – what is understood are the signals themselves. No such devices are allowed into Sorrentino's fiction without being so labelled, as in the passage with 'Anton Harley' above.

A self-conscious use (rather than intentional disabuse) of signals has been made by a group of writers who have taken full advantage of the revolt against the *conventions* of realism in order to return to realism itself with fresh enthusiasm, renewed purpose, and a new appreciation of what fiction's artifice can achieve. Unlike the self-proclaimed 'moral fiction' writer John Gardner (1933–82), who invoked Tolstoy's notion of God instructing, heroes enacting and writers recording for the edification of human kind, and most certainly unlike the 'mininalist' fiction of Anne Beattie (b. 1947) and Raymond Carver (b. 1938), which in Gardner's footsteps suspends all aesthetic innovation in favour of parsing out the most mundane concerns of superficial life (for fear of intruding with a humanly judgmental use of imagination), the 'experimental realists' such as Thomas McGuane (b. 1939), Grace Paley (b. 1922) and Stephen Dixon (b. 1936) construct a virtually new American novel of manners by allowing sign systems to grow naturally from their narrative materials – just as they do in life. The characters in these novels and short stories are often cast as readers of their culture; consider the neo-Western cowboy protagonist of Thomas McGuane's *Something to be Desired* (1984), who grows up on personal-survival narratives only to find his own adult life eclipsed by the stock lines people must speak in familiar situations. His man comes home from a life not on the cattle trail but with the United States Information Agency during the turmoil of the 1960s and 70s. He is pleased to note his experience 'in an epoch when it seemed to him there were actually signs, an era in which he could join the rest of the populace in the wonderful ongoing melodrama of inanimate objects. He thrilled to clothes and cars; he sat at an old tropical wicker desk which seemed to guarantee character in his work.' Back home in South-Western Montana, he delights in the tacky residue of popular culture, including 'such an early-day drive-in that it should have been one of the primary artifacts, alongside the buffalo jumps and Calamity Jane's favourite bar, of this good little town'. Seeing that so much of the world is manufactured, he tries to improve his own life, only to have this sense of 'something better' spoil the casually achieved happiness he has been lucky to enjoy.

This fiction of manners is not for everyone. Its themes and interests can be expressed in other ways, as writers who share similar concerns show; yet the difference in technique is essential, creating an entirely different form. The Canadian writer Margaret Atwood and the American Grace Paley have each devoted a certain portion of their work to issues of militarism, feminism and social welfare. Yet Atwood's basically political novel, *The Handmaid's Tale* (1985), is radically different from Paley's *Later the Same Day* (1985), a collection which draws on the formal techniques of the new American novel of manners. The grimly anti-utopian future of Gilead, Atwood's extrapolation of certain American political tendencies, is drawn quite differently from Paley's view of life as she sees it from her New York window, leaning out to shout some words of caution to a young father playing a bit too roughly with his little girl:

First I want to say you're about a generation ahead of your father in your attitude and behavior toward your child.

Really? Well? Anything else, ma'am?

Son, I said, leaning another two, three dangerous inches toward him. Son, I must tell you that madmen intend to destroy this beautifully made planet. That the murder of our children by these men has got to become a terror and a sorrow to you, and starting now, it had better interfere with any daily pleasure.

Speech, speech, he called.

I waited a minute, but he continued to look up. So, I said, I can tell by your general appearance and loping walk that you agree with me.

(p 101)

Paley's difference is to restrict her actual speeches to the PEN Congress and the White House lawn, while using her fiction to create a character who is prompted to cry out against some specifically dangerous behaviour and in the normal course of events relate it to the greater issues of our world. Her narrators speak with a peculiar sense of animation – 'It is something like I am a crazy construction worker in conversation with cement', one of them admits – because their energy comes from hands-on experience with the signs of life. She will have a drunken and enraged husband wave a pistol before his eyes 'as though it could clear fogs and smogs', and see all things graphically, from the sun setting as 'a red ball falling hopelessly west, just missing the Hudson River, Jersey City, Chicago, the Great Plains, the Golden Gate – falling falling' to the success of her immigrant father before the American flag: 'Under its protection and working like a horse, he'd read Dickens, gone to medical school, and shot like a surface-to-air missile right into the middle class.'

Stephen Dixon's novels and short-story collections employ these techniques and more in order to keep the possibilities for fiction expanding. Unlike the entropic styles and themes, from Pynchon to Beattie, which have found such favour with academic critics, his work is expansive rather than constricting, showing how within the range of familiar narrative techniques there remains a fresh world of discovery. The stories collected in *No Relief* (1976) enlarge situations which would otherwise be limiting: breaking up with a lover, saying farewell to a dying father, and having to tell people how large such vacancies loom. Dixon's first novel, *Work* (1977), confirms this method for his full-length fiction: how intricate a supposedly menial job can be, creating a virtual intertext of exponentially increasing meanings. Dixon's subsequent books extend these writerly tendencies. His finest short stories are found in the volumes *14 Stories* (1980), *Movies* (1983) and *Time to Go* (1984), where the motive to interconnect is kept within each text's bounds, with the result that these boundaries of the text generate the possibilities of narrative. A suicide's bullet crashing through the hotel window and initiating other stories all around town, a couple's parrying relationship as they attend a film, the memory of a father physically haunting (and guiding) a son's and his fiancée's trip to the jeweller for wedding rings – these title stories of the three collections show how Dixon views limits and conventions not as inhibitions but rather as invitations to write. The roots for such technique are comic, as in 'Love Has Its Own Action' (from *14 Stories*), where the event of a meeting and separation is replicated several times, each time becoming faster and less justified, until by the story's final paragraph the narrator is sundering old alliances and forming new ones at the rate of one per sentence. Yet there is ample opportunity for pathos as well as humour, as 'The Sub' (from this same collection) demonstrates in its intricacies of fantasy and reality. The narrator has had a casual meeting with a young woman and fills Dixon's story with his optatives and subjectives for success, climaxing with a final run-through of what he could imagine happening after a first date:

The weekend after that we could plan to camp out. I'd bring the sleeping bags and just in case there's a bug problem I'm sure I could borrow a tent. In a month I could ask to move in with her or if she's with her parents or roommate we could look for our own place. But I'd prefer going abroad with her for around six weeks. Ancient hotels, inexpensive bistros and cafés. Light and dark native beers and stouts and all the time drawing a chronicle of our trip: everything from the rickety buses and flying buttresses to Judy dressing, undressing, sipping cafés au lait in big fluffy beds. We could return by ship if the fare's not too steep, rent a flat in this neighborhood so I could be near by school and folks. And maybe after a while we could get married and have a child or get married without having a child or have a child without getting married but living together, loving one another, subbing for most of the year and drawing, engraving, maybe trying my hand at woodcuts and aquatints.

(p 53)

One sees how Dixon allows his narrator to create a life out of the very conventions of syntax and verbal mood which other writers have found constricting. His story has proceeded this way for nearly twenty pages, and even its conclusion remains open ended: 'I think this will happen one day though I don't think the woman it will happen with will necessarily be her.'

In McGuane's, Paley's and Dixon's writing, such apt verbal structures grow naturally from the social behaviour they have observed. As signs of value and meaning, they themselves are the elements which create stories which are tellable in imaginatively valid ways. Their verbal music takes its melody from the semiotically and syntactically traceable actions of their characters – the key is not just observation but animation, showing how lives are lived within the generating terms of social intercourse and behaviour. As such, this style of fiction helps solve the problem created when anti-mimetic innovative fiction set itself against the assumptions of conventional realism twenty years ago. A wealth of talented Experimentalists have in the meantime pushed the novel to its limits: Raymond Federman (b. 1928) striving in *Double or Nothing* (1971) to articulate the unspeakable by conveying the sense of absence in his subject (the act of writing about a family lost to the Holocaust), Walter Abish (b. 1931) struggling against the limits of a strictly alphabetical structure in *Alphabetical Africa* (1974) and a phenomenologically resistant narrative surface in *How German Is It* (1980), Michael Stephens (b. 1946) exploiting the undulations of language itself in *Paragraphs* (1974), and Kenneth Gangemi restricting language to the form of a cinematic treatment in *The Interceptor Pilot* (1980). Yet life-studies still demand their space on the novel's canvas, and a self-apparent use of signs as the material of fiction has achieved the same end as the abstract experiments and elaborate typology of the innovators named above. Such signs are not lifeless entities, for man is the sign-making animal who places the essence of his soul in the media by which he communicates. In this way the literary concerns of the new American fiction remain identical with the way we most truly live.

14

LITERATURE AND SOCIETY

Marcus Cunliffe

Changes since 1900

The main emphasis of this book has been the literature of successive avant-gardes. In other words, upon 'highbrow' writing, to use
the annoying term first popularized by Van Wyck Brooks early in
the century; and – two similarly unlikeable but convenient labels –
upon 'creative' or 'imaginative' writing. Our nineteenth-century
ancestors might well find such an emphasis puzzlingly incomplete.
Ralph Waldo Emerson, for example, hardly ever read novels and
hardly ever liked those that did come his way. Poetry was more
important to him, and it figured prominently in bygone histories of
literature. So did a mass of writing of the kind our own age is apt to
lump together, somewhat dismissively, as 'non-fiction': the essay,
the sermon, the political tract, prose satire, philosophy, economics,
anthropology, biology, memoirs, historical biography and narrative,
travel and exploration.

My essay is concerned with the shift that has taken place in the
definition of 'literature', since about 1900. As a field of serious
study, in the 'creative' sense, it has come to mean primarily fiction,
poetry and drama – in that order. Fiction – the novel and the short
story – has attracted the greatest amount of attention. Generalizations about the American character and the American psyche
often use fiction as their basic material. Poetry too is taken
seriously, but by a more limited audience, and has not been required to bear quite so heavy an interpretative burden. Drama
comes a poor third. There has been less of it, a less continuous
advance, and the complicating factor that the impact of a play
depends not only upon the text but upon acting and stagecraft.
Waiting upon these three creative forms comes literary criticism:
their servant, though at times a rather imperious one, like a butler in
what he views as a parvenu household.

I wish to discuss first the changing atmosphere of such literature in the America of the twentieth century; then to relate it to other types of writing, and to the mechanisms by which all kinds of literature have been merchandized. Next we can consider whether the imaginative avant-garde literature of the past decades deserves to be considered as profoundly representative of American society as a whole. This will lead to some comments on the nature of American society, the links between 'highbrow' and 'middlebrow' culture during the century, and finally to a sketch of thought-patterns I believe to underlie many of the hopes and fears of American citizenry at all levels.

First the changes since 1900. These are so conspicuous that we might seem to be talking about two (or perhaps several) different worlds. If the fiddles were tuning up between 1890 and the First World War, the main sound of the orchestra was still brass and woodwind. Or, to put the matter differently, American literature was dominated by the standards of the educated, Protestant, Europe-oriented middle class. The Wild West was only beginning to be discovered as the presumed true source of Americanness; and the discovery owed a good deal to the promotional efforts of such Harvard-trained Easterners as Theodore Roosevelt and Owen Wister. Frederick Jackson Turner's celebrated paper on 'The Significance of the Frontier in American History', which he delivered in 1893, took some years to make its way among the rest of his profession. The guiding 'germ theory' among historians, eventually ousted by Turner's 'Frontier thesis', was that American institutions derived from European origins. The vital element was the source, not the outcome.

Literary modes were similarly derivative. The American vernacular was thought only to be suitable for humorous effects. In one of her early review-essays Willa Cather scolded Mark Twain for his vulgarity. The uncouthness of *Pudd'nhead Wilson*, she suggested, marred the tone of the distinguished *Century* magazine in which it was serialized. Twain himself adopted a very different style, of the limpid-archaic variety, for his fictional biography *Joan of Arc* (1896) – a work he may privately have felt was his masterpiece. The editors he wished to impress were men like Richard Watson Gilder of the *Century*. Gilder was a fluent versifier, a worker for respectable good causes, a recipient of honorary degrees, and the author among many other works of *Grover Cleveland, a·Record of Friendship* (1910). Van Wyck Brooks has recalled pre-war undergraduate days at Harvard. Brooks and other budding writers feasted upon English and Continental authors; American literature they ignored as an inferior local product. T. S. Eliot, also a Harvard student, may never quite have escaped this early conviction that the best authors were probably long dead, and for that reason unlikely to be American. There were of course grounds for such a prejudice, since the sum total of American literary achievement was not yet gigantic; and it was reinforced by the vogue for historical romance that coexisted with the rise of realism. Before 1914, American intellectuals were well aware of the sly dig in the jest by Thomas Wentworth Higginson that 'the man who is really cosmopolitan feels at home even in his own country'. In general American literature of the period resembled that of England, but with less assurance and with rather less robustness.

The instinct of sex was, as Henry Adams remarked, almost absent from the American novel. Thomas Hardy, not to mention French novelists, could get away with intimations of sexuality that led to semi-suppression in the case of Theodore Dreiser's *Sister Carrie* (1900). One common argument was that the American novel ought to differ from the European because American life itself differed. Unlike the French, American men did not have sex on the brain. They did not scheme incessantly on how to seduce women. American women, married or unmarried, made plain that they were not sexually available. Another common argument, not easily compatible with the theory of superior American morals, was that literature had a didactic effect. The writer might claim he had a duty to portray how people actually think and behave. This could be conceded to a degree; after all, the Bible was full of stories about fornication. But the writer also had a duty to implant moral lessons. Retribution must overtake the sinner, especially in the case of sexual depravity. Thus the gravest charge against *Sister Carrie* was that the heroine continued to prosper in spite of her immoral ways. Naturally enough, the same didactic code operated in the theatre. Scoundrels and cads must get their come-uppance before the final curtain. The code was made explicit by Hollywood's Hays Office in the 1920s. This censoring body announced a rule of 'compensating values', according to which reprehensible conduct had to be conspicuously reprehended. Virtue must triumph over vice.

Traces of Comstockery – the censorship of literature by zealous committees and individuals – still remain in the United States. But to an even greater degree than in Europe the public restraints on sexual candour have disappeared. The process can be traced from the end of the First World War with the emergence of the 'flapper' and the new college generation. In 1919 James Branch Cabell's

Jurgen, a whimsical novel of erotic adventure, both shocked and titillated. During the next twenty years an increasing casualness and frankness in describing sex was apparent. The licence claimed by avant-garde writers – Ernest Hemingway, E. E. Cummings, John Dos Passos, James T. Farrell – was fairly soon incorporated in popular best-sellers such as Hervey Allen's *Anthony Adverse* (1933) and Margaret Mitchell's *Gone With the Wind* (1936), and still more in the next decade by books like *Forever Amber* and *Peyton Place*. By 1948 it was just possible (Gore Vidal's *The City and the Pillar*) to introduce homosexuality as an overt theme. William Burroughs, Allen Ginsberg, John Rechy and others went further in saying the hitherto unsayable. In various essays of the 1950s Leslie Fiedler outraged an older generation of critics by asserting that homo-erotic relationships were a central aspect of American 'classics' – *Moby Dick, Huckleberry Finn* and so on. At the beginning of the century 'dirty books' were always by foreign authors, usually under a Paris imprint. Wartime GIs discovered that their expatriate countryman Henry Miller (*Tropic of Cancer*, 1934; *Black Spring*, 1936; *Tropic of Capricorn*, 1939) had been producing a series of attractively scabrous confessions. Back from Paris too came Terry Southern's parody-pornography *Candy*, and in the same year (1955) Vladimir Nabokov's *Lolita*, which dwelt on the sexual appeal for older men of the 'nymphet'. A ferocious obscenity characterized Norman Mailer's 'The Time of Her Time', *An American Dream* (1965) and *Why Are We in Vietnam?* (1967). Gore Vidal's *Myra Breckinridge* (1968) exposed its hero/heroine to a change of sex. *Portnoy's Complaint* (1969), by Philip Roth, explained the thrills of adolescent masturbation. During the 1960s the public could gaze upon topless waitresses in California and live sex-shows on New York's West 42nd Street. Underground magazines and cartoon-books took for granted that their readers were mainly concerned with sex and drugs; *Fritz the Cat* was light-years away from the innocent frolics of *Krazy Cat* in the 1920s. Fiedler among others argued that an entire substitution of values was taking place, away from the old ethic of he-man competitiveness towards a new, relaxed, communal style: a shift symbolized by the transference from a 'whisky' to a 'pot' culture.

Certainly the repudiation of the old, sententious, genteelly cautious American culture of 1900 has been mirrored in the nation's literature. In 1900 the typical author was a Protestant, probably of British descent. During the next decades this Gilderish man of letters mutated into many different forms. He might well be

Jewish or black or avowedly homosexual. He might be living almost anywhere from Seattle to Casablanca. He might be teaching in a university – a striking development since 1945. And of course 'he' might be a 'she', though until the 1980s most of the prizes were still being borne off by male authors.

As in most Western countries, American twentieth-century literature has been increasingly one of 'alienation'. In avant-garde fiction one can trace the gradual disappearance of the qualities of worthiness formerly attributed to the main characters. Even the strongest (as in Hemingway) go down to defeat. The majority are either victims or slobs. Decency may still be a preserve of childhood (Sherwood Anderson's story, 'I Want to Know Why'; J. D. Salinger's *The Catcher in the Rye*, 1951), but the adult world is repugnantly gross. On the other hand, American literature has discarded diffidence along with reticence. In all its main branches, though still with greatest felicity in comedy and satire, American creative writing has absorbed the vernacular. Indeed, by the 1930s English authors were beginning to envy Americans their abundance of demotic styles, and to lament the relative insipidity of 'English English'. American literature by then enjoyed at least equal status with that coming from Britain; and much of the best 'English' literature was in any case either Irish (James Joyce, W. B. Yeats) or American (T. S. Eliot). By the 1960s the old Anglo-American cultural relationship was decisively reversed: the major contribution, in quantity and in quality, was American. A generation earlier it was still fairly usual for American intellectuals to lament the vulgarities of their spiritual climate. By 1970 their quarrel with American society was tinged with a certain relish – as if to say: America is uniquely monstrous, and *therefore* the best place for the writer; this is where the action is. Neither the grumble nor the boast would have made much sense in 1900. By the 1980s American culture, however defined, was so omnipresent, on every continent, that it was influencing if not establishing the standards of taste at every level – from Nobel-prize economics and medicine to architecture and blue jeans, from abstract art and music to hamburgers and cola.

The Sociology of Literature

There is a resultant query that Emerson might have raised and which has arisen in the different contexts of our own time. How far can we understand avant-garde literature without placing it in its society as a whole? Does it deserve to be regarded as representative of that society?

The answer turns on how we define 'literature'. Leaving aside for the moment the genres of 'non-fiction' that Emerson would have thought significant, literature in the broadest sense could include everything that is sung, spoken or put into print. Some aspects of this vast realm – Pop lyrics, for example, or movie techniques – may exert a direct influence upon the avant-garde writer. There could be something foolishly blinkered about discussing twentieth-century novels without any reference to the cinema. Some writers have worked in Hollywood, willingly or sheepishly. Many of their stories and novels have been made into films, usually to the financial benefit of the author though not always to his aesthetic satisfaction. In some instances though, such as John Steinbeck's *Of Mice and Men* and *The Grapes of Wrath*, the films may actually have been better than the books. A number of novelists have dreamed of making films; Norman Mailer is one of those who took the plunge. In the case of playwrights – Arthur Miller, Tennessee Williams, Sam Shepard, David Mamet – stage and screen have powerfully influenced one another. For both writer and reader, awareness of the cinema has affected the entire situation. Style and expectations have tended to become more cinematic. In a full evaluation of creative literature, the film of Jack Kerouac's *Pull My Daisy* (1961), those from the Andy Warhol stable, or a mass of older movies (whether appreciated seriously or in a 'camp' way), may be as important a determinant as books in book-form.

Or, if we confine ourselves to the printed word, it is salutary to reflect that avant-garde writing is only a tiny proportion of an immense, heterogeneous output. Print, with or without accompanying illustrations, provides information, advertisement, entertainment, uplift. Writing is a commodity handled by the brand of business enterprise known as publishing. The commonest form of reading is probably the newspaper, together with a medley of magazines. The average student of literature may, among these, have heard of *Reader's Digest*, which started in 1922. Scores of other magazines catering for specialized audiences – women, car-owners, teenagers, hobbyists – are probably unknown to him, though their combined circulation in a single month vastly exceeds that of all the highbrow publications in a decade.

Publishers, being businessmen, have had to reckon with these elementary facts. The twenty or so principal commercial firms (as distinct from university presses) which have constituted serious publishing could never forget the need to show a profit. The frequent failures and mergers that make up publishing history are a sufficient reminder of market realities. A publisher might be proud to have the most talented authors on his list. But talent and profitability have not been synonymous. Twentieth-century poetry, with the exception of an occasional book like S. V. Benét's *John Brown's Body* (1928), could be expected to lose money. This was true also of volumes of short stories, and to a growing extent of the majority of novels. The publisher's best hope, in the case of avant-garde writing, was that an author's reputation might enlarge over the years. Few of the names that bulk large in good critical histories of twentieth-century American literature, such as those by Alfred Kazin, appeared initially on best-seller lists. Sinclair Lewis was unusual in this respect: *Main Street* (1920) was a best-seller and so were most of his books in the next fifteen to twenty years. But even he had published several novels before he achieved fame and wealth with *Main Street*. Scott Fitzgerald established a reputation and made some money with *This Side of Paradise* (1920), when he was in his early twenties. Up to his death in 1940 he earned a sizeable income by knocking off short stories for popular magazines like the *Saturday Evening Post*, and later by collaborating on film scripts in Hollywood. He did not however (to his dismay) gain much income from *The Great Gatsby* (1925) or *Tender Is the Night* (1934). Edith Wharton had written a dozen books before she climbed into 'best-sellerdom' with *The Age of Innocence* (1920). Hemingway did not appear on the best-seller list until the publication of *For Whom the Bell Tolls* (1940). William Faulkner was never a favourite with the general public. The most successful novel of the 1920s in America, in sales, was *The Sheik* (1921), an abduction-fantasy by an obscure Englishwoman named Edith M. Hull. It became the 'book-of-the-film' when Rudolph Valentino starred in a movie version, and sold over a million copies. The most discussed 'college novel' of the early 1920s was not *This Side of Paradise* but the best-selling *Plastic Age* (1924) by Percy Marks. In the nine years 1917–25 the most consistently popular American writer was a former New York dentist, Zane Grey, who hit his stride with *Riders of the Purple Sage* (1912) and subsequently climbed high on the lists with such Western sagas as *The Mysterious Rider* and *The Call of the Canyon*. A generation later, the public bought several million copies of *Vengeance Is Mine, Kiss Me, Deadly* and other pieces of detective fiction by Mickey Spillane. Its favourite novels in 1951 were James Jones's *From Here to Eternity* and Herman Wouk's *The Caine Mutiny*: more book-of-the-film examples.

The point is not that best-sellers were necessarily trash. Some were:

Spillane's thuggish hero Mike Hammer was far inferior to Dashiell Hammett's Sam Spade or the best of Raymond Chandler's stories of Philip Marlowe. But James Gould Cozzens's *By Love Possessed* (1957) and William Styron's *Confessions of Nat Turner* (1967) were at first acclaimed by critics before they changed their minds. There was a tendency on the part of little-magazine reviewers to assume that any widely read book was *per se* worthless. Their disdain could be extravagant. The important consideration is that, unless writers were prepared to confine themselves to avant-garde publications, able to pay little or nothing, they had to survive in the realm of commercial publishing.

To stay in business a publisher had to hit upon profitable items. Simon and Schuster, two aspiring young publishers, launched themselves in 1924 with a series of crossword-books. Viking Press in 1927 began to prosper by issuing *Ask Me Another* quiz books. In fiction, publishers were obliged to hunt for answers to the formula parodied in one recommendation: 'it has everything – horror, sex, madness, and depravity, all handled with dignity and restraint'. The foundation of the Book-of-the-Month Club in 1926, followed by a number of others including the Literary Guild, increased the chance of income at the risk of standardizing the desired product. After 1945 the prodigious expansion of paperback publishing threw conventional publishing and bookselling into chaos. Optimists declared with some justification that more good literature than ever was now available to the public. If poetry and drama did not greatly benefit, the writer of fiction could see his work resurrected long after it had disappeared in hard cover from the display of new fiction and then the melancholy piles of remaindered books. The fortunate handful of well-known novelists could now hope for paperback advances big enough to make them millionaires in a couple of years. Pessimists, however, predicted the disappearance of the old-style publisher, and the swamping of the paperback market through overproduction. Publishing, they said, was a frantic and unstable industry. Gone for ever was the possibility that editors of the calibre of Maxwell Perkins would have time and inclination to grapple with recalcitrant geniuses, as Perkins did with Thomas Wolfe. Books were now, revealingly, classified either as 'college' or as 'trade'. The former were aimed at adoption for required texts; the latter, a dismally miscellaneous category, covered everything else.

As this division suggests, imaginative writing was somewhat peripheral to the publishing industry – and indeed had been through most of the century. Again, best-seller lists put the situation in perspective. In the United States three books sold more than a million copies during the 1920s. One was *The Sheik*. The other two were H. G. Wells's *Outline of History* and Will Durant's *Story of Philosophy*. Other leading non-fiction best-sellers of the decade were Emily Post's *Etiquette* (1923), Emile Coué's *Self-Mastery Through Conscious Auto-Suggestion* (also 1923), Lulu Hunt Peters's *Diet and Health* (1924) and Ernest Dimnet's *Art of Thinking* (1929). Now and then a fiction best-seller gladdened a publisher's heart, as *Anthony Adverse* and *Gone With the Wind* did in the severe Depression of the 1930s. The most reliable mainstay however was non-fiction: self-help, popular religion, sexology, health, cookery, history and biography, advice on investments, documented scandal, accounts of adventure, reminiscences. Among conspicuous examples were Bruce Barton's *The Man Nobody Knows* (1925), a portrait of Jesus Christ as a pioneer businessman; Dale Carnegie's *How to Win Friends and Influence People* (1937); *A Guide to Confident Living* (1949) by Norman Vincent Peale, who brought more comfort to America with his subsequent *Power of Positive Thinking*; and Dr Benjamin Spock's *Common Sense Book of Baby and Child Care* (1946). Some, like Dr Spock's, were deserved successes. Some enterprises, such as the ghost-written memoirs of ex-presidents, actresses and other celebrities, were deserved failures. A number of best-sellers such as Charles Reich's *The Greening of America* (1970) engrossed attention for a reason and were then forgotten. Non-fiction admittedly could not as a rule be translated into movies or Broadway shows, though Woody Allen made a brave attempt with his film of Dr Reuben's *All You Wanted to Know About Sex but Were Afraid to Ask*. But they were the publisher's standby; and the many reputable titles on publishers' lists, to which we shall return, helped to substantiate the simple fact that cumulatively non-fiction was more essential than fiction or of course poetry and drama to publishers' balance-sheets. A few writers of mediocre books became rich on the proceeds. So did a few authors of considerably greater talent. Most authors, highbrow or middlebrow, survived in the interstices of a complicated precarious industry, which in turn survived through an intricate dependence upon agents, publicity and other 'media' (also a revealing term) – newspapers and magazines, radio and television, the live theatre, and above all Hollywood. We come back to the question: has twentieth-century avant garde literature been truly representative of American society when, judged by numbers, that society has preferred to read other

things, or not to read at all? By 1960 the annual American consumption of comic books had passed the billion mark; expenditure
on them, estimated at $100 million a year, was four times as large as
the combined budgets of all the public libraries.

The Truthfulness of Literature

One obvious response is that, in the United States as elsewhere,
'good' writing has always been a minority enterprise. If works are
assessed merely by their popularity, Nathaniel Hawthorne was
overshadowed by what he called 'a damned mob of scribbling
women'. So were Emily Dickinson, Walt Whitman and Herman
Melville. Best-sellers operate at one level, and may tell us things of
some value – usually things the author was not trying to convey –
about the approved or concealed appetites and aversions of their
day. According to this argument, the popularity of Zane Grey would
be a guide to the average American's nostalgic fondness for simple,
heroic behaviour. The continuing audience for crime and detection
stories, from Sherlock Holmes to Ian Fleming, and John Le Carré,
could have several explanations: appreciation for cleverness combined with courage, delight in vicarious violence, escape from
everyday problems, the insatiable curiosity of human beings to find
out what happened – greater than their desire to puzzle out why it
happened. The consolatory appeal of books entitled *Smile or Perish*
or *How to Live With Your Ulcer* is evident enough. Laughter seems to
be another basic need, though the sociologist of popular culture
might speculate on the increasingly conspicuous display of
happiness in twentieth-century America. One sociologist has indeed measured the growing width of the smile on the faces in
advertisements; and anyone who overhears a radio or TV programme is likely to be struck by the frequency of the mechanical
bursts of laughter that punctuate it.

The easy explanation, then, is that popular literature caters to
immediate enthusiasms or anxieties, generally in a superficial or
calculated way. As fiction it deals in stereotypes, which may actually
be anachronistic as well as bigoted. One would therefore expect to
find that popular melodrama, in print or in the cinema, would
persist in portraying heroes and heroines as traditional 'WASP'
Americans when avant-garde fiction had already come closer to the
truth of national diversity. One would also expect stereotyped
villains and buffoons – scheming Orientals, foreign-born radicals,
English dudes, black Sambos. Popular poetry ought to obey similar

dictates: that is, to be easily comprehensible and heavily rhythmic, and to embody popular precepts, as in the daily verse Edgar A. Guest used to churn out for the Detroit *Free Press* ('It takes a heap o' livin' in a house t'make it home').

The implication of this contrast between highbrow and lowbrow is between work written for its own sake, and work produced on commission: between something created and something manufactured. The genuine imaginative writer, we gather, may appear to be totally out of step with his time but is in fact acutely perceptive. Since he is not being paid to flatter or amuse his audience, he writes without fear or favour. He is merely out of his time in the sense of being in the vanguard of consciousness. The main body of opinion will in due course reach the position he has attained, though he himself will no doubt have moved on again. He is thus a prophet. Though he may seem to be without honour, he is not ignored. What bohemia thinks today, the suburbs will think they think tomorrow. In the history of artistic innovation the innovator is invariably vindicated. The book banned in one year will be applauded or taken for granted a few years afterwards. The violent disapproval that typically greets a new imaginative statement is a sign of its power to stir an audience; anger is the beginning of wisdom. One might add that our hypothetical truthteller is distinguished by his feeling for language. He is intensely preoccupied with words and endlessly ready to experiment with them. The run-of-the-mill writer, on the other hand, is often merely fluent. At its worst his prose is simply wordage. His artifices are apt to be rhetorical tricks, conventional stimuli to evoke a conventional response. In consequence, the manipulative element very quickly becomes apparent to even a casual reader, let alone a connoisseur of *kitsch*. A bad popular book, scrutinized a few years after publication, seems like a poorly staged puppet show – all jerks and dangling threads. Even a competent best-seller tends to go stale before long. If so, this may be because it is basically insincere or inauthentic. Nothing puts the wary reader more on his guard than a paragraph that begins 'Sincerely . . .' or 'Frankly . . .'

The trouble is that the highbrow-lowbrow contrast is much too neat, especially as applied to the literature of recent years. American men of letters have never as a group felt comfortable with the 'elitist' proposition that good art is and can only be appreciated by a small proportion of people. Democracy is based on the theory that issues are best decided by numbers. If the majority is right in politics, why not in literature? The notion of 'giving the public what it wants' has seemed ideologically as well as commercially sound. One objection to the dominant genteel tradition of the early twentieth century was that it entrusted cultural judgments to an unresponsive minority of snobs for whom 'the wind blew from the East'. In other words, they were anglophiles who sought to impose English class-values upon a pluralistic, aspiringly democratic native culture. They were 'alienated' from the imaginative life of their own land. This condemnation was for instance vigorously expressed by H. L. Mencken in many essays between about 1915 and 1930. American political conservatism, as a body of doctrine, is singularly thin and discontinuous. Cultural conservatism has found more defenders, though until the 1970s their complaints have often been muted and oblique. In the earlier twentieth century such traditionalists as Irving Babbitt, Paul Elmer More and the Southern Agrarians were certainly outside the mainstream of intellectual discourse.

The American democratic creed asserts that the majority is always right, or at any rate that minority-dictates are ultimately unacceptable. The spokesmen for avant-garde culture, however, have for a good many years believed that in matters of taste the majority is nearly always wrong. The discrepancy is easy to detect in Mencken's work. He was consistent in resisting any form of cultural overlordship, whether that of the old high priests of the genteel persuasion or that of censuring bodies – officially charged or self-appointed. But in his view, made heretically clear in *Notes on Democracy* (1926), the mass of Americans were 'boobs', and bigoted, conformist boobs at that. Which public then was he addressing? Why try to protect Americans against things most of them approved of? Mencken no doubt would have said that democracy was the least bad of the conceivable polities, and that it had to be defended from its own more foolish products (compare the remark of John Adams, more than a century earlier: 'Democracy is Lovelace and the people is Clarissa'). But his argument did not hang together. Ordinary Americans after all had contributed the profusion of slang he chronicled with such relish in *The American Language* (1919). Which were the desirable and which the harmful forces in American life? Could they be separated?

Various answers have been offered in the twentieth century. Mencken and some contemporaries singled out particular tendencies, notably 'Puritanism', for reprobation. Or they poured scorn on particular types of Americans. In Mencken's case the villains included politicians (he agreed with the dictum that 'the politician is the courtier of democracy'), most clergymen, and most college professors and presidents. These more or less correspond to the guardians of culture and ideology whom Coleridge called the 'clerisy'. Mencken rejected their claims because he thought them pompous asses, and because he repudiated the very principle of a civic culture maintained by recognized arbiters. Matthew Arnold had said of England (*Culture and Anarchy*, 1869): 'Our society distributes itself into Barbarians, Philistines, and Populace', these roughly equivalent to upper, middle, and lower class; 'and America is just ourselves, with the Barbarians quite left out, and the Populace nearly so'.

Similar statements are fairly common, among American as well as European analysts. There was wide agreement that the United States was a society of the middle, without a coherent aristocracy at the top or a self-conscious proletariat at the bottom. Yet, from Emerson to Mencken, there was also agreement that the vital spark of American culture was kept alive by America's plain folk – unsophisticated, unawed, quick, intuitive. So the enemy of the 'highbrow' in the good sense was not the 'lowbrow': these two extremes of culture needed one another. The insidious threat arose from the inhabitants of America's Philistia – Middle America, as it came to be known in the 1960s. The essential clash in the nation's culture was thus between highbrow and middlebrow. Mass-culture was awful, in some respects. But sometimes a folk-style pushed through, in jazz, in vaudeville, in popular verbal humour, in the silent-film era of Charlie Chaplin, Buster Keaton and Harry Langdon, and later in the slapstick comedies of the Marx Brothers. The pace, the freshness and the fantasy of this side of American life were praised as early as 1924 in *The Seven Lively Arts*, a book by the Harvard-educated critic Gilbert Seldes. Edmund Wilson and the poet E. E. Cummings shared some of Seldes's enthusiasm. The curse of mass-culture, in their view, was its increasing passivity and commercialism. But it was always capable of producing its own grass-roots material. The customer quickly got wise to attempts to manipulate him, as one could tell from the popularity of *Mad* magazine and comparably sassy publications during the 1950s and 1960s. And even the crassest of commercial offerings were at least unpretentious. The wooing of the mass-culture market is an open covenant openly arrived at. Indeed with the 1950s popular culture as pop culture became an intellectual vogue. This might seem quite unconnected with the old didactic American assumption that art ought to spring democratically from the people – the People with a capital P. Sometimes it was a chic in-joke, as with the 'camp' admiration for the musicals of Busby Berkeley or the tough-guy films of Humphrey Bogart. In general it was *Against Interpretation* – the title of a book of intelligently modish essays (1966) by the critic (or anti-critic) Susan Sontag. One reason for looking askance at high culture was the suspicion in some intellectual quarters that the orthodox novel was an exhausted genre – irritatingly 'fictitious' and not sufficiently imaginative. Nevertheless the indulgent acceptance of popular culture was in line with an old American tradition, and easily compatible with political radicalism.

Middlebrow culture – 'midcult' in Dwight MacDonald's coinage – was handled more sharply. But the nature of the complaint against it altered. The accusation in Mencken's day was that the middlemen who regarded themselves as the nation's clerisy were obtuse, anachronistic and repressive. Thirty years later, the unforgivable sin of middlebrow taste was said to be not its imperviousness but, on the contrary, its own frantic desire to be chic, to be in the swim, to keep up with the way-out Joneses (LeRoi – as he then was: subsequently transformed into Imamu Amiri Baraka – in preference to James Jones). With each year the time-lag between avant-garde and main body diminished. The United States always prided itself on being the newest country, the one most ready to welcome change. Changes in style are commercially essential to a consumer society; the rise of Modernism in the arts is paralleled by the rise of advertising as an institution, itself claiming to be the chief authority on the 'media' by which manufacturer and artist alike seek to communicate with their public. Once the notion of Modernism in the arts was accepted, the middling American was perfectly ready to look at, and perhaps profit by purchasing, Action painting, Pop art, Op (for 'optical') art, Magic realism, or whatever brand was 'in'. Madison Avenue advertising agencies helped to keep him culturally on his toes; so did magazine articles that regularly explained what was in and what was out. Hippy, yippy and later yuppy, modes were imitated overnight by hordes of youngsters. In the 1960s undergraduates began to 'drop out' in quantity, though afterward many dropped in again and went on to graduate school to qualify for respectable professional careers. A group sharing rooms in a rented house of the sixties might well call it a 'commune'. Jeans and long hair became so universal among the youth of both sexes – a new theme for cartoonists – that the observable differences between culture or class levels became still harder to distinguish. Magazines that had once been clear about which segment of the public constituted their readership began desperately to modify their house-style. *Life*, *Harper's*, the *Saturday Review*, the *Saturday Evening Post* and other pillars of middlebrow culture changed direction or disappeared.

In keeping with the curious American mix of commercial and ideological motives, midcult was swift to revise its stereotypes. In 1930 Owen Wister could without apparent embarrassment stigmatize the 'Broadway Jew' as a menace to cleancut American entertainment. By 1950 anti-Semitism of that openly casual sort was no longer tolerable in ordinary literature. Little by little the American Indian, hitherto usually the villain or victim of Western fiction, was metamorphosed into hero and sometimes even winner. Publishers and the other media hastened to do the same office for the Negro American. A generation that had been taught to use 'Negro' as the polite designation now tried to re-educate itself into substituting 'black', and into paying at least lip-service to the proposition that black was beautiful. Early in the century one could almost take for granted that the 'good' characters in a novel would have Anglo-Saxon names. The 'bad' characters were likely to be halfbreeds, foreigners, Orientals. Mr Moto, the Japanese sleuth in John P. Marquand's *Saturday Evening Post* stories of the 1930s, was the first unequivocally virtuous and accomplished Oriental hero to be portrayed in American literature. By 1970 the process had gone so far that the good guys in popular fiction were likely not to be Anglo-Saxon while, to avoid giving offence to minority groups, the villains were often allotted Anglo-Saxon names. Women were likewise redefined, in an evolution far from concluded (and discussed again later in this chapter). The American history shelves in paperback bookstores were dominated by Indian, black, 'ethnic' and feminist material.

The lines between highbrow, middlebrow and lowbrow prove so hard to draw that one is tempted to conclude that these categories are hopelessly artificial. We have seen that avant-garde culture has tended to assert a kinship with lowbrow or popular culture, and to deny affinities with midcult. But the embrace of midcult has been close, if stultifying. If avant-garde literature is recognizable mainly through a brief precedence *in time*, then a lead of a year or two may not seem of much significance. If sales and celebrity are an index to quality, what are we to make of the Nobel prizes, the Guggenheim fellowships, the Pulitzer awards, and the sheer income accruing to a number of 'serious' authors, especially novelists, ever since Sinclair Lewis? By the test of sensitiveness to racial prejudice, there is not much to choose between highbrow and middlebrow writing. Jack London, realist and socialist, was capable of a repellent short story that foretold the slaughter of the entire population of China by means of germ warfare. Ezra Pound's *Cantos*, masterly as poetry, revealed an obsession with 'Jewish' usury. Though William Styron's *Confessions of Nat Turner* (1968) enraged a number of black readers, the issue was not really whether his novel had literary merit but rather whether he had shown his black hero in an unfavourable light. If it had appeared a few years earlier it might have been acclaimed as brilliant and sympathetic.

A Sick Society?

Even so, many students of America believed and perhaps still believe there is a gulf between two cultures in America. In Lionel Trilling's terminology, it is the gulf between the 'adversary culture' and the middle, mainstream, or official culture. This sense of mutual antagonism, artistic and political, goes back at least sixty years. The little magazines of the 1920s proclaimed an aesthetic revolt. The controversy over the Italian-born anarchists Sacco and Vanzetti, arrested for murder in 1920 and finally executed in 1927, symbolized the division. On one side were the authorities, in the shape of the Governor of Massachusetts, the judge who heard the case and the President of Harvard who was asked to review it. On the other side were most of America's intellectuals under the age of forty – convinced that Sacco and Vanzetti were being tried for their presumed opinions and not for their unprovable actions, and that America was, in the words of John Dos Passos, 'two nations'.

Seen in such a perspective, the adversary culture is or was quite rightly alienated from middle America. America according to this position is a sick society, increasingly given over to violence, aggression, greed, corruption and falsehood. To the extent that middlebrow culture imitates the adversary culture, it is in effect therefore supposedly admitting the truth laid bare by serious novelists, poets and dramatists. After all, a more reputable clerisy than the ignoramuses derided by Mencken has also produced searching criticisms. Revelations of actual American behaviour in Vietnam seemed to validate Joseph Heller's *Catch 22* (1961) and Terry Southern's film script for *Dr Strangelove; or, How I Learned to Stop Worrying and Love the Bomb* – as if fiction's challenge was to rival the lunatic dimensions of reality. America-boosters in the 1950s could draw no great comfort from such sociological surveys as David Riesman's *The Lonely Crowd*, William H. Whyte Jr's *The Organization Man* and C. Wright Mills's *The Power Elite*. A decade later they were beginning to be confronted with books like *The End of the American Era*, by the historian Andrew Hacker. Hacker maintained that the United States had lost its way since the Second World War, by following out its creed of acquisitive individualism to the logical, inescapable conclusion. Every American institution – business, education, government, the family – was a failure, signalled by anger, inefficiency and sterility.

Nevertheless, Lionel Trilling and some other spokesmen for the clerisy took issue with the – to them – aggrandizing claims of the adversary culture. To attack abuses was one thing. The error, they felt, was in confining one's viewpoint to ridicule, hysteria, apocalypse. Mencken had merely supposed that politicians were bores and fools. The new mode presented politicians as vicious conspirators. *MacBird*, for example, a play that enjoyed a *succès-de-scandale* in 1968, hinted that President Lyndon Johnson had plotted the death of John F. Kennedy in 1963, just as Macbeth had schemed to usurp the throne by murder. Why not try to talk sensibly about America's condition? Why refuse to consider that the nation possessed an alternative, 'responsible culture'? In the 1960s Daniel Bell and Irving Kristol launched a periodical named *The Public Interest*. As the title implied, they believed there was such a thing as the public interest which needed to be identified and strengthened. The responsible culture accused the adversary culture of operating within a hermetic tradition of Modernism (or Post-Modernism). Adversary literature tended to imitate other adversary literature, generating its own clichés of futility and nightmare. The pressure to innovate impelled the avant-garde into more and more extreme essays in outrage.

The 'responsible' position was difficult to sustain without sounding complacent or officious. The adversary culture was widespread and closely attended by big-city representatives of middlebrow America. It was supported by a large proportion of Americans under thirty. The atmosphere of the national capital, Washington, in the 1960s and early 1970s from the Vietnam protests to the Watergate imbroglio and eventual forced resignation of President Nixon, served to convince the adherents of the adversary culture that they were now not so much nay-sayers as doom-watchers. Yet many Americans, especially those of older generations, expressed increasing dissatisfaction with the creative writing that purported to represent the age. The historian Richard Hofstadter, who died in

1970, was one such. In books like *Anti-Intellectualism in American Life* (1963) and *The Paranoid Style in American Politics* (1965) he had sharply dissected the weaknesses in his country's thinking. But in 1967, writing in *The Public Interest*, he asked:

is it not quite possible that the responsible society will get little or no nourishment from modern literature, but will have to draw mainly on history, journalism, economics, sociological commentary? Art, as it more ruthlessly affirms the self, as it more candidly probes the human abyss, may in fact have less and less to tell us about the conditions of a responsible society.

His contention was not that the United States was an admirable, still less an ideal society. What he saw was an absence of contact between adversary and responsible modes. He believed that any society must think socially if it is to work, and that adversary culture had abandoned that task. He suspected that adversary historians would fail to interpret the nation's past, except as a grim caricature; and that for the best picture of recent events one would turn not to poets or novelists, black or white, but to columnists like Walter Lippmann, Richard Rovere and James Reston, to economists like John Kenneth Galbraith and Paul Samuelson, to sociologists like Nathan Glazer and Daniel P. Moynihan.

Phases of the Zeitgeist

Generalizations about literature and thought are apt to exasperate. The categories seem grossly to oversimplify, and to carry signs of approval or disapproval. To contrast an adversary with a responsible culture appears – though this was not Lionel Trilling's or Hofstadter's intention – to mean that the adversary culture has been 'irresponsible'. This echoes a controversy started by Archibald MacLeish with his book *The Irresponsibles* (1940), and followed by Mike Gold's *The Hollow Men* (1941) and Bernard DeVoto's *The Literary Fallacy* (1944). Each condemned American writers, particularly of the 1920s, for having taken too frivolous or too gloomy a view of their society. They were excessively 'literary', DeVoto complained: they 'begin with study of literature; most of them employ literary data exclusively. Practically all of them who extend their inquiry beyond literary data extend it by means of primarily literary ideas'. Van Wyck Brooks joined in, maintaining that creative writers had been blind to moral values; they had shirked the duty of giving a spiritual lead to America, and left it ill-equipped to deal first with the Depression and then with the military régimes of Germany, Italy and Japan.

Mention of this bygone polemic ought to make us cautious – in part because authors like Brooks reversed their own previous positions. Since we are discussing a span of almost ninety years, it is useful to subdivide the period into shorter sequences. It then becomes easier to see American society as a whole – indeed, to perceive that despite the existence of two or more levels of culture the unifying features, with the passage of time, strike one as more important than the differentiating features. Again, to chop up the time-continuum is to oversimplify. But the culture itself has revealed an almost excessive awareness of successive phases of the *Zeitgeist*, and has tended to identify these with decade-units. Thus we can think of a first phase from 1900 to 1920; a second lasting from 1920 to 1940; a third from 1940 to 1960; a fourth *c*.1960–75; and the latest phase, since about 1975. Within each, common preoccupations can be recognized, and each has tended to reject the assumptions of its predecessor. A comparable though not identical idea, put forward by the historian Arthur M. Schlesinger, Sr, was that the national past comprised a cyclical alternation between periods of reform and periods of quiescence.

The phase from 1900 to 1920 could certainly be called a period of reform. It was, in a word much employed by contemporaries, 'progressive'. Progressives emphasized the newness of the problems facing an urbanized, industrialized, expansive, polyglot nation. As we have seen, the genteel tradition prevailed in literary circles, though challenged by new developments in Naturalistic and Imagistic literature. But in all fields there was an earnest search for fresh and appropriate ways of apprehending reality. By the eve of the First World War what Morton White has called the 'revolt against formalism' was being attempted not only by Ezra Pound and the prime spokesman for Youth, Randolph Bourne, but by lawyers, educators, philosophers and historians – some of whom excited Bourne through their teaching when he was an undergraduate at Columbia. In 'sociological jurisprudence', Oliver Wendell Holmes Jr, Louis D. Brandeis and others contended that legal precedent could not be absolutely binding. Social circumstances, and expert knowledge of them, changed; the law must take account of the actual needs of people whose jobs and homes were quite different from those of their parents. In education (and also in philosophy), John Dewey poured out books and articles (*The School and Society*,

1899; *How We Think*, 1909; *Democracy and Education*, 1916; *Reconstruction in Philosophy*, 1920) which argued a similar pragmatic case. Men must learn by experience, so they must be flexible. The lore of the past might or might not be relevant. It had to be tested by its appropriateness to the present; and the finest formative laboratory was the school, since education was the key to the enlightenment of the coming generation. The good American must be a constant questioner. In history the message was communicated by two Columbia colleagues, James Harvey Robinson and Charles A. Beard. Robinson (*The New History*, 1911) claimed that what had 'happened' in the past was shaped by what interested the historian, who would select facts accordingly. Robinson thought this was a liberating admission: the historian was now free to serve the social needs of his own day. Beard concurred. A vigorous reformer, he published *An Economic Interpretation of the Constitution* (1913), in the same year as President Woodrow Wilson's inauguration, to show that America's revered Founding Fathers were as keenly concerned as their descendants with personal economic benefit. In the following year Herbert Croly, Walter Lippmann and others founded the weekly *New Republic* 'less to inform or entertain its readers than to start little insurrections in the realm of their convictions'. The overriding assumption of the Progressive era was that America needed to honour its historic promises, but also to put the democratic ideology in a modern context. This was what Croly meant by *The Promise of American Life* (1909), or Lippmann by his book *Drift and Mastery* (1914). Central government was to become a decisive force; the intellectual was to arouse and enlighten the public, partly through well-documented 'muckraking' journalism that exposed malpractices in business and politics. The resourceful, hardhitting, fearless reporter – sometimes depicted as cynical, sometimes as a Candide who caught on to the trick – began to emerge as a stock figure in the repertory of American fiction. No one did more to encourage the process than the engagingly active and self-assured journalist Lincoln Steffens, seconded by David Graham Phillips (*The Treason of the Senate*, 1906), Ray Stannard Baker (*Following the Color Line*, 1903), John Reed and others. In American folklore the reporter was a kind of 'private eye', of essentially the same breed as the lone-ranger cowboy hero and, somewhat later, the self-employed city detective.

The second phase (1920–40) built upon the first, in the act of denouncing its *naïvetés*. The 1920s emphasized experiment and insurrection, though without much faith in political protest or social reform. Politicians were not only laughed at by the avant-garde; in this respect almost the whole culture was 'adversary'. The popular humorist Will Rogers compared Congress to Hollywood, with scenario and cutting departments: 'Now, Folks, why patronize California-made Productions? The Capitol Comedy Co. of Washington, DC have never made a failure. They are every one, 100 per cent funny, or 100 per cent sad.' The historians continued to be influenced by theories of Relativism, and with the First World War in mind began to depict all previous conflicts including the American Civil War as unnecessary and futile. No doubt there were deep antagonisms inside the society. Rural and small-town America, committed to Prohibition and religious fundamentalism, was bitterly at odds with the city sophisticates. Yet in retrospect the sophistication seems genially innocent. The *New Yorker* began publication in 1925 with the announcement that it was intended for a cosmopolitan audience, not for a hypothetical old lady in Dubuque, Iowa. Its editor Harold Ross was however himself a small-towner from Colorado, adamantly opposed to material he found even remotely suggestive. Expatriates might castigate America; they were annoyed when Europeans did the same thing, and sometimes offended by home-produced denigration. Kenneth Burke, writing in *Vanity Fair* in 1923, described the United States as 'the purest concentration point for the vices and vulgarities of the world'. His friend Malcolm Cowley rebuked him from Paris. 'America is just as god-damned good as Europe – worse in some ways, better in others, just as appreciative, fresher material . . . New York is refinement itself beside Berlin. French taste in most details is unbearable. London is a huge Gopher Prairie.' With an incomplete gesture towards self-mockery he added: 'I'm not ashamed to take off my coat anywhere and tell these degenerate Europeans that I'm an American citizen. Wave Old Glory! Peace! Normalcy!'

When the Depression hit America at the beginning of the 1930s the expatriates nearly all came home. The mood of the whole country was sombre and penitential. For a little while writers aligned themselves with left-wing politics, and debated the possibilities of a genuinely proletarian literature. Here too they were more or less in accord with majority feeling. In 1933 the United States at last agreed to give diplomatic recognition to Soviet Russia. In the words of Will Rogers:

We would recognize the Devil . . . if he would contract for some pitchforks. The shape we are in right now we would be glad to receive a good will tour from Alibaba and his Forty Thieves, if they needed enough tooth paste and radio tubes. . . . Nothing will bring a nation off its moral horse like poverty. Poverty is a terrible handicap but a great humanizer.

Writers rediscovered the textures of the American past, many of them working on projects improvised by the federal government. Constance Rourke wrote an affectionate study of *American Humor* (1931) and biographies of Davy Crockett and the naturalist John James Audubon. Van Wyck Brooks began his nostalgic chronicle of America's literary past with *The Flowering of New England* (1936). James Agee's *Let Us Now Praise Famous Men* (a 1936 magazine assignment, not published until 1941), illustrated with photographs by Walker Evans, was an equivocally moving account, both indignant and lyrical, of the lives of a group of Southern sharecroppers. F. O. Matthiessen's *American Renaissance* (1941), a labour of love by a Harvard professor, sought to explain why so many masterpieces had been written in the 1850s. A note of fashionable 'solidarity' crept into the work of Ernest Hemingway. The dying hero of his *To Have and Have Not* (1937) gasps out a final message: 'A man . . . ain't got no . . . hasn't got any can't really isn't any way out. . . . One man alone ain't got . . . no chance.'

With the third phase (1940–60) new moods supervened. The coming of the Second World War, which the United States formally entered in December 1941, after the Japanese bombing of its Pearl Harbor base, pushed the preoccupations of the Depression years into the background. The former dramas of economic collapse and radical resolve were replaced by new scenes, set to energetic martial airs. One heard bugles, trumpets, gunfire and explosions. John Wayne the cowboy was now a Seabee of a marine. March of Time newsreels revelled in stories of welders and riveters (women as well as men), tanks and bombers coming off assembly lines, Liberty cargo ships tumbling into the water in multiple launches, convoys, thumbs-up aviators, plucky war-brides choking back emotion, their men stoically wading ashore on once-picturesque beaches – postcard images defaced with scrawls of wire and blotches of shrapnel.

Had the Depression ever existed? That seemed doubtful, in the plethoric new age when everyone had a job to do and a war to win. Established talents, sure enough, were enlisted in the enterprise. John Steinbeck wrote of enemy-occupied Europe and of bomber missions. Ernest Hemingway turned from hunting submarines in the Caribbean to liberating Paris (his own 'diamond as big as the

Ritz', to borrow the title of a Scott Fitzgerald story). In poetry and in prose fresh talents – Karl Shapiro, Peter Viereck, Harry Brown, Alfred Hayes, Randall Jarrell – began to appear in print with the grand finale of 1945. The publication of the most famous of all the 'war novels', Norman Mailer's *The Naked and the Dead*, came in 1948. Three years after came two more books that ran it close in acclaim, both of them subsequently filmed: *The Caine Mutiny* by Herman Wouk and James Jones's *From Here to Eternity*, about the regular army in Hawaii on the eve of Pearl Harbor.

Some of this writing, retrospectively immersed in service life, or in combat's bad dreams, was in its nature apolitical. After 1945, a number of other authors unconcerned either with war or with social and political questions, immersed themselves instead in the discovery of self. For some of these Henry Miller provided a congenial example. Back from Europe, installed on California's Big Sur coastline, Miller offered himself as a guru of the benevolently outrageous, linking ego and cosmos with a neo-Emersonian relish. During the 1950s California, and the North-West of Oregon and Washington State (followed subsequently by Alaska), became the latest of America's succession of Last Frontiers, where individuals could still seek open space in which to 'be themselves'. The 'Beat' authors associated with California, and especially with San Francisco, were perhaps more important as poets than as prose narrators (see the comments of Eric Mottram, in Chapter 9). For the public, however, the 'Beat' author was the Jack Kerouac of *On the Road* (1957) and *The Dharma Bums* (1958), who at his best caught the unwilled compulsions of the decade's foot-on-the-gas nomadic cronies. 'Beat' and 'beatitude' in this respect had the same root. The epiphanies announced in Kerouac's non-stop chronicle combined golden exuberance and black (or blue?) dejection. The Beat vocabulary, with its talk of 'highs', 'speed', 'crashing' and the like, may have soon seemed limited and repetitive. For a while, though, it possessed an odd, ambivalent rightness.

Or rather, it did for those who cared to listen. A dominant quasi-political drama for many others was represented by the anti-foreign, anti-communist campaigns of Senators Pat McCarran and Joseph McCarthy. Supporters of these 'populist' crusades believed that subversives were sapping the nation's strength with a diabolically disguised malignity akin to that of the super-villains of American comic-books. Patriots, it was implied, must counter underhandedness with the equally audacious highhandedness displayed by the comic-books' supermen heroes.

Not surprisingly, in face of the denunciations and blacklists of the early 1950s, anti-anti-communism absorbed a good deal of the energy of American authors (such as Lillian Hellman and Arthur Miller) and liberal academics (Richard Hofstadter, Daniel Bell, Arthur M. Schlesinger, Jr.) But their protest was weakened in a few instances (Hellman's is one) because they were not entirely candid about their own current or previous beliefs, or else because they too experienced a revulsion from radicalism. They were no longer enthralled by European civilization; the Old World's intellectualizing had led to Hitler, Mussolini and Stalin. Most of them could see no future in communism, and not much in the impoverished socialism of the British variety. 'Consensus' became a favourite word, not only among politicians. A few writers clamantly dissented, Mailer among them, but aroused little response even among the potentially adversary culture. What they faced was a combination of jadedness and qualified optimism. Holden Caulfield, the boy-narrator of *The Catcher in the Rye* (1951), seemed to speak for an era which distrusted public attitudes but had nothing very certain to put in their place. His elder brother works in Hollywood:

He just got a Jaguar. One of those English jobs that can do around two hundred miles an hour. It cost him damn near four thousand bucks. He's got a lot of dough, now. He didn't use to. He used to be just a regular writer, when he was home.

The optimism came from the feeling that the nation was in reasonably good working order – the theme of Max Lerner's *America as a Civilization* (1957). The economy was prospering; race-prejudice was dwindling. Historians supplied the moral that 'consensus' – the middle way – was the fundamental rule of American evolution. In *The Genius of American Politics* (1953), Daniel J. Boorstin found a new answer for the old lament that the United States had never nurtured great political thinkers (or for that matter, theorists of international repute in most of the speculative fields). The reason, Boorstin argued, was simple and cheering. There was no American equivalent of men like Marx and Engels because America had never needed them. Happy countries can dispense with ideology. The American genius was to have no geniuses, but to arrange affairs on a practical basis of give-and-take. There had not been a true revolution in America; the War of Independence and the Civil War were profoundly conservative in outlook. Richard Hofstadter, drawing upon sociological and psychological approaches, inclined to the view that the issues in American elections boiled down to either 'status' or 'interest' politics – neither of which left room for ideological passion. David Donald put forward the theory that abolitionist campaigns against slavery sprung from buried 'status' resentments among the American clerisy, and Hofstadter made a similar point about the gentleman-reformers of the century's end. Allan Nevins and a number of economic historians maintained that tycoons like John D. Rockefeller had been maligned by scholars of the Progressive stamp. They were 'industrial statesmen' rather than 'robber barons'. In *People of Plenty* (1954) David M. Potter, considerably modifying the Turner Frontier thesis, presented economic abundance as the central feature of American history, and the expectation of abundance as the main determinant of national character.

The fourth phase, dating from about 1960, to the mid-1970s, saw an extraordinary change. In *The End of Ideology* (1960) the sociologist Daniel Bell admitted that while the old ideologies were dead for his generation, 'the young intellectual is unhappy because the "middle way" is for the middle-aged, not for him; it is without passion and is deadening'. With the 1939–45 war a fading memory, the young awoke to a new militancy all over the Western world. In the United States the rise of Black Power was one manifestation. Protest against the 'military-industrial complex' and the Vietnam War was another. Horror and hatred of the political scene seemed about to boil over in 1968, the year when Lyndon Johnson acknowledged defeat and Martin Luther King and Robert F. Kennedy were murdered. Now once again, as before 1940, the adversary culture seemed a reality – indeed a more belligerent and articulate force than ever before. College campuses, which only a few years before had been criticized by professors for their lethargy, sprouted revolt. Academics and creative writers – Noam Chomsky, Mailer, Robert Lowell – vied with one another in insisting that the state of the Union was dreadful. The *New York Review of Books* became indispensable reading for the avant-garde. In professional conferences radical pressure-groups clamoured for a hearing. Maverick dissenters such as I. F. Stone and Paul Goodman (author of *Growing Up Absurd*, 1960) suddenly won a following. The younger generation of American historians, with some collaboration from their elders, started to revise the national record. Far from being a peaceful, classless, conflict-free society, the United States in their version was endemically violent; social mobility was a myth;

radicalism had persisted, though in face of reactionary oppression, ever since colonial times. In the 1940–60 phase a historian might note, for instance, that the socialist candidate in the 1912 presidential election, Eugene V. Debs, got only 6 per cent of the popular vote. In the next phase, a historian might stress how well Debs had done in securing 900,000 votes in spite of the immense handicaps he faced. Black historians concentrated upon Negro resistance and separateness. Scholars concerned with immigration now retreated from the idea that America was a unitary society; the new idea about the national melting-pot was that it had *not* melted different people into one. Foreign-policy revisionists contended that the United States, not Russia, was to blame for the onset of the cold war. Every received opinion seemed to be in the discard. In the 1940s and 1950s it had often been assumed that literature's great period of excitement was already over: where could the writer go beyond *Finnegan's Wake?* But then innovation was again in the air. Projective verse had staked out fresh territory and its claims began to be respected. Surrealism was reborn in the fantasy-fiction of Donald Barthelme, Richard Brautigan and others. Tom Wolfe (not to be confused with the novelist Thomas Wolfe) galvanized documentary journalism with the hectic Pop-prose of *The Kandy-Kolored Tangerine-Flake Streamline Baby* (1965) and *The Electric Kool-Aid Acid Test* (1968). The adversary culture ran the gamut from the Maoist to the psychedelic.

Some of these developments, it is clear from the perspective of the 1980s, proved not to be of lasting significance. Certain among them had the well-nigh irresistible allure of vogues in popular music or dress, and the same essential temporariness. In crudely simplified terms, the vogue for 'protest' ended for two reasons. First, being a vogue or fad, it was necessarily short-lived. Its prophets became bored with the slogans they had recently proclaimed; so did their restless followers. Abbie Hoffman had got married, it was said; he had named his baby 'America', a big responsibility for a little child, and for a parent with entrepreneurial instincts. Though Allen Ginsberg's sincerity was not in question, cynics also noted that his platform appearances were frequent and regular enough to constitute a profession; and that he was said to be investing surplus income, with advice from his father, on the stock market.

Second, we are told, came the socio-economic changes that ultimately determine the rise and fall of all fashions, whether in ideas or in skirt-lengths. Draft evasion ceased to be an issue in the mid-1970s; all but the most hardened sceptics were willing to believe that the United States was in fact pulling its troops out of South-East Asia. Whether or not the economy suffered in direct and immediate consequence, the long post-war boom was apparently ending. The oil shortages of the period indicated that America was no longer able to count on an infinite supply of mineral resources. Books of the 1950s had stressed abundance; for the historian David M. Potter, Americans were a *People of Plenty*. Twenty years later, Potter's successors began to contemplate the effects upon national character not of opulence but of scarcity.

In the early 1970s, the revelations of Watergate scandalized all but diehard Republicans and the palace guard of President Nixon. Alarmed Americans, including the writer Philip Roth, hypothesized or fantasized that Richard Nixon might attempt a *coup d'état*, or perhaps a managed plebiscite, to prolong and intensify his stay in power, as Louis-Napoleon had once contrived to promote himself from President to Emperor of France. Arthur M. Schlesinger Jr argued in *The Imperial Presidency* (1974) that recent White House incumbents had enlarged their prerogative with dangerous lack of scruple. Since this was perceived as a particularly Republican stratagem, encouraged by the venal attitudes of old-guard politicians, it was widely hoped in 1976 that the election victory of the Democrat Jimmy Carter, a Southerner never involved in Washington's power-game, would signal a new era of honest and modest executive conduct.

Such hopes however were not borne out. Before long, President Carter was under fire as weak, sanctimonious, negative – a 'wimp'. Commentators switched overnight from denunciations of a 'runaway' presidency, to a demand for more inspiring leadership. To judge from the large majority secured by the Republican Ronald Reagan in 1980, and again in 1984, the nation had repudiated the repudiations of the previous decade. Radicalism was 'out': the in-thing was patriotism, a build-up of the military, an end to the 'spend and spend, tax and tax' philosophy of the welfare state. Conservative economics were certainly in vogue – preached for example by Michael Novak and George Gilder, who perceived in private enterprise not only invigorating competition but deeply altruistic, civilizing elements. The Chicago monetarists Milton Friedman and George Stigler, and the 'public-choice' advocate James Buchanan, all became Nobel laureates, at the behest of the Swedish Academy, so globally *à la mode* were the new creeds of the market economy and the reduced welfare state.

There was, after the mid-1970s, far more talk of a return to traditional values – self-help, prayer, family. Non-fiction best-sellers of the mid-1980s featured the memoirs of Lee Iacocca, the brash automobile tycoon; *Fatherhood* by the winsome black TV star Bill Cosby; and *You're Only Old Once* by the juveniles' bard Dr Seuss. University campuses were certainly more restrained. Postgraduate enrolments were greatly reduced in history, literature, sociology, as the supply of fellowships and posts dried up. The same shrinkage was evident among undergraduates; students were turning away from the humanities toward sound vocational investments such as accountancy. Newspapers and magazines teemed with articles on these trends, agreeing generally that today's youth possessed memories as astoundingly short as those of their parents. Had there ever been a Depression – a McCarthy era (if so, which McCarthy – Joe or Eugene?)? – a man named John Fitzgerald Kennedy and another called Lee Harvey Oswald? – a vast, ragged conflict in Vietnam (if so, who had won?)?

Acts of amnesia, yes. But basic changes in American thought and feeling? That was doubtful. Analysts of modern times are driven to exaggerate the extent of change – true change, that is, as distinct from the sort of technological innovation that replaces the radio with television, black-and-white with colour, the typewriter with the personal computer. Carter himself was after all more steeped in born-again Christianity than Reagan and hardly less conservative in other respects. Reagan's 'leadership' was logically at odds with his insistence that the country was suffering from too much government. Despite the talk of renewed decency, drug-taking, bad language in print and in the movies, premarital and extramarital sex, and acceptance of 'gay' behaviour, showed no signs of abatement. If rumour could be believed, or such novels as Jay McInerney's *Bright Lights, Big City* (1984), cocaine was a standard diversion in smart society.

Again, although the bookstores were less given over than in a previous decade to racial, ethnic, gender and economic protest, publishers' lists continue to embody such material. Some of the most admired historians still offered quasi-Marxist interpretations. If Reagan was personally popular, public opinion – according to the polls – still approved the social changes begun in the New Deal. Black literature was in some ways less excitedly discussed than in the 1960s; not many of the Afro-American university programmes launched at that time were flourishing, and fresh creative work from the senior male authors (Ralph Ellison, James Baldwin) was no longer eagerly anticipated. LeRoi Jones, in his metamorphosed existence as Imamu Amiri Baraka, now concerned himself with activist local politics rather than with literature. Other warrior-spokesmen of the sixties, notably Eldridge Cleaver, fell silent or announced their conversion to the values of mainstream America. The underrated black novelist Chester Himes, long expatriated in Paris, died in 1984. The dazzlingly gifted exponent of 'black Dada', Ishmael Reed, seemed less certain of his direction after the appearance of such sharp fantasies as *Yellow Back Radio Broke-Down* (1969) and *Flight to Canada* (1976). Negritude, as realized by some of these black authors (and discussed by Arnold Goldman, in Chapter 10), was an intricate concept: each apparent solution, when reached, was liable to disclose yet another, concealed yet unavoidable dilemma. But if these were difficulties for male writers, there was an astonishing burst of creativity among black women, not only from older writers like Gwendolyn Brooks and Paule Marshall, but from such younger figures as Nikki Giovanni, Toni Morrison, Ntozake Shange, and the even more popular author Alice Walker – poets and dramatists as well as novelists. Feminist literature and scholarship as a whole was strikingly vigorous, and likely to expand yet further into the foreseeable future, whatever the pundits might say of an anti-feminist backlash, or of reduced militance on the part of a Betty Friedan (*The Second Stage*, 1981).

Native American (Indian) literature had likewise built considerably upon the achievements of such 1960s figures as N. Scott Momaday (*The House Made of Dawn*, 1968). One might now add – noting too the prominence of women in the tally, and their versatility in poetry as well as fiction – the names of Leslie Marmon Silko (e.g. *Ceremony*, 1977), Gerald Vizenor (*Darkness in St Louis Bearheart*, 1978), James Welch (*The Death of Jim Loney*, 1979), Louise Erdrich (*Love Medicine*, 1984; *Beet Queen*, 1986), and Janet Campbell-Hale (*The Jailing of Cecelia Capture*, 1985).

The unceasing appetite for crime and detection, on the printed page and in the cinema, also contributed to a more permissive acceptance of genres hitherto excluded from academic literary analysis. As Dashiell Hammett and Raymond Chandler were more and more readily accorded 'classic' status, so was there a greater readiness to pay heed to the inventiveness, the fast pace and accurate ear for American 'tough' speech, displayed by an Ed McBain, a George V. Higgins, a William Kennedy or an Elmore Leonard. Leonard, for instance (b.1925), achieved international celebrity in 1985 with the publication of his novel *Glitz*. But he had already built up a large and technically adept *oeuvre*. His skills could be defined, and so perhaps shrugged off as 'formulaic' (a useful term in popular culture developed by John G. Cawelti). A typical Leonard hero is obscure and outwardly unimpressive, yet possessed of a tenacious courage and intelligence that enable him to overcome numerous and brutal enemies with an almost Rambo-like assurance. However, Leonard (like George Higgins) is a master of low-life idiom, including the trick of dispensing with 'whens' and 'ifs'. Here is an example from *LaBrava* (1983):

I see 'em come in with no socks on, I know they've got a portfolio of social commentary.

The hero of *LaBrava*, a one-time security guard, is making a second career as a photographer of street scenes. He derives a wry amusement from the jargon of art-criticism (and reveals the author's sophistication): 'The review in the paper said, "The aesthetic sub-text of his work is the systematic exposure of artistic pretension." I thought I was just taking pictures.' LaBrava reacts in the same way to a second review: 'They say, "His work is a compendium of humanity's defeat at the hand of venture capital."'

Recognitions of this sort might, it is true, not commend themselves to the elegantly intellectual Nobelist Saul Bellow (b.1915), whose disdain for vox pop was manifest in *The Dean's December* (1982), or *Him With His Foot in His Mouth* (1984), nor possibly, at another extreme, to the exegesists of Thomas Pynchon's rarefied fiction, or that of John Barth. Nevertheless, Bellow as VIP was willy-nilly incorporated into the culture of the gossip-column. He was joined there by a miscellany of writer-celebrities, some of whom like Bernard Malamud (1914–84) had been grouped with Bellow as in some sense fundamentally 'Jewish'. They would undoubtedly include, whether or not that assignment was stipulated, Philip Roth (b.1933) of the *Zuckerman* trilogy, and Joseph Heller (b.1923), whose *God Knows* (1984) featured the King David of the Old Testament as a garrulous streetwise old American; and of course Norman Mailer. With them would be put several other figures of established importance – John Updike, William Styron, John Irving, and perhaps some women novelists; a handful of scholars and commentators; the durable dramatist Arthur Miller; but, since the demise of Robert Lowell, no poets, with the possible exception of John Ashbery. The scene lacked the coherence attributed to other national cultures – say, to that exemplified in the Académie Française. By and large, there was no clearcut division between 'high' and 'low'. Into which, for instance, should one fit the deservedly best-selling *Lake Wobegon Days* (1985), the drolly heartfelt confessional of Garrison Keillor, based on his weekly St Paul, Minnesota radio show?

American Homogeneities

Much probably remains to be said in this particular debate. Still, taking the century as a whole, one is aware both of swings and of the recurrences inherent in the very nature of a 'swing': the implication is of a sort of pendular motion, oscillating about some central line. In this regard, the homogeneous feature of American society, the behaviour linking, say, all the presidents and nearly all the thinkers and imaginers since 1900, is – taken for better and for worse, in sickness and in health – the 'propertarian' or democratic-capitalist creed on which it has long been based. Technologically the United States has undergone constant change. Ideologically it has remained remarkably static. The creed upholds individual enterprise: on this, in different ways, all segments of the society can agree. There is also a majoritarian emphasis. The avant-garde has often had cause to complain of the resultant pressure to conform, but has not been happy with alternative theories – including cultural elitism. America has been ideologically sluggish, yet susceptible to campaigns for reform that appeal either to the notion that America is itself an avant-garde society, or else to the historic conception of America as a land of liberty and equality. In consequence, adversary attacks on departures from the ideal have occurred at regular intervals. They appear to die away before any fundamental improvements have been introduced. This was true of Progressivism, of the New Deal in the 1930s, and probably of the radicalism of the 1960s. One reason is the readiness of middlebrow America, after some initial hostility, to join the crusade. Radicals, in literature as in politics, have been smothered by this indiscriminate embrace. 'Beware of imitations' might be their warning slogan.

A more important reason is that the ideology imposes its own limits. According to Louis Hartz (*The Liberal Tradition in America*, 1955) the nation has never had any full-scale creed except liberalism. Though this might seem to be a 'consensus' proposition, it makes sense when applied to adversary situations. Liberalism has been assailed from all sides in twentieth-century America. An example by a semi-conservative writer is *Nixon Agonistes* (1970), by Garry Wills, who takes Nixon to reveal the bankruptcy of liberal ideology. But Wills cannot offer a conservative substitute that would fit the American context; so his lively diatribe closes in anticlimax. Nor can radicals frame a constructive programme. For one thing, it would have to abridge private property rights to a far greater extent than would be tolerated – even by more than a minority of the adversary culture. American democracy and private property have become indissolubly bonded. If radical protest cannot therefore be constructive, it finds an outlet in being 'destructive'. To say this is not to indict the adversary culture, but merely to explain how American radicalism tends to be driven into extreme fantasies of corruption and overthrow. As imaginative statements they often show remarkable ingenuity and eloquence. But they remain fantasies, even if at times actual American conduct seems to bear out Oscar Wilde's aphorism that nature imitates art. In this sense they lose touch with reality. The tendency has been accentuated, as the adversary culture has enlarged and followed its own leapfrog logic of developing provocation. But the outcome is curiously inconclusive. Writers and readers weary of their task. They abandon apocalypse – temporarily.

BIBLIOGRAPHY

1. The American Risorgimento: The United States and the Coming of the New Arts

General

Anderson, Margaret, *The Fiery Fountains*, London, 1953.
Bourne, Randolph, *The History of a Literary Radical*, ed. V. W. Brooks, New York, 1920.
Bradbury, Malcolm, *The Modern American Novel*, Oxford, 1983.
Brooks, Van Wyck, *America's Coming-of-Age*, 1915: repr. New York, 1958.
——*The Confident Years, 1885–1915*, New York, 1959.
Dell, Floyd, *Intellectual Vagabondage*, New York, 1926.
Duffey, Bernard, *The Chicago Renaissance in American Letters*, East Lancing, Mi., 1954.
Fletcher, John Gould, *Life Is My Song*, New York, 1937.
Frank, Waldo, *Our America*, New York, 1919.
——*et al.*, eds, *America and Alfred Stieglitz*, New York, 1934.
Geismar, Maxwell, *Rebels and Ancestors: The American Novel, 1890–1915*, Boston, 1953.
Goldman, Eric, *Rendezvous With Destiny: A History of Modern American Reform*, New York, 1952.
Hoffman, F., *et al.*, *The Little Magazine*, Princeton, N.J., 1946.
Kazin, Alfred, *On Native Grounds: An Interpretation of Modern American Prose Literature*, New York, 1942; rev. edn, 1966.
——*An American Procession: The Major American Writers from 1830 to 1930*, New York, 1984.
Kenner, Hugh, *The Pound Era*, New York, 1971.
——*A Homemade World: The American Modernist Writers*, New York, 1975.
Lasch, Christopher, *The New Radicalism in America, 1889–1963*, New York, 1965; London, 1966.
Luhan, Mabel Dodge, *Movers and Shakers*, 4 vols, New York, 1933–7.
Martin, Jay, *Harvests of Change: American Literature, 1865–1914*, Englewood Cliffs, N.J., 1967.

May, Henry F., *The End of American Innocence, A Study of the First Years of Our Own Time, 1885–1915*, New York, 1959.

Monroe, Harriet, *A Poet's Life*, New York/London, 1938.

Parry, Albert, *Garrets and Pretenders*, New York, 1933.

Santayana, George, 'The Genteel Tradition,' in *Winds of Doctrine*, New York, 1913.

Stead, C. K., *The New Poetic: Yeats to Eliot*, London, 1964.

Trachtenberg, Alan, *The Incorporation of America: Culture and Society in the Gilded Age*, New York, 1982.

Walcutt, Charles C., *American Literary Nationalism: A Divided Stream*, Minneapolis, 1966.

Individual Authors

Sherwood Anderson (1876–1941)

TEXTS

Cowley, Malcolm, ed., *Winesburg, Ohio*, London, 1967.

Gregory, Horace, Introduction to *The Portable Sherwood Anderson*, New York, 1949.

Rosenfeld, Paul, ed., *The Sherwood Anderson Reader*, Boston, 1947.

CRITICAL–BIOGRAPHICAL

Howe, Irving, *Sherwood Anderson*, Stanford, 1966.

Schevill, James E., *Sherwood Anderson: His Life and Work*, Denver, 1951.

White, Ray L., ed., *The Achievement of Sherwood Anderson: Essays In Criticism*, Chapel Hill, 1966.

Theodore Dreiser (1871–1945)

TEXTS

Kazin, Alfred, Introduction to *Sister Carrie* (a restored edition based on the ms), Pennsylvania/Penguin, 1981.

CRITICAL–BIOGRAPHICAL

Kazin, Alfred, and Shapiro, Charles, eds., *The Stature of Theodore Dreiser*, Bloomington, Ind., 1955.

Lyndenberg, John, ed., *Theodore Dreiser: A Collection of Critical Essays*, Englewood Cliffs, N.J., 1971.

Matthiessen, F. O., *Theodore Dreiser*, New York, 1951.

Pizer, Donald, *The Novels of Theodore Dreiser: A Critical Study*, Minneapolis, 1976.

Robert Frost (see bibliography to Chapter 4)

Ellen Glasgow (1874–1945)

TEXTS
Collected Works, New York, 1938.
Meeker, R. K., ed., *Collected Stories of Ellen Glasgow*, Baton Rouge, 1963.
Rouse, Blair, ed., *Letters of Ellen Glasgow*, New York, 1958.

CRITICAL–BIOGRAPHICAL
Auchinloss, Louis, *Ellen Glasgow*, Minneapolis, 1964.

Vachel Lindsay (1879–1931)

TEXTS
Collected Poems, rev. edn, New York, 1966.

CRITICAL–BIOGRAPHICAL
Harris, Mark, *City of Discontent*, Indianapolis, 1952.
Massa, Anna, *Vachel Lindsay*, Bloomington/London, 1970.
Ruggles, Eleanor, *The West-Going Heart: A Life of Vachel Lindsay*, New York, 1959.

Edgar Lee Masters (1868–1950)

TEXTS
Spoon River Anthology, reissue Collier, New York, 1965.

CRITICAL–BIOGRAPHICAL
Masters, Edgar Lee, *Across Spoon River* (autobiography), New York, 1936.

Ezra Pound (see bibliography to Chapter 4)

Carl Sandburg (see bibliography to Chapter 4)

Gertrude Stein (1874–1946)

TEXTS

The Yale Edition of the Unpublished Writings, 8 vols, New Haven, 1951ff.

Meyerowitz, Patricia, ed., *Look at Me Now and Here I Am: Writings and Lectures 1909–45*, London, 1967; Penguin Modern Classics, 1979.

Three Lives, 1909; Penguin Modern Classics, 1979.

CRITICAL–BIOGRAPHICAL

Brinnin, John Malcolm, *The Third Rose: Gertrude Stein and Her World*, New York, 1959; London, 1960.

Sprigge, Elizabeth, *Gertrude Stein: Her Life and Work*, New York, 1957.

Sutherland, Donald, *Gertrude Stein: A Biography of Her Work*, New York, 1951.

Weinstein, Norman, *Gertrude Stein and the Literature of the Modern Consciousness*, New York, 1970.

Wallace Stevens (see bibliography to Chapter 4)

Edith Wharton (1862–1937)

TEXTS

Auchinloss, Louis, ed., *The Edith Wharton Reader*, New York, 1965.

Andrews, Wayne, ed., *The Best Short Stories of Edith Wharton*, New York, 1958.

Lewis, R. W. B., ed., *The Collected Short Stories*, New York, 1958.

CRITICAL–BIOGRAPHICAL

Auchinloss, Louis, *Edith Wharton: A Woman in Her Time*, New York, 1971.

Howe, Irving, ed., *Edith Wharton: A Collection of Critical Essays*, Englewood Cliffs, N.J., 1962.

Lewis, R. W. B., *Edith Wharton*, New York, 1975.

Nevius, Blake, *Edith Wharton: A Study of Her Fiction*, Berkeley, 1953.

2. *The Language of American Fiction between the Wars*

General

Aaron, Daniel, *Writers on the Left*, New York, 1961.
Bradbury, Malcolm, *The Modern American Novel*, Oxford, 1983.
Bryer, Jackson R., ed., *Sixteen Modern American Authors: A Survey of Research and Criticism*, Durham, N.C., 1974.
Cooperman, Stanley J., *World War I and the American Novel*, Baltimore, 1967.
Cowley, Malcolm, *Exile's Return*, rev. edn, New York, 1959.
——*A Second Flowering: Works and Days of the Lost Generation*, New York, 1973.
——*The Dream of the Golden Mountains: Remembering the 1930s*, New York, 1980.
Frohock, Wilbur M., *The Novel of Violence in America*, rev. edn, Dallas, 1957.
Geismar, Maxwell, *Writers in Crisis: 1925–1940*, Boston and London, 1947.
Hoffman, Frederick J., *The Modern Novel in America: 1900–1950*, Chicago, 1951.
——*The Twenties: American Writing in the Post-War Decade*, rev. edn, New York, 1962.
Kazin, Alfred, *On Native Grounds*, New York, 1942.
——*Bright Book of Life: American Novelists and Storytellers from Hemingway to Mailer*, New York, 1973; London, 1974.
Millgate, Michael, *American Social Fiction: James to Cozzens*, Edinburgh and London, 1964.
Munson, Gorham, *The Awakening Twenties: A Memoir-History of a Literary Period*, Baton Rouge and London, 1985.
Wilson, Edmund, *A Literary Chronicle, 1920–1950*, New York, 1956.
——memoirs, ed. Leon Edel, *The Twenties*, New York, 1975; *The Thirties*, 1980; *The Forties*, 1983.

Individual Authors

Sherwood Anderson (see bibliography for Chapter 1)

John Dos Passos

Carr, Virginia S., *Dos Passos: A Life*, Garden City, New York, 1984.
Ludington, Townsend, *John Dos Passos: A Twentieth-Century Odyssey*, New York, 1980.

F. Scott Fitzgerald

Fitzgerald is published in the US by Scribners and in the UK by Cape; he is also well represented in Penguins and other good paperback lists.

Bruccoli, Matthew J., *Some Sort of Epic Grandeur: The Life of F. Scott Fitzgerald*, New York, 1981.
Kazin, Alfred, ed., *F. Scott Fitzgerald: The Man and his Work*, New York, 1951.
Latham, Aaron, *Crazy Sunday: F. Scott Fitzgerald in Hollywood*, New York, 1971.
LeVot, Andre, *F. Scott Fitzgerald: A Biography*, transl. from the French, Garden City, New York, 1983.
Piper, H. Dan, *F. Scott Fitzgerald: A Critical Portrait*, New York, 1965.
Turnbull, Andrew, *Scott Fitzgerald*, New York and London, 1962.
——ed., *The Letters of F. Scott Fitzgerald*, New York, 1963.

Ernest Hemingway

Published in the US by Scribners and in the UK by Cape; many paperback editions also.

Baker, Carlos, *Hemingway: The Writer as Artist*, rev. edn, Princeton and London, 1963.
Fenton, Charles A., *The Literary Apprenticeship of Ernest Hemingway*, New York, 1954.
Griffin, Peter, *Along With Youth: Hemingway, the Early Years*, New York, 1985.
Meyers, Jeffrey, *Hemingway: A Biography*, New York, 1985.
Raeburn, John, *Fame Became of Him: Hemingway as Public Writer*, Bloomington, Indiana, 1984.

Sinclair Lewis

Babbitt was published in the US by Harcourt, Brace and in the UK by Cape. With *Main Street* and two or three other Lewis novels it is readily available in paperback.
Schorer, Mark, *Sinclair Lewis: An American Life*, New York, 1961; London, 1963.
Dooley, David J., *The Art of Sinclair Lewis*, Lincoln, Neb., 1967.

John Steinbeck

Steinbeck's American publisher was Viking, his British one Heinemann. There have been a number of paperback editions of *Cannery Row, The Grapes of Wrath* and other Steinbeck favourites.
Benson, Jackson J., *The True Adventures of John Steinbeck, Writer: A Biography*, New York, 1984.
French, Warren, *John Steinbeck*, 2nd edn, Boston, 1975.
Timmerman, John H., *John Steinbeck's Fiction: The Aesthetics of the Road Taken*, Norman, Okla. and London, 1986.

Thomas Wolfe

Wolfe was published in the US by Scribners and later by Harpers; *Look Homeward, Angel* was also reprinted by the Modern Library. The length of his novels has sometimes discouraged paperback publishers from maintaining them in print.
Donald, David H., *Look Homeward: A Life of Thomas Wolfe*, Boston, 1987.
Fiedler, Leslie A., ed., *Thomas Wolfe: Three Decades of Criticism*, New York and London, 1968.
Holman, C. Hugh, *The Loneliness at the Core: Studies in Thomas Wolfe*, Baton Rouge, 1975.
Nowell, Elizabeth, *Thomas Wolfe*, New York, 1960.
——, ed., *Letters of Thomas Wolfe*, New York, 1956; London (as *Selected Letters*), 1958.

3. *American Theatre: The Age of O'Neill*

Abramson, Doris E., *Negro Playwrights of the American Theatre*, New York, 1969.

Anderson, John, *The American Theatre*, New York, 1938.

Anderson, Maxwell, *Eleven Verse Plays*, New York, 1940.

——*Off Broadway*, New York, 1947.

Atkinson, Brooks, *Broadway*, London, 1970.

Bailey, Mabel Driscoll, *Maxwell Anderson: The Playwright as Prophet*, New York, 1957.

Bigsby, C. W. E., *A Critical Introduction to Twentieth-Century Drama*, Vol. 1, 1900–40, Cambridge, 1982.

Broussard, Louis, *American Drama*, Norman, 1962.

Brown, John Mason, *Two on the Aisle*, New York, 1938.

Brown, John Russell and Harris, Bernard, eds, *American Theatre*, Stratford-upon-Avon Studies 10, London, 1967.

Cargill, Oscar and others, eds, *O'Neill and His Plays*, New York, 1962.

Carpenter, Frederic I., *Eugene O'Neill*, New York, 1964.

Carter, Huntly, *The New Spirit in the European Theatre*, London, 1925.

Clark, Barrett H., *Eugene O'Neill: The Man and His Plays*, New York, 1947.

Clurman, Harold, *The Fervent Years*, New York, 1957.

Deutch, Helen and Hanau, Stella, *The Provincetown Players*, New York, 1931.

Downer, Alan S., *Fifty Years of American Drama, 1900–1950*, Chicago, 1951.

—— ed., *American Drama and Its Critics*, Chicago, 1965.

Eaton, Walter P., *The Theatre Guild, The First Ten Years*, New York, 1929.

Engel, Edwin A., *The Haunted Heroes of Eugene O'Neill*, Cambridge, 1953.

Eustis, Morton, *Broadway, Inc: The Theatre as Business*, New York, 1934.

Falk, Doris V., *Eugene O'Neill and the Tragic Tension*, New Brunswick, N.J., 1958.

Flanagan, Hallie, *Shifting Scenes of the Modern European Theatre*, London, 1929.

——*Arena*, New York, 1940.

Flexner, Eleanor, *American Playwrights 1918–1938*, New York, 1939.

Floan, Howard R., *William Saroyan*, New York, 1966.

Gagey, Edmond, *Revolution in American Drama*, New York, 1947.

Gassner, John, ed., *Twenty Best Plays of the Modern American Theatre*, New York, 1939.

Gelb, Arthur, and Gelb, Barbara, *O'Neill*, New York, 1962.

Green, Paul, *Five Plays of the South*, New York, 1963.

Haberman, Donald, *The Plays of Thornton Wilder*, Middletown, Conn., 1967.

Hellman, Lillian, *Four Plays*, New York, 1942.

Hewitt, Barnard, *Theatre, USA: 1688 to 1957*, New York, 1959.

Himmelstein, Morgan, *Drama Was a Weapon*, New Brunswick, 1963.

Hughes, Glenn, *History of the American Theater, 1700–1950*, New York, 1951.

Kernan, Alvin B., ed., *The Modern American Theater*, Englewood Cliffs, N.J., 1967.

Kinne, Wisner Payne, *George Pierce Baker and the American Theatre*, Cambridge, 1954.

Knox, George A., and Stahl, Herbert M., *Dos Passos and 'The Revolting Playwrights'*, Uppsala, 1964.

Krutch, Joseph Wood, *The American Drama Since 1918*, New York, 1957.

Langner, Lawrence, *The Magic Curtain*, London, 1952.

Leuchtenburg, William E., *Franklin Roosevelt and the New Deal, 1932–1940*, New York, 1963.

MacGowan, Kenneth, *The Theatre of Tomorrow*, New York, 1921.

—— *Footlights Across America*, New York, 1929.

—— and Jones, Robert Edmond, *Continental Stagecraft*, London, 1923.

Mathews, Jane DeHart, *The Federal Theatre 1935–39*, Princeton, 1967.

Mickle, Alan D., *Six Plays of Eugene O'Neill*, New York, 1929.

Miller, Jordan Y., *Playwright's Progress: O'Neill and the Critics*, New York, 1965.

Mersand, Joseph, *The American Drama Since 1930*, Port Washington, New York, 1968.

Meserve, Walter, *Discussions of Modern American Drama*, Boston, 1965.

Mordden, Ethan, *The American Theatre*, New York, 1981.

Odets, Clifford, *Six Plays*, New York, 1935.

O'Neill, Eugene, *Plays*, 3 vols, New York, 1954.

Rabkin, Gerald, *Drama and Commitment*, Bloomingdale, Indiana, 1964.

Raleigh, John Henry, *The Plays of Eugene O'Neill*, Carbondale and Edwardsville, 1965.

Rice, Elmer, *Plays*, London, 1933.

Rohan, Pierre de, ed., *Federal Theatre Plays*, 2 vols, New York, 1938.

Saroyan, William, *The Time of Your Life*, London, 1942.

——*The Beautiful People*, London, 1943.

Scanlon, Tom, *Family Drama and American Dreams*, Westport, Conn. and London, 1978.

Shuman, R. Baird, *Clifford Odets*, New York, 1962.

Simonson, Lee, *The Stage is Set*, New York, 1932.

Skinner, Richard Dana, *Eugene O'Neill: A Poet's Quest*, New York, 1935.

Smiley, Sam, *The Drama of Attack*, Columbia, Missouri, 1972.

Taubman, Howard, *The Making of the American Theatre*, London, 1967.

Taylor, Karen Malpede, *People's Theatre in Amerika*, New York, 1972.

Tiusanen, Timo, *O'Neill's Scenic Images*, Princeton, 1968.

Valgemae, Mardi, *Accelerated Grimace: Expressionism in the American Drama of the 1920s*, Carbondale, 1972.

von Szeliski, John, *Tragedy and Fear*, Chapel Hill, 1971.

Waldau, Roy S., *Vintage Years of the Theatre Guild 1928–1939*, Cleveland and London, 1972.

Whitman, Wilson, *Bread and Circuses*, New York, 1937.

Wilder, Thornton, *Three Plays*, London, 1958.

4. American Poetry and the English Language, 1900–45

General

Allen, D. M., and Tallman, T., eds, *Poetics of the New American Poetry*, New York, 1970.

Allen, Gay Wilson, *American Prosody*, New York, 1935.

Alvarez, A., *The Shaping Spirit* (American ed.: *Stewards of Excellence*), London, 1958.

Berg, S., and Mezey, R., eds, *Naked Poetry*, 1969.

Berke, Roberta, *Bounds out of Bounds*, New York, 1981.

Bernetta Quinn, M. *The Metamorphic Tradition in Modern Poetry*, New Brunswick, NJ, 1955.

Bewley, Marius, *The Complex Fate*, London, 1952.

Bigsby, C. W. E., ed., *The Black American Writer: Volume 2. Poetry and Drama*, London, 1969.

Blackmur, R. P., *Language as Gesture*, New York, 1954.

Bode, Carl, *The Great Experiment in American Literature*, London, 1961.

Bogan, Louise, *Achievement in American Poetry 1900–1950*, Chicago, 1951.

Bové, Paul A., *Destructive Poetics: Heidegger and Modern American Poetry*, New York and Guildford, 1980.

Bradbury, J. M., *The Fugitives: A Critical Account*, Chapel Hill, 1958.

Brooks, Cleanth, *Modern Poetry and the Tradition*, Chapel Hill, 1939.

Cambon, Glauco, *The Inclusive Flame: Studies in American Poetry*, Bloomington, 1963.

Carroll, Paul, *The Poem in its Skin*, Chicago, 1968.

Ciardi, John, *Mid-Century American Poets*, 1950.

Coffman, Stanley K., *Imagism, A Chapter for the History of Modern Poetry*, Norman, Okl., 1951.

Cook, Bruce, *The Beat Generation*, 1971.

Davenport, Guy, *The Geography of the Imagination*, London, 1981.

Dembo, Lawrence S., *Conceptions of Reality in Modern American Poetry*, Berkeley, 1966.

Deutsch, Babette, *Poetry in Our Time*, New York, 1952, rev. 1963.

Dodsworth, Martin, ed., *The Survival of Poetry: A Contemporary Survey by Donald Davie and Others*, London, 1970.

Donoghue, Denis, *Connoisseurs of Chaos: Ideas of Order in Modern American Poetry*, New York, 1965.

Duberman, Martin, *Black Mountain: An Experiment in Community*, London, 1972.

Ellmann, Richard, and Feidelson, Charles, Jr, eds, *The Modern Tradition: Backgrounds of Modern Literature*, New York, 1965.

Faas, Ekbert, *Towards A New American Poetics*, Santa Barbara, 1979.

Feidelson, Charles, Jr, *Symbolism and American Literature*, Chicago, 1953.

Fender, Stephen, *The American Long Poem*, London, 1977.

Frankenberg, Lloyd, *Pleasure Dome*, New York, 1949.

Fussell, Edwin, *Lucifer in Harness: American Meter, Metaphor and Diction*, Princeton, 1973.

Gayle, Addison, Jr, *The Black Aesthetic*, 1971.

Gibson, D. B., *Five Black Writers*, New York and London, 1970.

Ginsberg, Allen (ed. Donald Allen), *Composed On The Tongue*, Bolinas, Cal., 1980.

Gregory, Horace, and Zaturenska, Marya, *A History of American Poetry, 1900–1940*, New York, 1946.

Hamilton, Ian, ed., *The Modern Poet: Essays from 'The Review'*, Oxford, 1968.

Howard, Richard, *Alone with America: The Art of Poetry in the United States since 1950*, 1969.

Hughes, Glenn, *Imagism and the Imagists: A Study in Modern Poetry*, London, 1941.

Hungerford, Edward B., ed., *Poets in Progress: Critical Prefaces to Ten Contemporary Americans*, Evanston (Northwestern University Press), 1962.

Jarrell, Randall, *Poetry and the Age*, London, 1953.

Jones, Peter, *Imagist Poetry*, Harmondsworth, 1973.

Kenner, Hugh, *A Homemade World*, New York, 1975.

Kherdian, David, ed., *Six San Francisco Poets*, Fresno, 1969.

Koch, K., and Farrell, K., *Sleeping on the Wing*, 1981.

Lee, Don L., *Dynamite Voices: Black Poets of the 1960s*, 1971.

Levertov, Denise, *The Poet in the World*, 1973.

Lowell, Amy, *Tendencies in Modern American Poetry*, Boston and New York, 1927.

Ludwig, Richard M., ed., *Aspects of American Poetry*, 1963.

Lutyens, David Bulwer, *The Creative Encounter*, London, 1960.

Mazzaro, Jerome, ed., *Modern American Poetry: Essays in Criticism*, Urbana and London, 1970.

——*Postmodern American Poetry*, Urbana and London, 1980.

Meltzer, David, ed., *The San Francisco Poets*, New York, 1971.

Mills, Ralph J., Jr, *Contemporary American Poetry*, New York, 1965.

Molesworth, Charles, *The Fierce Embrace*, Columbia and London, 1979.

Nemerov, Howard, ed., *Poets on Poetry*, New York and London, 1966.

Norman, Charles, ed., *Poets on Poetry*, New York and London, 1962.

O'Connor, W. V., *Sense and Sensibility in Modern Poetry*, Chicago, 1948.

Ossman, David, *The Sullen Art: Interviews with Modern American Poets*, New York, 1963.

Ostroff, Anthony, ed., *The Contemporary Poet as Artist and Critic*, Boston and Toronto, 1964.

Paris Review, Writers at Work: 'The Paris Review' Interviews, First series, 1950; Second series, 1963; Third series, 1967.

Parkinson, Thomas, ed., *A Casebook on the Beat*, New York, 1961.

Pearce, Roy Harvey, *The Continuity of American Poetry*, Princeton, 1961.

Pound, Ezra, *Make it New*, London, 1934.

——*Polite Essays*, London, 1937.

——*Literary Essays of Ezra Pound*, London, 1953.

Raiziss, Sonia, *The Metaphysical Passion: Seven Modern American Poets and the Seventeenth-Century Tradition*, Philadelphia, 1952.

Rajan, B., *Modern American Poetry*, London, 1950.

Revell, Peter, *Quest in Modern American Poetry*, London, 1982.

Rexroth, Kenneth, *American Poetry in the Twentieth Century*, New York, 1971.

Rosenthal, M. L., *The Modern Poets: A Critical Introduction*, New York, 1960.

——*The New Poets, American and British Poetry since World War II*, New York, 1967.

Schlauch, Margaret, *Modern British and American Poetry: Techniques and Ideologies*, London, 1956.

Shaw, Robert B., ed., *American Poetry Since 1960: Some Critical Perspectives*, Cheadle, 1973.

Simpson, Louis, *Three On The Tower*, New York, 1975.

Solt, Mary Ellen, ed., *Concrete Poetry: A World View*, London, 1968.

Southworth, J. G., *Some Modern American Poets*, Oxford, 1950.

——*More Modern American Poets*, Oxford, 1954.

Spears, Monroe K., *Dionysus and the City: Modernism in Twentieth Century American Poetry*, New York, 1970.

Stepanchev, Stephen, *American Poetry Since 1945*, New York, 1965.

Tate, Allen, ed., *Six American Poets from Emily Dickinson to the Present*, Minneapolis, 1969.

Taupin, René, *L'Influence du symbolisme Français sur la poésie Américaine*, Paris, 1929.

Tomlinson, Charles, *Some Americans*, Berkeley and London, 1981.

Turner, Darwin T., *Black American Literature: Poetry*, Ohio, 1969.

Wager, Willis, *American Literature – A World View*, London, 1970.

Waggoner, Hyatt H., *American Poets: From the Puritans to the Present*, Boston, 1968.

Wagner, Jean, *Black Poets of the United States: Racial and Religious Feeling in Poetry from P. L. Dunbar to L. Hughes, 1890–1940*, Paris, 1963.

Wagner, Linda W., *American Modern*, New York and London, 1980.

Wakoski, Diane, *Toward a New Poetry*, Ann Arbor, 1981.

Waldman, Anne, and Webb, Marilyn, *Talking Poetics From Naropa Institute*, Vols 1 and 2, London, 1978.

Weatherhead, A. Kingsley, *The Edge of the Image: Marianne Moore, William Carlos Williams, and Some Other Poets*, Seattle and London, 1967.

Weirick, B., *From Whitman to Sandburg in American Poetry*, New York, 1924.

Wells, Henry W., *The American Way of Poetry*, New York, 1943.

Williams, Stanley T., *The Beginnings of American Poetry, 1620–1855*, Uppsala, 1970.

Williams, William Carlos, *Selected Essays*, New York, 1954.

Wilson, Edmund, *Axel's Castle*, London and Glasgow, 1936.

Winters, Yvor, *In Defense of Reason* (including *Maule's Curse, Primitivism and Decadence*, and *The Anatomy of Nonsense*), London, 1947.

Individual Poets

Hart Crane (1899–1932)

TEXTS
White Buildings, 1926.
The Bridge, Paris, 1930.
Collected Poems, New York, 1933.
Seven Lyrics, Cambridge, Mass., 1966.
The Complete Poems and Selected Letters and Prose, New York, 1966.
Ten Unpublished Poems, New York, 1972.

CRITICISM

Butterfield, R. W., *The Broken Arc: A Study of Hart Crane*, Edinburgh, 1969.

Dembo, L. S., *Hart Crane's Sanskrit Charge: A Study of The Bridge*, Ithaca, 1960.

Hazo, Samuel, *Hart Crane: An Introduction and Interpretation*, New York, 1963.

——*Smithereened Apart: A Critique of Hart Crane*, 1977.

Landry, Hilton, *A Concordance to the Poems of Hart Crane*, Metuchen, NY, 1973.

Lane, Gary, *A Concordance to the Poems of Hart Crane*, 1972.

Lewis, R. W. B., *The Poetry of Hart Crane: A Critical Study*, Princeton, 1967.

Leibowitz, Herbert A., *Hart Crane: An Introduction to the Poetry*, New York and London, 1968.

Perry, Robert L., *The Shared Vision of Waldo Frank and Hart Crane*, Lincoln, Nebraska, 1966.

Quinn, Vincent, *Hart Crane*, New York, 1963.

Schwartz, Joseph, and Schweik, Robert C., eds, *Hart Crane: A Descriptive Bibliography*, Pittsburgh, 1972.

Spears, Monroe K., *Hart Crane*, Minneapolis, 1965.

Sugg, R. P., *Hart Crane's 'The Bridge'*, Alabama, 1977.

Uroff, Margaret Dickie, *Hart Crane: The Patterns of his Poetry*, Urbana, Illinois, 1974.

E. E. Cummings (1894–1962)

TEXTS

Tulips and Chimneys, New York, 1923.
&, New York, 1925.
is 5, New York, 1926.
CIOPW, New York, 1931.
ViVa, New York, 1931.
no thanks, New York, 1935.
One Over Twenty, New York, 1936.
Collected Poems, New York, 1938.
50 Poems, New York, 1940.
1 × 1, London, 1944.
XAIPE: 71 Poems, New York, 1950.
Poems, 1923–1954, New York, 1954.
95 Poems, New York, 1958.
100 Selected Poems, New York, 1959.
73 Poems, London, 1963.
Complete Poems, London, 1973.

CRITICISM

Baum, S. V. ed., *EΣTI: eec: E. E. Cummings and The Critics*, East Lansing, 1962.

Friedman, Norman, *E. E. Cummings: The Art of His Poetry*, London and Baltimore, 1960.

——, ed., *E. E. Cummings: The Growth of a Writer*, Carbondale, 1964.

——(ed), *E. E. Cummings: A Collection of Critical Essays*, Englewood Cliffs, NJ, 1972.

Lane, G., *I Am: A Study of E. E. Cummings' Poems*, 1976.

Marks, Barry A., *E. E. Cummings*, New York, 1964.

Rotella, Guy L., *E. E. Cummings: A Reference Guide*, Boston, Mass., 1979.

Triem, Eve, *E. E. Cummings*, Minneapolis, 1969.

Wegner, Robert E., *The Poetry and Prose of E. E. Cummings*, New York, 1965.

HD (Hilda Doolittle) (1886–1961)

TEXTS

Sea Garden, London, 1916.

Hymen, London, 1921.

Heliodora and Other Poems, London, 1924.

Collected Poems, New York, 1925.

Red Roses for Bronze, New York, 1931.

The Walls Do Not Fall, London, 1944.

Tribute to Angels, London, 1945.

The Flowering of the Rod, London, 1946.

By Avon River, New York, 1949.

Selected Poems, New York, 1957.

Helen in Egypt, New York, 1961.

Hermetic Definition, Oxford, 1972.

Trilogy, Cheadle Hulme, 1973.

The Poet and the Dancer, 1975.

CRITICISM

Quinn, Vincent, *H.D.*, New York, 1967.

Swann, Thomas B., *The Classical World of H.D.*, Lincoln, Nebraska, 1962.

T. S. Eliot (1886–1965)

TEXTS
Prufrock and Other Observations, London, 1917.
Poems, New York, 1919.
Ara Vos Prec, London, 1920.
The Waste Land, New York, 1922.
Poems 1909–1925, London, 1925.
Ash-Wednesday, New York, 1930.
Collected Poems, 1909–1935, London, 1936.
Old Possum's Book of Practical Cats, London, 1939.
The Waste Land and Other Poems, London, 1940.
East Coker, London, 1940.
Burnt Norton, London, 1941.
The Dry Salvages, London, 1941.
Little Gidding, London, 1942.
Four Quartets, London, 1943.
Poems Written in Early Youth, Stockholm, 1950.
The Complete Poems and Plays, New York, 1952.
Collected Poems 1909–1962, London, 1963.
The Waste Land [Facsimile of MS], London, 1971.

CRITICISM
Aldritt, Keith, *Eliot's Four Quartets: Poetry as Chamber Music*, London, 1978.
Brady, Ann Patrick, *Lyricism in the Poetry of T. S. Eliot*, London, 1978.
Bradbrook, M. C., *T. S. Eliot*, London, 1951.
Braybrooke, N., *T. S. Eliot*, 1967.
——, (ed), *T. S. Eliot: A Symposium for His Seventieth Birthday*, 1958.
Daiches, D., and others, eds, *'The Waste Land' by T. S. Eliot: Critical Analysis*, 1971.
Drew, E., *T. S. Eliot: The Design of His Poetry*, New York, 1949.
Freed, Lewis, *T. S. Eliot: Aesthetics and History*, West Lafayette, 1977.
Frye, N., *T. S. Eliot*, London and Edinburgh, 1963.
Gardner, H., *The Art of T. S. Eliot*, London, 1950.
——*The Composition of Four Quartets*, London, 1978.
Gish, Nancy K., *Time in the Poetry of T. S. Eliot*, London, 1981.
Gordon, Lyndall, *Eliot's Early Years*, Oxford, 1977.
Kenner, Hugh, *The Invisible Poet*, London, 1959.
——, ed., *T. S. Eliot: A Collection of Critical Essays*, Englewood Cliffs, NJ, 1962.
Kirk, R., *Eliot and His Age*, 1972.

Knoll, R. E., ed., *Storm Over the Waste Land*, Chicago, 1964.

Lobb, Edward, *T. S. Eliot and the Romantic Critical Tradition*, London, 1981.

March, R., and Tambimuttu, T., eds, *T. S. Eliot*, 1949.

Martin, J., ed., *Twentieth-Century Interpretations of 'The Waste Land'*, Englewood Cliffs, NJ,1968.

Martin, M., *A Half-Century of Eliot Criticism: An Annotated Bibliography*, London, 1972.

Matthiessen, F. O., *The Achievement of T. S. Eliot*, New York, 1947.

Maxwell, D. E. S., *The Poetry of T. S. Eliot*, London, 1952.

Miller, James E., *T. S. Eliot's Personal Waste Land: Exorcism of the Demons*, London, 1977.

Moody, Anthony D., *Thomas Stearns Eliot, Poet*, Cambridge, 1979.

——, ed., *The Wasteland in Different Voices*, London, 1974.

Morris, D. B., *The Poetry of Gerard Manley Hopkins and T. S. Eliot in the Light of the Donne Tradition*, 1953.

Musgrove, Sydney, *T. S. Eliot and Walt Whitman*, Wellington, New Zealand, 1952.

Rajan, Balachandra, *The Overwhelming Question: A Study of the Poetry of T. S. Eliot*, Toronto, 1976.

Schneider, Elizabeth, *T. S. Eliot: Pattern in the Carpet*, Berkeley and London, 1975.

Sinha, Krishna, *On 'Four Quartets' of T. S. Eliot*, 1963.

Smith, Grover, *T. S. Eliot's Poetry and Plays: A Study in Sources and Meaning*, Chicago, 1956.

Spender, S., *Eliot*, Harmondsworth, 1975.

Tate, A., ed., *T. S. Eliot: The Man and His Work*, 1966.

Thomas, C. T., *Poetic Tradition and Eliot's Talent*, Bombay, 1979.

Thormahlen, Marianne, *The Wasteland: A Fragmentary Wholeness*, Lund, 1978.

Traversi, D. A., *T. S. Eliot: The Longer Poems*, London, 1976.

Unger, L. *T. S. Eliot*, Minneapolis, 1961.

——*T. S. Eliot: Monuments and Patterns*, London and Minneapolis, 1965.

——, ed., *T. S. Eliot: A Selected Critique*, New York and Toronto, 1948.

Williamson, G., *A Reader's Guide to T. S. Eliot*, New York, 1965.

Robert Frost (1874–1963)

TEXTS
A Boy's Will, New York, 1913.

North of Boston, London, 1914.

Mountain Interval, New York, 1916.
New Hampshire, New York, 1923.
Selected Poems, London, 1923, rev. 1928 and 1934.
West-Running Brook, New York, 1928.
Collected Poems, London, 1930.
A Further Range, New York, 1936.
Selected Poems, London, 1936.
Collected Poems, London, 1939.
A Witness Tree, London, 1942.
A Masque of Reason, London, 1945.
Poems, New York, 1946.
A Masque of Mercy, New York, 1947.
A Sermon, 1947.
Steeple Bush, New York, 1947.
Complete Poems, New York, 1949.
Aforesaid, 1954.
In the Clearing, New York, 1962.
The Poetry of Robert Frost, New York, 1969.

CRITICISM
Brower, Reuben, *The Poetry of Robert Frost: Constellations of Intention*,
    New York, 1963.
Clymer, W. B. S., *Robert Frost: A Bibliography*, 1972.
Cook, Reginald L., *The Dimensions of Robert Frost*, New York, 1958.
Cox, James M., ed., *Robert Frost: A Collection of Critical Essays*,
    Englewood Cliffs, NJ, 1962.
Doyle, John R., Jr, *The Poetry of Robert Frost: An Analysis*, New York,
    1962.
Francis, Robert, *Robert Frost: A Time to Talk*, London, 1973.
Gerber, Philip L., *Robert Frost*, New York, 1966.
Greenberg, Robert A., and Hepburn, James G., eds, *Robert Frost:
    An Introduction*, 1961.
Isaacs, Elizabeth, *An Introduction to Robert Frost*, Denver, 1962.
Jennings, Elizabeth, *Robert Frost*, London and Edinburgh, 1964.
Kemp, John C., *Robert Frost and New England: The Poet as Reg-
    ionalist*, Princeton and Guildford, 1979.
Lentricchia, Frank, *Robert Frost: Modern Poetics and the Landscape of
    Self*, Durham, N Carolina, 1975.
Lynen, John F., *The Pastoral Art of Robert Frost*, New Haven, 1964.
Nitchie, George W., *Human Values in the Poetry of Robert Frost*,
    Durham, N Carolina, 1960.
Poirier, W. R., *Robert Frost*, New York, 1977.

Potter, James L., *Robert Frost: Handbook*, London, 1981.
Sell, Roger D., *Robert Frost: Four Studies*, 1980.
Squires, Radcliffe, *The Major Themes of Robert Frost*, Ann Arbor, 1963.
Thompson, Lawrance R., *Fire and Ice: The Art and Thought of Robert Frost*, New York, 1942.
——*Robert Frost*, New York, 1964.
Thornton, Richard, ed., *The Recognition of Robert Frost*, 1970.

Robinson Jeffers (1887–1962)

TEXTS

Flagons and Apples, Los Angeles, 1912.
Californians, New York, 1916.
Tamar and Other Poems, New York, 1924.
Roan Stallion, London, 1925.
The Woman at Point Sur, New York, 1927.
Poems, 1928.
Cawdor and Other Poems, London, 1928.
Dear Judas and Other Poems, London, 1929.
Descent to the Dead: Poems Written in Ireland and Great Britain, New York, 1931.
Thurso's Landing, New York, 1932.
Give Your Heart to the Hawks and Other Poems, New York, 1933.
Solstice and Other Poems, New York and San Francisco, 1935.
Such Counsels You Gave to Me and Other Poems, New York, 1937.
Poems Known and Unknown, 1938.
Selected Poetry, New York, 1938.
Be Angry at the Sun, New York, 1941.
The Double Axe and Other Poems, New York, 1948.
Hungerfield and Other Poems, New York, 1954.
The Beginning and the End, New York, 1963.
Selected Poems, 1965.
Scott, Robert, ed., *What Odd Expedients and Other Poems*, 1982.

CRITICISM

Alberts, Sydney S., *A Bibliography of the Works of Robinson Jeffers*, 1933.
Antoninus, Brother, *Robinson Jeffers: Fragments of an Older Fury*, 1970.
Coffin, Arthur B., *Robinson Jeffers: Poet of Inhumanism*, Madison, Wisconsin, 1971.

Shebl, J., *In this Wild Water: the Suppressed Poems of Robinson Jeffers*, Pasadena, 1976.
Squires, Radcliffe, *The Loyalties of Robinson Jeffers*, Ann Arbor, 1966.
Verdamis, Alex A., *The Critical Reputation of Robinson Jeffers*, 1972.
White, Kenneth, *The Coast Opposite Humanity*, Llanfynydd, 1975.

Vachel Lindsay (1879–1931)

TEXTS
The Tramp's Excuse and Other Poems, 1909.
General William Booth Enters into Heaven and Other Poems, New York, 1913.
The Congo and Other Poems, New York, 1914.
The Chinese Nightingale and Other Poems, New York, 1917.
The Golden Whales of California and Other Rhymes in the American Language, New York, 1920.
The Daniel Jazz and Other Poems, London, 1920.
Going-to-the-sun, New York and London, 1923.
The Candle in the Cabin: A Weaving Together of Script and Singing, New York and London, 1926.
Going-to-the-Stars, New York and London, 1926.
Johnny Appleseed, New York, 1928.
Every Soul is a Circus, New York, 1929.
Selected Poems, 1931, rev. New York, 1963.

CRITICISM
Harris, M., *City of Discontent: An Interpretive Biography of Vachel Lindsay*, 1952.
Massa, Ann, *Vachel Lindsay: Field Worker for the American Dream*, Bloomington and London, 1970.
Masters, H. L., *Vachel Lindsay: A Poet in America*, New York and London, 1935.
Scouffas, George, *Vachel Lindsay: A Study in Retreat and Repudiation*, 1951.

Amy Lowell (1874–1925)

TEXTS
A Dome of Many-Colored Glass, Boston, Mass. and London, 1912.
Sword Blades and Poppy Seeds, London, 1914.
Men, Women and Ghosts, 1916.

Can Grande's Castle, Oxford, 1918.
Pictures of the Floating World, Boston, Mass. and New York, 1919.
Legends, Boston, Mass. and New York, 1921.
Fir-Flower Tablets, 1921.
A Critical Fable, Boston, Mass. and New York, 1922.
What's O'Clock, Boston, Mass. and New York, 1925.
East Wind, Boston, Mass. and New York, 1926.
Ballads for Sale, Boston, Mass. and New York, 1927.
Selected Poems, Boston, Mass. and New York, 1928.
The Complete Poetical Works of Amy Lowell, Boston, Mass., 1955.

CRITICISM
Damon, S. Foster, *Amy Lowell: A Chronicle*, Boston, Mass. and New York, 1935.
Flint, F. C., *Amy Lowell*, Minneapolis, 1969.
Gregory, H., *Amy Lowell: Portrait of a Poet in Her Time*, New York, 1958.

Archibald MacLeish (1892–1982)

TEXTS
Songs for a Summer's Day, 1915.
Tower of Ivory, New Haven and London, 1917.
The Happy Marriage, Boston, Mass. and London, 1924.
Streets in the Moon, Boston, Mass. and New York, 1926.
The Hamlet of A. MacLeish, Boston, Mass. and New York, 1928.
New Found Land, Paris, 1930.
Conquistador, London, 1932.
Before March, New York, 1932.
Poems 1924–1933, Boston, Mass. and New York, 1933.
Frescoes for Mr Rockefeller's City, New York, 1933.
Public Speech, London, 1936.
Land of the Free, London, 1938.
America Was Promises, London, 1939.
Act Five, London, 1948.
Collected Poems, Boston, Mass., 1952, rev. 1963.
Songs for Eve, Boston, Mass., 1954.
The Wild Old Wicked Man and Other Poems, London, 1967.
The Human Season: Selected Poems, 1926–1972, 1972.
New and Collected Poems 1917–1976, Boston, Mass., 1976.

CRITICISM
Falk, Signi, *Archibald MacLeish*, New York, 1965.
Mullaly, Edward J., *Archibald MacLeish: A Checklist*, Kent, Ohio, 1973.
Smith, G., *Archibald MacLeish*, Minneapolis, 1971.

Edgar Lee Masters (1869–1950)

TEXTS
The Book of Verses, Chicago, 1898.
The Blood of the Prophets, 1905.
Spoon River Anthology, London and Norwood, Mass., 1915.
Songs and Satires, London and Norwood Mass., 1916.
Toward the Gulf, New York, 1918.
Starved Rock, New York, 1919.
Domesday Book, New York, 1920.
The New Spoon River, New York, 1924.
Selected Poems, 1925.
The Fate of the Jury: An Epilogue to 'Domesday Book', New York and London, 1929.
Lichee Nuts, New York, 1930.
The Serpent in the Wilderness, New York, 1933.
Invisible Landscapes, New York, 1935.
The Golden Fleece of California, New York, 1936.
Poems of People, New York and London, 1936.
The New World, New York and London, 1937.
More People, New York and London, 1939.
Illinois Poems, 1941.
The Sangamon, New York and Toronto, 1942.

CRITICISM
Flaccus, Kimball, *The Vermont Background of Edgar Lee Masters*, New York, 1955.
Hartley, Lois Teal, *Edgar Lee Masters: A Study*, 1950.

Edna St Vincent Millay (1892–1950)

TEXTS
Renascence and Other Poems, New York, 1917.
A Few Figs from Thistles, New York and London, 1920.
Second April, New York, 1921.
The Harp-Weaver and Other Poems, New York and London, 1923.

The Buck in the Snow, New York and London, 1928.
Fatal Interview, New York and London, 1931.
Wine from These Grapes, London, 1934.
Conversation at Midnight, London, 1937.
Huntsman, What Quarry?, London, 1939.
Make Bright the Arrows, New York and London, 1940.
Collected Sonnets, New York and London, 1941.
Collected Lyrics, New York and London, 1943.
Mine the Harvest, New York, 1954.
Collected Poems, New York, 1956.

CRITICISM
Atkins, Elizabeth, *Edna St Vincent Millay and Her Times*, Chicago, 1936.
Britten, Norman A., *Edna St Vincent Millay*, 1967.
Gould, Jean, *The Poet and Her Book: The Life and Work of Edna St Vincent Millay*, New York, 1969.
Gray, James, *Edna St Vincent Millay*, Minneapolis, 1967.
Yost, Karl, *A Bibliography of the Works of Edna St Vincent Millay*, New York and London, 1937.

Marianne Moore (1887–1972)

TEXTS
Poems, London, 1921.
Observations, New York, 1924.
Selected Poems, London, 1935.
The Pangolin, London, 1936.
What Are Years?, New York, 1941.
Nevertheless, New York, 1944.
Collected Poems, London, 1951.
Like a Bulwark, London, 1956.
O To Be a Dragon, New York, 1959.
The Arctic Ox, London, 1964.
Tell Me, Tell Me, New York, 1966.
Complete Poems, London, 1967.

CRITICISM
Abbot, Craig S., *Marianne Moore: A Descriptive Bibliography*, London and Pittsburgh, 1977.
Costello, Bonnie, *Marianne Moore: Imaginary Possessions*, London and Cambridge, Mass., 1981.

Engle, Bernard F., *Marianne Moore*, New Haven, 1963.
Garrigue, Jean, *Marianne Moore*, Minneapolis and London, 1965.
Hadas, P. W., *Marianne Moore: Poet of Affection*, Syracuse, 1977.
Hall, Donald, *Marianne Moore: The Cage and the Animal*, 1970.
Lane, Gary, *A Concordance to the Poems of Marianne Moore*, 1972.
Nitchie, George W., *Marianne Moore: An Introduction to the Poetry*, New York and London, 1969.
Sheehy, Eugene P., and Lohf, Kenneth A., *The Achievement of Marianne Moore*, New York, 1958.
Stapleton, Lawrence, *Marianne Moore: the Poet's Advance*, Princeton and Guildford, 1978.
Tomlinson, Charles, ed., *Marianne Moore: A Collection of Critical Essays*, New York, 1969.

Ezra Pound (1885–1972)

TEXTS
A Lume Spento, Milan, 1908.
A Quinzaine for This Yule, 1908.
Personae, London, 1909.
Exultations, 1909.
Provença: Poems Selected from Personae, Exultations and Canzoniere, Boston, Mass., 1910.
Canzoni, London, 1911.
Ripostes, 1912.
Lustra, New York, 1916.
Quia Pauper Amavi, London, 1919.
Umbra: The Early Poems, London, 1920.
Hugh Selwyn Mauberley, 1920.
Poems, 1918–1921, New York, 1921.
A Draft of XVI Cantos, London, 1925.
Personae: Collected Poems, New York, 1926, rev. 1949.
Selected Poems, London, 1928.
A Draft of The Cantos 17–27, London, 1928.
A Draft of XXX Cantos, Paris, 1930.
Homage to Sextus Propertius, London, 1934.
Eleven New Cantos: XXXI–XLI, New York, 1934.
The Fifth Decad of Cantos, London and Norfolk, Conn., 1937.
Cantos LII-LXXI, London, 1940.
The Cantos, New York, 1948, 1965, 1971.
The Pisan Cantos, London, 1948.
Selected Poems, London, 1949, rev. 1957.

Seventy Cantos, London, 1950.
Selected Shorter Poems, London, 1952, rev. 1973.
Section: Rock-Drill: 86–95 de los cantares, Milan, 1955.
Thrones: 96–109 de los cantares, New York, 1959.
A Lume Spento and Other Early Poems, London, 1965.
Selected Cantos, 1967.
Drafts and Fragments of Cantos CX to CXVII, New York, 1969.
The Cantos of Ezra Pound, London, 1975.
King, M. J., ed., *Collected Early Poems*, London, 1977.

CRITICISM

Agenda Special Issue, London, 1980.
Alexander, Michael, *The Poetic Achievement of Ezra Pound*, London, 1979.
Baumann, Walter, *The Rose in the Steel Dust: An Examination of the Cantos of Ezra Pound*, Berne, 1967.
Bell, Ian F. A., *Critic as Scientist: the Modernist Poetics of Ezra Pound*, London, 1981.
Bernstein, Michael André, *The Tale of the Tribe: Ezra Pound and the Modern Verse Epic*, Princeton, 1980.
Brooke-Rose, Christine, *A ZBC of Ezra Pound*, London, 1971.
Brooker, Peter, *A Student's Guide to the Selected Poems of Ezra Pound*, London, 1979.
Bush, R., *The Genesis of Ezra Pound's Cantos*, Princeton and Guildford, 1976.
Davie, Donald, *Ezra Pound: Poet as Sculptor*, London, 1964.
——*Pound*, London, 1975.
Dekker, George, *Sailing After Knowledge: The Cantos of Ezra Pound*, London, 1963.
Christoph de Nagy, N., *The Poetry of Ezra Pound: The Pre-Imagist Stage*, Berne, 1960, rev. 1968.
Dilligan, Robert J., *A Concordance to Ezra Pound's Cantos*, 1981.
Durant, Alan, *Ezra Pound: Identity in Crisis*, Brighton, 1981.
Edwards John H., and Vasse, William W., Jr, eds, *Annotated Index to the Cantos of Ezra Pound* (to Canto 84), 1957.
Eliot, T. S., *Ezra Pound: His Metric and Poetry*, 1917.
Emery, Clark, *Ideas into Action: A Study of Pound's Cantos*, 1958.
Epsey, John, *Ezra Pound's 'Mauberley'*, 1955.
Flory, Wendy S., *Ezra Pound and the Cantos: a Record of Struggle*, New Haven and London, 1980.
Fraser, G. S., *Ezra Pound*, 1961.
Gallup, Donald, *A Bibliography of Ezra Pound*, London, 1964.

Goodwin, K. L., *The Influence of Ezra Pound*, London, 1966.

Hesse, Eva, ed., *New Approaches to Ezra Pound*, London, 1969.

Heymann, C. D., *Ezra Pound*, London, 1976.

Homberger, Eric, *Ezra Pound: The Critical Heritage*, London, 1972.

Jackson, Thomas H., *The Early Poetry of Ezra Pound*, Cambridge, Mass., 1968.

Kearns, George, *Guide to Ezra Pound's Selected Cantos*, Folkestone, 1980.

Kenner, Hugh, *The Poetry of Ezra Pound*, London, 1951.

——*The Pound Era*, 1972.

Lane, Gary, *A Concordance to the Poems of Ezra Pound*, 1972.

Leary, Lewis, *Motive and Method in the Cantos of Ezra Pound*, New York, 1954.

Makin, Peter, *Provence and Pound*, Berkeley and London, 1979.

Nassar, Eugene P., *The Cantos of Ezra Pound: The Lyric Mode*, London and Baltimore, 1975.

O'Connor, William Van, *Ezra Pound*, Minneapolis, 1963.

——, ed., with Stone, Edward, *A Case Book on Ezra Pound*, 1959.

Pearlman, Daniel D., *The Barb of Time: On the Unity of Pound's Cantos*, New York, 1969.

Reck, Michael, *Ezra Pound: A Close-up*, 1973.

Rosenthal, M. L., *A Primer of Ezra Pound*, New York, 1960.

Russell, Peter., ed., *An Examination of Ezra Pound*, New York, 1950.

Ruthven, K. K., *A Guide to Ezra Pound's 'Personae'*, Berkeley and Los Angeles, 1969.

Sullivan, J. P., *Ezra Pound and Sextus Propertius: A Study in Creative Translation*, London, 1964.

——*Ezra Pound: A Collection of Critical Essays*, 1963.

Surette, Leon, *A Light from Eleusis: A Study of Ezra Pound's Cantos*, Oxford, 1979.

Terrell, Carroll F., *A Companion to the 'Cantos' of Ezra Pound*, London and Berkeley, 1981.

Wilhelm, J. J., *The Later Cantos of Ezra Pound*, 1977.

Witemeyer, Hugh, *The Poetry of Ezra Pound: Forms and Renewal, 1908–1920*, Berkeley, Los Angeles and London, 1969.

Woodward, Anthony, *Ezra Pound and the Pisan Cantos*, London, 1980.

John Crowe Ransom (1888–1974)

TEXTS

Poems About God, New York, 1919.

Chills and Fever, New York, 1924.

Grace After Meat, London, 1924.
Two Gentlemen in Bonds, New York, 1927.
Selected Poems, New York, 1945, rev. 1963.
Poems and Essays, New York, 1955.

CRITICISM

Buffington, Robert, *But What I Wear Is Flesh*, Nashville, 1967.
Knight, Karl F., *The Poetry of John Crowe Ransom: A Study of Diction, Metaphor, and Symbol*, The Hague, 1971.
Parsons, Thornton H., *John Crowe Ransom*, New York, 1969.
Stewart, John L., *John Crowe Ransom*, Minneapolis, 1962.
Young, Thomas H., ed., *John Crowe Ransom: Critical Essays and a Bibliography*, 1968.

Edwin Arlington Robinson (1869–1935)

TEXTS

The Torrent and the Night Before, 1896.
The Children of the Night, Boston, Mass., 1897.
Captain Craig, London and Cambridge, Mass., 1902.
The Town down the River, 1910.
The Man Against the Sky, New York, 1916.
Merlin, New York, 1917.
Lancelot, New York, 1920.
The Three Taverns, New York, 1920.
Avon's Harvest, New York, 1921.
Collected Poems, London, 1921.
Roman Bartholow, London, 1923.
The Man Who Died Twice, London, 1924.
Dionysus in Doubt, New York, 1925.
Tristram, London, 1927.
Collected Poems, New York, 5 vols, 1927.
Sonnets: 1889–1927, New York, 1928.
Cavender's House, London, 1929.
Collected Poems, London, 1929.
The Glory of the Nightingales, New York, 1930.
Selected Poems, New York, 1931.
Matthias at the Door, New York, 1931.
Nicodemus, New York, 1932.
Talifer, New York, 1933.
Amaranth, New York, 1934.
King Jasper, New York, 1935.
Collected Poems, 1937.

CRITICISM

Anderson, Wallace L., *Edwin Arlington Robinson: A Critical Introduction*, Cambridge, Mass., 1967.

Barnard, Ellsworth, *Edwin Arlington Robinson: A Critical Study*, New York, 1952.

——, ed., *Edwin Arlington Robinson: Centenary Essays*, Athens, Georgia, 1969.

Cary, Richard, ed., *An Appreciation of Edwin Arlington Robinson*, 1969.

Cestre, Charles, *An Introduction to Edwin Arlington Robinson*, New York, 1930.

Coxe, Louis O., *Edwin Arlington Robinson*, Minneapolis, 1962.

——*Edwin Arlington Robinson: The Life of Poetry*, New York, 1968.

Franchere, Hoyt C., *Edwin Arlington Robinson*, New York, 1968.

Fussell, Edwin S., *Edwin Arlington Robinson: The Literary Background of a Traditional Poet*, Berkeley and Los Angeles, 1954.

Hogan, Charles B., *A Bibliography of Edwin Arlington Robinson*, New Haven, 1936.

Murphy, Francis, ed., *Edwin Arlington Robinson: A Collection of Critical Essays*, 1970.

Neff, Emery, *Edwin Arlington Robinson*, London, 1948.

Robinson, W. R., *Edwin Arlington Robinson: A Poetry of the Act*, 1967.

White, William, *Edwin Arlington Robinson: A Supplementary Bibliography, 1936–1970*, Kent, Ohio, 1971.

Winters, Yvor, *Edwin Arlington Robinson*, Norfolk, Conn., 1946.

Carl Sandburg (1878–1967)

TEXTS

In Reckless Ecstasy, 1904.
Chicago Poems, New York, 1916.
Cornhuskers, New York, 1918.
Smoke and Steel, New York, 1920.
Slabs of the Sunburnt West, New York, 1922.
Selected Poems, London, 1926.
Good Morning, America, New York, 1928.
The People, Yes, New York, 1936.
Complete Poems, New York, 1950, rev. 1970;
Wind Song, New York, 1960.

CRITICISM

Allen, Gay Wilson, *Carl Sandburg*, Minneapolis, 1972.
Crowder, Richard, *Carl Sandburg*, New York, 1963.

Golden, Harry, *Carl Sandburg*, Cleveland and New York, 1961.
Longo, Lucas, *Carl Sandburg: Poet and Historian*, 1972.
Shaw, Thomas S., *Carl Sandburg: A Bibliography*, 1948.

Wallace Stevens (1879–1955)

TEXTS
Harmonium, New York, 1923.
Ideas of Order, New York and London, 1935.
Owl's Clover, 1936.
The Man with the Blue Guitar, New York and London, 1937.
Transport to Summer, New York, 1947.
The Auroras of Autumn, New York, 1950.
Selected Poems, London, 1953.
Collected Poems, London, 1954.
Opus Posthumous, New York, 1957.
The Palm at the End of the Mind, New York, 1971.

CRITICISM
Baird, James, *The Dome and the Rock: Structure in the Poetry of Wallace Stevens*, Baltimore, 1968.
Beckett, Lucy, *Wallace Stevens*, London, 1974.
Benamou, Michel, *Wallace Stevens and the Symbolist Imagination*, Princeton, 1972.
Blessing, Richard, *Wallace Stevens, Whole Harmonium*, 1970.
Bloom, Harold, *Wallace Stevens: The Poems of our Climate*, London and Ithaca, 1977.
Borroff, Marie, ed., *Wallace Stevens: A Collection of Critical Essays*, Englewood Cliffs, NJ, 1963.
Brown, Ashley, and Haller, Robert, eds, *The Achievement of Wallace Stevens*, New York and Philadephia, 1962.
Brown, Merle E., *Wallace Stevens: The Poem as Act*, Detroit, 1971.
Burney, William, *Wallace Stevens*, New York, 1968.
Buttel, Robert, *Wallace Stevens: The Making of 'Harmonium'*, Princeton, 1967.
Doggett, Frank, *Stevens' Poetry of Thought*, Baltimore, 1966.
Enck, John J., *Wallace Stevens: Images and Judgments*, 1964.
Fuchs, Daniel, *The Comic Spirit of Wallace Stevens*, Durham, NC, 1962.
Hines, T. J., *The Later Poetry of Wallace Stevens*, London and Lewisburg, 1976.
Kermode, Frank, *Wallace Stevens*, London and Edinburgh, 1960.

Kessler, Edward, *Images of Wallace Stevens*, 1972.

Litz, A. Walton, *Introspective Voyager: The Poetic Development of Wallace Stevens*, New York, 1972.

Morris, A. K., *Wallace Stevens: Imagination and Faith*, Princeton, 1974.

Morse, Samuel French, *Wallace Stevens: Life as Poetry*, 1970.

——*A Wallace Stevens Checklist* and *Bibliography of Stevens Criticism*, 1963.

Nassar, Eugene P., *Wallace Stevens: An Anatomy of Figuration*, Philadelphia, 1965.

O'Connor, William Van, *The Shaping Spirit: A Study of Wallace Stevens*, Chicago, 1950.

Pearce, Roy H., and Miller, J. H., eds, *The Act of the Mind: Essays on the Poetry of Wallace Stevens*, Baltimore, 1965.

Perlis, Alan, *Wallace Stevens: A World of Transforming Shapes*, Lewisburg, 1976.

Riddell, Joseph N., *The Clairvoyant Eye: The Poetry and Poetics of Wallace Stevens*, Louisiana, 1965.

Stern, Herbert J., *Wallace Stevens: Art of Uncertainty*, Ann Arbor, 1966.

Vendler, Helen H., *On Extended Wings: Wallace Stevens' Longer Poems*, Cambridge, Mass., 1969.

Walsh, Thomas F., *A Concordance to the Poetry of Wallace Stevens*, University Park, Penn., 1963.

Wells, Henry, *Introduction to Wallace Stevens*, 1964.

Weston, S. B., *Wallace Stevens: An Introduction to the Poetry*, New York and Guildford, 1977.

Allen Tate (1899–1979)

TEXTS

Mr Pope and Other Poems, New York, 1928.

Poems, 1928–1931, 1932.

The Mediterranean and Other Poems, New York, 1936.

Selected Poems, New York and London, 1937.

The Winter Sea, Cummington, Mass., 1944.

Poems, 1920–1945, London, 1947.

Poems, 1922–1947, 1948.

Two Conceits for the Eye to Sing, If Possible, Cummington, Mass., 1950.

Poems, New York, 1960.

Poems, Denver, 1961.

The Swimmers and Other Selected Poems, London and New York, 1970.

Collected Poems 1919–1976, New York, 1977.

CRITICISM
Arnold, Willard Burdett, *The Social Ideas of Allen Tate*, 1955.
Bishop, Ferman, *Allen Tate*, New York, 1967.
Hemphill, George, *Allen Tate*, Minneapolis, 1964.
Meiners, R. K., *The Last Alternatives*, Denver, 1963.
Squires, Radcliffe, *Allen Tate: A Literary Biography*, Minneaplois, 1971.
——, ed., *Allen Tate and His Work: Critical Evaluations*, Minneapolis, 1972.

Robert Penn Warren (b. 1905)

TEXTS
Thirty-Six Poems, 1936.
Eleven Poems on the Same Theme, Norfolk, Conn., 1942.
Selected Poems, 1923–1943, New York, 1944.
Brother to Dragons, London, 1953.
Promises: Poems, 1954–1956, New York, 1957.
You, Emperors and Others: Poems 1957–1960, New York, 1960.
Selected Poems: New and Old, 1923–66, New York, 1966.
Incarnations, New York, 1968.
Audubon: A Vision, New York, 1969.
Or Else: Poem/Poems 1969–1974, 1974.
Selected Poems 1923–1975, London, 1977.
Now and Then: Poems 1976–78, 1978.
Being Here: Poetry 1977–80, London, 1980.

CRITICISM
Bohner, Charles H., *Robert Penn Warren*, New York, 1964.
Casper Leonard, *Robert Penn Warren: The Dark and Bloody Ground*, Seattle, 1960.
Huff, Mary N., *Robert Penn Warren, A Bibliography*, New York, 1968.
Longley, John, ed., *Robert Penn Warren*, 1964.
Strandberg, Victor, *A Colder Fire*, Lexington, Kentucky, 1965.
——*The Poetic Vision of Robert Penn Warren*, Lexington, Kentucky, 1977.
West, Paul, *Robert Penn Warren*, Minneapolis, 1964.

William Carlos Williams (1883–1963)

TEXTS
Poems, 1909.
The Tempers, 1913.

Al Que Quere!, Boston, Mass., 1917.
Kora in Hell, London and San Francisco, 1920.
Sour Grapes, Boston, Mass., 1921.
Spring and All, Dijon, 1923.
Collected Poems, 1921–1931, New York, 1934.
An Early Martyr, New York, 1935.
Adam and Eve and the City, 1936.
The Complete Collected Poems, 1906–1938, Norfolk, Conn., 1938.
The Wedge, Cummington, Mass., 1944.
Paterson, Book I, New York, 1946.
Paterson, Book II, New York, 1948.
The Clouds, New York, 1948.
Selected Poems, New York, 1949.
Paterson, Book III, New York, 1949.
The Collected Later Poems, London, 1950, rev. 1963.
The Collected Earlier Poems, Norfolk, Conn., 1951.
Paterson, Book IV, New York, 1951.
The Desert Music, New York, 1954.
Journey to Love, New York, 1955.
Paterson, Book V, New York, 1958.
Pictures from Brueghel, Norfolk, Conn., 1962.
Paterson, New York, 1963.
Imaginations, New York and London, 1970.
Selected Poems, Harmondsworth, 1976.

CRITICISM

Breslin, James, *William Carlos Williams: An American Artist*, New York, 1970.
Brinnin, John Malcolm, *William Carlos Williams*, Minneapolis, 1963.
Coles, Robert, *William Carlos Williams: The Knack of Survival in America*, New Brunswick, 1975.
Conarroe, Joel, *William Carlos Williams' 'Paterson': Language and Landscape*, 1970.
Dijkstra, Bram, *The Hieroglyphics of a New Speech: Cubism, Stieglitz, and the Early Poetry of William Carlos Williams*, Princeton, 1968.
——*A Recognizable Image: William Carlos Williams on Art and Artists*, 1978.
Doyle, Charles, ed., *William Carlos Williams: The Critical Heritage*, London, 1980.
Engels, John, *Checklist of William Carlos Williams*, Columbus, Ohio, 1969.

Guimond, James, *The Art of William Carlos Williams: A Discovery and Possession of America*, London and Urbana, 1968.

Lloyd, Margaret Glynne, *William Carlos Williams' 'Paterson'*, Rutherford, 1981.

Mariani, Paul L., *William Carlos Williams: The Poet and his Critics*, Chicago, 1975.

Mazzaro, Jerome, ed., *Profile of William Carlos Williams*, Columbus, Ohio, 1971.

——*William Carlos Williams: the Later Poems*, 1973.

Miller, J. Hillis, ed., *William Carlos Williams: A Collection of Critical Essays*, Baltimore, 1966.

Paul, Sherman, *The Music of Survival*, Urbana and London, 1968.

Peterson, Walter Scott, *An Approach to 'Paterson'*, London and New Haven, 1967.

Riddel, Joseph N., *The Inverted Bell: Modernism and the Counter-Poetics of William Carlos Williams*, Baton Rouge, 1974.

Sankey, Benjamin, *A Companion to William Carlos Williams's 'Paterson'*, Berkeley and London, 1971.

Tashjran, D., *William Carlos Williams and the American Scene 1920–1940*, Berkeley and London, 1978.

Townley, R., *The Early Poetry of William Carlos Williams*, London and Ithaca, 1975.

Wagner, Linda W., *The Poems of William Carlos Williams: A Critical Study*, Boston, Mass., 1964.

——*William Carlos Williams: A Reference Guide*, Boston, Mass., 1978.

Wallace, Emily Mitchell, *A Bibliography of William Carlos Williams*, New York, 1968.

Weaver, M., *William Carlos Williams: The American Background*, London, 1977.

Whitaker, Thomas, *William Carlos Williams*, New York, 1968.

Whittemore, R. *William Carlos Williams: Poet from Jersey*, Boston, Mass., 1975.

5. *Poetry 1945–60: Self versus Culture*

General

See also some titles in bibliography for Chapter 4

Daiches, David, 'The Anglo-American Difference: Two Views', *The Anchor Review*, Number One, Garden City, New York, 1955.

Deutsch, Babette, *Poetry in Our Time*, Garden City, New York, 1963.

Fein, Richard J., 'Major American Poetry of World War II', *Dissertation Abstracts*, Ann Arbor, Michigan, 21, 1961: 2292 (New York University 1960).

Hall, Donald, 'American Poets Since the War,' *World Review*, Vol. 2, London, 1952.

——'The New Poetry: Notes on the Past Fifteen Years in America', *New World Writing*, Seventh Mentor Selection, New York, 1955.

——Introduction to *Contemporary American Poetry*, Baltimore, 1962.

Hungerford, Edward, ed., *Poets in Progress*, 1962; 1967.

Mills, Ralph J., Jr, *Contemporary American Poetry*, New York, 1965.

National Poetry Festival, held in the Library of Congress October 22–24, 1962, Proceedings, Library of Congress, Washington, DC, 1964.

Nemerov, Howard, ed., *Poets on Poetry*, New York and London, 1965.

Ostroff, Anthony, ed., *The Contemporary Poet as Artist and Critic*, Boston and Toronto, 1964.

Rosenthal, M. L., *The Modern Poets*, New York, 1960.

——*The New Poets*, London, Oxford and New York, 1967.

Stepanchev, Stephen, *American Poetry Since 1945*, New York, Evanston and London, 1965.

Vendler, Helen, *The Harvard Book of Contemporary American Poetry*, Cambridge, Mass., 1985; as *Faber Book of Contemporary American Poetry*, London, 1986.

Waggoner, Hyatt H., *American Poets From the Puritans to the Present*, Boston, 1966.

Richard Wilbur

COLLECTIONS OF POEMS
Poems 1943–1956, London, 1956.
The Poems of Richard Wilbur, New York, 1963.

OTHER WORKS
A Bestiary, New York, 1955.
The Misanthrope, by Molière (translation), New York, 1955.
Tartuffe, by Molière (translation), New York, 1963.

CRITICISM
Asselineau, Roger, 'Les "Fleurs de Verre" de Richard Wilbur', *Critique*, 819–38, Oct. 1960.
Ashman, Richard (Review, *Things of This World*), *Talisman*, No. 10, 61–69, Winter 1956.
Gustafson, Richard, 'Richard Wilbur and the Beasts', *Iowa English Yearbook*, No. 11, 59–63, Fall 1966.
Hill, Donald, *Richard Wilbur*, New York, 1967.
Southworth, James G., 'The Poetry of Richard Wilbur', *College English*, XXII, 24–29, 1960.
Warlow, Francis W., 'Richard Wilbur', *Bucknell Review*, VII, 217–33, May 1958.

Randall Jarrell

COLLECTIONS OF POETRY
Randall Jarrell, The Complete Poems, New York, 1969.
Randall Jarrell, Selected Poems, Including The Woman at the Washington Zoo, New York, 1964.

OTHER WORKS
Pictures from an Institution, A Comedy (novel), New York, 1954.
Poetry and the Age (essays), New York, 1953; London, 1955.
A Sad Heart at the Supermarket; Essays and Fables, New York, 1962.

CRITICISM
Adams, Charles M., comp., *Randall Jarrell: A Bibliography*, Chapel Hill, 1958.
Analects (Woman's College, University of North Carolina), I, ii, (essays on Jarrell, incl. Adams, Charles M., 'A Supplement to *Randall Jarrell: A Bibliography*'), Spring 1961.

Bell, Vereen M., *Robert Lowell: Nihilist as Hero*, Cambridge, Mass., 1983.

Calhoun, Richard J., 'Randall Jarrell. Towards a Reassessment', *South Atlantic Bulletin*, 32, iv, 1967, 1–4.

Flint, R. W., 'On Randall Jarrell', *Commentary*, XLI, ii, 79–81, 1966.

Kobler, J. F., 'Randall Jarrell Seeks Truth in Fantasy', *Forum*, III, vi, 17–20, Houston, 1961.

Lowell, Robert, *et al.*, ed., *Randall Jarrell: 1914–1965*, Straus and Giroux, New York, 1967.

Rundman, Mark, *Robert Lowell: An Introduction to the Poetry*, New York, 1983.

Shapiro, Karl, *Randall Jarrell: A Lecture*, with a bibliography of Jarrell materials in the Library of Congress, Washington, DC, Library of Congress, 1967.

John Berryman

COLLECTIONS OF POEMS
The Dispossessed, New York, 1948.
Homage to Mistress Bradstreet, New York, 1956.
Short Poems, New York, 1967.
Berryman's Sonnets, London, 1968.
The Dream Songs, New York, 1970.

CRITICISM
Anon., 'Zoo-Maze. The World in Vaudeville', *Times Literary Supplement*, 292, Apr. 15, 1965.

Haffenden, John, *The Life of John Berryman*, London and Boston, 1982.

Hamilton, Ian, 'John Berryman', *London Magazine*, IV, 93–100, Feb. 1965.

Jackson, Bruce, 'Berryman's Chaplinesque', *The Minnesota Review*, 5, No. 1, 90–94, Jan./Apr. 1965.

Johnson, Carol, 'John Berryman and Mistress Bradstreet: A Relation of Reason', *Essays in Criticism*, XIV, 388–96, Oct. 1964.

Meredith, William, 'Henry Tasting all the Secret Bits of Life: Berryman's "Dream Songs"', *Wisconsin Studies in Contemporary Literature*, VI, 21–33, Winter-Spring 1965.

Nims, John Frederick, 'Homage in Measure to Mr Berryman', *Prairie Schooner*, 32, 1–7, Spring 1958.

Stitt, Peter A., 'Berryman's Vein Profound', *The Minnesota Review*, VII, 3–4, 356–9, 1967.

Karl Shapiro

COLLECTIONS OF POEMS
The Bourgeois Poet, New York, 1964.
Selected Poems, New York, 1968.
White-Haired Lover, New York, 1968.

OTHER WORKS
Essay on Rime, New York, 1945.
A Primer for Poets (essays), Lincoln, 1965. Original title, *Beyond Criticism*, 1953.
In Defense of Ignorance (essays), New York, 1960.

CRITICISM
Bradley, Sam, 'Shapiro Strikes at the Establishment', *University of Kansas City Review*, XXIX, 275–9, 1963.
Chari, V. K., 'Karl Shapiro and New Romanticism', *Criticism and Research* (Benares Hindu University), 124–35, 1964.
Eckman, Frederick, 'Karl Shapiro's "Adam and Eve"', *Texas Studies in English*, XXXV, 1–10, 1956.
Fussell, Edwin, 'Karl Shapiro: the Paradox of Prose and Poetry', *Western Review*, 18, No. 3, 225–44, Spring 1954.
Glicksberg, Charles I., 'Karl Shapiro and the Personal Accent', *Prairie Schooner*, XXII, 44–52, Spring 1948.
Rubin, Louis D., Jr, 'The Search for Lost Innocence: Karl Shapiro's "The Bourgeois Poet"', *The Hollins Critics*, I, iv, 1–16, 1964.
Slotkin, Richard, 'The Contextual Symbol: Karl Shapiro's Image of the Jew', *American Quarterly*, XVIII, No. 2, Pt. 1, 220–26, summer 1966.
Southworth, James G., 'The Poetry of Karl Shapiro', *English Journal*, LII, 159–66, Mar. 1962.
White, William, *Karl Shapiro: A Bibliography*, Detroit, 1960.

Theodore Roethke

COLLECTIONS OF POEMS
The Collected Poems of Theodore Roethke, Garden City, New York, 1966.

OTHER WORKS
On the Poet and His Craft, Selected Prose, ed. Mills, Ralph J., Jr, Seattle, 1965.
Selected Letters of Theodore Roethke, ed. Mills, Ralph J., Jr, London, 1970.

CRITICISM
Burke, Kenneth, 'The Vegetal Radicalism of Theodore Roethke', *Sewanee Review*, LVIII, 68–108, Winter 1950.
Eberhart, Richard, 'On Theodore Roethke's Poetry', *Southern Review*, 1, 612–20, 1965.
Gustafson, Richard, 'In Roethkeland', *The Midwest Quarterly*, VII, No. 2, 167–74, Winter 1966.
Hollenberg, S. W., 'Theodore Roethke, Bibliography', *Twentieth Century Literature*, 12, 216–21, Jan. 1967.
Kramer, Hilton, 'The Poetry of Theodore Roethke', *Western Review*, XVIII, 131–46, Winter 1954.
Kunitz, Stanley, 'Roethke: Poet of Transformations', *The New Republic*, CLII, 23–29, 23 January 1965.
Malkoff, Karl, *Theodore Roethke, An Introduction to the Poetry*, New York and London, 1966.
Mills, Ralph J., Jr, 'Keeping the Spirit Spare', *Chicago Review*, XIII, No. 4, 114–22, Winter 1959.
——*Theodore Roethke* University of Minnesota Press, (Pamphlets on American Writers, No. 30), 1963.
Seager, Allan, *The Glass House* (biography), New York, 1968.
Southworth, James G., 'The Poetry of Theodore Roethke', *College English*, XXI, 326–38, 1960.
——'Theodore Roethke's *The Far Field*', *College English*, XXVII, 413–18, 1966.
Staples, Hugh B., 'The Rose in the Sea Wind: A Reading of Theodore Roethke's "North American Sequence"', *American Literature*, XXXVI, 189–203, 1964.
Stein, Arnold, ed., *Theodore Roethke: Essays on the Poetry*, Seattle and London, 1965.
Wain, John, 'Theodore Roethke', *Critical Quarterly*, VI, 322–38, Winter 1964.

Robert Lowell

COLLECTIONS OF POEMS
Lord Weary's Castle and The Mills of the Kavanaughs, New York, 1961.
Poems, 1938–49, London, 1950.

Life Studies and *For the Union Dead*, New York, 1967.
Life Studies, London, 1969.
For the Union Dead, London, 1965.
Imitations, New York, 1961; London, 1962.
The Old Glory, New York, 1965; London, 1966.
Near the Ocean, New York, 1967; London, 1967.
Notebook 1967–68, New York, 1969.
History and *For Lizzie and Harriet* [reworking of material in *Notebook*], London, 1973.
The Dolphin, London, 1973.

OTHER WORKS

Racine's *Phèdre* (translation) in *Phaedra and Figaro*, New York.
The Voyage and other versions of poems by Baudelaire, New York; London, 1968.

CRITICISM

Bell, Vereen M., *Robert Lowell: Nihilist as Hero*, Cambridge, Mass., 1983.
Brumleve, Sister Eric Marie, SSND, 'Permanence and Change in the Poetry of Robert Lowell, *Texas Studies in Literature and Language*, 10, 143–53, 1968.
Calhoun, Richard James, 'The Poetic Metamorphosis of Robert Lowell, *Furman Studies*, XIII, i, 7–17.
Cambon, Glauco, 'Dea Roma and Robert Lowell', *Accent*, XX, 51–61, Winter 1960.
——'Robert Lowell and the Sense of History', *PMASAL* (Publications of the Michigan Academy of Science, Arts and Letters), XLVII, 571–8, 1962.
Carruth, Hayden, 'A Meaning of Robert Lowell', *Hudson Review*, 20, 429–47, 1967.
Cooper, Philip, Jr, 'Lyric Ambivalence: An Essay on the Poetry of William Butler Yeats and Robert Lowell', *Dissertation Abstracts*, 1492A (Columbia), 28, 1967.
Fein, Richard, 'Mary and Bellona: The War Poetry of Robert Lowell, *Southern Review*, I, 820–34, 1965.
Hamilton, Ian, *Robert Lowell: A Biography*, New York, 1982.
Hoffman, Daniel, 'Robert Lowell's *Near the Ocean*: The Greatness and Horror of Empire', *The Hollins Critic*, 4, i, 1–16, 1967.
Jones, A. R., 'Necessity and Freedom: The Poetry of Robert Lowell, Sylvia Plath, and Anne Sexton', *Critical Quarterly*, VII, 11–30, Spring 1965.

Knox, Stephen H., 'Robert Lowell: Lyric Strategy and Dramatic Narrative In the Poems Leading Up to "Skunk Hour",' *Dissertation Abstracts*, 1052A (Penn. State), 28, 1967.

Mazzaro, Jerome L., *The Achievement of Robert Lowell, 1939–1959* (bibliography), Detroit, 1960.

——*The Poetic Themes of Robert Lowell*, Ann Arbor, 1965.

——'The World of Robert Lowell', *Dissertation Abstracts*, 4640A (Wayne State), 28, 1968.

Parkinson, Thomas, *Robert Lowell: A Collection of Critical Essays*, Englewood Cliffs, N.J., 1968

Perloff, Marjorie, 'Death by Water: The Winslow Elegies of Robert Lowell', *Journal of English Literary History*, 34, 166–40, 1967.

Rudman, Mark, *Robert Lowell: An Introduction to the Poetry*, New York, 1983.

Staples, Hugh B., 'Robert Lowell: Bibliography 1939–1959, with an Illustrative Critique', *Harvard Library Bulletin*, XIII, 292–318, 1959.

——*Robert Lowell: The First Twenty Years*, New York and London, 1962.

6. *Literary Criticism to 1965*

This selective list does not include items mentioned in the text. It is offered as a preliminary guide for further reading: most of the works cited include bibliographies and/or notes.

Aldridge, John W., ed., *Critiques and Essays on Modern Fiction, 1920–1951*, New York, 1952.

Basler, Roy P., *Sex, Symbolism, and Psychology in Literature*, New Brunswick, N.J., 1948.

Blackmur, R.P., *Selected Essays*, ed. Denis Donoghue, New York, 1987.

Bradbury, John M., *The Fugitives: A Critical Account*, Chapel Hill, N.C. and London, 1958.

Brombert, Victor H., *The Criticism of T. S. Eliot*, New Haven, Conn., 1949.

Brown, Clarence Arthur, ed., *The Achievement of American Criticism*, New York, 1954.

Brown, Merle E., *Kenneth Burke*, Minneapolis, 1969.

Chase, William M., *Lionel Trilling: Criticism and Politics*, Stanford, Cal., 1980.

Clark, Harry H., ed., *Transitions in American Literary History*, Durham, N.C. and Cambridge, 1954.

Comito, Terry, *In Defense of Winters: The Poetry and Prose of Yvor Winters*, Madison, Wisc., 1986.

Cowan, Louise, *The Fugitive Group: A Literary History*, Baton Rouge, La. and Toronto, 1959.

Dakin, Arthur Hazard, *Paul Elmer More*, Princeton and London, 1960.

Davis, Dick, *Wisdom and Wilderness: The Achievement of Yvor Winters*, Athens, Ga., 1983.

Denham, Robert D., *Northrop Frye and Critical Method*, University Park, Pa., 1978.

Elton, William, *A Guide to the New Criticism*, Chicago, 1953.

Foerster, Norman, McGalliard, John C., Wellek, René, Warren, Austin, and Schramm, Wilbur Lang, *Literary Scholarship: Its Aims and Methods*, Chapel Hill, N.C., 1941.

Forgue, Guy, *H. L. Mencken: l'homme, l'oeuvre, l'influence*, Paris, 1967.

Foster, Richard, *The New Romantics: A Reappraisal of the New Criticism*, Bloomington, Ind. and Toronto, 1962.

Fraser, Russell, *A Mingled Yarn: the Life of R. P. Blackmur*, New York, 1981.

Frye, Northrop, *The Great Code: The Bible and Literature*, New York, 1982.

Glicksburg, Charles, ed., *American Literary Criticism, 1900–1950*, New York, 1951.

Goldsmith, Arnold, *American Literary Criticism, 1905–1965*, Boston, 1979.

Gomme, Andor, *Attitudes Towards Criticism*, Carbondale, Ill. and Toronto, 1966.

Grebstein, Sheldon N., ed., *Perspectives in Contemporary Criticism*, New York and London, 1968.

Hartman, Geoffrey, *Beyond Formalism: Literary Essays, 1958–1970*, New Haven, 1970.

Hirsch, E. D., Jr, *Validity in Interpretation*, New Haven, Conn., 1967.

Hoffman, Frederick J., *Freudianism and the Literary Mind*, Baton Rouge, La., 1945.

Hyman, Stanley Edgar, *The Armed Vision: A Study in the Methods of Modern Literary Criticism*, New York and Toronto, 1968.

Jones, James T., *Wayward Skeptic: the Theories of R. P. Blackmur*, Champaign, Ill., 1987.

Karanikas, Alexander, *Tillers of a Myth: The Southern Agrarians as Social and Literary Critics*, Madison, Wis., and Toronto, 1966.

Knox, George, *Critical Moments: Kenneth Burke's Categories and Critiques*, Seattle, 1957.

Krieger, Murray, ed., *Northrop Frye in Modern Criticism*, New York and London, 1966.

Lawall, Sarah N., *Critics of Consciousness*, Cambridge, Mass., 1968.

Lemon, Lee T., *The Partial Critics*, New York, 1965; London, 1966.

Lu, Fei-Pai, *T. S. Eliot: The Dialectical Structure of His Theory of Poetry*, Chicago, 1966.

McKean, Keith F., *The Moral Measure of Literature*, Denver, 1961.

Nolte, William H., *H. L. Mencken, Literary Critic*, Middletown, Conn. and Toronto, 1966.

O'Connor, William Van, *An Age of Criticism, 1900–1950*, Chicago, 1952.

Paul, Sherman, *Edmund Wilson: A Study of Literary Vocation in Our Time*, Urbana, Ill., 1965.

Powell, Grosvenor, *Yvor Winters: An Annotated Bibliography, 1919–1982*, Metuchen, N.J., 1983.

Pritchard, J. P., *Criticism in America*, Norman, Okla. and Toronto, 1956.

Ransom, John Crowe, ed., *The Kenyon Critics*, New York and Toronto, 1951.

Rueckert, William H., ed., *Critical Responses to Kenneth Burke, 1924–1966*. Minneapolis and London, 1963.

——*Kenneth Burke and the Drama of Human Relations*, Minneapolis and London, 1963.

Ruland, Richard, *The Rediscovery of American Literature: Premises of Critical Taste, 1900–1940*, Cambridge, Mass. and London, 1967.

Schwab, Arnold T., *James Gibbons Huneker, Critic of the Seven Arts*, Stanford, Cal. and London, 1963.

Shafer, Robert, *Paul Elmer More and American Criticism*, New Haven, Conn., 1935.

Spiller, Robert E., *et al.*, eds, *A Literary History of the United States*, New York and London, 3 vols, 1948; 4th rev. edn, 2 vols, 1974.

Spingarn, J. E., ed., *Criticism in America, Its Function and Status*, New York, 1924.

Stallman, Robert W., ed., *Critiques and Essays in Criticism, 1920–1948*, New York, 1949.

Stovall, Floyd, ed., *The Development of American Literary Criticism*, Chapel Hill, N.C., and London, 1955.

Sutton, Walter, ed., *Modern Criticism: Theory and Practice*, New York, 1963.

Vickery, John B., ed., *Myth and Literature: Contemporary Theory and Practice*, Lincoln, Neb., 1966.

Wain, John, ed., *Edmund Wilson: The Man and His Work*, New York, 1978.

Wasserstrom, William, *The Legacy of Van Wyck Brooks: A Study of Maladies and Motives*, Carbondale, Ill., 1971.

——ed., *Van Wyck Brooks: The Critic and His Critics*, Port Washington, New York, 1979.

Webster, Grant, *The Republic of Letters: A History of Postwar American Literary Opinion*, Baltimore, 1979.

Wellek, René, *Concepts of Criticism*, ed. Stephen G. Nichols, Jr, New Haven, Conn., and London, 1963.

——*American Criticism, 1900–1950*, Vol. 6 of *A History of Modern Criticism, 1750–1950*, New Haven, 1986.

——and Warren, Austin, *Theory of Literature*, New York, 1942; London, 1949; 3rd edn, New York and London, 1966.

White, Hayden, and Brose, Margaret, *Representing Kenneth Burke*, Baltimore, 1982.

Wimsatt, William K., Jr, and Brooks, Cleanth, *Literary Criticism, A Short History*, New York, 1957; London, 1958.

Zabel, Morton D., ed., *Literary Opinion in America*, rev. edn, New York and London, 1951, 1962.

7. *William Faulkner and the Southern Renascence*

General
Cowan, Louise, *The Fugitive Group. A Literary History*, Baton Rouge, 1959.
Jones, Anne Goodwyn, *Tomorrow is Another Day: The Woman Writer in the South 1859–1936*, Baton Rouge, 1981.
Rubin, Louis D., Jr, *A Bibliographical Guide To the Study of Southern Literature*, Baton Rouge, 1969.
——*et al.*, eds, *The History of Southern Literature*, Baton Rouge and London, 1985. Appendix A contains a bibliographical essay.
——and Jacobs, Robert D., eds, *Southern Renascence: The Literature of the Modern South*, Baltimore, 1953.
——and Jacobs, Robert D., eds, *Modern Southern Literature in its Cultural Setting*, Westport, Conn., 1961.
——*A Gallery of Southerners*, Baton Rouge and London, 1982.

William Faulkner
There exists as yet no critical edition of Faulkner's complete work. Most of his novels are available in various paperback editions.

A bibliography of his work (except the latest) is contained in:
Meriwether, James B., *The Literary Career of William Faulkner: A Bibliographical Study*, 1961.

A comprehensive biography is:
Blotner, Joseph, *Faulkner, A Biography*, 2 vols, New York, 1974.

CRITICISM
Bassett, John, ed., *William Faulkner: An Annotated Checklist of Criticism*, New York, 1972.
——*An Annotated Checklist of Recent Criticism*, Kent State University, 1983.
Ricks, Beatrice, *William Faulkner: A Bibliography of Secondary Works*, Metuchen, N.J., 1981.

Faulkner's own views can be found in the following volumes:
Blotner, Joseph, ed., *Selected Letters of William Faulkner*, New York, 1977.
Cowley, Malcolm, ed., *The Faulkner–Cowley File: Letters and Memoirs: 1944–1962*, New York, 1966.

Gwynn, Frederick L., and Blotner, Joseph L., eds, *Faulkner in the University: Class Conferences at the University of Virginia 1957 to 1958*, Charlottesville, Va., 1959.

Jelliffe, Robert A., ed., *Faulkner at Nagano*, Tokyo, 1956.

Meriwether, James B., and Millgate, Michael, eds, *Lion in the Garden. Interviews with William Faulkner*, New York, 1968.

Stein, Jean, 'The Art of Fiction XII: William Faulkner', *The Paris Review 12*, 1956, pp. 28–52; also contained in *Writers at Work. The Paris Review Interviews*, introd. Malcolm Cowley, London, 1958.

The listing of Faulkner criticism has reached book-length; from this long list, only the most important and useful works can be mentioned:

Cowley, Malcolm, ed., *The Portable Faulkner*, New York, 1946.

Hoffman, Frederick J., and Vickery, Olga W., eds, *William Faulkner: Three Decades of Criticism*, Michigan State University Press, 1960. (This volume contains a selection of important essays and thereby also gives a survey of the development of Faulkner criticism.)

Help in unravelling the difficulties and obscurities of Faulkner's work is provided by:

Kirk, Robert W., and Klotz, Marvin, *Faulkner's People: A Complete Guide and Index to Characters in the Fiction of William Faulkner*, Berkeley and Los Angeles, 1963.

Volpe, Edmond L., *A Reader's Guide to William Faulkner*, New York, 1964.

The following monographs are essential contributions to Faulkner criticism:

Brooks, Cleanth, *William Faulkner: The Yoknapatawpha Country*, New Haven and London, 1963.

——*William Faulkner: Toward Yoknapatawpha and Beyond*, New Haven, 1978.

Millgate, Michael, *The Achievement of William Faulkner*, London, 1966.

Reed, Joseph W., Jr, *Faulkner's Narrative*, New Haven, 1973.

Slatoff, Walter J., *A Quest for Failure: A Study of William Faulkner*, Ithaca, New York, 1960.

8. *American Theatre Since 1945*

Arthur Miller, *Plays*, London.
Tennessee Williams, *Plays*, London.
Ardrey, Robert, *Plays of Three Decades*, London, 1968.
Bentley, Eric, *What is Theatre?*, London, 1969.
Biner, Pierre, *Le Living Théâtre*, Lausanne, 1968.
Blau, Herbert, *The Impossible Theatre*, New York, 1965.
Brustein, Robert, *Seasons of Discontent*, London, 1966.
Clurman, Harold, *The Fervent Years*, New York, 1957.
Eight Plays from Off-Off-Broadway, New York, 1966.
Golden, Joseph, *The Death of Tinker Bell*, Syracuse, 1967.
Guthrie, Tyrone, *A New Theater*, New York, 1964.
Jones, LeRoi, *Dutchman & The Slave*, London, 1964.
Kostelanetz, Richard, ed., *The Theater of Mixed Means*, New York, 1968.
Kourilsky, Françoise, *Le Théâtre Aux Etats-Unis*, Paris, 1967.
Leverett, James, ed., *New Plays USA I*, New York, 1982. (Contains work and introductions by Adele Edling Shank, David Henry Hwang, Emily Mann and Tom Cole.)
Novik, Julius, *Beyond Broadway: The Quest for Permanent Theaters*, New York, 1968.
Spoto, Donald, *The Kindness of Strangers: The Life of Tennessee Williams*, London, 1985.
Strasberg, Lee, *Strasberg at the Actors' Studio*, London, 1966.
Terry, Megan, *Four Plays*, New York, 1967.
Theater Arts Anthology, New York, 1961.
van Itallie, Jean-Claude, *The Serpent*, New York, 1969.

10. *A Remnant to Escape: The American Writer and the Minority Group*

Saul Bellow

TEXTS
Dangling Man, New York, 1944; London, 1946.
The Victim, New York, 1947; London, 1948.
The Adventures of Augie March, New York, 1953; London, 1954.
Seize the Day, New York, 1956; London, 1957.
Henderson the Rain King, New York and London, 1959.
Herzog, New York, 1964; London, 1965.
Mr Sammler's Planet, New York and London, 1970.

Bernard Malamud

TEXTS
The Natural (novel), New York, 1952; London, 1963.
The Assistant (novel), New York, 1957; London, 1959.
The Magic Barrel (stories), New York, 1958; London, 1960.
A New Life (novel), New York, 1961; London, 1962.
Idiots First (novel), New York, 1966; London, 1964.
The Fixer (novel), New York, 1966; London, 1967.
Pictures of Fidelman (stories), New York and London, 1969.

Philip Roth

TEXTS
Goodbye, Columbus (novella and stories), New York, 1958; London, 1959.
Letting Go (novel), New York and London, 1962.
When She Was Good (novel), New York and London, 1967.
Portnoy's Complaint (novel), New York and London, 1969.
Zuckerman Bound: A Trilogy and Epilogue (fiction), New York and London, 1985.
The Counterlife (fiction), New York, 1986; London, 1987.
A Philip Roth Reader, New York, 1980.

Ralph Ellison

TEXTS

Invisible Man (novel), New York, 1952; London, 1953.
Shadow and Act (essays), New York, 1964; London, 1967.

Richard Wright

TEXTS

Uncle Tom's Children (short stories), New York, 1938; London,
   1939.
Native Son (novel), New York, 1940; London, 1940.
Twelve Million Black Voices (documentary), New York, 1941.
Black Boy (autobiography), New York, 1945; London, 1947.
The Outsider (novel), New York, 1953; London, 1954.
White Man, Listen! (essays), New York, 1957.
The Long Dream (novel), New York, 1958; London, 1960.
Eight Men (stories), Cleveland and New York, 1961.
Lawd Today (novel) (written *c.*1937), New York, 1963; London,
   1965.

James Baldwin

TEXTS

Go Tell It on the Mountain (novel), New York, 1953; London, 1954.
Notes of a Native Son (essays), New York, 1955; London, 1964.
Giovanni's Room (novel), New York, 1956; London, 1957.
Nobody Knows My Name (essays), New York, 1961; London, 1964.
Another Country (novel), New York, 1962; London, 1963.
The Fire Next Time (two essays), New York and London, 1963.
Blues for Mister Charlie (play), New York, 1964; London, 1965.
Going to Meet the Man (short stories), New York and London, 1965.
Tell Me How Long the Train's Been Gone (novel), New York and
   London, 1968.
The Evidence of Things Not Seen, New York, 1985.
The Price of The Ticket: Collected Non-Fiction, 1948–1985, New York,
   1985.

CRITICISM

Bone, Robert, *The Negro Novel in America*, New Haven, Conn.,
   1958 and 1965.

Bloom, Harold, general ed., *Modern Critical Views*, New York, 1986, vols on Saul Bellow, Norman Mailer, Bernard Malamud, Philip Roth.

Bradbury, Malcolm, *Saul Bellow*, London, 1982.

Fiedler, Leslie A., *No! in Thunder*, Boston, 1960.

——*Waiting for the End*, New York, 1964; London, 1965.

——*To the Gentiles*, New York, 1972.

Guttmann, Allen, *The Jewish Writer in America*, New York and London, 1971.

Klein, Marcus, *After Alienation*, Cleveland and New York, 1964.

Lee, A. Robert, *Black American Fiction since Richard Wright*, London, British Association for American Studies pamphlet, 1983.

Lewis, David L., *When Harlem Was In Vogue*, New York, 1981.

Salzberg, Joel, *Bernard Malamud: A Reference Guide*, Boston, 1985.

Tanner, Tony, *Saul Bellow*, Edinburgh and New York, 1965.

Warshow, Robert, *The Immediate Experience*, Garden City, New York, 1962.

For a classic evocation of the traumas of immigration see Oscar Handlin, *The Uprooted*, Boston, 1951; 2nd edn, 1973. See also such careful studies as Maldwyn A. Jones, *American Immigration*, Chicago and London, 1960; Philip Taylor, *The Distant Magnet: European Emigraton to the U.S.A.*, London, 1971; New York, 1974; John Higham, *Send These to Me; Jews and Other Immigrants in Urban America*, New York, 1975; and ed. Cynthia Jaffee McCabe, *The Golden Door: Artist-Immigrants of America, 1876–1976*, Washington, D. C., 1976.

11.   *Literary Criticism Since 1965*

This selective list supplements items mentioned in the essay and is offered as a preliminary guide to further reading.

Arac, Jonathan, *et al.*, *The Yale Critics: Deconstruction in America*, Minneapolis, 1983.
Culler, Jonathan, *Ferdinand de Saussure*, New York, 1977.
——*On Deconstruction*, Ithaca, 1982.
de Man, Paul, *Allegories of Reading*, New Haven, 1979.
——'The Resistance to Literary Theory', *Yale French Studies*, 63, 1982.
Derrida, Jacques, *Dissemination*, Chicago, 1982.
——*Writing and Difference*, Chicago, 1978.
Fish, Stanley, *Is There a Text in This Class?*, Cambridge, Mass., 1980.
Foucault, Michel, *The Archeology of Knowledge*, New York, 1972.
——*Madness and Civilization*, New York, 1965.
Hartman, Geoffrey, *Beyond Formalism*, New Haven, 1970.
——*The Fate of Reading*, Chicago, 1975.
Jameson, Fredric, *The Prison-House of Language*, Princeton, 1972.
Johnson, Barbara, *The Critical Difference*, Baltimore, 1980.
Krieger, Murray, and Dembo, Larry, eds, *Directions for Criticism: Structuralism and Its Alternatives*, Madison, 1977.
Lacan, Jacques, *Ecrits*, New York, 1977.
Macksey, Richard, and Donato, Eugenio, eds, *The Structuralist Controversy: The Languages of Criticism and the Sciences of Man*, Baltimore, 1970.
Mileur, Jean-Pierre, *Literary Revisionism and the Burden of Modernity*, Berkeley, 1985.
O'Hara, Daniel T., *The Romance of Interpretation*, New York, 1985.
Riffaterre, Michael, *Semiotics of Poetry*, Bloomington, 1978.
Said, Edward, *Beginnings: Intention and Method*, New York, 1975.
——*The World, the Text, and the Critic*, Cambridge, Mass., 1983.
Scholes, Robert, *Structuralism in Literature*, New Haven, 1974.
White, Hayden, *Tropics of Discourse: Essays on Cultural Criticism*, Baltimore, 1978.
Wilden, Anthony, *The Language of the Self*, Baltimore, 1968.

[For bibliography to Chapter 12, see bibliography to Chapter 14 which covers both chapters.]

13. *The New Fiction*

General Studies

Beidler, Philip, *American Literature and the Experience of Vietnam*, Athens, Ga., 1982.

Bellamy, Joe David, *The New Fiction: Interviews with Innovative American Writers*, Urbana, Ill., 1974.

Davis, Douglas M., ed., *The World of Black Humor*, New York, 1967.

Friedman, Bruce Jay, ed., *Black Humor*, New York, 1965.

Hassan, Ihab, *The Postmodern Turn*, Columbus, Oh., 1987.

Herzinger, Kim A., 'Introduction: On the New Fiction', *Mississippi Review*, No. 40–41 (Winter 1985: 'Minimalism' Issue), pp 7–22.

Karl, Frederick R., *American Fictions 1940–1980*, New York, 1983.

Klinkowitz, Jerome, *The American 1960s*, Ames, Ia., 1980.

——*Literary Disruptions*, Urbana, Ill., 1975.

——*The New American Novel of Manners*, Athens, Ga., 1986.

——*The Self-Apparent Word*, Carbondale, Ill., 1984.

LeClair, Tom, and McCaffery, Larry, *Anything Can Happen: Interviews with Contemporary American Novelists*, Urbana, Ill., 1983.

McCaffery, Larry, *The Metafictional Muse*, Pittsburgh, Pa., 1982.

Mellard, James M., *The Exploded Form*, Urbana, Ill., 1980.

Scholes, Robert, *Fabulation and Metafiction*, Urbana, Ill., 1979.

——*The Fabulators*, New York, 1967.

Stevick, Philip, *Alternative Pleasures: Postrealistic Fiction and the Tradition*, Urbana, Ill., 1981.

Tanner, Tony, *City of Words*, London and New York, 1971.

Wilde, Alan, *Horizons of Assent*, Baltimore, 1981.

Zavarzadeh, Mas'ud, *The Mythopoeic Reality: The Postwar American Nonfiction Novel*, Urbana, Ill., 1976.

Selected Works (Including Criticism) by Fiction Writers

Abish, Walter, *Alphabetical Africa*, New York, 1974.

——*How German Is It*, New York, 1980.

Barth, John, *The Friday Book*, New York, 1984.

Barthelme, Donald, *Sixty Stories*, New York, 1981.

——*Snow White*, New York, 1967.

Brautigan, Richard, *So the Wind Won't Blow It All Away*, New York, 1982.

——*Trout Fishing in America*, San Francisco, 1967.
Capote, Truman, *In Cold Blood*, New York, 1966.
Coover, Robert, *The Public Burning*, New York, 1977.
Dixon, Stephen, *14 Stories*, Baltimore, 1980.
——*Movies*, San Francisco, 1983.
——*No Relief*, Ann Arbor, Mich., 1976.
——*Time to Go*, Baltimore, 1984.
——*Work*, Ann Arbor, Mich., 1977.
Doctorow, E. L., *Ragtime*, New York, 1975.
Federman, Raymond, *Double or Nothing*, Chicago, 1971.
——*Surfiction*, Chicago, 1975.
Gangemi, Kenneth, *The Interceptor Pilot*, London and Salem, N.H., 1980.
Gass, William H., *Fiction and the Figures of Life*, New York, 1970.
——*Willie Masters' Lonesome Wife*, Evanston, Ill., 1968.
Hawkes, John, *Adventures in the Alaskan Skin Trade*, New York, 1985.
——*The Cannibal*, New York, 1949.
——*The Lime Twig*, New York, 1961.
——*The Passion Artist*, New York, 1979.
——*Virginie: Her Two Lives*, New York, 1982.
Irving, John, *The World According to Garp*, New York, 1978.
Kosinski, Jerzy, *Being There*, New York, 1971.
——*The Devil Tree*, New York, 1974.
——*The Painted Bird*, Boston, 1965.
——*Steps*, New York, 1968.
Mailer, Norman, *The Armies of the Night*, New York, 1968.
McGuane, Thomas, *Something to be Desired*, New York, 1984.
Ondaatje, Michael, *Coming Through Slaughter*, New York, 1976.
Paley, Grace, *Enormous Changes at the Last Minute*, New York, 1974.
——*Later the Same Day*, New York, 1985.
Pynchon, Thomas, *Gravity's Rainbow*, New York, 1973.
Reed, Ishmael, *God Made Alaska for the Indians*, New York, 1982.
——*The Terrible Twos*, New York, 1982.
Sorrentino, Gilbert, *Imaginative Qualities of Actual Things*, New York, 1971.
——*Something Said: Essays*, San Francisco, 1984.
——*Splendide-Hôtel*, New York, 1973.
Sukenick, Ronald, *The Death of the Novel and Other Stories*, New York, 1969.
——*In Form: Digressions on the Act of Fiction*, Carbondale, Ill., 1985.
Stephens, Michael, *The Dramaturgy of Style*, Carbondale, Ill., 1986.

——*Paragraphs*, Amherst, Mass., 1974.

——*Season at Coole*, New York, 1972.

Thompson, Hunter S., *Fear and Loathing in Las Vegas*, New York, 1972.

Vonnegut, Kurt, *Mother Night*, Greenwich, Conn., 1961; New York, 1966.

——*Slaughterhouse-Five*, New York, 1969.

Wolfe, Tom, and Johnson, E. W., eds, *The New Journalism*, New York, 1973.

14. *Literature and Society*

Abbott, Jack Henry, *In the Belly of the Beast: Letters from Prison*, introd. by Norman Mailer, New York, 1981.

Bagdikian, Ben H., *The Media Monopoly*, Boston, 1983.

Bartlett, Mary D., *The New Native American Novel: Works in Progress*, Albuquerque, New Mexico, 1986.

Baumbach, Jonathan, *The Landscape of Nightmare: Studies in the Contemporary American Novel*, New York, 1965.

Bell, Daniel, *The End of Ideology*, New York, 1960.

——, ed., *The Radical Right*, Garden City, New York, 1963.

Bellamy, Joe D., *The New Fiction: Interviews with Innovative American Writers*, Urbana, Ill., 1974.

Berman, Ronald, *America in the Sixties: An Intellectual History*, New York and London, 1968.

Bittner, James W., *Approaches to the Fiction of Ursula LeGuin*, Ann Arbor, Mich., 1984.

Boorstin, Daniel J., ed., *American Civilization*, London, 1972.

Carroll, Peter N., *It Seemed Like Nothing Happened: The Tragedy and Promise of America in the 1970s*, New York, 1982.

Cawelti, John G., *Adventure, Mystery, and Romance: Formula Stories as Art and Popular Culture*, Chicago, 1976.

Conlin, Joseph, *The Troubles: A Jaundiced Glance Back at the Movements of the Sixties*, New York, 1982.

Cowart, David, *Thomas Pynchon: The Art of Allusion*, Carbondale, Ill., 1980.

Cunliffe, Marcus, *The Literature of the United States*, Harmondsworth and New York, 4th edn, revised, 1986.

Fiedler, Leslie, *The Return of the Vanishing American*, New York and London, 1968.

——*What Was Literature? Class Culture and Mass Society*, New York, 1982.

Friedan, Betty, *The Second Stage*, New York, 1981.

Gates, Henry L., Jr, *Black Literature and Literary Theory*, New York and London, 1984.

Harrington, Michael, *The Accidental Century*, New York, 1965; London, 1966.

Hart, Jeffrey, *When The Going Was Good: American Life in the Fifties*, New York, 1982.

Hellmann, John, *American Myth and the Legacy of Vietnam*, New York, 1986.

Howe, Irving, *Beyond the Welfare State*, New York, 1982.

Jackson, Kenneth T., *Crabgrass Frontier: The Suburbanization of the United States*, New York, 1985.

Kazin, Alfred, *Contemporaries*, Boston, 1962.

Klein, Marcus, *Foreigners: The Making of American Literature, 1900–1940*, Chicago, 1980.

Lasch, Christopher, *The New Radicalism in America*, New York, 1965; London, 1966.

Long, Elizabeth, *The American Dream and the Popular Novel*, London and Boston, 1985.

Lynn, Kenneth S., *The Airline to Seattle: Studies in Literary and Historical Writing About America*, Chicago, 1983.

Macdonald, Dwight, *Against the American Grain*, New York, 1962; London, 1963.

Machlup, Fritz, *The Production and Distribution of Knowledge in the United States*, Princeton, N.J., 1962.

Mitchell, Arnold, *The Nine American Lifestyles: Who We Are and Where We're Going*, New York, 1983.

Newman, Judie, *Saul Bellow and History*, London, 1984.

North, Joseph, ed., *New Masses: An Anthology of the Rebel Thirties*, New York, 1969; Berlin, 1972.

Phillips, William, *A Sense of the Present*, New York, 1967.

Podhoretz, Norman, *Doings and Undoings*, New York, 1964.

Rahv, Philip, *Image and Idea*, Norfolk, Conn., 1949.

——*The Myth and The Powerhouse*, New York, 1965.

Rose, Barbara, *American Art Since 1900*, New York and London, 1967.

Rosenberg, Harold, *The Tradition of the New*, New York, 1961.

Shils, Edward, *The Intellectuals and the Powers, and Other Essays*, Chicago and London, 1972.

Sims, Norman, ed., *The Literary Journalists*, New York, 1984.

Sontag, Susan, *Against Interpretation and Other Essays*, New York, 1965; London, 1967.

Strelow, Michael, and the staff of the *Northwest Review*, eds, *Kesey*, Eugene, Oregon, 1977.

Tanner, Tony, *City of Words: American Fiction, 1950–1970*, New York and London, 1971.

Tilman, Rich, *C. Wright Mills: A Native Radical and his American Intellectual Roots*, University Park, Pa., 1984.

Tipple, John, *Crisis of the American Dream: A History of American Social Thought, 1920–1940*, New York, 1968.

Toffler, Alvin, *The Culture Consumers*, New York, 1964.

Trilling, Diana, *Claremont Essays*, New York, 1964; London, 1965.

Trilling, Lionel, *Beyond Culture*, New York, 1965; London, 1966.

——*Sincerity and Authenticity*, New York and London, 1973.

Updike, John, *Hugging the Shore* (literary essays), New York, 1984.

Vidal, Gore, *The Second American Revolution; and Other Essays, 1976–1982*, New York, 1982.

Walker, Alice, *In Search of Our Mothers' Gardens: Womanist Prose*, San Diego, California, 1983.

Warshow, Robert, *The Immediate Experience*, New York, 1962.

Webster, Grant, *The Republic of Letters: A History of Postwar American Literary Opinion*, Baltimore, 1979.

Wiget, Andrew, *Native American Literature*, Boston, 1985.

Wilkinson, Rupert, *American Tough: The Tough-Guy Tradition and American Character*, 1984; repr. New York, 1986.

Winchell, Mary R., *Leslie Fiedler*, Boston, 1985.

TABLE OF DATES

1923	D. H. Lawrence, *Studies in Classic American Literature*; Wallace Stevens, *Harmonium*; death of Harding (followed as president, to 1929, by Calvin Coolidge).
1925	Dos Passos, *Manhattan Transfer*; Scott Fitzgerald, *The Great Gatsby*; Scopes (evolution) trial in Dayton, Tennessee.
1926	Ernest Hemingway, *The Sun Also Rises* (published in England as *Fiesta*).
1927	Lindbergh flies the Atlantic; Sacco and Vanzetti executed in Boston.
1928	Talking pictures; first Mickey Mouse cartoon.
1929	Hemingway, *A Farewell to Arms*; William Faulkner, *The Sound and the Fury*; stock market crash in New York; inauguration of President Herbert Hoover.
1930	Hart Crane, *The Bridge*; Dos Passos, *42nd Parallel* (first vol. of *USA* trilogy); Sinclair Lewis wins Nobel prize.
1931	O'Neill, *Mourning Becomes Electra*.
1932	Erskine Caldwell, *Tobacco Road*; several million unemployed.
1933	Inauguration of Franklin D. Roosevelt (president until death in 1945); beginning of New Deal.
1935	Clifford Odets, *Waiting for Lefty*; Federal Writers Project (until 1939).
1936	Margaret Mitchell, *Gone With the Wind*; O'Neill wins Nobel prize; civil war in Spain (to 1939).
1937	John Steinbeck, *Of Mice and Men*.
1938	Thornton Wilder, *Our Town*; Czechoslovakian crisis in Europe.
1939	Steinbeck, *The Grapes of Wrath*; Frost, *Collected Poems*; war begins in Europe.
1940	Hemingway, *For Whom the Bell Tolls*; US population 132 million; fall of France.
1941	Germany invades Russia (June); Japanese attack on Pearl Harbor (December), and American declaration of war on Japan, Germany and Italy.
1942	Campaigns in the Pacific and North Africa; Alamein and Stalingrad.
1943	Eliot, *Four Quartets*; more heavy fighting on Russian front and in Pacific, North Africa, Sicily and Italy.
1944	US landings in Philippines; Allied invasion of Normandy (June) and liberation of France and Belgium.

1945   Tennessee Williams, *The Glass Menagerie*; collapse of
        Germany; surrender of Japan after atomic bombing of
        Hiroshima and Nagasaki.
1946   Robert Penn Warren, *All the King's Men*; W. C. Williams,
        Paterson.
1947   Truman Doctrine and Marshall Plan (development of the
        Cold War and of European reconstruction).
1948   Norman Mailer, *The Naked and the Dead*; T. S. Eliot wins
        Nobel prize.
1949   Arthur Miller, *Death of a Salesman*.
1950   Faulkner receives Nobel prize; beginning of war in
        Korea; anti-communism rife in US (culminating in
        McCarthy hearings, 1954).
1951   Marianne Moore, *Collected Poems*; J. D. Salinger, *The
        Catcher in the Rye*.
1953   Dwight D. Eisenhower inaugurated as president (to
        1961).
1954   Faulkner, *A Fable*; Hemingway receives Nobel prize.
1956   Allen Ginsberg, *Howl*.
1957   Jack Kerouac, *On the Road*; school integration crisis in
        Little Rock, Arkansas.
1958   Vladimir Nabokov, *Lolita*; Alaska admitted as 49th state
        (Hawaii enters as 50th state, 1959).
1959   Saul Bellow, *Henderson the Rain King*; Robert Lowell, *Life
        Studies*.
1960   John F. Kennedy defeats Richard M. Nixon in pres-
        idential election; US population 180 million.
1961   James Baldwin, *Nobody Knows My Name*; Bay of Pigs
        (Cuban invasion) fiasco.
1962   Edward Albee, *Who's Afraid of Virginia Woolf?*
1963   Assassination of President Kennedy (November;
        succeeded, to 1969, by Lyndon B. Johnson).
1964   Bellow, *Herzog*; growing US involvement in Vietnam
        (protest mounting to a peak in 1968).
1965   Assassination of Malcolm X; spread of Black Power con-
        cepts.
1968   Murder of Martin Luther King (April) and Robert
        F. Kennedy (June); Richard Nixon defeats Hubert
        Humphrey in presidential election; Mailer, *Armies of
        the Night*.
1969   Kurt Vonnegut, *Slaughterhouse-Five*; US lands two men
        on the moon.

1972   Nixon re-elected as president.
1973   Thomas Pynchon, *Gravity's Rainbow*; unfolding of the Watergate psychodrama.
1974   Ursula LeGuin, *The Dispossessed*.
1975   John Ashbery, *Self-Portrait in a Convex Mirror*; Cambodian seizure of merchant ship *Mayaguez* and recapture by marines.
1976   US bicentennial festivities; Saul Bellow receives Nobel prize; Alex Haley, *Roots*.
1977   Jimmy Carter inaugurated as president (defeated in 1980 campaign by Ronald W. Reagan).
1978   Isaac B. Singer wins Nobel prize; Pulitzer drama award to Sam Shepard, *Buried Child*.
1979   American hostage crisis in Iran; Norman Mailer, *The Executioner's Song*; William Styron, *Sophie's Choice*.
1980   US population 225 million; Walker Percy, *The Second Coming*.
1981   Reagan assassination attempt; John Updike, *Rabbit Is Rich*; Philip Roth, *Zuckerman Unbound*; Tracy Kidder, *The Soul of a New Machine*.
1982   Fears of US recession; Alice Walker, *The Color Purple*; Paul Theroux, *The Mosquito Coast*; Leslie Fiedler, *What Was Literature?*
1983   David Mamet, *Glengarry Glen Ross* (awarded Pulitzer drama prize, 1984); William Kennedy, *Ironweed*.
1984   Ronald Reagan re-elected as president, defeating Democrat candidate Walter (Fritz) Mondale; Gore Vidal, *Lincoln*.
1985   Elmore Leonard, *Glitz*.
1986   US federal tax legislated (first major change since 1913); abortive disarmament talks between USA and USSR; John Updike, *Roger's Choice*.
1987   Two hundredth anniversary of Federal Constitution (drawn up in Philadelphia, 1787, ratified 1788, put into effect 1789); Saul Bellow, *More Die of Heartbreak*.
1988   Presidential election year.

INDEX

Socin, Jay, 262
Solt, Mary Ellen, 257
Something Else Press, 253
Sondheim, Stephen, 235
Sontag, Susan, 382
Sorel, Georges, 8
Sorrentino, Gilbert, 261, 361, 362, 363-4
sound-text poetry, 247-8, 253-4
Soupault, Phillippe, 238
Southern, Terry, *Candy*, 341, 372; *Dr Strangelove; or, How I Learned to Stop Worrying and Love the Bomb*, 384
'Southern Agrarians', 177-8, 239, 380; *see also* 'Fugitives'
Spellman, A. B., 278
Spender, Stephen, 14, 84, 111
Spicer, Jack, 266
Spillane, Mickey, 251, 375, 376
Spingarn, J. E., 148, 151, 155-6; 'The American Critic', 150; 'The Growth of a Literary Myth', 150; 'Scholarship and Criticism', 150; *Critical Essays of the Seventeenth Century*, 155; *History of Literary Criticism in the Renaissance*, 155; *Literature and the New Era*, 155; 'The New Criticism', 155; 'Scholarship and Criticism', 155; 'Politics and the Poet', 156
Spock, Dr Benjamin, *Common Sense Book of Baby and Child Care*, 377
Stanislavsky, Konstantin, 68, 212, 213
Stauffer, Donald, 157-8
Stead, C. K., 19
Stearns, Harold, 4, 159
Stedman, E. C., 148
Steffens, Lincoln, 388
Stein, Gertrude, 1-3, 9, 27, 224, 240; influence on American writers, 4, 5, 9, 12-15, 40; influenced by William James, 7-8; on American

Modernism, 10, 12; influenced by painters, 12-13; language, 31-2; *Paris France*, 1; *Quod Erat Demonstrandum* (*Things As They Are*), 12; *The Making of Americans*, 13, 17-18; *Tender Buttons*, 13; *Three Lives*, 13; *The Autobiography of Alice B. Toklas*, 21
Stein, Jean, 188
Stein, Leo, 8, 12-13
Steinbeck, John, 18, 390; *The Grapes of Wrath*, 38, 39, 374; *Of Mice and Men*, 374
Stella, Frank, 241
Stephens, James, 81, 84
Stephens, Michael, *Paragraphs*, 367
Stevens, Wallace, 25, 84, 104, 108-9; in *Poetry* magazine, 11; influenced by Modernism, 20, 24; on differences between American and English literature, 79, 106; language, 93-4, 96, 97-9; in *Others* magazine, 238; 'Credences of Summer', 98, 258; 'Sunday Morning', 97; 'Notes Toward a Supreme Fiction', 97-8; *Harmonium*, 106; 'Esthétique du Mal', 258
Stevenson, Robert Louis, 334
Stevick, Philip, 354
Stewart, Ellen, 229
Stickney, Trumbull, 83
Stieglitz, Alfred, 8
Stigler, George, 395
Still, Clyfford, 250, 254, 265
Stoddard, Richard Henry, 148
Stone, I. F., 393
Storer, Edward, 19
Strasberg, Lee, 212, 213, 214, 233
Structuralism, 313-14, 320
Styron, William, 180-1, 398; *Lie Down in Darkness*, 180;